More Advance Praise for *The Myth of the Strong Leader*

"The best analysis of the nature of true leadership I have read. Turning his considerable erudition on Russia and communism to the vaguely-discussed but seldom qualitatively defined question of political leadership, Professor Brown dismantles the myth that power equals strength and that strength guarantees positive outcomes. Genuine leadership, he cogently argues, redefines national directions and social agendas and transforms entire political systems as the means to move nations forward. History, experience, and wisdom underwrite his case."

—Gary Hart, Former United States Senator

"A magnificent achievement, *The Myth of the Strong Leader* combines bold conceptual analysis with vivid descriptions of leaders ranging from Stalin and Hitler to Roosevelt and Churchill, from Mao Zedong and Fidel Castro to LBJ and Nelson Mandela. Archie Brown examines the types of power and leadership amassed by such diverse figures as Lenin, Ataturk, de Gaulle, Gorbachev, and Margaret Thatcher. This is a book which will be read with sheer pleasure by the general reader for its riveting insights and by students throughout the world as a lucid and witty guide to distinctive kinds of political leadership."

—Wm. Roger Louis, University of Texas, Past President of the American Historical Association

"This book badly needed to be written, and only Archie Brown—with his unique breadth of scholarly knowledge combined with a finger-tip feel for real-world politics—could possibly have written it. It turns out that there are fewer strong leaders in the world than is often supposed and that many of them, far from being desirable, are positively dangerous. Perhaps the best political systems are those that are effectively 'leader-proofed.'"

—Anthony King, Professor of Government at the University of Essex and co-author of *The Blunders of Our Governments*

"For nearly a half century, Archie Brown has been one of our most perceptive observers of world leaders and their contexts, from Mikhail Gorbachev's Soviet Union to Margaret Thatcher's Britain and beyond. His message is that our virtues are in fact our vices. Being decisive, staying the course, and having a clear vision are lauded as the core requirements of good leadership—yet they have just as often blinded those in authority to the folly of their own choices. Established leaders as well as aspiring ones should heed the lessons in Brown's timely book."

—Charles King, Professor of International Affairs and
Government, Georgetown University

"This is a real triumph of scholarship and intellect—and brilliantly written. Archie Brown demonstrates how dangerous is the myth of the strong leader and he pinpoints the disservice it does to society. The book is awesome in the depth of its analysis and in providing truly indispensable insights."

—Lilia Shevtsova, Chair, Russian Domestic Politics and
Political Institutions Program at the Carnegie Moscow Center

THE MYTH
OF THE STRONG
LEADER

ALSO BY ARCHIE BROWN:

The Rise and Fall of Communism
Seven Years that Changed the World
The Demise of Marxism-Leninism in Russia
The Gorbachev Factor

THE MYTH
OF THE STRONG
LEADER

Political Leadership in the Modern Age

Archie Brown

BASIC BOOKS

New York
A Member of the Perseus Books Group

Published by Basic Books,
A Member of the Perseus Books Group

First published in Great Britain in 2014 by
The Bodley Head
Random House, 20 Vauxhall Bridge Road,
London SWIV 2SA
ISBN 978-1-84792-175-8 (British edition)

Books published by Basic Books are available at special discounts for bulk purchases in the United States by corporations, institutions, and other organizations. For more information, please contact the Special Markets Department at the Perseus Books Group, 2300 Chestnut Street, Suite 200, Philadelphia, PA 19103, or call (800) 810-4145, ext. 5000, or e-mail special.markets@perseusbooks.com.

Library of Congress Control Number: 2014931301
ISBN 978-0-465-02766-8 (hardcover)
ISBN 978-0-465-08097-7 (e-book)

10 9 8 7 6 5 4 3 2

Contents

Preface

This is an argumentative book and one of the main contentions is already suggested by the title. The central misconception, which I set out to expose, is the notion that strong leaders in the conventional sense of leaders who get their way, dominate their colleagues, and concentrate decision-making in their hands, are the most successful and admirable. While some leaders who come into that category emerge more positively than negatively, in general huge power amassed by an individual leader paves the way for important errors at best and disaster and massive bloodshed at worst. Although the book also examines many other aspects of political leadership, what I call *the myth of the strong leader* is a central thread which unifies the discussion of democratic, revolutionary, authoritarian and totalitarian leaders. Those in the first of these categories can do far less damage, precisely because there are constraints upon their power from outside government. It is, nevertheless, an illusion – and one as dangerous as it is widespread – that in contemporary democracies the more a leader dominates his or her political party and Cabinet, the greater the leader. A more collegial style of leadership is too often characterized as a weakness, the advantages of a more collective political leadership too commonly overlooked.

The evidence is drawn from many different democracies – with Great Britain and the United States bulking large – and from a variety of authoritarian and totalitarian systems. When I turn to such dictatorial regimes, Communist leaders, as well as Hitler and Mussolini, get special attention. The scope is much broader, though, than the countries and leaders already mentioned. The chapter on revolutions in authoritarian systems ranges from Mexico to the Middle East. In its historical reach, the book aims to cover the whole of the twentieth century and what has happened thus far in the twenty-first. Notwithstanding the necessary element of selectivity, the conclusions I come to are intended to be of some general validity. The book's arguments are addressed to any citizen who thinks about how we are governed. My hope is that they may have an impact also on politicians themselves and on those who write about politics.

During the writing, and especially in the longer-term gestation, of this book, I have drawn not only on political memoirs, archives, newspapers and other mass media, and on the work of historians, political scientists and social psychologists, but also on many of my own meetings with politicians from different countries. These have included ad hoc consultation by prime ministers and secretaries of state for foreign affairs from different political parties in Britain, participation in the 1980s in policy seminars in Britain and the United States, taking part in twenty-first-century conferences with former heads of government, and meetings with senior figures within ruling Communist parties (usually, but in the case of some Communist reformers not only, after they had left or had been removed from office).

The book is a product of more than fifty years of study of politics, and of research and lecturing on the subject in different parts of North America, Europe and Asia. Great Britain apart, the country in which I have spent most time has been the United States where I have learned much during teaching and research spells as a Visiting Professor of Political Science at Yale, the University of Connecticut, Columbia University (New York) and the University of Texas at Austin, as well as during a Visiting Fellowship at the Kellogg Institute for International Studies of the University of Notre Dame (Indiana). I have spent almost as much time in Russia, in both the Soviet and the post-Soviet periods. I first arrived in Moscow on a British Council exchange scholarship in January 1966. That three-month visit was followed by an academic year in Moscow State University in 1967–68, also under the auspices of the British Council. I have made some forty visits to Russia since then.

Political leadership is an important subject and one I have been concerned with for a very long time. One of my earliest articles for an academic journal – in the 1960s – was on the powers, and especially the constraints upon those powers, of the British prime minister.[1] It drew not only on library research but also on my interviews with senior politicians – in that case prominent members and former members of the Cabinet from both of the major British political parties. As long ago as 1980 I taught a graduate course in the Department of Political Science at Yale which compared chief executives, especially American and French presidents, British prime ministers and leaders of the Communist Party of the Soviet Union.

My interest in studying the powers – and their limitations – of democratic leaders was already aroused when I was a student at the London School of Economics. Indeed, when I was being interviewed for an undergraduate place there, the chair of the admissions committee, Reginald Bassett (a specialist on British politics), recommended the reading of politicians' memoirs. I followed that advice, and in the years since then have acquired a large collection of political autobiography (as well as biography) from different countries. Their purchase during my student days was greatly facilitated by the fact that so many memoirs by politicians were remaindered and could be bought for next to nothing. The selective recollections and reminiscences of politicians have their limitations, but they can also be revealing, and not always in ways that their authors intended.

An engagement with leadership politics was further provoked when, in my first teaching post at Glasgow University, a departmental colleague during the 1964–65 academic year was John Mackintosh (later a Member of Parliament) who had recently published his influential book, *The British Cabinet*. It was because I disagreed with Mackintosh's – and Richard Crossman's – central thesis that the British political system could best be described as 'prime ministerial government' that I came to write the long response to which I have already referred. That old debate – on whether the UK has prime ministerial or Cabinet government – is not, however, what concerns me in this book. I am interested in whether democratic leaders more generally are as powerful as they are often assumed to be and whether, for example, it is leaders who determine electoral outcomes. I am still more concerned with questioning the tendency to assume that one person, the head of the government, is *entitled* to have the last and most decisive word on all important issues. Some leaders, more than others, have been eager to foster this view and to act as if it were true. I argue that this is neither sensible, in terms of effective government and judicious political outcomes, nor normatively desirable in a democracy.

There are numerous books on political leadership, and many more on leadership in the business world. The focus in this work is very much on party and government leaders, although some of the argument has a bearing on leadership more broadly. Leadership styles matter in all organizations. Even in one as hierarchical as the Catholic Church, the defects of government by one man have been voiced – and from the very top of that hierarchy. In an interesting self-criticism, and statement of intent, Pope Francis observed in a recent interview that when he was appointed the superior of a Jesuit province in Argentina 'at the "crazy" young age of 36', his leadership style had been too autocratic. It was, he said, 'my authoritarian way of making decisions that created problems', giving the misleading impression that he was a 'right-winger' or even 'ultraconservative'. Now, said the Pope, he prefers a more consultative style. He had, accordingly, appointed an advisory group of eight cardinals, a step urged on him by the cardinals at the conclave which elected him to the papacy. They had been demanding reform of the Vatican bureaucracy. Therefore, he intends his meetings with the eight to be 'a real, not ceremonial, consultation'.[2]

An unusual feature of the pages that follow is that they pay almost as much attention to totalitarian and authoritarian regimes as to democracies. Since there are nearly as many people in the world today living under some form of dictatorship as under democratic rule, that is appropriate. Real autocratic rule, moreover, puts in different and useful perspective the talk from time to time of 'an imperial presidency' in the United States or of 'prime ministerial government' in Britain, Canada or Australia. A leader who comes to power in an authoritarian system has not only the possibility of wreaking havoc and imposing suffering within his own country on a scale that could not be perpetrated by even the worst democratic leader but also, with rare individuals and in conducive circumstances, a greater chance of making qualitative change for the better. Some leaders, it goes without saying, are much more consequential than others. And, as I shall argue, those who deserve the greatest respect are frequently not the most domineering. Good leadership requires many attributes, whose relative importance varies according to time, place and context. It should never be confused with the overmighty power of overweening individuals.

Introduction

In democracies there is quite broad agreement that a 'strong leader' is a good thing.[1] Although the term is open to more than one interpretation, it is generally taken to mean a leader who concentrates a lot of power in his or her hands, dominates both a wide swath of public policy and the political party to which he or she belongs, and takes the big decisions. The idea that the more power one individual leader wields, the more we should be impressed by that leader is, I shall argue, an illusion, whether we are talking about democracies, authoritarian regimes or the hybrid regimes which fall in between. Effective government is necessary everywhere. But process matters. When corners are cut because one leader is sure he knows best, problems follow, and they can be on a disastrous scale. Due process means involving all the senior politicians with relevant departmental responsibilities in the decision-making process. It also naturally means that the government's actions should be in conformity with the rule of law, and the government democratically accountable to parliament and the people.

No one ever says, 'What we need is a weak leader.' Strength is to be admired, weakness to be deplored or pitied. Yet the facile weak– strong dichotomy is a very limited and unhelpful way of assessing individual leaders. There are many qualities desirable in a political leader that should matter more than the criterion of strength, one better suited to judging weightlifters or long-distance runners. These include integrity, intelligence, articulateness, collegiality, shrewd judgement, a questioning mind, willingness to seek disparate views, ability to absorb information, flexibility, good memory, courage, vision, empathy and boundless energy. Although incomplete, that is already a formidable list. We should hardly expect most leaders to embody *all* of those qualities. They are not supermen or superwomen – and they should never forget it, even though it would be a requirement too far to add modesty to this inventory of leadership desiderata.

Yet, for all its limitations, the strong–weak theme has become a constant in discussions of leadership in democracies, not least in Great Britain. When he was Leader of the Opposition, Tony Blair liked to portray the British prime minister, John Major, who had inherited a divided parliamentary party, as 'weak'. Contrasting himself with Major, Blair said: 'I lead my party. He follows his.'[2] David Cameron, as prime minister, adopted similar tactics with Ed Miliband from the outset of his Labour leadership, hoping to make the 'weak' epithet stick.[3] Miliband was able to retaliate when a large rebellion of Conservative back-benchers in July 2012 blocked an attempt to make the House of Lords a mainly elected, rather than appointed, legislative chamber. He said that Cameron had 'lost control of his party' and that the backbenchers' defiance of the party whips showed that the prime minister was 'weak'.[4] Since then efforts of the one leader to depict the other as weak and himself as strong have resurfaced with boring regularity. Such attempts to portray the person who heads a rival party as a 'weak leader' have become common in a number of countries. In Canada, for example, shortly after Stéphane Dion was elected Leader of the Liberal Party in 2006, the Conservatives launched a sustained campaign to define him as weak.[5] (Among Commonwealth countries which have adopted the 'Westminster model', including Great Britain where it originated, it is Canadian prime ministers who appear to be the most dominant over their parties, even though they tend to be 'pragmatic, non-charismatic and even dull'.[6]) It is evident that politicians believe that if they can pin the 'weak' label on their principal opponent, this will work to their advantage with voters. How leaders are perceived is, indeed, of some electoral significance, but it is a great exaggeration to suggest that this is the basis on which 'elections are now won and lost'.[7]

Far more desirable than the model of political leader as master is *collective leadership*. Placing great power in the hands of one person is inappropriate in a democracy, and it would be an unusually lacklustre government in which just one individual was best qualified, as distinct from sometimes feeling entitled, to have the last word on everything. In the case of authoritarian regimes, oligarchic leadership is usually a lesser evil when compared with the dictatorship of one man. Moreover, strong individual leadership means different things in different contexts. It is not only less appropriate than is widely believed, it is often very different from what it claims to be. Leaders are also followers, and while they may take pride in standing up to one group, even (in some cases *especially*) their own political party, they may be kowtowing to another. In other words, there can be a wide gulf between the image of the strong leader which many politicians have liked to project and the more complex reality. If one element of the myth of the strong leader is the use of strength as the criterion of desirable leadership, another is that – in a democracy – the leader's advertised strength is often an artifice or illusion.

In countries making a transition from highly authoritarian rule either to democracy or to a variety of intermediate hybrid regimes, the idea of the strong leader can take a still more dangerous form than in a fully fledged democracy. A survey conducted in thirteen countries of post-Communist Europe in 2007 investigated reactions to the statement that 'it would be worthwhile to support a *leader* who could solve the problems facing [that particular country] today *even if he overthrew democracy*'.[8] In eight of the countries more than a third of respondents supported these 'strong leader' and anti-democratic sentiments. Agreement with the statement was above 40 per cent in Hungary, Russia and Latvia and reached over 50 per cent in Bulgaria and Ukraine. Acceptance of the proposition was lowest – in other words, support for democracy was highest and scepticism about the strong leader as saviour most widespread – in the Czech Republic (16 per cent) and Slovakia (15.3 per cent). It is probably not accidental that, as Czechoslovakia, these countries had rather more experience of genuine democracy in the twentieth century, especially between the two World Wars, than any of the other countries surveyed. However, one of the few other states in which *less than a quarter* of the population preferred the strong leader to democracy was Belarus (24.6 per cent), which, as part of the Soviet Union, had scarcely any experience of democracy. Moreover, in its post-Soviet existence, it has been the most authoritarian country in Europe. In this particular case, it may be the actual, continuing and unpleasant experience of autocracy – that of Alexander

Lukashenka who has ruled the country increasingly dictatorially since 1994 – which has inoculated citizens against the idea that the answer to their problems was a strong leader.*

There are occasions – in war and crises – when inspirational leadership is needed. It is sometimes pined for even in periods when a more prosaic leader would suffice. More often than not, inspirational leadership is described, loosely, as charismatic. Originally, *charisma* meant a god-given talent. As the concept was developed by Max Weber, the charismatic was a 'natural leader', one with special, even supernatural, gifts whose leadership did not depend in any way on institutions or on holding office. The charismatic leader was seen as a prophet and hero and he was followed as an act of faith. For Weber the concept of charisma was 'value-neutral'.[9] Charismatic leaders may, indeed, do either appalling harm or great good. If we take two examples from later in the twentieth century than Weber's lifetime (the great German social theorist died in 1920), they can be an Adolf Hitler or a Martin Luther King. While a wariness of charismatic leadership is justified, for followers should not suspend their critical faculties, how such leaders are ultimately assessed depends, in large part, on how we judge the causes that their inspirational speeches and example serve.

Moreover, the idea that charisma is a special quality a leader is born with needs to be severely qualified. To a large extent, it is *followers who bestow charisma on leaders*, when that person seems to embody the qualities they are looking for.[10] During a good deal of his political career Winston Churchill was as much derided as he was admired. In the 1930s he was widely considered to be a failure who had not lived up to early promise. His inspirational presence and memorable speeches during the Second World War would appear to qualify him for the status of charismatic leader. More important than whether or not he fitted the hazy criteria of 'charismatic', though, was the fact that he was the right leader in the right place at the right time. Yet his success between 1940 and 1945 was heavily dependent on the specific

---

* At the other end of the scale, the very high proportion of people ready in Bulgaria and Ukraine to embrace a strong leader, even if that person were to overthrow democracy, may reflect extreme dissatisfaction with the quality of what has passed for democracy in these countries. In the Bulgarian case it is likely to be associated with the manifest public anger (including sit-ins in parliament) about the level of corruption.

political context – a grim and global war in which Churchill embodied the spirit of resistance to which a majority of British citizens aspired. No sooner was the war over than the party which Churchill led was comprehensively defeated in the 1945 general election. That illustrates the important point that democratic parliamentary elections are not primarily contests between leaders. We do not have survey data on the comparative popularity of Churchill and the Labour Party leader Clement Attlee at that time, but it is likely that in the immediate aftermath of the war Churchill would have been ahead in such a personality contest. Nevertheless, his 'charisma' was insecure. From being supremely 'one of us' during the war, Churchill was becoming again, in the eyes of at least half the nation, 'one of them'.

Charismatic leadership can be won and lost, and is not generally a lifetime endowment. It is often dangerous, and frequently overrated. More useful categories of leadership, I suggest, are the *redefining* and the *transformational*. Each of them is the subject of a chapter in this book. *Redefining leadership*, as I use the term, means stretching the limits of the possible in politics and radically altering the political agenda. It can be exercised by the leadership of political parties, collectively as well as individually. Parties which aspire to win elections generally feel a need to seek the 'centre ground'. However, *redefining leaders, whether as individuals or collectively, seek to move the centre in their direction.* They aim to alter people's thinking on what is feasible and desirable. They redefine what is the political centre, rather than simply accept the conventional view of the middle ground at any particular time, then placing themselves squarely within it. Franklin D. Roosevelt, with the New Deal, and Lyndon B. Johnson with his 'Great Society' reforms and civil rights legislation, provided twentieth-century American examples of redefining administrations. In Britain Margaret Thatcher ranks as a redefining leader. She cited her mentor, Sir Keith Joseph, complaining that 'post-war politics had become a "socialist ratchet"', with successive Labour governments 'moving the country a little further left'. Even if 'the Tories stood pat', their 'accommodationist politics' meant that they had connived in moving the centre of political gravity leftwards.[11] The Labour governments headed by Tony Blair from 1997 to 2007 and Gordon Brown from 2007 to 2010 occupied the new centre (as redefined by Thatcher) in a comparable way to that in which the Conservative governments of Harold Macmillan and

Edward Heath (so Thatcher complained) had occupied the previous middle ground which had been shifted leftwards by the redefining Labour government of 1945–1951, headed by Clement Attlee.

Transformational leaders are the rare people who make a still bigger difference. By a transformational leader I mean one who plays a decisive role in changing the economic system or political system of his or her country or who, even more remarkably, plays a crucial part in changing the international system. That is setting the bar high, but it enables us to make a distinction between even seriously reforming and redefining leaders, on the one hand, and those who play an indispensable role in effecting *systemic transformation*, on the other. The political context is all important. A transformational leader is extremely rare in a democracy for the simple reason that democracies do not normally undergo sudden transformations. Change tends to be sufficiently gradual that no one leader can be seen to have played a definitive part in systemic change. *Fundamental* change – for better or worse – tends to occur more rapidly within authoritarian regimes. It can be seen most clearly in the course of transition to or from authoritarian rule. When, however, we speak of transformational leaders, the focus is on systemic change that is for the better.

There is, then, a normative element in the use of the term. Transformational leaders are distinguished in this book from *revolutionary leaders* (the subject of Chapter 5), even though they, too, change the system after attaining power. They do so, however, relying on duress. Vladimir Lenin in Russia, Josef Broz Tito in Yugoslavia, Mao Zedong in China, Fidel Castro in Cuba, and Ho Chi Minh in Vietnam played decisive roles in the achievement of fundamental change of both the economic and the political systems of their countries. So, in that sense, they were also transformational leaders, but revolution, as commonly understood, involves the violent overthrow of state structures and more often than not inaugurates new forms of authoritarian rule. Revolutionary leaders are, therefore, to be distinguished from those who play a decisive role in transforming the political or economic system of their country without resort either to violent seizure of power or to the physical coercion of their opponents.

The notion that there is, or should be, one leader who stands head and shoulders above his or her colleagues and dominates the political process is common enough in democracies. As a description of the reality of the leader's power, it is often misleading, and as an aspiration it is misguided. As British prime minister from 1997 to 2007, Tony Blair aspired to dominance of the policy process and undoubtedly set the tone of the government. However, his lasting impact is easy to exaggerate. A number of the major policy decisions taken by the government had little to do with the prime minister. Its most significant legacy was constitutional reform, much of which resulted from policies Blair inherited and for which he lacked enthusiasm. This package included Scottish and Welsh devolution, power-sharing in Northern Ireland, House of Lords reform, Human Rights legislation and a Freedom of Information Act.[12] In his memoirs, Blair describes the last-named legislation as 'imbecility', adding: 'Where was Sir Humphrey when I needed him?'[13] Of the constitutional change, only the negotiated sharing of power in Northern Ireland was an area in which Blair played a leading role – although others, too, were decisively important there – and the Northern Ireland settlement may be regarded as his most signal achievement.

That Blair's dominance as prime minister was less than he wished was borne out by the nature of his uneasy – and often far from peaceful – co-existence with an authoritative and assertive Chancellor of the Exchequer. It was that minister, Gordon Brown, who was the dominant figure in the crucially important area of economic policy. Blair and those closest to him were eager to promote British membership of the common European currency, but Brown prevented this by insisting upon five tests which had to be successfully met before Britain could sign up to the euro. They were deliberately designed either *not* to be met or, at least, to give the chancellor the sole right to determine whether they had been.[14] Alistair Darling, a Cabinet minister throughout the years of Labour government between 1997 and 2010 (and Chancellor of the Exchequer in the government headed by Gordon Brown during the last three of those years) has confirmed that economic policy during the Blair premiership was largely in the hands of Brown, and that the one economic issue on which Blair 'expended a great deal of energy, including exceptional Cabinet consultation' was that of the single currency, 'trying to get us to join'.[15] In this endeavour, of course, Blair failed. Darling is not alone in expressing relief that the Chancellor prevailed in that contest with the Prime Minister.

Relations between Blair and Brown deteriorated to the point at which the prime minister and his closest advisers had great difficulty in finding out what the chancellor was going to put in the annual Budget. Blair's principal aide, Jonathan Powell, notes that Brown 'saw off' two 10 Downing Street economic advisers 'by starving them of information and forbidding Treasury officials to meet them'.[16] In key areas of economic policy Blair, ever eager to project the image of the strong leader, actually had less influence than had many of his predecessors in their time. Foreign policy was another matter. Here Blair was much more dominant, especially on relations with the United States and on Middle Eastern policy. Time and again in his memoirs, Blair emphasizes that the decision to take Britain into war in Iraq in 2003 was his, that as prime minister he was entitled to take it, and that, even if people disagreed with the military intervention, they 'sympathised with the fact that *the leader* had to take the decision' (italics added).[17]

The push for one leader as ultimate decision-maker is still more prevalent, and more frequently pernicious in its consequences, within *authoritarian* and *totalitarian* regimes. They, of course, place far more power in the hands of leaders than is politically possible in a democracy. There may be some checks from within the executive on what the authoritarian leader can do, but legislatures provide, at best, a façade, judges are subservient to the political leadership, and the mass media are controlled and censored with varying degrees of severity. It goes without saying that there is no accountability of the top leadership of an authoritarian or totalitarian regime to the citizenry as a whole. Even in these cases, though, it makes a difference (as will be argued in Chapter 6) whether authoritarian power is wielded individually or collectively. In a totalitarian system, one man (and all such systems have been male-dominated) holds preponderant, and frequently overwhelming, power. Authoritarian regimes, in contrast, can be either autocracies or oligarchies. Some, in other words, are ruled by a single dictator and others have a more collective leadership. The more collective it is, the more points of access there are for privileged groups to lobby members of the top leadership team. The freer the deliberation and argument in a collective leadership, the less likely are the worst extremes of policy. Even in an authoritarian regime with a collective leadership, such as the Soviet Union in the second half of the 1980s, the personality and values of the top leader can make a vast difference, as Mikhail Gorbachev did in the Soviet case.

The potential impact of the leader is greater than that of his counterpart in a democracy, in light of the more numerous constraints on the ability of a democratic leader to impose his or her will.

INDIVIDUAL AND COLLECTIVE LEADERSHIP

'Strong' leadership is, then, generally taken to signify an *individual* concentrating power in his or her own hands and wielding it decisively. Yet the more power and authority is accumulated in just one leader's hands, the more that leader comes to believe in his or her unrivalled judgement and indispensability. The more decisions are taken by one individual leader, the less time that person has for thinking about the policy and weighing up the evidence in each case. Since there are only twenty-four hours in the day of even the strongest leader, that person's aides find themselves (often to their great satisfaction) taking decisions in the name of the leader. That is just one reason why the allure of 'strong leadership' being exercised by a single person at the top of the political hierarchy should be resisted.

In democracies collective leadership is exercised by political parties. Although parties often get a bad name, and their membership has greatly declined in most countries over the past half-century, they remain indispensable to the working of democracy, offering some policy coherence, significant political choice and a measure of accountability.[18] If, as is widely believed, electorates vote primarily for a particular leader rather than for a political party or policies, then there may be nothing so very wrong with the top leader's aides exercising greater influence than senior members of the governing party. However, as has already been touched upon and will be demonstrated in Chapter 2, it is at best a huge oversimplification and usually misleading to see votes in a democratic general election as being mainly for or against an *individual leader*.

When a leader of a democratic party, knowing full well that it will be politically embarrassing to remove him or her, says, in effect, 'either back me or sack me', that leader is normally asserting a claim to superior judgement.[19] Yet, the idea that one and the same person should be best equipped to adjudicate in all areas of policy is an odd belief to hold in a democracy. The former British prime minister Tony Blair has written that 'a strong leader needs loyal supporters' and added: 'If you think the leadership is wrong or fundamentally misguided, then change leaders, but don't have a leader and not support their leadership.'[20] Blair's chief of staff Jonathan Powell has devoted an entire book to elaborating the ways in which a political leader can and should maximize his power in relation to his colleagues and his political party.[21] The more the leader is set apart from other elected politicians, the greater the independent influence of his or her non-elected advisers – such as Powell. Indeed, the latter's personal role in the making of ministerial appointments emerges from his memoir-cum-handbook as remarkably extensive, although he is committed to the idea of the 'strong leader' and at pains to portray Blair in that light. Viewing Machiavelli's maxims for a prince operating within an authoritarian political system as no less applicable, with suitable updating, to a democracy, Powell writes: 'Each time weak prime ministers succeed strong ones they invariably announce they are reintroducing Cabinet government, but all they really mean is that they do not have the power to lead their government effectively by themselves.'[22]

Few people today would admit to agreeing with Thomas Carlyle that 'the history of what man has accomplished in this world' is 'at bottom the History of the Great Men who have worked here'.[23] And that is not only because Carlyle forgot about the great women. Yet, the eagerness of politicians and journalists to focus their hopes and expectations on just one person within a government has echoes of Carlyle's deeply flawed conception of history. The extent to which both the 'political class' and broader public opinion in many countries accept the idea of the elevation of one leader far above others within a democratic government is puzzling. The expectations they generate thereby mean that heads of government may acquire still greater political authority than that already granted by the powers of the office they hold. Changing perceptions of what is acceptable behaviour by a president or prime minister can redefine the powers of the office in the absence of any overt constitutional change.

This has occurred even in the United States where the Constitution is venerated to a unique degree. Article 1 of that Constitution gives the American Congress the power to declare war. The president, as commander-in-chief, can respond with force if and when the United States is invaded, but otherwise, if the Constitution is strictly adhered to, he has the power to conduct war only after it has been authorized by Congress.[24] Louis Fisher, who worked for Congress for four decades as a senior specialist on the separation of powers, has been the most notable and consistent critic of the drift of war-waging powers from Congress to the presidency.* He sees Harry Truman, Lyndon Johnson, Ronald Reagan and George W. Bush as presidents who exceeded their constitutional powers by waging war before they had congressional approval. The Vietnam War, from 1964 to 1975, and the twenty-first-century wars in Afghanistan and Iraq are among the cases in point. Congress, Fisher contends, has been far too supine in ceding an extra-constitutional power to the president, in failing to assert its own prerogatives, and in critical scrutiny of operations involving the US military. He argues that both Republicans and Democrats 'need to rethink the merits of presidential wars' and that legislators 'must be prepared, and willing, to use the ample powers at their disposal'.[25]

However, foreign policy, including major issues of war and peace, is an area in which heads of government generally – not only in the United States – have played an enhanced role from the middle decades of the twentieth century onwards. One development which greatly contributed to this, and had a big impact on political leadership, has been the unprecedented increase in the speed of communications. Of huge importance

---

* Against the Fisher viewpoint, two general objections may be made. The first is that Congress as a whole remains one of the most powerful legislatures in the world. As a result of the separation of powers, it can frustrate the executive – admittedly, especially in domestic policy – more than can the great majority of its counterparts elsewhere. The second objection is that the presidency has a greater *democratic* legitimacy than has the Senate (as distinct from the House of Representatives). Among powerful second chambers, the Senate is exceptionally unrepresentative of the population of the country as a whole. (The British House of Lords, formerly a hereditary chamber and now a predominantly appointed body, clearly has still less popular legitimacy. However, it is a revising and advisory chamber, no longer possessing the power of veto.) Equal representation of every state in the US Senate means that a vote for a senator in Wyoming has almost seventy times more weight than that for a senator in the vastly more populous California. See Alfred Stepan and Juan J. Linz, 'Comparative Perspectives on Inequality and the Quality of Democracy in the United States', *Perspectives on Politics*, Vol. 9, No. 4, 2011, pp. 841-856, esp. 844 and 846. Moreover, the Senate has great influence on federal appointments (much more than has the House of Representatives), and more impact on the filling of government posts than have most legislatures elsewhere. This includes federal appointments to senior foreign and defence policy positions.

was the establishment of international telephone links. The first trans-atlantic telephone conversation did not take place until 1915 and it was the late 1920s before a regular intercontinental service was established. Air transport has impinged even more strongly on the conduct of foreign policy. When British prime minister Neville Chamberlain flew to Munich for his ill-fated meeting with Adolf Hitler in 1938, such travel for the specific purpose of one head of government meeting another was still a fairly unusual undertaking. Chamberlain's predecessor, Stanley Baldwin, never once boarded a plane. Baldwin was, though, the last UK prime minister to eschew air transport. During the Second World War there were important meetings of the leaders of the Allied opposition to Hitler in Casablanca, Tehran and Yalta, and just after victory over Nazi Germany had been secured, at Potsdam. In the post-war era 'summit talks' between potential adversaries and face-to-face meetings with foreign allies have become commonplace. Once it was technically easier for heads of government to meet more often in person, an increase in diplomacy conducted at the highest political level meant that not only parliaments but also ambassadors and even foreign ministers found their own international policy roles somewhat downgraded.

Technological developments that made possible instant communication between top leaders have, then, profoundly affected the way business is conducted between governments internationally. The internet has added a vast new dimension to the stream of instant information being thrust at national politicians, and especially their leaders. Cumulatively, these developments have tended to reduce the role of legislatures in war-related policy and have also meant that even a head of government who might wish to leave diplomacy almost entirely to the foreign ministry is not able to do so. Nevertheless, the increase in the speed of communication is an inadequate reason for focusing diplomacy and especially decisions involving war or peace in the person of the head of government, whether the president of the United States or the premier in a European country. It takes time to assemble a military force and there is a strong element of special pleading on the part of chief executives when the argument is made that the peculiar dangers of the contemporary world, together with the need for speedy action, mean that they are uniquely entitled to decide on military action. In the American context, Fisher has argued, too much emphasis has been placed on speed and too much trust in the judgement of the president. If, he has written, 'the current risk to national security is great, so is the risk of presidential miscalculation and aggrandizement – all the more reason for insisting that military decisions be thoroughly examined and approved by Congress. Contemporary presidential judgements need more, not less, scrutiny'.[26]

Most unusually, President Barack Obama sought congressional approval in September 2013 for an attack on selected Syrian targets following the Assad regime's use of chemical weapons in its civil war. This had little, however, to do with interpretations of the American constitution and more with a concern to seek domestic legitimacy and shared responsibility for a military intervention about which there was widespread public scepticism, following the embroilments in Iraq and Afghanistan. The precedent of seeking the legislature's approval had already been set by British Prime Minister David Cameron. The House of Commons, in an almost unheard-of rebuff of the government on a major foreign policy issue, refused to back military action, thus ruling out British participation in any military strike against Syrian targets. The referral of the decision to Congress stimulated wider debate on the issue in the United States and it became far from clear that the White House would prevail. Apart from members of both houses, and from both parties (but especially the Democrats), who feared that US military strikes on Syria might make a bad situation even worse, there were Republicans eager to inflict a defeat on Obama, whatever the issue.

Secretary of State John Kerry, speaking at a press conference in London on 9 September, said that the only way President Bashar al-Assad could avoid military strikes, was to turn over his entire stock of chemical weapons within the next week ('But he isn't going to do it. And it can't be done obviously'). The remarks were, however, seized upon by Kerry's Russian counterpart, Foreign Minister Sergey Lavrov, who promptly announced an initiative to persuade Assad to give up all his chemical weapons. Russia was the country with the greatest influence over Syria and President Vladimir Putin had been in the forefront of opponents of the proposed American military action. Obama responded willingly, suspending the proposed missile strike and, accordingly, the congressional vote. Inaugurating a process of disarming Syria of its chemical weapons under international super-vision, following agreements hammered out between Kerry and Lavrov, had two beneficial effects for the US president (in addition to being something of a diplomatic coup for Russia). It meant avoiding a potentially damaging rejection by Congress of a big presidential foreign policy decision and, more importantly, raised the possibility of attaining the limited goal of removing Syria's chemical weapons without the wholly unpredictable consequences of unilateral military intervention. This outcome was in itself an unintended result of the referral of the issue to Congress, but that decision provided more time for reflection and, ultimately, negotiation. It did not end the civil war in which the overwhelming majority of people who perished had been killed by non-chemical weapons. By leading, however, to US–Russian cooperation on the issue, it brought the prospect of a negotiated end to the conflict at least somewhat closer than military strikes, with inevitable civilian casualties, was likely to have done.[27]

The Truman Example

Harry Truman is among the presidents criticized for sending troops into battle without congressional approval, and of being, indeed, the president who set in motion the executive power's claim to be the initiator of war with the decision in 1950 to deploy troops in Korea.[28] Crucially, however, this was not unilateralism on the part of the United States. Truman had clear United Nations authorization for the military action. American troops were the main contingent within a broader UN force sent to defend non-Communist South Korea from attack by the Communist North in a mission that benefited from its international legitimacy.[29] Truman was, moreover, the kind of leader very ready to draw upon the collective wisdom within the broader leadership. It goes without saying that most politicians who attain high office, especially the highest, are ambitious and enjoy wielding power and authority. Yet some of the partial exceptions to that generalization are among the most effective heads of government. Truman was one of them. He was neither a redefining nor, still less, a transformational leader, but he was a successful one. If the desire for 'strong leadership' on the part of one individual is the pursuit of a false god, that is not to decry the need for *leadership*. It can, and often must, come from the chief executive, but it can and should come also from other members of a democratically elected government.

Truman was a reluctant vice-president of the United States and subsequently a reluctant president. Brought to the highest office by the death of Franklin Roosevelt in 1945, he is a president whose reputation has grown over the years, and he headed an administration that laid solid foundations for the post-war order in both America and Europe.[30] Being far from overbearing, Truman was prepared to cede great authority in foreign policy to his successive secretaries of state, General George Marshall and Dean Acheson. He had begun his presidency distrusting the department they headed, observing in his diary that 'the striped-pants boys' or 'smart boys' in 'the State Department, as usual, are against the best interests of the US'.[31] In this respect, Truman was like Margaret Thatcher who – as her foreign policy adviser, Sir Percy Cradock, remarked – saw the British Foreign Office as 'defeatists, even collaborators', sharing the view Cradock attributed to her close Cabinet ally Norman Tebbit that they were 'the ministry that looked after foreigners, in the same way that the Ministry of Agriculture looked after farmers'.[32] Truman's view changed, however, in a way in which Mrs Thatcher's did not. While the American president's right to determine foreign policy (war powers apart) is much more constitutionally entrenched than that of a prime minister in a parliamentary system, Truman treated Marshall and Acheson with great respect, doing nothing to detract from their authority.

In his famous study of presidential power, Richard E. Neustadt began by stressing the limits on the power of an American president, and it was Truman's perception of this on which he especially drew. Truman said: 'I sit here all day trying to persuade people to do the things they ought to have sense enough to do without my persuading them . . . That's all the powers of the President amount to.'[33] Speaking in 1952 just before General Eisenhower was elected to the presidency, Truman observed that Eisenhower would be sitting at his desk, saying: 'Do this! Do that! *And nothing will happen*. Poor Ike – it won't be a bit like the Army.'[34] (Italics in original.)* While collegial in his style, Truman was, nonetheless, prepared to exert his authority when senior

---

* Eisenhower was, however, better prepared for government by consent than another military man-turned-politician, the Duke of Wellington. Following his first Cabinet meeting as British prime minister in 1828, he said: 'An extraordinary affair. I gave them their orders and they wanted to stay and discuss them.' Peter Hennessy, *Cabinet* (Basil Blackwell, Oxford, 1986), p. 121, notes that the story was told in after-lunch speeches by Peter Walker, Secretary of State for Energy in the government headed at that time by Margaret Thatcher. After a pause, Walker would add: 'I'm so glad that we don't have Prime Ministers like that today.'

subordinates became intractable. He was not afraid to dismiss popular figures, even when their removal was liable to damage him in the eyes of public opinion. When in 1946 Secretary of Commerce Henry Wallace began to pursue what amounted to an independent foreign policy – less critical of the Soviet Union and more critical of Britain – Truman fired him, albeit after some initial vacillation between supporting Wallace or his secretary of state at the time, James F. Byrnes. In a letter to his mother and sister, Truman wrote: 'Charlie Ross [the President's press secretary] said I'd shown I'd rather be right than President and I told him I'd rather be anything than President.'[35] Truman was equally undaunted in 1951 when he recalled General Douglas MacArthur from his command in Asia for airing his discordant views on foreign policy in a manner which the president regarded as 'rank insubordination'. MacArthur had been speaking in increasingly apocalyptical terms in 1950 and early 1951 about how the Korean War could only be won by taking the fight into China and with the possible use of nuclear weapons. He insisted that 'if we lose the war to Communism in Asia the fall of Europe is inevitable'.[36]

The dismissal of MacArthur, Truman recorded in his diary, produced 'quite an explosion'; and 'telegrams and letters of abuse by the dozens'.[37] The mailbag soon contained not 'dozens', but some eighty thousand communications on the subject of MacArthur's firing, with a substantial majority in favour of the general. Telegrams to Congress were ten to one on the side of MacArthur. Even the (far more representative) Gallup Poll showed 69 per cent support for MacArthur against 29 per cent who approved of Truman's decision.[38] The attacks on Truman in the Senate were venomous. Senator William Jenner of Indiana declared that secret Soviet agents were running the government of the United States, and Richard Nixon – at that time also a senator – interpreted MacArthur's dismissal as appeasement of Communism. Senator Joseph McCarthy – whose attempts to find Communists in every governmental closet, not to mention within the military and Hollywood, gave rise to the term 'McCarthyism' – said that Truman must have been drunk when he made the decision and that 'the son of a bitch ought to be impeached'.[39]

The political system of the United States is such that choosing and, on occasion, changing Cabinet members; taking responsibility for the most senior military appointments, and making foreign policy rank as the president's areas of greatest power. But it was characteristic of Truman's style that the most outstanding foreign policy achievement of his presidency is known as the Marshall Plan, not the Truman Plan.[40] The countries of Western Europe, both those on the side of the victors in the Second World War and those that were defeated, had been devastated economically by the conflict. There was a fear that democratic government would be undermined by economic collapse at a time when the Soviet Union had overseen the creation of a number of client states in the Eastern half of the continent. The policy of economic bolstering of democracy, put together by Secretary of State Marshall, with the strong backing of Truman and the help of Acheson (at that time Marshall's right-hand man in the State Department), was decisively important for European recuperation and revival. In the words of the British foreign secretary at the time, Ernest Bevin, it was 'like a lifeline to sinking men'.[41]

LEADERSHIP AND POWER

It is said that all political careers end in failure – an exaggeration but one containing a grain of truth. Many hitherto successful political lives end with electoral defeat, but for a leader to lose an election, after some years in government, is normal in a democracy. Having led a party to defeat at the polls, a politician will often voluntarily relinquish its leadership. In the UK, for example, Sir Alec Douglas-Home resigned after the Conservatives lost the British general election of 1964. Neil Kinnock did so, having never held governmental office and after leading the Labour Party to defeat both in 1987 and in 1992. Gordon Brown resigned following the election of 2010 when no party won an overall majority but the Conservatives did much better than Labour. Failure of a more profound kind is when a leader is forced out by his or her governmental or party colleagues. It tends to be the fate of overweening leaders who try to concentrate power in their hands and treat colleagues high-handedly. Among British prime ministers, David Lloyd George, Neville Chamberlain, Margaret Thatcher and Tony Blair all left office, in their own view prematurely, through failure to retain sufficient support from their own side in parliament.

There remains, nevertheless, a widespread assumption that placing greater power and authority in the hands of one individual leader is worth doing in a democracy.[42] That is despite the evidence (some of which will be found in Chapters 2 and 7 of this book) that both their countries and such leaders themselves pay a price for it in the end. This is not for a moment to deny that in political reality some individual leaders – and in a democracy, not only the top leader – can make an enormous difference, either for better or for worse. Even if eventually ousted by her or his own party colleagues, such a leader may have a big impact on public policy and her country while in office. Margaret Thatcher's prime ministership in Britain from 1979 until 1990 is an obvious example. Thatcher may be regarded as one of a minority of party leaders and prime ministers within democracies who radically redefined the terms of the political debate, but whose style of leadership, nevertheless, led to hubris and her downfall.

There is no need, then, to endorse the 'Great Man' or 'Great Woman' conception of history to be aware that *some* leaders matter greatly. Economists and economic historians are often to be found among those who go to the opposite extreme from the 'Great Man' notion and embrace the view that history is made by impersonal forces. It would be foolish to deny the importance of fundamental shifts in the way human beings acquire the means of subsistence, of technological change, or of the significance of a series of international economic crises in recent years which came as a surprise to leaders – and, for that matter, to most economists. Political leaders have also appeared comparatively helpless in the face of globalization as industry has moved from one country and continent to another and left some of the world's most advanced economies needing major structural adaptation. Yet, it would be absurd to claim that the policies of governments or of international institutions can make no difference to the way technological change is managed or financial turmoil dealt with. These phenomena do require leadership, but collegial and collective leadership. However, when economic depression occurs, this has often merely strengthened the myth of the strong leader – a belief that a strong, and preferably charismatic, individual will provide the answer to these and other serious problems. The rule of Benito Mussolini in inter-war Italy and, still more, the rise in popularity of Adolf Hitler in the Great Depression election in Germany of 1930, and his subsequent ascent to power, are sombre illustrations of this tendency.[43]

Most of the leaders I write about in this book have wielded governmental power. When the term 'strong leader' is used of politicians, it is a party leader, premier or president who is being talked about. The image projected is of a head of government surrounded by advisers who will provide information and make suggestions, but who will ultimately defer to the top leader. Too much deference, however, makes for bad policy. A leader needs colleagues of political stature who will stand their ground and not hesitate to disagree with the judgement of the person who formally or informally presides over their deliberations. This will seldom amount to a leader being overtly overruled by the cabinet or shadow cabinet, for a democratic leader, aware that his or her colleagues remain unconvinced, will generally draw appropriate conclusions. Only leaders of autocratic temperament, too sure of the superiority of their own judgement, will attempt to railroad a policy through against the wishes of a majority of their colleagues. Since heads of government usually have some discretion in deciding whether to promote or demote cabinet colleagues, they can, however, more often than not rely on the compliance of many of the latter who hope to earn points for conformity with the leader's wishes. That is a significant instrument of power, but it has its limits. A leader who loses the confidence of a large proportion of senior colleagues can hardly survive within a democratic political party.

The difference between accountable or despotic, honest or corrupt, effective or inefficient government has a huge impact on the lives and well-being of ordinary people. So what the politicians who head these governments do – and how they are held responsible for their actions and style of rule – is clearly worth our close attention. Institutional power adds enormously to the potential impact of a leader. Yet it is worth keeping in mind that having your hands on levers of power is not the same as leadership in its purest form. The most authentic political leadership is to be seen when large numbers of people are inspired by someone who has neither power nor patronage to dispose of, but whose message strikes a chord with them. Such leadership can be provided by an emergent or rising political party, by a group, or by an individual. It is the readiness of others to embrace the message and take part in a movement that defines the effectiveness of such political leadership. The leader of the Indian struggle for independence from British imperial rule, Mahatma Gandhi, and the American civil rights leader, Martin Luther King, were outstanding twentieth-century examples. Both chose the path of non-violence (King himself was influenced by Gandhi) and showed the world that it was not to be confused with non-resistance.

The twenty-first century has seen no more remarkable example of leadership – or of courage – than that offered by Malala Yousafzai, a schoolgirl from the Swat valley of Pakistan who became an internationally renowned campaigner for girls' education. She was shot in the head by the Taliban in October 2012 in an attempt to kill her which came very close to succeeding. This was intended not only to put an end to her personal campaign but also to frighten off other female pupils from daring to attend school. From the age of eleven, Malala Yousafzai was championing education for girls. She wrote a blog for the BBC Urdu service which described her struggle to attend classes in the face of Taliban obscurantism and its hostility to female education. Aged fifteen when she was shot (injuries which led to multiple operations, first in Pakistan and then in Britain, to save her life), she became the youngest person ever to be nominated for the Nobel Peace Prize.[44] On her sixteenth birthday, 12 July 2013, she addressed the United Nations in New York, with the Secretary General of the UN, Ban Ki-moon, presiding.[45] By this time more than four million people had signed a 'stand with Malala' petition that called for education for the fifty-seven million children around the world (girls a high proportion of them) who are not able to go to school.[46] This, it is worth reiterating, is leadership of a purer form than that exercised by heads of government with jobs and favours to dispense.

Not all leadership that attracts spontaneous followers is, needless to say, of comparable moral worth. That provided by Benito Mussolini in Italy immediately after the First World War and by Adolf Hitler in Germany from the 1920s to the early 1930s was effective enough in attracting disciples. These were years when Mussolini and Hitler did not yet have instruments of state power at their disposal. This was, therefore, leadership in a more unalloyed sense than their subsequent rule, however morally reprehensible in the eyes of posterity. Mussolini and Hitler are among those who have been widely, and understandably, regarded as charismatic leaders on the strength of their oratory and ability to attract a spontaneous following. They also made the transition from one form of leadership to the other – from that which people were inspired to follow when they still had a choice to leadership backed by coercive state power.

There are many other examples of individuals who moved on from being leaders who had to rely on force of argument and example to establish their leadership to positions of state power. Nelson Mandela's journey from leading opponent of white minority rule in apartheid South Africa, via a scarcely imaginable twenty-seven years of imprisonment, to the South African presidency was among the most inspiring examples of leadership of the twentieth century. Lech Wałęsa's trajectory from strike leader in the Gdansk shipyards to leader of a massive unofficial trade union, Solidarity, in Communist Poland to the presidency in post-Communist Poland is another notable instance of spontaneous political leadership turning, in due course, into the formal authority and accoutrements of the highest office of state.

Choosing Leaders in Democracies

Many heads of government, however, have not attracted vast followings before becoming a leader of a party and subsequently a government – sometimes hardly any at all outside their immediate entourage. They have been selected for a variety of reasons and by a variety of means. In non-democratic regimes, they have quite often chosen themselves, as in the case of a military coup. Within parliamentary democracies – including, until recently, Australia – the choice may be restricted to a selectorate consisting only of members of the party who have seats in the legislature. In many countries, the choice is made by wider constituencies, including the party membership as a whole. (This may, as in the UK, involve parliamentarians' votes being weighted much more heavily than that of the individual party member, since the MPs will generally have a more intimate knowledge of the rival candidates.) The leaders chosen should not assume that they have been picked because of qualities so special that colleagues and party members have delegated responsibility to them for taking the big decisions. Yet, from the way some of them, a number of their colleagues, and the mass media alike discuss politics, it often seems as if just such an assumption has been made.

The idea that leaders of a political party or heads of a government have been chosen because they have already demonstrated such remarkable leadership that people are eager to follow them is, with few exceptions, far-fetched. Within a party which is sharply divided on policy, the choice may alight on someone who is seen as a unifier or, alternatively, as a representative of the majority standpoint in the battle of ideas. Often, the vote goes to the person who is viewed as the most articulate and persuasive advocate of the party's line. Sometimes, but far from always, the party members vote for the person who, opinion polls suggest, is most popular with the wider electorate. A leader may also be chosen because he or she is deemed to be inclusive in political style and good at coalition-building, whether within his or her political party (for serious parties are never homogeneous) or within the legislature. If we take the example of two especially notable women leaders, the last point has been as clearly true of the German chancellor Angela Merkel as it was spectacularly untrue of the former British prime minister Margaret Thatcher. In a parliamentary system, it is a major plus for a leadership candidate to be an effective performer on the floor of the legislature. This strengthens the morale of the parliamentary party and feeds through to the electorate in media reports. In all democracies it has become increasingly important over the past half-century for a leader to come over well on television. None of that means that such politicians are, or need be, charismatic.

Most prime ministers in parliamentary systems come to that office, having previously held ministerial posts. They have already, therefore, some experience of governing at the national level. Tony Blair in 1997 and David Cameron in 2010 were two British exceptions to that general rule, as a result of their relative youth and the lengthy periods their parties had been out of power. American presidents, much more often, have not previously held office in the federal government before being thrust into the highest post of all within the executive. A seat in the Senate provides very limited experience of coordinating policy and none of controlling a vast bureaucracy. A state governorship is a poor apprenticeship for the foreign policy role that an American president is expected to play. Presidential candidates do, though, test some of their leadership skills on the campaign trail. Their ability to communicate effectively and to make an emotional connection with a wider public comes under scrutiny in the drawn-out system of primary elections and then in the presidential campaign itself. The entire process is extremely long in comparison with other countries. Both the extraordinary length of time candidates have to spend traversing the country and the cost of running, which is greater than in any other democracy, puts off many able potential candidates. Large-scale personal wealth or good connections to corporate and rich individual donors have been in danger of becoming prerequisites of entering the race as a serious contender, thus depriving the country of leaders from outside a charmed circle.

Nevertheless, the two most recent Democratic presidents, Bill Clinton and Barack Obama, did not come from privileged family backgrounds. They both went to elite universities, but through scholarships and loans and as a result of their own abilities and endeavours. While striving for the party nomination and as presidential candidates, they still had to raise vast sums of money. Obama, in particular, succeeded in attracting a wide array of small and moderate donations, as well as large ones from wealthy individuals of liberal views, thus reducing his dependence on corporate interests. The long and arduous process of gaining, first, the party nomination and then the presidency is also, in significant ways, a school of leadership. As Obama put it in an interview during his first term as president:

I do think that two years of campaigning under some pretty high-pressure situations in a perverse way does prepare you for the pressures involved in the office, because you're used to being on the high-wire, you're used to people scrutinizing you, you're used to – in some ways – a lot of folks depending on you. This is just at a different level. It's not politics, its governance, so there's an added weight there. But . . . there was not a moment when I suddenly said, Whoa, what have I gotten myself into?[47]

*

Too frequently all leadership is reduced to a dichotomy, although the pairs themselves come in many variants.[48] 'Charismatic leaders' are set against 'mere office-holders', 'innovators' compared with 'bureaucrats', 'real leaders' contrasted with 'managers', while 'transforming leaders' are distinguished from 'transactional leaders'.[49] Then there are 'great leaders' and 'ordinary leaders', 'good' or 'bad', and, of course, 'strong' and 'weak' leaders. Such an either-or distinction invariably entails vast oversimplification. In this book I focus on the inadequacy of the 'strong'–'weak' dichotomy in particular and highlight the dangers of believing that strength and domination are what we should look for, and expect to find, in a paragon of a leader. There are a lot of different ways of exercising effective political leadership as well as different ways of failing. Many of the failures of leaders who are confident they know best, and brook no disagreement, have been monumental.

In paying particular attention to redefining, transformational, revolutionary, authoritarian and totalitarian leaders, I am focusing on categories of leadership and exercise of power which have had an especially significant impact on people's lives. Yet they are far from occupying the entire spectrum of political leadership. There are, as we have seen, remarkable leaders who never held governmental office. And there are presidents, of whom Truman was one, as well as prime ministers (some of whom figure in the chapters that follow) who were effective enough heads of government, although they did not introduce radical change. And sometimes, as has already been touched upon and will be further explored, the most significant of a government's achievements have less to do with the person at its head than with other members of the top leadership team. Too much is expected of the individuals at the top of the hierarchy and too much attributed to them. That is especially so in a democracy where there are, quite properly, many constraints on the top leader, even though an excessive focus on the person occupying the highest rung of the ladder has become all too common. Political leadership is multifaceted. It must be seen in different contexts and from different perspectives. That is what the chapter that follows sets out to do.

1

Putting Leaders in Context

Some of the attributes desirable in a modern leader (suggested on the first page of the Introduction) have proved valuable in political leadership throughout the ages – intelligence, good memory, courage, flexibility and stamina, among them. But leadership must be placed in context if it is to be better understood. In this chapter I'll look at four different, but interconnected, frames of reference for thinking about leadership – the historical, cultural, psychological and institutional. Leadership is highly contextual and what is appropriate or possible in one situation may be inappropriate or unattainable in another. Leadership styles differ in war and peace and in a crisis as compared with calmer times. Within a democracy the opportunities open to a head of government are very different when the leader's political party has a large majority in the legislature, a knife-edge majority, or no majority at all. What is conventionally hailed as strong leadership is not identical with good leadership, and the latter is not an abstract attribute but an appropriate response in a distinctive setting – in a particular time and place.

The times, moreover, are different in different places. This truth was well understood by a number of eighteenth-century scholars when they began to reflect seriously on the development of human society. Enlightenment thinkers in Scotland and in France first elaborated in the 1750s a four-stage theory of development which they believed went a long way to explaining the laws and institutions at each phase.[1]

Although excessively schematic in their approach – human development has been much less unilinear than their analyses suggested[2] – these thinkers offered many pertinent insights. It was a theory of development which summed up existing knowledge and allowed for exceptions at each of the stages.[3] Its most original exponent, Adam Smith, was a far from dogmatic thinker – one, indeed, who took a delight in finding exceptions to his every rule.[4]*

THE EVOLUTION OF GOVERNMENT AND OF THINKING ABOUT LEADERSHIP

Concerned to study 'the progress of government', Enlightenment thinkers attempted, among other things, to account both for the emergence of chieftains and monarchs and for the subsequent nature of leadership and followership. While intent on imposing a pattern on history, they drew on a wide variety of sources, ranging from the Old Testament to the literature of ancient Greece and Rome (especially the Roman historian Tacitus), and moving on to the accounts of travellers who had acquired familiarity with hunter-gatherer societies of their own time. Native American tribes were accorded particular attention. Some eighteenth-century writers suggested that leadership in the earliest stage of development of primitive societies went to the strongest or tallest man in the tribe. And other things being equal (a crucial qualification), higher than average height has continued to be a helpful attribute for the would-be leader.†

---

* Similarly, Smith's defence of political and economic freedom had nothing in common with an indiscriminate defence of business interests. On the contrary, it was Smith who wrote: 'People of the same trade seldom meet together, even for merriment and diversion, but the conversation ends in a conspiracy against the public, or in some contrivance to raise prices.' (Adam Smith, *An Inquiry into the Nature and Causes of the Wealth of Nations*, edited by R.H. Campbell and A.S. Skinner, Clarendon Press, Oxford, 1976, Vol. 1, p. 145.) For twenty-first-century examples of the kind of phenomenon Smith had in mind, we need look no further than the world of high finance and the cosy relationships involved in determining remuneration of those at the top of their hierarchies.

† The last American president to be elected who was below the height of the average American man was William McKinley at the end of the nineteenth century. (See Tim Harford, 'Since you asked', *Financial Times*, 11 May 2013.) In American

During the first phase of social development – that of subsistence based on hunting animals and living on 'the spontaneous fruits of the earth' – there was, Adam Smith observed, little that deserved the name of government.[5] 'In the age of hunters,' he said, 'there can be very little government of any sort, but what there is will be of the democratical kind.' Smith recognized that leadership was not the same as power. Thus, in such very different settings as groups of hunter-gatherers and members of a club or assembly in eighteenth-century Britain, there would be some people of greater weight than others, but their influence would be due to 'their superior wisdom, valour, or such like qualifications' and it would be up to the other members of the group to choose whether or not to be guided by them. Thus, leadership, as distinct from power, was to be observed where all the members were 'on an equal footing', yet where there was 'generally some person whose counsel is more followed' than that of others.[6] This is leadership in its purest form, defined as someone other people *wish* to be guided by and to follow.

It was the acquisition of property that led to a need for government,[7] and in the second stage of development, that of shepherds, people began to acquire property in the form of animals. In the third stage they became husbandmen, cultivating the soil and gradually becoming owners of property in the form of land.[8] The fourth phase of development for Adam Smith was the commercial stage, at which people began to engage in mercantile activity. (He never used the term 'capitalism'. That was a mid-nineteenth-century coinage.) Smith's somewhat younger near-contemporary, the French nobleman and government administrator Anne-Robert-Jacques Turgot, who developed a rather

---

presidential elections since then, victory has gone to the taller of the two main candidates approximately 60 per cent of the time. The point about the successful candidate being taller than the average male in the United States over the past 110 years probably relates at least as much to the relatively privileged social background of a majority of presidents (although with some notable exceptions) as compared with most Americans. Insofar as the generalization that height matters has any merit at all, it refers to leaders who are chosen by a wider group – a tribe, a political party or an electorate. The most frequently cited counter-examples of leaders who are small in stature are of authoritarian rulers, and thus of no relevance to the issue of the electoral advantage of greater height. Famous small leaders include, for example, Napoleon Bonaparte, Josif Stalin and Deng Xiaoping as well as hereditary monarchs such as Queen Elizabeth I and Queen Victoria.

similar theory of stages of development, surmised that when 'quarrels first took place in nations, a man who was superior in strength, in valour, or in prudence persuaded and then forced the very people whom he was defending to obey him'.[9]

For David Hume, nothing was 'more surprising to those who consider human affairs with a philosophical eye, than the easiness with which the many are governed by the few'.[10] He believed it probable that the ascendancy of one man over a great many began during 'a state of war; where the superiority of courage and of genius discovers itself most visibly, where unanimity and concert are most requisite, and where the pernicious effects of disorder are most sensibly felt'.[11] Moreover, Hume surmised that 'if the chieftain possessed as much equity as prudence and valour', he would become 'even during peace, the arbiter of all differences, and could gradually, by a mixture of force and consent, establish his authority'.[12]

Adam Smith devoted still more attention to the problem of how some people gained ascendancy over others and of how both leadership and power developed alongside the growth of differentiation in social rank. In *The Wealth of Nations*, he noted four ways in which authority and subordination came about. Initially, personal qualifications, including strength and agility, were important. However, 'the qualities of the body, unless supported by those of the mind, can give little authority in any period of society'.[13] The second source of authority was age. 'Among nations of hunters, such as the native tribes of North America,' Smith wrote, 'age is the sole foundation of rank and precedency.'[14] But age also counts for much in 'the most opulent and civilized nations', regulating rank among people who are in other respects equal, so that a title, for example, descends to the eldest member (or eldest male) of the family. The third source of authority was 'superiority of fortune'. Riches were an advantage for a leader at every stage of society, but perhaps especially in the second phase of development – the earliest which permitted great inequality.[15] 'A Tartar chief', Smith observed, possessing herds and flocks 'sufficient to maintain a thousand men' will, in fact, rule over them:

The thousand men whom he thus maintains, depending entirely upon him for their subsistence, must both obey his orders in war, and submit to his jurisdiction in peace. He is necessarily both their general and their judge, and his chieftainship is the necessary effect of the superiority of his fortune.[16]

In the commercial stage of development, a man could have a much greater fortune and yet be able to command not more than a dozen people, since apart from family servants, no one would depend on him for material support. Yet, Smith observes, the 'authority of fortune' is 'very great even in an opulent and civilized society'.[17] In every stage of development in which inequality of wealth existed, it had counted for still more than either personal qualities or age.[18] The fourth source of authority, which followed logically from the wide differentiation of wealth, was 'superiority of birth'.[19] By this Smith did not mean 'old families', a concept he ridicules, observing:

All families are equally ancient; and the ancestors of the prince, though they may be better known, cannot well be more numerous than those of the beggar. Antiquity of family means everywhere the antiquity either of wealth, or of that greatness which is commonly either founded upon wealth, or accompanied by it.[20]

Smith is highly sceptical of vast power being placed in the hands of an individual, noting that the apparent stability created by absolute monarchs is an illusion. Perverse and unreasonable behaviour by rulers establishes the right of the people to oust them, and an individual ruler is more likely to be guilty of this than a more collective government. As Smith puts it: 'single persons are much more liable to these absurdities than large assemblies, so we find that revolutions on this head are much more frequent in absolute monarchies than anywhere else'.[21] The Turks, Smith contends, 'seldom have the same sultan (though they have still the same absolute government) above 6 or 8 years'.[22] Addressing his student audience at the University of Glasgow in March 1763, Smith adds: 'There have been more revolutions in Russia than in all Europe besides for some years past. The folly of single men often incenses the people and makes it proper and right to rebel.'[23]

The person who becomes a ruler in a primitive society – or 'the chief of a rude tribe', in the language of one of Smith's pupils and later professorial colleague, John Millar – earns such a position in the first instance by becoming commander of their forces. This leads, though, to an attachment to his person and a desire to promote his interest.[24] Millar, who adopted and elaborated the four-stages framework of analysis, followed Smith in arguing that differentiation of wealth became significant already in the second stage 'after mankind had fallen upon the expedient of taming pasturing cattle', and this had implications for social and political hierarchy:

The authority derived from wealth, is not only greater than that which arises from mere personal accomplishments, but also more stable and permanent. Extraordinary endowments, either of mind or body, can operate only during the life of the possessor, and are seldom continued for any length of time in the same family. But a man usually transmits his fortune to his posterity, and along with it all the means of creating dependence which he enjoyed. Thus the son, who inherits the estate of his father, is enabled to maintain the same rank, at the same time that he preserves all the influence of the former proprietor, which is daily augmented by the power of habit, and becomes more considerable from one generation to another.[25]

This applied very forcefully in the case of chiefs. As a man became more opulent, he was the better able to support his leadership and in many cases make it hereditary. Being richer than others, he had 'more power to reward and protect his friends, and to punish or depress those who have become the objects of his resentment or displeasure'.[26] Thus, other people had reason to court his favour, leading to an increase in the immediate followers of the 'great chief, or *king*'.[27]

Monarchy, usually hereditary, and under a variety of names – kings, tsars, emperors, khans, chiefs, sultans, pharaohs, sheikhs, among others – became, indeed, the archetypal mode of political leadership across millennia and continents.[28] There was huge variation among them in terms of despotism, arbitrariness, respect for law, and willingness to share some power.[29] Before Napoleon Bonaparte came to power in France, monarchs in Europe as a whole (although no longer in Great Britain) claimed that their rule was based on 'divine right'. However, as S.E. Finer observed: 'Once Napoleon acceded, this hoary old political formula was on the defensive. It now appeared that any Tom, Dick, or Harry might come forward and seize the state, provided he had taken sufficient pains to make it appear that he had done so as the result of a call from the People.'[30]

British 'Exceptionalism'

Limited monarchy and widespread civil rights and freedoms were relatively rare prior to the nineteenth century. The most striking exception was England – and subsequently Britain – which provided the classic case of very gradual transformation of hereditary rule from absolute power to limited monarchy and, by the twentieth century, to symbolic authority. It has been called 'democracy on the installment plan', although those who made concessions at each stage rarely had in mind a goal of full democracy. More often than not – as in the passing of the acts of parliament which widened the suffrage in nineteenth-century Britain – they believed that this latest step of reform was as far as one could go while still preserving liberty and the rule of law.[31] Britain, nonetheless, saw over several centuries a gradual reduction in the power of monarchs and a leisurely rise in the power of parliament and of the accountability of politicians to an ever wider public.

Yet gradualism was not a smooth and uninterrupted process. It was most spectacularly interrupted in the middle of the seventeenth century. Civil war between 1642 and 1649 ended with the victory of parliamentary forces over those of the king and in the beheading of Charles I. Between 1649 and 1660, the British state was a republic. From 1653 until 1658 Oliver Cromwell ruled the country as Lord Protector, relying on his command of the New Model Army. The bickering that followed Cromwell's death, however, led to the dominant grouping within the army favouring recall of the monarchy (in the shape of Charles II) – and a restoration of gradualism. But the short-lived 'English Revolution' left an imprint on the monarchy. When James Boswell's father, Lord Auchinleck, was challenged by Samuel Johnson to say what good Cromwell had ever done, he responded (in Scots vernacular): 'He gart kings ken that they had a lith in their neck' (He made kings aware they had a joint in their neck).[32]

Parliamentary power was given a substantial fillip by the 'Glorious Revolution' of 1688. Charles II and especially his successor James II, having attempted to bypass and downgrade parliament, succeeded instead in putting an end to the Stuart dynasty. The belief that James, a Roman Catholic, was biased in favour of Catholics – and possibly attempting to reimpose Roman Catholicism as the country's religion

– was just one of a number of reasons for growing opposition to him. When influential opponents of James decided to present the monarchy to James's Protestant daughter Mary, her Dutch husband William of Orange insisted that if she were Queen, he would be King, not merely the Queen's consort. The 'revolution', although it was hardly that, was termed 'glorious' largely because it was bloodless in England (although it was far from bloodless in Ireland and Scotland). James II fled the country, and William III and Mary became his successors. The trend towards greater parliamentary power and in the direction of enhanced governmental independence from the monarchy continued during the short reign of Queen Anne – which saw the creation of Great Britain with the union of English and Scottish parliaments in 1707 – and under her Hanoverian successors from 1712. By the twentieth century the gradual development of constitutional monarchy had come close to turning Britain into a 'crowned republic'.

The American Constitution and its Legacy

The two most momentous breaks with monarchy in the history of government were the American Revolution and the French Revolution. The Founding Fathers of the United States who signed the Declaration of Independence of 1776 and the framers of the American Constitution in Philadelphia in 1787 disagreed on many matters, but were virtually united on one crucial issue – that the government of the United States must be republican, not monarchical or aristocratic.[33] They took pains to enshrine a rule of law and protection for the freedoms of those who enjoyed the rights of citizenship. The American Constitution, however, was neither democratic nor intended to be by most of its framers. It did not outlaw slavery and it implicitly denied the vote to more than half the population – women, African-Americans and Native Americans.*

---

* John Millar, one of the more radical representatives of the Scottish Enlightenment and a fierce opponent of slavery wherever it was to be found, did not feel the need to alter any word of a paragraph he first committed to print in 1771 when he published the third edition of his *Origin of the Distinction of Ranks* in 1779, three years after the American Declaration of Independence. Nor would the American Constitution subsequently diminish the force of his argument about the gulf between rhetoric and reality. Millar wrote: 'It affords a curious spectacle to observe that the same people who talk in a high strain of political liberty, and who consider the privilege of

It also deliberately tried to insulate the presidency from both 'popular majorities and congressional rule'.[34] It was the growth of support for greater democracy on the part of the American people, not the Constitution, which gradually turned the electoral college, set up to choose a president indirectly, into a de facto popular election, albeit one that was imperfectly democratic. As Robert A. Dahl has observed:

. . . the electoral college still preserved features that openly violated basic democratic principles: citizens of different states would be unequally represented, and a candidate with the largest number of popular votes might lose the presidency because of a failure to win a majority in the electoral college. That this outcome was more than a theoretical possibility had already occurred three times before it was displayed for all the world to see in the election of 2000.[35]

The designers of the Constitution, in creating a presidency, made that person the embodiment of executive power, which he remains, in a way in which a prime minister within a parliamentary system is not, even though some holders of that office aspire to it and their placemen may encourage it. The American Constitution, however, is unambiguous. Article II, Section 1, begins with the sentence: 'The executive Power shall be vested in a President of the United States of America', and the first sentence of Section 2 of the same article makes the president the commander-in-chief of the armed forces. Yet, to reiterate: the framers of the Constitution never intended that the president should be chosen by popular election. Their aim was to put the choice of president into the hands of men of exceptional wisdom, rather than let the great mass of the people make such a momentous decision. They also took pains to ensure that the president would not be able to turn himself into a monarch in citizen's clothing. By enshrining a separation of powers within the Constitution, and by placing serious constraints on the president's ability to determine policy, they guaranteed that the president (in contrast

imposing their own taxes as one of the inalienable rights of mankind, should make no scruple of reducing a great proportion of their fellow-creatures into circumstances by which they are not only deprived of property, but almost of every species of right. Fortune perhaps never produced a situation more calculated to ridicule a liberal hypothesis, or to show how little the conduct of men is at the bottom directed by any philosophical principles.'

with England's first and last republican ruler, Oliver Cromwell) would not acquire the equivalent of kingly powers.

The participants in the Convention which met in Philadelphia in 1787 came up with two innovations in the practice of government – a written constitution and a federal division of powers. Thus, the president's power was limited by a codification of law on the political system which set out the powers of various institutions. This document, the Constitution, became, in the words of de Tocqueville, 'the fount of all authority' within the republic.[36] Presidential power was limited also by the way the Constitution divided authority between the federal government and the states, with each entitled to autonomy in their own separate spheres. This was qualitatively different from mere decentralization – that could be found in some other countries – since it meant that, in principle, neither could encroach on the jurisdiction of the other. As the first country consciously and deliberately to embrace both constitutionalism and federalism, the USA significantly influenced the adoption of those broad principles elsewhere, although the actual institutional arrangements outlined in the American Constitution remained unique to the United States.

The constitution and the federal division of powers in the USA put novel limits on the power of chief executives, as did the special place accorded to law in the practice of American politics, with the rule of law coming close at times to the rule of lawyers. The 'most legalistic constitution in the entire world', as Finer described it,[37] has meant that decisions that could quite properly be taken by a popularly elected government anywhere else in the world have aroused legal challenge in the United States. Thus, when President Barack Obama succeeded in 2010 in getting a comprehensive healthcare bill passed, albeit one that still did not bring medical provision for the whole population up to the level taken for granted in other advanced democracies, the Supreme Court took it upon itself to consider the constitutionality of the Patient Protection and Affordable Health Care Act.[38] Since the votes of most of the members of the Court could be predicted on the basis of their political and social predilections, it was only the surprising decision of the conservative Chief Justice John Roberts which enabled the healthcare legislation to be deemed constitutional by five votes to four.[39] Many of the Supreme Court's decisions appear to be a continuation of politics by other means. The distinguished legal theorist Ronald Dworkin even suggested that Roberts wished to uphold the act 'for public relations reasons' rather than on genuine legal grounds.[40] Nevertheless, the Supreme Court it was which took the ultimate decision. More than a century and a half ago, de Tocqueville wrote: 'There is hardly a political question in the United States which does not sooner or later turn into a judicial one.'[41]

The French Revolution

Large though the international impact was of the American Revolution, that of the French Revolution was still greater.[42] Whereas the Americans had asserted the right to govern themselves, the French revolutionaries made larger claims. They believed that they were creating a model for the rest of the world – for Europe in the first instance. Even twentieth-century revolutionaries, such as the Russian Bolsheviks, often themselves invoked comparisons with the French Revolution and its aftermath – from identification with the Jacobins to fear of Bonapartism.[43] The French Revolution was, in principle, democratic and egalitarian in a way in which the American Revolution was not. There was, however, an important contrast between the American Constitution and its Bill of Rights, on the one hand, and the French Revolution and its Declaration of Human Rights, on the other, that was in the longer term to the advantage of the former. The American rights were specific and legally enforcible, the French rights were general and declarations of intent.[44]

French monarchical rule had been inefficient and oppressive, but not more so than in many another European country, and there was already more freedom in France than in most of Europe. An essential added ingredient which inspired many of the revolutionaries was the ideology of popular sovereignty and equality, the ideas of the 'radical Enlightenment', which are part of the explanation of why the revolution took the form it did. Among the changes the French Revolution inaugurated were a transformation of the legal system, the removal of feudal privileges, the ending of ecclesiastical authority, proclamation of the universal suppression of black slavery, changing the laws of marriage and introducing the possibility of divorce, and emancipation of Jews.[45] There is still lively argument not only about the causes of the French Revolution but also about when it began and ended, although the storming of the Bastille on 14 July 1789 has come to symbolize the destruction of the authority of the old regime and the forcible assertion of popular sovereignty.

Some of the political innovations which came with the French Revolution have had a lasting impact – including the notions of 'left' and 'right' in politics, based on the seating arrangements in France's National Assembly and the concept (or slogan) of 'liberty, equality and fraternity'. Of continuing influence also has been the French revolutionary assertion of secular and anti-clerical values, going beyond an attempt to replace one religion, or branch of a religion, by another. Whether religious or secular authority should be politically supreme is still a live leadership issue in many parts of the world today, but nowhere in contemporary Europe are religious leaders able to dictate the policy of governments. Notwithstanding a general hostility to religion, the French Revolution was soon creating its own rituals and myths, and it subsequently employed the use of terror on a scale that dampened an initial enthusiasm elsewhere in Europe for the French example and went some way to discredit the ideas it had embodied. That process of disillusionment continued when the early chaotic egalitarianism gave way to revivified hierarchy, military adventurism and a new autocracy. This was especially so after the collective executive, the Directory, which had come to power in 1795, was overthrown in 1799 by Napoleon Bonaparte who went on to establish his dictatorial power. In a reversal of many of the ideals of the revolution, Napoleon was crowned emperor by the Pope in 1804. The French Revolution was the first serious attempt to refound a state on the basis of radical ideas of equality and democracy. It was not to be the last time that a revolution galvanized by similar beliefs would end in autocratic rule by a strongman.

The Evolution of Democracy and of Democratic Leadership

In the course of the nineteenth century ever more social groups acquired a foothold in the political system in much of Europe and in America as economic status ceased to be a determinant of the right to vote. Even in America, however, property requirements long restricted the right to vote, and universal male white suffrage took place at different times in different states. By the 1860s it was largely complete. Non-white males were debarred from voting until 1870 when the passing of the Fifteenth Amendment to the Constitution enfranchised them – in principle. It came just five years after the Thirteenth Amendment had abolished slavery. The Fifteenth Amendment was not, however, sufficient to prevent southern states putting obstacles in the way of black Americans' exercise of their voting rights. Even in the later years of the twentieth century, a number of states still found ways of restricting the voting opportunities of their fellow citizens of African descent. The best response to the bigots was the election of the son of a white American woman and black African father as president in 2008 and the re-election of Barack Obama in 2012. In the first of these elections Obama won a higher percentage of white voters (43 per cent) than did John Kerry (41 per cent) in 2004.[46]

In many countries of Europe the last third of the nineteenth century saw important extensions of the right to vote, as it was delinked from property ownership. France had universal male suffrage from 1871 and Switzerland followed suit in 1874. In Britain the extension of the suffrage was so gradual that almost a quarter of adult men were still voteless at a time when they were being conscripted for service in the First World War. It was the lack of votes for women, however, which ensured that an absolute majority of the adult population throughout Europe and America were disenfranchized prior to the twentieth century. It is, therefore, hardly appropriate to call any European country or the United States of America democratic earlier than the last hundred years or so. That is notwithstanding the fact that some countries, not least the United States and Britain, were notable in the nineteenth century (and, indeed, well before then) for the extent of their freedoms and political pluralism and the existence (however flawed) of a rule of law. More generally, there was in Europe and America a gradual but uneven growth of government by persuasion.[47] At a time, however, when both women and African-Americans were denied the vote in the nineteenth-century United States, Alexis de Tocqueville was premature, albeit in many other ways prescient, in calling the remarkable book he wrote in the 1830s *Democracy in America*.

The development of democracy in the twentieth century, with the advent of female suffrage, had important implications for political leadership. Not the least of these was the entirely new possibility of a woman being chosen to head an elected government. It was as late as 1893 that the right of full adult suffrage was extended to women, and even then in one country only – New Zealand. Within Europe, it was from Scandinavia (characteristically) that the lead came in extending women's rights, Finland and Norway being in 1907 pioneers of women's suffrage. In most countries, the United States and Britain among them, women got the vote only after the First World War. Enfranchisement of women in the US came in 1920 with the passing of the Nineteenth Amendment. Unlike the constitutional amendment of half a century earlier, abolishing the colour bar to voting, states did not seek to circumvent this new provision. In the UK votes for women came in two stages – for those over the age of thirty in 1918 and for women aged twenty-one or older in 1928. At long last, that brought them into electoral equality with men.

The political advance of women has been an essential component of democracy, but it took some time for votes for women to pave the way for their elevation to positions of political leadership. Sirimavo Bandaranaike in 1960 became the world's first woman prime minister. She acquired this position in Ceylon (now Sri Lanka), having been persuaded by the Sri Lanka Freedom Party to become their leader, following the assassination of her husband who had been the party's founder. Centuries earlier women had, of course, at times held the highest political office, but as hereditary monarchs, with none more illustrious than Elizabeth I in sixteenth-century England and Catherine II in eighteenth-century Russia. Until the second half of the twentieth century, however, women had not headed governments as leaders of political parties which had won popular elections. Yet by 2013 more than eighty women had held the highest elected governmental office in a wide variety of countries, spanning every continent of the world. These included Golda Meir, Israeli Prime Minister from 1969 until 1974; followed by (to take only some of the more notable European examples) Margaret Thatcher in Britain in 1979; Gro Harlem Brundtland in Norway in 1981; Angela Merkel as Chancellor of Germany in 2005; Helle Thorning-Schmidt in Denmark (2011); and Norway's second woman prime minister, Erna Solberg, in 2013.

Contrary to most people's expectations, women leaders emerged earlier and more often in patriarchal Asian societies than in Europe or North America (where, although Canada has had a woman premier, the United States awaits its first woman president). Indira Gandhi became Indian prime minister as early as 1966. However, in all the

Asian cases, there has been a family connection to an important male politician – father or husband. Thus, significant breakthrough though this was, the emergence of women leaders on the Asian continent can also be seen as a new variation on the theme of hereditary rule and dynastic politics. Bandaranaike took the place of her slain husband. Mrs Gandhi was the only child of the first prime minister of independent India, Jawaharlal 'Pandit' Nehru. Corazón Acquino, President of the Philippines from 1986 to 1992, was the widow of Benigno 'Ninoy' Acquino, the most respected political opponent of the authoritarian and corrupt Ferdinand Marcos who paid for his opposition to Marcos with his life. Benazir Bhutto, prime minister of Pakistan from 1988 to 1990 and again from 1993 to 1996, was the country's first woman head of government. Her father, Zulfikar, had been successively president and prime minister of Pakistan in the 1970s. Their deaths were emblematic of the violence and volatility of Pakistani politics, with Zulkifar hanged in 1979 for the alleged political murder of an opponent, and Benazir killed by a bomb while she was election campaigning in December 2007. The first woman president of South Korea, Park Geun-hye, was democratically elected in December 2012 and took office in February 2013. She is the daughter of Park Chung-hee, the authoritarian president of South Korea in the 1960s and 1970s who was killed by his intelligence chief in 1979. Even the remarkable Burmese opposition leader, Aung San Suu Kyi, whose leadership of the democratic resistance to the military dictatorship led to long years of house arrest, owed her initial prestige to being the daughter of Aung San, the assassinated leader of the Burmese independence struggle.

The family connection was important also in the emergence of the earliest women leaders in Latin America. Without ever holding the highest political office, Evita Perón, the second wife of Argentina's first post-World War Two president, Juan Perón, became influential both during her life and after her death. In particular, she was a significant influence on the achievement of female suffrage in Argentina in 1947. And it was Perón's third wife, Isabel, who became the first woman President of Argentina, on her husband's death in 1975. More recently, however, women leaders have been elected in Latin America without needing any dynastic connection. Although Christina Fernández in Argentina conforms to the earlier pattern, having succeeded her late husband, Néstor Kirchner, neither Dilma Rousseff in Brazil nor Michelle Bachelet in Chile needed any such family connection. They came to prominence entirely on the basis of their own efforts and abilities and to power as a result of their high standing within their parties and countries. Bachelet, who belonged to the essentially social democratic Chilean Socialist Party, was President of Chile from 2006 to 2010, and Rousseff, a member of the Brazilian Workers' Party, was elected President in succession to Lula da Silva in the latter year. One thing the two women did have in common is that they had been active opponents of military dictatorship and that both were subjected to persecution, including torture, when they were militants resisting authoritarian rule in their countries.

CULTURAL CONTEXT

Recent anthropological research has expanded our understanding of the development of leadership over time and in different societies. It has fleshed out with new evidence, and simultaneously modified, some of the ideas of Enlightenment theorists outlined earlier in this chapter. It is clearer than ever that there has been a wide variety of ways of reaching decisions in pre-modern communities. There are many egalitarian hunter-gatherer societies in which no one person has been designated as leader and others which have chiefs.[48] Moreover, since hunter-gathering has been the mode of subsistence of human beings during 99 per cent of their existence on earth, it is unsurprising that there should have been variation at different times and in different places in the ways these groups reached agreement and resolved disagreements.[49] The American scholar Jared Diamond has noted that the size of the group is important. If it consists of several hundred people, in which not only does everyone know everyone else but they also form a kinship group, they can get by without a chief. Diamond writes:

Tribes still have an informal, 'egalitarian' system of government. Information and decision making are both communal . . . Many [New Guinean] highland villages do have someone known as the 'big-man', the most influential man in the village. But that position is not a formal office to be filled and carries only limited power. The big-man has no independent decision-making authority . . . and can do no more than attempt to sway communal decisions. Big-men achieve that status by their own attributes; the position is not inherited.[50]

In some instances, however, big-men could over time transform themselves into chiefs and when they did so, the anthropologist Marshall Sahlins argued, they used their leadership to subvert the egalitarian norms of the tribe, demanding economic dues and forcing people to produce more than was needed for subsistence. Initially such chiefs were constrained by the belief that all the members of the tribe were part of an extended family, but some of their number went on to repudiate the ties of kinship and to engage in more ruthless exploitation.[51] Thus, what began as leadership and persuasion turned into power and coercion. Chiefdoms, as distinct from bands or tribes with no one granted supreme authority, appear to have first arisen some 7,500 years ago.[52] Tribal associations of people tended to develop into societies headed by chiefs when 'the local population was sufficiently large and dense' and there was 'potential for surplus food production'. The larger the group, the more difficult it was to avoid the emergence of a leader who was in some, but not all, cases authoritarian. Different pre-modern societies have had their own distinctive features.[53]

Political life in African states, which have generally come under indigenous rule only from the later decades of the twentieth century, frequently bears the imprint of earlier forms of social organization. When British colonies were accorded independent statehood (usually following political struggle) and presented with a constitution based on the 'Westminster model', deeper cultural traits often trumped formal institutions, and any similarity to Westminster became increasingly difficult to discern. Thus, African leaders have tended to operate 'through highly personalized patron-client networks' that are usually, but not always, based on ethnic and regional groupings. Within these networks there are generally 'Big Men' who wield disproportionate influence and 'circumvent the formal rules of the game'.[54] A persistent problem of African states has been the fact that boundaries that are a legacy of colonial conquest forcibly brought together peoples of different ethnic identities and religion who had little in common. One of the most challenging tasks of political leadership was to create a sense of national identity. Presidents Julius Nyerere in Tanzania and Nelson Mandela in

South Africa were unusually successful in doing so.[55] Good institutions clearly are important, but much depends on the quality and integrity of leadership. If leaders themselves circumvent the institutions and thus undermine their legitimacy, then sound structures will not be enough.

Thus, leadership matters, but it is visionary and inclusive leadership which the poorest and most divided societies need, not a strongman. Many of the most impoverished countries of the world are among the most ethnically diverse. This compounds the problem of making electoral competition work, for there is a strong tendency for voting (to the extent that the election is reasonably free) to be along lines of ethnic loyalty. The temptation is to conclude that what is needed by the kind of ethnically diverse society in which most of the bottom billion of the world's poor live *is* 'a strongman'.[56] On the basis of long observation of African states and of statistical analysis of factors conducive to inter-communal violence, Paul Collier begs to differ. Noting the damage that violence does to the prospects for economic growth, in addition to its devastating immediate effects on people's lives, Collier concludes that 'bad as democracy is' in ethnically diverse failing states inhabited by the world's poorest people, 'dictators are even worse'.[57]

Political Culture

My main concern in the present context is, however, with locating political leadership within the political cultures of modern societies. A focus on political culture means attending to those aspects of culture which bear relevance to politics. It also provides a link between history and politics, for deep-seated cultures, as distinct from ephemeral attitudes, are a product of the historical experience of nations and groups (although less history as distilled by professional historians than history as popularly perceived). The concept of political culture and, still more, its parent concept of culture have been defined in a great many different ways.[58] In essence, however, a political culture embodies what people take for granted as appropriate or inappropriate behaviour on the part of governments and citizens; people's understandings of the means by which political change may be brought about; their perceptions of the history of their group or nation; and their values and fundamental political beliefs.[59] Students of values accept that they can alter over time, but contend that, as a rule, they change only gradually.[60] Fundamental political beliefs refer not to whether people support one or another political party, but to something more basic – whether, for example, they believe that all citizens have the right to influence their leaders and help determine political outcomes or, on the contrary, they hold that what happens in government must be left in the hands of their rulers who, like the winds and the waves, are not (and should not be) subject to the sway of ordinary mortals.

Political cultures in complex, modern societies are not homogeneous. *Most* countries are, in fact, ethnically diverse and contain also people of different religious faiths and of none. In the more successful of them, value is attached to what they, nevertheless, have in common. They are characterized also by broad agreement on the ways in which political change may be brought about, even though, in a democracy, the content and direction of the change will remain objects of contention. It is always an oversimplification to speak about *the* political culture of a particular nation. Nations and states contain a number of sub-cultures. In some cases, even allegiance to a political party can be a signifier of this. Members of the Communist Party or of a conservative Catholic party in Fourth or Fifth Republic France belonged to very different sub-cultures. Yet, there are often some beliefs broadly accepted in one society which are by no means taken for granted in another.[61] In one country there may, for example, be a widespread willingness to accord a leader uninhibited power for the sake of 'order' (seen as the supreme value), whereas in another the emphasis is on constraining the power of the top leader and making him or her legally and politically accountable. Historically, Russia has been an example of the first and the United States of America of the second.

Leaders, then, operate within political cultures which are not immutable but which tend to change slowly. Suppression of freedom of the press by an American president, Canadian prime minister or French president would meet cultural as well as institutional resistance. Indeed, during his single term of office as President of France, Nicholas Sarkozy came under strong domestic attack for an alleged willingness to use the security services to investigate critical journalists.[62] Italy has been a flawed democracy in the post-Second World War period, but a democracy nevertheless.[63] Thus, there was substantial opposition within the society to Prime Minister Silvio Berlusconi's use of his media empire to curtail criticism and debate. In Russia, there has never been a fully fledged democracy, although a vigorous political pluralism emerged in the second half of the 1980s. Over the past two decades that has become progressively attenuated. There was, though, a break with the passivity and conformism of the previous decade in 2011 and 2012 when rigged parliamentary elections brought tens of thousands of protesters on to the streets of Moscow and (in much smaller numbers) in other cities. The twenty-first-century harassment of opposition leaders, accompanied by state-enforced conformism of the mass media, have, however, evoked protests from only a small minority of the population. A democratic political culture grows out of lengthy democratic experience, and such experience in Russia has been both incomplete and short-lived.

Yet political cultures change over time in an interaction between institutions and values. It is a two-way relationship. Long experience with democratic institutions helps to mould and consolidate democratic values. But there are instances where the predominant influence is from the other direction. They may arise when an authoritarian regime has been imposed on a country and the new rulers promote an ideology which is at odds with well-established and widespread beliefs within the society. A good example of this was Czechoslovakia, which existed from 1918 until the end of 1992 (following which the Czech Republic and Slovak Republic became separate states). It was the most democratic state within central Europe between the two world wars, and was led for most of that time by its main founder, Thomas Masaryk. In the years immediately after the Second World War that First Republic was denigrated by Communists and linked in many people's minds with the unemployment of the 1930s and, above all, with the collapse of the republic in the face of Nazi aggression. Yet Czechs (more than did Slovaks) perceived their inter-war democracy much more positively after two decades of Communist rule than they had done in the early post-war period. A 1946 survey asked Czech citizens to say which period of Czech history they considered to be the most glorious. The First Republic (1918–1938) was named by only 8 per cent of respondents and came fifth from the top of 'glorious' periods. When the question was repeated in 1968, the First Republic topped the list with the support of 39 per cent of Czechs.[64] By the 1960s many Czech and Slovak Communists were themselves re-evaluating the advantages of political pluralism, and also the moral and political stature of Masaryk, after their experience of Soviet-style oppressive rule.

In the early post-war years there had been genuine enthusiasm in Czechoslovakia for 'building socialism'. Yet bureaucratic authoritarian rule, accompanied by political police surveillance and repression, was not what the more idealistic of young Czech Communists had sought or expected. The contrast between the depressing reality and their ideals led over time to some serious rethinking. Reform was also stimulated by Nikita Khrushchev's attack on Stalin in a closed session of the Twentieth Congress of the Communist Party of the Soviet Union in Moscow in 1956 and then again, openly, at the Twenty-Second Congress in 1961. What became known as the Prague Spring was the culmination of a reform movement inside the Communist Party of Czechoslovakia itself. However, in the more tolerant and rapidly changing atmosphere of 1968 the broader society was revitalized. Civic groups representing the non-Communist majority of the population sprang up. The process – especially the political reforms endorsed by the Communist Party leadership – so alarmed the Soviet Politburo that they sent half a million troops in August of that year to put a stop to it.

The top party leader, Alexander Dubček (a Slovak by nationality), was not himself a radical reformer, but he was a good listener who preferred persuasion to coercion and tolerated critical discussion and a partial pluralization of the system. In the eyes of senior Soviet leaders, he became 'the Number One Scoundrel'.[65] Although Dubček's role was that of facilitator rather than driving force, his succeeding the hardline Antonín Novotný as party leader at the beginning of 1968 was of great importance. In a highly authoritarian, strictly hierarchical political system, a change at the top of the hierarchy to a leader possessing not only a different style but also more humane values could make a huge difference. In general, *the more power is concentrated in the office, the greater the potential significance of the change of leader occupying it.*

Cultural influence, an important fact of political life, should never be taken to mean cultural determinism. Transnational influences, cutting across national cultures, have been important for centuries and seldom more so than in the last decades of the twentieth century and in the twenty-first when the means of instant communication between countries and continents are more numerous than ever before. Within any modern state, moreover, there is a variety of cultural traditions that can be drawn upon. Czechs were fortunate in having a past leader who embodied democratic values and who could become a potent symbol for those seeking change. Photographs of Masaryk were being sold on the streets of Prague in 1968 (I bought one there myself in that year), then banned for the next twenty years, only to re-emerge in late 1989. And this time, what became known as the 'Velvet Revolution' met no resistance from Moscow.

Some countries under authoritarian or totalitarian rule have a less usable past than that which Czechs could draw upon. It helps to have had past experience of democracy and to have symbols of democracy and freedom to quarry. A less propitious political cultural inheritance, from a democratic standpoint, does not, however, mean that nations are destined to spend the rest of time under dictatorial rule. Far from it. Every country in the world today which is regarded as democratic was at one time governed by authoritarian warlords or by an absolute monarch.

Leaders can be especially important at times of transition from authoritarianism to democracy. The depth of their commitment to democratic values is liable, in periods of political turmoil, to be decisively important both in securing such a breakthrough and in sustaining it. Mikhail Gorbachev, as I shall argue in Chapter 4, was a transformational leader, but he and his allies in the Soviet Union had an uphill struggle. There were not only powerful vested interests opposed to the radical changes which the last leader of the Soviet Union initiated, but also important strands in Russian political culture that could be drawn upon by his opponents. They have been among the underpinnings of the rule of post-Soviet Russian leaders as they whittled away checks on the power of the top leadership, which had emerged in the last years of the Soviet Union, and retained democratic forms while depriving them of most of their democratic substance. There has been a relapse into modes of conformist thinking whereby it becomes natural as well as prudent not to challenge the authority of the powers that be. In Russia a leader's supposed 'popularity' is often an effect of 'his perceived grip on power'. An interview with a woman voter in the run-up to the 1996 presidential election provided an apt illustration of this. Asked whom she supported, she named the Communist Party candidate, Gennady Zyuganov, but said she would be voting for Boris Yeltsin. To the question why, she replied: 'When Zyuganov is president, I will vote for him.' Power is deemed to confer authority and, in turn, commands respect and allegiance. As Ivan Krastev and Stephen Holmes have observed, if Putin ever becomes 'just one of several genuinely plausible candidates for the post of president, he would no longer be the Putin for whom an opportunistically deferential electorate was eager to vote'.[66]

Survey research has provided much evidence of attachment to a tradition which links legitimate government to the rule of a strongman. In the year 2000 the institute headed by Yuriy Levada (until his death in 2006 the respected doyen of Russian public opinion researchers) polled fellow citizens on which of their leaders in the twentieth century they considered the most outstanding. The top five who emerged were different personalities in many ways, but the one thing they had in common was hostility to democracy. They were, at best, authoritarian and, at worst, totalitarian leaders. Josif Stalin came top with Vladimir Lenin in second place. Third was Yuriy Andropov who headed the KGB for fifteen years and was leader of the Communist Party of the Soviet Union from 1982 until his death in early 1984. Leonid Brezhnev, Soviet leader from 1964 until 1982, occupied the fourth slot, and in fifth place came the last tsar, Nicholas II, who was overthrown in 1917.[67]

There have been other surveys, it is important to add, which suggest that there is more support for democratic principles among the population of Russia than is evinced by the political elite. Only a minority of Russians believe that they are living under democracy, but a majority regard it as an appropriate way to govern their country. Yet, in reporting these results, Timothy Colton and Michael McFaul note also the less encouraging findings that when Russians were forced to choose between democracy, on the one hand, and a strong state, on the other, only 6 per cent preferred democracy.[68] Consonant with such a preference, three surveys conducted in the Russian city of Yaroslavl in 1993, 1996 and 2004 found over 80 per cent of respondents agreeing with the statement that 'talented, strong-willed leaders always achieve success in any undertaking', while some three-quarters agreed that 'a few strong leaders could do more for their country than all laws and discussion'.[69]

Not only, however, are there different sub-cultures within Russia, as within any modern state, there are particularly striking generational differences. In the Levada survey already cited, respondents were allowed to name only one person as the greatest leader of their country in the twentieth century. Those who chose Stalin and those who named

Gorbachev clearly belonged to very different sub-cultures, given the chasm between the values and policies of these two men. Gorbachev occupied sixth place in that survey, named by 7 per cent of respondents. There were, however, very significant differences linked to age and education. Stalin's support was highest among those aged fifty-five and over and lowest among the eighteen- to twenty-four-year-olds. Of the three levels of educational attainment – higher, middle or 'less than middle' – Stalin's support was lowest among those with higher education. With Gorbachev it was the other way round in terms of both educational level and age groups. He was seen as the greatest leader of the century by 14 per cent of respondents with higher education, the same percentage from that highly educated section of the population as chose Stalin as the greatest.[70] In a survey conducted in 2005 there were similar age-related differences in Russian attitudes to the unreformed Soviet system. Asked whether it would have been 'better if everything in the country had remained as it was before 1985' (the year Gorbachev became leader), 48 per cent agreed with that statement. Whereas, however, 66 per cent of the over-fifty-fives agreed, only 24 per cent of the eighteen to twenty-four age group accepted that proposition.[71]

Political cultures are historically conditioned, but we should never underestimate the impact of the history that people themselves actually live through. Yet, how they interpret that experience is likely to be heavily influenced by the values and beliefs they have imbibed in childhood and youth. Studies of the acquisition of political outlooks in established democracies have shown that parental political partisanship 'has a major effect on the flow of political information to offspring'.[72] The same is doubtless true within societies under authoritarian rule. Especially in states where Communist regimes were imposed from without, socialization within the family could be a decisively important counterweight to the state educational system and the official mass media. In the case of Poland, the influence of parents – and, linked to this, the influence of the Catholic Church – was greater than that of a party-state which never overcame the obstacle to its legitimacy of having been imposed, essentially, by Soviet force of arms. A mighty secular leader was far less likely for Poles than for Russians to be seen as the answer to their problems, still less their prayers.[73]

PSYCHOLOGICAL DIMENSIONS

The pursuit of power and wealth is often seen as a game played by rational actors in defence of their self-interest, especially by many contemporary economists and their fellow-travellers among political scientists. Paradoxically, though, even the motivation for money-making – except for those so poor that it is closely related to survival – often is not primarily economic. In the words of Daniel Kahneman (a psychologist who was awarded the Nobel Prize in Economics): 'For the billionaire looking for the extra billion, and indeed for the participant in an experimental economics project looking for the extra dollar, money is a proxy for points on a scale of self-regard and achievement.'[74] As usual, Adam Smith was wiser than those who interpret his theories as an unalloyed defence of economic self-interest and who view that as *the* governing principle of society. Smith was well aware of the non-rational element in life generally, including the way people react to major political events. He noted, for example, that 'all the innocent blood that was shed in the civil wars, provoked less indignation than the death of Charles I'.[75] 'A stranger to human nature,' Smith observed, 'would be apt to imagine, that pain must be more agonizing, and the convulsions of death more terrible to persons of higher rank, than to those of meaner stations.' He turns this reflection into a psychological explanation for social and political hierarchy, one which complements his ideas about the relationship of forms of government to the means of economic subsistence. Writing in *The Theory of Moral Sentiments*, Smith contends:

Upon this disposition of mankind, to go along with all the passions of the rich and powerful, is founded the distinction of ranks, and the order of society. Our obsequiousness to our superiors more frequently arises from our admiration for the advantages of their situation, than from any private expectations of benefit from their good-will. Their benefits can extend but to a few; but their fortunes interest almost every body.[76]

It is mainly the wise and virtuous – who form, Smith observes, 'but a small party' – who are 'the real and steady admirers of wisdom and virtue'. In contrast: 'The great mob of mankind are the admirers and worshippers, and, what may seem more extraordinary, most frequently the *disinterested* admirers and worshippers, of wealth and greatness' (italics added).[77]

To that disposition to admire 'wealth and greatness' may be added a tendency of many observers to take individual rulers – whether monarchs, presidents or prime ministers – at their own high value of themselves, sustained, as it is, by flattery and the hopes of preferment of some of those around them. A number of books on leadership do now pay more attention than in the past to followers and their complex relationship with leaders.[78] Timid and gullible followers, it is postulated, get the bad leaders they deserve. Leaders rely on 'true-believer' followers who will recruit other followers to promote their heroic image and to spread their message. Therefore, 'to the extent that leaders' reliance on followers is ignored, so the autonomy of the leader is exaggerated'.[79]

Obeisance to authority figures can allow 'toxic leaders' in many professions – not only politics – to survive in office when they should be driven from it. Jean Lipman-Blumen has noted a widespread tendency to 'prefer toxic leaders to those disillusioning leaders, who would press our noses to the dark window of life'.[80] Many leaders, of course, are neither 'toxic' nor gloom-laden. Indeed, a leader needs to be able to instil hope and provide reasons for optimism, even while being honest about the scale of problems to be overcome. Winston Churchill performed that task *par excellence* as British wartime prime minister. As American president, Jimmy Carter identified many of the problems facing the United States, but was much less successful at boosting morale. An intelligent and upright leader, Carter has, nevertheless, been characterized as 'slightly too pious and nearly joyless'.[81] He tried to do too much himself, and placed excessive reliance on rationality, uncluttered by emotional appeal or political sentiment, to be effective in achieving his policy goals. While Carter was still in the White House, one of his former aides identified as a problem of his leadership a failure 'to project a vision larger than the problem he is tackling at the moment'.[82] Carter had a far more detailed grasp of the issues than his successor, Ronald Reagan, but the latter's sunny optimism went a long way towards helping him win the 1980 presidential election. There is much evidence from studies of American politics that 'people vote for the candidate who elicits the right feelings, not the candidate who presents the best arguments'.[83]

Leaders often give themselves credit for a particular success, even when there is no evidence that they have done anything in particular, or even anything at all, to bring it about.[84] As social psychologists Alexander Haslam, Stephen Reicher and Michael Platow put it: 'There is no mystery as to why leaders themselves are attracted to the idea of heroic leadership. First, it legitimates their position by providing a rationale for claims that they, rather than anyone else, should hold the reins of power, . . . Second it frees them from the constraints of group traditions, from any obligations to group members . . . Third, it allows leaders to reap all the benefits of success while often avoiding the pitfalls of failure.'[85] Pronouns can be revealing. Thus, the more self-regarding of leaders' accounts of their exploits can be summarised as 'I lead, you blunder, we fail.'[86] More generally, as Kahneman has observed: 'We know that people can maintain an unshakable faith in any proposition, however absurd, when they are sustained by a community of like-minded believers.'[87]

The recent attention paid to followers as well as leaders is welcome. A focus, however, only on the one person at the top of the hierarchy and on people who may reasonably be described as his or her followers leaves out an important category of leaders. Within a democratic government – and even in some authoritarian regimes – *there are people of substance within the leadership group who should not be regarded as 'followers' of the top leader.* They may, indeed, have played as important – or sometimes even more important – a part in such successes as the government enjoys as did the official leader. That would not be news to serious biographers of some of the major figures in governments who became neither president nor prime minister. Yet it is much less discernible in books that seek to generalize about political leadership.

It is an axiom of institutional analysis that within bureaucracies *where you stand depends on where you sit*.[88] And it is true up to a point. To take the most obvious example, officials within a government's Department of Health or Department of Education (still more the politician in charge of the department) will generally seek substantially increased budgets for their respective spheres of health or education. The primary preoccupation of a Treasury official, in contrast, will be to keep government spending within the bounds of financial prudence. Winston Churchill is not generally regarded as a politician who favoured reducing military expenditure, but when he was Chancellor of the Exchequer, he demanded (in 1925) deep cuts from the Admiralty and called for a smaller navy, although as First Lord of the Admiralty before the First World War, he had successfully pressed for a huge increase in naval expenditure.[89] More generally, what is a major concern for one department may be a matter of little interest or low priority for another.

One of the many suggestive findings, however, of social and political psychology, which complements what we know about institutional roles, is that *where you stand depends also on what you see*.[90] Misperception of facts feeds back into values and helps to shape particular views.[91] Thus, in the 1990s a fifth of Americans thought that what the government spent most money on was foreign aid – at a time when it took about 2 per cent of the budget.[92] This strengthened hostility to spending money for that purpose. It is well known that in their perceptions people tend to screen out information that is at odds with their pre-existing beliefs and will find a variety of imaginative means to view decisions they have made as reasonable and justified, including those which display inconsistency between their actions and professed principles.[93] People selectively process and interpret information so that it does not challenge their previous assumptions in uncomfortable ways. Perceptions of political reality are 'inextricably intertwined with citizen's political preferences and identity'. Thus, studies of televised American presidential and vice-presidential debates found that 'people's perceptions of who "won"' were 'strongly colored by their prior opinions about the candidates'.[94]*

A large body of evidence testifies to the fact that emotions matter greatly in politics.[95] To such an extent that we need to add to the other determinants of political stance: *where you stand depends on what you feel*. Rationality and people's perceptions of their interests are far from being irrelevant to the choices they make in elections; but material self-interest plays a less major role for a significant number of voters than might be expected. There is a particularly rich body of research

---

* There are, though, limits to this when a candidate's performance falls well short of expectations. In early October 2012, in the first of the three televised presidential debates of the campaign that year, Barack Obama's performance was unusually lacklustre. By a substantial majority, viewers thought that Mitt Romney had done the better of the two. Romney also got a significant bounce in the polls tracking voting intentions. (*Financial Times*, 6–7 October and 8 October.) In the remaining two debates, with Obama more than holding his own against Romney, perceptions of who prevailed once again tended strongly to reflect the viewer's political predilections.

on this in the context of American politics. The paradox whereby many people will cast their vote for a representative or leader on grounds far removed from their immediate economic interests is well summed up by Drew Westen, a clinical psychologist and political strategist: 'How gay people express their commitment to one another doesn't affect the marriages of 95 per cent of Americans, who aren't likely to start dashing off with their fishing buddies in droves if given the opportunity to tie the gay knot. Whether a few dozen murderers a year get a life sentence or the chair doesn't make much difference to the day-to-day experience of most of us.'[96] What is remarkable, Westen suggests, is the extent to which emotional reaction on such social issues influences many American votes. That is in spite of the fact that what affects people's everyday lives much more is 'who gets tax breaks and who doesn't; whether they can leave one job and begin another without fear of losing their health insurance because of a pre-existing condition; whether they can take maternity leave without getting fired'.[97]

INSTITUTIONS OF LEADERSHIP

I have already made the point that leaders in the purest sense of the term are those who attract followers and make an impact on society and politics while not holding any vestige of state power. Mahatma Gandhi during India's quest for independence from Britain, Nelson Mandela in the South African anti-apartheid struggle for majority rule, and Aung San Suu Kyi as the acknowledged leader of the campaign for democracy in Burma are outstanding examples from the twentieth and twenty-first centuries.[98] And leaders such as these are surely no less deserving of the adjective 'great' than monarchs in earlier centuries who were given that accolade on account of military victories, however inadequate 'great man' (or great woman) narratives may be as exclusive, or general, explanations of historical change.

Even for these three leaders, however, institutions – albeit non-governmental – have mattered in the furtherance of their cause. Gandhi became head of the Indian National Congress, the main institution of opposition to British rule long before it became a governing party in independent India. Mandela was the most renowned figure in the leadership of the African National Congress, the organization that led the struggle against institutionalized white supremacy in South Africa over many decades until, eventually, it had the opportunity of forming a government. Aung San Suu Kyi has been the longstanding leader of the National League for Democracy, an organization that had to resort to an underground existence for years on end under Burma's oppressive military dictatorship. Yet these leaders needed neither patronage nor governmental power to bolster their moral authority and political appeal.

Most political leaders who become renowned at a national level in their own countries are not like that. Their leadership is very dependent on the office they hold, most obviously as head of the government, whether President, Prime Minister or (in the case of Germany) Chancellor. Even talented politicians with a strong personality may achieve notable success in one office and find themselves powerless to influence events in another. The institutional setting, and its scope or limitations, more often than not determines what they can do. Some leaders, however, find ways of expanding their influence, even from relatively unpromising offices. Lyndon B. Johnson, as majority leader of the US Senate from 1955 (and before that minority leader), overcame the constraints of the seniority system (less flatteringly known as the 'senility system'), whereby promotion to committee chairs depended on how long someone had been in the Senate. Johnson, by mixing persuasion, inducements and sometimes intimidation, was able to fill slots on key committees and win votes as a ruthlessly effective Senate leader. Indeed, he virtually reinvented legislative leadership. In the words of his outstanding biographer, Robert A. Caro, he bent to his will an institution that had been 'stubbornly unbendable' and was 'the greatest Senate leader in America's history'. He was 'master of the Senate – master of an institution that had never before had a master, and that . . . has not had one since'.[99] Later, as US president, he became that rare thing – a redefining leader (discussed in Chapter 3). He left a much greater legislative legacy than his predecessor, John F. Kennedy. In particular, Johnson was able to get civil rights legislation approved that went far beyond what Kennedy was capable of persuading Congress to pass. Johnson's achievement in the White House depended not only on his tactical acumen and virtuoso cajolery but also on a combination of his consummate Senate know-how and presidential power.

Yet in between holding the Senate leadership, which he had turned into a major power base, and (as a result of Kennedy's assassination) acceding to the presidency, Johnson had been Kennedy's vice-president. The charisma which Johnson appeared to radiate as Senate Majority Leader, and which was to reappear in the earliest months of his presidency, was obscured to the point of non-existence in the early 1960s when he was vice-president. In that role he was frozen out of the inner circle of most significant decision-makers. The latter included the president's brother, Robert Kennedy, whose hatred of Johnson was heartily reciprocated. Johnson's leadership talents had no chance to emerge, so severely were they limited by the office he held. An earlier Texan vice-president, John Nance Garner, had described the job as not worth 'a bucket of warm piss'.[100] Johnson himself added:

The vice-presidency is filled with trips around the world, chauffeurs, men saluting, people clapping, chairmanships of councils, but in the end it is nothing. I detested every minute of it.[101]

An American vice-president *can* become a hugely influential figure – another leader, in fact – but only if the president chooses to repose great trust in him, as George W. Bush did with Dick Cheney.[102] For Johnson, in harness with Kennedy, it was a very different story. While Johnson had been wrong in imagining that much of the authority he had acquired in the Senate would be transferable to the vice-presidency, he had also made another calculation which turned out to be more realistic. Convinced that no candidate from a southern state would be elected President during his lifetime (the last one, Zachary Taylor, had been in 1848), he noted that one in five presidents had acceded to that office on the death of the elected incumbent. When Kennedy, aiming to strengthen his electoral chances in the south, invited the Texan to be his running-mate, Johnson (who had aspired to the presidency from an early age) reckoned those odds were as good as he was now likely to get.[103]

Institutions are both enabling and constraining. They help leaders to get policy implemented. Their rules, procedures and collective ethos, however, limit his or her freedom of action. An American president has more power *within* the executive than is normally the case for a prime minister in a parliamentary system. Johnson, like Franklin Delano Roosevelt, was among those who used it to the full. Yet, in comparison with a prime minister whose party has an overall majority in parliament (as is usual in Britain, the coalition government formed in 2010 being the UK's first since the Second World War), the president is much weaker vis-à-vis the other branches of government – the legislature and the judiciary. Johnson's vast Senate experience, allied to the vice-presidency, availed him nothing. But when as president he called every senator in turn, it counted for a great deal. Moreover, the US president is head of state as well as head of government and, as a result, has traditionally been treated with more deference in interviews and press conferences than a British prime minister, not to speak of the way the latter may be scorned at question-time in the House of Commons. The especially strict separation of powers in the United States has an effect on the way that presidential leadership is exercised. Hence the use of the presidency as a 'bully pulpit', appealing to the public over the heads of other branches of the political system in the hope of persuading voters to put pressure on Congress. Franklin D. Roosevelt and Ronald Reagan, in their different ways, were effective practitioners of what, as noted in the previous chapter, Truman regarded as the president's main power – the power to persuade.

Leaders and Political Parties

In a democracy, a head of the executive who leads a political party has the backing of its organization and the advantage of its campaigning support. He or she had better, however, take account of opinion within the party – and in the parliamentary party in the first instance – if the relationship is to remain a happy one. It is because being a party leader in a democracy means persuading senior party colleagues and the broader membership that a policy is desirable, rather than simply decreeing it, that the party role is constraining as well as enabling. A party leader who espouses policies at odds with the core values of the party or with overwhelming party opinion on any particular issue is courting trouble. For the President of the United States, the constraints imposed by his own party are generally less than in parliamentary democracies, although they are not absent. Thus, President George H.W. Bush deemed it necessary to impose a lengthy pause in the constructive and increasingly friendly relationship with Gorbachev's Soviet Union which had been developing under his predecessor, Ronald Reagan. Brent Scowcroft and his National Security Council staff set up a series of policy reviews with the aim of showing that Bush's foreign policy would not simply be a continuation of Reagan's. Condoleezza Rice, who managed two of the reviews, said that the purpose was 'in the case of European and Soviet policy, to slow down what was widely seen as Ronald Reagan's too-close embrace of Mikhail Gorbachev in 1988'. Only the subsequent 'rapid collapse of communism got our attention in time to overcome our inherent caution'.[104]

In the view of the American ambassador to Moscow, Jack Matlock, it was not simply a matter of the wrong experts giving the wrong advice in Washington, but Bush's need to shore up his political support where it was weakest. Whereas Reagan's good standing with right-wing Republicans had left him more (though not entirely) immune from criticism from within his own party, Bush, as Matlock put it, felt a need 'to reassure the right wing of the Republican Party' and 'put on a show of toughness to insulate himself from right-wing criticism'.[105] While foreign policy issues do, in some cases, still divide the parties, they are less prominent than during the Cold War. The growing salience of social issues in American politics – abortion, school prayer, gay marriage – has contributed to a weakening of party structures.[106] Even before those trends became pronounced, the American comedian Will Rogers remarked: 'I do not belong to any organized political group – I'm a Democrat.'[107]

Other than through impeachment, American presidents cannot be removed in between elections. Prime ministers in parliamentary democracies have no such guarantee. If they lose the confidence of their party, especially the parliamentary party, they can be replaced. Mobilizing a large enough group to challenge a leader is a simpler task if only the parliamentary party has a vote on the leadership, as distinct from an electoral college comprising a wider electorate, including rank-and-file party members. Australia is a striking example of a country where these decisions have been exclusively in the hands of members of parliament and where there has been no shortage in modern times of party leaders being forced out by their own party, even when that person is prime minister.[108]

The most recent instance was the replacement of Julia Gillard by Kevin Rudd as Labor leader, and hence as prime minister, in June 2013, thus reversing Rudd's ouster by Gillard, who was deputy leader at the time, just three years earlier.[109] Following his removal as party leader and prime minister in 2010, Rudd went on to serve as foreign minister, but resigned that post in February 2012 and provoked a leadership contest in an attempt to regain the premiership. He was comprehensively defeated by Gillard, even though Rudd was by this time more popular in the country than was Australia's first woman prime minister. Senior ministers attacked Rudd's record and style as prime minister 'with a candour and vehemence' which suggested that 'the majority of his cabinet did not want him as prime minister under any circumstances'.[110] Still not accepting Julia Gillard's leadership, Rudd and his supporters mounted another challenge just over a year later. Minutes before the vote was to be taken in March 2013, however, Rudd 'announced he would not run, saying he did not have the numbers'.[111] He also said that this would be his last attempt to regain the party leadership. Yet, a mere three months later, convinced that he now did have the numbers, Rudd renewed his challenge and won the party vote. A Chinese-speaking former diplomat, Rudd is regarded as 'ferociously bright', but his 'autocratic leadership style' when he was prime minister earlier led to his being 'despised by large sections of his own party'.[112]

As was entirely predictable, Labor's change of leadership did not affect the overall outcome of the general election when it took place in September 2013. Immediately after his return to the prime ministership in late June, Rudd was ahead not only of Gillard in the opinion polls but also of the Leader of the Opposition, Tony Abbott, although as a party Labor still trailed, albeit with the gap temporarily narrowed. By the time of the election in early September, Abbott's ratings were higher than Rudd's, but in neither case was the popularity or unpopularity of the leader decisive. The vote was against the Labor government at a time when it had been weakened by the extent of its public infighting and when Australia's sustained economic success had begun to show signs of fragility. The opposition Liberal Party was able to make the most of these issues, striking a chord also with its harder line on immigration. Rudd's return to the premiership had proved to be singularly pointless, dividing his party once again and failing to impress the country. In the wake of the electoral defeat, he announced his resignation as party leader.

Rudd's problems during his first stint as premier were foreshadowed by his announcement that when in government he, and not members of the parliamentary party, would choose members of the Cabinet.[113]* The change in Australia was criticized on the grounds that it turned both Cabinet members and those who aspired to governmental office into 'sycophants'. An Australian senator observed that 'under the old system, everybody owned the front bench. At the moment, the front bench is wholly and solely the property of the leader.' A Cabinet minister who served during Kevin Rudd's first premiership said: 'In his [Rudd's] perfect world, he would have decided everything himself.'[114] More complex voting systems for choosing a new party leader provide somewhat greater protection for heads of government in many other parliamentary democracies, but they put their future in jeopardy if they lose the support of their parliamentary party. It is, therefore, unwise as well as undemocratic for a prime minister to wish to decide everything himself or herself.

It is because they do not wish to be hemmed in by their senior colleagues and, still less, by rank-and-file party members that some leaders, whose commitment to democratic norms is less than whole-hearted, make a virtue of *not* joining a political party. This is extremely rare in an established democracy. General Charles de Gaulle is the exception who proved the rule – not only by being 'above party' but by ultimately enhancing, rather than undermining, French democracy. Leaders professing to be above party are more liable to be found in countries emerging from authoritarian rule and their distancing themselves from party helps to ensure that the transition from authoritarianism is, to say the least, incomplete. Boris Yeltsin and Vladimir Putin in Russia each made much of the boast that they were president of the whole people and not shackled or tainted by party membership. In so doing, they unknowingly, or knowingly, did a disservice to the development of democracy in post-Soviet Russia. (Putin was, for a time, the designated leader of the pro-Kremlin political party, United Russia, but without actually joining it.) A president or prime minister in a democracy is no less the national leader, acting in the interests of the people as a whole as he or she perceives them, for belonging to a political party. It is not a chief executive's party membership that

---

* In Britain both Labour and Conservative prime ministers select their Cabinet colleagues, but in opposition the Labour Shadow Cabinet was until 2011 elected by the parliamentary party. A year after Ed Miliband succeeded Gordon Brown, this choice was placed in the hands of the leader.

is a threat to an emerging democracy, but weak or ineffective political parties. And for the head of the government *not* to be a party leader, or even a party member, devalues political parties and hence democratic institution-building.

Leaders and Forms of Government

Institutions clearly make a difference to what leaders can do and leaders' choices have an impact on institutions. What form of government – whether presidential, parliamentary or semi-presidential – a country in transition from highly authoritarian rule chooses is of some consequence. There is a large literature on the relative merits of presidential and parliamentary systems for the development of democracy. The bulk of the evidence suggests that parliamentarism is more conducive to the flourishing of democracy than either a presidential or a semi-presidential system, the latter being one in which the highest executive power is divided between a president and a prime minister.[115] Semi-presidential systems occupy an increasingly important place in the constellation of governments. More than fifty countries have such dual executives.[116]

Moreover, within these dual executive systems, there is an important distinction between the countries in which the prime minister and cabinet are responsible *only* to the legislature and those in which the prime minister and cabinet are responsible *both* to the president and to parliament. It is the latter type, in which the president is much the stronger partner, that is mainly responsible for the statistics that show semi-presidential regimes to be less democratic than parliamentary systems.[117] In a semi-presidential system that is, nevertheless, democratic there is the possibility of awkward 'cohabitation' – a president who was elected at a different time from the legislature having to find a way of working with a prime minister and a parliamentary majority of a different political persuasion. That can lead to tension that is potentially destabilizing for the system, although the French Fifth Republic has survived such electoral outcomes remarkably smoothly.

In Russia, in contrast, parliament was gradually reduced to a condition of docile deference and dependency during the presidency of Vladimir Putin. Earlier, the system generated serious conflict between the legislature and the executive, with Boris Yeltsin employing tanks and shells to quell the most intransigent of his parliamentary opponents in 1993 – an extreme version of 'strong leadership' that elicited hardly a murmur of criticism from most Western governments. This was, in fact, a fateful step towards restoration of 'strongman' government, taking Russia in a more authoritarian direction. The choice of Putin as Yeltsin's successor consolidated a trend that was already underway.[118] This also raises the chicken-and-egg question about whether leaders and political elites in countries with a tradition of authoritarian rule opt for a strongly presidentialized semi-presidentialism, leading to an excessive concentration of power in the hands of the chief executive. We have to be careful not to make institutional design explain too much. Indeed, the Russian tradition of personalized power meant that when Putin ceded the presidency to his protégé Dmitriy Medvedev for a period of four years, because the constitution did not allow him more than two *consecutive* terms, he remained in political reality the stronger partner while holding what had hitherto been (and has again become) the less powerful post of prime minister within the dual executive.[119] Putin was the patron, Medvedev the client, and everyone knew it.

★

Leaders everywhere operate within historically conditioned political cultures. In the way they lead, they cannot rely on reason and argument alone, but must be able to appeal to emotion, sharing in the sense of identity of their party or group. In government, the minority of leaders who come to be revered and who retain the admiration of posterity, are those who have also fostered a sense of purpose within their country as a whole, who have provided grounds for trust and have offered a vision that transcends day-to-day decision-making. There are, though, many different styles of leadership within democracies and even within authoritarian regimes. The personality and beliefs of the leader matter – and some leaders matter much more than others. That does not mean that the more power the leader accumulates in his or her own hands, as distinct from those of governmental colleagues, the more outstanding is the person and the more effective the leadership. It does not imply, in other words (as I argue in greater detail in other chapters), that the optimal model for a head of government is that of the leader as *boss*.

2

Democratic Leadership: Myths, Powers, Styles

Tony Blair gets no further than the second page of the introduction to his memoirs before announcing: 'I won three general elections.'[1] He later adds: 'Political analysts and practising politicians love to speculate on this or that voting trend – and very often there is much truth in it – but there is always a tendency to underplay the importance of the leader.'[2] But is it a case of 'underplaying' or of recognizing that some political leaders are *not quite as important as they think they are*? If leaders are perceived by themselves and others to have played the decisive role in the winning of elections, this will have an impact on the way the government operates. Leaders who believe that election victories are more their personal triumphs than victories for their parties are inclined to take this as an entitlement to concentrate power in their hands. These quotations from Tony Blair (which could be multiplied from answers he has given in interviews) raise two questions. The first, and more important, is a general one: when people in parliamentary democracies cast their ballots, are they voting primarily for (or against) particular party leaders? Presidential systems, in which the chief executive is directly elected by citizens, are a separate case. The second question is more specific: how justified is Blair in using the first person singular when he refers to the Labour Party's victories in the British general elections of 1997, 2001 and 2005?

Of still greater concern than either of these questions is the issue of how we assess democratic leaders once the elections are over. That raises different questions. Is it true that heads of governments in democracies have become more dominant over time? Are calls for more power to be placed in the hands of the individual who heads the government justified? Or is there more to be said for collective leadership, in which at the national level authoritative figures in a political party are firmly in charge of government departments, but on major issues require the support of a group of their senior colleagues, to whom they are accountable (as well, of course, as being accountable to parliament and, ultimately, to the electorate)?

LEADERS AND ELECTION OUTCOMES

The political scientist Anthony King has described the 'near-universal belief' that leaders' and candidates' personalities are hugely important factors in determining the outcomes of elections as 'simply wrong'. That is not, King observes, to deny that leaders' personal characteristics count for something, simply that it is 'not for nearly as much as is generally supposed'. Summing up a study of modern elections in six countries, King concludes that 'it is quite unusual for leaders' and candidates' personalities and other personal traits to determine election outcomes'.[3] Among specialists who have made serious studies of the role of leaders in the determination of electoral outcomes – and their number has increased in the decade since King's work was published – there is no consensus. Some attribute more electoral significance to leaders than do others. Their work contains little, however, to justify certain political leaders' attribution of election victories primarily to themselves.

Given that there has been a general decline in the membership of political parties in democracies, and a decline also in long-term party allegiance, it might be supposed that the characteristics of the party leader will have become increasingly influential. Some evidence has, indeed, been adduced to support the proposition that leaders have become more important in the minds of voters, in substantial part as a result of change over the past half-century in the way the mass media report politics.[4] Quite often an increased 'personalization' has been turned into a case for the 'presidentialization' of politics within parliamentary systems.[5] Yet, while a greater focus on the top leader by parties and the mass media can be observed in many countries, this does not mean that voters are as obsessed with the top leader as are many politicians and most political journalists.[6] Not only is the idea that leaders everywhere have become more important for the outcome of elections highly questionable, but the portrayal of prime ministers as increasingly 'presidential', and more autonomous in the performance of their duties, has been overdrawn.

A recent scholarly monograph by Lauri Karvonen on the 'personalization' (as distinct from 'presidentialization') of politics brings together research on almost all of the world's most stable parliamentary democracies. This Finnish political scientist found 'no clear evidence for the notion that the importance of party leader evaluations for party choice has increased over time'. And contrary to some earlier speculation that people with a weak sense of party identification would set more store on the personality of the leader, the evidence pointed the other way.[7] It is party loyalists who have more intense support for particular leaders, suggesting that it is loyalty to the party that determines support for the captain of the team rather than the leader having great influence over the uncommitted. Another recent study underlines the point that the 'party label gets applied as a stereotype when voters are confronted by party leaders, and determines (to a large extent) how leaders will be perceived by voters'.[8] Thus, if you are already well disposed to the Christian Democrats in Germany, to the Liberal Party in Australia, to the French Socialists or to the Labour Party in Britain, you will be likely in the run-up to an election to approve of the leader of those parties, whoever he or she may be.

A focus on leaders is hardly an entirely new phenomenon, especially when the people in question were particularly formidable. William Gladstone and Benjamin Disraeli, rival politicians of legendary standing in nineteenth-century Britain, are obvious cases in point. In the second half of the twentieth century, however, television added a new dimension to the personalization of politics. The appearance and performance of the leader, as a significant component of the party image, became a more prominent feature of the electoral contest than it was in the century's earliest decades. As a source of information on the rival candidates, TV has, however, almost certainly passed its peak – especially in the majority of democracies, which do not allow money to determine who gets television time. The United States, with its paid TV political advertisements, is a partial exception here. Many people watching programmes far removed from ideological debate are not able entirely to escape from political propaganda in the advertising breaks, but, even then, only if they are watching live rather than recorded TV. More generally, however, the vast increase in the number of television channels has enabled those viewers who are not already politically engaged to avoid politicians and their debates. Still more important – and here the USA is very far from being an exception – has been the rise of the internet and the huge array of alternatives to political discussion that it offers, while at the same time providing opportunities for political argument unrelated to the views and personalities of leaders.

While no serious analyst suggests that the assessment of leaders is irrelevant to voters' choice, 'this effect is dwarfed by such "usual suspects" as party identity and preferences, as well as by socio-economic factors'.[9] Overall, neither the personalities of leaders nor citizens' evaluation of political leaders have become the main determinants of voter choice or of electoral outcomes.[10] A study of the impact of leaders in nine different democracies over half a century of elections concluded that the leader counted for something in all of them, but – unsurprisingly – more in presidential than in parliamentary systems. In particular, the impact of the leader on the outcome of presidential elections was found to be substantial in the United States.[11] Yet, even in America, the significance of the personality of the presidential candidates and the minutiae of the campaign, including presidential debates, can be overstated. If we take the examples of two highly articulate presidential candidates, with attractive personalities, who ran successful campaigns – John F. Kennedy in 1960 and Barack Obama in 2008 – it is tempting to attribute the electoral victories to their magnetism. On the basis of relevant survey research, Anthony King is dismissive of the view that Kennedy's narrow victory over Richard Nixon was due 'to his youth, charm, and elegance compared with Nixon's five-o-clock shadow and generally shifty demeanor'. King observes that 'Kennedy won because he was the Democratic Party's candidate in a year when the Democrats were almost certainly going to regain the White House anyway, not least because a substantial plurality of American voters were Democratic Party identifiers'.[12]

Obama also won in a propitious year for a Democratic contender for the presidency. The outgoing Republican president was exceptionally unpopular. One pollster in 2008 quipped that George W. Bush's 'job approval is almost as poor as that of King George III among the colonists 240 years ago'.[13] In a country where money matters much more in elections than in Europe – and where the sums involved are vastly greater – the Democrats, most unusually, outspent the Republicans. In their campaign advertisements, they successfully portrayed John McCain, who wished to distance himself from the unpopular Bush, as more of the same. When the campaign ended, McCain, as a major study of the 2008 election put it, was 'more likely than before to be seen as McSame, in part because, abetted by the media, the Democrats scraped the maverick label from him and sutured the name and face of the Republican incumbent in its place'.[14] The condition of the economy in late 2008, as the financial crisis began to manifest itself, also meant that this was not a good time to be repre- senting the party which had occupied the White House for the previous eight years. The *Wall Street Journal* characterized the US economy's performance in the closing months of 2008 as the worst in a quarter of a century.[15] That was all the more damaging for the Republicans, since the eight years when the last Democratic president, Bill Clinton, had occupied the White House were recalled as a time of economic buoyancy. Obama won convincingly in 2008 notwithstanding the fact that in surveys he scored no more highly than McCain in 'leadership qualities' or 'trustworthiness'. Only in empathy was his rating signifi- cantly higher than that of his Republican opponent.[16]

While the personality of the leader tends to count for more in presidential than in parliamentary systems, it is usually far from being the overwhelming determinant of voter choice. Thus, a survey-based study of French presidential elections between 1965 and 1995 found only one out of six in which the candidate's personality had a very substantial impact on the outcome – the election of General Charles de Gaulle in 1965 – as well as one in which it *probably* had a substantial impact. This was the next presidential election, that of 1969, which resulted in the victory of Georges Pompidou. The election had been triggered by the resignation of de Gaulle after he lost a referendum.[17] Discussing de Gaulle's earlier electoral victory, Roy Pierce noted: 'It requires a large imbalance in perceptions of leadership attributes to attract people away from a candidate whom they are predisposed to support on grounds of established political orientations. Such an imbal- ance existed in France in 1965.'[18]

Within parliamentary democracies with majoritarian (first-past-the-post) electoral systems, the impact of leaders is somewhat more of a factor in electoral choice than in countries that have proportional representation. PR makes coalition government more probable, and the electorate is further removed from the decision as to who will be prime minister. That will have to be agreed among the parties who are becoming coalition partners. There is also a modest general tendency for the electoral effect of leaders to be greater when the policy differences between parties are small. This leads two scholars to conclude: 'If parties abdicate, leaders may take over. However, if party polarization increases in the future, we would expect to see decreasing effects of party leader popularity on the vote.'[19] The same authors find some long-term increase in the impact of leaders on electoral outcomes in the United States and Sweden and a small downward trend in Canada. Importantly, however, their comparative study does *not* provide 'any clear confirmation of the hypothesis that the influence of party leaders [on elections] is generally on the rise'.[20]

Leaders' Influence on Electoral Outcomes in Britain

Before we turn specifically to the assertion of former British prime minister Tony Blair with which this chapter opened – and his role in the determination of victories in the British general elections of 1997, 2001 and 2005 – it is worth putting it in the context of post-Second World War elections. (Prior to that period, serious studies of elections, based on contemporary interviewing and survey research, did not exist.) In a very close-run election, since evaluations of leaders do count for something in voters' minds, the comparative standing of the two main rival party leaders may at times be of decisive importance for the victory of one party rather than the other. But it is very rare for this to occur. If any post-war British party leader made just that difference between victory and defeat for his party, it was Harold Wilson. It is even possible that Wilson did this twice, but only because the gap between the two main political parties was very close in these elections and his personal ascendancy over the Conservative Party leaders then was particularly wide. The first occasion was in 1964 when opinion polls showed Harold Wilson to be vastly preferred to Sir Alec

Douglas-Home, and the other time was February 1974 when Wilson had a large personal lead over Edward Heath. Labour ended only 0.7 per cent ahead of the Conservative Party in the 1964 election and had a majority of just four seats. In February 1974, the first of two general elections that year, Labour were 0.8 per cent ahead, but did not achieve an overall majority in the House of Commons.[21]*

Referring to the second of the two general elections of 1974, the director of a conservative think tank Policy Exchange wrote in 2012: 'No sitting prime minister has increased his or her share of the vote since 1974.'[22] Wilson's popularity no doubt played its part in that October 1974 victory when Labour won eighteen more seats than in February, but it was hardly decisive. The real point here is that 'prime minister' is being used as if it were a synonym for political party. As a plain statement of fact it is wrong. If we are to go no further back than the 2010 general election, we find that the sitting prime minister, Gordon Brown, *increased* his share of the vote by more than 6 per cent in the only election in which people were casting their ballots directly for or against him – the voters in his constituency of Kirkcaldy and Cowdenbeath.[23] The use of 'prime minister' as a substitute for 'party' is both misleading and an astonishingly widespread confusion.

It is, indeed, quite possible for a political party to win a general election even though its leader is less popular than the person heading the rival party. Thus, for example, when the Conservative Party comfortably won the British general election of 1970, the poll ratings of their leader Edward Heath were far below those accorded their party, and Heath was less popular than the Labour leader (and prime minister for the previous six years), Harold Wilson.[24] And when the Conservatives still more convincingly won the 1979 election, Margaret Thatcher trailed well behind the Labour leader and outgoing prime minister, James Callaghan, in popularity. The election took place on 3 May and in polling conducted on 28–30 April, Callaghan's lead over Mrs Thatcher was as much as 24 points. His personal lead appears to have declined somewhat in the last few days, but he remained far ahead of Thatcher, while his

* Wilson also happens to share with the Conservative Party leader throughout most of the inter-war years, Stanley Baldwin, the distinction of being the only British prime minister within the last hundred years to leave 10 Downing Street at a time unambiguously of his own choosing, neither forced out by the electorate nor – with varying degrees of gentle, or not so gentle, pressure – eased out by his own party.

party went down to defeat.[25]* Other parliamentary democracies offer similar examples, including Australia with its Westminster-type system. John Howard led the Australian Liberal Party (its name notwithstanding, the equivalent of the Conservative Party in Britain) to four successive election victories between 1996 and 2004. In two of these elections Howard's principal opponent, Labor Party leaders Paul Keating in 1996 and Kim Beazley in 1998 scored more highly in surveys of leadership qualities than did Howard.[26]

So what of Tony Blair's claim that *he* won three general elections? In an interview with the editor of the *Financial Times* in 2012, he said: 'Sometimes the way the media talks, you'd think that I'd lost three elections rather than won them . . .'[27] In fact, it has been much more common for journalists and many others unthinkingly to go along with Blair's belief that these victories were, above all, his than to question this repeated assertion. The extent to which attributing electoral outcomes to party leaders, not least in the case of Blair, has become commonplace but illusory has been brought out by the political scientists John Bartle and Ivor Crewe, the joint authors of a study of party leaders and general elections in Britain. Crewe (former Vice-Chancellor of the University of Essex and now Master of University College, Oxford) and Bartle write: 'We have experienced at first hand the stunned disbelief, bordering on hostility, of a non-academic audience on being told that the impact of Blair's and [John] Major's personalities on the 1997 election was negligible.'[28]

Although party loyalties are more fluid in Britain and in most democracies than they were half a century ago, it is still the case that people vote for a political party. In the general election of 1997 the main opposition party had an overwhelming advantage. It is very difficult in a genuine democracy for a governing party to win four, never mind five, elections in a row. The Conservatives had, against the odds, won four, but 'time for a change' sentiments militated strongly against them winning a fifth. Moreover, they had lost their reputation for economic competence, which had traditionally been one of their perceived strengths. While Margaret Thatcher was still

---

* The size of Callaghan's popularity advantage over Thatcher has done nothing to inhibit journalists from referring to the 1979 election as Mrs Thatcher's rout of James Callaghan.

prime minister, they had joined in 1990 a European economic project that was to be a forerunner of the common currency, the Exchange Rate Mechanism (ERM). On 16 September 1992, a day that became known as Black Wednesday, there was such a run on the pound sterling that the government had to make an ignominious exit from the ERM in order to devalue the currency, having first hiked interest rates to a level that would have been devastating for the domestic economy. The prime minister at the time, John Major, was later, quite correctly, to observe: 'On that day, a fifth consecutive Conservative election victory, which always looked unlikely unless the opposition were to self-destruct, became remote, if not impossible.'[29]

Until his sudden death in May 1994, John Smith was destined to be the next British prime minister. He had served in a Labour Cabinet under the leadership of James Callaghan and was a formidable politician known for his wit and common sense. He was not likely to 'self-destruct', to use Major's term.* However, Peter Mandelson – who had been close to Smith's predecessor, Neil Kinnock, and was to become still closer to Tony Blair, but was kept at arm's length by Smith – is just one of the politicians from Blair's circle to suggest that a Labour victory would have been less likely under Smith. He cites as evidence that at the end of 1992, Smith's satisfaction rating in opinion polls had fallen 'to plus 4'. He notes that at the same time Major's ratings were '*minus* 30 per cent'.[30] There was, in other words, a gap between the two leaders of 34 points. While the gulf between Blair and Major was to become still wider, no serious study of the leadership effect in the 1997 election has indicated that Labour would have had less than an overwhelming victory in Blair's absence.

The landslide – an overall Labour majority of 178 – itself owed much to an electoral system which translates a fairly modest percentage increase in popular votes into a disproportionately great advantage in seats. Labour's share of the popular vote was lower in 1997 than in all elections between 1945 and 1966, including those which Labour lost. The Conservatives, however, fared catastrophically. They had their

---

* Sir Leo Pliatzky was the most senior civil servant – Permanent Secretary – at the Department of Trade when John Smith was Secretary of State for Trade in 1978–79 and the youngest member of James Callaghan's Labour Cabinet. In a conversation I had with Pliatzky at a time when Smith was Leader of the Opposition, he said: 'John Smith was a very good minister, and he'll be an even better prime minister.'

lowest share of the vote of the century, as well as their worst result since 1906 in terms of seats.[31] They had become so unpopular that any Labour leader who did not 'self-destruct' would have led the party to an overall majority of well over a hundred seats in the House of Commons. Bartle and Crewe calculate that had Major and Blair 'been evaluated equally favourably, Labour's majority would have been cut from 11.9 to 11.0 points, altering the outcome in just four seats'.[32]

Labour's second successive election victory – in 2001 – owed a great deal to the perception that they had, in contrast with their predecessors, been running the economy competently. As the major study of this election noted, that 'was crucial as a determinant of voting choice'.[33] It was loss of confidence in the Conservatives' economic competence which contributed greatly to their electoral defeat in 1997, while doubts on this score about Labour had been disadvantageous to them in the past. The person who was running the economy in the government led by Blair was the Chancellor of the Exchequer, Gordon Brown. Treasury ministers in virtually all governments in any country are important, but it is generally agreed that Brown's dominance over economic policy was more than usually great. No doubt in 2001, as in 1997, Blair was still an electoral asset, but it is no less clear that he was a far from decisive one in securing the party's electoral victory.

By 2005 the increasing unpopularity of the war in Iraq, launched two years previously, meant that Blair was even further from being the reason for Labour's election victory. As was widely known to the electorate, Blair had taken a lead in backing the administration of George W. Bush in their desire to initiate military action against Saddam Hussein's Iraq, and in committing British troops to this war of choice. Since, however, the main opposition party, the Conservatives, had also given vociferous support to the invasion of Iraq, it was the Liberal Democrats who were able most effectively to tap into popular discontent with Labour's Middle East policy. Their share of the vote increased by almost four percentage points to 22 per cent and their number of parliamentary seats from fifty-two to sixty-two.[34] This was far less dangerous to Labour than any addition to the swing to the Conservatives would have been. Neither of the main political parties could generate much public enthusiasm. In their victory, the Labour Party received just over nine and a half million votes, more than two million fewer than they obtained in 1992 when, on a higher turnout and under Neil Kinnock's leadership, they lost the election to the Conservatives.* Taken as a whole, the evidence suggests that Blair's electoral value was less than has been widely assumed. And, contrary to what appears to be his own belief, it did not make the difference between victory and defeat in any of the three elections which the Labour Party won during his leadership.

HAVE DEMOCRATIC LEADERS BECOME MORE DOMINANT OVER TIME?

In the course of the twentieth century most central governments in democracies acquired more powers. The dominance of the central executive, to the extent that it has occurred, is not, however, the same thing as the domination of the head of government within the executive, even though there is some limited evidence to support the idea that democratic leaders have become more powerful over time. That applies most unambiguously to the role played by heads of government internationally. They have, as was noted in Chapter 1, been thrust into the forefront of foreign policy-making as a result of the growth in the speed of communications. That has facilitated both the ease of interaction among prime ministers and presidents and the expectation

---

* A separate issue is how much the emphasis on change within the Labour Party, and the use of the term 'New Labour', of which Blair, Peter Mandelson and Gordon Brown were the main progenitors, contributed to the scale of the electoral victory in 1997. The crude dichotomy between 'New Labour' and 'Old Labour' had some appeal for conservative newspaper proprietors, but it was oddly indiscriminating. Blair, in particular, seemed to distance himself from his party's history – with the term 'Old Labour' apparently embracing such major Labour figures as Clement Attlee, Ernest Bevin, Hugh Gaitskell, Harold Wilson, James Callaghan and Denis Healey, as if they belonged under the same label as Trotskyists, 'trendy lefties' or socialist fundamentalists who had been among the party's members in the past but who had no influence on the policies of previous Labour governments. By 2005 any novelty value that the image of 'New Labour' may have possessed had worn off. More fundamentally, although Blair and some of his colleagues continued to talk about 'Old Labour' and 'New Labour', no party called 'New Labour' ever appeared on the ballot paper in a general election, and the significance of the notion can easily be exaggerated. Voters cast their ballot for the candidates of the Labour Party, albeit by 2005 in far smaller numbers than in the past. In any event, this attempt at rebranding was quietly abandoned by Blair's successor but one as Labour leader, Ed Miliband.

that this would take place. Wise heads of government pay great heed to the expertise accumulated in their foreign ministries and work closely with the senior politician who heads it, for even those whose interest hitherto has been mainly in domestic politics cannot avoid the international stage. Most of them come quite quickly to enjoy it. As Harold Macmillan – the British prime minister whose period of office coincided with Dwight D. Eisenhower (in his last years in the presidency) and John F. Kennedy in the United States, General Charles de Gaulle in France, Nikita Khrushchev in the Soviet Union and Chancellor Konrad Adenauer in West Germany – wryly observed, he was a 'politician' at home but a 'statesman' whenever he went abroad.[35] (Harry Truman put it differently, but no less ironically, when he said that 'a statesman is a dead politician'.)[36]

The Constraints of the American Presidency

One of the reasons why the term 'presidentialization' is misleading when used to describe the role of prime ministers in parliamentary democracies is because the best known presidency of all, that of the United States, is an office which constrains its leader domestically more thoroughly than do the limitations on the power of most European premiers. That results, above all, from the strictness of the American separation of powers. A different electoral cycle for presidency and legislature means that Congress can be under the control of a different party from that of the president, and there are times when, with Congress responding to different pressures and lobbies, even a majority in the legislature belonging to his own party has been no guarantee that the president will get his way. In recent years, however, the split between the party represented in the White House and that controlling the House of Representatives has become a still greater limitation on presidential power than in the past. This results from a rise in unyielding partisanship, with fewer members of Congress voting independently.

The autonomous political power of the US Supreme Court, willing on ostensibly legal grounds to strike down presidential decisions or legislation which had the president's backing, is also a greater judicial impediment than most prime ministers have to contend with. And though the American president *is* the embodiment of the central executive power in a way in which a prime minister in a parliamentary democracy is not, the sheer size and complexity of the federal government makes it difficult for the president to determine government policy. Indeed, it has even been argued that 'the White House staff constitutes the *only* organization in the federal government on which the president can put his personal imprint, and from which he can expect accountability and loyalty'.[37] As a former US government official turned scholar, Harold Seidman, observed, even if an American president dislikes members of his cabinet, disagrees with them, and suspects their loyalty, 'he cannot destroy their power without seriously undermining his own'. Seidman adds:

The occupant of the 'most powerful office on earth' quickly learns the harsh truth. His executive power has a very frail constitutional foundation – the power to appoint officers of the United States. Appointing authority may be so hedged with qualifications as to limit severely his discretion. He can fire officers performing administrative duties but here again his power is limited. Dismissal of a high official is a measure of last resort which can be utilized only under extreme provocation.[38]

The limitations on the power of appointment were well illustrated by Bill Clinton's difficulty in appointing an Assistant Attorney General for Civil Rights in 1993. His first choice was Lani Guinier, a University of Pennsylvania professor who had been one of his Yale Law School classmates. It soon became clear that there was sufficient opposition to her from within the Senate that her nomination was unlikely to be ratified and, rather than suffer a drawn-out defeat, Clinton abandoned the effort. His next candidate for the same post, another African-American lawyer, John Payton, also encountered opposition from within Congress, and he himself withdrew from contention. 'Eventually', as Clinton notes, he nominated Deval Patrick, 'another brilliant African-American lawyer with a strong civil rights background' and 'he did a fine job'. But Clinton was left to regret that he had lost the friendship of Guinier.[39] More recently, President Barack Obama ran into trouble, trying to fill a much higher governmental office. His first choice to succeed Hillary Clinton as Secretary of State in 2013 was the US ambassador to the United Nations (and his long-time foreign policy adviser), Susan Rice. Fierce Republican opposition led the president reluctantly to agree to her withdrawing her candidacy.[40] And these are just a small sample of the limitations on what is regarded as one of the president's main prerogatives, 'the power to appoint officers of the United States'.

No one doubts that in the USA, if not quite to the same degree as in European democracies, more power over the past century has accrued to central government collectively. However, if we look at the past hundred years and more, it is a great oversimplification to see the power of the chief executive in America following an upward curve of *increased* power *within* the government. Theodore Roosevelt was a more dominant figure than such inter-war presidents as Warren Harding, Calvin Coolidge and Herbert Hoover. Franklin D. Roosevelt, Hoover's successor, brought about an upsurge in presidential dominance through political skill and his popular appeal. It was he who first took advantage of radio as a way of influencing public opinion with his highly effective 'fireside chats'. Roosevelt had a supremely confident leadership style, but the instant impact he made was based also on concrete actions, including an impressive inaugural address, his calling Congress into emergency session, and his tackling of the financial crisis. He was sensitive to public moods and adept in the timing of his initiatives. He was an unusually forceful president and made dramatic use of his power of veto.* So much so that by the end of his second term his vetoes amounted to 'more than 30 per cent of all the measures disallowed by presidents since 1792'.[41] For a time there was an assumption that Roosevelt's incumbency heralded a long-lasting increase in the power of what was to be dubbed 'the modern presidency'. The advent of it has generally been dated to the late 1930s and FDR's second term. It was at that very time, however, that Roosevelt overreached himself by trying to expand the membership of the Supreme Court in order to change the political balance within it. Having won a landslide victory in 1936, Roosevelt appeared to be at the height of his powers when he tried to increase the size of the Court in order to add justices who would be supportive of New Deal

---

* When Congress presents the president with a bill to sign into law, he has the option of vetoing it. The presidential veto can, however, be overridden if both chambers of Congress vote by a two-thirds majority to overturn it. The very fact that the veto exists can lead to bargaining between the different branches of government in order to avoid a presidential veto. Use of the veto, however, carries risks, since much depends on whose side the public takes. A president who is popular at the time, as Roosevelt was, may use the veto more profusely than one who is unpopular.

policies. His bill not only failed to pass, it also consolidated a coalition of opponents of Roosevelt's domestic agenda. As a leading specialist on the American presidency observed:

Some members of Congress who broke with FDR in 1937 never again would accord him the same degree of loyalty they had in his first term. Similarly, the dispute produced divisions among reformers of many types, undermining the bipartisan support for the New Deal and confirming for Republican progressives their suspicions that the New Dealers were interested in self-aggrandizement and concentrating power in Washington.[42]

Truman, as already noted in Chapter 1, reposed greater trust in his cabinet secretaries than had been characteristic of Roosevelt and was generally more supportive of them. His successor, Dwight D. Eisenhower, was also a less dominant policy-maker than Roosevelt and was readier to devolve responsibility to his subordinates, and to trust them, than FDR had been. Eisenhower's Second World War career, which had involved a good deal of diplomacy, had given him incomparably better preparation for his international role than is afforded presidents who move directly from state governorships to the White House. When, for example, his foreign counterparts were French president Charles de Gaulle and British prime ministers Winston Churchill, Anthony Eden and Harold Macmillan, in each one of these cases he was dealing with people whom he had known during the war. Yet, Eisenhower allowed his secretary of state, John Foster Dulles, great leeway. Much disliked in Western Europe, Dulles was described by Churchill as 'a dull, unimaginative, uncomprehending, insensitive man' and, more pithily on another occasion, as 'Dull, Duller, Dulles'.[43]

Presidential Powers and Leadership Styles – the American Case

The Supreme Court can be a real obstacle to a president's ambitions, as Harry Truman found when, during the Korean War, the Court stopped him from temporarily nationalizing the steel industry, which was undergoing at the time a major industrial dispute. However, the Supreme Court at its best can on occasion add lustre to a presidency. This was surely the case with Dwight Eisenhower. He wished to avoid conflict over civil rights and reluctantly accepted, rather than welcomed, the Supreme Court's landmark verdict in *Brown v. the Board of Education of Topeka* in 1954, which desegregated schools and presaged conflict between the federal government and southern states wishing to maintain separate and unequal education. The driving force behind federal support for civil rights was Eisenhower's attorney general, Herbert Brownell, and the most crucial judgements were those of the Supreme Court, headed by the liberal Republican, Earl Warren, whom Eisenhower himself had nominated. So far as civil rights – those of black Americans, most specifically – were concerned, Eisenhower's recent and sympathetic biographer, Jim Newton, observes that 'Eisenhower's record in that area reflected a triumph of leadership style over personal conviction: he trusted Brownell to lead'. Thus, while Eisenhower 'balked occasionally, the administration made progress despite Ike's own reservations'.[44]

Although the Supreme Court's ruling brought about the backlash in southern states which Eisenhower had feared, he was determined to uphold the federal law. When a white supremacist mob tried to prevent black students from attending school in Little Rock, Arkansas, the mayor, Woodrow Wilson Mann, appealed for federal troops to 'restore peace and order'. Deliberately bypassing the state government, the mayor was only too well aware that they were fully supporting the violent opposition to integration. The response of the federal government was much more receptive. In addition to his commitment to the rule of law, Eisenhower was acutely conscious of how damaging it was to America's reputation internationally to have pictures going round the world of a white mob bullying black pupils who were doing no more than asserting their legal right to attend school. The president sent in federal troops and their presence enabled the law to be implemented. As Eisenhower's biographer notes: 'The racists who were brave enough to confront defenceless high school students shrank back in the face of the U.S. Army.'[45]

Although styles of presidential leadership vary, and some have found more time for leisure pursuits than others, they have in common the fact that every American president comes under immense pressure. Throughout the twentieth century the United States was a major power, then one of the two 'superpowers', and subsequently, following the dissolution of the Soviet Union, indisputably the world's most politically influential and militarily powerful state. While American presidents have also encountered – sometimes to their surprise – the very real limitations on their authority worldwide, it remains the case that their international policy decisions tend to matter more than do those of their foreign contemporaries. They would all, no doubt, have felt able to sympathize with Eisenhower when, following a serious heart attack, he expressed some exasperation with the medical profession in a letter to a friend: "'I am to avoid all situations that tend to bring about such reactions as irritation, frustration, anxiety, fear and, above all anger", Ike wrote. "When doctors give me such instructions, I say to them, 'Just what do you think the Presidency is?'"'[46]

Of the presidents who have held office since Franklin Roosevelt, perhaps only Lyndon B. Johnson has exercised as much power both within the executive and vis-à-vis the other branches of government as FDR, albeit over a much shorter period and with far less popular acclaim.* One of Johnson's major biographers describes him as 'the most ardent presidential lawmaker of the twentieth century', outdoing even the hyper-activist Roosevelt.[47] In foreign policy, too, LBJ personally took big decisions, though with much less positive outcomes than those of FDR. Johnson's domestic achievements were ultimately overshadowed by the great loss of American lives – and far greater Vietnamese losses – in an unnecessary war which the United States lost. Although Johnson considered American involvement in Vietnam to be a poisoned chalice he had inherited from Kennedy, he also believed that once the USA was committed there, it could not afford to fail.[48]

Ronald Reagan's presidency has been described as one of 'extreme delegation', which worked well when he had appointed highly competent people with strong political skills – George Shultz as Secretary of State was a notable example – but which 'turned into a disaster' in the persons of Donald Regan, John Poindexter and Oliver North.[49] Reagan's background as a film actor had led to scepticism about his qualifications for the presidency – although they had been bolstered by his governorship of California – but his response, as his second term of office drew

---

* While Roosevelt had more followers than Johnson, he was scarcely less lacking in enemies. A Connecticut country club is supposed to have banned mention of his name as a precaution against apoplexy. In Kansas a man disappeared into his cellar, announcing that he would not come up until Roosevelt was out of office, although before he had a chance to re-emerge, his wife seized the opportunity to go off with a travelling salesman.

to a close, was to say that 'there have been times in this office when I've wondered how you could do the job if you hadn't been an actor'.[50] It was generally agreed that Reagan conducted the ceremonial aspects of the presidency with aplomb. He was also an effective communicator in set speeches, although much less so in open-ended press conferences when his lack of detailed knowledge was a serious handicap. Speaking in 1984, Reagan said: 'FDR, Kennedy, and Teddy Roosevelt loved the Office of the Presidency and the bully pulpit it afforded them. And so do I.'[51]

Reagan focused on a few big issues that he felt strongly about. These were, most notably, cutting taxes, promoting his Strategic Defense Initiative, aiding anti-communist guerrillas in Central America, and fighting the Cold War both rhetorically and through increased defence spending, while looking for a Soviet leader with whom he could begin a dialogue. In principle, he was in favour of small government, low taxes and balanced budgets. However, any idea that he achieved this is wholly fanciful. The tax reductions benefited mainly the wealthy, and as a share of national income, federal income tax remained steady throughout the 1980s. As for 'small government', there were more people employed in the federal government by 1989 than there were in 1981. And, having poured scorn on the federal budget deficit left by the Carter administration, Reagan bequeathed a vastly greater deficit to his successor, George H.W. Bush.[52] On most issues, Reagan was 'exceptionally detached from details' and even his closest aides frequently had to guess what he wanted them to do.[53] He was lucky in two respects. One was that the 1980s saw a sharp decline in the price of oil, which helped the American economy and damaged that of the Soviet Union. The other was the emergence of Mikhail Gorbachev as Soviet leader early in Reagan's second term. During his first term, relations with the Soviet adversary had gone from bad to worse and Gorbachev's fortuitous elevation, after the deaths of three aged Soviet leaders in quick succession, had nothing whatsoever to do with Reagan's policies.

Nevertheless, just as Napoleon liked lucky generals, so millions of Americans decided they liked a lucky president. Reagan also made some of his own luck. He was unlucky to be shot in the 1981 assassination attempt – although fortunate that the bullet narrowly missed his heart. However, Reagan's 'Honey, I forgot to duck' to his wife, and saying to the medical staff when he was wheeled into the operating theatre, 'I hope you are all Republicans', confirmed his sense of humour and enhanced his popularity. Reagan's charm and optimism, which many Americans appreciated, served him well when he approved a deal which on the face of it was duplicitous and later more or less shrugged it off as an oversight. Admittedly, this 'Iran and Contras affair' saw Reagan's approval ratings fall to 47 per cent, but that was not a bad level of support in the circumstances. He fared much better than the charmless Richard Nixon did when, with the Watergate break-in and cover-up, he committed what could be considered a somewhat lesser offence. Reagan, for his part, had authorized secret arms deliveries to Iran in the hope that this would lead to the freeing of American hostages being held in Tehran. Oliver North came up with the 'neat idea' of overcharging the Iranians and siphoning the profits to support the Nicaraguan Contras.[54] The enterprise was not only against the law, but also botched. The illegal arms went not to Iranian 'moderates' but to hardliners who had supported the taking of American hostages in the first place.[55]

Yet, this discreditable episode paled into insignificance compared with a major achievement – the part Reagan played in the ending of the Cold War in the second half of the 1980s, once a Soviet leader had arrived on the scene with whom, in Margaret Thatcher's words, it was possible to 'do business'. The idea that Reagan could take a friendly stroll alongside the General Secretary of the Communist Party of the Soviet Union in Red Square or deliver a stirring and well-received speech to Moscow State University students, standing underneath a framed portrait of Vladimir Lenin, would have seemed preposterous in 1980. Yet these things happened in the summer of 1988. In the final analysis, Reagan's popularity both during and since his presidency is further testimony to the importance for a political leader of being able to tap into emotions and feelings, since they often count for more than the most cogent arguments.

If one possible criterion of a successful presidency is popularity at the end of two terms of office, then Bill Clinton qualifies as the most successful of the last half-century. It is not a wholly satisfactory standard of judgement, for Truman's up-and-down poll ratings were particularly low in his last two years in office, yet his stock has risen with the passage of time.[56] Clinton, for his part, was not 'strong' in the LBJ sense, for he had far less sway over Congress. For much of the time he faced an unremittingly hostile Republican majority, with Newt Gingrich at its head. To win over the likes of Gingrich was impossible, but Clinton also failed to forge good relations with the veteran Democrat, Daniel Patrick Moynihan, at a time when Moynihan still chaired the Senate Finance Committee.[57] In his first term, Clinton's Health Care flagship legislation – the detailed preparation of which had been entrusted to his wife, Hillary – came a cropper. Clinton's foreign policy record was mixed, but he did have much more success in his second term in getting incremental domestic change through Congress. And while safeguarding such programmes as Medicaid (which provided safeguards for the poor, whereas Medicare, which he also supported, benefited mainly the middle class), he, nevertheless, was able to leave his successor the gift of a balanced budget.

Especially from 1998, with the revelation of the Monica Lewinsky affair, Clinton was battered by unremitting attention to his personal life from the mass media, his Republican opponents and an obsessively hostile Special Prosecutor (or 'special persecutor'), Kenneth Starr. Yet, he ended his second term of office with the highest presidential approval ratings at the close of a presidency since Kennedy's at the time of his assassination.[58] Clinton combined intelligence and an impressive grasp of policy detail with enormous skill as a campaigner and speaker. He was able to radiate optimism. He had an empathetic and emotional appeal, which goes quite a long way towards explaining not only the survival of his presidency (in the face of attempts to impeach him) but also of his popularity while he was under prurient and sustained onslaught from press, television and rampaging political opponents. His focus on the economy, and the sense of economic well-being in the United States in the 1990s, was a major buttress of Clinton's popularity. Yet his presidency in the immediate aftermath of the end of the Cold War was also one of missed opportunities. His basically sympathetic biographer, Joe Klein, concludes his appraisal with the back-handed compliment: 'He remains the most compelling politician of his generation, although that isn't saying very much.'[59]

The constraints upon the American president, the variations in power relations from one president to another, and the oversimplification involved in seeing a linear increase in presidential power within the system are not only important in themselves. They give grounds for caution about using 'presidentialization' as a way of describing a conjectured increase in the power of prime ministers in parliamentary democracies. Another reason why this is a misleading term to apply is that in the many dual-executive systems that now exist, there is a wide variation in the distribution of power between the president and the prime minister. In some, including France, the president is very much the senior partner in determining policy, although that applies significantly more to foreign than to domestic policy. In other countries, including Germany, Israel and Ireland, it is the chancellor in the German case, the prime minister in Israel, and the Taoiseach (prime minister) in the Irish case who is the undisputed head of the government, while the president, as head of state, has high status but negligible power.

PRIME MINISTERIAL POWERS AND LEADERSHIP STYLES – THE BRITISH CASE

If we turn to the other main case (besides the United States) explored in this chapter, namely the United Kingdom, it is also an oversimplification, if we look at the past hundred years and more, to see the head of executive following an upward curve of increased prime ministerial power. There have been a great many zigzags. If we take the popular view that a strong prime minister is one who intervenes frequently in a variety of policy areas, imposes his or her will on colleagues and takes many important decisions personally, then David Lloyd George, not only during the First World War but also as head of the government which followed it, was more powerful than any of the three prime ministers (Arthur Bonar Law, Ramsay MacDonald and Stanley Baldwin) who held that office between his removal in 1922 and the elevation to the premiership of Neville Chamberlain in 1937.

When Lloyd George wished to come to an economic and political settlement with the new Communist regime in Russia, he took with him Lord Swinton, then the Secretary for Overseas Trade, rather than Lord Curzon who, as Foreign Secretary, might have been expected to conduct the negotiations and who was, at the very least, entitled to be present. Swinton recognized this, and once said to Lloyd George: 'If you treated me as you do Curzon, I would quit. I cannot understand why Curzon does not resign.' Lloyd George replied: 'Oh, but he does, constantly. There are two messengers in the Foreign Office: one has a club foot, he comes with the resignation: the other is a champion runner, he always catches him up.'[60] Curzon liked office too much to relinquish it voluntarily. His arrogance meant that he was little liked not only by Lloyd George but also by his Conservative colleagues in the coalition government, so he contented himself with letting off steam to close friends and to his wife. Writing to Lady Curzon about Lloyd George, he complained: 'I am getting very tired of trying to work with that man. He wants his Forn. Sec. to be a valet, almost a drudge . . .'[61]

Lloyd George achieved his dominance with a mixture of guile and sheer force of personality. Even in a Cabinet that contained some outstanding people, none seemed to rival the brilliance of the prime minister. Neville Chamberlain, prime minister from 1937 to 1940, had none of Lloyd George's sparkle, and whereas Lloyd George never lived in fear of other strong personalities or of being outshone, Chamberlain kept out of his Cabinet able critics. There was no place for Winston Churchill, Leo Amery or Harold Macmillan who would have challenged his views. Churchill, as late as 1936, was still distrusted by most Conservatives because of his intemperate position on India, and he lost further ground within the House of Commons in that year with his championship of Edward VIII during the abdication crisis. (The film *The King's Speech* could not have been further removed from historical reality when it portrayed Churchill as an early ally of King George VI. The mutual esteem between the two men developed only after Churchill became prime minister in 1940.)[62] Chamberlain lost his Foreign Secretary when Anthony Eden did what Curzon had merely threatened to do and resigned because of the way Chamberlain was conducting personal diplomacy. 'It was,' said Swinton, 'an increasingly impossible position for a Foreign Secretary to be in, especially for one as sensitive about his importance and private feelings of pride as Eden was.'[63] Even before he became prime minister, however, Chamberlain had regarded himself as the strong man of the government at a time when he was Chancellor of the Exchequer under MacDonald and Baldwin and nominally number three after them. The kind of prime minister he intended to become is foreshadowed in his comment to his sister in March 1935: 'As you will see I have become a sort of Acting P.M. – only without the actual power of the P.M. I have to say "Have you thought" or "What would you say" when it would be quicker to say "That is what you must do".'[64]

Churchill and Attlee

The principal difference between Mr Churchill and a cat, as Mark Twain might say, is that a cat has only nine lives. By all the laws of mortality, Mr Churchill should have perished a score of times, sometimes in laughter, sometimes in anger, sometimes in contempt; but the funeral has always been premature, the grave always empty. You may scotch him for a moment, but you cannot kill him, and we grow weary of pronouncing his obsequies . . . His failures are monumental, but the energy of his mind and the sheer impetus of his personality make his failures more brilliant than other men's successes.[65]

So wrote the journalist and essayist, A.G. Gardiner – in a book published in 1926. At that time Churchill was a senior member of the Conservative government led by Stanley Baldwin. Churchill had first stood for parliament in 1899, successfully in 1900. At first a Conservative, in 1904 he switched to the Liberal Party, and by 1910 held the senior Cabinet post of Home Secretary. He was in government for most of the years between then and 1922 when the Lloyd George coalition government fell. Soon after that Churchill rejoined the Conservative Party. By the time Gardiner wrote so perceptively about him, Churchill was Chancellor of the Exchequer. Throughout the 1930s he was at odds with the leadership of his party, and only with the start of the Second World War in 1939 did he rejoin the government. A major issue which had caused the rift was India. Within government and out of it, Churchill objected to even tentative steps towards Indian self-government, a subject on which he felt strongly. In the second half of the 1930s, he also became increasingly critical of the government's policy of making concessions to Nazi Germany, in the hope of averting war, and was a strong critic of the 1938 Munich agreement between Hitler and Chamberlain, which led to the dismemberment of Czechoslovakia. When Germany invaded Poland in September 1939 and Britain declared war on Germany, the policy of appeasement had manifestly failed to prevent major conflict. Churchill's warnings were more widely seen as prescient and he was invited by Chamberlain to join the War Cabinet – as First Lord of the Admiralty, a post he had first held in 1911.

There was, nevertheless, an accidental element in Churchill's becoming prime minister in May 1940. Chamberlain still commanded the support of a substantial majority of Conservative MPs but was thoroughly disliked by the main opposition Labour Party. In sharp contrast with his predecessor, Baldwin, he had treated them with disdain. When a significant minority of Conservative MPs criticized Chamberlain and the conduct of the war in a House of Commons debate on 7 and 8 May 1940, the Labour opposition took the opportunity to press a vote. The government majority dropped from 213 to 81 and Chamberlain's position was fatally weakened. It was clear that the government had to be reconstructed, and under someone else. However strange it may appear today, had Lord Halifax, Eden's successor as Foreign Secretary, wished to be prime minister, the post could have been his, notwithstanding the serious disadvantage of his being in the House of Lords, not the Commons.

It was not until 1965 that Conservative MPs elected their leader, and the constitutional convention (which still prevails) that the monarch asks a person who can count on the support of a majority in the House of Commons to form a government left, in 1940, some discretion in the hands of King George VI. The king made clear his preference for Halifax who was also the choice of Chamberlain. All the indications are that Halifax was also favoured by most Conservative members of parliament. The leading historian of the Conservative Party, Robert Blake, wrote: 'By May 1940 there was a small minority of Conservative MPs who saw in Churchill the one hope of injecting purpose, energy, and originality into the war, but there can be little doubt that the party would have chosen Halifax had there been an election. But there was not; the question turned on advice to the Crown rather than counting of heads . . .'[66]

However, Labour made clear that they would not enter a coalition government led by Chamberlain, and, no less crucially, Halifax made it plain that he did not want the premiership. He recognized that Churchill's talents were more suited to the task of mobilizing a nation than were his own.[67] Churchill proceeded to form a coalition government with strong Labour and some Liberal representation. The Labour leader, Clement Attlee, became his deputy, chairing meetings during Churchill's not infrequent absences. Neville Chamberlain remained in the Cabinet, and also as Leader of the Conservative Party, but by late summer 1940 he was terminally ill. He resigned from the Cabinet in October and died the following month. Only with Chamberlain's departure was Churchill able to add the leadership of his party to the prime ministership. On this issue, Blake observes: 'There was no lack of high minded persons to advise Churchill that he would be better placed to unify the nation if he was not tied to the leadership of a party. Churchill had more sense. He had seen the fate of Lloyd George . . . He at once indicated that he would accept the leadership, and by now his prestige made his unanimous election a certainty.'[68]

Churchill was the dominating figure in the government and in particular charge of defence and foreign policy. He had invented for himself the post of Minister of Defence, to accompany the prime ministership, just in case anyone should be in doubt about who was in charge of that area. A War Cabinet was formed which initially consisted of just five members, three Conservative and two Labour. By 1945 its membership had increased to eight. Other ministers attended when there were important matters arising from their departments. This smaller than usual Cabinet was supplemented, as had already become normal in peacetime, by a system of Cabinet committees. In the earlier days of his premiership Churchill read Cabinet documents more assiduously than later in the war. His focus, his private secretary, John (Jock) Colville, noted, was on 'defence, foreign affairs and party politics', much less on 'domestic problems or the home front except when he was aroused for sentimental reasons'.[69]

While some aspects of Winston Churchill's wartime prime ministership are still a matter for debate, there is no disputing the inspirational quality of his leadership during those years. In the words of the great American broadcasting journalist, Ed Murrow, who was in London throughout the Blitz, Churchill 'mobilized the English language and sent it into battle'. It was not just Churchill's eloquence and the manner of delivery which, in both his parliamentary speeches and his radio broadcasts, were so galvanizing, but, as the writer Vita Sackville-West put it, 'the whole massive backing of power and resolve behind them'.[70] Moreover, aristocratic lineage notwithstanding, Churchill established during the five years of his wartime leadership a closer rapport with the British people, including those in bomb-devastated working-class areas of London and other cities, than did the more middle-class representatives of his party in government. He also had the sense, in consultation with Attlee, to give highly visible Cabinet posts to two very able Labour politicians of humble origins,

Ernest Bevin, who was Minister of Labour from the outset of Churchill's government, and Herbert Morrison who, from October 1940, was Home Secretary and Minister of Home Security.[71]

These two leading figures in the Labour Party – who strongly disliked each other – were more in the public eye than Attlee. His work was behind the scenes (as a coordinator, chairman of Cabinet committees and of the War Cabinet itself when Churchill was ill or away) but all three of them were particularly important members of the coalition government. From the outset, Attlee was de facto deputy prime minister and from 1942 had that title officially. An outstanding administrator, Sir John Anderson (Viscount Waverley), who late in his career had become an Independent MP, was also to become a key member of the Cabinet. The most prominent Conservative within the coalition government was Anthony Eden who returned to the Foreign Secretaryship, from which he had resigned under Chamberlain, succeeding Halifax in late 1940. In the course of the war, he became the number-two figure within his party after Churchill. However, as the voice of his country at home and abroad, and in his detailed involvement with military operations, there is no doubt about Churchill's wartime dominance.

Churchill's very preoccupation with military strategy and interaction with the military high command and with foreign leaders meant, however, that the whole of domestic policy was more influenced by Attlee and the Labour members of the coalition government than by the prime minister. Among their Conservative colleagues within the government, R.A. (Rab) Butler played a significant role, both as the architect of the 1944 Education Act and as an important member of the Reconstruction Committee, established in 1943. Churchill's interest in the domestic agenda was at best sporadic, and the observations of Colville on this are supported in a recent scholarly study by an author, Robert Crowcroft, whose findings are coloured neither by admiration of Churchill nor by any iota of sympathy for the British Labour Party. Absurdly, he describes Attlee as 'an English Stalin' who 'would have thrived in the Byzantine politics of the Soviet Union'.[72] Yet, the evidence Crowcroft adduces shows the limitations (much more understandable, given the circumstances, than the author allows) of Churchill's control over the government. From 1943 the senior Labour members of the Cabinet were increasingly in charge of planning for post-war reconstruction and with laying the foundations of the welfare state. When he did get involved, Churchill had to concede a lot of ground. After one Cabinet meeting in October 1943, he complained that he had been 'jostled and beaten up by the Deputy Prime Minister'.[73] That hardly accords with the popular perception of Churchill and Attlee. Their personalities could not, indeed, have been more different. One was among the most theatrical of politicians, the other the least flamboyant.

Attlee, while notably loyal to every institution to which he belonged – including, naturally, the coalition government – was never a pushover. He was also a stickler for procedure. At the beginning of 1945, he typed with two fingers a two-thousand-word letter of protest to Churchill, doing so himself in order that his criticism would remain strictly between the two men themselves. This was an unusually long letter from Attlee, of whom it was aptly said that he would never use one word when none would do. He observed that it was 'very exceptional' for Churchill to have read Cabinet committee conclusions when these papers went to the Cabinet. Consequently, half an hour or more would be wasted 'explaining what could have been grasped by two or three minutes reading of the document'. Moreover: 'Not infrequently a phrase catches your eye which gives rise to a disquisition on an interesting point only slightly connected with the subject matter.' But, said Attlee, there was 'something worse'. Churchill paid far too much attention to two ministers who were not members of the War Cabinet, Lord Beaverbrook and Brendan Bracken. (These were Churchill's personal cronies. However, far from spelling that out, Attlee did not even refer to them by name – only by their official titles, the Lord Privy Seal and the Minister of Information.) Attlee strongly asserted the supremacy of the Cabinet, writing: 'There is a serious constitutional issue here. In the eyes of the country and under our constitution the eight members of the War Cabinet take responsibility for decisions.'[74]

Although Attlee had taken such pains to keep his missive confidential, Churchill read the letter over the telephone to Beaverbrook who the following day unexpectedly described it as 'a very good letter'. According to the private secretary, and excellent diarist, Colville, this was the 'last straw' for Churchill.[75] Clementine Churchill, the prime minister's wife (whose judgement on a number of issues was better than that of her husband), had already reached a similar conclusion. She told Colville that she thought Attlee's letter was 'both true and wholesome'. Colville's own response on the day the letter arrived was to write in his diary:

'Greatly as I love and admire the P.M. I am afraid there is much in what Attlee says, and I rather admire his courage in saying it. Many Conservatives and officials . . . feel the same.'[76] Churchill had been outraged by the letter. On first reading it, he 'drafted and redrafted', Colville's diary records, 'a sarcastic reply', which he did not send. He went on at some length about 'a socialist conspiracy' and 'harped on nothing but the inadequate representation of Tories in the Cabinet, in spite of their numerical weight in the House'. His private secretary's diary entry noted that was 'beside the point'.* By the following day, however, Colville believed that Churchill, while still 'sorely piqued', was 'not unmoved by Attlee's arguments' and by the response to them of Mrs Churchill and, more surprisingly, Beaverbrook.[77] In the end he sent a terse, formal but not impolite letter to Attlee in which he wrote: 'You may be sure I shall always endeavour to profit by your counsels.'[78]

Churchill's dominance as prime minister between 1940 and 1945 was very great, so far as the prosecution of the war was concerned, but negligible in the entire field of domestic policy. During his only spell as a peacetime prime minister, he was still further from dominating the policy agenda. This was understandable, given that military matters were

---

* One of Churchill's most misguided speeches was his first broadcast in the general election campaign of 1945 when, after five years of successful collaboration with Labour ministers in the war with Nazi Germany, he said that 'No Socialist Government conducting the entire life and industry of the country could afford to allow free, sharp, or violently-worded expressions of public discontent. They would have to fall back on some form of Gestapo . . .' Mrs Churchill, when she read the speech in advance, advised her husband to cut that passage out, but he preferred the advice of 'party advisers who had excitedly been reading Hayek's *The Road to Serfdom* and that of Lord Beaverbrook . . .' (Geoffrey Best, *Churchill: A Study in Greatness*, Penguin, London, 2002, p. 268.) Geoffrey Best describes this as an example of Churchill's 'impetuous liability to go over the top at the wrong moment' and Clementine 'as usual the more commonsensical of the two'. Attlee's response, in his first broadcast of the election campaign the following day, was, as Roy Jenkins observes, 'quietly devastating'. He said that the prime minister wanted 'the electors to understand how great was the difference between Winston Churchill, the great leader in war of a united nation, and Mr Churchill, the party Leader of the Conservatives'. Churchill had feared, said Attlee ironically, that 'those who had accepted his leadership in war might be tempted out of gratitude to follow him further', adding: 'I thank him for having disillusioned them so thoroughly. The voice we heard last night was that of Mr Churchill, but the mind was that of Lord Beaverbrook.' (Roy Jenkins, *Churchill*, Pan Macmillan, London, 2002, p. 793.)

no longer the top priority, and also because of Churchill's advanced age and, for a time, serious ill-health (including a stroke), later to be extensively and indiscreetly documented by his physician, Lord Moran.[79] R.A. Butler, when I interviewed him in 1966, said that when he was Chancellor of the Exchequer in that government, Churchill 'did not interfere at all', except to hope, for example, that 'you will be doing something for the pensioners' or 'I hope you are not going to forget the poor' or 'I hope it's not just going to be more dividends for the rich'.[80] In contrast with his vast knowledge of foreign affairs and especially defence, Churchill was, in Butler's view, ignorant of economic policy, but 'he was very tender-hearted'.[81] (On a rare occasion, somewhat illustrative of Butler's last point, Churchill did bypass the Chancellor on an economic issue, in the company of Walter Monckton, the Minister of Labour. One morning in 1954 Butler was summoned by the prime minister and told: 'Walter and I settled the rail strike in the early hours of this morning on their terms. We did not think it necessary to keep you up.'[82])*

While Churchill's personality could be overpowering, he remained convinced of the central importance of the Cabinet, while also upholding the rights and substantial autonomy of individual ministers. He remarked to Moran in 1953: 'We had 110 Cabinet meetings in the past year; while the Socialists had only 85 in a year – and that in a time of great political activity. I am a great believer in bringing things before the Cabinet. If a Minister has got anything on his mind and he has the sense to get it argued by the Cabinet he will have the machine behind

---

* R.A. Butler had been strongly opposed to Churchill becoming prime minister in 1940 and tried hard to persuade Halifax to allow his name to go forward. Later he became more appreciative of Churchill's strengths, while remaining far from uncritical. To put in fuller context the quotation above from my interview with Butler on 23 September 1966, he said: 'Churchill is someone whose reputation has been grossly inflated, especially with the recent spate of books of adulation. Of course, he was a great leader. He was a great lion – I am a mouse in comparison – and he was absolutely straight. But he could be extraordinarily stupid. He knew practically nothing about economic policy. He scarcely understood the meaning of inflation. But he was very tender-hearted.' In his memoirs, Butler writes of Churchill telling him, after his 1953 Budget, that 'I like the spirit in which you conduct our affairs', and adds: 'I record with strong emotion that however exasperated one became at times, a word of commendation from him always set one up cheerfully.' (Lord Butler, *The Art of the Possible: The Memoirs of Lord Butler, K.G., C.H.*, Hamish Hamilton, London, 1971, p. 165.)

him.'[83] Ministers were allowed a great deal of freedom to get on with their jobs, subject to their accountability to the Cabinet. Even in Churchill's special domain of foreign policy, Anthony Eden, thanks to his long experience and to Churchill's respect for his judgement, enjoyed more autonomy than might have been expected. Sometimes, though, Churchill felt he should have been consulted more by Eden. 'Anthony tells me nothing,' he complained to Moran in June 1954. 'He keeps me out of foreign affairs, treats them as a private reserve of his own.'[84]

In between Churchill's wartime and peacetime premierships came the Labour government headed by Clement Attlee. The most impressive of Labour prime ministers was also the most self-effacing, and the fact that his government set the course of British foreign policy for the next half-century had much to do with the political skills and judgement of the Foreign Secretary, Ernest Bevin. That this first post-war government also laid down the main lines of domestic policy for a generation was a collective achievement, in which a number of ministers of different political dispositions played important roles, among them Herbert Morrison, Stafford Cripps, Hugh Dalton and Aneurin Bevan. The leader–follower dichotomy does not begin to do justice to this relationship. None of these people were followers of Attlee. Indeed, the deputy leader, Morrison, wished to take his place. Dalton also actively conspired to remove Attlee from the party leadership and premiership. Bevan was the most inspirational politician in this group. He came from the left of the Labour Party – unlike Attlee who was a party centrist – and had been a strong critic at times of Attlee's moderate leadership and of the coalition government during the war. Later, in opposition, he was again to be at odds with many of his colleagues and was the acknowledged leader of a left-wing group within the party who became known as Bevanites. Furthermore, Ernest Bevin, who was loyal to Attlee, was not a follower of the prime minister, but a formidable leader in his own right who between the wars had built up the largest trade union in Europe. He had broadened his high standing within the Labour movement by serving as a highly effective Minister of Labour in the wartime government. Of all the Labour ministers in the coalition, he was Winston Churchill's favourite – Attlee's, too, for that matter.

Bevin, who grew up in poverty in West of England villages and left school at the age of eleven, quickly won the admiration of Foreign

Office officials who were from a very different social background. Apart from his obvious ability, natural assurance and the 'imaginative quality of his mind', one reason for this, writes Bevin's biographer, Alan Bullock, was his total absence of snobbery and lack of interest in 'placing' anyone socially: 'Untroubled by any sense of class distinction he treated everyone he met, from the King to the office doorkeeper (both equally admirers of Bevin), in exactly the same way and always as human beings.'[85] Arthur Deakin, Bevin's successor as leader of the Transport and General Workers' Union, said of him: 'Ernie had no more ego than he needed to get where he did', while the American ambassador to London, Lew Douglas, remarked: 'He had no need, like Eden, to show that he was in the top class: he was, and knew it.'[86] Bullock himself notes that while Bevin obviously had none of the 'aristocratic pride of family' of one of his twentieth-century predecessors, Lord Curzon, 'he enjoyed a self-confidence which was positively imperial'[87] – and, it hardly needs adding, he was a much more formidable and successful Foreign Secretary than Curzon.

Attlee's strength as prime minister was to enable a team of ministers with hard-earned life experience to get on with the job and to preside over the coordination of their efforts. They did not all get on with each other, whether on political or personal grounds, but Attlee kept them together. As Bullock observed:

No politician ever made less effort to project his personality or court popularity; in place of Churchill's heroic style, his speeches were dry, matter of fact and often banal. He preferred understatement to rhetoric, and his most effective weapon in debate was a gift for deflation which more than once took the wind out of Churchill's sails . . . Attlee's unassuming manner and laconic habit of speech, however, were deceptive . . . There were half-a-dozen men in the Government with more obvious talents than his own; it was Attlee's strength as Prime Minister that he turned this to his advantage. Unaffected by vanity and with a shrewd eye for the strengths and weaknesses of his colleagues, he left them a free hand in carrying out their different jobs and made little or no attempt to impose his own views on departmental policy.[88]

A prime minister in the twentieth and twenty-first centuries has rarely been only a first among equals, although Attlee came closer than most, provided we add that some government ministers were 'more equal than others'. Attlee did not hesitate to dismiss ministers he regarded as 'not up to the job', but would – and could – not have dreamt of doing so with such senior colleagues as Bevin, Morrison, Stafford Cripps, Aneurin Bevan or (later) Hugh Gaitskell. Bevin and Cripps were removed by illness and death, and Bevan when he resigned from the Cabinet, along with Harold Wilson, after clashing with the Chancellor of the Exchequer, Gaitskell. Attlee was ill in hospital at the time. He believed that he could have found a compromise that would have kept both ministers in the Cabinet had he, rather than the deputy leader of the Labour Party, Herbert Morrison, been presiding at the time.[89]

An extremely brisk and efficient chairman of the Cabinet and of its Defence Committee, Attlee was responsive to opinion within the parliamentary party and government. Speaking in 1948, and referring to meetings of Labour MPs, he said: 'They may not convince me that they are right, but I believe that the foundation of democratic liberty is a willingness to believe that other people may perhaps be wiser than oneself.'[90] In the same speech, Attlee emphasized the collective nature of government policy:

It is the practice of our opponents for obvious reasons to try to disrupt our team – and I am sorry to say that some of our own supporters are also led away – by ascribing particular policies to particular members: Thus they talk sometimes about 'Cripps's economic policy', or 'Dalton's financial policy', or 'Bevan's dealing with the doctors', or 'Bevin's foreign policy', as if there was no coordination in the Government. Nevertheless there is coordination. Whilst every Minister is responsible for his own departmental decisions the collective responsibility both in home and foreign policy is with the Cabinet. We share the blame or the credit for every action of the Government.[91]

In British politics it is now more common, although often still more misleading, for government policies to be attributed to the prime minister as distinct from individual ministers – a Thatcher, Blair, Brown or (to a lesser extent) Cameron deciding on this, that or the other.[92] Even in the 1960s, as Harold Wilson later complained, the headline of a regional newspaper attacked 'Wilson' for a local planning decision in Lancashire.[93] The main exception in political discourse, and not perhaps accidentally, is when the policies in question have become extremely unpopular. Then they are designated as those of the departmental minister. A case in point is Andrew Lansley, Secretary of State for Health in the Conservative–Liberal Democrat coalition government from 2010 until 2012. There was no shortage of references both from within the coalition and by commentators to 'Lansley's health reforms'.[94]

The Macmillan Premiership

In post-war Britain both Clement Attlee and Winston Churchill allowed departmental ministers and Cabinet committees to work out policy and only rarely countermanded them. Anthony Eden, who succeeded Churchill as head of the government in 1955 and led the Conservative Party to victory in the general election of that year, was a fussy, interfering prime minister. He was very sensitive to criticism and especially to articles in the Conservative press critical of his performance and that of the government he led. R.A. Butler has recorded, in his ironic style, that Eden paid him the compliment of holding him responsible for Conservative success in the country, and so 'I was therefore at the receiving end of those innumerable telephone calls, on every day of the week and at every hour of the day, which characterized his conscientious but highly strung supervision of our affairs.'[95] Eden had moved Butler from the Treasury to a non-departmental Cabinet post with the title of Lord Privy Seal.* Eden was especially preoccupied with foreign policy, particularly the Suez crisis, which is discussed in a later chapter, and he intervened less in economic policy than did his successor Harold Macmillan.

Macmillan succeeded Eden as prime minister in January 1957 and held that office for almost seven years – until his resignation in October 1963. He was the son-in-law of an English duke, the great-grandson of a Scottish crofter, and the grandson of the founder of the Macmillan publishing company. (Daniel Macmillan, the last of these, was the son of the crofter, and he himself left school at the age of ten.) For good measure, Macmillan's mother (like Churchill's) was an American. Harold Macmillan mixed contentedly in aristocratic circles. As Rab

---

* With kind intentions, Attlee had given that office to Ernie Bevin when his health had deteriorated too much for him to continue as Foreign Secretary. It was not much appreciated by Bevin who said he was not a lord, or a privy, or a seal.

Butler said of him, he had 'the soft heart for and the strong determination to help the underdog, and the social habit to associate happily with the overdog'.[96] Which of Macmillan's diverse backgrounds he chose to emphasize depended on where and to whom he was speaking. In Scotland the humble crofter was always well to the fore. On visits to his mother's home state of Indiana, he projected himself as 'one of their own, a home-town boy descended from a simple, pioneer family', although he may have struck his enthusiastic audiences as a rather implausible 'Hoosier'.[97] He came to the prime ministership with a wealth of governmental experience exceeded only by his rival for the post, Butler. Macmillan had been a wartime minister, representing the British government in North Africa. In the Conservative governments led by Churchill and Eden, he had been, successively, Minister of Housing, Secretary of State for Defence, Foreign Secretary and Chancellor of the Exchequer.

As Prime Minister, Macmillan naturally played a major role in foreign policy, but had strong views also on the economy. His expansionist impulse, and willingness to risk inflation rather than increased unemployment, led to the resignation in early 1958 of all of his Treasury ministers, headed by Peter Thorneycroft. His next Chancellor, Selwyn Lloyd, was often at odds with Macmillan on economic policy, but when Lloyd objected to a policy supported by the prime minister on the grounds of its cost, as he did on a number of occasions, making clear that he regarded it as resigning matter, both Macmillan and the spending ministers gave way.[98] In an interview in 1966 (non-attributable at the time), Lloyd remarked: 'If in June 1962 I had said I proposed to resign because the Prime Minister was not giving me adequate support, Macmillan might have fallen.'[99] Ever loyal, Lloyd did not do that and just one month later he became the most prominent name within the third of the Cabinet summarily dismissed by Macmillan in his 'night of the long knives'. That was an attempt by the prime minister to refresh the government's image and improve its standing after a series of by-election reverses. It backfired, and in the words of Macmillan's most recent biographer, it showed him 'at his most ruthless, and, ultimately, his most ineffectual'.[100] Macmillan had cultivated an air of unflappability which his sudden and sweeping use of his power of dismissal undermined.

More than once in his diaries, Macmillan himself commends ruthlessness as a worthwhile attribute of a leader. Thus, he wrote of the

Indian Prime Minister, Pandit Nehru, that 'he is able, full of charm, cultivated, and ruthless – all great qualities in a leader'.[101] Ruthlessness, of course, means something different for a democratic leader (Nehru included) from what it connotes in an authoritarian regime. Nevertheless, Macmillan's dismissal of a third of his Cabinet in one fell swoop in 1962 did him much more harm than good. If illness and tiredness had not caused his resignation in 1963, it is likely that he would have been replaced as party leader (and prime minister) before the next election, for the 'night of the long knives' had increased the number of his opponents. One of the ministers who survived Macmillan's cull, Reginal Bevins, wrote: 'This was making enemies on a grand scale, enemies of those dismissed, enemies of their friends in Parliament, and shattering confidence in the Party at large.' He added: 'Of one thing I was then convinced: no Conservative Prime Minister could behave like that and survive. In July 1962 Harold Macmillan committed political suicide more certainly than if he had himself resigned.'[102] The backlash against his dismissal of colleagues illustrated the limits of ruthlessness in a democracy.

Thatcher and Blair

No British prime ministers in the years since the Second World War have aspired to more control over wide areas of policy than did Margaret Thatcher and Tony Blair. Thatcher made the greater impact of the two. Her period of office was linked to foreign policy successes, most notably the end of the Cold War. The part she played in East–West diplomacy was greater than that of any other post-war British prime minister. It was of real significance that she maintained cordial relations with both Ronald Reagan and Mikhail Gorbachev, while never hesitating to argue with either one of them. Her foreign policy adviser, Sir Percy Cradock, took a dim view of Gorbachev's becoming for her 'something of an icon', complaining that 'she acted as a conduit from Gorbachev to Reagan, selling him in Washington as a man to do business with, and operating as an agent of influence in both directions'.[103] Cradock himself, however, was slower than Thatcher to grasp the extent of the change in the Soviet Union after 1985 and the scale of Gorbachev's radicalism. In reality, the constructive role Margaret Thatcher played in East–West relations in the 1980s became her most notable foreign policy achievement. Her foreign policy instincts were far from uniformly impressive. During the years of Nelson Mandela's incarceration in Robben Island prison, she was more sympathetic to the South African apartheid regime than to Mandela. She had a soft spot also for the authoritarian Chilean leader Augusto Pinochet, partly in gratitude for his support during the Falklands War of 1982. That war is generally regarded as a foreign policy success, since it prevented the Falkland Islands passing to Argentina by force. Although the sovereignty of the islands is still a live issue in Argentina (known there as the Malvinas), the British military victory did the Argentinians a good turn at the time. A major reason for counting this as a foreign policy achievement is that the success of the British forces in recapturing the islands led to the fall of Argentina's military dictatorship, headed by Leopold Galtieri, and the restoration of democracy.

Domestically, although Thatcher's policies were extremely divisive, she was a redefining leader – one who redefined the rules of the political game. (As such a leader, she is discussed more fully in the next chapter.) The policies she vigorously espoused, enthusiastically backed during most of her premiership by a clear majority within her own party, broke with much that had been taken for granted (including the great power of trade union leaders) in the post-war period. When a political party is electorally popular, the leader's senior colleagues and backbenchers will tolerate more high-handedness from their leader than they will when the party is losing ground. That is partly because, like many political commentators, they too readily believe that the leader plays a decisive role in determining election outcomes.

The growing unpopularity by the end of the 1980s of Conservative Party policies – most notably, the community charge, or 'poll tax' – made it easier for those who disliked Margaret Thatcher's style of rule to rebel against it. Geoffrey Howe, one of the most outstandingly capable members of the government led by Thatcher, finally lost patience with her increasing belief that she alone knew best and, with his resignation speech in the House of Commons, precipitated her downfall in November 1990. Mrs Thatcher's response, even following a lengthy period of reflection, was to observe that Howe would be remembered not for his achievements but only for 'this final act of bile and treachery'.[104] Following Howe's quietly devastating resignation speech, Thatcher was subsequently abandoned by a majority of the

Cabinet. She later wrote that 'a prime minister who knows that his or her Cabinet has withheld its support is fatally weakened'.[105]

That was an understatement. Leaders who are disdainful of senior colleagues or of their parties will in due course be ousted. Margaret Thatcher and Tony Blair are notable examples of prime ministers who came to believe themselves indispensable to their party and country and to be convinced of their destiny to lead. They differ inasmuch as Thatcher, unlike Blair, did not try to define herself against her party, although her domineering style in Cabinet and in her relations with Cabinet ministers helped to ensure that when her leadership hung by a thread in 1990, she lacked allies precisely where she most needed them. 'My biggest area of weakness', she noted, 'was among Cabinet ministers.'[106] Surveying her colleagues and finding most of them wanting, and anxious about her 'legacy', she decided that John Major was the person most likely to 'secure and safeguard' it, although she detected 'a certain ambiguity' even in his stance.[107]

Tony Blair took a much more dismissive view of his party than Mrs Thatcher did of the Conservative Party. On his talks with the Liberal Democrat leader Paddy Ashdown (whom he had wished to include in the Cabinet in 1997 but could not because of the size of Labour's victory) Blair wrote of 'our cavalier attitude to our parties'.[108] Blair has noted that in order 'to circumvent' his party, 'what I had done was construct an alliance between myself and the public', an alliance that especially in the first three years of his leadership 'was firm and unshakeable'.[109] Blair's patronizing attitude to the people who had elevated him to a position of authority and privilege – the party members who, unlike the electorate as a whole, had voted directly for him – comes out most clearly when he writes that in a pre-election period 'the party people, exiled for years in the Siberia of party drudgery far from the centre of government, suddenly re-emerge in the halls of the Kremlin with renewed self-importance . . .'[110]

Reform of public services, with an increasing market and private sector component, was one of Blair's priorities, along with foreign policy. He also devoted much time to seeking a compromise resolution of the Northern Ireland impasse, and there was general – and well-merited – praise for the part he played in that process. On domestic 'reform', however, if the party disagreed with Blair's views, it was the party that had to give way, not the person they had elected leader. As Blair puts it: 'I didn't choose to have rows with the party; I chose to reform. But if the reform was resisted, then you couldn't avoid the row.'[111] Like Margaret Thatcher, Blair worried about his 'legacy'. As his relations with Gordon Brown during his final incomplete term of office went from bad to worse, Brown 'felt I was ruining his inheritance and I felt he was ruining my legacy'.[112] From time to time, Blair thought of taking the risk of removing his most formidable rival within the government, but when it came to the point, he refrained, being aware that it might merely hasten his own exit from 10 Downing Street. Observing also that Brown's 'energy, intellect and political weight were undeniable', he believed that his presence was 'a massive plus' for the government, notwithstanding the tensions between the two men. The longer Blair was in office, the surer he became of his own stature and the superiority of his judgement. 'If there was a clash,' Blair wrote of his relationship with Brown, 'it was at least a clash of the titans.'[113] He had become confident he could recognize a titan when he looked in the mirror.

During Blair's prime ministership his chief of staff Jonathan Powell and press secretary Alastair Campbell were, in a break with British tradition (discontinued by Brown and Cameron, his successors), given the authority to instruct civil servants, a power previously reserved for ministers. They also had a great deal of authority vis-à-vis ministers and (in Campbell's case, especially) backbench Labour MPs, since they were so close to Blair. Lesser figures than Campbell and Powell also, however, acquired an enormous sense of their own importance from working in 10 Downing Street. Just as in the United States, where a vast growth since the Second World War in the size of the Executive Office of the Presidency has led to complaints from those at the receiving end of 'too many people trying to bite me with the President's teeth', so ministers and MPs have found themselves being patronized or scolded by persons who assume the authority of the prime minister. Tony Wright was a Labour MP much respected by fellow parliamentarians. When he became Chair of the Public Administration Committee of the House of Commons, he turned what had been a little regarded committee into a body which produced high-quality reports that were taken unusually seriously. Before Wright acquired that position, which gave him a greater independence from the executive, he made his views known on a variety of subjects, drawing on knowledge of political and constitutional issues acquired during his previous career as a university teacher. On one such occasion, a message appeared on his pager which read: 'The prime minister is pissed off with you. Phone No. 10 at once.'[114] Wright observed later that his offence had no doubt been to express a view that was regarded as 'unhelpful'. However: 'what really shocked and appalled me was that some No. 10 apparatchik had thought it appropriate to put such coarse language in the name of the prime minister, who almost certainly knew nothing about it, and that it was acceptable to communicate with a Member of Parliament in this way'.[115] The underlying problem was the assumption that the prime minister was a general who stood so far above his party that it was his prerogative to determine policy and strategy. Thus, even senior parliamentarians should jump to attention at the command of a Downing Street lance-corporal.

*

A number of conclusions from the points elaborated in this chapter may be briefly stated. Party leaders have some effect when people are thinking about voting, but only very rarely are they of decisive importance in securing election victories. It is also largely a myth that over time their electoral influence in Western democracies has grown stronger.[116] In office, presidents and prime ministers have shared in an increase of power which has accrued to central executives in modern states. However, other than in foreign policy, there are insubstantial grounds for supposing that their personal power vis-à-vis their colleagues has become significantly greater over the past hundred years, although some are more presumptuous than others in staking a claim to domination. There has been wide variety in the style of leadership from one president and prime minister to another and great oscillations in the extent of the power they have personally been able to wield. The evidence, taken from the United States and the United Kingdom in particular, does not suggest a graph or marked trend of ascending power on the part of democratic leaders. Finally, those prime ministers, such as Lloyd George, Neville Chamberlain, Margaret Thatcher and Tony Blair, who aspire to equate headship of government in a democracy with personal hegemony, pay a serious political price – removal from office as a result of alienating a sufficient number of their own colleagues rather than by the more usual form of rejection at the hands of the electorate.

3

Redefining Leadership

Not all political leaders who become heads of government make much of a difference. This chapter is primarily about those leaders within a democracy who do – *redefining leaders* who challenge previous assumptions, who redefine what is thought to be politically possible, and who introduce radical policy change.[1] Redefining leadership does not always come primarily from the head of the government. It is not unusual for the most important policy innovation to be very much a product of collective leadership. At other times there is an individual within the top team, other than the head of government, who is the prime mover. However, presidents and prime ministers have greater opportunities than their colleagues to set the tone of government and to influence its priorities. When redefining leaders emerge, more often than not this person is, indeed, the head of the executive. The political resources available to that leader are greater than those accruing to any other member of the top team.

AMERICAN PRESIDENTS AS REDEFINING LEADERS

The twentieth-century American presidents with the strongest claim to be regarded as redefining leaders were Franklin D. Roosevelt and Lyndon B. Johnson (although a case could also be made for Theodore Roosevelt).[2] The unusual legislative success of FDR and LBJ has already been illustrated in the previous chapter. Both were formidable leaders in the sense that they used to the full the powers of the office of president and were more than usually dominant in the policy process. Both of them during their presidencies radically changed policy as well as the assumptions about what was possible within the American system. Successful outcomes, I argue throughout this book, are rarely associated with the kind of leadership in which one person tries to dominate the entire policy-making process. Indeed, as we have seen, this is impossible in the American system. Redefining presidents tend, therefore, to be those who maximize the use of the political resources they do have. In the United States the impediments in the way of radical change in domestic policy are especially formidable.

Franklin D. Roosevelt

Franklin Roosevelt did not attempt systemic change, nor did he preside over a qualitatively new order. He does not, therefore, fit the criteria of *transformational* leader, but he is a notable example of a *redefining* one.[3] Roosevelt's imaginative response to economic depression in the 1930s contributed to a revival of the existing economic and political system at a time when it was falling into some disrepute, although the USA was by no means on the verge of revolutionary change. The power of the presidency, especially over foreign policy, had been consolidated by his older relative, the early-twentieth-century president Theodore Roosevelt. It was carried much further by FDR. One important measure was the creation in 1939 of the Executive Office of the President, which, not without difficulty, he persuaded Congress to approve. Henry L. Stimson, Roosevelt's Secretary of State for War, confided to his diary his dissatisfaction with Roosevelt wanting 'to do it all himself' and his irritation that Roosevelt tolerated, or perhaps even encouraged, an atmosphere in Washington 'full of acrimonious disputes over matters of jurisdiction'.[4] Roosevelt was reluctant to delegate power. Even his sympathetic biographer, James MacGregor Burns, describes Roosevelt as a 'prima donna' who 'had no relish for yielding the spotlight for long'.[5] But playing off officials and factions against one another was a mechanism for hoarding as much power as he could in a system in which authority was highly fragmented.

Roosevelt used his powers, not least his power of persuasion, to good effect. He did his best to prepare American public opinion for possible involvement in a war against Nazi Germany at a time when

Joseph Kennedy, the American ambassador to London from 1938 to 1940 and father of the future American president, was saying that 'democracy in Britain was finished, and that the same fate might well await the United States if she foolishly entered the war'.[6] After the German invasion of Poland in 1939, Roosevelt persuaded Congress to remove the ban on exports of armaments, which, under the Neutrality Act of 1937, had prevented the US from supplying any arms to allies.[7] Following the Japanese attack on the American fleet in Pearl Harbor in December 1941, which brought the United States into the Second World War, Roosevelt, as commander-in-chief, took charge of the American war effort in a way comparable to Churchill's wartime prime ministership in Britain – with the difference that the United States was by this time far the stronger of these two major powers in the democratic component of the anti-fascist alliance with the Soviet Union. Two War Powers Acts gave Roosevelt a remarkably free hand for an American president, enabling him to establish a host of wartime agencies, including an Office of Censorship, and extensive control over the domestic economy. In one of his radio 'fireside chats' of 7 September 1942, Roosevelt laid claim to additional regulatory economic powers and indicated that he would not tolerate inaction by Congress in conferring them, for 'in the event that Congress should fail to act, and act adequately, I shall accept the responsibility, and I will act'.[8] The extraordinary powers he planned to exercise would, said Roosevelt, 'automatically revert to the people after the war'. Writing in 1946, the constitutional specialist Edward Corwin observed that the president appeared to have been claiming 'some peculiar relationship between himself and the people – a doctrine with a strong family resemblance to the Leadership principle against which the war was supposedly being fought'.[9] Many, though not all, of the powers that Roosevelt accumulated during the war were, however, explicitly delegated to him by Congress.

Unusually powerful war leader though he was, it was, above all, his domestic policy which made Roosevelt a redefining leader. That he held as many as 337 press conferences during his first period of office, which began in 1933, and 374 in his second term (1937–1941) reflected, as did his radio 'fireside chats', the high priority he placed on communicating with the electorate and with restoring public morale. With Roosevelt's backing, Congress passed within the space of a hundred days in 1933 a wide range of legislation aimed at overcoming the economic depression. The measures included the National Industrial Recovery Act, the Agricultural Adjustment Act, the Federal Emergency Relief Act, the Tennessee Valley Authority Act (TVA), the Emergency Farm Mortgage Act, the Home Owners' Loan Act and the Railway Coordination Act. The TVA in particular has been described as 'Roosevelt's most unalloyed example of presidential leadership'.[10] It brought together public and private bodies, linking industry and agriculture, forestry and flood prevention, and provided an example of social and economic planning at the regional level. It was a policy which Roosevelt 'authored, proposed, and oversaw to passage'.[11]

Although a number of the specific New Deal measures fell by the wayside in subsequent years, Roosevelt's presidency, it has convincingly been argued, 'removed psychological and political obstacles to using government to protect people from the vicissitudes of the marketplace'.[12] The New Deal was, however, a collective enterprise. Much of it was conceived by people other than Roosevelt, but his beliefs and political popularity underpinned it. Its programmes required legislation, which meant that in addition to their enactment by Congress, these measures were subject to continuing congressional oversight and investigation. That might have been enough to scupper them had it not been for the popularity both of the programmes and of the president. Roosevelt deliberately kept himself in the spotlight and took full political advantage of the high esteem in which he was held by many voters (even though he was loathed by others).[13]

To get the New Deal through Congress, Roosevelt required the support of Southern Democrats who formed a solid bloc of votes and he took pains to cultivate and flatter them. They willingly went along with policies that placed constraints on business and the stock market, supported large-scale public infrastructure projects, backed the National Industrial Relations Act of 1935, which broadened the possibilities of unions to organize, and approved the Revenue Act of the same year, which raised the surtax on incomes over $50,000 from 59 to 75 per cent.[14] The support of Northern Democrats and of liberal Republicans would not alone have been enough to enact what were in the American context such radical measures. Yet the same Southern Democrats opposed every attempt to extend the citizenship rights of black Americans. The South remained in Roosevelt's time white supremacist.

Thus, at the heart of the New Deal, as Ira Katznelson has put it, lay a 'rotten compromise'. Roosevelt did little to challenge the 'rights' of Southern states to treat African-Americans abominably. Yet, without the economic measures of the New Deal, including some political support for the advance of labour unions, the conditions of black Americans would have been even worse. These policies – especially when taken in conjunction with the subsequent participation of black servicemen in the American war effort – created preconditions for the civil rights movement and advances of the post-war era.[15]

Among the most significant influences during Roosevelt's presidency was his politically active wife who was, in many respects, more radical than her husband. Eleanor Roosevelt admitted that if her husband had not been running for the presidency in 1932, she would have voted for the Socialist candidate, Norman Thomas.[16] She diligently sought to improve opportunities for women and for African-Americans. She tried hard to get more women appointed to public offices and was especially active in attempting to counter the institutionally embedded racism which pervaded American politics. Her husband felt too constrained by the need for the votes of Southern Democrats, both in popular elections and in Congress, to offer much more than tepid support for civil rights. Eleanor Roosevelt resigned from the Daughters of the American Revolution in 1939 when they refused to allow the great black American singer Marian Anderson to sing in Constitution Hall. That American society as a whole was less bigoted than that organiza-tion was suggested by a Gallop poll, which showed 67 per cent approval of her decision.[17] Yet every step towards securing civil rights – even the anti-lynching legislation that Roosevelt supported during his second term – encountered fierce opposition in the South. It was approved in the House of Representatives by a large majority, but did not survive a six-week filibuster of late 1937 in the Senate at a time when that body had an overwhelming Democratic majority.[18] Very cautiously, however, Roosevelt backed incremental improvements in the civil rights of black Americans, for whom the New Deal brought some gains socially and economically. By the end of the 1930s, black Americans constituted 'a key element of the Roosevelt vote in northern states'.[19]

In a broadcast in November 1934, Roosevelt declared that 'we must make it a national principle that we will not tolerate a large army of unemployed'.[20] Public works to reduce unemployment were at the heart of the New Deal. Yet, we should not exaggerate Roosevelt's role as an initiator of the new policy. The president was at first very cool towards the idea of public works. That they became an important part of the National Industrial Recovery Act, one of the notable pieces of legislation in FDR's first hundred days, in large measure resulted from the pressure and persuasion of Secretary of Labor Frances Perkins and of New York Senator Robert F. Wagner.[21] Roosevelt's successes with Congress were greatest during his first three years as president – and, then again, in the special circumstances of the Second World War. In the second half of the 1930s he had greater difficulties with the legislature. A conservative coalition gradually formed that was capable of thwarting him, and he increasingly resorted to the use of the presidential veto.[22]

Lyndon B. Johnson

If Roosevelt was a complex personality but undoubtedly a redefining leader and successful president, Lyndon Baines Johnson was a man of still more contradictions and greater deviousness. Moreover, Roosevelt's presidency ended only with his death, Johnson's in failure. The bitterness caused by the unsuccessful Vietnam War, in which the United States was enmeshed, eventually led Johnson not to seek a second term. Yet, what he achieved domestically was remarkable. It owed a good deal to the political environment in which he entered the White House. The shock of the assassination of his predecessor gave a fillip to causes Kennedy had espoused but on which he had made little headway with Congress – most notably civil rights. Pressures from below were strong, particularly from black Americans, for whom Martin Luther King was an inspirational leader. They came also from a broader society, especially educated youth that was more politicized than in the 1950s, partly as a result of the Vietnam War and its concomitant military draft, but also in response to the leadership of King and other civil rights activists. On the opposite side stood many Republicans and their allies on the civil rights issue, the Southern Democrats. No more sympathetic to the causes Johnson embraced was the long-serving Director of the FBI, J. Edgar Hoover whom, Dean Acheson told Harry Truman, 'you should trust as much as a rattlesnake with the silencer on its rattle'. While paying scant attention to the murder of peaceful black protesters, Hoover did all in his power to discredit

the civil rights movement by spreading rumours of Communist pene-
tration of its ranks. King's response was to say that it would be
encouraging 'if Mr Hoover and the FBI would be as diligent in appre-
hending those responsible for bombing churches and killing little
children, as they are in seeking out alleged communist infiltration in
the civil rights movement'.[23]

Unlike many other southern Democrats, Johnson had supported
the Supreme Court's *Brown v. the Board of Education* decision, during
the Eisenhower administration, which mandated the desegregation of
schools. As president, Johnson's supreme achievement was to get the
most important civil rights legislation passed, overcoming sustained
Senate resistance. He also introduced Medicare – and Medicaid for the
poor, which was to be administered by the states – and within two
years of accidentally ascending to the presidency, his legislative accomplishments had put real substance into his rhetoric about the Great
Society and the War on Poverty. The lowest level of inequality ever
recorded in the United States was achieved in 1968.[24] Johnson has a
good claim to be regarded as the greatest American lawmaker of the
twentieth century, even if we consider his presidency on its own –
unquestionably so, if his years as Senate Majority Leader are added
in. Focusing on Johnson's first two years in the White House, Stephen
Graubard has observed: 'Although Wilson, Roosevelt, and Truman
established credible records that gave proof of their ability to collabor-
ate with Congress, to secure passage of the domestic legislation they
insisted on, none was master of the arts of persuasion in the way
Johnson proved to be in 1964 and 1965.'[25] How did he do it? One of
his major biographers, Randall Woods, notes that the telephone was
the 'true instrument of the Johnson legislative will', adding:

From late 1963 through 1966, Lyndon Johnson interacted with senators and
representatives on a daily and even hourly basis. He became personally familiar
with the details of the more than one thousand major bills Congress considered
during this period. His memory banks were still full of information concerning
the personal characteristics of the various congressional and senatorial districts
and the personal peccadilloes of those men and women who served them.
'There is but one way for a President to deal with the Congress', Johnson
would observe, 'and that is continuously, incessantly, and without interruption
. . . He's got to know them even better than they know themselves . . .'[26]

LBJ was living proof that the president's greatest 'power' was 'the power to persuade'. Nevertheless, his reputation was low among the highly educated advisers who surrounded Kennedy, and Johnson himself felt keenly the inadequacies of his education compared with 'the Harvards', as he called them.[27] His ruthlessness and lack of scruples, as he made his political ascent, have been thoroughly documented, not least by Robert Caro in his magisterial multi-volume biography. In the summer of 1957 Johnson, as Majority Leader, pushed through the Senate a Civil Rights Act which made only modest advances, but which, nevertheless, extended black voting rights and paved the way for the major Civil Rights Acts of 1964 and 1965 when he was president. It was against all expectations that Johnson used his influence in 1957 in favour of civil rights, for he had voted over a twenty-year period both in the Senate and before that in the House of Representatives in the same way as other Southern Democrats – against improvement in the civil rights of black Americans.[28] Any other course of action would have put an end to the rise of a Texan politician.

Even when Johnson was pursuing a liberal policy, he displayed, writes Caro, 'a pragmatism and ruthlessness striking even to Washington insiders who had thought themselves calloused to the pragmatism of politics'. He was 'deceitful and proud of it', as he talked 'first to a liberal, then to a conservative, walked over first to a southern group and then to a northern', telling 'liberals one thing, conservatives the opposite, and asserting both positions with equal, and seemingly total, conviction'.[29] But his deviousness went alongside 'political genius'.[30] Considering Johnson's career in the round, Caro is able to conclude: 'Abraham Lincoln struck off the chains of black Americans, but it was Lyndon Johnson who led them into voting booths, closed democracy's sacred curtain behind them, placed their hands upon the lever that gave them a hold on their own destiny, made them, at last and forever, a true part of American political life.'[31]

Johnson had learned during the contest for the Democratic presidential nomination in 1960 (which John F. Kennedy secured) that the state governors could be effective in putting pressure on senators and representatives. Immediately after the funeral of President Kennedy in November 1963, before the governors had a chance to leave Washington, Johnson called them to a meeting in his office. He told them that he had spent two and a half hours the previous day with

Eisenhower, 'the great President who led our forces to victory' who made him realize that no party has 'a single mortgage on patriotism' and that, regardless of party, they should help him to save the country. He got more and more passionate as he spoke. They had to do something to stop the hate and tackle the injustice, inequality, poverty and unemployment 'that exists in this land'. The best way to deal with these problems, Johnson said:

is to pass the tax bill and get some more jobs and get some more investments and, incidentally, get more revenue and taxes, and pass the civil rights bill so that we can say to the Mexican in California or the Negro in Mississippi or the Oriental on the West Coast or the Johnsons in Johnson City that we are going to treat you all equally and fairly, and you are going to be judged on merit and not ancestry, nor on how you spell your name.[32]

Johnson had always been concerned with the fate of the poor, not least the injustices suffered by poor blacks, but he had been concerned, above all, with his own political advancement. Roy Wilkins of the National Association for the Advancement of Colored People (NAACP) had long been ambivalent about him. 'With Johnson,' he said, 'you never quite knew if he was out to lift your heart or your wallet.'[33] He finished up admiring him. When Johnson's ambition and compassion had been in conflict, then it was compassion that came off second best. From the moment he became president, however, that conflict was over and, as Caro observes, the cause of social justice 'moved forward under the direction of this master at transmuting sympathy into governmental action'.[34]

Of course, the contrast between Johnson's domestic successes and his foreign policy failures could not have been starker. His inability to understand nationalism and Communism in Asia was shared by his immediate predecessor and also by his advisers, and it was fear of 'losing' Vietnam (which was never America's to lose) that brought about his political downfall. Yet Johnson was a redefining leader. He changed the terms of political debate, not only making American poverty a salient political issue but tackling it head on, while playing a decisive role in ending the virtual disenfranchisement of black voters in a number of southern American states. In his State of the Union address to Congress in January 1964, Johnson said that 'many Americans live on the outskirts of hope – some because of their poverty, and some because of their color, and all too many because of both'. The task, he said, was to 'replace their despair with opportunity', adding: 'This administration today, here and now, declares unconditional war on poverty in America.'[35] At the time of Johnson's death in 1973, the black writer Ralph Waldo Ellison acknowledged that Johnson had been widely despised both by conservatives and by many liberals. He would 'have to settle for being recognized as the greatest American President for the poor and for the Negroes', which, Ellison added, was 'a very great honor indeed'.[36]

Ronald Reagan – Redefining Leader?

The United States has had some notable presidents since Johnson, but none who was a redefining leader in the sense in which both Roosevelt and Johnson were. Ronald Reagan is sometimes accorded great significance, but there has been a tendency to exaggerate the difference he made. Leaders and especially their most enthusiastic supporters are prone to assume that momentous events which occur during their time in power are attributable to them. Such arguments have frequently been advanced on behalf of Reagan, but he did not make things happen in the way that Johnson did. Notwithstanding the importance of the United States in world politics, fundamental change can occur internationally, as it did during the presidencies of Ronald Reagan and George Bush the elder, without it being primarily a result of contemporaneous American policy. The liberalization of the Soviet Union, democratization of East-Central Europe and the end of the Cold War were very largely the result of change in Moscow to which Reagan and Bush were responsive but for which they were not responsible. More specifically, the transformation of Soviet domestic and foreign policy in the second half of the 1980s owed little or nothing to Washington hardliners, triumphalist Western accounts notwithstanding.

Domestically, neither Reagan nor (still more obviously) Bush comes into the category of a redefining leader, although Reagan, while less knowledgeable than Bush, was more successful in imparting a distinctive tone to his presidency as well as, in further contrast with his successor, comfortably winning a second term. There was, as noted in the previous chapter, a large gulf between Reagan's rhetoric and the realities of his presidency. His legislative achievements were modest and 'in spite of promises to shrink federal spending, the size of government and the deficit, all grew larger under Reagan'.[37] The biggest difference he made in moving the United States in a more conservative direction was almost certainly through judicial appointments – more than four hundred federal judges with lifetime tenure and four Supreme Court appointments, with William Rehnquist promoted to Chief Justice and Sandra Day O'Connor, Antonin Scalia and Anthony Kennedy becoming Supreme Court judges.[38]

BRITISH REDEFINING LEADERS

Within a democracy there can on occasion be a fine line between leaders and governments we would wish to call redefining and those not meeting the criteria. Changes of government will almost invariably produce *some* difference: democratic leaders do not last long unless they have a political party behind them, and parties offer policy *choices*. Yet, if we turn to the British case, there have been just three governments in the twentieth and twenty-first centuries with strong claims to be regarded as redefining – the Liberal government of 1905 to 1915 (when a wartime coalition was formed) and which was led by Herbert Asquith from 1908; the Labour government headed by Clement Attlee from 1945 to 1951; and the Conservative government during Margaret Thatcher's premiership from 1979 to 1990. That is not, of course, to say that there was no significant policy innovation by other UK governments over the last century. The Conservative government led by Harold Macmillan between 1957 and 1963, the Labour government of 1964 to 1970 during the prime ministership of Harold Wilson, and the Labour government headed by Tony Blair from 1997 until 2007 witnessed quite substantial change – and we shall come to them shortly.

The Pre-First-World-War Liberal Government

During the first four decades of the twentieth century the only redefining British government was that formed by the Liberal Party in December 1905 and confirmed by that party's landslide victory in the 1906 election. In its first two years it was headed by the cautious Henry

Campbell-Bannerman, but it was especially after his ill health (and death shortly thereafter) led to his replacement as prime minister by Asquith in 1908, that most of the far-reaching change took place. It included a raft of legislation which constituted the building blocks of what would become known as the welfare state. The driving force behind much of this legislation was David Lloyd George who succeeded Asquith as Chancellor of the Exchequer when the latter became Prime Minister. Old age pensions had already been planned by Asquith when he was Chancellor, but they were carried into law by Lloyd George in 1908.

The government was open to ideas from elsewhere. Pensions for the aged had already been introduced in New Zealand, which Asquith described as a laboratory for political and social experiments that provided instruction for 'the older countries of the world'.[39] Lloyd George's enthusiasm for unemployment insurance was sparked by a visit to Germany where some of the earliest welfare state measures had been brought in by Bismarck.[40] The National Insurance Act of 1911 introduced compulsory health and unemployment insurance in Britain, paid for out of taxation of both employers and employees. Earlier (in 1909) Winston Churchill, as President of the Board of Trade, had established labour exchanges to boost employment. He, too, had been influenced by German experience. As the youngest Cabinet minister for a generation (he was thirty-three at the time of his appointment in April 1908), he wrote to the prime minister, Asquith: 'Germany with a harder climate and far less accumulated wealth has managed to establish tolerable basic conditions for her people. She is organized not only for war, but for peace. We are organized for nothing except party politics.'[41]

A major constitutional reform was the reduction in the power of the House of Lords. The upper house was no longer allowed to hold up financial legislation or permitted to delay *any* bill for more than two years. This was a fundamental change whereby 'a chamber of veto was forced to reinvent itself as a chamber of scrutiny'.[42] The clash with the House of Lords was triggered by Lloyd George's 'People's Budget' of 1909. Among other measures, it raised income tax, increased death duties on the larger estates, imposed land taxes, and introduced a tax on petrol and motor-car licences at a time when cars were owned only by the rich. The revenue was used partly to pay for substantially increased defence expenditure. Although the House of Lords had long accepted a convention that it did not block a Budget approved by the House of Commons, the overwhelming Conservative majority in the hereditary chamber, outraged by what they saw as an attack on the rich and on landed interests, rejected this legislation. Feelings ran high. The Duke of Beaufort said he would 'like to see Winston Churchill and Lloyd George in the midst of twenty couples of dog hounds'. The Duke of Buccleuch informed a small Scottish football club that because of the land tax he would be cancelling his subscription to them of just over a pound a year.[43] Asquith called an election at which the Budget and the need to reduce the power of the Lords were major issues. Surprisingly, the Liberals lost over a hundred seats in that election of January 1910 and became dependent for the continuation of their government on the support of Labour and Irish Nationalist MPs. The portrayal of the government as extremist evidently resonated with an electorate in which many male workers and all women still did not have a vote.

Trade Union rights to raise money for political purposes, which had been undermined by the judiciary, were extended by the government in 1913. Now workers who did not wish to contribute to the political levy had to contract out, rather than contract in. Domestic pressures on the government were still more decisive than foreign example. Much suffering that had previously been accepted as an unavoidable by-product of capitalism began to be tackled from fear of socialism and as a result of the demands of an increasingly organized labour movement. Trade union membership more than doubled in size between 1900 and 1913 (to over four million members), and from 1910 the influence of Labour Members of Parliament was greatly enhanced by the government's dependence on their votes.

What makes this Liberal government a redefining one was, above all, its laying the early foundations of the welfare state. In that enterprise, as well as in its attack on the hereditary privileges of the House of Lords, it owed at least as much to Lloyd George as to Asquith, the Prime Minister. Asquith was not a domineering prime minister and the more important of the changes introduced were very much the achievement of the government collectively, in which, however, two members were of particular consequence. The Cabinet Asquith headed benefited from the driving force provided by Lloyd George and Churchill, two magnetic personalities who have been described, not unreasonably, as 'the two British politicians of genius' in the first half of the twentieth century.[44]

The Post-Second World War Labour Government

The government led by Clement Attlee from 1945 until 1951 was an especially clear case of redefining leadership. As the previous chapter has already touched upon, it was no less striking an example of that leadership being provided by senior ministers collectively rather than by the prime minister individually, important though his contribution was in managing large egos and playing a calm, coordinating role. Of the Labour Cabinet of twenty (nineteen men and one woman) formed in 1945, none had been born in the twentieth century. The youngest, Aneurin Bevan, who had been regarded as an incorrigible rebel and who was Attlee's surprise choice as Minister of Health, was forty-seven. They had accumulated a lot of experience in different walks of life, and a number of them had the advantage of having served in the wartime coalition government – in the cases of Attlee, Ernest Bevin, Herbert Morrison, Stafford Cripps and Hugh Dalton at a very high level. Attlee's wartime role as deputy prime minister, chairing Cabinet committees and the Cabinet when Churchill was absent, had not put him in the public eye as much as Bevin and Morrison, and the latter aspired to take Attlee's place as Labour leader and potential prime minister when the war ended.

Harold Laski, who held the main Chair of Political Science at the London School of Economics, happened to be Chairman of the National Executive Committee of the Labour Party in 1945 (it was an office which rotated), and he tried both then and later to have Attlee replaced as Labour leader, since he believed him to be insufficiently socialist, excessively anti-Soviet, and lacking the ability 'to reach out to the masses'.[45]* Laski wrote to Attlee during the 1945 election

---

* It is almost an iron law that intellectuals who speak of 'the masses' are out of touch with real people. That would, though, be unfair to Laski who was generous with his time and sympathetic attention, whether addressing South Wales miners and staying in their homes, or with his students, to whom he was endlessly helpful. See Kingsley Martin, *Harold Laski: A Biography* (Jonathan Cape, London, new edition, 1969), pp. xiv, 95, 127 and 250–251. He was, though, a poor judge of opinion beyond the ranks of party activists and of the intellectual circles in which he moved.

campaign to tell him that his leadership was 'a grave handicap to our hopes of victory in the coming election' (in which Labour was soon to gain a huge majority over all other parties, winning 183 more seats than the Conservatives and their allies).[46] For the most part, Attlee put up with the constant stream of criticism patiently. As early as 1941, after Laski had accused him of being in danger of following in the footsteps of Ramsay MacDonald (the Labour leader who was expelled from the party when he became head of a predominantly Conservative coalition government in 1931), Attlee replied: 'I am sorry that you suggest that I am verging towards MacDonaldism. As you have so well pointed out, I have neither the personality nor the distinction to tempt me to think that I should have any value apart from the party which I serve.'[47] When, however, Laski used his position in 1945 to speak in the name of the recently elected Labour government in interviews to foreign newspapers, Attlee wrote to him that 'Foreign affairs are in the capable hands of Ernest Bevin', that the Foreign Secretary's task was 'quite sufficiently difficult' without the embarrassment of Laski's irresponsible statements, and that 'a period of silence on your part would be welcome.'[48]

The Labour government did introduce a substantial number of socialist measures, nationalizing the Bank of England, the railways, long-distance transport, the electricity and gas industries, the coal mines, civil aviation, and the iron and steel industries. These concerns remained in public ownership for at least a generation after the defeat of the Labour government in 1951 with the exception of the iron and steel enterprises, which were denationalized by Churchill's Conservative government. Since the House of Lords had been determined to delay the Iron and Steel Nationalization Bill, a new Parliament Act was passed, reducing their 1911 powers of delay from two years to one.[49] The government pursued egalitarian and redistributive policies. Britain had been devastated economically by the war, and as shortages were still severe, food and petrol rationing continued for the remainder of the 1940s, with only the rationing of clothes ending in 1949. Free milk for schoolchildren and other welfare benefits, however, saw a steady improvement in the standard of health of all ages as compared with the inter-war years.[50] The National Insurance Act of 1946 provided vastly extended benefits for the sick and unemployed and 'remained a basis of the welfare state for the next thirty years or more'.[51] Most important of all was the creation of the National Health Service, under Bevan's leadership – a service that was to become so popular that governments a generation and more later who wished to introduce a greater element of private health provision had to do so by stealth, after swearing fealty to the NHS. As recently as 2010, Attlee's latest biographer contended: 'The National Health Service remains today, with its central principle of healthcare free at the point of delivery, almost entirely intact.'[52] Its iconic status in post-war Britain was reflected when a substantial part of the Opening Ceremony of the 2012 London Olympic Games, no doubt puzzling for American viewers, consisted of artistic homage to the National Health Service.

Margaret Thatcher as Redefining Leader

Many of the principles established by the first post-war Labour government remained a basis for policy until the advent of the government headed by Margaret Thatcher. Britain's first (and, thus far, only) woman prime minister, Mrs Thatcher undoubtedly ranks as a redefining leader. Her eleven years as prime minister from 1979 to 1990 constituted also the longest stint of any premier in the twentieth or twenty-first centuries. She was hyper-active in both foreign and domestic policy. Although she was by no means displeased with the term the 'iron lady', first conferred on her by Soviet journalists, in practice her foreign policy was more nuanced than her belligerent image suggests. It was also rather different in government from what it was before she became prime minister and from what appeared in some of her retrospective observations after she had been forced out of the premiership.

In office she was influenced by able civil servant advisers in 10 Downing Street, by government colleagues, including successive Foreign Secretaries, as well as by outside academic specialists, consulted on an ad hoc basis. (Along with her strong convictions, she had a prodigious appetite for relevant facts and the capacity to work an exceptionally long day, sleeping for only four hours a night.) Out of office, she had less expert advice and was more prone to listen to zealots. As prime minister, she became an early proponent of the idea that Mikhail Gorbachev was a different kind of Soviet leader from any of his predecessors. She was the most vigorous advocate among conservative politicians, whether in Europe or in North America, of the view that his reforms were of far-reaching significance. Thatcher's political instincts had not led her to suppose that fundamental change could be initiated from within the upper echelons of a ruling Communist Party. Rather than rely purely on her gut feelings, however, she listened to a broad spectrum of specialist opinion and reassessed some of her previous views on the prospects for change in the Soviet Union and Eastern Europe.[53]*

Contrary also to her belligerent reputation, Thatcher took a sceptical view of American military strikes in Lebanon and Libya, saying: 'Once you start to go across borders, then I do not see an end to it and I uphold international law very firmly.'[54] Her willingness to use force to take back the Falkland Islands, following their seizure by Argentinian troops, should not obscure her extreme reluctance to endorse military intervention where there had been no external attack on Britain or on

---

* Throughout the period when Margaret Thatcher's prime ministership overlapped with Mikhail Gorbachev's Soviet leadership, she benefited also from having excellent British ambassadors to the Soviet Union – Sir Bryan Cartledge (who had worked with Thatcher earlier in 10 Downing Street) from 1985 to 1988 and Sir Rodric Braithwaite from 1988 (to 1992). I took part in two seminars on the Soviet Union and Eastern Europe, held at Chequers, the weekend residence of British prime ministers. They were presided over by Mrs Thatcher and attended by Foreign Secretary Sir Geoffrey Howe and other senior members of the government. The first of these, in September 1983, was especially significant. In the words of Sir Percy Cradock (*In Pursuit of British Interests: Reflections on Foreign Policy under Margaret Thatcher and John Major*, John Murray, London, 1997, p. 18) who very shortly after that seminar became the Prime Minister's Foreign Policy Adviser, it 'inaugurated a more open approach to Eastern Europe and led eventually to the first meeting with Gorbachev'. Especially at that stage of her premiership, Mrs Thatcher listened to what outside specialists had to say. At the 1983 Chequers seminar she interrupted her colleagues, especially Geoffrey Howe, frequently and the academics rarely. In their memoirs, both Thatcher and Howe devote several pages to this seminar with differing accounts of its genesis, and both attach importance to it. Howe notes that 'in discussion with the experts on the Soviet Union' the prime minister was 'unusually restrained'. See Geoffrey Howe, *Conflict of Loyalty* (Macmillan, London, 1994), pp. 315–17; and Margaret Thatcher, *The Downing Street Years* (HarperCollins, London, 1993), pp. 451–3. The second Chequers seminar on the Soviet Union was held in February 1987, as part of the preparation for Thatcher's high-profile and successful visit to the Soviet Union the following month. In between, I was one of four academics invited to 10 Downing Street for an informal briefing meeting with Thatcher and Howe on the eve of Gorbachev's first visit to Britain in December 1984, three months before he became Soviet leader.

a British dependency. She was enraged by the American invasion of Grenada in October 1983 to reverse an internal coup. This was an especially sore point since Grenada was a former British colony and remained part of the Commonwealth. Thatcher, however, speaking on a BBC World Service phone-in, drew a much broader conclusion, saying:

We in . . . the Western democracies use our force to defend our way of life . . . We do not use it to walk into independent sovereign territories . . . If you're going to pronounce a new law that wherever Communism reigns against the will of the people, even though it happened internally, there the USA shall enter, then we are going to have really terrible wars in the world.[55]

Although Thatcher took a very dim view of the British Foreign and Commonwealth Office as an institution (making exceptions for several of its distinguished members who worked for her in 10 Downing Street as close aides), on a number of issues her policies were not out of line with those of the FCO and of her last two Foreign Secretaries, Sir Geoffrey Howe and Douglas Hurd. Her views on dealing with the South African apartheid regime, the European Union and the unification of Germany were among the major exceptions. On those issues she lived up to her ultra-conservative stereotype, and on them she and the Foreign Office were far apart.[56]

It is, though, the domestic policy of the Thatcher government which makes it one of the three redefining administrations of twentieth-century Britain. And in this case, unlike that of the Attlee government, it is entirely reasonable to single out the prime minister individually as a redefining leader.[57] On the economy, trade unions and the welfare state, Thatcher came to the premiership with very firm views which she was determined would become government policy. The contrast between the programmes of the Attlee and Thatcher governments could hardly be greater. Moreover, the difference between her Cabinet meetings and those of Attlee was at least as striking. Unlike Attlee, Thatcher stated her opinion on issues on which she had a strong point of view (and they were many) at the outset, thus biasing the discussion in the direction of her convictions. Many important issues did not even come to the Cabinet table. In the words of a highly critical member of her first Cabinet, Ian Gilmour: 'Collective decision-making was severely truncated and with it, inevitably, collective responsibility'.[58]

At least half the members of Mrs Thatcher's first Cabinet were people whose outlook was very different from her own – among them, the Foreign Secretary Lord Carrington, Michael Heseltine, Jim Prior, Peter Walker and Gilmour himself. At that time Geoffrey Howe, as Chancellor of the Exchequer, was a close ally of the prime minister. Gradually, individual resignations and prime ministerial reshuffles changed the composition of the higher echelons of the government, but Thatcher succeeded in alienating even some of her earlier supporters. Howe's resignation triggered her downfall in 1990, but it had been preceded by the departure of other very senior ministers who were explicitly critical of Thatcher's style of rule. This was notably true of Michael Heseltine's resignation as Secretary of State for Defence in 1986 and of Nigel Lawson's as Chancellor of the Exchequer in 1989.[59] Lawson, like Howe (but unlike Heseltine), had initially seen eye to eye with Thatcher on economic policy, but their views increasingly diverged, not least on Britain's membership of the European monetary system, the independence of the Bank of England, and on taxation.[60]

An important attribute of Thatcher as prime minister was the thoroughness with which she did her homework and her insistence on being well briefed. She was not much given to self-criticism, but her official biographer notes that in old age there was nothing for which she would rebuke herself more than the thought that 'I had not prepared thoroughly enough for something'.[61] She had an excellent memory and absorbed a great deal of information in the course of methodical preparation, whether it was for a meeting with Gorbachev or for the more routine twice-weekly prime minister's questions.[62] Although she kept officials on their toes and could even be feared in government departments – 'she sent tremors through the whole of Whitehall'[63] – she gleaned a great deal from the civil service. In some ways, she preferred them to her Cabinet colleagues, since, in addition to supplying the facts she wanted, they could be more relied upon to do her bidding. So much so, that Thatcher said to her principal private secretary Clive Whitmore: 'Clive, I'd be able to run this Government much better if I didn't have ministers, only permanent secretaries.'[64]

Although her style of government was to be her ultimate undoing – with practically her entire Cabinet telling her in 1990 that she could not survive as prime minister – it makes it easier to classify Thatcher as a redefining leader and not simply the head of a redefining government. There is surprisingly broad agreement, among both critics of Thatcher's policies and those sympathetic to them that she was a leader who altered the terms of political debate, changed opinion on what was politically possible, and introduced radical change.[65] She was also a highly divisive leader who polarized opinion within England and became especially unpopular in Scotland. She ultimately lost the support of most of her Cabinet colleagues (as a direct result of treating them much less than collegially) and she left the Conservative Party more divided than it had been for many decades. One outcome of her foreign policy, which no one would have dared to predict at the start of her premiership in 1979, is that she made many more friends in Eastern Europe than she did in Western Europe, and finished up popular in Moscow, Prague and Warsaw and a bugbear in Bonn, Paris and Brussels.

Thatcher's predecessor as Conservative Party leader (and prime minister from 1970 to 1974), Edward Heath, had adopted a rather similar style of domineering leadership, but the only major mark he left was to lead the United Kingdom into the European Community (later called the European Union). As Anthony King has written: 'Despite his frequent changes of policy direction, Heath undoubtedly exercised a more complete, more continuous control over his administration than any other prime minister since 1945 . . . The fact that the Tories lost in February 1974 – and the fact that, apart from Britain's entry into the European Community, almost the whole of Heath's policy legacy soon lay in ruins – does not mean that Heath was not a domin-ant prime minister. It merely means that not all dominant prime ministers are successful.'[66] It is worth adding that prior to becoming prime minister, Heath was 'considered "weak" by a large section of the population'.[67] His case illustrates three points. The first is that before a leader has held the premiership, it is harder for that person to be perceived as 'strong'. The second is that popular opinion about whether a leader *is* strong or weak, in the sense of being a dominat-ing or domineering decision-maker, can be extraordinarily wide of the mark. The third is that there is no reason to suppose that 'strength' of a prime minister's leadership (in the sense of domineering relation-ship with Cabinet colleagues) leads to successful government.

While the leadership styles of Thatcher and Heath were not all that far apart, they differed significantly on important issues. Heath, who never forgave Thatcher for displacing him as Conservative leader, did not share her admiration for unfettered capitalism. One of the senior figures in the Thatcher government argued that 'the two key principles' for which the Attlee government had stood, 'big interventionist government and the drive towards equality', had remained effectively unchallenged for more than a generation – until, in fact, Mrs Thatcher entered 10 Downing Street.[68] The Thatcher government removed many of the regulations on commercial institutions (including banks), freed capital markets, and acted on the belief, for which the prime minister was an evangelist, that there was no substitute for market forces. Part and parcel of such an approach was a programme of privatization, with two-thirds of state assets being sold off within a decade. More traditional Tories disapproved of this. When Harold Macmillan was invited back to 10 Downing Street at the time of the Falklands dispute to advise Mrs Thatcher on 'how to run a war', he looked around a room which had been partly emptied to make space for an evening function. 'Where's all the furniture?' he wanted to know. 'You've sold it all off, I suppose.'[69] Thatcher defeated a prolonged strike by coal miners (whose union solidarity had helped earlier to bring down the Heath government) and drastically curtailed trade union power. She allowed council house occupiers to buy their properties at favourable prices as part of a policy of encouraging greater home ownership and reducing the size of the publicly owned sector.

More generally, the Thatcher government shifted the public–private balance within the British state substantially in the direction of the private. This included bringing business experience into the civil service and introducing measures which reversed the egalitarian policies that had first been introduced by the Attlee government. Income tax rates paid by the wealthy were reduced, and a new local tax, officially called the community charge but universally known as the poll tax, was brought in. Since it was designed to take the place of a tax on property (the rates), and was based instead on a head-count, its opponents objected that the same sum would be paid by a duke and a dustman. It provoked fierce opposition, and contributed to Mrs Thatcher's growing unpopularity during her later years in office. Her Chancellor of the Exchequer at the time, Nigel Lawson, believed that it had been 'a colossal error of judgement on her part to seek to turn a form of taxation which had been notorious throughout the ages into the flagship of her Government'. Lawson concedes, nevertheless, that with this particular policy, despite 'her profound personal commitment, she observed the proprieties of Cabinet government throughout'.[70] The Chancellor opposed it vigorously, noting in an internal memorandum of May 1985 that a 'pensioner couple in Inner London could find themselves paying 22 per cent of their net income in poll tax, whereas a better off couple in the suburbs would pay only 1 per cent'.[71] However, Thatcher carried the Cabinet with her and the measure was approved in 1986. The tax was introduced a year earlier in Scotland than in England and Wales. It proved to be a gift to the Scottish National Party as well as to Labour and added to the already high level of Scots' disenchantment with the Conservative Party.[72]

Significantly Innovative British Governments

There are three other British governments in the period with which we are concerned that, while falling short of providing redefining leadership, were responsible for especially noteworthy innovation – those led by Harold Macmillan, Harold Wilson and Tony Blair. However, the most important changes brought about during the lifetime of the Labour governments led by Wilson and Blair were not primarily the doing of these two prime ministers.

The government headed by Macmillan came to terms, however hesitatingly, with decolonization. This sparked outrage directed at the Colonial Secretary Iain Macleod and, to a lesser extent, at Macmillan himself – both for his 'wind of change' speech in South Africa and for appointing the relatively liberal Macleod to the office responsible for colonial policy. The attacks came not only from fringe organizations such as the League of Empire Loyalists but from a substantial body of opinion on the right of the Conservative Party. In economic policy, there was less of a sharp break with the Churchill and Eden governments in which Macmillan had served, latterly as Chancellor of the Exchequer. Macmillan himself took a dim view of Treasury orthodoxy, was Keynesian in his economic philosophy, and sceptical of some of the activities of the City of London, privately referring to bankers as 'banksters'.[73]

Constitutionally, the most significant change brought in by the Macmillan government was the Life Peerages Act of 1958. This created a new category of non-hereditary peers who were subsequently to include people with impressive achievements in different walks of life, as well as notable politicians who were 'kicked upstairs'. The legislation gave a new lease of life to the House of Lords, raising the quality of many of the debates. The Labour Party, it should be added, had been in no particular hurry to abolish the second chamber, having hitherto been reasonably content that its hereditary basis made it indefensible and no possible threat to the supremacy of the House of Commons. In another measure of long-term significance, the Conservative government headed by Macmillan set up in 1961 a prestigious committee to investigate the condition and future of higher education in Britain under the chairmanship of the economist Lord (Lionel) Robbins. The government's subsequent acceptance of the Robbins Report, published in 1963, led to a great expansion in the number of British universities.[74]

The most important achievement of the Labour governments led by Harold Wilson in the 1960s was – contrary to the stereotype of Conservative and Labour governments – a substantial widening of personal freedoms. Wilson presided over very important social change, including a liberalization of the divorce laws, the legalization of homosexual acts between consenting adult males (which brought the law for men into line with that for women), the abolition of the death penalty and the legalization (subject to certain safeguards) of abortion. In order to increase the likelihood of criminals being convicted in trials by jury, the need for a unanimous verdict, which had existed in England since the fourteenth century, was ended.[75] The right of the Lord Chamberlain to censor theatre productions was abolished.[76] This cluster of liberalizing measures was the most lasting legacy of the Labour government of the 1960s, and its main promoter and driving force was not Wilson (who was socially rather conservative), but the Home Secretary, Roy Jenkins – another example of why we should stop speaking of prime ministers as if they are synonymous with governments.

Of the legislation mentioned, only one item – the vote to abolish the death penalty – was carried while Jenkins's Labour predecessor, Sir Frank Soskice, was Home Secretary.[77] That bill was sponsored by the backbench Labour MP Sydney Silverman, and was the culmination of decades of parliamentary endeavour by him to end capital punishment.[78]

All the other changes (as well as the abolition of capital punishment) had been advocated by Jenkins in a book he published in 1959. He had the ability and drive to push them through when offered the Home Secretaryship by Wilson who expressed surprise that Jenkins wanted that job.[79] Even when a bill was introduced by a backbencher, as was the case with abortion law reform – on which Members of Parliament had a free vote – the Liberal MP who sponsored the bill, David Steel, benefited from a 'strongly favourable ministerial speech' by Jenkins.[80] Neither that bill nor the Sexual Offences Act (which freed 'homosexuals over twenty-one from the rigours of the criminal law', and of which the backbench sponsor was the Labour MP Leo Abse) would have got through the legislative process but for the support of Jenkins as Home Secretary.[81]

One other major initiative of that government was, however, very much Harold Wilson's idea. He regarded it with pride and it was the achievement for which he most wished to be remembered. This was the foundation of the Open University, which made use of radio and television in teaching and aimed to extend higher educational opportunities to many who had missed out when they were younger. The use of the broadcasting mass media was combined with innovative teaching materials and part-time personal instruction to enable adults of all ages, working from home, to study at their own pace up to degree level. Wilson entrusted the task of turning into concrete reality what he had initially called a 'University of the Air' to a politician who became by far the most formidable 'junior minister' in the government of 1964–70. This was Jennie Lee, who won numerous battles with the Treasury (as well as with her own nominal immediate superior, the Secretary of State for Education) through imperious political will, her standing with party members nationally, and Wilson's respect for her and for her late husband, Aneurin Bevan, the minister in the Attlee government who had introduced the National Health Service.[82] In her dual capacity of Minister for the Arts and minister charged with bringing the Open University into being, Jennie Lee aroused the envy of colleagues of Cabinet rank (which she was not) with her ability to obtain vastly increased funding, even in difficult times, because she could, whenever the need arose, call the prime minister and enlist his support.[83]

The Asquith, Attlee and Thatcher governments were redefining across a broad spectrum of policy. The only lasting impact of the Labour government led for a decade by Tony Blair (continuing fallout from the Iraq war apart) is likely to be the constitutional change which was enacted. But that was on a scale which made it not far short of redefining. House of Lords reform was carried much further, with a radical reduction in the number of hereditary peers – 90 per cent of them removed in one fell swoop. A Human Rights Act, which has been described by Vernon Bogdanor as 'the cornerstone of the new British constitution',[84] and a Freedom of Information Act were introduced. A Scottish parliament and Welsh assembly were created and there was both executive and legislative devolution to Northern Ireland in a power-sharing agreement between the divided communities. Many people – including previous British and Irish prime ministers, successive Secretaries of State for Northern Ireland, Blair's chief of staff Jonathan Powell, Senator George Mitchell and even President Bill Clinton – had been involved in the last of these achievements, but Blair's role was recognized by the principal protagonists in Northern Ireland, and by the Irish Republic premier Bertie Ahern, to have been important. Northern Ireland apart, constitutional reform (as was noted briefly in an earlier chapter) was a result of policy Blair inherited and for which he showed little fervour. Later, indeed, he viewed the Freedom of Information Act, in particular, as a mistake which benefited mainly journalists and as something that would in future inhibit people within government giving frank advice, for fear of early disclosure of what they had said.[85] Devolution of decision-making to Scotland and Wales, the Human Rights Act and the Freedom of Information Act contributed in their various ways also to a diminution of Blair's own powers. That, together with the fact that they were not policies for which the prime minister could take personal credit, meant that the most momentous achievements of the Labour government during the decade in which it was led by Blair were not trumpeted from 10 Downing Street.[86]

The leading historian of twentieth-century British politics (and of the Labour Party especially), Kenneth Morgan, has noted that *only* in respect of constitutional reform was the government led by Blair bolder than was Asquith's ninety years earlier. Morgan appositely observes that in this area of policy Lord (Derry) Irvine's influence was 'of central importance'.[87] One change of constitutional significance which Blair backed – Britain's entry into the European common currency (the euro) – did not happen, for the prime minister was easily outmanoeuvred by the Chancellor of the Exchequer, Gordon Brown.[88] In 2000 Blair asserted: 'I will decide the issue of monetary union', but he was unable to do so.[89] He went so far as to indicate to Brown that he would retire earlier, to make way for him, if he would 'take a more sympathetic view of the euro', but to no avail.[90]

In the Introduction to this book, I noted that *redefining* leaders, individually or collectively, seek to move the centre in the direction of their party rather than simply trying to place the party in the centre ground as defined by others. Blair chose the latter course. It is fair to say that he and, to a lesser extent, Brown, as Chancellor for a decade and as prime minister from 2007 until 2010, allowed a genuinely re-defining leader, in the shape of Thatcher, to establish different limits of what was politically possible and desirable.[91] There were, however, distinctions between the political convictions of Blair, on the one hand, and of Brown, on the other, which were somewhat obscured by 'New Labour' rhetoric. Robin Cook, one of the leading figures in the government led by Blair until he resigned from it in protest against the Iraq war, praised Brown (with whom his relations had in the past been frosty, to say the least) for taking 'millions of children and pensioners out of poverty'. But he told Blair, Brown and other ministers at a Chequers meeting that 'when I talk proudly of what we've done for the poor, inside I feel vaguely uneasy as if I've somehow gone off message'.[92]

Blair describes Brown in his memoirs as the more thoroughgoing 'public service guy' of the two of them and notes his concern that Brown would not, if he succeeded him, carry on with an 'authentic New Labour' agenda.[93] Given the extent to which manufacturing industry had left Britain's shores, the financial sector was a very import-ant source of tax revenues. That was a major reason why Labour Chancellors (Brown for the decade when Blair was prime minister and Alistair Darling during the three years of Brown's premiership) treated it gingerly. Nevertheless, the 'light touch regulation' of the City of London was in the tradition of the Thatcher government – or, at least, in the post-Thatcher centre ground. Until the financial crisis struck in 2008, revealing a host of dubious practices, 'the Conservative opposition was arguing for even less regulation'.[94]

Alex Salmond – and the Possible Break-up of Britain

There is one candidate for redefining leader in contemporary British politics – the leader of the Scottish National Party, Alex Salmond. *If* – and it is a big if – Scotland were to vote in a referendum for separate statehood, thus ending a political union which has been remarkably stable and comparatively successful for over three hundred years, this would, indeed, constitute systemic change. Salmond, in such circumstances, could even be counted as a transformational leader, although opinion in Scotland and in the UK as a whole would doubtless remain divided on whether this was a positive development. It would certainly be consequential, and not all of those consequences foreseeable. Although there are a number of important reasons for the rise of the Scottish National Party quite apart from the debating skill, personality and persuasiveness of Salmond, he is recognized by his adversaries as well as his supporters to be a formidable politician. It is also the case that a political party which is a latecomer on the political scene depends more than do long-established parties on the particular talents of its leadership, including their ability to attract public and mass media attention.

Founded in 1934, but with minimal representation in the House of Commons until the 1970s, the Scottish National Party has benefited from the creation of a Scottish parliament, for Scots have voted for the SNP in much larger numbers for the Edinburgh parliament than for the House of Commons.* Just eight years after the first election for the Scottish parliament in 1999, the SNP, led by Salmond, formed a minority administration, and having demonstrated that they could govern (and were more than a one-man band), secured an absolute majority four years later in the election of 2011.[95] And that, moreover, in a highly proportional electoral system, deliberately designed to make it difficult for any one party (not least the SNP) to gain an overall majority.

Many factors are involved in an explanation of the Scottish Nationalists' rise. The international context is one. There has been a

---

* The SNP might have seen an even greater upsurge in its support if the promise of a devolved Scottish parliament had been broken by the UK government elected in 1997. For decades there has been a very clear Scottish majority in favour of more 'Home Rule' and a devolved parliament, whereas support for separate statehood for Scotland in opinion surveys has rarely risen above a third of the electorate.

proliferation of new states, with seats at the United Nations, in recent decades. The end of Communist rule in the Soviet Union and Eastern Europe saw the re-establishment of statehood of countries which had formerly been independent and the creation of many new states with far less continuity of national institutions or tradition of national consciousness than Scotland. The Labour Party, the strongest in Scotland from the end of the 1950s onwards, lost some of its popularity north of the border during the Blair years. Part of the new support the SNP gathered came from voters attracted to policies that were closer to those of the Labour Party prior to its 'New Labour' makeover.

Alex Salmond himself came originally from the left of his party, and the Scottish Nationalists were by this time far removed from the days when they could be dismissed as the 'Tartan Tories'. The SNP benefited also after 2003 from the unpopularity of the Iraq war, of which Salmond, a Westminster MP at the time, was one of the most effective critics. Salmond led the SNP from 1990 to 2000 and then took a break from the leadership for four years. Its support lessened during that period. Having earlier announced that he was 'fed up with going up like a rocket and down like a stick', he presided over the party's most spectacular rise when he resumed its leadership in 2004.[96] Salmond has described himself as 'a great fan of Harold Wilson', and, like Wilson, he has been adept at lacing invective with humour and at talking himself out of tricky situations.[97] Not the least of these has been jettisoning an earlier strong commitment to the idea of the euro as Scotland's post-independence currency once the euro ran into severe difficulties and its popularity plummeted. Forced to fall back on using the pound and accepting the ministrations of the Bank of England in a hypothetically independent Scotland, Salmond consoled himself by reminding everyone that the Bank had been founded by a Scotsman. He has exemplified the contention that detailed arguments are less decisive for political success than making emotional contact with the electorate.[98]

REDEFINING LEADERSHIP IN POST-WAR GERMANY

Post-war West Germany and – from 1990 – the unified Germany have been success stories, both economically and politically. The country has prospered and the quality of its democracy has been high, as has that of its leaders. It is reasonable to see a linkage between good leadership and democratic consolidation, even if this connection is less overwhelmingly obvious than the link between Germany's 'strong' and charismatic leadership in the 1930s and the country's oppressive totalitarian political system from 1933 until 1945. Three of the post-war chancellors, Konrad Adenauer, Willy Brandt and Helmut Kohl, have persuasive claims to be regarded as redefining leaders. The chancellor is not head of state in Germany – that is the role of the president who is a political figurehead. A holder of that office can provide significant moral leadership, as Richard von Weizsäcker, in particular, demonstrated in the 1980s and '90s. But it is the chancellor who heads the government and wields more power than anyone else in the country. He or she – for Germany's first woman chancellor Angela Merkel, another talented politician and astute leader, was elected in 2005 – is not chosen directly by the electorate but by the German parliament. Each party nominates its candidate for the Chancellorship in advance, and so this knowledge is a significant consideration in voters' choice. Party allegiance is sufficiently strong, however, that the candidate is hardly ever the decisive factor. A major study of post-war German elections found 'the role of party identification' to be 'by far the most important single determinant of voter choices'.[99]

Once in office, the chancellor has very substantial authority, although it is greater (as is true of many other heads of government) in foreign than in domestic policy. The chancellor is granted the right to determine the broad guidelines of policy – in a way in which the British prime minister is not, even if some holders of the office attempt to act as if they were – and is responsible to the legislature for government policy outcomes. Nevertheless, ministers in Germany enjoy quite a high degree of autonomy, which is constitutionally enshrined. Even while operating within general lines laid down by the chancellor, they are in full charge of their own departments, and the chancellor is not constitutionally permitted to issue specific orders to ministers. In cases of conflict between one department and another, the Cabinet has a role to play in reconciling the differences, but the main political actor in the conciliatory process is the chancellor.[100] The Constitution for a democratic Germany had been drawn up by representatives of the various parties who came together in a Parliamentary Council in 1948. They were intent on creating institutions that would avoid not only the totalitarianism of the Third Reich but also the weakness of the Weimar Republic that had preceded it.[101] Thus, they made it difficult to dissolve parliament and to overthrow governments between elections. That could only be done through a 'constructive vote of no confidence'. This meant that a chancellor would be forced to resign only if a parliamentary majority had agreed on the name of his or her successor – quite a high hurdle.

Two of the main constraints upon the chancellor's powers follow from the nature of the electoral system and the federal character of German government. Germany's system of proportional representation rarely gives any one political party an overall majority and so most German governments since the end of the Second World War have been coalitions. The chancellor, whether a Christian Democrat or a Social Democrat, has, therefore, to do deals with the other party in the coalition – usually the Free Democrats, although, when the Social Democrats are the largest party, it can be the Greens.*

The Christian Democrats did so well in the September 2013 general election, in which they made the most of the popularity of Angela Merkel, that they came close to winning an outright majority, but still fell short of it. Although Merkel thereby was assured of a third term as Chancellor, the electoral system presented her with a major problem. The Free Democrats failed to reach the quite demanding 5 per cent threshold for parliamentary representation, thus leaving her little option but a 'grand coalition' with the Social Democrats, to which the SPD responded warily, since the Christian Democrats would be very much the senior partner. A deal was struck between the party leaderships in late November and ratified by the SPD membership the following month.

Konrad Adenauer

The top leader of a political party obviously has special opportunities to set the tone for the party he or she leads, and for the country when

---

* Political power is also less centralized in Germany than in England (*England* as distinct from the United Kingdom, for there is now substantial devolution of power to Scotland, Wales and Northern Ireland). The federal components of Germany's political system – the regional *Länder* – each have their own Constitution, parliament, government and administration.

that person becomes chancellor. This applied to an exceptional degree to the first chancellor of post-war Germany, the Christian Democrat Konrad Adenauer, whose responsibility for re-establishing German democracy, following more than a decade of Nazi rule, and in a country in ruins, was profound. Support for democracy was shaky, to say the least, in the early post-war years. It was a time when 'many West Germans still assented to the statement that Hitler would have been one of the greatest statesmen there had ever been, if only he had not lost the war'.[102] Adenauer was already seventy-three when he became Chancellor of the Federal Republic of Germany in 1949. He had become Mayor of Cologne as long ago as 1917, an office he held until 1933 when he was removed by the Nazis, becoming Cologne's mayor again, briefly, in 1945, before going on to become Chairman of the Christian Democratic Union.[103]

The recovery of the German economy, over which Adenauer presided and from which his popularity benefited, owed a great deal to his Economic Minister, Ludwig Erhard, the architect of what was called the 'economic miracle'. Adenauer himself put the idea of the Social Market Economy into the Christian Democrats' programme in 1949, and may have been influenced by Roman Catholic social teaching. The same is often – and wrongly – said of Erhard. Along with most of the economists who supported him, Erhard was a Protestant and a politician who believed that sweeping away the bureaucratic controls that had been put in place by the Nazis and which had continued under the Allied occupiers would itself promote social welfare. The resultant policy of the government, however, combined private enterprise and competition with a consensus-seeking approach to industrial relations and with the construction of a welfare state (whose origins went back much further – to Bismarck's social insurance legislation of the 1880s).[104] Although he was to serve as chancellor from 1963 to 1966 as Adenauer's successor, Erhard was less effective in that role than he had been as a key member of Adenauer's administration, helping to lay economic foundations for democracy. Growing prosperity underpinned support for democratic norms, reversing the pattern of German democracy after the First World War when economic failure, hyper-inflation and subsequent unemployment had much to do with the demise of the Weimar Republic and the rise of Hitler.

If Erhard helped to make Adenauer a redefining leader domestically, it was Adenauer himself who radically redefined West Germany's foreign policy. Given the division of Germany, and the fact that the United States emerged from the war (and the early post-war occupation of Germany) as clearly the strongest Western power, Adenauer unsurprisingly established and maintained good relations with the Americans. Moreover, he welcomed their continued presence in Europe as a bulwark against possible Soviet expansionism. What was more distinctive and momentous, in the context of German history, was his establishment of good relations with France – not least, with General de Gaulle after his return to power in Paris in 1958. Adenauer was strongly in favour of European economic and political cooperation, and supported a joint European military organization. He also, however, wished the Federal Republic of Germany to have access to nuclear weapons, and in retirement he was vehemently opposed to German acceptance of the nuclear non-proliferation treaty, the signing of which was one of Willy Brandt's first acts as chancellor. Under Adenauer's leadership, West Germany joined NATO in the mid-1950s, and in 1957 was a founder signatory of the Treaty of Rome, which created the European Economic Community, the forerunner of the European Union. Adenauer was able to claim: 'I am the only German Chancellor in history who has preferred the unity of Europe to unity of the Reich.'[105] He has also been described as 'the first German statesman who was able to overcome the unconscious tendency of his countrymen to believe that leaders could only be taken seriously if they wore uniforms'.[106] Adenauer, however, stayed in the office of chancellor for far too long, and to diminishing effect. Like many leaders, he increasingly thought of himself as indispensable and could see no one worthy to take his place. When he was finally persuaded in 1963 to retire from the most powerful political post in West Germany, he was aged eighty-seven.

Willy Brandt

The conservative Catholic, Adenauer, could also be ruthless in the way in which he fought electoral battles. Willy Brandt noted that the Chancellor spent 'half an election campaign on the issue of my birth' and the day after the Berlin Wall went up in August 1961 referred to him as 'alias Frahm'.[107] Brandt's mother was an unmarried salesgirl who gave birth to him in 1913. The boy grew up as Herbert Frahm, taking his mother's name, and not knowing who his father was. Both his mother and her father, who shared in his upbringing, were active members of the Social Democratic Party, and they enrolled him in the children's section of the party's sports club 'almost as soon as I could walk'.[108] He grew up, and remained, a socialist of a social democratic kind, tempted by neither Communism nor fascism. In 1933, when anti-Nazi activity had become increasingly dangerous, necessitating clandestine activity, he took the name Willy Brandt. He was an active anti-Nazi before and after Hitler came to power, working mainly from other European countries, especially Norway, but also spending a dangerous period back in Germany in the guise of a Norwegian student. Brandt escaped again to Norway in 1938, and after Nazi Germany invaded the country in 1940, he moved to neutral Sweden. Although Brandt had been working not for the defeat of his homeland but for its liberation, in the early post-war years he was regarded by many of his fellow countrymen as a traitor. He was still a Norwegian citizen when he returned to Germany in 1945. He rejoined the SPD, and regained his German citizenship in 1948.

Brandt's rise in German politics was quite rapid. He proved no less resolute in standing up to Communist than to Nazi repression. He was a leading figure in the government of Berlin by 1948–49 when the Soviet blockade took place, and the city survived thanks mainly to the allied airlift of food and other supplies. When the Berlin Wall went up in 1961, Brandt had already been Mayor of Berlin for four years, and he did more than anyone to maintain the morale of the city's residents. During almost a decade as mayor of divided Berlin, he continued to provide inspirational leadership. It was his years as Chancellor, however, from 1969 to 1974 which firmly established him as a redefining leader. His political style was not only more collegial than that of Adenauer, but also relaxed, conciliatory and 'patient enough to permit the building of an authentic cabinet consensus'.[109] Collegiality, however, was not incompatible with an outstanding personal initiative on an issue of major international, as well as inter-German, importance – West Germany's relations with East Germany and, more generally, with the Eastern part of the European continent. This *Ostpolitik* was the major achievement of Brandt's chancellorship. The policy led to an acceptance of Germany's post-war borders in the east, an amelioration of relations between East and West Germany and recognition (without legitimation) of the status quo that they had become two separate states. Human contacts between the two Germanies became more frequent, and Brandt was greeted with great enthusiasm by the East German public when he visited the German Democratic Republic (GDR) in March 1970. Taking advantage of a period of détente during the Nixon presidency between the United States and the Soviet Union, Brandt also became the first West German leader to establish a working relationship with Moscow.*

There was serious opposition within Germany to Brandt's *Ostpolitik*, not only from Christian Democrats, but from some of the Free Democrats who were in coalition with Brandt's SPD. A number of them defected from the coalition and at one point Brandt survived a parliamentary vote of no confidence by only two votes.[110] Brandt's acceptance that Germany would not regain territory that had belonged to it before the war – Silesia and East Prussia – enraged his political opponents as well as influential associations of expellees. Moreover, it appeared to many, both in Germany and abroad, that Brandt was giving up on the ultimate goal of reunification of East and West Germany and getting little or nothing in return. Reasonable as that objection sounded at the time, it could not have been further from the truth. Hatred and fear of Germany, for understandable reasons, was still rife in Russia in the mid-1960s. It had greatly dissipated by the mid-1970s.[111] Brandt's lifelong anti-fascism and his anti-Nazi activities during the Second World War earned him the respect of East Germans, of ordinary Russians, and even of the Soviet leadership, headed by Leonid Brezhnev. Brandt was especially highly regarded by the most reformist members of the ruling parties of Communist

---

* None of that prevented the GDR intelligence service – in a decision requiring highest-level political approval – from planting an East German spy, Günter Guillaume, as a senior aide in Brandt's entourage. When this espionage was discovered, Brandt resigned the chancellorship, once again setting an honourable example. See Mary Fulbrook, *History of Germany 1918–2000: The Divided Nation* (Blackwell, Oxford, 2002), pp. 168–71.

Europe.* That became particularly relevant with the arrival in 1985 as Soviet leader of Mikhail Gorbachev, whose own political evolution during the second half of that decade was very much in the direction of social democracy.[112] Gorbachev established excellent relations with Brandt who by then was President of the Socialist International, the organization of social democratic parties which had for long been regarded by Communists as the most dangerous of their enemies.[113] Most fundamentally, it is inconceivable that the Kremlin leadership would have quietly accepted the fall of the Berlin Wall in 1989 and acquiesced in the unification of Germany in 1990, had Germany still been seen as the kind of threat it was perceived to be a little over two decades earlier before Brandt became West German leader.

The public image of Brandt most vividly remembered is of him on his knees in front of the Warsaw memorial dedicated to the Jewish ghetto and the countless Polish Jews who died at the hands of the Nazis. On this visit to Poland in December 1970, the German chancellor had not planned that gesture. It took even his closest colleagues by surprise. Brandt later wrote: 'From the bottom of the abyss of German history, under the burden of millions of victims of murder, I did what human beings do when speech fails them.'[114] A journalist put it no less aptly at the time when he wrote that 'he who does not need to kneel knelt, on behalf of all who do need to kneel, but do not'.[115]

Domestically, Brandt's record both in resistance to fascism and in the post-war reconstruction of a divided country played an important part in the consolidation of democracy in Germany. But his contribution internationally was even more redefining. He put it fairly himself:

Circumstances, my office, and also, I am sure, the experiences of my youth, gave me a chance – first as Mayor of Berlin, then as Foreign Minister and as Federal Chancellor – to reconcile the idea of Germany with the idea of peace

* It was in the company of two distinguished Hungarian historians on Visiting Fellowships, Ivan Berend and György Ránki, that I met Brandt in Oxford. Both were members of the Communist Party, as they had been from their youth, but serious reformers who worked for change from within the Hungarian system. Both were also of Jewish origin. Berend, as a teenager, spent the last year of the war in a German concentration camp. I remember the warmth of Brandt's personality during the conversation, but recall just as vividly how moved, almost to tears, were the two Hungarian scholars in meeting him.

in the minds of large parts of the world. After all that had happened, that was no small matter . . ."[116]

There have been other Social Democratic leaders in post-war Germany apart from Willy Brandt who were impressive – above all, Helmut Schmidt, a politician with a commanding presence who had been Minister of Defence and Minister of Economics and Finance in Brandt's government before serving for eight successful years as chancellor (1974–1982). Schmidt's historical significance, however, hardly matched that of Brandt. His personal biography was very different. As a relatively apolitical young man, he served as an officer in the German army during the Second World War, and won the Iron Cross, fighting on the Russian front. His sharp intellect, brusque manner and more conventional views contrasted with the imagination, charm and political daring of Brandt. Schmidt was a controversial figure in the early 1980s when his readiness to accept American Pershing and cruise missiles on German soil met with widespread protests. In terms of ability, though, he remains another outstanding example of how well, by international standards, Germany has been served by its post-war leaders.

Helmut Kohl

Two things are remarkable about the chancellorship of Helmut Kohl. One is the length of time during which he held that office – sixteen years, from 1982 until 1998 – and the other is the skill and alacrity with which he seized an opportunity to pursue the unification of Germany at a time when other leaders advised caution. Kohl was underestimated as a politician during much of his time in office, and he fell under a cloud following his retirement when evidence emerged of party funding scandals in which he had been involved. He also had to overcome a very bad start in his relations with Gorbachev, being far slower than Margaret Thatcher to spot the potential for change brought about by the new Russian leader. As late as October 1986, a year and a half into the Soviet perestroika, Kohl told *Newsweek* that he did not consider Gorbachev to be a liberal but a 'modern communist leader who understands public relations', adding: 'Goebbels, who was one of those responsible for the crimes in the Hitler era, was an expert in public relations, too.'[117] The implied comparison with Goebbels offended Gorbachev and those around him, and it meant that Kohl was kept waiting – until the autumn of 1988 – for a meeting with the Soviet leader, even after he had come to realize his mistake. He then made up for lost time and went on to establish surprisingly warm relations with Gorbachev. Since the future of a divided Germany still depended heavily on what happened in Moscow, this was politically wise. But the connection was personal and emotional as well as prudential. What might have fundamentally divided the two men brought them together – their memories of being children, growing up on opposite sides of a war in which their countries were the major European antagonists. The devastation and suffering on the victorious side was no less than in that of the vanquished, and the war left indelible marks on both Gorbachev and Kohl.

At the beginning of 1989, unification still seemed a distant dream for Germans. Emboldened, however, by the radical changes in Moscow, the peoples of Eastern Europe pushed aside their Communist rulers in the course of that year. Until then it had been assumed that, as in Hungary (1956) and Czechoslovakia (1968), Soviet military force would be used to ensure that no European country that was within the Communist camp would be allowed to slip out of it. This was taken to apply, above all, to the GDR, the East German state where 350,000 Soviet troops were stationed. Yet, when massive demonstrations took place in East German cities in October and November, and when the Berlin Wall was suddenly opened – as a result of a misunderstanding of a Politburo decision to ease travel restrictions – on the night of 9 November 1989, Soviet soldiers did not intervene. East German citizens who demonstrated in October had chanted, 'We are the people.' After the fall of the Wall, this became, 'We are *one* people.'[118]

The popular desire for unification could not have been clearer, but many leading politicians, in Germany as well as in the rest of Europe, thought the issue so delicate that the process could only be a gradual one. Kohl took a different view. He believed, not without reason, that Gorbachev might be deposed by conservative Soviet Communists, alarmed by the domestic and international repercussions of his policies. In that event, a once-in-a-lifetime opportunity for reunification would have been missed. With strong American backing, Kohl hammered out a deal on reunification with Gorbachev, ignored the objections of Margaret Thatcher, and was ready to pay the price demanded by French President François Mitterrand for securing his agreement to German unification. It involved acceptance of closer European unity and, most specifically, undertaking to give up the Deutschmark in order to join a new, common currency to be created for EU members – the euro. Kohl himself was much more relaxed about the idea of both economic and monetary union than was the Bundesbank.

Before the common European currency could be created, Kohl worked for monetary union in Germany, offering a one-to-one exchange of the West German Deutschmark for East German marks, an attractive offer to those on the Eastern side of the divide, whose currency had been worth far less than that on the black market. In the process, Kohl ignored expert advice that the East German economy needed some years to be brought up to a comparable level with that of the West and that only then would a common currency make sense.[119] Kohl's focus was entirely on short-term attraction with a view to pushing through unification at the fastest possible speed. It was important within Germany, for if union had not gone ahead quickly, and on generous terms for citizens of the GDR, there would have been a real possibility of breakdown of order in East Germany. If that had led to bloodshed and internal repression, it would have posed very serious problems for Gorbachev and his allies in the Soviet leadership. The relationship Kohl had established with Gorbachev was of huge importance. In a meeting on 10 February 1990, the Soviet leader came to a provisional agreement with Kohl that unification would go ahead, although many details still had to be worked out. President George Bush the elder played a supportive role during the process, acting carefully so as not to undermine Gorbachev. He did not, however, share some of the apprehensions of a number of European leaders about the potential strength of a reunited Germany.[120]

Kohl's seizing of the historic moment, and his skilful diplomacy in both inter-German and international relations, brought a speedy reward. The first was an election victory in East Germany when the Christian-Democrat-led 'Alliance for Germany' emerged as the most successful coalition of parties, getting almost half of all votes in March 1990. The last part of the process was completed in just eight weeks of the summer of that year – in the 2 + 4 negotiations, in which the representatives of the two Germanies sat down with those of the countries that had earlier constituted the four occupying powers: the Soviet Union, the United States, the United Kingdom and France. The Treaty on German Unity was signed on 31 August 1990. No doubt, German unification would have taken place at some point, for the East German economy was collapsing, and almost 350,000 of its citizens had left the country in the course of 1989. Public opinion, which could now be freely expressed in the East, was clearly in favour of national unity. Yet, something that had seemed inconceivable just a few years earlier would not have proceeded so smoothly, speedily and peacefully had any one of Gorbachev, Bush and Kohl acted either more rashly or with significantly greater caution. It would be going much too far to say that there would have been no unification without Kohl, but, in his absence it could hardly have happened so quickly in 1990. As one student of inter-German relations appositely observed, it was Helmut Kohl who pushed reunification through 'with verve, determination and an invincible – some would say finally disastrous – capacity to suppress economic and social misgivings in the cause of the final political goal'.[121] For all the problems that were to come later, not least the vicissitudes of the euro, the part Kohl played in the unification of his country which had been divided for forty-five years gives him a strong claim to be regarded as a redefining leader.

REDEFINING LEADERS IN PERSPECTIVE

The focus in this chapter has been on redefining leadership in just three, albeit major, democracies. Not many generalizations can be based on such a small sample, although a close look at American presidents suggests the conclusion that it is very difficult to be a redefining leader (and almost impossible to be a transformational one) in twentieth- or twenty-first-century USA. Even those presidents who use to the full their political resources generally have less leverage within the domestic context than have the German chancellor and British prime minister. If we were to bring in additional redefining leaders from other democracies, whether presidential or parliamentary, the constraints on the occupant of the White House would doubtless still bulk large in comparison.[122] Redefining the limits of the possible, changing the way people think about politics, and introducing radical policy change is a very tall order for any American president. A combination of the strictness of the separation of powers, the fact that Congress is by comparative standards an unusually strong legislature, the willingness of the Supreme Court to pass judgement on the constitutionality of presidential actions, not to speak of the existence of powerful and lavishly funded lobbies, mean that the American president's scope for action is far more limited than the prestige of this apparently ultra-powerful office would suggest.

The widespread belief in a vast growth over time of presidential power within the political system of the United States is an oversimplification. It is, for one thing, contradicted by the finding that there has been a historic decrease in the rate of presidential vetoes of legislation as measured against congressional output.[123] Richard Rose has observed that in Washington 'there is a simple answer to the inquiring journalist's question: Who's in charge here? The correct constitutional answer is: No one.'[124] The demanding nature of international politics, in which more is expected of the American president than of other heads of government, severely restricts the time available for implementation of a domestic agenda, quite apart from the constitutional and political constraints. In a nicely paradoxical phrase, Rose captures the practical limitations on presidential response to the endless problems that come his way when he characterizes it as 'influencing organized anarchy'.[125] A leading specialist on American government, Hugh Heclo, sees the presidential use of the 'bully pulpit' (first associated with Theodore Roosevelt) as a diminishing asset. The president's capacity to rally public opinion has been reduced by 'the proliferation of news sources, sites for contending political commentaries, and the ordinary citizen's information overload'.[126]

Perhaps, then, it is not surprising that the only two clear examples of redefining leaders to occupy the White House in the twentieth and twenty-first centuries ceased to be president almost seventy years ago in the one case and more than four decades ago in the other. Presidential power, though, remains vastly greater in foreign than in domestic policy. This, indeed, is an area where the president's power and influence have grown in the period that began with the Second World War, and where he (or, one day, she) can make an enormous difference.* In the international sphere, the president wields more power, both politically and militarily, than any other politician on earth. Yet, the limits of power are all too evident even here. While contenders for the American presidency may announce that the Middle East or some other part of the world is crying out for American leadership, the sober reality is that a majority of people in the area concerned are often disinclined to follow. Moreover, the use of American military power has in major instances been followed by profound unintended political consequences – from the Vietnam War to the wars in Afghanistan and Iraq. The hopes and expectations vested in the American president in the twenty-first century are so high and, in many respects, contradictory that they are impossible for any holder of that office to meet.[127]

Redefining leaders are rare within the entire constellation of political leaders, but examples of them could be multiplied if we move beyond the three countries from which the illustrations in this chapter have been drawn. One special category of redefining leaders consists of those who, as transitional leaders, pave the way for the transformation of the political or economic system of their countries, opening up space for that fundamental change without going on to play the leading role in the transformation themselves. The reforming leader can, in some cases, redefine the scope of legitimate political activity and stimulate either more radical leadership or movement from below, and sometimes a mixture of both, going beyond the intentions of the reformer. Not every transformational leader is, however, immediately preceded by a redefining one. Even his kindest obituarist could hardly have called Konstantin Chernenko a redefining leader. The main advantage for Mikhail Gorbachev in following this colourless apparatchik was in the immediate contrast he provided with Chernenko, under whom the only slight political movement was backwards.[128]

* I do not follow the fashion, begun by Joseph Nye, of using the terms 'hard power' and 'soft power'. They may be a useful shorthand for newspaper columnists and politicians, but the vocabulary of authority, leadership, influence, persuasion, prestige, political power, economic power and military power remains perfectly serviceable. Although these terms are also open to more than one interpretation, they are somewhat more precise than the hard power–soft power dichotomy. Nye does not, of course, confine himself to such a division and his work contains many cogent arguments, but it retains a strong paternal attachment to his coinage of 'soft power'.

There are also quite different, and surprising, cases where leaders of a racially repressive or authoritarian regime have moved from being pillars of resistance to change to paving the way for the new, and not simply by unwittingly provoking collapse. F.W. de Klerk in South Africa and Chiang Ching-kuo, the son of Chiang Kai-shek, in Taiwan are examples of such transitional leadership. Adolfo Suárez in Spain could be seen as another, but for the fact that in Spain's transition from authoritarianism to democracy, the part he played was *so* significant – overseeing the transition from a regime in which there were no pluralistic political institutions all the way to one in which democracy, with free elections, prevailed – that he should be considered as a transformational leader, and is treated as such in the next chapter.

Fernando Henrique Cardoso

A striking example of a redefining leader was Fernando Henrique Cardoso who played a crucial part in the development and consolidation of democracy in Brazil, especially but not only after he became president in 1995. A social scientist-turned-politician, he redefined the limits of the possible in Brazil. When he became Minister of Finance in 1994, Brazil's inflation rate was running at over 3000 per cent annually. When asked for his leadership philosophy in the face of this national disaster, Cardoso said: 'I looked to exercise the art of politics which consists precisely in creating conditions in which one can realize an objective for which conditions do not yet exist.'[129] In one year Cardoso had reduced the inflation rate to less than 10 per cent and hyperinflation has not in subsequent years returned to Brazil. The secret of his success was to delay the implementation of his anti-inflation plan until he had persuaded the trade unions by cogent argument that wage earners (as distinct from the wealthy taking advantage of high real interest rates) had most to gain if inflation were controlled. It is notable that Lula, Cardoso's presidential successor who had been not only a trade union leader but also a long-term opponent of Cardoso, praised this achievement, observing that the lesson had been learned that low inflation was beneficial for a society where the great majority of people live on their wages.

When Lula succeeded Cardoso as president in 2003, this was Brazil's first democratic succession in forty-three years. Lula himself was followed by a democratically elected president, Dilma Rousseff, in 2011. Cardoso's leadership altered perceptions of the limits of what politicians could achieve in a number of important ways. In addition to successfully combating hyperinflation, he showed great diplomatic skill in his dealings with the military and in subordinating them to civilian control. Through dialogue and persuasion, he won the armed forces over to acceptance of democracy, including the creation of a Ministry of Defence under civilian political leadership. Cardoso laid foundations whereby democratic electoral succession became the new normality in Brazilian politics. Taken in the round, his achievements were a notable example of stretching the limits of the attainable.

F.W. de Klerk

South Africa had a pluralist political system with real competition between the political parties of the white minority, but its racist basis meant that it was, in many respects, an international pariah state, subject also to a partially effective economic and sporting boycott. What tilted the balance was a new international context, brought about by the dramatic change within the Soviet Union and in Soviet foreign policy in the second half of the 1980s. The South African apartheid regime had long justified its existence by portraying itself as a bastion against the spread of Communism, citing the strong influence of the Communist Party of South Africa within the main black opposition movement, the African National Congress. The ANC, for its part, received economic as well as political backing from the Soviet Union, although it attracted much moral support also from democratic governments and liberal opinion in Western countries. When a liberalization of the Soviet Union itself took place, leading to much improved relations between it and the United States and the countries of Western Europe, the flimsy political pretext for apartheid appeared thinner than ever. Added to this was the change in Soviet foreign policy away from support for armed struggle and in favour of peaceful reconciliation of political differences in South Africa and elsewhere. Thus, the ANC, too, had reason to be responsive to serious overtures from the South African government in the hope of reaching agreement on peaceful transition to majority rule.[130]

By the time F.W. de Klerk succeeded P.W. Botha as South African president in 1989, the change in the international climate had become so great that it was clear to de Klerk that the moment had come for major domestic change. Embarking on a process of political reform, he took the risk of holding a referendum of white voters on whether this process should continue. More than two-thirds of them backed the policy. The key interlocutor – and the person who unquestionably was the transformational leader in the South African context – had to be Nelson Mandela, who had been demonized in the Afrikaner press for decades, and who was in his twenty-eighth year of imprisonment. Mandela himself has written that nothing in de Klerk's past had 'seemed to hint at a spirit of reform', but he decided that the new president was 'not an ideologue but a pragmatist', and on the day he was sworn in wrote him a letter requesting a meeting.[131] Negotiations between Mandela and de Klerk took place, Mandela was released from prison, the ban on the ANC (and also on the Communist Party of South Africa) was lifted, and a new constitution, according equal political rights to all citizens, was promulgated in 1993. Mandela, for his part, had agreed to renounce violent means for the achievement of majority rule, convinced by now that it was possible to reach that goal peacefully. Following free elections in 1994, in which the ANC-led coalition of parties gained more than 60 per cent of the votes, Mandela became South Africa's first black president. Given the extent to which he personally had suffered at the hands of the oppressive apartheid regime, his magnanimity and inspirational leadership were decisive. Nevertheless, de Klerk earned the title of 'enlightened conservative' by seizing the moment when a negotiated settlement had become possible. It was a break with past policy, which paved the way for relatively peaceful systemic change in a country where many had assumed it would take much longer and end more bloodily.[132]

The Case of Taiwan

A still more surprising redefining leader than de Klerk was Chiang Ching-kuo, first the head of the secret police and later prime minister in Taiwan (or the Republic of China, as the Taipei government terms that country). He was the son of an unremittingly authoritarian leader, Chiang Kai-shek. The elder Chiang died in 1975 and three years later Chiang Ching-kuo moved from the premiership to the presidency which his father had held. Throughout the period between the demise of Chiang Kai-Shek and Chiang Ching-kuo's own death in 1988, the younger Chiang's was by far the most authoritative voice in Taiwan as the regime gradually liberalized and moved towards pluralist democracy. Again there was a hugely important international stimulus. From the time Chiang Kai-shek set up his Chinese government in exile in Taiwan, it had been recognized by only a minority of countries in the world and relied very heavily on political and military support from the United States. The biggest single incentive to Chiang Ching-kuo's rethinking was the United States announcement in 1978 of normalization of its relations with mainland China.[133]

Rapprochement between the USA and the People's Republic of China (mainland China where more than a billion people lived, compared with Taiwan's population at the time of some twenty million) was bound to lead to a weakening of America's ties with Taiwan. The process of improving American–Chinese relations was started by President Nixon's visit to Beijing in 1972 and taken up again with some zest in the late 1970s by President Carter, whose National Security Adviser, Zbigniew Brzezinski, was especially keen to play the China card against the Soviet Union.[134] Cultivation of mainland China continued under President Reagan. In early 1982 it was announced that the Reagan administration would not sell the advanced FX fighter jet aircraft to Taiwan, so as not to jeopardize Sino-American relations.[135]

Taiwan had been developing economically and educationally at an impressive rate already in Chaing Kai-shek's time, but the younger Chiang realized that this was not enough. If his country was to achieve greater recognition in the outside world, earn renewed respect from the United States, and, ultimately perhaps become a model for mainland China itself (since the party he led, the Kuomintang, favoured eventual union with China, but as a non-Communist state), then movement towards democracy had to begin. Having come to believe that democracy would suit Taiwan's interests better than dictatorship, Chiang Ching-kuo pushed through a series of liberalizing reforms in the mid-1980s, and ended dynastic rule by saying that members of the Chiang family 'could not and would not' compete for the presidency in subsequent elections. The reforms also ended martial law and legalized opposition political parties.[136] It took almost a decade for all this to reach fruition, and fully democratic (although often turbulent) politics emerged only after Chiang's death. It was he, however, who took the decisive steps to redefine the nature of the political system and pave the way for genuinely competitive elections in which the Kuomintang would not be guaranteed victory.

*

What these examples illustrate is that in the process of liberalizing and democratizing an undemocratic political system, innovative political leadership from within the old regime can be extraordinarily important. When there is a change of opinions, beliefs and even goals of leaders who already hold positions of institutional power, that can decisively facilitate democratization of an authoritarian regime. If a leader in a democracy changes his or her opinions while holding office, this often does the politician concerned more harm than good, earning fierce criticism for U-turns, intellectual flip-flopping and political inconsistency. An authoritarian leader, however, can use the levers of power he controls to introduce liberalizing or even democratizing measures, although these will pose risks for the existing holders of bureaucratic power. The cases with which this chapter has concluded underscore also the need always to understand leadership in its political context. What they have in common is that they refer to regimes which were becoming increasingly isolated, both politically and economically, although that in itself does not guarantee redefining change. North Korea has experienced economic failure and international contempt over decades, and yet the regime survives.

Within democracies (as in authoritarian regimes) redefining leadership is the exception rather than the rule. Sometimes it does come from leaders who are very dominant within their political parties – a Thatcher or an Adenauer – but it can just as readily come from a leadership in which the head of the government is far less assertive and there are a number of authoritative ministers playing decisively important roles, as in the case of the Asquith and Attlee governments in twentieth-century Britain. American presidents, despite the immense prestige of their office, find it difficult to dominate the political process, given the nature of the political system in which they operate.

When they do dominate, as Franklin Roosevelt and, much more briefly, Lyndon Johnson did, this depends less on their actual powers (although veto and power of appointment matter) than on influence and authority. Roosevelt's success was in persuading a broader public of the need for legislation which was radically innovative in the American context and of using that public opinion to help persuade Congress of the necessity of these measures. It depended also, however, on one of the messy compromises of politics – tacit concessions to Southern Democrats that there would be no drastic federal interference with ethnic segregation in the South. Johnson's persuasion, more directly focused on Congress, drew on his excellent memory and intimate knowledge of the type of argument that would carry weight with each Senator or Representative. In these cases, as in other instances of redefining leadership, the circumstances in which the leaders came to the highest office were decisively important. A crisis by definition poses problems but it also presents opportunities. Roosevelt's New Deal was a response to the economic depression of the 1930s, and he exercised his greatest power when the United States was engaged in a global war. Johnson came to the White House when his country had just suffered the trauma of assassination of a young and popular president. He seized the moment to persuade Congress to pass legislation which redefined citizenship for many hitherto deprived Americans and constituted at least as significant a breakthrough as Roosevelt's New Deal.

4

Transformational Political Leadership

By a transformational political leader, I mean one who plays a decisive role in introducing *systemic change*, whether of the political or economic system of his or her country or (more rarely) of the international system. The word 'transformational' generally has a positive connotation. It suggests profound change, but a fundamental reconstruction of the system into one that is qualitatively better than what has gone before. Largely for that reason, I distinguish it from revolutionary leadership. Some revolutions against oppressive rulers produce regimes that are an improvement in certain respects, and worse in others, than their predecessors. They are generally characterized, however, by the use of force to overthrow the pre-existing regime and by the subsequent use of coercive power to impose and sustain their rule over the whole population. However egalitarian and democratic their revolutionary rhetoric may be, they also have a strong tendency to create not only authoritarian regimes but also a cult of the strong individual leader within the post-revolutionary system. Leaders who play a decisive role in transforming the political or economic system of their country, without resort either to violent seizure of power or to the physical coercion of their opponents, are different from such revolutionaries. They are likely to do more lasting good and certainly less harm. It is rare, of course, for *all* of the aspirations of transformational leaders to be fully realized. And the systemic change they introduce may only partially survive the rule of their successors. However, the gulf between the utopian rhetoric of revolutionaries and the subsequent authoritarian reality is generally much wider.

Although the list is not intended to be exclusive, and though mention will be made of other leaders who have made significant contributions to promoting transformative change, the major focus of the chapter will be on five leaders from different countries – General Charles de Gaulle, Adolfo Suárez, Mikhail Gorbachev, Deng Xiaoping and Nelson Mandela. Only France was a democracy at the time when transformational change took place, but de Gaulle was responsible for a profound switch from one kind of democratic political system to another. Within a democracy such transformative change is likely to occur only when the existing system is in severe crisis. Change in Britain has been sufficiently gradual that there was no place for a transformational leader in the twentieth century (or in the twenty-first thus far). In the United States, the last president with a strong claim to be regarded as a transformational leader was Abraham Lincoln, and it is no accident that nineteenth-century America was in deep internal crisis at the time.

CHARLES DE GAULLE

Usually leaders who think of themselves as being above politics, and who regard politicians with disdain, are bad for democracy. It is an outlook to which some military men have been particularly prone. General Charles de Gaulle, too, believed that he had a higher understanding and conception of France than mere politicians, and he was disparaging of political parties. Yet, in spite of fears to the contrary, he strengthened French democracy, rather than undermining it, and played the decisive role in replacing an ailing democratic political system with a more robust one.

De Gaulle had an indomitable belief in France's grandeur. Very early in his memoirs he writes of his feeling that 'France is not really herself unless in the front rank' and that 'France cannot be France without greatness.'[1] An army general who was a junior minister of defence at the time France surrendered to Nazi Germany in 1940, he saw Marshal Pétain's collaborationist government as a stain on his country's honour. Departing for London, he immediately took upon himself the role of commander of the Free French. He came to be accepted as such by the allied leaders, especially by Churchill, although the relationship between these two exceptional and strong-willed men was, to say the least, prickly. De Gaulle attributed this, in large part, to the greater distrust of him felt by Roosevelt and to Churchill's believing that, under wartime conditions, he had to keep in step with the American president. The British prime minister, de Gaulle wrote, 'did not mean to adopt towards Free France an attitude that would be in conflict with the White House'. And, since 'Roosevelt showed himself distrustful towards General de Gaulle, Churchill would be reserved'.[2]

In spite of stubbornness on both sides, with de Gaulle in much the weaker position but determined not to show it, there was also mutual respect. Churchill's first encounter with de Gaulle was in France at a meeting with leading figures in the French government just three days before German troops occupied Paris on 14 June 1940. The British prime minister flew in secret to a small airstrip near Orleans. Marshal Pétain, Churchill noted, 'had quite made up his mind that peace must be made', for 'France was being systematically destroyed', and Pétain believed it to be his duty to save Paris and the rest of the country from that fate.[3] De Gaulle made clear how different was his conception. He was in favour of carrying on guerrilla warfare against the German occupying troops.* Already aged forty-nine, de Gaulle appeared youthful

---

* De Gaulle's unwillingness to go along with his senior governmental colleagues and accept defeat was on a par with the spirit of the British prime minister. At that June 1940 meeting in France, which de Gaulle attended, Churchill (as reported by another participant, General Ismay) said: 'If it is thought best for France in her agony that her Army should capitulate, let there be no hesitation on our account, because whatever you may do we shall fight on for ever and ever and ever.' (Churchill, *The Second World War: Volume II: Their Finest Hour*, Cassell, London, 1949, p. 138.) De Gaulle's most interesting observations on his relations with Churchill appear in the passage in his memoirs when he reflects upon the abrupt removal of the Prime Minister from 10 Downing Street as a result of the 1945 British general election. De Gaulle valued the fact that 'this great politician had always been convinced that France was necessary to the free world; and this exceptional artist was certainly conscious of the dramatic character of my mission'. He admitted to envy of the fact that Churchill had the resources of a state, 'a unanimous people', an intact territory, 'a tremendous Empire' and 'formidable armies' at his disposal, whereas he, de Gaulle, had to answer alone for the destiny of a nation. 'Yet,' de Gaulle concludes, 'different though the conditions were under which Churchill and De Gaulle had had to accomplish their tasks, fierce though their disputes had been, for more than five years they had nonetheless sailed side by side, guiding themselves by the same stars on the

to Churchill who had become prime minister one month earlier at the age of sixty-five. Churchill wrote of him: 'He was young and energetic and had made a very favourable impression on me.' Churchill himself saw de Gaulle as the potential leader of the French struggle for liberation.[4] In London, de Gaulle had to work hard to gain recognition from the French Resistance that he was their leader in exile. His radio broadcasts to France during the war helped to consolidate that leadership and it was symbolically confirmed when, with the liberation of France in August 1944, he led the march of Free French troops into Paris.

De Gaulle's great physical height was accompanied by an equally high conception of himself as a man of destiny. He was not only convinced that he had a momentous role to play, but also saw himself as a performer. During the Second World War, he once said, he had become aware that 'there existed in people's spirits someone named de Gaulle', and 'I knew that I should have to take account of that man . . . I became almost his prisoner.' Therefore: 'Before every speech or decision I questioned myself: is this the way in which the people expect de Gaulle to act? There were many things I should like to have done, but that I did not do because they would not have been what they expected of General de Gaulle.'[5]

Such an elevated sense of duty and destiny did not fit comfortably with the messiness and compromises of everyday peacetime politics. De Gaulle, however, by the end of the war had established himself as a leader with an appeal to French democrats from different parts of the political spectrum. With his impeccable wartime record and anti-Nazi credentials, he was a natural choice to head the French provisional government in the immediate aftermath of the Second World War. Eschewing at each stage of his career any attempt to rule by force, de Gaulle chose a democratic path. In 1946 that meant resigning from the premiership and retiring to his home in the village of Colombey-les-deux-Eglises, from where, nevertheless, he hoped that before long he would be called back to Paris to lead the nation. It was to be another twelve years before the call came.

---

raging sea of history.' Above all, de Gaulle acknowledged that without Churchill, 'my efforts would have been futile from the start, and that by lending me a strong and willing hand when he did, Churchill had vitally aided the cause of France'. (De Gaulle, *The Complete War Memoirs of Charles de Gaulle*, Carroll & Graf, New York, 1998, pp. 900–901.)

De Gaulle's main complaint against the constitution of the Fourth Republic that had been created just after the war was that it did not provide a powerful executive. In particular, it lacked the strong presidency which he craved. Most French democrats were extremely wary of a powerful executive. Having lived under authoritarian rule during the war and having seen the havoc wreaked by totalitarian and authoritarian governments elsewhere in Europe over the previous two decades, they tended, too readily, to associate a strong executive with despotism. In reality, there can be no democracy without an authoritative – as distinct from authoritarian – executive.

De Gaulle set out his critique of the Fourth Republic constitution in 1946. Not all of it was well founded – in particular, his disparagement of political parties. There were too many of them in France at that time, and they were too divided internally, but competing parties are an indispensable component of a democracy. In his prediction of instability, as a result of an executive insufficiently powerful vis-à-vis parliament, de Gaulle was more prescient. During the thirteen years of the Fourth Republic (1945–1958) there were as many as twenty-five governments and fifteen premiers, during a time when Britain had just four prime ministers. Governmental crises were frequent, and in the last year of the Fourth Republic's existence, France was ruled by caretaker governments for one day out of every four.[6] Yet, it is possible to exaggerate the failures of those thirteen years. The French Communists were supported by about a quarter of the electorate, but the country remained democratic. Relations with Germany – a country whose forces had invaded France twice in the first half of the twentieth century – had been repaired, and France had become a founder member of the European Economic Community. French industrial production expanded faster than did that of the United States and Britain in the 1950s, and France had an impressive social security system. Living standards had risen quite rapidly.[7] So the Fourth Republic was not without its achievements.

Yet the system and the country were, by 1958, in crisis. Governments were falling with increasing frequency. They struggled to come to terms with loss of empire, and, in particular, they found themselves incapable of resolving the Algerian problem. On the French right, in the army and, still more, among the French settler population in Algeria, there was a determination that Algeria would remain French (as it had been since 1830), whatever might happen to other former colonies. The army had entered the Algerian war in a 'never again' mood, believing that this was the last place 'where they could feel useful and respected' and that loss of Algeria would be disastrous for both them and their homeland.[8] Already in 1956, France had 400,000 troops in Algeria, many of them conscripts, combating the Front de Libération Nationale (FLN), the radical Arab nationalist movement for Algerian independence. Tensions over this colonial war poisoned French politics. Even Socialist governments maintained the attempt to keep Algeria French, while critics of the war – and of the use of torture in its prosecution – were treated vindictively.[9] Successive French governments were caught between the incompatible demands of Algerians for independence and of the large white settler population insistent that Algeria was an integral part of France. Added to this was the highly questionable loyalty of the army, should any government in Paris make too many concessions to the FLN. Indeed, a French government which was even suspected of being willing to grant independence for Algeria risked being overthrown in a military coup.

It was not a new uprising of indigenous Algerians but of the French settlers which brought developments to crisis point in May 1958. It was they who sacked government offices in Algiers. Partly from qualified sympathy with the French settlers, but mainly in order to control the situation, the commanding officer of the troops in Algiers, General Jacques Massu, set up a 'committee of public safety'. On 15 May he ended a speech with the words, 'Vive de Gaulle!' Increasingly, the army, the settlers and many members of the political class in Paris began to think of de Gaulle as the one person who could get them out of the impasse. The assumption within the army and among the settlers was that he would be the most formidable defender of *Algérie Française*. On the same day as Massu's speech, de Gaulle issued a brief statement in which he spoke about the degredation of the state, the alienation of the people, turmoil in the army, and of France being on a road to disaster thanks to the 'regime of parties'. He announced his willingness 'to assume the powers of the Republic'.[10] Four factors facilitated his return – his status as war hero who had returned to France in 1944 and restored the integrity of the French state on a democratic and republican basis; the memory of his dramatic and voluntary withdrawal from French public life in 1946; the publication in the recent past of his several volumes of war memoirs, which not only heightened people's consciousness that de Gaulle was still waiting in the wings but also made a great impact with their evocative language and emotional appeal;[11] and, above all, the fact that by 1958 the authority of the French state had reached a low ebb and appeared to be at risk of a *coup d'état*.[12]

Before the end of May the National Assembly had voted to ask de Gaulle to form a government. He then moved quickly towards getting the kind of political system he had long favoured – one in which there would be a dual executive of president and prime minister, but with the president very much the senior partner. The detailed new Constitution was drafted by de Gaulle's loyal follower, Michel Debré, who was to become the first prime minister of the Fifth French Republic after de Gaulle had become its president. The constitution contained most of what de Gaulle had wanted, though it was Debré, who shared his views, who was left to negotiate it.[13] Eighty-five per cent of the electorate came out to vote in a referendum on the constitution, held on 28 September 1958, and of that large turnout 80 per cent voted 'yes'. This was, essentially, a 'yes' to the person of de Gaulle.[14] The new constitution made it much harder for the legislature to make and unmake governments and the presidency was substantially strengthened, even though the prime minister retained significant policy-making powers. The president was particularly responsible for foreign and defence policy, and de Gaulle made full use of his powers, devoting especial attention to Europe, to colonial and French Community questions and, above all, to Algeria, which, until 1962, was the most pressing issue on the political agenda.[15] De Gaulle would also intervene in other areas when he so wished, but he did not try to exercise detailed control over day-to-day policy. In particular, economic policy and financial matters were largely left to his successive prime ministers and finance ministers.[16]

In order to avoid the recurrence of a multiplicity of political parties, the voting system was radically changed, with various forms of proportional representation rejected. The system adopted was a two-round electoral process in which there was a run-off election a week after the first round, in which only the leading candidates (usually just two of them) were left in the contest. This made for majorities in the National Assembly capable of sustaining a government, although deputies remained as free as ever to criticize the executive. The new electoral system worked well for the freshly created Gaullist party, the Union for a New Republic (UNR) and much less well for the Communist Party. De Gaulle did not allow the new party to use his name, but his apparent distance from it was no more than a careful contrivance.[17] He was aware that without the support of a major party he would over time lose ground. The one other major constitutional change desired by de Gaulle, but for which he was content to wait, was direct election of the president by the electorate rather than the legislature. This he obtained by referendum in 1962, as well as agreement on a seven-year term of office. This clearly enhanced the independent authority of the presidency not only for de Gaulle but for future incumbents, although the term was reduced to five years in 2002.[18]

Most importantly, the institutions created at de Gaulle's behest have stood the test of time. This form of dual executive – or semi-presidentialism – has been much copied by other countries, not least in former Communist states, but has rarely produced as satisfactory a combination of effective governance and democratic accountability as it has in France. There has been stable government during the five and a half decades of the Fifth Republic and its institutions have gained widespread acceptance within the country. That endorsement extends to the Socialist and Communist parties, although many of the former and all of the latter were opposed to the new political system at the time of its introduction. After he had become French President in the 1980s, François Mitterrand remarked that 'the institutions were not made with me in mind, but they suit me very well'.[19]

General de Gaulle's achievements did not lie only in far-reaching institutional change. Making masterly use of ambiguity as a political device, he resolved the Algerian issue. When de Gaulle told the settlers in 1958 'I have understood you', they took that to mean that he was committed to keeping Algeria French, yet what he had said was both ambiguous and non-committal. De Gaulle was not strongly for or against Algerian union with France, but he aimed, above all, to end the war and the festering sore which the Algerian problem had become. He skilfully 'exploited the divisions of his opponents, the loyalty of his own supporters (Michel Debré, the prime minister, was notably lukewarm about Algerian independence) and the war-weariness of a frustrated French population'.[20] De Gaulle's position, and along with it French public opinion, ever more obviously shifted further away from that of the French settlers and their military backers. In 1959 de Gaulle reminded the army that they were not an autonomous body: 'You are the army of France. You only exist by her, because of her, and for her. You are at her service, and that is your *raison d'être*.'[21] Both the army and the settlers realized that, even if they had played a crucial role in bringing de Gaulle to power in May 1958, his standing with the French public had in the meantime become so enhanced that a new insurrection would have a slimmer chance of success. Nevertheless, there was an army revolt in Algeria in 1961, and de Gaulle, with superb aplomb, got most of the French people on his side, and the insurrection fizzled out. As Vincent Wright noted, de Gaulle's television appeal to the nation 'was as moving and as resolute as it was effective, a rare combination of high drama and deep sincerity'.[22] By 1962 Algeria had become an independent state. De Gaulle also oversaw the granting of independence to twelve other French overseas territories.

In many respects deeply conservative, de Gaulle was also, argues Sudhir Hazareesingh (the author of an illuminating book on the Gaullian mythology and legacy), 'moving in the direction of history'. The big questions on which his judgement was vindicated by posterity were the need to continue the war after 1940 and to unify the Resistance; his assessment of the weaknesses of the electoral and party systems in the Fourth Republic; his determination to create the new institutions which have worked well in the Fifth Republic; and his acceptance of the need for decolonization.[23] Not only did de Gaulle change the political system, Hazareesingh argues, but he also made an important contribution to changing the political culture of France, reconciling 'the Right with the Republic and the Left with the nation'. At the same time he gave new meaning to older values – 'heroism, sense of duty, the feeling of belonging, defiance of fate, and contempt for materialism'.[24] The heroism is worth underlining. Especially in the period up to the end of the Algerian war, there were repeated attempts to assassinate de Gaulle. He was constantly being warned by security advisers to reduce his contact with crowds. In any gathering he towered above those around him and appeared to present all too vulnerable a target. Yet de Gaulle rejected with disdain the warnings of danger and admonitions not to take unnecessary risks.[25]

On foreign policy, de Gaulle recognized Communist China and was critical of the American war in Vietnam, believing (on the basis of

French experience) that it would end in failure.[26] He played an important part in maintaining the good relations with West Germany already
established by Fourth Republic politicians. He withdrew France from
the integrated command system of NATO and, although resolutely
anti-Communist, established better relations with the Soviet Union,
having asserted his independence from American foreign policy. An
animus against both the Americans and the British was easily discernible, and he twice vetoed Britain's application to join the European
Community (accepted only during the presidency of his successor,
Georges Pompidou). The deeply divided and ambivalent attitudes of
the British to joining European institutions were such that de Gaulle
received many letters from the UK telling him to carry on the good
work of keeping Britain out of the Common Market.[27] De Gaulle could
be a difficult partner for American and British governments, but there
is no doubt that France's international prestige was enhanced during
the years of his presidency.

   One of the more questionable elements of the constitution of the
Fifth Republic was the introduction of the referendum, since referendums on particular issues tend to become plebiscites on the government or person initiating them. They are also open to abuse. In
principle, the president could not initiate a referendum; it was the
government and parliament which had the right to do so. They were
also not to be held on a reform which was in conflict with the constitution. Yet both of those provisions were to be breached by de Gaulle
and by later presidents. Referendums were also a double-edged sword.
To the extent that they amounted to a vote of confidence in the
president and his judgement, they helped de Gaulle in January 1961
and April 1962 on Algeria-related questions and in October 1962 when
there was a referendum on what was clearly a constitutional issue –
direct election of the president.[28] However, social unrest, including
violent clashes between police and demonstrators on the streets of
Paris in 1968, saw de Gaulle lose some of his earlier authority. This
was reflected when he lost a referendum in April 1969 on issues of
regionalism and the reorganization of the upper house of the legislature, the Senate.[29] Reacting as if this were, indeed, a withdrawal of
confidence in him by the French public (although the referendum was
lost quite narrowly), de Gaulle immediately resigned and retired for
the last time to Colombey. He died eighteen months later, aged eighty.

In the years since then he has come to be widely regarded, both in his homeland and abroad, as the greatest Frenchman of the twentieth century.

ADOLFO SUÁREZ

Six years before his death in 1975, the Spanish dictator, General Francisco Franco, decided that, after he had gone, monarchy would be restored in the person of Juan Carlos. This duly occurred, and one year after his accession to the throne, the king appointed Adolfo Suárez as prime minister to replace Franco's last appointee in that office, Admiral Carerro Blanco. There were many in the military who had no intention of giving up the privileged place which the Franco dictatorship had accorded them, but the king, even though he was Franco's choice as head of state, selected Suárez to lead the government in the expectation that he would take Spain on a democratic path. Suárez, who was to be prime minister from 1976 until his resignation in 1981, appeared to many observers as an unlikely agent of radical change. He had been a high-level bureaucrat in the Franco regime, rising to be head of radio and television in the late 1960s and early 1970s. Yet, he was to exceed the expectations of democrats by playing a decisive role in the transition.

Suárez's achievement must be put in context. He was in part responding to a strong feeling within Spanish society that change was necessary, although the levers of coercive power were in the hands of those opposed to a dramatic break with the previous regime. On the one side, there were powerful pressures from interests served by a continuation of authoritarian rule. On the other side, there were the demands for radical change coming from the anti-Francoist Left, both Socialists and Communists. It was Suárez's consensus-building style that was to be decisively important in reconciling, to a remarkable degree, apparently irreconcilable differences. He did not achieve widespread popularity. In that respect he was far outshone by the Socialist leader, Felipe González.[30] It was, though, a working relationship with the Communist leader, Santiago Carrillo, to which Suárez gave priority. Carrillo was a veteran of the Spanish Civil War who had recently earned some international renown as the head of one of the two major 'Eurocommunist' parties (the Italian Communist Party, led by Enrico

Berlinguer, being the other).³¹ Yet Suárez's decision to seek the legalization of the Communist Party in 1977 was unquestionably the most dangerous moment for the emerging democracy. It could easily have led to a military *coup d'état* to put a stop to the democratizing process. That threat was constant throughout Suárez's years in power, and it was a major achievement on his part that he staved off a major coup attempt until as late as 1981.

If a Francoist bureaucrat may be regarded as a surprising agent of democratic change, the same would be no less true of a Communist leader. Yet, at an early stage of the transition, Carrillo (who died as recently as September 2012 at the age of ninety-seven), turned out to be one of Suárez's most important partners in the negotiation of a new political order. Once the democratic breakthrough had taken place, the Socialists gained far more support than the Communists, but at the time of Franco's death, the Communist Party, although still illegal, had significant backing within Spanish society. While the legalization of that party infuriated many in the high command of the military, its continued suppression could have had serious repercussions. A direct clash between the Communist Party and the new government would have given the military the excuse to put a brake on the democratization process.

Thus, the long-exiled Communist leader had a pivotal role to play. Following his return to Spain, Carrillo was imprisoned in December 1976, but Suárez had conversations with him as early as February 1977. The Communist leader was responsive to the prime minister's overtures. Carrillo agreed to recognize the monarchy, the flag and the unity of the Spanish state, thus somewhat assuaging conservative fears.³² To persuade the Communists to accept a constitutional monarchy was a major achievement on Suárez's part. It took far longer for the Socialists to agree to this, for the basic division since the civil war had been between Francoists and Republicans, with the unacceptability of a monarchy taken for granted on the left. However, Suárez saw it as fundamentally important to bring the Communists within the system, and his negotiations with Carrillo achieved this. The senior officer corps did little to disguise their anger at the acceptance of the Communist Party as a legitimate participant in Spanish political life, yet they were persuaded to swallow this bitter pill. Suárez boldly and publicly proclaimed his belief that the Spanish people were mature enough 'to assimilate their own pluralism', that to continue making the Communist Party illegal would mean repression, and that he did not think the population should feel 'obliged to see our jails full of people for ideological reasons'.[33]

Even more remarkable than encompassing the Communist Party within the new order was Suárez's success in persuading the corporatist parliament that had been appointed (not elected) under the Franco regime, the Cortes, to agree to its own abolition. If Suárez had simply announced that he was closing it down, the security forces would surely have arrested him. Instead, he set about building a coalition for change. In a major speech to the Cortes, he made a forceful case that if they wanted to avoid conflict and subversion in Spain, they should begin to recognize the 'pluralism of our society' and that meant opening up the opportunity of legality for groups and political parties. As he put it: 'The aims of parties are specific and not the least of them is to assume power. So, if the road is not opened by the legality which is being proposed by the state itself, there will be an apparent peace, below which will germinate subversion.' He played on his audience's desire to avoid 'subversion' and said he was sure that they would understand that there 'cannot be, and will not be, a constitutional vacuum, and still less a vacuum of legality'.[34] The night before the Cortes voted on the Law on Political Reform in November 1976, just five months after Suárez had been appointed prime minister, many observers remained uncertain of the outcome. The vote, however, was 425 in favour and only fifty-nine against. Suárez had displayed skilful leadership not only by recognizing and responding to demands from within the broader society but by winning support for consensual solutions even from within the ranks of the old elite. To consolidate the new foundations, he put the Law on Political Reform to a national referendum, obtaining an impressive 94 per cent approval for the law.

Suárez succeeded also in forming a moderate conservative alliance called the Union of the Democratic Centre, which emerged in 1977 as the most successful party in what was Spain's first general election since 1936. One effect of democratization was to give hope, and new opportunities, to separatist movements in the Basque country and Catalonia. It was, therefore, of real significance for the consolidation of Spanish statehood in its democratic form that these first competitive elections were national, rather than regional. Nationalist and regional parties tend to perform better in regional elections in their own territory than they do when the same citizens are voting for a government of the entire country. In the Spanish case, they have polled between 15 and 25 per cent higher in regional elections than in those at state-wide level.[35] Thus, the parties which benefited most from holding, in the first instance, free elections for the country-wide legislature were those whose appeal was to the whole of Spain. These were, most notably, Suárez's centre-right coalition and the Socialist Party, led by González. In the earliest post-Franco years, it was important for the development of democracy that moderate, non-nationalist parties emerged as the strongest.

Nationalist and separatist movements continue to be a serious issue in Spanish politics in the second decade of the twenty-first century, but they no longer present such a threat to democratic government.[36] Had they appeared to risk break-up of the state in the immediate post-Franco years, this would, in all likelihood, have provoked a return to authoritarian rule. The military would have formed the backbone of a regime whose coercive crushing of separatism (although that would have been only a short-term solution) would have been accompanied by suppression of the fledgling Spanish democracy.* Suárez, in contrast, took early steps to reassure moderate opinion in Catalonia and the Basque country, with particular success in Catalonia. The Basque National Party and representatives of Catalan nationalism took part in negotiations in 1977, and the 1978 Spanish Constitution offered significant devolution of power to both regions, with Catalan and Basque becoming official languages in both territories, alongside Castilian (standard Spanish).

The first Suárez government was beset by severe economic and social problems in the wake of the 1973 oil crisis. The newly elected prime minster initially considered introducing an economic stabilization plan by executive decision. After reflection, however, he decided

---

* The Spanish scholar, Sonia Alonso, has noted the growing support in Catalonia in recent years for secession, while stressing that this is not an argument against the kind of devolution of power that has taken place (in the years since democracy was restored in Spain) to territories where there is a strong sense of local national identity, since the experience of 'systematically ignoring the grievances from the periphery' and 'imposing a centralized homogeneous state . . . guaranteed neither the territorial integrity of the state nor the survival of democracy'. (Sonia Alonso, *Challenging the State: Devolution and the Battle for Partisan Credibility. A Comparison of Belgium, Italy, Spain, and the United Kingdom*, Oxford University Press, Oxford, 2012, pp. 247–248.)

that it would be more legitimate and more effective if he could get agreement on a consensual 'pact' in support of policies that measured up to the scale of the problems. The 'Moncloa Pact' (the name is that of the prime minister's residence) is widely considered to be one of the most effective agreements in the history of democratic transitions. Faced by the threat of widespread worker unrest, Suárez understood that he must engage in give-and-take negotiations with the Communist and Socialist opposition if the government were to get union leaders to understand and tolerate painful wage control policies and anti-strike agreements for the first year of the democratic experiment. He invited the leaders of every party with seats in the new parliament which had been generated by free elections in June 1977, Communists included, to a series of private meetings in Moncloa.

Only after these extensive negotiations and resultant agreements did Suárez bring the Moncloa Pact to both houses of parliament. With the parties having already made their difficult concessions, there was only one vote against acceptance of the pact in the Lower House and only three votes against (and two abstentions) in the Upper House. The Pact which the unions and the major political parties had signed up to included, in return for moderating wage demands to lower inflation and public debt, a range of political and social reforms from guarantees for freedom of expression to the legalization of contraception. The agreement prepared the way for a fuller democratization of Spanish society.[37] The fruits of Suárez's inclusive political style were seen also when Spain applied in 1977 for membership of the European Community (as the European Union was then known). This had the support of all the parliamentary parties. In Spain, as in other countries moving away from authoritarian rule, EU membership helped to solidify democratic rule (notwithstanding tensions caused in more recent years by the international economic crisis and the problems of the common currency).

Recognizing the need for a new constitution which would underpin the emerging democratic order, Suárez was aware of the dangers of imposing it by a simple majority. In a parliamentary speech in April 1978, he said that 'the Constitution, as an expression of national concord, must be obtained by consensus, for which it is necessary to take into account the diverse political forces now present'.[38] Although the Communists had already conceded that the monarch would be head of state, the Socialists took more persuading and, until late in the day of drawing up the constitution, were insisting that the Spanish state should become, and be defined as, a Republic. However, they eventually agreed to the idea of a constitutional monarchy in return for abolition of the death penalty and reduction of the voting age to eighteen.[39] In large measure as a result of Suárez's leadership, Spain made a negotiated transition to democracy. The draft constitution received close to unanimous assent in the parliament and was endorsed by almost 90 per cent of the population, the Basque region being the one major exception.[40]

In elections in 1979, Suárez's Union of the Democratic Centre had a narrow lead over the Socialist Party, but did not have an overall majority. Throughout his time in office, Suárez never achieved popular acclaim. He was too closely associated with the Franco regime to be admired by the democratic left, and far too liberal and conciliatory to anti-Francoist opinion for the taste of the most conservative forces (including many in the senior officer corps). Terrorist attacks by the Basque extremist organization, ETA, were by the beginning of the 1980s threatening the stability of the political system. In each successive year since the mid-1970s there had been more deaths, including those among the armed forces, which fuelled military discontent with the emergent democracy. Suárez was very conscious of an erosion of his own political authority and believed that if he attempted to hold on to power for a full parliamentary term, this would endanger democratization. More concerned with the fate of Spanish democracy than with prolonging his time in office, he resigned from the premiership in late January 1981.

Just a few weeks later, on 23 February, when the Cortes was in session to confirm the choice of his successor as premier, a military contingent, led by Lieutenant-Colonel Antonio Tejero, interrupted the parliamentary session, fired several rounds, and ordered all the deputies to be silent. Almost all of them crouched on the floor. Suárez was in the small group who did not. Along with Santiago Carrillo, Felipe González and another leading member of the Socialist Party, he was separated from the other deputies and destined for imprisonment if the coup had been successfully implemented. The role played by King Juan Carlos was pivotal in making certain this did not happen. Tanks had gone on to the streets in other cities at the same time as the military incursion into the country's parliament. The king telephoned the main commanders and ordered them to get their tanks and men back to their barracks.

The next day, wearing his uniform of Captain General, the highest military rank, Juan Carlos appeared on television and announced that he would not tolerate this attempt to interrupt the democratic process. Although there was a substantial majority of Spanish public opinion opposed to the coup, the king's stance was hugely important in ensuring its collapse. The military were much more responsive to commands from the king as head of state than they were to politicians or to public opinion. The coup failed and a number of the officers involved in it were arrested and subsequently imprisoned. The revived monarchy had not been a particularly popular institution. Such legitimacy as it was accorded was – and remains – fragile and highly dependent on the behaviour of the occupant of the throne. Juan Carlos, by appointing Suárez in the first place, by accepting that Spain should become a democracy and that his role would be that of a constitutional monarch, and, above all, by his stance at the time of the February 1981 coup, earned respect. As Juan Linz and Alfred Stepan observed, Juan Carlos 'legitimated the monarchy more than the monarchy legitimated the king'.[41]

Of all those who had accepted the Franco regime, and prospered under it, it was, however, Suárez who played the most decisive part in the speedy transformation of the Spanish political system from authoritarianism to democracy. The fact that he came from the heart of the old establishment meant that he was able to carry enough of that body of opinion with him, even as he legalized hitherto banned political parties and wasted no time in holding genuinely democratic elections. He was by no stretch of the imagination a charismatic leader. (Felipe González came closest to that description among Spain's post-Franco politicians.) Nor was he a 'strong' leader in the sense of one who dominated all those around him. He sought consensus and his style was collegial. He made concessions and compromises, but in pursuit of a goal he steadfastly pursued – that of democracy. In this he was astonishingly successful.

MIKHAIL GORBACHEV

Mikhail Gorbachev was a leader who was responsible for still more dramatic change than what occurred under Suárez. For one thing, he came to power in a country that was, in military terms at least, a 'superpower' and which had for decades ensured that Communist rule prevailed not only in the multinational Soviet state but also throughout most of Central and Eastern Europe. Systemic change in the Soviet Union would, accordingly, have much wider repercussions than fundamental change in Spain.* Yet, there are important parallels between the cases of Suárez and Gorbachev. Both had risen through the ranks of the old regime, and most Soviet dissidents, as well as foreign leaders, assumed that any reforms that Gorbachev might undertake would be within fairly narrow limits. It was taken for granted that Gorbachev would not do anything that would risk the monopoly of power of the Communist Party of the Soviet Union or undermine its internal hierarchical power structure. Equally, it was assumed, he would never risk undermining Soviet hegemony in Eastern Europe. There could be no question of 'losing' any of the countries which the leaders of the Soviet party-state – not to speak of its military-industrial complex – regarded as their country's legitimate geopolitical gains from victory in the Second World War.

Gorbachev is a pre-eminent example of a political leader who individually made a profound difference, even though there were many good reasons why change should be embarked upon in the Soviet Union in the second half of the 1980s.[42] There had been a long-term decline in the rate of economic growth. The military-industrial complex flourished, but at the expense of the rest of the economy. Living standards, while much higher than in Stalin's time, remained well below those enjoyed in neighbouring Scandinavian countries and in Western Europe. Even one of the successes of the Communist period, the rise in educational standards – including a strong higher education sector containing many well-qualified specialists in research institutes and universities – harboured the seeds of change and provided a potential constituency supportive of radical reform.

Yet the Soviet system was one in which there was a sophisticated array of rewards for political conformism and a hierarchy of sanctions and punishments for nonconformity and dissent. For Soviet power-holders,

---

* Democratization in Spain and Portugal was, however, a stimulus and encouragement to the spread of democracy in Latin America – what has been called the Third Wave of democratization. What happened in the late 1980s, and which began in the Soviet Union, was unconnected with the earlier change in southern Europe and Latin America. It constituted a Fourth Wave of democratization.

in particular, the risks of radical reform appeared to far outweigh the potential benefits. If their highest priority was to keep intact both the Communist system and the Soviet Union, they could plausibly argue by 1992 – by which time neither the one nor the other existed – that their caution had been fully justified. While at some stage in the future, the Soviet Union would have reached a crisis point, it remained stable in the mid-1980s, its underlying problems notwithstanding.* Even during the thirteen dreary months when Konstantin Chernenko was general secretary of the Communist Party – and, therefore, the country's leader – there was no public unrest, only private grumbling. While the limitations of the Soviet command economy (despite its successes in military technology and space research and development) were among the stimuli to change, the Soviet Union was *not* in crisis in 1985. It was radical reform which produced crisis, rather than crisis that dictated reform. The idea that the Soviet economy was in such a parlous condition that it *forced* reform on Gorbachev is a misleading explanation of the profound change which occurred. If the economic imperative was so overwhelmingly strong, it does not explain why Gorbachev before long – certainly by the beginning of 1987 – was giving priority to political over economic reform. It is arguable that political reform was required to overcome entrenched bureaucratic opposition to the introduction of a market. However, Gorbachev pursued liberalizing and democratizing change for its own sake, and was later to admit: 'In the heat of political battles we lost sight of the economy, and people never forgave us for the shortages of everyday items and the lines for essential goods.'[43]

No less wide of the mark is the notion that the hardline rhetoric and increased arms expenditure of the Reagan administration left the Soviet leadership with no option but to concede defeat in the Cold War.† From the end of the war to the 1960s the United States had

---

* A fundamental lurking problem was the nationalities issue. Among the non-Russian nations of the Soviet Union, and especially in Estonia, Latvia and Lithuania, there was a majority of the indigenous population who would have welcomed independent statehood, had this been an option. Prior to the perestroika years, however, citizens of those Baltic republics knew that to assert a demand for independence led to nowhere but the Gulag or, in earlier years, to execution.
† The Soviet leadership prior to Gorbachev's coming to power reacted to the policies of the first term of the Reagan administration in the traditional manner. There was no dissent from the view of the veteran Soviet Minister of Defence, Dmitriy Ustinov,

enjoyed military superiority over the Soviet Union, but that did not produce a more conciliatory Soviet foreign policy. On the contrary, these were years of Soviet-backed Communist expansion – and of the crushing of both the Hungarian revolution and the Prague Spring. It was from the early 1970s that the Soviet Union acquired a rough military parity with the USA, each side having enough nuclear weapons, and the means of their delivery, to wipe the other off the face of the earth. Although the possible technological spin-offs from investment in Reagan's favoured Strategic Defense Initiative (SDI) caused some Soviet concern, it was talked up by leading members of the Soviet military-industrial complex mainly as a device to avoid the cuts in defence expenditure which Gorbachev was pursuing.[44] Reagan himself later conceded that 'SDI might take decades to develop' and that it would not be 'an impenetrable shield', for 'no defense could ever be expected to be one hundred per cent effective'.[45] The SDI aspiration was unveiled by Reagan to the world in March 1983 when Andropov was Soviet leader. Yet, under both Andropov's and Chernenko's leadership, the Soviet response to stepped-up military spending in the United States was to follow suit. It was Gorbachev who changed Soviet foreign and defence policy, not Reagan or SDI.

Gorbachev took a more critical view of the condition of Soviet society in the mid-1980s than did any of his colleagues in the leadership. He was also more concerned than they were about the possibility of catastrophic nuclear war occurring through miscalculation, accident or technical malfunction. However, in March 1985, when Chernenko died, Gorbachev was the *only* reformer in the Politburo and the only one of them seriously intent on ending the Cold War. The other members of the Politburo formed the selectorate who nominated one of their number to the Central Committee to be general secretary, effectively thus choosing the next leader of the Soviet Union. How did Gorbachev become that person within twenty-four hours of Chernenko's death?

---

when he told a Politburo meeting in May 1983: 'Everything that we are doing in relation to defence we should continue doing. All of the missiles that we've planned should be delivered . . .' (*Zasedanie Politbyuro TsK KPSS, 31 maya 1983 goda*, Hoover Institution Archives, Fond 89, Reel 1.1003, Opis 42, File 53.) Even in 1986 the Chairman of the KGB at that time, Viktor Chebrikov, insisted at a Politburo meeting that 'the Americans understand only strength'. (*Zasedanie Politbyuro TsK KPSS 14 oktyabrya 1986 goda*, Volkogonov Collection, R9744, National Security Archive, Washington, DC.)

Given the composition and conservatism of the Soviet top leadership team, he was obviously not chosen *because* he was a reformer. He had not shared his more radical reformist ideas with his Politburo colleagues, and several of them were later to complain that they had no inkling that he would pursue the policies he did.[46] He was also the youngest member of the Politburo, intellectually its most agile and physically its most robust, at a time when three aged top leaders had died within a period of less than three years. Annual state funerals had become an embarrassment to the Soviet state. Moreover, Gorbachev was already number two within the leadership. (Yuriy Andropov, in particular, had been impressed by his intelligence and energy and had extended his responsibilities during his fifteen months as Soviet leader.) Gorbachev was in a position to seize the initiative when Chernenko died in the early evening of 10 March 1985. He called and chaired a meeting of the Politburo which convened at 11 p.m. that same day, was effectively 'pre-selected' as leader there and then, and by the following afternoon was general secretary.[47]

What is especially important is that Gorbachev's views continued to evolve once he became Soviet leader. In 1985 he believed not only that the Soviet Union needed reform but also that the system was, indeed, *reformable*. By the summer of 1988 he had come to the conclusion that reform was inadequate and that the system needed to be comprehensively *transformed*. His speech to the Nineteenth Conference of the Soviet Communist Party in that year was, as he later wrote, nothing less than an attempt to make a 'peaceful, smooth transition from one political system to another'.[48] In the same speech Gorbachev said that every country should have the freedom to choose its own way of life and social structure, and that any attempt to impose these from without, especially by military means, was 'from the dangerous armoury of past years'.[49] In that June 1988 report, and again in a speech at the United Nations six months later, Gorbachev made clear that this was a universal principle, allowing no exceptions. That gave a green light to the peoples of Eastern Europe to take him at his word the following year. Had Gorbachev already believed in 1985 that reform was not enough and that systemic change was required, it would not have been sufficient to be as circumspect as he was; he would have needed to be a consummate actor to succeed in being chosen as general secretary. It was of decisive importance that Gorbachev's political goals – not merely many of his specific attitudes – changed while he held the most powerful office within the highly authoritarian Soviet system.[50]

The strictly hierarchical nature of the Communist Party, the political resources (including substantial power of appointment) concentrated in the general secretaryship, and the superior authority of the top leader in relation to the party bureaucracy, the government machine, the KGB and the armed forces meant that the general secretary had a far greater chance of introducing fundamental change than had any other political actor. Nevertheless, no Soviet leader after Stalin had the power of life and death over his colleagues, and if he alienated them sufficiently, he could be overthrown, as Nikita Khrushchev discovered to his cost in 1964. To weaken the authority of institutions long accustomed to wielding great power was extremely dangerous. Therefore, Gorbachev had to use the powers of his office with immense political skill in order to introduce radical change that undermined existing institutional interests. As he later wrote: 'Without political manoeuvring, it was no good even to think about moving aside the powerful bureaucracy.'[51] One of Gorbachev's closest reformist allies during the first four years of perestroika, Aleksandr Yakovlev (to whom he had given accelerated promotion) put it more strongly: 'A consistent radicalism in the earliest years of perestroika would have destroyed the very idea of all-embracing reform. A united revolt of the bureaucracies – party, state, repressive and economic – would have returned the country to the worst times of Stalinism.' The political context, he added, was utterly different in the mid-1980s from what it was later to become.[52]

Gorbachev, especially during the first few years of his leadership, was very careful to get the approval of the Politburo for each reformist step he wished to take. The meetings became much longer than they were in Brezhnev's time, with members feeling free to contribute and to disagree with the party leader. On many occasions, documents which, under Gorbachev's supervision, had been prepared by his aides and brought to the Politburo, had to be amended, even though Gorbachev had already approved them. For example, when the draft of the speech he was to make in November 1987 on the seventieth anniversary of the Bolshevik revolution was submitted to the Politburo for its approval, several members objected strongly to the statement within it that an 'authoritarian-bureaucratic model of socialism' had been built in the Soviet Union. Gorbachev characteristically responded by making a tactical retreat, saying that the word 'model' should, perhaps, be replaced by 'methods' or 'means'. At the same Politburo meeting there were objections to the use of the phrase, 'socialist pluralism', with 'pluralism' being condemned as an alien concept.[53] Gorbachev's flexibility meant that each document that became official policy, even though some of the formulations he had jointly developed with his advisers were lost in the process, nevertheless broke new ground – and, crucially, the Politburo had taken collective responsibility for it. No matter what doubts they harboured, they could not easily disassociate themselves from the final product.

Gorbachev never had a majority of like-minded people in the Politburo. In common with many other heads of government, including those in democratic countries, he had more leeway over foreign policy than he had in relation to the economy. He was able to replace the entire top foreign policy-making team within a year of becoming general secretary.[54] Promotion to the Politburo, however, could only be from the ranks of people who were already members of the Central Committee. The general secretary had more influence than any other Soviet politician on those promotions, but in the post-Stalin era did not have a completely free hand. The Politburo collectively co-opted new members. One of the important reforms eventually adopted was the creation of a state presidency in March 1990, to which Gorbachev was elected by the legislature.*

Especially in the period up until March 1990, Gorbachev had to handle the predominantly conservative membership of the Politburo

---

* According to the law passed at that time, future elections of the President of the USSR were to be by the whole people. However, the Soviet Union had ceased to exist before any such election could take place. From March 1990 onwards, Gorbachev governed more through that state office than through the general secretaryship and proceeded to bypass the Politburo even on many major issues. Until 1990 the Soviet Union had remained a party-state, and the Politburo had the power to frustrate a general secretary and, if he overstepped the mark, to depose him. By the last two years of the Soviet Union's existence, power had been transferred from party to state institutions. When I had a meeting with the deputy head of the Ideology department of the Central Committee in January 1991, he said that he thought he had just about enough power left to get coffee delivered to us in his room. It was only in the last two years of the Soviet Union's existence, when power had essentially left the Central Committee building, that a foreign non-Communist scholar could gain access to that secular temple of the Communist Party.

with finesse. One of them, Vitaliy Vorotnikov, described how he did it. Gorbachev's style, according to Vorotnikov (whose testimony is supported by that of several of his colleagues), was 'democratic and collegial'. Everyone who wished to speak in the Politburo was given the chance to do so, and Gorbachev would listen carefully to their arguments. If there was significant disagreement, Gorbachev would say that 'we need to think a bit more about it, do some more work'. He would find a form of words that would reassure those who had expressed concerns or would postpone a decision until a later meeting. But in the final analysis, Vorotnikov ruefully observes, Gorbachev would get his way, sometimes accepting a middle position which he would then move away from at an opportune moment.[55] From his different standpoint, Yakovlev notes in his memoirs that Gorbachev found himself in 'a circle of people much older than him and more experienced in underhand games who at any moment could reach an agreement to cast him aside'.[56] He stresses the fact that Gorbachev was powerful only up to the point at which he encroached on the interests of the 'most powerful elites and clans at that time'.[57]

The Power of Persuasion

The more Gorbachev liberalized the Soviet system, the more he needed to rely on his powers of persuasion rather than on the authority of the general secretaryship. Vorotnikov admits to having been swept along for some time by Gorbachev's arguments. He often spoke in the Politburo, expressing doubts about Gorbachev's reforms and argued against them not only orally but sometimes also in writing. 'But in the end,' he says, 'I often yielded to the logic of his [Gorbachev's] conviction. That was also my fault.'[58] He and his colleagues were too late in seeing that Gorbachev was engaged in a process of democratization, moving power away from Communist Party officials, and replacing Marxism-Leninism by competitive elections as the source of political legitimacy. By embracing freedom of speech, Gorbachev at the same time substantially liberated publishing houses and the mass media and galvanized Soviet society, putting conservative Communists, in particular, on the defensive. The same point is made differently by Vorotnikov: 'The train of pseudo-democracy had gathered such speed that to stop it was beyond our powers.'[59]

Gorbachev was not, in the conventional sense, a 'strong leader'. He was not overbearing and was willing both to make tactical retreats and to absorb criticism. In particular, he did not fit Russians' traditional image of a strong leader. The head of Soviet space research, Roald Sagdeev, had opportunities to observe Gorbachev in small group discussions in the early years of perestroika.[60] He noted that there were 'only a few people who did not fall under the spell of Gorbachev's personal charm and the magnetism of his verbal talent'. Admiring his zeal as 'a genuine born missionary', Sagdeev remarked, however, on Gorbachev's tendency to overestimate what he could achieve with his formidable powers of persuasion. He had come to believe that 'he could persuade anyone in the Soviet Union about anything'.[61] Yet what was especially important about Gorbachev's leadership, Sagdeev adds, was precisely that he attempted to *persuade* his interlocutors, albeit in 'a most impassioned and eloquent way'. That, said Sagdeev, was 'a sign of great progress in the political culture of my country', for this approach 'was in sharp variance to the tradition that bosses usually adopted'. Hitherto, they had 'never tried to change people's genuine opinions or beliefs, but simply issued an instruction and demanded that it be followed'.[62]

That Gorbachev's style of leadership was at odds with traditional Russian political culture, in the way Sagdeev suggested, attracted that eminent scientist, but it was not of universal appeal in Soviet society. Gorbachev's popularity declined quite steeply between the spring of 1989 and the end of the Soviet Union in December 1991 (although it was as late as May 1990, more than five years after he became general secretary, that Boris Yeltsin overtook him as the most popular politician in Russia).[63] Gorbachev's aide and adviser on political reform, Georgiy Shakhnazarov, argued that his authority was undermined from the spring of 1989 when he presided over the new legislature, the Congress of People's Deputies – and its inner body, the Supreme Soviet – which had come into being as a result of the first genuinely competitive national elections in the history of the USSR, held in March of that year.[64] Wishing to encourage the development of 'a culture of parliamentarism', Gorbachev spent whole days chairing the legislature, in effect becoming its speaker as well as the head of state and leader of the Communist Party. Well-wishers, says Shakhnazarov, told Gorbachev that by taking upon himself the role of speaker, he was contributing to the decline of his personal authority: 'When millions of people, sitting in front of their

television, witnessed some unknown young deputy engaging in argument with the head of state who patiently explained himself and even
took in his stride patent insults', they concluded that nothing good lay
in store for the country. 'In Russia,' said Shakhnazarov, 'from time
immemorial people have admired and even loved severe rulers.' It was
difficult for them to accept mild and tactful people as leaders. How
could they expect such a leader to provide order and security, in exchange
for which they would willingly serve him?[65]*

The person who was in charge of management of the Soviet
economy for most of the perestroika period was Nikolay Ryzhkov,
Chairman of the Council of Ministers from 1985 to 1990. At first a
conditional ally of Gorbachev, he later became a stern critic. He
deplored, in particular, Gorbachev's pursuit of democratization at the
expense of what he saw as more pressing economic problems. In fact,
Ryzhkov's own technocratic approach to the economy was a major
reason why marketizing reform was not embraced earlier. In the
present context, however, it is Ryzhkov's observation of Gorbachev's
leadership style which matters most. By nature and character, Ryzhkov
observed, Gorbachev was incapable of being a Machiavellian prince,
even though it was an error to believe him to be indecisive.[66] But 'long
before our native parliamentary games began', said Ryzhkov, Gorbachev
'was a leader of a parliamentary type', adding: 'How he was thus
formed in a party-bureaucratic system, God alone knows.' Gorbachev,
observed Ryzhkov, had become that kind of a leader in spite of the
fact that from his earliest youth he had risen, rung-by-rung, up the
traditional career ladder of Komsomol (Communist Youth League)
and the Communist Party.[67] He had neither the temperament nor the
desire to rule by making himself feared, as Machiavelli taught and
Stalin imbibed.† That does not mean that Gorbachev lacked ambition

---

* Russia was, and remains, a diverse country, and the attitudes Shakhnazarov attributed to the population were far from universal. Nevertheless, there were a great
many Russians for whom the sight of a leader reacting calmly to public criticism
signified weakness.
† A Russian scholar, Dmitriy Furman, observed that people who would be regarded
as monsters in everyday life, among whom he numbers Ivan the Terrible and Peter
I, have traditionally been regarded as 'great' in Russia, whereas the tsar who ended
serfdom, Alexander II, was *not* 'great'. Where, he asks, does Gorbachev fit into that
system of evaluation? Nowhere at all is his answer: 'In a system of evaluation in

to lead. On the contrary. In conversation with a close friend, he remarked: 'From my earliest days I liked to be a leader among my peers – that was my nature. And this remained true when I joined the Komsomol . . . and later when I joined the party – it was a way of somehow realizing my potential.'[68]

Gorbachev was, as already noted, the most popular politician in the country for the first five out of the almost seven years in which he was Soviet leader. That owed a great deal to his openness, to removing the fear of war (which in a country that lost twenty-seven million people during the Second World War counted for a great deal), and to his presiding over the introduction of a host of new freedoms, including freedom of speech, religious freedom, and elections with choice. What was especially important – a weakness for some observers, a strength in the eyes of others – was the extent to which he was willing to change his mind when presented with new evidence or persuasive arguments. Much of the change was startlingly obvious. Other changes in Gorbachev's outlook were disguised by some linguistic continuity. Some of his radical critics downplayed the extent of the evolution of Gorbachev's thinking by seizing on his continuing attachment to 'perestroika' and to 'socialism'. They missed the fundamental point that in the course of his first five years in the Kremlin what he meant by those terms changed utterly. 'Perestroika' had begun as a euphemism for reform of the Soviet system at a time when the very word 'reform' was taboo. It gradually came to stand for the root-and-branch transformation of the Soviet system which Gorbachev sought – a system of pluralist democracy founded on a rule of law, not the guaranteed rule of the Communist Party. As for 'socialism', Gorbachev moved from being a Communist reformer in 1985 to a socialist of a social democratic type by the end of that decade – a qualitative change.[69]

By the spring of 1990 the Soviet Union no longer had a Communist system, but one characterized by political pluralism, a burgeoning civil society, a developing rule of law which was replacing arbitrariness,

---

which the great are Ivan the Terrible, Peter and Stalin, Gorbachev not only is "not great", he is the antithesis of greatness.' (Dmitriy Furman, *Nezavisimaya gazeta*, 1 March 2011.) However, Furman goes on to contend that in a system of evaluation 'normal for the contemporary developed world, Gorbachev is simply a great ruler and politician, perhaps the very greatest in Russian history'.

and rapidly advancing democratization. The political system, in short, had been transformed. For the first four years of perestroika, this was very much a 'revolution from above', one dependent on Gorbachev's tranquillizing the hardliners, even as he radicalized the political agenda, thus avoiding the kind of internal coup that would have turned the clock backwards with a vengeance. There is a parallel here with Suárez. Gorbachev, too, managed to postpone the coup by the hardliners for so long – until August 1991 in his case – that by the time it came, there were institutions in place and enough people who had turned from obedient subjects into active citizens successfully to resist it. It was especially important that just two months earlier Boris Yeltsin had been elected President of Russia (as distinct from the Soviet Union) by universal suffrage in a competitive election and had, therefore, democratic legitimacy to defy the putschists at a time when Gorbachev and his family were under house arrest in their holiday home on the Crimean coast.[70]

By playing the principal role in the transformation of Soviet foreign policy, Gorbachev had also been the key figure in changing the international system. The Cold War had begun with the Soviet takeover of Eastern Europe. It ended when the countries of East and Central Europe became, one by one, independent and non-Communist and Gorbachev calmly accepted that outcome. So far as the economic system is concerned, Gorbachev in the course of 1990–91 accepted the *principle* of a market economy, but one of a social democratic type. Cooperatives were legalized in 1988 and many of them rapidly became thinly disguised private enterprises. Yet, Gorbachev was much later in accepting the market as the main regulator of the economy than he was in accepting the need for democracy. He was also faced by powerful bureaucratic opposition to marketization. As a result, the economy was in limbo when the Soviet Union came to an end – no longer a command economy but not yet a market one.

Gorbachev has been regarded by some as a 'weak' leader, or even a failure, because the country over which he presided – the Soviet Union – ceased to exist at the end of 1991. The state could have been held together for many more years had he not embarked on the liberalization and democratization of the Soviet system and the transformation of Soviet foreign policy. The relevance of foreign policy was that when the most disaffected of Soviet nationalities – especially

Estonians, Latvians and Lithuanians – saw the peoples of Eastern Europe acquiring independent statehood in 1989, this raised their aspirations from seeking greater autonomy within a Soviet state to demanding full independence. Gorbachev consciously sought the dismantling of the Soviet *system*, but he sought to prevent the dissolution of the Soviet *state*. He was not, however, prepared to resort to the kind of sustained use of force that would have been required to crush independence movements once expectations were aroused. Before his policies had generated the belief that national independence for Soviet union republics might be possible, the status quo could have been maintained by the pre-existing system of rewards and severe punishments. Gorbachev tried to keep a union together – in its ultimate proposed form not even a renewed USSR (Union of Soviet Socialist Republics) but a USS, a Union of Sovereign States – through a process of negotiation, persuasion and compromise. That was already several steps too far for many party and state officials, military leaders and the KGB. Gorbachev was accused by them of being far too conciliatory to radicals and nationalists, and too reluctant to use the coercive power at his disposal to preserve the Soviet Union intact.*

He was later told by a leading Russian nationalist that he did not have the historic right to allow either the Warsaw Pact or the Soviet Union itself to be dissolved. If he had not been prepared to use force to prevent these things, he should have made way for a 'more decisive patriot'.[71] Yet, the fact that the Soviet Union was dissolved largely peacefully (in contrast with another multi-national Communist state, Yugoslavia) was also in some ways an achievement on Gorbachev's part. For him it was very much an unintended consequence of systemic change, but he resisted repeated calls to declare a state of emergency, meaning martial law, and put a stop to the fissiparous processes. Most fundamentally, it was Gorbachev's liberalization and democratization that made pursuit of independence movements possible. His 'guilt' in relation to the break-up of the Soviet state lay in replacing fear by freedoms and in an aversion to shedding blood.

---

* It was in order to reverse the process of disintegration and, in the first instance, stop Gorbachev and at least five of the fifteen leaders of Soviet republics from signing a treaty to form a new, voluntary and loose federation in place of what had been the Soviet Union, that the August coup of 1991 (which collapsed within a few days) took place.

Ideas were important for Gorbachev and for the demise of Communism, just as they had been in its rise. But especially in a highly authoritarian system, ideas – if they are to be politically effective – require institutional bearers. It was the combination of ideas that were radically new in the Soviet context, innovative leadership, and political power (of a general secretary with a different mindset from that of any of his predecessors) which was decisive in producing transformative change in the Soviet Union – and, as a consequence, metamorphosis in that part of Europe whose sovereignty had been strictly limited by an unreconstructed Soviet leadership over the previous four decades. Aleksandr Yakovlev, who by the 1990s had become a far from uncritical admirer of Gorbachev, said, nevertheless, in 1995: 'I consider Gorbachev to be the greatest reformer of the century, the more so because he tried to do this in Russia where from time immemorial the fate of reformers has been unenviable.'[72] It is certainly difficult to think of anyone in the second half of the twentieth century who had a larger (and generally beneficent) impact not only on his own multinational state but also internationally. By temperament a reformer rather than revolutionary, he, nevertheless, pursued (as he put it) 'revolutionary change by evolutionary means'.

DENG XIAOPING

Deng Xiaoping was a transformational leader of a very different kind from Gorbachev. Deng was the key political figure in the transformation of the Chinese *economic* system, while Gorbachev transformed the Soviet *political* system. Of an older generation (he was born in 1904, Gorbachev in 1931), Deng was one of those who made the Chinese revolution, whereas Gorbachev emerged into a Communist order that had already been established. Both men were born in villages far from the capital, but Deng Xiaoping into an established landlord family, Gorbachev in a peasant household. Both Deng and Gorbachev placed a high value on education and on listening to well-informed specialists. Unlike Gorbachev (who unusually for a boy from a peasant family studied in Russia's leading university), the Chinese leader did not have access to higher education. Deng Xiaoping spent the first half of the 1920s in France, where he had hoped to study as well as to work, but spent his time as a low-paid worker before moving to office tasks on a Communist journal, produced by young Chinese who had become radicalized during their time in France. Deng's immediate superior there was Zhou Enlai, who was six years older – later to become, after Mao Zedong, the second most prominent member of the Communist government of China. Believing in January 1926 that he was about to be arrested and deported for his political propaganda work, Deng escaped to the Soviet Union. There he studied for a year at the Sun Yat-sen University, which had been established by the Comintern to train members both of the Chinese Communist Party and of the Kuomintang, the Chinese Nationalist Party. The fact that activists of these two parties were brought together under one roof led Deng to have as one of his classmates Chiang Ching-kuo, the son of Chiang Kai-shek. (During the years when Deng Xiaoping was the paramount leader of China and Chiang Ching-kuo his equivalent in Taiwan, Deng tried to meet with him, but Chiang refused.)[73]

Deng was one of those who took part in the famous Long March with Mao Zedong in the mid-1930s, as the Communists retreated, under attack from the Chinese Nationalists, to a new base in Shaanxi province in north-west China. Only one in ten of the 80,000 men and 2,000 women who embarked on the march reached their destination.[74] Although at times in later years he incurred Mao Zedong's wrath, Deng early on earned Mao's respect for his intelligence and organizational ability. Long before the Second World War Deng had, accordingly, established good personal relations with both Mao and Zhou. In the Chinese civil war, which ended with the Communists taking power in 1949, Deng was a political commissar and the effective leader of some half a million troops in one of the decisive campaigns of the conflict.[75] As early as 1956, Deng was appointed general secretary of the Communist Party. In most Communist countries, that would have been the top position, but in China Mao had the title of Chairman of the party and there was no questioning his supreme authority. Nevertheless, Deng was in charge of the day-to-day administration of the party and also a member of the Standing Committee of the Politburo, the inner sanctum of the party leadership.[76]

Mao combined ruthless power-seeking, vindictiveness towards those who thwarted him, and encouragement of the cult of his personality with romantic revolutionary ideas of surging ahead to some kind of full communism, in the process overtaking the Soviet Union, which had started earlier, in the pursuit of that wholly fanciful goal. Deng, although he never wavered in his belief in the absolute power of the Communist Party and of strict hierarchy and discipline within it ('democratic centralism'), was much more of a pragmatist than Mao in his approach to governmental organization and economic modernization. Thus, it was not difficult for Mao Zedong, in his later years, to suspect that Deng had serious reservations about the wisdom of his 'Great Leap Forward' and the 'Cultural Revolution'. Both of these Maoist initiatives were disasters. The Great Leap Forward – between 1958 and 1960 – saw the creation of enormous 'people's communes' in the countryside with mass mobilization turning out to be a very poor substitute for the smaller agricultural cooperatives and for professional expertise. The calamitous loss of life caused by the Great Leap into communization of Chinese society is discussed more fully in Chapter 6.

Whatever his private thoughts at the time, Deng Xiaoping loyally and ruthlessly helped to implement on Mao's behalf that policy which led to massive famine.[77] During the Cultural Revolution in the second half of the 1960s and first half of the 1970s, Deng's distaste was more immediately discernible for what was in effect an anti-intellectual, anti-educational and anti-cultural mobilization of young radicals against almost all authoritative institutions, other than Mao's inviolable supreme leadership. Deng himself became a target of abuse and was condemned as a 'capitalist roader'. He was exiled to the countryside in 1969 and worked for a time as a fitter, a job that he had done some forty years earlier in a Renault factory in France. Deng's elder son, trying to escape from Red Guard persecutors, was crippled for life when he jumped from a high dormitory window of Peking University.[78]

Although Mao fully approved Deng's removal from the political leadership and his exile to the countryside, he did not endorse demands for his expulsion from the Communist Party. Had that occurred, it would hardly have been possible for Deng to make a political come-back. Mao, however, retained a residual respect for Deng who had been his strongest supporter in factional struggles in the 1930s and had proved himself in war and peace. Deng and his family were allowed to return to Beijing in February 1973 and the following month Deng was restored to the post he had held on the eve of his expulsion, that of Vice Premier.[79] Nevertheless, he was dismissed again in 1975. When Deng met the American Secretary of State Cyrus Vance in 1977, by which time he was back in high office, he recalled that they had last met just before his dismissal two years earlier. Deng joked that if he was well known internationally, it was 'because I have been three times up and three times down'.[80] After Mao's death in 1976, Deng, who was highly respected by a great many senior party officials (although he was bitterly opposed by the 'Gang of Four' who had led the assault in the Cultural Revolution), quite rapidly consolidated his position within the leadership.

Deng never held the top post of party Chairman, nor did he again become general secretary of the party. Yet, by the end of the 1970s, he was more powerful than Mao's chosen successor as party Chairman, Hua Guofeng.[81] This was a rare case in a Communist system where a leader's individual authority became more important than his rank within the party. However, it was not a personal rule over the party, but governance through it, and it reflected Deng's high standing with influential party officials. His dominance grew as he was able to bring an increasing number of allies into key positions. By February 1980, there was a majority of Deng supporters in the Politburo. By 1981 Deng himself held three posts – vice premier, vice chairman of the party, and, not least, Chairman of the Central Military Commission. Formally, he was not the country's leader, but informally from the late 1970s and throughout the 1980s he unquestionably was. Deng did nothing to create a cult of his personality. In contrast with Mao, there was no question of students having to waste time memorizing quotations from his writings.[82]

Having attained a position of ascendancy, although not of dictatorial power, Deng proceeded to pursue economic policies that were to change utterly the character of the Chinese economic system. Mao in 1957 had described Deng to Soviet leader Nikita Khrushchev as a 'little man' (Deng was barely five feet tall) who was 'highly intelligent' and had 'a great future ahead of him'.[83] Mao was right, but he hardly imagined that Deng's greatest legacy would be to destroy the essentials of Maoism. Deng did not encourage frontal attacks on Mao, for that would mean 'discrediting our Party and state'.[84] Mao, after all, was China's Lenin and Stalin rolled into one. He had led the Chinese party to victory in revolution and had then been the country's ruler for the greater part of its existence as a Communist state. Deng Xiaoping's policies, however, marked a fundamental break with Maoism. Deng began with agricultural reform, and in the early 1980s collectivization gave way to a return to peasant household farming, stimulating a dramatic improvement in agricultural productivity. Four special economic zones were set up in coastal areas and gradually opened up to inward investment from international companies. Deng's approach was 'consistent experimentation before widespread adoption of a particular policy',[85] although with the firm intent of introducing far-reaching change into the economy as a whole.

The transformation of the economic system since the late 1970s has enabled China to experience one of the most remarkable periods of economic growth in human history.[86] An economy of state, or public, ownership became a mixed economy with a substantial private sector. A command economy was gradually turned into an essentially market economy, albeit one in which there was a close relationship between private enterprise and state institutions. Over time, although Deng was not personally implicated in this, cosy relationships developed between high officials and business enterprises (including those with multiple offshoots abroad), with many of the party-state cadres acquiring immense wealth.[87] The growth of corruption and of extreme inequality were among the results of the systemic changes in the economy which Deng set in train. They are also an Achilles heel of the system, for in the absence of democratic accountability, popular anger about these outcomes is potentially dangerous for the regime.

Nevertheless, it is not only a new category of super-rich who have benefited from China becoming the workshop of the world and emerging as a key player in the international economic system. Economic growth rates of 10 per cent annually raised the standard of living of hundreds of millions of people. Urbanization has proceeded at a remarkable pace. Whereas 80 per cent of the Chinese population still lived in the countryside at the time of Mao's death in 1976, by 2012 almost half the population of 1.3 billion people lived in cities.[88] A majority of the urban population are now factory workers, but there has also been a huge growth of a well-to-do middle class. In spite of the extremely uneven distribution of the rewards for fast economic growth, the fruits of Deng's reforms have brought far more concrete benefits to the many than did Mao's penurious egalitarianism.

Under Deng and his successors there has also been some political relaxation. His policies of encouraging young Chinese to study abroad and opening the country to foreign direct investment could not avoid bringing in a greater knowledge of the outside world, including of other political systems. The limits of the possible in political discussion have become broader than they were during most of the Mao years. Nevertheless, while embracing systemic change of the economy, Deng firmly resisted qualitative change of the political system. He remained committed to the monopoly of power of the Communist Party and was prepared to act ruthlessly against those who challenged it in the name of democracy. Thus, when hundreds of demonstrators (as well as some mere bystanders) were massacred in the vicinity of Tiananmen Square on 4 June 1989, it had been Deng more than anyone else who was insistent on calling in the army and tanks to put an end to the protests at whatever cost in blood.[89] The general secretary of the Communist Party, Zhao Ziyang, who had earlier as premier implemented Deng's economic reforms with skill and enthusiasm, opposed this introduction of martial law on the streets of Beijing. As a result, from that time until his death in 2005, he was kept under house arrest.[90]

Deng Xiaoping and Mikhail Gorbachev remain the two great transformers of Communist systems, but their achievements were very different. How these are weighed against each other depends ultimately on the values of the assessor. Gorbachev played a decisive role in facilitating a host of personal freedoms (of speech and publication, assembly, religion, communications, civil association and travel) of several hundred million people – the population of the Soviet Union and Eastern Europe. Deng Xiaoping played a no less significant part in raising the material living standards of even more millions without according them any of the above-mentioned freedoms other than that of foreign travel. China today is a hybrid, having a Communist political system and a non-Communist economic system. Although he preserved the former, Deng's credentials as a transformational leader are well established by the decisive role he played in the transition to the latter. Deng's legacy is, indeed, more visible in contemporary China than is Gorbachev's in contemporary Russia. China today is, in many respects, what Deng Xiaoping made it. If it continues to combine fast economic growth with relative political stability, the China which Deng

4

The end of the apartheid regime in South Africa has already been touched upon in the previous chapter in the context of viewing F.W. de Klerk as a redefining leader. As we saw, the rapid transition to majority rule in South Africa in the early 1990s owed much to the changes in the Soviet Union, especially the transformation of Soviet foreign policy and the end of the Cold War. For white supremacists to play up the spectre of Communism, which, they claimed, a transition to majority rule would mean for South Africa, had become more implausible than ever by the end of the 1980s. F.W. de Klerk acknowledged this, although he puts the point differently, writing that, without the changes initiated by Gorbachev, 'our own transformation process in South Africa would have been much more difficult and might have been delayed by several years'.[91]

Nelson Mandela had long been the most internationally recognized opponent of the apartheid regime. The son of a minor chief, he was born in the Transkei territory of South Africa in 1918. Mandela was only nine years of age when his father died, and Jongintaba Dalindyebo, the paramount chief of the Themu people, to which Mandela belonged, took him into his own household and became his guardian. His style of leadership, which (as Mandela recollected it) was more collective than individual, had a significant impact on South Africa's future president. From time to time chiefs and headmen, but also many others, from miles around would be summoned to a meeting at the Great Place where they would be welcomed by Jongintaba who would explain why he had called them together. 'From that point on,' says Mandela, 'he would not utter another word until the meeting was nearing its end.'[92] Mandela, who as a boy sat fascinated through these meetings, describes them thus:

Everyone who wanted to speak did so. It was democracy in its purest form. There may have been a hierarchy of importance among the speakers, but everyone was heard: chief and subject, warrior and medicine man, shopkeeper and farmer, landowner and labourer. People spoke without interruption and the meetings lasted for many hours. The foundation of self-government was that all men were free to voice their opinions and were equal in their value as citizens. (Women, I am afraid, were deemed second-class citizens.)[93]

Apart from the reference to women's subordination, Mandela may, in his old age, have had a somewhat gilded memory of the degree of democracy. But perceptions and selective memory of personal experience can influence later conduct more than an objective account by a dispassionate historian or anthropologist. Both Mandela's experience of tribal culture and his anglicized education in South African schools and colleges contributed distinctive elements to his sense of identity. He notes that the regent (as the paramount chief was also known) was often criticized, sometimes vehemently, but he 'simply listened' and showed 'no emotion at all'. The meetings continued until either a consensus was reached or all agreed to disagree, leaving a solution to the problem for a subsequent meeting. There was, Mandela says, no question of a minority being crushed by a majority. The regent would speak only at the end of the meeting, summing up what had been said. Mandela adds: 'As a leader, I have always followed the principles I first saw demonstrated by the regent at the Great Place. I have always endeavoured to listen to what each and every person in a discussion had to say before venturing my own opinion.' Often, he adds, what he himself subsequently said represented no more than 'a consensus of what I heard in the discussion'.[94]

Mandela was educated at mission schools, and at the major higher educational institution for Africans, the University College of Fort Hare (from which he was expelled for organizing a strike), and subsequently at the University of Witwatersrand. Distinguished by his height (he was almost as tall as de Gaulle), Mandela soon acquired other features that set him apart. He became one of the few black lawyers in South Africa, and he was politically active from the early 1940s. Along with his friends and long-term leading colleagues in the African National Congress (ANC), Walter Sisulu and Oliver Tambo, he founded the ANC Youth League in 1944. This was, in many respects, a radical offshoot of the moderate ANC. Initially, it espoused a racial nationalism, its members being suspicious of cooperation with whites, which included white Communists who had exercised some influence in the

African National Congress. Mandela in 1949 called for their expulsion from the ANC. However, when the South African government introduced the Suppression of Communism Act in 1950, they drafted it sufficiently broadly that it could be used to outlaw any organization or individual opposed to the authorities.[95] The shared threat encouraged Mandela to make common cause with the Communists in the struggle against white minority rule. Addressing a South African court in 1964, Mandela distinguished the goals of the Communist Party from those of the ANC. The Communists, he said, aimed to remove the capitalists and bring the working class to power, whereas the ANC sought to harmonize class interests. However, he added:

Theoretical differences amongst those fighting against oppression are a luxury we cannot afford at this stage. What is more, for many decades communists were the only political group in South Africa who were prepared to treat Africans as human beings and their equals; who were prepared to eat with us; talk with us, live with and work with us. Because of this, there are many Africans who, today, tend to equate freedom with communism.[96]

Mandela made clear his position was different. He stressed his admiration for the British parliament, for the separation of powers in the United States, and for the independence of the judiciary in particular. Against the argument that the ANC had become an instrument of the Communist Party, he drew the comparison of American and British cooperation with the Soviet Union in the struggle against Nazi Germany during the Second World War, adding that only Hitler would have dared 'to suggest that such cooperation turned Churchill or Roosevelt into communists or communist tools'.[97]

Mandela and Tambo in 1952 opened one of the first legal practices to be run by black lawyers. Throughout that decade Mandela was frequently banned and sometimes arrested. At one point when there was a warrant for his arrest, he moved from house to house and evaded the police for long enough to become known as the 'Black Pimpernel'. When sixty-nine African protesters were shot dead and many more wounded at Sharpeville, south of Johannesburg, on 21 March 1960, further outraging the black African majority as well as opinion abroad, the apartheid government declared a state of emergency and banned the African National Congress.[98] The ANC resolved to become an underground organization and formed a five-member coordinating committee, with Mandela chosen as one of its members. He was allotted the task of explaining these decisions in secret meetings with the rank and file.[99] Mandela spent the evening of the Sharpeville massacre, discussing the ANC response to it, in the company of Walter Sisulu at the home of Joe Slovo, one of their white colleagues who was also a leading figure in the South African Communist Party. They decided to call for a nationwide burning of the passes that black Africans were legally obliged to carry. Mandela burned his pass on 28 March in front of a specially invited group of journalists. Two days later he was arrested and he spent the next five months in prison.[100]

From the time the organization went underground, Mandela began to look like its future leader. The President of the ANC, Chief Albert Luthuli, was widely respected abroad – in 1961 he became the first African to receive the Nobel Peace Prize – but he was regarded as too moderate by the ANC's more radical members, partly because of his willingness to cooperate with whites and partly because of his strong commitment to non-violence. Mandela was one of those who decided, following Sharpeville, that the continuing intransigence of the regime and its violence against the black majority would have to be met with armed struggle. He became the principal founder of an offshoot from the ANC, *Umkhonto we Sizwe* (Spear of the Nation). It adopted a policy of economic sabotage rather than of terrorism against persons on the grounds that this offered more hope of later reconciliation. *Umkhonto*, the joint creation of the ANC and the South African Communist Party, was headed by Mandela who appointed Slovo as his chief of staff.[101] During 1962 Mandela, wanted by the South African police, slipped out of the country and spent half a year visiting different African leaders to garner support for the ANC and the new phase of the struggle. He also had military training in Ethiopia and Morocco.[102] Before going back to South Africa, he visited London where he had meetings with Oliver Tambo, his old friend and leader of ANC members in exile, with Labour and Liberal Party leaders and with Christian fundraisers for the ANC.[103] Shortly after his return to South Africa, Mandela was arrested on 5 August 1962. He spent the next twenty-seven and a half years in prison, not being released until 11 February 1990, nine days after the South African government's ban on the ANC was lifted.

Originally, Mandela was sentenced to five years of imprisonment. However, when evidence was uncovered of his leadership of *Umkhonto*, he was tried again in 1964 and narrowly escaped being sentenced to death, receiving instead a life imprisonment sentence. Mandela ended his four-hour address to the court on that occasion by saying:

During my lifetime I have dedicated myself to this struggle of the African people. I have fought against white domination, and I have fought against black domination. I have cherished the ideal of a democratic and free society in which all persons live together in harmony and with equal opportunities. It is an ideal which I hope to live for and to achieve. But if needs be, it is an ideal for which I am prepared to die.[104]

Many of Mandela's years of imprisonment were spent in the extremely harsh conditions of Robben Island, although later he was transferred to more normal prisons, albeit isolated in separate sections. From 1985 the South African government began making contact with him, with President P.W. Botha offering him release from prison if he would renounce violence as a political strategy. Mandela, however, refused such terms and it cost him almost five more years in prison. He continued to show almost superhuman patience, having become increasingly conscious by the 1980s that one day he would be released. He was determined that it would be on his, and the ANC's, terms.

Mandela's resilience, together with the growing pressures on the South African government (including capital flight), meant that de Klerk and his National Party (NP), both before Mandela's release in 1990 and in the period of negotiations which followed it, were able to get only a little of what they wanted – protection of minority rights, property rights and agreements on electoral rules. Essentially, however, 'the NP leadership could only bargain on how it would give up power'.[105] Mandela was elected President of the ANC in 1991 at its first national conference in South Africa since its banning in 1960 and in 1993 he and de Klerk were jointly awarded the Nobel Peace Prize. Even as President of the ANC, and with the heroic status conferred upon him by his long imprisonment, during which he had become the major symbol of opposition to apartheid, Mandela did not always get his way in the ANC's policy discussions. With South Africa's first democratic election in the offing, he proposed, for example, that the voting age be lowered to fourteen, but he retreated in the face of strong opposition from members of the ANC's National Executive Committee.[106] During those years Mandela was reflecting on the nature of political leadership. He wrote in a notebook: 'The leader's first task is to create a vision. His second is to create a following to help him implement the vision and to manage the process through effective teams. The people being led know where they are going because the leader has communicated the vision and the followers have bought into the goal he had set as well as the process of getting there.'[107]

There was a tension between Mandela's belief in principle in collective leadership and his heroic status. Against the odds, he won the respect and even affection of the majority of the white South African population after he became the country's first black president, democratically elected in 1994. He resented, however, the share of credit for the South African transition to democracy which had been accorded de Klerk.[108] After what he had been through, that was more than understandable. He chaired Cabinet meetings rather in the manner of the regent at the Great Place. According to one of its members, Mandela 'listened impassively, taking in everything and then intervening'.[109] He sometimes took a different line from the ANC. They, for example, had been critical of the findings of the Truth and Reconciliation Commission, which Mandela had set up. His own response was to say that 'they have not done a perfect but a remarkable job and I approve of everything they did'.[110] Mandela devolved the making of economic policy to others, especially his deputy Thabo Mbeki, but was himself active in foreign policy, taking delight 'in personal diplomacy, telephoning heads of state in blithe disregard of international time zones'.[111]

Mandela was devoted to the advancement of human rights, greater socio-economic equality, non-racialism and reconciliation among South Africa's different ethnic groups. Some of these aims were realized in practice more than others. What was especially remarkable was the extent to which Mandela won over a great many Afrikaners, embracing cultural symbols that had in the past been regarded as deeply alien by black South Africans. An especially notable occasion was when he appeared at the World Cup Rugby finals wearing a Springbok jersey, winning the warm appreciation of the players and the wholehearted approval of the crowd. The task of building a harmonious multiracial society and new forms of national unity, especially in conditions of continuing great inequality, was never going to be other than arduous. It is hard, though, to imagine anyone making a better or more gracious start than Mandela, especially in the light of all that had gone before in the history of the country and in his own life. He himself played by the new rules of the democratic game and, on a continent which has seen too many 'presidents for life', he set a worthy example by standing down in 1999 after just one five-year term. He died, aged ninety-five, in December 2013. More than anyone else, Mandela had been instrumental in producing the transformation of the political system which turned South Africa from a country of white minority rule, with the great majority of the population disenfranchised, into a democracy. Apartheid would have ended sometime, but without Mandela it is very unlikely that the transition to democracy could have been so relatively peaceful and ultimately accepted by the white minority who had lost political power.

TRANSFORMATIONAL AND INSPIRATIONAL LEADERS

The criteria for counting someone as a transformational leader, set out at the beginning of this chapter, are very demanding. The five examples considered here are of people who held the highest executive posts in their respective countries (in Deng Xiaoping's case, de facto rather than de jure), and it would be difficult to meet the criteria without doing so. It is *extremely rare*, however, for a head of government to make that degree of difference and play an indispensable part in introducing systemic change. A transformational leader is not the same as an inspirational leader, although these are not, of course, mutually exclusive categories. It would be hard to think of a more politically significant example of an inspirational leader than Mahatma Gandhi, though he never held governmental office. He not only played a crucial part in the Indian struggle for independence from Britain but his example of non-violent resistance was an inspiration to countless protest movements in different countries. A contemporary inspirational leader who might yet become also a transformational leader is Aung San Suu Kyi, the leader of the democratic opposition to the Burmese military regime.

If the modest liberalization of that regime were to develop into systemic change, she would have played a huge part in bringing it about and would surely be regarded as the founding mother of Burmese democracy. In South Korea Kim Dae Jung was an inspiration for those opposed to the authoritarian rule that prevailed until well into the 1980s. Having been imprisoned and at one time sentenced to death, Kim did as much as anyone to give substance to the development of democracy in Korea and was eventually elected to the presidency in 1998. During that time he freed many political prisoners and initiated a 'sunshine policy' towards North Korea, aimed at unfreezing the relations between the two parts of the peninsula, with some limited but temporary success. Since the democratization process was already underway in South Korea before he came to power, Kim Dae Jung was not quite a transformational leader, but a courageous and important figure, nonetheless, in Asian politics. (He was awarded the Nobel Peace Prize in 2000.)

There are other leaders who may be considered both charismatic and politically important but who did not play the decisive role in systemic change. One such person is Boris Yeltsin who was sometimes, and quite wrongly, portrayed as 'the father of Russian democracy'. Yeltsin had broken with the Communist Party leadership in 1987 (although he remained a member of the party until 1990) and was without influence when the most important decisions – not least, to move to contested elections – were taken by Gorbachev and his inner circle in 1988. American President Bill Clinton said it preyed on Yeltsin's mind that he 'got so little credit for starting a democracy'.[112] There was, however, a good reason for that: he did not initiate the process of democratization and was in no position to do so. What Yeltsin did do with great initial success was to move into political space which the Gorbachev reforms had created.

The nearest Yeltsin came to being a transformational leader was in the sphere of economic change. The idea of a market economy had already been accepted in the last years of the Soviet Union and the country had ceased to have anything that could be called a planned or command economy. However, a number of practical steps to creating a market were taken during Yeltsin's years in power, starting with the very important freeing of most prices in January 1992. But what was built in the 1990s was less a market economy than 'a bad case of predatory capitalism', as the title of a book by the Swedish scholar Stefan

Hedlund puts it.[113] Russia's natural resources were handed over at a frac-
tion of their international market value in rigged auctions to people
who were 'appointed billionaires'. Popular discontent with this, and with
the extremes of inequality and corruption which developed, undermined
support in Russia for democracy. Yeltsin in the last years of the Soviet
Union had acquired a large following. He had a commanding presence
and an impulsive political style which fitted Russian notions of a 'strong
leader'. Long before the year 2000, when Yeltsin handed power over to
Vladimir Putin, who promised him and his family immunity from prosecution, his early popularity had largely evaporated, and he had done
the cause of democracy more harm than good.*[114]

A somewhat stronger candidate to be considered as a transformational leader is Lech Wałęsa. In the 1970s he emerged as a leader of
Polish shipyard workers, and in 1980–81 he was an inspirational and
politically astute leader of Solidarity, the workers' mass movement that
rocked the foundations of the Polish party-state. There was a de facto
political pluralism in Poland from the summer of 1980 until December
1981 and a vibrant civil society, of which Solidarity and the Catholic
Church, overlapping bodies with many millions of members, were the
most visible and authoritative components. Had the Polish regime not
succeeded in introducing martial law in December 1981, arresting
Wałęsa and other leading figures in Solidarity, and reducing that movement to a shadow of its former self, Wałęsa would, indeed, have been
a transformational leader. However, the transition to democracy in
Poland came not at the beginning of the 1980s – for a Communist
order was re-established – but at the end of that decade, by which time
external influences were decisively important. When Solidarity was
legalized again – in 1989 – and went on to win a stunning victory in a
national election, the Polish Communist leadership was responding to
the changes in Moscow, the rising expectations of Polish society engendered by those changes, and the drawing to an end of the Cold War.
Wałęsa remained for a time a focus of identification for Poles – and in

* As the Russian political analyst Lilia Shevtsova has observed: 'It is paradoxical that
the degeneration of Yeltsin's leadership strengthened demands, not for independent
institutions as a means of avoiding a repetition of that leadership, but for more
powerful, authoritarian rule.' (Lilia Shevtsova, *Russia – Lost in Transition: The Yeltsin
and Putin Legacies*, Carnegie Endowment for International Peace, Washington, DC,
2007, p. 32.)

late 1990 was elected president (after which his popularity began to decline) – but even without him, Poland would very rapidly have become non-Communist and independent. All that was required for that to happen was for Poles to believe that if they cast aside their domestic Communist rulers, this would not lead to Soviet military intervention.*

The same point applies to Václav Havel and to Czechoslovakia's 'Velvet Revolution' of late 1989. Havel was a leader of great moral authority, since he was a distinguished writer who had chosen a life of harassment and frequent imprisonment rather than accept the rules of the game laid down by the conservative Communist regime put in place after the crushing by Soviet tanks of the Prague Spring of 1968. The overwhelming majority of the population of Czechoslovakia, however, in the years between 1969 and 1988, had opted for a quiet life. Having the dubious honour of being the last European country to experience a Soviet invasion (to reimpose Communist orthodoxy and Moscow-approved leaders), they were extremely cautious about risking a repeat intervention. Before the invasion of August 1968, Communists were in a minority in Czechoslovakia, but a very much larger minority than they were in Poland. Following the invasion, there were far fewer Communist believers in either the Czech lands or Slovakia than before. People simply retreated into their private lives. There was no reason to doubt that Czechoslovakia would become non-Communist very quickly indeed if and when it became clear that

---

* We now know from Soviet Politburo transcripts that an invasion of Poland was being seriously considered in August 1980, but that by 1981 the Soviet leadership had turned firmly against this. They were in increasing trouble in Afghanistan, Poland was the largest of the East European countries, and its people had a tradition of standing up to invaders. This was also early in the Reagan administration's first term and an invasion of Poland would have raised East–West tensions dangerously. The Poles, however, were unaware in 1981 that the Soviet leadership, who were putting intense efforts into persuading the Polish Communist leader Wojciech Jaruzelski to institute his own domestic crackdown, had decided against invasion. By 1989, with Gorbachev having already publicly declared that every country, including 'socialist' countries, had the right to choose the kind of system their people wanted, Poles could be much more confident that by removing their own Communist leaders they would not be paving the way for foreign intervention, thus making a bad situation worse.

to do so would not lead to foreign troops on the streets of Prague and Bratislava. It was fortunate for the population of the country that they had someone of the moral authority of Havel, even though he was not a natural politician, to call on when that time came. He was an impressive leader, both in the eloquent expression of his ideas and his willingness to take the consequences of disseminating them. He was not, however, a transformational leader, for in his absence Czechs and Slovaks would still have made a rapid transition to democracy, once they had observed Poles and Hungarians moving undisturbed in that direction and even East Germans getting away with mass demonstrations against their unpopular regime.

★

Transformational leaders play that role not only because of exceptional personal qualities, for a leader such as Havel had those, too, and there have been many inspirational leaders who have never held any kind of governmental office. Of the five transformational leaders examined in this chapter, the least exceptional in personal attributes was Suárez and the most remarkable, in terms of endurance of suffering and magnanimity in victory, was Mandela. In dignity and charisma, he is rivalled only by de Gaulle. The two who made the biggest differences to most lives were Gorbachev and Deng Xiaoping. In the one case, this was through facilitating the democratization of half of Europe; in the other, it was by raising the living standards of even more millions of people through transforming the economy of the world's most populous state. What they *all* had in common was that time, place and circumstance put them in a position where they had just a chance, which they seized, to *make the decisive difference in changing the system.*

5

Revolutions and Revolutionary Leadership

Transformational leaders are not the only ones who produce systemic change. So do revolutionary leaders, provided they are successful in carrying through the revolution. Compared with those who succeed, however, there are many more revolutionary leaders who fail to dislodge the powers that be. In an authoritarian regime, the reward for failure is execution or, at best, imprisonment. In established democracies, revolutionaries have experienced *only* failure. Fortunately for them, however, the consequences of leading or belonging to a revolutionary party or movement, unless they have reached the point of employing violence, are generally nothing worse than marginalization. The explanation for the failure of revolutionary leaders and revolutionary parties in democracies is straightforward. The very fact that governments are held responsible for their decisions by an enfranchised citizenry places constraints upon what they may do. It gives them a strong incentive to pay some heed to people's views and interests, rather than bring them to a boiling point of indignation. Most crucially, free and honest elections mean that governments can be removed, and hopes for significant policy change maintained, without the need for either violent upheaval or sudden systemic change. As the Czech writer, Ludvík Vaculík, observed in a speech in Prague in June 1967 (which incurred the wrath of the Communist authorities), the rules and norms of democracy are 'a human invention which makes the job of ruling considerably harder'. They have obvious advantages for the ruled – the citizens of the country – by enabling them to hold governments accountable for their actions. As Vaculík noted, however, they bestow benefits also on those in power, since when a government falls, democratic rules 'save its ministers from being shot'.[1]

To examine revolutionary leadership presupposes clarity on what we mean by a revolution. In its derivation, the term points to a circular movement, as the verb 'to revolve' suggests. And, in practice, more often than not, a revolution replaces one form of authoritarian rule by another. However, in the years since the French Revolution, the notion has acquired a connotation different from that of government rotating in a full circle. For Samuel Huntington, revolution 'involves the rapid and violent destruction of existing political institutions, the mobilization of new groups into politics, and the creation of new political institutions'.[2] For John Dunn, 'Revolutions are a form of massive, violent and rapid social change.'[3] Moreover, even when, as is generally the case, authoritarian rule follows the overthrow of a despotic regime by revolution, it is no less usual for it to be a type of authoritarianism quite distinct from the pre-revolutionary order. There will be different political institutions, different winners and losers within the society, and, in the case of Communist revolutions, a different economic system.

Some authors do not include violence as one of the defining characteristics of revolution.[4] When it is excluded, however, the notion of revolution is made to cover too many disparate political phenomena. It is better to make a clear distinction between revolution, in the sense in which thinkers as very different in other respects as Huntington and Dunn use the term, and such occurrences as civil disobedience, passive resistance, state breakdown and *coups d'état*. Excluding civil resistance and non-violent demonstrations (even when they lead to the replacement of one regime by another) from the definition of revolution is not to downplay their significance, still less their merits. On the contrary, non-violent resistance to authoritarian regimes on the part of large numbers of citizens more often succeeds in overturning dictatorships than does violent resistance, and it has a much better record in establishing democracy thereafter.[5] It is useful also to distinguish revolution from splits within the ruling elite, with one faction overthrowing and outlawing another. When a group within an elite replaces another in a palace coup, they themselves may call it a revolution (since 'revolution' retains a romantic aura, whereas *'coup d'état'* is almost invariably a pejorative term), but that is stretching the concept unhelpfully.

CHARACTERISTICS AND CONSEQUENCES OF REVOLUTION

What are the main characteristics of a revolution as distinct from peaceful transition from authoritarianism to democracy? The nature of regime change is most distinctively revolutionary when it is characterized by: (1) large-scale popular involvement; (2) the overthrow of existing institutions; (3) the establishment of a new legitimizing ideology for the post-revolutionary regime, and (4) the use of violence before, during or immediately after the change of regime. It is possible, naturally (as is true of other political concepts), to define revolution in different ways. Our starting point, however, remains the desirability of maintaining a distinction between peaceful systemic change and a negotiated transfer of power, on the one hand, and violent overthrow of a regime by a social and political movement, on the other.

There have been some attempts to study all known cases of revolution (often more broadly defined than here) and to delineate the social and political conditions in which they occur. Such efforts to find common features in, and parsimonious explanations of, the causes of revolution have failed, because the cases are too diverse.[6] While it is possible to outline some of the social and political conditions that are conducive to revolution – they include war, rulers' loss of faith in their own legitimating beliefs, the development of high educational levels within a closed political system, a heightened sense of relative deprivation, extreme inequality, the liberalization of a hitherto highly authoritarian regime, and rising expectations which state authorities lack the capacity to meet – we can find plenty of instances of these phenomena at times and in places where revolution did *not* occur. There is, moreover, sufficient variety in the causes and courses of different revolutions to limit the value of attempts to find factors that would explain them all.

The most ambitious general explanation remains that of Karl Marx. He saw the source of revolutionary transformation in the 'contradictions'

– meaning growing incompatibilities – between institutional relationships and the changing material forces of production.[7] State power was the power of a ruling class, and class conflict he regarded as the engine of historical change. It would culminate in proletarian revolution to overthrow capitalism and the bourgeoisie. Between capitalism and communism there would be a 'revolutionary dictatorship of the proletariat', but that would lead on to communism, which, in its higher phase, would take the form of a classless, stateless society.[8] This doctrine has inspired many a revolutionary movement, some of which were successful in overthrowing capitalism, although none came close to realizing Marx's dream of a communist society. Although Marx played down the importance both of leaders and of ideas – classes rather than individual leaders were what mattered and ideologies were epiphenomena of socio-economic development, not of autonomous significance – the international Communist movement in the twentieth century, paradoxically but spectacularly, provided a refutation of his doctrine. Ideas mattered a great deal to such people as Lenin and Mao Zedong, and these leaders in turn played decisive roles in effecting revolutionary change and establishing Communist systems both within the largest country on earth and in the world's most populous state.[9]

Not all revolutions are led by strong leaders. Some, indeed, are relatively leaderless, although that does not last for long once a revolution has succeeded in overthrowing the regime to which it is opposed. What the leaders get up to *after the revolution* figures in some cases in this chapter and in other cases in the next, for it is striking how often those revolutionary leaders who do manage to overturn an authoritarian regime go on to preside over one that is no less authoritarian, even if differently structured. Since political cultures are harder to change overnight than political institutions, much may depend on the new leaderships' political-cultural inheritance. A great deal depends also, however, on the values, political beliefs and style of rule of the top revolutionary leader once he (and it has been a male-dominated vocation) is ensconced in governmental office. Although no such leader starts off with an entirely blank sheet, he has a wider range of choices open to him than has a leader within a consolidated democracy. He may, of course, be constrained by circumstances, both domestic and foreign, but is, by definition, far less constrained by institutions and custom.

THE MEXICAN REVOLUTION

The revolutions in the twentieth century which had the greatest global impact were those which brought Communists to power. We shall come to them, and their leaders, later in the chapter. The Russian revolutions aside, there were three other revolutions in the first quarter of the twentieth century of long-lasting significance – in Mexico, China and Turkey. The Mexican revolution is the odd one out, not only because it was much less the product of a national and cultural movement than the other two but also because there was *no one leader* who was as distinctively significant in the revolutionary process as was Sun Yat-sen in China or, still more, Atatürk in Turkey.

Eric Hobsbawm observed that 'it is when the relatively modest expectations of everyday life look as if they cannot be achieved without revolutions, that individuals become revolutionaries'.[10] Even where this radicalization occurs, it does not follow that a revolution will succeed. The Mexican case, though, is one where a deterioration in the already modest quality of life in the countryside turned many peasants into revolutionaries and where the revolution eventually prevailed. It began in 1910 and involved violent struggle over the next decade. The authoritarian regime that provoked the popular uprisings was such that reformist goals, it seemed, could be achieved only by revolutionary methods. The aims included land and labour reform, access to education, and opposition to foreign economic domination and exploitation. The bulk of the fighting forces of the revolution were peasants who had seen their standard of living fall in the immediately preceding years. The revolution had a number of leaders, but rather than forming a cohesive revolutionary movement, they were geographically dispersed, politically heterogeneous, and during a decade of revolutionary war and turmoil often engaged in fighting each other.

The authoritarian ruler of Mexico at the time the revolution broke out in 1910, Porfirio Diaz, had come to power in a coup (as had many of his nineteenth-century predecessors). It was middle-class discontent with Diaz's dictatorship that triggered the movement. A wealthy and idealistic landowner, Francisco Madero, fired the first shot. He demanded that Mexico's 1857 constitution be observed, and he opposed Diaz in the 1910 presidential election. After Diaz had won a typically corrupt

contest, Madero was rewarded for his audacity by a spell of imprisonment. On his release, instead of returning quietly to his estates, he
called in November 1910 for the forcible overthrow of the Diaz regime.
There was a ready response to this appeal, especially from the rural
poor, some of them indigenous peoples who had been deprived of
their ancestral lands, while most were *mestizo* (of mixed ethnic ancestry).
The immediate goal of the revolution, the removal of Diaz, was
achieved when his advisers persuaded him to resign in 1911.

In a far freer election than that of the previous year, Madero was
elected president. This did not put a stop to the violence, for Madero
was too reformist for the old regime and too modest in the changes
he introduced to satisfy the forces that had been unleashed in rural
areas. The Madero presidency was ended by a military coup in 1913
and Madero himself was killed. The harsh military regime that followed
did not, however, halt the rebellion. Local leaders who had been active
in the revolutionary struggle since 1911 came to the fore in different
parts of the country, the most notable being Emiliano Zapata in the
south of Mexico and Francisco ('Pancho') Villa in the north. Zapata
had been among those dissatisfied with Madero, especially on account
of his failure instantly to hand back confiscated land to the peasantry.
Both Zapata and Villa were skilled in guerrilla warfare and attracted
armies of loyal followers. Their appeal was populist and egalitarian,
although lacking national political ambitions and sophisticated ideological underpinning. While still fighting a guerrilla war, Zapata was
lured into a trap in 1919 and shot. Villa survived until 1923, three years
after the revolutionary war had ended, before he, too, was assassinated.[11]

The revolution was not animated by a great idea in the way in which
three other major revolutions of the first quarter of the century were.
The Chinese revolution of the same period was inspired by the idea of
a modernized nation-state, the Turkish revolution spurred by concepts
of Westernization and secularization, and that of Russia in 1917 driven
by the goal of overthrowing capitalism as well as the autocracy and by
the aspiration to build communism. In Mexico it was not so much a
vision of the future as a demand to restore past rights that had been
lost which turned agricultural workers into revolutionaries. The removal
of local freedoms, the conversion of independent peasants into landless
labourers, and a growth of destitution in the countryside were stimuli
enough for people to fight. The Mexican revolution had, then, relatively

modest goals. It had no one authoritative leader, 'no great intellectual fathers', did not claim a universal validity, and was not utopian.[12]

It was much less an ideological revolution than those which occurred around the same time in China and Turkey, not to speak of Russia. If it is compared with one of the outstanding examples of radical change discussed in the previous chapter – the transformation of the Soviet Union in the second half of the 1980s – the contrast is especially sharp. In the Soviet case, there was (as Gorbachev put it) 'revolutionary' change by evolutionary and reformist means.[13] What happened in Mexico was the obverse – reformist change by revolutionary means.[14] Significant and concrete political and social innovation did, indeed, follow the decade of revolutionary turmoil and civil war when a post-revolutionary regime was established in 1920. Some of the change was not what the various revolutionary leaders intended. Their support had been local, regional and personal. The regime which was established was more centralized, statist and bureaucratic. Nevertheless, the post-revolutionary government facilitated agrarian reform and promoted secular education. New institutions were created in the 1920s, among them an education ministry in 1921, the central Bank of Mexico in 1925, the National Irrigation Commission in 1926 and the new official political party, the PNR in 1929.[15]

Many of the old pre-revolutionary elite were ousted. The president who made the most significant mark on Mexican politics of the early 1920s, Álvaro Obregón, had been a supporter of the moderate reformer Madero and an opponent of Zapata and Villa. Obregón was, however, no slouch when it came to populist and radical gestures. When he occupied Mexico City in the middle of the revolutionary wars, at a time when the people were going hungry, he distributed some of the Church wealth to the poor and forced rich merchants to sweep the streets.[16] Becoming president in December 1920, he put in place not only educational and labour reform but anticlerical policies, which were, ultimately, and in the most literal sense, to be fatal for him. His response to the desire for greater national economic autonomy put him on a collision course with the United States, which recognized his government only after he promised in 1923 not to nationalize American oil companies. Obregón was debarred by the new rules established by the revolution from seeking a second consecutive term of office in the election of December 1924, but returned to the fray four years later. He was re-elected to the presidency, but during a victory celebration in Mexico City he was assassinated by a Catholic fanatic who objected to his policies towards the Church.

The point has been made already that the leader of a country, immediately following a successful revolution, generally has a wider available range of policy options than has a president or prime minister within an established democracy. Nevertheless, a post-revolutionary leader in Mexico was far from unconstrained by factions, business interests and social institutions, among which the Church loomed especially large. But the social and economic policies pursued were, on the whole, in line with the main strands of the revolutionary movement. No one individual leader made all the difference. Had another of the revolutionary leaders emerged on top (Pancho Villa came close to doing so), the result, Alan Knight has argued, 'would have been – in broad *ideological* terms – much the same'.[17]

THE CHINESE REVOLUTION OF 1911–12

The Chinese revolution of late 1911 and early 1912 brought to an end not only the Qing dynasty, which had lasted for well over two and a half centuries, but also two thousand years of imperial rule. China became a republic in February 1912 when the Chinese court bowed to the strength of the revolutionary forces and announced the abdication of the boy emperor, the five-year-old Puyi. This outcome was a good illustration of de Tocqueville's dictum that the most dangerous time for an authoritarian regime is when it begins to reform itself. During the first decade of the twentieth century some significant reforms were introduced. In 1905 the empress dowager Cixi sent a Chinese delegation to Japan and the United States and to five European countries to study how their countries were governed. Constitutional changes and also educational reform were brought in, but the former did not noticeably reduce the power of the existing elite or the latter significantly counteract the advantages that still accrued to wealthy families. Moreover, the court and the government continued to be dominated by the Manchu minority who formed the Qing dynasty, largely to the exclusion of the Han majority of Chinese. The most important reform was the creation of provincial assemblies in 1909 and a new tolerance of public gatherings.[18] From some of the most highly educated members of these assemblies came calls for more far-reaching reform.

A series of uprisings took place in late 1911, led by local army commanders. The revolts reflected their anger at the extent to which China had fallen behind Japan militarily and economically. They also made clear the anti-Qing nationalist sentiments of these provincial military leaders. The belief that China badly needed to be modernized was held even more strongly by many within the educated middle class, especially those who had studied abroad. Revolts took place in one region after another, and by the end of the year a republic had been declared with its seat of government in the old summer capital, Nanjing, while the imperial government remained precariously in place in Beijing. The closest approximation China had to a 'leader of the opposition' was Sun Yat-sen who for many years, most of them spent abroad, had campaigned for an end to Manchu rule and for the establishment of a modern republican government in China. Sun was travelling in the United States when the Chinese revolution broke out and learned of the uprisings in his homeland from a newspaper in Denver. Rather than take the first boat back to China, Sun went to Paris and London. His mission was to persuade European governments to preserve neutrality as the conflict in China intensified and to withhold financial assistance to the imperial government. Arriving back in China on Christmas Day 1911, Sun's status as the political and intellectual leader of the revolutionary movement was underlined when he was chosen by delegates from sixteen provincial assemblies, meeting in Nanjing, to be the country's 'provisional president'.[19]

In November 1911 the Qing court had recalled to Beijing Yuan Shikai, a capable and ambitious military leader. Earlier he had antagonized the acting regent, Prince Chun, Puyi's father, and had been dismissed from the service of the court. The dynasty now believed that Yuan was the strongman best equipped to win the support of the rebellious military throughout the country – and, where unable to do so, to crush them. Appointed premier in November 1911, he formed a cabinet composed mainly of his own followers. The court was divided between those who thought the game was up for the Manchu dynasty and those who were counting on Yuan Shikai to preserve it. Yuan himself became increasingly unwilling to share power with the imperial dynasty – or, subsequently, with anyone else. A number of assassinations of royalists, which Yuan was suspected of encouraging, as well as the presence now of more Han troops than Manchu forces in Beijing, tilted the balance against those who wished to preserve the imperial throne. The abdication of the child emperor, and thus the end of the dynasty, was announced on 12 February 1912.[20]

Sun Yat-sen had already been chosen as provisional president, but he did not have forces at his disposal at all comparable with the number under the command of Yuan Shikai. Rather than prolong a period of 'dual power', Sun held on to his 'presidential' status for only six weeks before persuading the delegates to a National Council, which had been convened in Nanjing, to choose Yuan as the country's provisional president. For Sun, however, the 'provisional' qualification was important. He was in favour of both post-revolutionary constitutional government and the partial democratization of China. The drawing up of a draft constitution was completed by March 1912 and preparations made for parliamentary elections – both for a Senate to be chosen by the provincial assemblies and for a directly elected House of Representatives to be formed on the basis of one member for every 800,000 people. The influence of the political system of the United States was evident, since the Senate was to be numerically the smaller body with each Senator serving for a six-year term, whereas the House of Representatives would be much larger, with its members serving for only half as long before facing re-election. The electoral rules fell a long way short of embracing democracy. Women were disenfranchised and there was also a significant property qualification. It was calculated that about forty million men, at that time some 10 per cent of the population, would be able to vote.[21]

The election could, nevertheless, have been an important first step on a road to democracy. It was, at least, less undemocratic than any election that has subsequently been held on mainland China (as distinct from Taiwan in recent decades). Sun Yat-sen had converted his Revolutionary Alliance into a political party, the Kuomintang. The KMT, as this Nationalist party was known, was led in the electoral contest by a talented young politician, Song Jiaoren. He had served under Sun Yat-sen within the Revolutionary Alliance while they were both in exile. Although allied with Sun, Song was not an uncritical follower. The younger man and the older leader differed on constitutional issues. Song favoured an essentially parliamentary system in which parliament and a prime minister would be far more powerful than the president who would be a purely formal head of state. Sun, however, aspired to return to the presidency he had briefly and provisionally held, this time with full constitutional legitimacy. He had no desire to be a mere figurehead after the party he had founded had become electorally successful.[22]

The last expectation turned out to be well founded when the election results were announced in January 1913. Four political parties had taken part, and the KMT emerged in both houses as by far the largest, albeit just short of an overall majority. It seemed evident that the Kuomintang would have the major say in the composition of a new government and in the choice of premier. The expectation was that the choice of the latter would fall upon Song Jiaoren, given that he had led the most successful party. However, when he was standing on the platform of Shanghai railway station in March 1913, about to board a train for Beijing and talks with Yuan on the formation of a government, he was approached by a gunman and shot. Two days later he died in hospital. It was generally believed that Yuan, who had no desire to share his recently acquired authority, was behind the assassination.[23]

At any rate, Yuan lost little time in acquiring authoritarian power. Throughout 1913 the police, on his orders, harassed KMT members of parliament and their supporters, and in January 1914 he formally dissolved the parliament, following this up in February with the dissolution of the provincial assemblies. In 1915 he even made an attempt to have himself chosen as emperor and thereby become the founder of a new dynasty. A hand-picked 'Representative Assembly' unanimously begged him to accept that office. This, however, alienated some of his support in the capital, and there were large-scale protests in the provinces, many of which proceeded to declare their independence from Beijing. Yuan died of natural causes the following year and his death was followed by several years of chaos in which regional 'warlords' (some of whom had formerly been loyal to Yuan) held sway. With China divided, its central government was weak both administratively and militarily. This did nothing to help its cause at the Versailles Peace Conference in 1919, following the First World War. The victorious Allies paid lip service to Chinese interests but in the end treated China shabbily. Economic concessions that the Germans had enjoyed before the war were transferred to the Japanese, and Japan was also granted the right to station troops in two Chinese provinces.[24]

Protests in China against the weakness of its own government in face of the Versailles victors' high-handed disregard for Chinese sovereignty began with a demonstration by some 3,000 students in Beijing on 4 May 1919. That particular protest ended with some of the students ransacking and setting fire to the home of a government minister who had, in their view, made humiliating concessions to Japan. Another prominent politician was badly beaten, as were some of the students (one of whom died of his injuries) by the police. The students' actions gave a name of lasting resonance to the much broader current of critical thought which was already discernible in Chinese society. It became known as the May Fourth movement.[25] Many of its leading thinkers were associated with Peking University.*

Just as the revolutionary events of 1911 unfolded without any one person acquiring the role of leader (with the very important exception of Sun Yat-sen on his American and European political missions), the same applied to the May Fourth movement. Following Yuan's death and the lapse into regional warlordism, the main national leader was a military man, Duan Qirui, who became premier in 1916. Although he had earlier been promoted by Yuan Shikhai and had served him loyally, he did not support Yuan's bid to turn himself into an emperor.[26] In the face of Yuan Shikai's severe crackdown in 1913 (Duan Qirui was acting premier at the time), Sun Yat-sen had been forced into exile again, returning to China only after Yuan's death in 1916. During his latest sojourn abroad, he turned the Kuomintang into a hierarchical, disciplined party with a premium placed on personal loyalty to him. The next revolution, he argued, would be military in the first instance, and that would be followed by 'tutelage' of the Chinese people. Only after this process had run its course would the population as a whole be ready for self-government under a republican constitution.[27] Although Sun was no Communist, the Bolshevik Revolution made an impact on him, as it did on other revolutionary activists in China. In light of the shameful treatment China had received at Versailles, and European powers' preoccupation with protecting their economic interests in China, Sun was

* Although the city of Peking is now known in English as Beijing, an exception has been made for Peking University by the University itself. Because it already had an international reputation under that name, the University in its official communications in English continues to refer to itself as Peking.

willing to seek cooperation with the new Soviet leadership. They, in turn, while not believing that China was ripe for Soviet-style 'socialism', were happy to promote cooperation between the Chinese Nationalists led by Sun and the newly formed Chinese Communist Party. The Bolsheviks' desire to support anti-imperial, revolutionary forces in China was in harmony with considerations of realpolitik, since a friendly China would be a useful Soviet ally vis-à-vis Japan. In the Russo-Japanese war of 1904-05, the Japanese had emerged victorious, and though this could be blamed on the weakness of the pre-revolutionary Russian regime, it had left its mark on the consciousness also of the Bolsheviks.

From 1920 Sun Yat-sen was setting forth his central ideas, which, as he tried to broaden the appeal of his political party, he called the Three People's Principles. These were nationalism, democracy and 'people's livelihood'. All three were somewhat problematical or ambiguous. The first was the clearest, for Sun did, indeed, head a Nationalist party. From his return to China in 1916, he was attempting to promote the unification of China and to bring an end to warlordism. The problem lay in the fact that, though there was a large Han majority in China, there were, as Sun acknowledged, other nationalities with rights as well. It was also not entirely clear what Sun meant by democracy (it was certainly not much practised within the Kuomintang). It is, moreover, arguable that China was not ready for fully fledged democracy at the time, and Sun's support for a restricted franchise and a period of 'tutelage' of the Chinese people reflected that view. The third principle is sometimes translated as 'socialism' but more literally as 'people's livelihood'. It reflected Sun's desire not only to raise the standard of living but also to promote some equalization, including in the size of land holdings.[28] During 1921 Sun was granted the title of 'president' by remnants of the short-lived Beijing parliament, but this was far from receiving country-wide recognition. Based for the most part in Canton, the capital city of his native province, Sun remained, in his last years, the undisputed leader of the Nationalist party, but he had very little support from the warlords among whom the country was divided. Soon after he took part in a 'national reconstruction conference' in Beijing in November 1924, Sun discovered that he had terminal cancer, from which he died, at the age of fifty-nine, in March 1925.[29]

Sun Yat-sen, who came from an unprivileged peasant family, had a strong sense of his ability to lead and a personality that attracted adherents. Although he played no part in the breakout of revolution in 1911 and never presided over a unified Chinese state, he is, nevertheless, justly regarded as one of the main founding fathers both of the revolution and of the republic of China. It was he who insisted that revolution was the appropriate way to bring about change at a time when there were many with a preference for a reformist constitutionalist course. With his higher education and his knowledge of English, he was an effective international representative of the forces in China seeking an end to the Qing dynasty and the creation of a modern republic. He was the principal founder of the Kuomintang, the Nationalist political party which, under Sun's successor, Chiang Kai-shek, was to dominate China until the Communists came to power in 1949.* Although not as authoritarian as his successor – and, indeed, an advocate of democracy in principle – Sun was a reforming and modernizing, but hardly democratic, leader. He remained somewhat aloof from the May Fourth political and intellectual current. In the words of a recent historian of modern China, 'he generally disapproved of any movement he could not control'.[30] That Sun is still regarded in his homeland as the principal leader of the first of the two great Chinese revolutions of the twentieth century underlines the fact that revolutionary leadership does not necessarily mean leading a charge over the barricades at the moment a regime falls, but takes many different forms.

ATATÜRK AND THE TURKISH REVOLUTION

Born in 1881, Mustafa Kemal – better known as Atatürk (meaning father of the Turks), a title he officially adopted from 1934 – took part in the 'Young Turk' revolution of 1908 against the unconstitutional rule of Sultan Abdülhamid II. Although not yet the leader of the opposition to the sultanate, he already harboured the ambition to play that role and to lead his country. As a far from teetotal young army officer, he told a friend in the course of one drinking session that he would make him prime minister. 'And what will you be?' was his friend's response. 'The man who appoints prime ministers,' replied Kemal.[31] In a letter

---

* It can stake a claim to continuous existence up to the present day. Under the same name, it is one of the two major political parties in contemporary Taiwan.

to a woman friend in 1918, he wrote: 'If I ever acquire great authority and power, I think that I would introduce at a single stroke the transformation needed in our social life . . . After spending so many years acquiring higher education, enquiring into civilized social life and getting a taste for freedom, why should I descend to the level of common people? Rather, I should raise them to my level. They should become like me, not I like them.'[32] In the light of such sentiments, it is unsurprising that Turkey under Atatürk did not become a democracy but, rather, a relatively enlightened authoritarian regime.

Atatürk had distinguished himself as a soldier during the First World War, when Turkey fought on the German side, and he led the campaign in the years immediately following against Allied control of Turkey and against Greek occupation of part of the country. Throughout 1919 he gathered together both nationalist army officers and various independent groups that had risen spontaneously to protest against the Allied occupation, and succeeded in consolidating them into a movement of national resistance.[33] By 1920 he was elected head of government by the Turkish Grand National Assembly which he had convened, and a new Turkish state was proclaimed in January 1921 after Atatürk had arranged for the ministers of the previous Ottoman government to be, in effect, kidnapped. Although he was to establish friendly relations with the leaders of the new Soviet state, Atatürk was no more sympathetic to Turkish Communists than he was to the traditional authorities. A number of Communists were shot in 1922 with Atatürk's acquiescence.[34]

This was a revolution not only because it involved the violent overthrow of the pre-existing state authorities but inasmuch as it also altered the ideological foundation of the state. It put an end to the institutions that had prevailed when Turkey was at the heart of the Ottoman empire. Both the traditional political and the religious authorities – the sultanate and the caliphate – were replaced. (There was an element of continuity, even so. The Turkish nationalists, while believing that the attempt to sustain an empire had been misguided and that the sultans had stood in the way of progress, drew on the Ottoman bureaucracy and especially the army as linchpins of their new state.[35]) The sultanate was not instantly abolished, but by the autumn of 1922 Atatürk, strengthened by the military victory over the Greeks, was moving to get rid of the remaining domestic curbs on his authority. He had the support of the government of the Grand

National Assembly in Ankara, which wielded real power, while the sultan still headed the remnants of the Ottoman government in Istanbul. Atatürk announced: 'Sovereignty and kingship are never decided by academic debate. They are seized by force. The Ottoman dynasty appropriated by force the government of the Turks, and reigned over them for six centuries. Now the Turkish nation has effectively gained possession of its sovereignty.' He hoped that this would be agreed. If it was not, the facts would still prevail 'but some heads may roll'.[36] The sultanate was duly abolished and the sultan himself went into exile before the end of 1922. The following year the Republic of Turkey was proclaimed and Atatürk became its first president.

The religious authority – the caliphate – was allowed to survive for longer than the sultanate. However, by 1924 Atatürk argued that the religious leader, the caliph, was doing what the sultan had done – listening to critics of the government and being in touch with the representatives of foreign powers. In early March the palace of Caliph Abdülmecid was surrounded by police and the building's telephones were cut off. The caliph deemed it prudent to announce his resignation, although he rescinded that statement as soon as he had crossed from Turkey into Bulgaria. It did him no good. He never set foot in Turkey again and, following his death in 1944, his descendants' requests to have his remains returned to Turkey were rejected.[37] The abolition of the caliphate, however, contributed to a deterioration in relations between Turks and the Kurdish citizens of the new state. Kurds constituted 20 per cent of the population, and putting an end to the caliphate removed an important religious symbol that had been common to both Turks and Kurds.[38]

Atatürk was both the intellectual and the military leader of the Turkish revolution. It was one in which ideas were important and the ideas of Atatürk above all. He was very much a Westernizer, although there was sometimes a gap between ideals and behaviour. The rise of Kurdish nationalism – a new phenomenon – in the first quarter of the twentieth century posed a serious challenge to the idea of a Turkish nation-state. Promises of autonomy for the Kurds, made by Atatürk and other Turkish nationalists during the independence struggle, were not kept, and Kurdish rebellions in the mid-1920s were brutally suppressed.[39] Moreover, Atatürk's respect for democracy in principle led to no more than half-hearted attempts to introduce it. They were aborted when it became clear that the creation of parties other than his own People's Party (later the Republican People's Party) would lead to frustration of his wishes and reforms. In other respects, however, the Westernization was real. Atatürk's principal biographer, Andrew Mango, notes a series of decisions that 'amounted to a cultural revolution'.[40] Secular rule replaced religious hegemony and of particular importance was the secularization of the educational system. Religious courts, which had adjudicated on marriage and divorce, were closed down. The ban on alcohol, which Atatürk had conspicuously ignored even while it was operative, was ended.

The emancipation of women was greatly advanced, although Atatürk unilaterally divorced his own wife in a traditional manner. Women in inter-war Turkey acquired equal inheritance rights and new educational and career opportunities. Under Atatürk's rule, women were also discouraged, although not banned, from wearing the veil.[41] In foreign policy, Atatürk combined nationalism and anti-imperialism with a cautiously pragmatic neutrality. The revolution which he led, and the secular norms which it established, outlived him. Following his death in 1938, İsmet İnönü – who had been foreign minister and subsequently prime minister throughout most of the Atatürk era – became president and carried forward the modernization process. He went much further than Atatürk in one crucial respect, presiding over the country's democratization. The first free elections in the history of the republic were held in 1950 and when the Republican People's Party were defeated, İsmet accepted the result with good grace.[42]

COMMUNIST REVOLUTIONS IN EUROPE

The Russian Revolutions of 1917

Few could doubt that one of the pivotal events of the twentieth century was the 'Russian revolution' of 1917. By the end of that year Communists had taken power in the largest country on the planet, and the Soviet state that emerged over the following years was to have an immense impact on world politics over the next seven decades, especially from the Second World War onwards. There were, though, two quite distinct revolutions in Russia in 1917 which should not be conflated. They became known as the February and October revolutions – somewhat confusingly, since according to the Western calendar they took place in March and November.[43] The strikes and demonstrations that marked the beginning of the first of Russia's 1917 revolutions were launched on 8 March – International Women's Day.[44] That timing was not coincidental, for the protests began with a walkout from the textile mills of Petrograd by women workers, who deliberately chose this particular date to make public their anger about the war and their own hardships. Events then moved quickly. It took only another week before the tsarist autocracy had collapsed.

The revolution came as a complete surprise to Vladimir Lenin who was, however, to be the most influential advocate of a second revolution in the same year and instrumental in ensuring that it would bring *Communists* – not a coalition of liberals and socialists or even a coalition of different types of socialist – to power. Rightly regarded as the principal founder of the Soviet state, Lenin was a sufficiently orthodox Marxist to believe in the inevitability of socialist revolution and enough of a revolutionary by temperament and conviction to devote his entire adult life to speeding up that process. Yet at the beginning of 1917 Lenin was far from sanguine about the prospects for early success. In exile in Switzerland, he addressed a meeting of workers in Zurich in January 1917 and said: 'We of the older generation may not live to see the decisive battles of this coming revolution.'[45] At that time Lenin was aged only forty-six.

Russia had suffered huge losses in the First World War, a conflict which had become increasingly unpopular, especially among those who bore the brunt of the fighting – the 'peasants in uniform', as Lenin called them. The Bolsheviks (renamed Communist Party in 1918) – the section of the Russian revolutionary movement which Lenin led – played little part in the February revolution, for their leading ranks had been depleted by imprisonment and exile.[46] There had been growing opposition to the tsarist government on the part both of liberals and of a range of socialist parties and factions. Although the Bolsheviks had significant worker support in the capital city, Petrograd (as St Petersburg was then called), they were far from being the most widely approved political party nationally. The party with the largest number of members as well as the most popular – as was shown in November 1917 in Russia's first fully free election, which turned out also to be the country's last democratic election for more than seventy years – was the Socialist Revolutionaries (SRs) whose appeal was primarily to the peasantry.[47]

The decisive action of the revolutions, however – those of both March and November – took place in Petrograd. Peasants, on learning what had happened in the capital, also asserted themselves and began redistributing land to those who worked on it. Bread shortages combined with war weariness to increase the general discontent with the tsarist regime. It had been gathering momentum over several decades, but in the first quarter of 1917 reached the point of no return. Mass walkouts from factories culminated in a general strike, which brought Petrograd to a standstill. The Duma, a legislature with limited powers and restricted suffrage that had been set up following an earlier revolution in 1905, attempted to mediate between the demonstrators and the government, but the tsar, Nicholas II, did not respond to their call for the formation of a government that could command the Duma's confidence.[48]

The February revolution was a brief moment of cooperation between liberal and radical opponents of the tsarist autocracy. A Soviet of Workers' Deputies ('soviet' is simply the Russian word for council) had existed briefly during the revolutionary turmoil of 1905 and it was to be resurrected in Petrograd in 1917. Conscious of the support this body could attract from within the army, its members renamed it the Soviet of Workers' and Soldiers' Deputies. On the fourth day of the strikes and demonstrations against the old regime, the police made many arrests and hundreds of people were killed or wounded when soldiers fired on the crowds. But by the following day many regiments had mutinied and in Petrograd alone sixty-five thousand troops had joined the rebellion.[49] Losing the support of the army left the old regime powerless. A majority of ministers in the tsarist government were arrested, and Nicholas II abdicated on 15 March 1917. He and his wife, together with their four daughters and haemophiliac son, were put under house arrest; they would be shot by the Bolsheviks in the Urals city of Ekaterinburg in July 1918.

A provisional government was formed, composed mainly of liberals who were critics of the incompetence as well as the authoritarianism of the old regime. They sought to introduce constitutional government and to move towards democratic elections for a Constituent Assembly. A socialist but anti-Communist member of that government, Aleksandr Kerensky had been, unusually, a member of both the Duma and the Petrograd soviet. He was to be joined by other socialists – Mensheviks and SRs – in May, as the coalition government was broadened.[50] An impressive orator, Kerensky was successively in the short period between March and November minister of justice (in which capacity he freed all political prisoners), minister of war, and (from July) prime minister. At this time of turmoil, his biggest handicap was his commitment to continue fighting the war alongside Russia's allies. Lenin and the Bolsheviks had opposed the war from the outset and were prepared to sign a separate peace with Germany to get out of it. Indeed, Lenin's desire to end Russia's participation in that war led the German High Command to facilitate his return from Switzerland to Russia. A sealed railway carriage was provided, in which Lenin travelled through Germany, along with some of his comrades, to the Finland Station in Petrograd. He immediately set about undermining the provisional government, calling on those who welcomed him not to cooperate with it. The period between the two Russian revolutions of 1917 became known as one of 'dual power', as the soviets (especially the Petrograd soviet) and the provisional government each claimed a superior authority.

Among the slogans Lenin had coined on the journey back to Russia, as part of what he called his April Theses, was that of 'peace, land, and bread'. This broadened the Bolsheviks' appeal, and the call for unilateral withdrawal from the war and forcible redistribution of land distinguished the Bolshevik position clearly from that of the provisional government. With the aim of wresting power from this new and precarious government, Lenin also included in his April Theses the slogan, 'All power to the soviets!' He was, at the same time, cautious about that outcome. In particular, he did not wish such a power transfer to occur until the Bolsheviks had a majority in the Petrograd soviet. In the early months following the February revolution, the executive committee of the Petrograd soviet was dominated by Mensheviks and SRs.[51] It was not until the autumn that the Bolsheviks had a majority in both the Petrograd and the Moscow soviets, and from that moment Lenin was ready for immediate insurrection. There was, however, far freer discussion in 1917 within his party than was to be the case throughout almost the whole of the Soviet period, and the Central Committee initially rejected Lenin's argument that the time was ripe for the Bolshevik seizure of power because the working class was now firmly on the party's side.[52]

If the February revolution was a combination of spontaneous unrest and the withdrawal of support for the autocracy on the part of a substantial part of the elite, with no one person or group overwhelmingly responsible for the outcome, the same could not be said of the October revolution. Lenin, as the most authoritative of the Bolsheviks, played a more decisive role than any other revolutionary, but Leon Trotsky's participation was also of major significance. Trotsky had earlier kept his distance from both the Bolsheviks and the Mensheviks, but in 1917 joined forces with Lenin. He believed that Lenin had come round to his view of 'permanent revolution' by abandoning the more academic Marxist precept that a lengthy period of 'bourgeois democratic' rule would be required, following a bourgeois revolution (which, in their terms, the February revolution was).[53] Trotsky matched both Lenin's intellectual power and his ingenuity as a revolutionary. Like Lenin, he also possessed enormous self-belief. (Trotsky was, however, to be outmanoeuvred in the intra-party politics of the 1920s by a less intellectually sophisticated, but craftier and still more ruthless member of the Bolsheviks' ruling group, Josif Stalin.) Just like Lenin, Trotsky had been taken by surprise by the suddenness of the collapse of the tsarist regime. Whereas Lenin had been in Switzerland in March 1917, Trotsky was in New York, as were two other leading Bolsheviks, Nikolay Bukharin, and the only woman who was to become a prominent member of the first Bolshevik government, Alexandra Kollontai. Members of their party who did not go into exile had been rounded up in 1914 because the Bolsheviks not only opposed the war with Germany, but also hoped for a German victory. They argued that it would speed up the revolution if Russia were to be defeated.[54]

The Bolsheviks suffered a setback in July 1917 when newspapers reported that Lenin was a German agent. Since Lenin had, indeed, used German help to get back into Russia from Switzerland, the accusation was damaging, although in essence absurd. It coincided, however, with a move by some Bolsheviks, which Lenin had considered premature, to seize power, with twenty thousand sailors from the Kronstadt naval base joining workers in this demand. The provisional government, albeit temporarily, came out on top. Armed clashes left some four hundred people dead. Lenin, endangered both by these events and by the supposed German connection, went once again into exile, this time in Finland. Trotsky was temporarily imprisoned, while

Stalin gained in significance by remaining the most senior of the Bolsheviks still to be in Russia and at large.[55]

By the autumn of 1917 the Bolsheviks had a majority within the Petrograd soviet and Trotsky had been chosen as its leader. He regarded the soviet as the most appropriate instrument of the revolution which would bring the Bolsheviks (a party he had formally joined only in August 1917) to power. Lenin's slogan of 'All power to the soviets' had been coined primarily to undermine the provisional government rather than because he shared Trotsky's firm belief that the soviet rather than the Bolshevik party should organize the seizure of the reins of government. Lenin's overwhelming concern was to ensure that the Bolsheviks would have nothing less than full power. At the First Congress of Soviets, held in June 1917, when the Bolsheviks did not yet have a majority within that national body and had not emerged victorious in any election of consequence, he made this clear in an unexpected answer to a rhetorical question. One of the speakers had asked, assuming that the answer in the negative was too obvious to need stating, whether in the prevailing conditions of Russia any political party was capable of taking power *on its own*. Lenin called out: 'There is such a party.'[56] His political boldness was not entirely matched by his personal conduct in the run-up to the Bolshevik revolution, which erred on the side of caution – perhaps because he was convinced of his indispensability once the revolution had succeeded. Even after the provisional government had released the Bolsheviks arrested in July, Lenin remained in Finland for several more weeks, while urging his comrades in writing that the time had come for an armed uprising. The Bolshevik leadership were divided about the wisdom of this, but when some of them published their disagreement with the policy in newspapers, it alerted the government to the likelihood of another revolutionary insurrection. Since the authorities had been forewarned, more of the Bolsheviks came to believe that it would be dangerous to postpone the seizure of power.[57]

The Military-Revolutionary Committee of the Petrograd soviet, which had been created to organize resistance to a threat in August of military dictatorship under the command of General Lavr Kornilov, became the chosen instrument of the Bolshevik insurrection. Lenin came out of hiding only on the night of 6–7 November (or 24–25 October, according to the Russian calendar in 1917). On the sixth, the forces deployed by the Military-Revolutionary Committee had taken over strategic points in the capital and on 7 November (the anniversary of which was celebrated with great fanfare throughout the Soviet period), they seized the Winter Palace where a meeting of the provisional government was in progress. Kerensky escaped and lived abroad for the rest of his life. (He died in New York in 1970 at the age of ninety-one. Stalin was later to ensure that many of the revolution's victors – his fellow Bolsheviks who took part in the seizure of power – lived far shorter lives than the premier they forcibly ousted in November 1917.)

Trotsky had more to do than had Lenin with the actual organization and implementation of the Bolshevik revolution, but it was Lenin who had more influence than anyone else on the power structure and ideology of the new regime. Although sometimes regarded as no more than a coup, this was a revolution as defined earlier in the chapter. It led to a change of both the political and the economic system, achieved through violent insurrection, and with substantial (albeit not majority) popular backing. And it led to a regime that rested on a new ideological basis for its legitimacy. Soviets had spread throughout Russia during 1917 and a national congress had elected a central executive committee to represent them. For ordinary members of soviets, that body appeared to be the obvious replacement for the provisional government until such time as a government emerged following the election for a Constituent Assembly, to be held in November 1917. (The date of that election had been decided before the Bolshevik seizure of power.) This, however, did not happen. The Bolshevik leadership had other ideas. When the new government was announced, it was called the Council of People's Commissars (which had a more revolutionary ring to it than Council of Ministers, the more conventional name it was given in 1946), and it consisted entirely of Bolsheviks. Lenin became head of the government, Trotsky the People's Commissar for Foreign Affairs and Stalin People's Commissar for Nationalities.

In the election for the Constituent Assembly, non-Communist socialists did much better than the party led by Lenin. As a leading historian of the Communist Party of the Soviet Union put it: 'Half the country voted for socialism but against bolshevism.'[58] Such democratic niceties did not trouble Lenin or Trotsky. When the Constituent Assembly held its first session and defeated the Bolsheviks in a vote, the Bolshevik delegates and the left wing of the socialist revolutionaries withdrew from the Assembly. The following day Bolshevik Red Guards stopped the remaining delegates – the majority of the assembly's members – from entering the building, and that was the end of the Constituent Assembly. Lenin had opted for one-party authoritarian rule. Some Bolsheviks did favour a broader coalition and a greater role for the soviets, but even though soviets were to remain part of the constitutional form, as well as the name, of what from 1922 was called the Union of Soviet Socialist Republics (USSR or Soviet Union), these institutions never regained the power they briefly wielded in 1917.

Until 1921 the Bolsheviks were fighting a civil war, in which they ultimately prevailed, against opponents of their revolution. Both sides acted ruthlessly and as early as December 1917 the Bolsheviks created an All-Russian Extraordinary Commission for Fighting Counter-Revolution and Sabotage, which became better known as the Cheka. In later incarnations it was known under different sets of Russian initials, among them the OGPU, the NKVD and the KGB. The Bolshevik victory in the civil war owed much to superior leadership, that of Trotsky (who in March 1918 became war commissar) and of Lenin as head of the government and principal ideologist.

Both the economic and the political systems were rapidly changed. Industry and the banks were nationalized and, in place of the somewhat anarchic democracy of 1917, there was political repression not only of those who would have liked a return to tsarist rule but also of non-Bolshevik socialists. Lenin was ready to make tactical retreats in economic policy when confronted by popular unrest, as he did with his New Economic Policy, launched in 1921, which legalized small-scale private manufacturing and private trade. He made clear, however, that this did not involve political tolerance of Mensheviks or other critics. Lenin suffered a stroke in 1922 and, following growing incapacity, died in January 1924. In the last two years of his life major levers of power were moving from the government (the Council of People's Commisars) to the Central Committee of the Party and the Secretariat that headed it. Its General Secretary from April 1922 was Stalin who had been chosen with Lenin's full approval. By the end of the 1920s Stalin had put an end to the partial economic liberalization – the mixed economy that prevailed throughout most of the decade – and proceeded with the compulsory collectivization of agriculture, which caused immense suffering, including famine. By the early 1930s not only was the dictatorship of the Communist Party fully established, but it was accompanied by Stalin's dictatorship over the party as well as over every other institution within the society. Whereas Lenin had not hesitated to employ terror or to order executions when dealing with opponents of Bolshevism, Stalin had no compunction about using the same methods against real and imagined enemies within the Bolshevik ranks. He also sought, and increasingly gained, a supreme leadership role within the international Communist movement.

Communist Revolutions in South-Eastern Europe

A majority of Communist states in Europe either were essentially Soviet creations – as was the case also of the first Asian country to adopt a Communist regime, Mongolia, in the 1920s – or were formed with important Soviet participation. The rise of Communism in Eastern Europe was very much a consequence of the Second World War and of the success of the Soviet army, which played a far greater part than the armed forces of any other country in defeating Hitler's Germany in the land war. The two countries where the Communist seizure of power was most clearly an indigenous revolution rather than a Soviet imposition were in south-eastern Europe – Yugoslavia and Albania, although Yugoslav Communists gave important assistance to the Albanian Communist Party, and serious consideration was given to a merger of the two countries in a confederation or even federal union. In both countries the Communist Party used the major parts they played in the wartime resistance movement as a means of furthering their revolutionary aims. This was true, to a certain extent, of other East and Central European countries where Communists were active in the resistance – albeit only after Nazi Germany attacked the Soviet Union in June 1941 – but nowhere else in the continent did Communist-led partisans play such a large wartime role as in Yugoslavia.

Josip Broz, who became better known as Tito, an alias he adopted in 1934, fought in the First World War in the Austro-Hungarian army, was severely wounded in 1915, captured, and spent the next five years in Russia – as a prisoner until after the Bolshevik revolution.[59] Tito returned to what was the Kingdom of Yugoslavia as a Bolshevik sympathizer. He became an early member of the Yugoslav Communist Party, which had been founded shortly after the end of the First World War.

Tito was arrested several times in the 1920s and was in jail from 1928 until 1934. On his release he was co-opted into membership of the Politburo of the Yugoslav Communist Party. The following year he was summoned to Moscow to work in the Comintern, the organization of the International Communist Movement. The Comintern was ultimately an instrument of the Soviet Communist Party and of its dictatorial leader – the 'Stalintern' as an American former Communist dubbed it.[60] Nevertheless, the person who headed the Comintern from 1935 until the dissolution of the organization in 1943, the Bulgarian Communist Georgi Dimitrov, enjoyed a degree of authority and influence.[61] For a foreign Communist the call to serve in the Comintern could be a path to higher things – or to the grave. Many European Communists, based in Moscow, who were refugees from fascist or other right-wing authoritarian regimes, perished in Stalin's purges of the late 1930s. Tito survived largely because he was looked upon with special favour by Dimitrov. The choice of leader of an underground Communist party was essentially made in Moscow, and in 1937 that position was granted to Tito and formalized with the title of general secretary in 1939.[62]

Someone who was later to be a thorn in the side of the Soviet leadership thus owed his initial pre-eminence among Yugoslav Communists to the patronage of Moscow. He went on, however, to establish a personal authority in Yugoslavia that was not dependent upon Soviet support and which, indeed, later increased when he incurred Soviet wrath. His leadership qualities came to the fore during the war years and, again, following the break in Yugoslav–Soviet relations in 1948. The British army officer, Bill Deakin (later Sir William Deakin and the first Warden of St Antony's College, Oxford), who was parachuted into Montenegro in occupied Yugoslavia in 1943 to liaise with the Yugoslav Partisans, noted that Tito's authority depended on 'few words or gestures' and that he gained 'an instinctive and total respect from those around him'. Deakin regarded him as 'sure in judgement and deeply self-controlled'. He had expected to meet a rigid doctrinaire who would be impervious to open debate, but found him instead to be 'flexible in discussion, with a sharp and humorous wit, and a wide curiosity'.[63]

Milovan Djilas, at one time a close comrade-in-arms of Tito, became in subsequent years more critical of Tito than was the conservative British soldier-scholar, Deakin.[64] Djilas belonged to the leadership group of the Yugoslav partisans and was an important member of the post-war

Yugoslav government until he became a critic of the system. He was expelled from the Yugoslav party in January 1954 after calling for its democratization. Subsequently Djilas spent nine years in Yugoslav prisons after writing *The New Class* (the first of a number of important books on Communism of which he was the author), in which he observed that 'so-called socialist ownership' had become 'a disguise for the real ownership by the political bureaucracy'.[65] In a later book – a critical, but nuanced, biography of Tito – Djilas wrote of Tito's intellectual limitations, of his vanity and his growing desire for luxury. Such aspersions notwithstanding, Djilas emphasized that both during and after the war, Tito displayed 'a glittering political talent'. He had a mastery of timing, which enabled him to choose the right moment for 'critical courses of action'. He also had 'a strong sense of danger, as instinctive as it is rational; an unconquerable will to live, to survive, and to endure; a shrewd and insatiable drive for power'.[66] Tito's years as the dominating figure in post-war Yugoslavia until his death in 1980 will be touched upon in the next chapter. In the present context what is important is how he and the Communists achieved power in the first place.

During the war Tito was not only the leader of the Communist-dominated Partisan resistance movement to German and Italian invaders, he and his comrades were also engaged in civil war. The Partisans triumphed over both Croat fascists and Serb nationalists, and Tito became the leader of a provisional government of Yugoslavia in 1944. Under pressure from Western allies, he reluctantly included three royalist members, but they were discarded – along with the monarchy itself – the following year. Yugoslavia, which had been dismembered during the war, was reconstituted as a Federal People's Republic. By the end of 1945 the Communists in Yugoslavia had achieved a monopoly of power which their counterparts in other East European countries took several years to attain. They won it first on the battlefield, subsequently dealing ruthlessly with known collaborators with the occupying forces. They then legitimated their rule with an election in November 1945 in which the only choice was to be for or against the nominees of the Communist Party. Since power was already in their hands, and as they had gained real prestige among a substantial part of the population for their role in the liberation of Yugoslavia from the invaders, they might well have secured victory in a free election. In the event, however, anti-Communists had no confidence that they could safely register negative votes and Tito's movement secured a massive 96 per cent of the votes cast.[67] The coming to power of the Communists was a combination of war of liberation and of revolutionary struggle, with nothing left to chance thereafter.

Success on the battlefield and intimidation were not, however, the only reasons for the success of the Yugoslav Communists. Along with the attractive promise of social justice, they appeared to offer the best prospect of bringing harmony in place of inter-ethnic conflict. The Communists had the advantage that they were the most Yugoslav (a word that means southern Slavs) of all the political parties, the only one which united the various nationalities who during the war – as well as earlier and much later – were engaged in bitter strife. Tito himself transcended the national divide. His father was a Croat, his mother a Slovene, and he grew up in a Croatian village. Yet Serbs and Montenegrins were disproportionately well represented in the Partisan movement he led. (The Serbian population was itself deeply divided between support for the nationalist Chetniks and for the Communist-led Partisans.) Different nationalities were represented also in the inner core of the party leadership.[68]

A combination of national resistance movement against invading forces and revolutionary civil war was characteristic also of the coming to power of Albanian Communists. Within the resistance to the Axis powers, the Communists in Albania acquired a position of clear dominance. Mussolini's Italy invaded Albania in 1939 and from the outset Enver Hoxha, the son of a landowner who had become attracted to Communism while studying in France, was active in the resistance. When the Albanian Communist Party was founded in 1941, Hoxha became its leader. He retained that position until his death in 1985. By then he had become not only the longest-lasting East European party leader but had been head of government for longer than any other non-hereditary ruler in the twentieth century. That owed much to his cunning as well as to his ruthlessness and to the institutions which the Communists put in place.

The Albanian Communists received more direct advice from their Yugoslav than Soviet counterparts during the Second World War, but Hoxha even in the war years was warier of the Yugoslav embrace than were some of his colleagues. In 1944 the Communists overthrew the German-supporting government in Tirana. As in Yugoslavia, they had proved capable of redirecting a national liberation struggle to revolutionary ends. Hoxha, who played the most important role in the takeover, was both well read and intelligent (and the author in later years of interesting memoirs).[69] He was also a vindictive and dogmatic Stalinist, remaining an admirer of Stalin to the end of his life, long after Khrushchev had drawn attention to at least some of Stalin's mass murders. Before the war, Albania had been under the authoritarian rule of King Zog. Under Hoxha Albania moved not just from one type of authoritarian rule to another but to totalitarianism. Hoxha went further than most Communist leaders in the elimination of all elements of civil society, with religious institutions and the practice of religion totally outlawed.

COMMUNIST REVOLUTIONS IN ASIA

The Chinese Communists' Capture of Power

Apart from the Soviet puppet regime of Mongolia, the first Communist state in Asia was China. It was also the earliest example of successful indigenous Communist revolution on the Asian continent. When Communists came to power in China, this was far more important for global politics, especially in the long run, than what happened in south-eastern Europe, but there are some parallels with the events in the Balkans. In China, as in Albania and, still more, in Yugoslavia, a war of national liberation was combined with a revolutionary struggle for Communist power. During the Second World War, with Japanese forces occupying China, there were separate Nationalist and Communist resistance armies. The Nationalists, under the leadership of Chiang Kai-shek, bore the brunt of the struggle and their losses were enormous. The Communists focused mainly on guerrilla attacks on the Japanese, and suffered less severe casualties. For Mao Zedong the highest priority was preparing for the coming struggle with the Nationalists for the control of all of China. When the war against Japanese aggression began, the Chinese Communists controlled territory occupied by only four million people. By the time it ended that had grown to territories with more than ninety-five million inhabitants. During the same period the

Chinese Red Army had risen in size from one hundred thousand troops to some nine hundred thousand.[70]

Mao had been the acknowledged leader of the Chinese Communists since the 1930s. Neither he nor the Kuomintang leader Chiang Kai-shek were in the least receptive to American attempts to broker an agreement between them following Japan's surrender. A superficial rapprochement in late 1945 and early 1946 soon broke down.[71] Civil war continued until it ended in victory for the Communists in 1949. The Soviet leadership, like that of the United States, had been in favour of compromise. Stalin advised the Chinese Communist Party not to attempt to take over the whole country. In a rare admission (albeit not in public) that he had been wrong, Stalin said that 'when the war with Japan ended, we invited the Chinese comrades to agree on a means of reaching a *modus vivendi* with Chiang Kai-shek'. They consented at the time but 'did it their own way when they got home: they mustered their forces and struck. It has been shown that they were right, and we were not.'[72] The Communists had a number of advantages in the contest for the support of the peasantry who constituted at that time the overwhelming majority of the Chinese population. They appealed successfully, in particular, to the poorer peasants and to landless agricultural labourers.[73] They promised them land of their own, whereas the Nationalists were too dependent on large landowners and regional power-brokers to match them in any such offers. The Kuomintang were also severely damaged by widespread corruption and by rampant inflation which the government utterly failed to bring under control. Shopkeepers found themselves changing their prices several times a day. And this was in a country that had suffered dire poverty throughout the whole of the first half of the twentieth century.

Some of those who had fought for the Kuomintang in the war against Japan were willing to fight for, and be fed by, the Communists who also did not hesitate to recruit Chinese auxiliaries who had fought on the Japanese side. The Communists had artillery, mostly of Japanese origin, which had been handed to them by their Soviet allies. They also had as head of their People's Liberation Army a capable military man, Zhu De, although Mao headed the Revolutionary Military Committee and retained the highest political authority. His skilful leadership at that stage of his career and ruthless determination to extend Communist control to the whole of China played a major part in the successful capture of power.

During the first two years of the civil war which broke out in 1946 Chiang Kai-shek's Nationalists had vast superiority in both numbers and equipment over the Communists, and in the first year, in particular, they had a lot of military success. Between then and the defeat of the Kuomintang in 1949, however, the Communist leadership succeeded in inspiring the forces under their command more than the Nationalist leaders were able to do, and they mobilized greater support in the society. The Communist victory was both military and political. Mao had significant success in showing that the Nationalists could be challenged on their own ground of fostering national pride. Although the Communists' accession to power meant, in many respects, a break with Chinese tradition, they evoked patriotic aspiration and desire for a clean break with the humiliations of the previous century and a half. On declaring the foundation of the People's Republic of China at the beginning of October 1949, Mao said that the Chinese people had 'stood up'.[74]

Ho Chi Minh and the Vietnamese Communists' Ascent to Power

Communists in many countries had an influence in excess of their numbers because of the strength of their ideological belief and their hierarchical and disciplined organization. Revolutionary movements in Asia, however, had two assets that were absent in Europe where so few Communist parties came to power as a result entirely of their own efforts. Asian Communists were able to combine their revolutionary commitment to a new social and economic order with that of national liberation from colonial rule, thus broadening their appeal. Their other strength lay in their appeal to a largely uneducated peasantry who constituted overwhelmingly the largest social class. A focus on the grievances and aspirations of peasants meant playing down the classical Marxist belief that the industrial working class would be the social force making for revolutionary change. Both Mao Zedong and Ho Chi Minh, who were of a similar age (Ho was born in 1890, Mao in 1893) and who became Communists in the early 1920s, emphasized the revolutionary potential of the peasantry. The name Ho Chi Minh,

which means He Who Enlightens, was the last in a series of pseudo-
nyms (at least fifty) which Ho adopted, in this case from the time of
the Second World War.[75]*

As a young man, Ho spent a number of years away from Indochina,
working in a variety of jobs. He was in the United States immediately
before the First World War, and later claimed to have worked as a
pastry chef in Boston. He also spent time as a seaman, a junior chef
in London's Carlton Hotel, and as a photo retoucher in Paris. He was in
London from 1915 to 1917, but it was his six years in France from the
end of 1917 to 1923 which turned him into a Communist. Inspired by
the Bolshevik revolution and radicalized also by the Versailles Peace
settlement, which he condemned for failing to apply President
Woodrow Wilson's doctrine of national self-determination to the
peoples of Indochina, he joined the French Communist Party in 1920
at the age of thirty. Ho spent time in both the Soviet Union and China
in the 1920s and 1930s and became an agent of the Comintern in Asia.
He took the view, at odds with conventional Marxism, that Communism
could 'acclimatize itself more easily in Asia than in Europe', for in
Asia there was a traditional sympathy for 'the idea of community and
social equality'.[76] The Indian Communist, M.N. Roy, who was the most
prominent Asian to take part in the founding meeting of the Comintern
in Moscow in 1919, was another who believed that the chances of
Communism taking hold in Asia were better than in Europe and that
Asian revolutions would lead the way in the worldwide overthrow of
capitalism. The two men did not, however, get on. Ho was generally
liked both within the international Communist movement and even
by anti-Communists with whom he negotiated, but Roy, who knew
him in Moscow in the 1920s, disparaged him as unimpressive both
intellectually and physically.[77] Ho's subsequent career, which included
long treks from one guerrilla base to another, suggests that Roy was
wrong on both counts. Ho became the principal founder and leader
of the Vietnamese Communist Party, established in 1930. In October
of the same year, on Comintern instructions, it changed its name to

---

* Many revolutionary leaders, as rebels against, or as fugitives from, the conservative
authoritarian regimes they were intent on overthrowing, adopted a *nom de guerre.*
Thus, for example, Ulyanov became Lenin, Djugashvili became Stalin, Bronstein
became Trotsky and Broz became Tito.

Indochinese Communist Party, since it was to embrace, for some years, Cambodia and Laos as well as Vietnam.

During the Second World War, the Vietnamese Communists created a national liberation movement, the Vietminh, opposed to the Vichy regime which collaborated with the Japanese occupiers. It was their wartime resistance role which brought them to national prominence and gave them popular influence. Although dominated by Ho and his party comrades, the Vietminh put their emphasis on building a broad coalition and on the attainment of an independent Vietnam.[78] They themselves were able to seize power in Hanoi in 1945, although the opportunity had been created by American action – the atomic bombs dropped on Hiroshima and Nagasaki in August 1945, which were rapidly followed by the Japanese surrender. The Vietminh took over government buildings in Hanoi in the same month and established what they called the Democratic Republic of Vietnam, with Ho Chi Minh as its president. At that point Ho was intent on maintaining an international as well as a domestic coalition of supporters. Addressing a crowd of half a million people in Hanoi in early September 1945, he quoted from the American Declaration of Independence, clearly hoping that the aftermath of the Second World War would bring more support for Vietnamese self-determination from the United States than had occurred after the First World War, Woodrow Wilson's rhetoric notwithstanding.[79]

President Truman, however, gave a higher priority to having France as an ally than to supporting the independence of the Vietnamese. Although General de Gaulle would later conclude that the French war in Indochina was unwinnable and that the United States would find their war in Vietnam to be equally forlorn, in 1945 he played the card which would have most effect in Washington when he warned that if the US opposed the French attempt to regain their colonies in Indochina, that would push France 'into the Russian orbit'.[80] Although the American government remained unenthusiastic about the French attempt to re-establish their colonial rule in Vietnam, this changed when the Chinese Communists attained power in 1949. From then on, stopping the spread of Communism in Asia was still more of a prime concern in Washington.

Despite the fact that the Vietminh had succeeded in wearing down the French, the peace agreement of 1954 which formally ended the conflict, involved, to Ho Chi Minh's great disappointment, the partition of the country. Both the Chinese and Soviet leaderships (who had taken until 1950 to recognize the Democratic Republic of Vietnam, the Chinese doing so before the Soviet Union followed suit) favoured this compromise. Ho felt let down by them. He needed, however, their political support and relied on the Soviet supply of weapons. North Vietnam was never, though, simply a Soviet client state, for Ho managed at times to play off the Chinese and Russians against one another and yet to maintain good relations with the leaders of both countries during the most acrimonious years of the Sino-Soviet dispute. With North Vietnam, in its turn, supplying weaponry to their Viet Cong comrades in the South, the United States government had reason to believe that the whole of Vietnam was liable to become Communist. Already under President Kennedy, American military advisers were sent to South Vietnam to assist the forces under the command of the anti-Communist and authoritarian President Ngo Dinh Diem. It was only during the Johnson presidency that American combat troops, in ever-increasing numbers, were dispatched to Vietnam. Ho did not live to see the American withdrawal from Vietnam and the face-saving treaty that was signed in Paris in 1973 and provided a politically convenient pause before the unification of Vietnam under Communist rule in 1975. By the time the war ended fifty-eight thousand Americans had lost their lives in vain, but the Vietnamese losses were vastly greater. Around three million soldiers and civilians had been killed and the country was devastated, not least by the use of Agent Orange, the toxic compound the United States forces had used to defoliate the forests which were the hiding place of the Viet Cong. Long after the war ended, this was causing many birth defects and cancers in Vietnam.[81] The victory of the Vietnamese revolutionaries had been attained at a very high price.[82]

In Communist revolutions, as distinct from more spontaneous uprisings – such as the February/March revolution in Russia – leaders, ideas and organization were invariably important. In some cases more than others, one person played a more significant role than any of his colleagues. That was true of Ho Chi Minh if we focus on the long haul – the creation and development of the revolutionary movement in Vietnam, the foundation of the republic in 1945, and the guerrilla war against the French as they tried to re-establish control over their former colony and failed. By the time American troops entered Vietnam in the mid-1960s, Ho Chi Minh was hardly the most powerful decision-maker within the Vietnamese Communist leadership, although still much revered in North Vietnam. His standing in the outside world, which he understood better than his less-travelled comrades, remained an asset for the Vietnamese Communists. Ho had his ups and downs during the first quarter of a century of the party's existence, but by the early 1940s undoubtedly wielded more power within it than anyone else. Yet, his style of rule within the highest party echelons was consensual. He did not try to dominate in the manner of Stalin, Mao Zedong or North Korea's Kim Il Sung, but operated within a more collective leadership in which, rather than browbeat or dictate, he relied substantially on his powers of persuasion.[83] Ho deliberately cultivated an image of saintliness and in the 1940s and 1950s wrote two self-congratulatory 'biographies' of himself under assumed names.[84] Nevertheless, he was by nature more of a conciliator than an autocratic strongman and was ultimately a more successful Communist leader than those in the latter category.

Pol Pot and the Killing Fields of Cambodia

After the Cambodian ruler, Prince Sihanouk, had been removed in a palace coup in 1970, a vicious civil war between the Khmer Rouge Communists and anti-Communist forces got underway, with the Vietnamese minority in Cambodia the greatest sufferers. American bombing of Cambodia in the early 1970s, ordered by President Nixon, was directed at the Khmer Rouge, and at the trails through the jungles by which weapons reached Vietnam, but its consequences were more indiscriminate and counterproductive. The bombing 'ensured that there would never be a shortage of recruits [for the Khmer Rouge] in a countryside now filled with hatred for the Americans'.[85] Prince Sihanouk played his part, too. Outraged at having been ousted by General Lon Nol, he encouraged Cambodians, in a broadcast from Beijing in March 1970, to 'go to the jungle and join the guerrillas', thus giving a boost to what was at that time a very small Communist Party.[86] Even before coming to power, the Khmer Rouge provided a foretaste of their extreme ruthlessness in the civil war. After capturing Oudong, at one time the royal capital, they massacred tens of thousands of people.[87] When they took the capital, Phnom Penh, in 1975, they set about trying to establish a Communist regime like no other, in which cities were emptied, money was abolished, as were schools, courts and markets. Collectivization of agriculture was completed far faster than in any other state, with virtually the whole population forced to work on the land. Between 1975 and 1979, when a Vietnamese invasion ended Khmer Rouge dictatorship and replaced it by more 'normal' Communist rule, it is estimated that at least one in five of the Cambodians, possibly even a quarter of the population, had died an untimely death.

The principal leader of the Khmer Rouge was Pol Pot, whose real name was Saloth Sar. As a young man he studied in France and became a member of the French Communist Party. On his return to Cambodia he worked as a schoolteacher. He was later influenced by Mao and by the Chinese Cultural Revolution. However, his combination of utopianism and bloodthirsty pursuit of class war far exceeded even Mao's on both counts. In his mercifully brief period as the number-one person within the Khmer Rouge government, he kept a low public profile and, unlike Mao, was far from promoting a cult of his personality. Pol Pot (a name he took in 1976) appeared actually to believe in the construction of some kind of communism, built on the bones of the people his henchmen and acolytes killed, whether by having their throats cut (the fate of tens of thousands), beating to death with spades, shooting, or the famine that the Khmer Rouge policies induced. Among those arrested were close comrades who had thought of themselves as friends of their leader. They were tortured before being killed. By 1979, 42 per cent of Cambodian children had lost at least one parent. Throughout all this, Pol Pot appears to have retained an unshakeable belief in his own genius.[88] He believed that 'he would be enthroned higher than his glorious ancestors – Marx, Lenin, Stalin, Mao Zedong'.[89] After the Vietnamese had installed a government of their choosing in Phnom Penh, Pol Pot and his forces retreated to jungle camps on the border of Cambodia and Thailand and carried on a guerrilla war for another eighteen years. Remarkably, they continued to be recognized as the government of Cambodia by the United Nations, thanks to the continued support of China and of Western countries' willingness to view Cambodia through the distorting lenses of the Cold War in which the principal adversary was not China but the Soviet Union. Pol Pot died of natural causes in 1998, just a month short of his sixty-third birthday.

Kim Il Sung's Accession to Power in North Korea

Kim Il Sung, in spite of the legends that were created for him by his propagandists and the fertility of his own myth-making, was put in place as the leader of North Korea by his Soviet sponsors. His earlier mentors, however, had been Chinese. In late 1929 and the first half of 1930 he was in prison under suspicion of belonging to a left-wing group. He had spent much of his boyhood in China – in Manchuria – and it was the Chinese Communist Party he joined in 1931. At that time a separate Korean party did not exist.[90] In the course of the 1930s, when Korea was under Japanese rule, Kim took part in guerrilla activity against the occupiers. In common with most other Communist revolutionary leaders, Kim did not use the name he was given at birth. Kim Il Sung was a *nom de guerre*, his original name being Kim Song Ju. He spent the years 1940 to 1945 in the Soviet Union, a fact he suppressed when he set about embellishing his image as a great national liberator. It was when Soviet forces captured the northern part of the Korean peninsula, with the Americans in control of the south, that they put Kim, who had made a good impression as someone of sharp intelligence, in charge. Nevertheless, Kim was not the first choice of the Soviet authorities to be the top leader of the part of Korea which they occupied. They had in mind someone who would *appear* more independent, Cho Man Sik, who had led a non-violent reformist group. The problem, however, was that Cho proved in reality to be too independent for their taste. Before long he was at odds with the Soviet occupying forces and was subsequently arrested.[91]

The second-choice Kim, having already in December 1945 become chairman of the North Korean branch of the Korean Communist Party, was installed the following February, thanks to Soviet backing, as chairman of the Interim People's Committee. This embryonic state authority took over 90 per cent of industry in the course of 1946 and launched a far-reaching land reform.[92] In September 1948, less than a month after the Republic of Korea had been formally declared to exist in Seoul, a separate state in the north was announced in the shape of the Democratic People's Republic of Korea, with Kim Il Sung at its head. This was less a revolution than a Soviet imposition, although Kim, with his promise to free Korea from foreign tutelage (with the exception, at that time, of the Soviet Union) appears to have had more popular support than did several of the Soviet-imposed leaderships in Eastern Europe. He also went on to establish a regime which, following Stalin's death, deviated substantially from the Soviet model. Instead of copying their partial relaxation and cultural thaw, Kim's North Korea continued its development as a peculiar Communist hybrid, one that was both sultanistic and totalitarian. The personality cult of the 'Great Leader', as he was known, exceeded even those of Stalin, Mao Zedong and the Romanian Communist leader Nicolae Ceauşescu, improbable feat though that was.

THE CUBAN REVOLUTION

Although Cuba, several years after Fidel Castro came to power, became a Communist state, the revolution of 1959 was not a Communist revolution. The Cuban Communist Party had been dismissive of the middle-class revolutionaries, led by Fidel and Raúl Castro and Che Guevara, who had for several years been fighting a guerrilla war from the thick forests and mountainous terrain of the Sierra Maestra against the country's corrupt authoritarian regime. Its president was Fulgencio Batista who had seized power in March 1952 in a military coup which he called a revolution. In contrast with Batista's coup, the eventually successful struggle of Castro and his comrades, which began in 1953 with a failed attempt to seize the Moncada military barracks in Santiago de Cuba, was a genuine revolution. Castro and his comrades-in-arms called for social transformation as well as national independence, viewing their large neighbour, the United States, as an exploitative imperial power. The fact that Batista was hand in glove with crooked American businessmen, most notably the mafia boss Meyer Lansky who became his 'official adviser for casino reform', helped to stoke a quite widespread popular anti-Americanism.[93] During the 1950s the predominant influence on Castro was not Marx but the hero of the island's struggle for freedom from Spanish colonial rule, José Martí, who died in 1895 before that independence was achieved. Martí, although not a Marxist, was an advocate of a socially just democracy as well as of national self-determination. Castro continued to admire Martí. As he later put it: 'I was first a Martían and then a Martían, Marxist and Leninist.'[94]

Castro was the son of a relationship between his landowner father and the cook-housekeeper, whom Castro's father later married. Fidel, who was born in August 1927, wrote a letter as a boy to Franklin Roosevelt, congratulating him on his election victory in 1940 and asking if he would send him ten dollars 'because I have not seen a ten dollars bill American and I would like to have one of them'.[95] He received an acknowledgement of his letter from the State Department, but no dollars were enclosed. Castro later remarked that 'there are people who've told me that if Roosevelt had only sent me $10 I wouldn't have given the United States so many headaches!'[96] Castro attended a prominent Jesuit school and then entered the Law Faculty of Havana University in 1945. Years later he said he didn't know why he had decided to study law, adding: 'I partly associate it with those who said: "He talks so much he should become a lawyer."'[97] As a student, Castro was drawn into radical politics, but was unusual in that he managed to combine political activism with notable sporting achievements. Nine years after his request to Roosevelt for ten dollars, he turned down the offer of a $5,000 signing-on fee from the New York Giants, for American talent scouts had noticed his great promise at baseball.[98]

After he embarked on serious revolutionary activity, Castro on numerous occasions came close to being killed. When the attempt to capture the Moncada barracks in 1953 failed, many of those who took part in the attack were shot, in most cases after gruesome torture and mutilation. Castro escaped but was captured five days later. He was about to be killed on the spot when the black officer in charge of the army patrol, Lieutenant Pedro Manuel Sarria, ordered his men to stop. According to Castro, he then added: 'Don't shoot. You can't kill ideas; you can't kill ideas . . .'[99] When he was brought to trial in October 1953, Castro made a stirring speech to the court which lasted for several hours. He concluded it with the words: 'Condemn me, it does not matter. History will absolve me!'[100] He was sentenced to fifteen years of imprisonment, but served only one year and seven months of the sentence. Following both public pressure and the intervention of Archbishop Pérez Serantes, who suggested that Castro and his associates no longer posed a danger, he was released as part of a wider amnesty.[101] Less than two months after leaving prison, Castro left Cuba for Mexico where he joined his younger brother, Raúl who, unlike Fidel, was already attracted to Communism. He also met the young

Argentinian doctor and Marxist revolutionary, Ernesto (better known as 'Che') Guevara who, at twenty-seven, was two years younger than Fidel. Ordered out of Mexico in November 1956, this group of revolutionaries acquired an ancient boat, the *Granma* (which later became the title of the main Cuban Communist party newspaper) and, after overloading it with weapons and ammunition as well as eighty-two people in a vessel meant to accommodate twenty-five, they set off for Cuba. They came close to sinking in a storm in the Gulf of Mexico and took two days longer than they intended to reach Cuba, eventually running aground about a mile short of where they planned to dock.

After taking to the hills of the Sierra Maestra, they made steady progress in winning support for their cause from the rural population. It was not primarily the peasantry who provided their most solid support, but workers who earned a living wage from the sugar industry during the harvest season and hardly anything outside it. They were described at the time as 'semi-proletarianized labourers'. The revolution in due course brought in other social groups (including urban workers), for Cuba was, by Latin American standards, a relatively urbanized and literate society, with some significant trade unions. Thus, this was not simply a peasant uprising, but it began in the countryside under the leadership of middle-class revolutionaries.

Castro and his core group of rebels confiscated livestock from large landowners and distributed them to peasants with little or no property. In the earliest months of 1957 the group around Fidel, who was the acknowledged leader, numbered just eighteen. Castro already recognized the value of publicity and news management, and agreed to be interviewed by a *New York Times* correspondent, Herbert L. Matthews. After an arduous climb, and taking care to avoid Batista's soldiers, Matthews reached Castro's camp and interviewed him. Meantime, Raúl organized frenetic activity intended to convey the impression that the company of armed rebels was much larger than it actually was. This included a messenger arriving breathlessly with a report from a 'Second Column', which did not actually exist.[102] The interview provided a great boost to Castro, and the size of his group soon grew to around three hundred. In the piece he published, Matthews wrote of Fidel: 'The personality of the man is overpowering. It was easy to see that his men adored him and also to see why he has caught the imagination of the youth of Cuba all over the island. Here was an educated, dedicated fanatic, a man of ideals, of courage and of remarkable qualities of leadership.'[103] The *Times* published a photograph of Castro holding a telescopic rifle.

Fidel Castro had been the only person in the group who was known as *commandante*, but he conferred that title on Guevara who not only acted as the group's field doctor, but took an active part in their armed struggle. He personally shot dead one of their scouts who had accepted 10,000 dollars from Batista's army to lead the revolutionaries into an ambush.[104] After numerous skirmishes, Castro's group controlled a substantial part of eastern Cuba by the middle of 1958 and set up a radio station in that territory. When in July that year eight Cuban opposition parties and anti-Batista groups met in the Venezuelan capital, Caracas, and issued a 'Manifesto of the Civil-Revolutionary Opposition Front', they recognized Fidel as their leader. Castro's radio station was able to broadcast their statement. The Cuban Communist Party did not participate in the Caracas meeting, but shortly afterwards their leader, Carlos Rafael Rodríguez, belatedly realizing that this movement had more potential than he had hitherto appreciated, made his way to the Sierra Maestra for a meeting with Castro. They went on to establish good relations, and Rodríguez subsequently served in government under Castro's leadership.

By late 1958 Castro's fighting force had risen to some three thousand people, and the support for them was much more widespread. They met less and less resistance from an increasingly demoralized army. As the rebels moved towards Havana, Batista decided that his days as president were numbered. On 1 January 1959 he left by plane with his relatives and some friends for the Dominican Republic. Two other planes followed, filled not only with some of the people closest to Batista but with almost all of Cuba's gold and dollar reserves. By 3 January Castro had embarked on a victory parade across the island, and on 8 January he led his column into Havana to the sound of church bells and factory and ship sirens. Castro addressed a crowd of several hundred thousand people from the balcony of the presidential palace, characteristically speaking for several hours. To the British ambassador to Cuba, Fidel seemed to be 'a mixture of José Martí, Robin Hood, Garibaldi and Jesus Christ'.[105] At that time Castro and his followers were widely perceived to be radical democrats rather than Marxist revolutionaries, and that was not entirely a misconception, although Raúl Castro and Che Guevara, while knowing very little about the Soviet

Union, were already more sympathetic to Communism than was Fidel. Incorporation in the international Communist movement (and the alliance with the Soviet Union) was to come later.

The Cuban revolution is a clear case where leadership mattered a great deal. It was not the organizational discipline of a Communist party in this instance that brought revolutionaries to power, but something much closer to charismatic leadership in the person of Fidel Castro. He did not manufacture a cult of himself in the manner of some Communist leaders – there were no streets, buildings or parks named after him during his years as Cuban leader – but that was partly because his personality was so overwhelming that he did not need to. His style of rule was widely known as *fidelismo*, a very particular variant of the Latin American tradition of *caudillo*, a popular leader who comes to be trusted and obeyed as a father figure. Orthodox Communists, such as those reporting from the GDR embassy in Cuba, disapproved of the emotional component of his leadership, but it was one reason why Castro could evoke a warmth of response and at times touch hearts in a way that Walter Ulbricht and Erich Honecker never could. A confidential report from the GDR embassy to the political leadership in East Berlin in 1964 complained of Castro's 'nationalism and left radicalism', his 'subjective evaluation of trends and their causes' and of his propensity to 'guide the popular masses from a basically emotional point of view' and of his 'letting off steam' in difficult situations.[106]

Castro also had an eye for the theatrical gesture and knew how to project his personality. When he appeared at the United Nations in 1960 and addressed the General Assembly wearing his characteristic olive-green battledress, this made his impact all the greater. He also cocked a snook at the US administration and hostile American mass media by moving, with his eighty-five-person delegation, from an expensive New York hotel to one in the middle of Harlem, where he was cheered by black and Latino supporters. In that unusual setting for head-of-government diplomacy, he received the Soviet leader, Nikita Khrushchev, the Indian premier Jawaharlal Nehru and the Egyptian president Gamal Abdel Nasser as well as the radical black leader Malcolm X.[107] Ever attentive to symbolism, Castro succeeded in preserving at the same time a greater frankness and spontaneity than is typical of leaders who have spent many years in power. He was also untouched by material motives. As his major biographer observes: 'Not only those who claim to know him personally, but also his various opponents, think that he is one of the few absolute rulers who have not enriched themselves in office and salted away millions in Switzerland.'[108]

Some revolutions begin when huge numbers of people take to the streets or storm government buildings without waiting for a leader to spur them into action. Others depend much more on a particular leader or small leadership group. Cuba was clearly in the latter category. The audacity and ability to inspire of Castro and his comrades-in-arms, and their evident desire to redress the grievances of the rural population and to remove the scourge of corruption, won them increasing support. Castro himself later emphasized what a tiny group it was who set the revolutionary process in motion: 'If you look, it was just three or four of us who created the embryo of the movement that attacked the Moncada barracks. From the beginning – it's strange – we had a small corps of leaders and a small executive committee of just three people'. He went on to generalize the point: 'Radical revolutionary parties are often born in the underground, clandestinely – they're created and led by a very few people.'[109] At the time he led the Cuban revolution Castro was neither a Marxist nor a Leninist, but his view of the movement's origins is consistent with Lenin's idea that the mass of the people needed an avant-garde of professional revolutionaries who would lead them to understand that amelioration of the conditions of life was not enough (indeed, it could be dangerously distracting and seductive); what was required was the complete overthrow of the old regime and the creation of a fundamentally different system and new society.

THE DEMISE OF COMMUNISM IN EUROPE – *NOT* REVOLUTIONS

It may seem odd to discuss *non*-revolutions in a chapter on revolutions and revolutionary leadership. The reason for doing so is very simple. The myth of the East European 'revolution' of 1989 is very pervasive. Both within the countries that underwent dramatic change and in the rest of the world, the events of that year are frequently referred to as a revolution. It is a telling example of the romantic aura which has clung to the word ever since the French Revolution that people who have experienced something different from – and better than – revolutions still yearn for that old revolutionary élan and feel a need to bolster their belief that systemic change was all their own doing.

It makes sense, on the contrary, to differentiate revolutions, long understood to involve violence or the threat of violence, not only from peaceful transformative change but also from the collapse of a regime which has continued to exist only so long as it is backed by a foreign power. When the leadership of a regional hegemon decides that it will no longer impose a system of rule on other countries against the will of their own people, then the resultant collapse of the regimes in question does not amount to revolution. The transformation of Eastern Europe in 1989–91 was a case in point. Gorbachev and his allies in the Soviet leadership had made it clear that they would not use force to maintain Communist systems in Eastern Europe, the more so since they were in the process of dismantling the pillars of such a system at home.[110] The Communist states of East Europe (with the exceptions of Yugoslavia, Albania and Romania) were penetrated political systems, by no means fully autonomous. When the Soviet Union abdicated from determining and enforcing the limits of change in the region, national independence was quickly asserted. Gorbachev, as we have seen in the previous chapter, publicly declared in Moscow in the summer of 1988, and in New York at the United Nations in December of the same year, that the peoples of every country had the right to decide for themselves what kind of system they wished to live in. And in 1989 the Kremlin leadership had not only removed the threat of Soviet armed intervention, they also strongly advised Communist leaders in Eastern Europe not to resort to force either.[111] Large-scale peaceful demonstrations took place, but they were as much a symptom as a cause of systemic change. They did not constitute a revolution; they were better than that.

In Poland and Hungary, in particular, there was a negotiated transition to democracy. They were the first countries to take advantage of the new opportunities opened up by change in Moscow, and Poland led the way in installing a non-Communist prime minister, Tadeusz Mazowiecki, as early as August 1989. In Czechoslovakia there were massive demonstrations against the Communist regime in the last two months of the year, once it had become obvious that this would not produce another Soviet armed response. For two decades those who had written and distributed underground literature had numbered not more than a thousand people, a small circle persecuted by the authorities and ignored by the majority of the population.[112] The ranks of their overt supporters swelled in the course of 1989 and on 19 November of that year the embattled minority, who had created Charter 77 as an oppositional pressure group in 1977, converted their movement into one called the Civic Forum, whose informal leader was Václav Havel. Coming together in the Magic Lantern Theatre in Prague from mid-November to early December, they held meetings that were highly democratic, with each participant allowed to have his or her say and important issues decided by vote.[113] Yet Timothy Garton Ash, who was present throughout most of these discussions, noted also the individual standing Havel had acquired. While 'a less authoritarian personality than Havel would be hard to imagine', he often became the final arbiter, 'the one person who could somehow balance the very different tendencies and interests in the movement'.[114]

Large but peaceful protests against Communist rule put pressure on the government, but the final straw for them was a declaration from a Warsaw Pact summit meeting in early December that the 1968 invasion had been wrong and illegal. Since every member of the top leadership team ultimately owed his position to that earlier Soviet intervention, their position was now completely untenable. Within days the prime minister Ladislav Adamec and president Gustáv Husák resigned in quick succession and a predominantly non-Communist government was formed which included leading Chartists. Before the year's end – on 28 December 1989 – Alexander Dubček, who had been the reformist First Secretary of the Communist Party in 1968, was co-opted to be Chairman of the Federal Assembly (Speaker of the Parliament) and the following day that still otherwise unreconstructed body bent before the winds of change and elected Havel as President of Czechoslovakia.

In Bulgaria the long-serving Communist leader, Todor Zhivkov, was deposed in what was essentially a palace coup one day after the Berlin Wall was breached in November 1989. Between then and multi-party elections in October 1991, Bulgaria made a peaceful transition to democracy. So, too, did Albania, which over many years had been the most repressive country in Europe. Albania was outside the Soviet bloc, but not immune to contagion from what was happening within it. In December 1990 a meeting of the ruling Communist party agreed to the legalization of opposition parties, and the following day the Democratic Party of Albania (DPA) was formed. In elections held in 1991, the new party fared less well than the successor party to the Communists, the Socialist Party of Albania, but in 1992 the DPA won an overwhelming victory. Not one of these peaceful transformations of political systems in East-Central Europe amounted to a revolution in the normal sense of the term.[115]

Only in Romania, where the example of the changes in the Soviet Union influenced the popular mood but where the Soviet leadership had long ceased to have leverage, was there something that looked more like a revolution (but which, nevertheless, did not meet the criteria of Huntington or Dunn). The regime used brutal force in the attempt to suppress those who demonstrated against the dictatorial rule of Nicolae Ceauşescu. There was violence also from some of Ceauşescu's opponents within the system as well as more widespread non-violent resistance on the part of the population. There was a strong element of manipulation of the process with one section of the political elite seizing the opportunity to replace another.[116] East Germany and Yugoslavia were also, in their different ways, exceptions to what was happening elsewhere in Central and Eastern Europe, although in neither instance did it amount to revolution. In the case of the German Democratic Republic, as East Germany was officially known, demonstrations in favour of democratization of the GDR in 1989 were soon superseded by demands for the unification of Germany, leading to a process of negotiation between Mikhail Gorbachev and Helmut Kohl, as the principal actors, which bore fruit in 1990.

In Yugoslavia, national sentiments had the opposite effect. Whereas in Germany, the emphasis on the nation led two states to become joined in one – the enlarged Federal Republic – in Yugoslavia fervid emphasis on nationhood, at the expense of the multinational state, became a source of discord and civil war. By the end of the 1980s Marxism-Leninism had lost whatever appeal it once had, and ever since the death of Tito there had not been a leader who could command respect in all the very unevenly developed republics of Yugoslavia. The Serbian Communist leader Slobodan Milošević led the way in playing the nationalist card. Realizing that Tito's federation was unlikely to survive, he set about creating (or attempting to *recreate*) a Greater Serbia. The consequences were disastrous, but the proper name for that disaster is not revolution.[117]

The systemic change of 1989–91 in Eastern Europe had, then, some common elements, but also much diversity. Communist leaderships which had appeared firmly entrenched, so long as they could count on the backing of Moscow, stepped aside with varying degrees of resentment or resignation. Transnational influences, emanating in the first place from the Soviet Union but then from one Central and East European country to another, played a decisive role. Ideas were critically important – not only the idea of national independence but the aspiration for democracy. Where Moscow's writ had ceased to run years earlier than 1989, but where national Communist leaders had maintained their own domestic authoritarian or totalitarian regimes, the transition from Communism was much less smooth, especially in two of the three cases. The Communist Party of Romania split, more than a thousand people were killed in the clashes that took place between demonstrators and the authorities in December, and Ceauşescu, with the full connivance of some of his former Politburo colleagues, was shot by firing squad on Christmas Day 1989.[118] The Albanian Communists negotiated their own path to political pluralism in a country which was nationally more homogeneous than most. Multinational Yugoslavia disintegrated in bloody civil war, while its successor states over the next two decades felt their way, at very different speeds, to varying degrees of democracy.

LEADERLESS REVOLUTIONS

Whereas indigenous Communist seizures of power have been led by a ruling group within those parties, often with one especially authoritative figure playing a decisive role, many revolutions break out so suddenly that even the most organized of opposition groups are taken by surprise. Thus, Sun Yat-sen was in Colorado when the Chinese revolution of 1911 broke out and Lenin was in Switzerland when the first of Russia's two revolutions of 1917 occurred. Revolutions in the Middle East in more recent times have also been more leaderless than led. That is true even of the Iranian revolution of 1979 as well as of the revolutionary upheaval in the Arab world in the second decade of the twenty-first century.

The Iranian Revolution

The Iranian revolution of 1977–79 saw vast popular demonstrations against the rule of Shah Reza Pahlavi, with as many as two million people on some occasions taking to the streets, in defiance of the secret police. Although most of the demonstrations were peaceful, there was violence as well, especially from the side of the regime. Iran had a long tradition of street protests, going back at least to the late nineteenth century and, more recently, in support of Muhammad Mossadegh, the liberal nationalist Iranian prime minister who in the early 1950s clashed with the Shah (as well as with British commercial interests) and was ousted in a coup. A first attempt, thought up by the British intelligence service, failed, but MI6 then persuaded the American government that there was an imminent threat of Iran going Communist, and though there was little substance in the claim, it had the effect the British authorities wanted. A second coup, orchestrated by the CIA, succeeded in removing Mossadegh in 1953. It was not only the people of Iran who were the losers, but the Western countries who, by their actions, earned long-lasting Iranian mistrust. Moreover, no subsequent leader of Iran has been as liberal or as relatively democratic as was Mossadegh. The Shah, when no longer shackled by a popular prime minister in the shape of Mossadegh, headed an authoritarian regime. Until he was removed (in a revolution, rather than a coup, in 1979), he was, in contrast with Mossadegh, subservient to Western interests, but only when those were defined as narrowly and short-sightedly as they were in Washington and London.[119]

Crowds returned to the streets of Iran in 1963 in support of Ayatolla Ruhollah Khomeini when he denounced the Shah for granting American military personnel immunity from Iranian laws.[120] Khomeini was, however, exiled from Iran the following year and was not able to return until February 1979 after the revolution had succeeded in ousting the Shah. While for some of those who took part in the series of demonstrations against the Shah's regime, Khomeini and the idea of an Islamic Republic were an inspiration, there were many others who looked back with admiration to the liberal and secular government of Mossadegh. Human rights violations under the Shah came under increased Western scrutiny in the 1970s, and Jimmy Carter's victory in the American presidential election of 1976 gave an undoubted boost to opponents of the regime. During the electoral campaign Carter had referred to Iran as a country which should do more to protect human rights. The Shah was sufficiently concerned to order SAVAK, his secret police, to stop torturing prisoners.[121]

The Shah's partial liberalization allowed many old organizations to reappear – among them Mossadegh's National Front, the Writers' Association, the Association of Teachers, and the Tudeh Party (meaning 'the masses' but, in fact, the Communist Party) – and numerous new ones to appear, including a Committee for the Defence of Political Prisoners and a Committee for the Defence of Human Rights.[122] Demonstrations against the Shah's rule, its associated corruption, and his dependence on foreign interests began in Tehran in 1977 and became more widespread in 1978. There were riots in the city of Tabriz in February. The crowds were dispersed by the military who arrested 650 demonstrators and killed nine of those who had attacked police stations, luxury hotels and the offices of the Iran-American Society and Pepsi Cola. Most of the rioters were young people – students, school pupils and young factory workers. The unrest spread to other cities, and in August 1978 a cinema was burned down, killing the 430 people inside. After martial law was declared in eleven cities in September, the military governor of Tehran ordered troops to disperse the crowds which had gathered, chanting anti-Shah slogans. They fired indiscriminately at them, and even the regime put the number of deaths at eighty-seven. The opposition claimed that at least four thousand people had been killed, an overestimate in response to the authorities' understating the number of deaths. By November the demonstrators themselves were becoming more aggressive, and numerous buildings in Tehran were set alight or ransacked, among them the British Embassy. By the end of the year, many of the soldiers as well as the demonstrators were no longer prepared to put up with the repression. The Shah left Iran, never to return, in January 1979, having 'realized that he had lost control not only of the streets but also of the military', some of whom were refusing to obey orders, deserting, and even handing over weapons to the demonstrators or themselves 'firing at gung-ho officers'.[123]

The Iranian revolution was far from bloodless, although the figure of over sixty thousand 'martyrs' which became official after an Islamist regime was established seems to have been a great exaggeration and

contrasts with the estimate of two sociologists that some three thousand people were killed. Ervand Abrahamian, a specialist on modern
Iranian history, has emphasized that the revolution emerged spontaneously from below rather than being managed from above. He writes:

There were no statewide parties, no systematic networks, and no coordinated
organizations mobilizing the mass protests, meetings, and strikes. On the
contrary, the crowds were often assembled by ad hoc groups, grass-roots
organizations, and, at most, informal networks: classmates in high schools,
colleges, and seminaries; teenagers in the slums; guild members, shop assis-
tants, and occasionally, mosque preachers in the city bazaars.[124]

What happened after the revolution was another matter. Ayatolla
Khomeini and radical Islamists did not make the revolution, but they
were quick to seize the opportunity to become the main beneficiaries
of its success. Moreover, the radical pronouncements of Khomeini
were in tune with widespread public sentiments at the time of the
revolution's triumph. He himself returned to Iran on 1 February 1979,
seventeen days after the Shah had left the country. He was greeted by
an enthusiastic crowd of two million people. The final phase of the
revolution occupied only a few days. Crowds prevented the Shah's
ministers from reaching their offices and broke into armouries, using
the weapons obtained to fight with the only part of the military still
remaining loyal to the Shah's regime, the Imperial Guards.[125] Taken as
a whole, the process showed that revolutions can be made without
leaders but that, even when that happens, leaders will quickly emerge
in the aftermath of the revolution. In Iran that leadership was, and
remains, Islamist – a theocracy in which the religious authorities have
wielded more power than the secular – with Khomeini its most authoritative figure from the time of his return until his death in 1989.

Arab Revolutions of the Twenty-first Century

It is, however, misleading to conflate the diverse groups who made
the Iranian revolution of 1977–79 into radical Islamists, even though
the latter were to find themselves best placed to reap the fruits of the
successful rebellion. The same is even more true of the Arab revolutions that got underway a generation later. The popular uprisings

across much of the Arab world began in December 2010 with an apparently random event. Inspectors in Tunisia confiscated the produce, cart and weights of a poor trader, Mohamed Bouazizi, who was unregistered with the authorities because he did not have the money needed to bribe officials to obtain a permit. In despair about losing everything and at the injustice of his plight, he set fire to himself and died of horrific burns a little over two weeks later.

There were good grounds for revolution in the Arab world – repressive rule of dictatorial leaders, massive unemployment, nepotism, corruption, poverty combined with huge inequality, subjugation of women, sectarianism and intolerance among them. Many could identify with the despair which Bouazizi's self-immolation exemplified. What, for most of the time, had prevented revolution from occurring was justified fear of the terrible retribution that would be meted by the authorities on anyone who rebelled. The BBC's Middle East Editor, Jeremy Bowen, observed in his book, *The Arab Uprisings*:

When I did my first trip to the Middle East after Iraq invaded Kuwait in 1990 I heard some reporters with a lot more experience saying that Arabs like a strong leader. Apparently that trait explained the survival of the likes of Saddam Hussein, even though they imprisoned and often killed their subjects. I realised almost straight away that despots ruled through violence and fear, and that the notion that Arabs liked it was absurd, but I am ashamed to admit that the line might have crept into a few scripts before my brain kicked in.[126]

The uprisings, for which Bouazizi lit a fuse, led to the overthrow of the dictatorial rulers of Tunisia (Zine el-Abidine Ben Ali) and Egypt (Hosni Mubarak) and the capture and killing of Libya's Muammar Gaddafi. The uprising in Yemen led to the resignation of Ali Abdullah Saleh who had been president for more than thirty years, although the outcome has remained ambiguous. He stayed in the country and many security officials, still loyal to him and his family, remained in post.[127] The revolutionary upsurge affected the whole of the Middle East and North Africa, with contagion hugely assisted by the significance of Arabic being a common language across the region; the comprehensibility, accordingly, of the broadcasts of Al Jazeera (including the transmission of amateur videos); the internet; and the widespread availability and use of mobile phones. The Qatari-financed

Al Jazeera played an especially important role in circumventing the censorship of authoritarian regimes and in giving 'voice to the voiceless'.[128]

In virtually every country of the region there was a new belief in the possibility of change, a greater confidence engendered by the sheer numbers of those prepared to resist the regimes, and the energizing example of the overthrow of such firmly established autocracies as those of Ben Ali, Mubarak and Gaddafi. The first two leaders and their entourages were removed entirely by their own citizens. In Gaddafi's case, although Libyans themselves rose up against him and overthrew his regime, they benefited from the NATO air support which they requested and were granted, with the backing of the United Nations. As David Gardner, the former Middle East Editor of the *Financial Times*, has noted, both European and American governments had long been 'wedded to a network of regional strongmen'. The Arab revolutions were a serious challenge to such 'realists' and led to an incoherent response whereby, for example, Libyan rebels were given military help but Bahrain was just mildly rebuked for brutal suppression of unarmed protesters.[129] In most cases, when people first took to the streets against the regimes, the protests were entirely non-violent and that worked to their advantage in getting international opinion on their side. When the regimes predictably turned to repression, varying degrees of violence were used also by the protesters. In Syria, in particular, the result has been prolonged and tragic civil war. Monarchies in the region, although also authoritarian, have survived with fewer problems than the republics. That is partly because their leaders appeared to be accorded a somewhat greater legitimacy than were self-appointed republican despots. Their (nevertheless precarious) survival was also aided by their making some mildly liberal compromises as well as by more substantial material concessions which helped to dampen down discontent. In Jordan and Morocco, in particular, reforms were introduced in 2011 precisely to forestall radical demands or revolutionary upheaval.

The hereditary principle has been more readily accepted in states ruled by monarchs, in which it is a traditional and basic norm of the system, than in republics where it is seen as usurpers adding insult to injury. Thus, the fact that Mubarak, Gaddafi and Saleh all had plans to be succeeded by one of their sons only added to the popular clamour in Egypt, Libya and Yemen to remove them. The hereditary transfer of power had already taken place in Syria at the turn of the century and subsequent experience has hardly been an advertisement for this mode of political succession. Although initially Bashar al-Assad seemed an improvement over his ruthless father, Hafez al-Assad, the ferocity and indiscriminate character of the violence used against those who – peacefully in the first instance (although not for long) – rose up against his regime was reminiscent of the elder Assad. As a leading analyst of the Middle Eastern revolutions has noted, 'not only the dictators but their sons and heirs' have come to be 'regarded as evil and as symbols of the wickedness of the regime'.[130]

The Arab revolutions of 2011, both those which succeeded in toppling the old regime and those which did not, were essentially leaderless. Where there has been a prolonged struggle, as in Syria, organized groups, including Islamist ones, have come to play a more prominent role in the fight even while the old regime has remained precariously in place, but in the revolutions which succeeded most quickly – those of Tunisia and Egypt – massive resistance to the regime emanated from a wide variety of social groups and took the authorities by surprise. The very fact that leaders could not be identified – and accordingly eliminated – was confusing for the regimes under threat. If the young, educated and middle class played a disproportionately prominent part in the upheaval, the more successful revolutions benefited from the participation of the poor who provided the numbers and who had 'no stake in the old world and nothing to lose by rising up'.[131] There were, naturally, informal leaders even in street demonstrations, but they tended not to belong to formal structures such as political parties or trade unions, nor were they 'charismatic' leaders. Rather, they were internet activists who were committed to spreading word of the demonstrations and of the cruelties of the regime's response, thus helping to mobilize their friends and engage still wider circles.[132]

In the aftermath of those Arab uprisings which have succeeded in removing essentially secular autocrats (all of whom, however, paid varying degrees of lip-service to Islam), the advantages of a leaderless revolution turned into a disadvantage (as in Iran in 1979). The best-organized groups moved rapidly to fill the vacuum and the new leaders were more intent on imposing their will than on building consensus and democratic institutions. The 2012 election in Egypt (which was democratic at least to the extent that the votes were honestly counted and the result not known in advance) was reduced to a choice between two candidates who were not to the liking of a great many people who had risked much to demand the removal of Mubarak. They were asked to choose between Mubarak's last prime minister, Ahmed Shafiq, who was backed by the military, and a leading member of the Muslim Brotherhood, Mohammed Morsi, who won a narrow victory. Many secular Egyptians who were distrustful of the Brotherhood voted for Morsi on the grounds that to support a prominent member of the Mubarak regime would mean that the sacrifices of those who had died or been maimed in the revolution had been in vain.

In Egypt and elsewhere, the Muslim Brothers had gained prestige from the very fact that they had been imprisoned and persecuted by the secular autocracies, and had earned some popularity for the charitable services they provided to the poor. The fact that they had an existing organization meant that they were much better prepared than were secular liberals to flourish in the post-revolutionary political climate. Yet it appears, as Olivier Roy has argued, that the 'Arab Spring took the Brothers by surprise'.[133] Research on public opinion in the Arab world has shown deep divisions in most countries on the role religion should play in politics, with the exception of Lebanon where there is a consensus that its influence should be minimal, reflecting sectarian divisions and fears of a return to devastating civil war along religious lines.[134] In most of the Arab countries surveyed, there was an emerging consensus that the clergy 'should not seek to affect the political behavior of ordinary citizens' but significant disagreement on how much influence religious officials should have on governmental decisions. For a majority of Arab respondents, though – and this was quite notably so in Tunisia and Egypt – economic issues were at the top of people's agenda. Unemployment and inflation were the problems that most worried them, followed in order of importance by corruption.[135]

Although the Muslim Brotherhood were not the prime movers in carrying out the revolution of 2011, they were its main initial beneficiaries. Those who worried about their capacity to govern democratically but gave Morsi the benefit of the doubt at the time of the presidential election soon had their doubts rather than their hopes amply reinforced. Morsi's popularity had dropped from 57 per cent at the time of his election in mid-2012 to 28 per cent by May 2013.[136] What was more fundamental was his use of a narrow majority to push through partisan changes rather than build consensus. A new constitution was ratified in a turnout of only 32 per cent of eligible voters. There could scarcely have been a sharper contrast between the manner in which Mohammed Morsi proceeded to govern and the way that Adolfo Suárez used the powers conferred upon him in the Spanish transition to democracy (discussed in Chapter 4). Morsi had, of course, a host of problems to contend with, quite apart from the teetering economy, which was the biggest issue for many Egyptians. The institutions of the 'deep state' that had developed in Mubarak's time – the army, the security forces, a significant part of the judiciary and of big business – were distrustful of the Muslim Brotherhood. The military had managed to emerge from the revolution of 2011 with its authority enhanced, since it had acquiesced in the removal of Mubarak. Opponents of the Morsi government were to be found on several different flanks. It had even disappointed more extreme Islamists, the Salafis, who had briefly formed an alliance with it. So far as they were concerned, the government was *too* liberal and insufficiently committed to a rigid interpretation of their religion. Above all, the secular liberals had every reason to be disappointed with Morsi's use of his small electoral majority to exclude them from the political process.

These failures meant that there was widespread support from many sections of society for the military coup that toppled the government in early July 2013 and placed Morsi under arrest. Not for the first time, those who had played a major part in overturning an unpopular autocratic regime felt that the revolution had been betrayed. Both the way Morsi governed and the manner in which he was, in turn, removed from power illustrated the advantages of a pact-making process whereby in some of the most successful transitions from authoritarianism to democracy – most notably Spain – very broad agreement was reached, as a result of bargaining and compromise, on the new rules of the game. The Morsi government showed little interest in or understanding of the need for 'societal' as distinct from 'majoritarian' legitimacy. Interestingly, a scholarly opinion survey conducted in Egypt in December 2011 found strong support for democracy, rejection of the idea that what the country needed was a strong leader even if that person overthrew democracy, *and* this was accompanied by more than 60 per cent of the population rejecting also the statement 'the military should withdraw entirely from political life for good'. That last opinion might seem, on the face of it, to be at odds with the first two. It appears, though, that with their recent experience in mind, many Egyptians had come to see the military as the ultimate guardians of the democracy they desired.[137] The majority who were ready to concede a political role for the military would include also people who were content with Egypt the way it was under Mubarak.

This helps to explain the breadth of the alliance in support of the forcible overthrow of the Morsi government in July 2013. It embraced those nostalgic for the Mubarak regime and determined to hold on to their former privileges and some of that old regime's most dedicated liberal and democratic opponents. Yet it is hard to see how the overturning of the result of a reasonably democratic presidential election will promote legitimate rule. It is equally difficult to comprehend how the banning of Egypt's largest social movement, the Muslim Brotherhood, is compatible with democracy. For the military elite who seized power, and who did not hesitate to kill hundreds of Brotherhood protesters, these may not be issues that particularly trouble them, but for the 'liberals' who cheered them on it seems all too likely that disillusionment with the results of violent overthrow of a regime will once again follow.

★

Some revolutions, then, are led – as in Russia in November 1917 or Cuba in 1958–59 – and others are relatively leaderless, as in Tunisia and Egypt in 2011. It is clear that regime change of itself does not necessarily require an established organization, an outstanding leader or even a handful of leaders but can, in a revolutionary situation, be a much wider, looser and unstructured movement. That is not to deny that in *some* revolutions particular leaders have been so important that the system would not have changed *when* it did, or would have changed in *very different ways*, in their absence. When the opportunity of holding leaders and regimes accountable for their misdeeds is absent, the case for systemic change is overwhelming. When that can be done by peaceful means, as it was in post-Franco Spain or in Eastern Europe in 1989, this is hugely preferable to revolution. In the last resort, however, there is justification for violent revolution – the forcible removal of tyrants from power – when all attempts to change an oppressive system by peaceful means have failed. What follows, however, seldom lives up to the rhetoric and hopes of the more idealistic of the revolutionaries, as most of the cases examined in this chapter and the next illustrate all too clearly.

6

Totalitarian and Authoritarian Leadership

The first, and perhaps only, dictator to use the adjective 'totalitarian' as one of warm approval was Benito Mussolini in inter-war Italy. It had been employed as early as 1923 by the Duce's opponents, but two years later was embraced by his supporters and by Mussolini himself. He spoke of 'our fierce totalitarian will' and continued: 'We want to make the nation fascist, so that tomorrow Italians and Fascists . . . will be the same thing.'[1] Mussolini liked to describe the system constructed under his leadership as *lo stato totalitario*, the totalitarian state.[2] He had borrowed the term from the Italian philosopher Giovanni Gentile who became an ideologist of fascism. Gentile's German equivalent was Carl Schmitt, an academic lawyer who provided some of the intellectual foundation for Hitler's dictatorship, arguing that 'the *Führer*' stood higher than any state institution and that he was 'the highest judge of the nation and the highest lawgiver'.[3] Schmitt, too, approved of the notion of the 'totalitarian state', but Hitler rarely used the term and, when he did so, prefaced it with 'so-called'.[4] Communist leaders and ideologists never applied 'totalitarian' to their own systems and only occasionally when referring to fascist states.[5]

Although the notion of totalitarianism predated both 'high Stalinism', a term coined to describe the Soviet Union from the early 1930s until Stalin's death in 1953, and the coming to power of Hitler, it was critics of both fascist and Communist systems who most commonly spoke of totalitarianism. What gave the term traction was the observation in the 1930s that, obvious differences of policy and goals notwithstanding, there were a number of notable similarities between the Soviet and Nazi regimes headed by Josif Stalin and Adolf Hitler, even though they claimed to be polar opposites. Both in the Soviet Union and in Germany there was a hierarchical single party which existed in parallel with, but had a superior authority to, governmental institutions at all levels.[6] There was in both countries a political police force which in the 1930s employed terror and violence, although more selectively in pre-war Germany than in the Soviet Union where at times it was on a mass scale. Each of these regimes had also a body of doctrine which purported to explain both history and contemporary society, providing a framework into which all social phenomena could be fitted. The doctrines themselves were very different, of course, with the ideas of Marx and Lenin (even in their Stalinist codified version) much the more sophisticated of the two. Each ideology offered a vision of the future – in the Nazi case that of a racially pure and powerful greater Germany and in the Soviet case of a harmonious, classless society. These imaginary futures were of far less consequence than scapegoating and violent repression in the present. In Germany millions responded to propaganda which portrayed Jews as the source of the world's ills and of Germany's misfortunes most specifically, while in the Soviet Union millions approved of the punishment of class enemies and bought into the myth that Stalin's tyrannical rule meant that the working class had gained power in what was represented as a 'dictatorship of the proletariat.'* Both regimes were also characterized by a cult of personality of the Great Leader.

The term 'totalitarian' gained still wider currency after the Second World War when it was often applied indiscriminatingly to all Communist states, although there were significant changes over time

---

* Whether those millions constituted a majority or a minority of Soviet citizens remains a subject of debate. The collectivization of agriculture created deep unhappiness in the countryside, and peasants in the 1930s still made up the majority of the population. However, the fact that even in the twenty-first century Stalin frequently tops the poll when citizens of post-Soviet Russia are asked to name the greatest leader of their country in the twentieth century suggests that propaganda which associated all the country's successes – above all, victory in the Second World War – with him and blamed failures, oppression and atrocities on others had a profound impact and left its mark on the consciousness of a substantial part of the population.

within these countries as well as substantial differences between one and another. There is, for example, a vast dissimilarity between contemporary China and contemporary North Korea. And to apply the same undifferentiating label of 'totalitarian' to Poland and Hungary when they were under Communist rule, to Tito's Yugoslavia in the 1960s and 1970s and to North Korea under any of the three successive Kims is unhelpful. In these three European Communist countries some elements of civil society existed (the Church was especially important in Poland), while being entirely absent in North Korea. Communist political systems were – and, where they still survive, are – never less than highly authoritarian, but to put them all in the more extreme totalitarian container is to obscure important differences.[7]

The very notion of totalitarianism is controversial. There are scholars who reject its application even to the Soviet Union from the early 1930s (by which time Stalin had consolidated his power) until Stalin's death or to Hitler's Germany from the mid-1930s to the country's defeat in 1945, making the point that not everything was controlled from above. If, however, totalitarianism were to be defined as a system in which one person decides everything, then there has never been such a system. That, however, is no more a reason for completely eschewing the term than the imperfections of all actually existing democracies are a reason for refusing to call any country democratic. It is evident that total control, especially over people's thinking, existed only in the pages of George Orwell's *Nineteen Eighty-Four*.[8] But Orwell himself was well aware that in depicting tendencies he observed in Communism and fascism, he was not providing a precise description of social reality but was drawing out 'totalitarian ideas . . . to their logical consequences'.* For Orwell, totalitarianism was what Max

* The fuller context is that of Orwell's distress about the misunderstanding, especially common in the United States, of *Nineteen Eight-Four* as an attack on socialism. Orwell made clear that he was, and remained, a 'democratic Socialist'. (He continued to spell 'Socialism' with a capital 'S'.) Thus, he wrote to an official of the United Automobile Workers in the USA, who had been troubled by the good reception *Nineteen Eighty-Four* had received in right-wing American publications: 'My recent novel is NOT intended as an attack on Socialism or on the British Labour Party (of which I am a supporter) but as a show-up of the perversions to which a centralized economy is liable and which have been partly realized in Communism and Fascism. I do not believe that the kind of society I describe necessarily *will* arrive, but I believe (allowing of course for the fact that the book is a satire) that something resembling

Weber called an 'ideal type' (by which, needless to say, Weber was not in any way implying a positive evaluation). Weber argued that it was analytically useful to express in extreme or pure form what was meant by a particular political or social category – as, for example, bureaucracy, the subject of one of his most famous analyses.[9]

It makes sense, similarly, to present the features of totalitarianism in stark and extreme terms. Particular countries can then be studied to see if they come sufficiently close to the ideal type to be meaningfully described as totalitarian. This is preferable to constantly changing the definition (as tended to happen during the Cold War years), so that Communist states generally, or the Soviet Union specifically, would always remain 'totalitarian', no matter how much they might change internally. That tendency led, in turn, to another confusion, most clearly exemplified by the American scholar, Jeane Kirkpatrick, who was the Reagan administration's ambassador to the UN in the first half of the 1980s. She helped to popularize the view that all Communist regimes were totalitarian and that whereas authoritarian systems, or what she called 'right-wing autocracies', could be changed from within, totalitarian regimes could not.[10] Thus, the Soviet Union, in particular, would be impervious to change emanating from inside the system or from Soviet society. Proponents of this widespread view confused the abstract notion of totalitarianism with actual Communist states. They failed to see that a number of Communist systems had in the post-Stalin era become more authoritarian than totalitarian and that within the ruling Communist parties themselves, there was diversity of view behind the monolithic façade they presented to their own societies and to the outside world.

Adherents of the totalitarian-and-impervious-to-change school overlooked also the importance of educational advancements under Communism – the development not only of universal literacy but also of substantial higher education sectors within these societies. If Communism contained 'the seeds of its own destruction' (to use Marx's phrase about capitalism), it was through educating people to

---

it *could* arrive. I believe also that totalitarian ideas have taken root in the minds of intellectuals everywhere, and I have tried to draw these ideas out to their logical consequences.' (Cited by Bernard Crick, *George Orwell: A Life*, Penguin, Harmondsworth, 1980, p. 569.)

the point at which they were open to new ideas and less inclined to accept outdated dogmas uncritically. Those who thought that Communist systems were immune to change from within also overlooked the fact that *leadership* – which played an important part in the transition to Communist rule, as well as in sustaining it – could be an instrument of transformative change.

In political and social reality totalitarian and authoritarian regimes are located on a continuum. At one end there is the totalitarian extreme of Enver Hoxha's Albania or Kim Il Sung's North Korea and at the other end the mild authoritarianism of Singapore, which, while not a democracy, has a vibrant market economy and, for most practical purposes, a rule of law. In between there are countries about which there can be legitimate argument as to whether they come close enough to ideal-typical totalitarianism to be called totalitarian or whether they are better described as authoritarian. There may be some dispersal of power within the group at the apex of the hierarchy, but in a *totalitarian* as distinct from authoritarian system, one man (and all such regimes have been male-dominated) holds preponderant, and often supreme, power. *Authoritarian* regimes, in contrast, can be *either* autocracies or oligarchies. In other words, some are ruled by a single dictator and others have a more collective leadership. Even within the oligarchies, a leader's personality and values have the potential to make a bigger difference to the system than is open to a leader in a democracy where power is more dispersed and both institutions and public opinion impose stricter limits on what a leader may do.

STALIN'S DICTATORSHIP AND SOVIET OLIGARCHIES

Adam Smith noted that 'gross abuse' of power, as well as 'perverseness, absurdity, and unreasonableness' were more liable to be found under the rule of 'single persons' than of larger assemblies.[11] While it would be foolish to deny – and Smith did not do so – that groups are also capable of coming to stupid decisions or of sponsoring dreadful actions, unconstrained personal rule is more dangerous. In the experience of the two major Communist states, the Soviet Union and China, periods of more collective leadership were far less devastating and murderous than those during which Stalin and Mao Zedong wielded their greatest individual power. In the Soviet case there was a basically collective leadership for at least a decade after the 1917 Bolshevik revolution, first under Lenin and then under Stalin, while the latter was still gradually strengthening his power base. So long as Lenin was alive, he was the most influential figure in the Communist Party, although his highest formal position was as head of the government (Chairman of the Council of People's Commissars) rather than of the party. Within the party leadership, however, Lenin relied on his political prestige, natural authority and powers of persuasion to carry the day. Inside his own party, he did not employ the type of coercion and terror he visited on those who stood in the way of the Communists' consolidation of their power. The fact, however, that Stalin became the most notorious mass murderer in the last hundred years of Russian history does not absolve Lenin from creating many of the preconditions for Stalin's tyranny. It was Lenin who played a decisive role in destroying a fragile political pluralism and in laying the foundations of future dictatorship with his emphasis on centralization of power within a single party, his contempt for parliamentary politics, his rejection of judicial independence, and the creation of punitive political police organs.

Until the late 1920s Stalin, as Lenin's successor, was gradually consolidating his authority, siding first with one group and then another in the leadership of the Communist Party, while avoiding the appearance of seeking dictatorial power. By 1929 Stalin was clearly the predominant Soviet leader, although some elements of collective leadership were still present even at the beginning of the 1930s. By 1933, however, as a leading specialist on this period of Soviet history has observed, Stalin 'was already a personal dictator, whose proposals were apparently never challenged in the Politburo'.[12] The most notable of Stalin's rivals, Leon Trotsky, had been successively expelled first from the top leadership and then from the party (in 1927), sent into internal exile in 1928, and expelled from the Soviet Union in 1929. Later, many of the leading revolutionaries of 1917, including Nikolay Bukharin, were to be killed at Stalin's behest. For a majority this meant execution following Moscow show-trials in 1936–38; for Trotsky it involved assassination with an ice-pick by one of Stalin's NKVD agents in Mexico in 1940.

Most of the 1920s, in contrast with the 1930s, were a time when some debate still took place within the Communist Party of the Soviet Union, although other political parties had been outlawed. After the Russian Civil War Lenin's New Economic Policy included economic concessions to the peasantry which persisted during the period of more collective leadership until the late twenties. From 1929 Stalin spearheaded the campaign of compulsory collectivization of agriculture, which by the end of 1933 had resulted in the deportation from their locality of more than two million peasants. Famine, which was a consequence of the high grain procurement quotas the state demanded from the collectivized peasantry, brought about the deaths of more than five million people in Ukraine, southern Russia and the North Caucasus.[13] Stalin took a particularly close interest in the collectivization process, and personally insisted on the introduction of the death penalty (by a decree issued on 7 August 1932) for theft of grain from collective farm fields.[14]

Stalin was determined to achieve the speedy industrialization of the country and, accompanied by rapid social mobility, this made great strides in the 1930s, but at a terrible price. It was obviously impossible for Stalin personally to take every major decision in the Soviet Union, even when he was at the height of his power. Power was wielded not only by Stalin but by bureaucracies at different levels of the system, and these bodies acquired, and attempted to defend, institutional interests of their own. Stalin, however, did succeed in destroying 'the oligarchical system' that had developed in the 1920s and, as the Russian scholar who has studied his rule most closely observes, at the root of his personal dictatorship was his 'limitless power' over 'the fate of any Soviet official, including the members of the Politburo'.[15]

Stalin took a more detailed interest in some institutions than others. In particular, he kept the organs of state security – the political police – under his close control, and supervised the repression. In two years alone, 1937–38, more than 1.7 million people were arrested and at least 818,000 of them were shot.[16] They included vast numbers of imaginary enemies of the Soviet state and of Stalin, and somewhat smaller numbers of real anti-Communists. Among the victims were several members of the Politburo as well as a large proportion of the senior army officer corps. The latter included, as an especially notable casualty, Marshal Tukhachevsky who had fought on the Bolshevik side in the civil war and later played a key role in the modernization of the Red Army. With his tight control over the NKVD, Stalin wielded a power of life and death over his 'colleagues'. He also spread his net far wider.

Some social groups were targeted more than others. The old nobility, clerics, intellectuals and peasants were, in proportion to their numbers, more likely to be arrested than were industrial workers. By the later 1930s, when Stalin was increasingly looking for the enemy within, high party and state officials were frequent victims of his chronic distrust. And successive heads of the political police, the very body that carried out the purges, stood exceptionally high chances of being executed. No social group or individual could feel immune from the risk of arrest for crimes that (unlike those of the NKVD) were often more imaginary than real. It has been rightly observed that Stalin's use of mass repression 'set his regime apart from its Leninist predecessor and from the selective use of repression employed by successive Soviet regimes'.[17]

Nikita Khrushchev, Stalin's successor, illustrated both the potential and the pitfalls of leadership within a system that some would still regard as totalitarian but by then is more aptly described as post-totalitarian authoritarianism. Like Stalin, he used the most senior position in the party – the General Secretaryship, renamed First Secretaryship during the Khrushchev era – to bring his supporters into the top leadership team and thus gradually enhanced his already strong position. It did not, however, become anything like the grotesque power that Stalin accumulated. Khrushchev, whose own hands in the Stalin era were very far from bloodless, displayed courageous leadership when he attacked Stalin, whose genius and godlike infallibility had been hailed for three decades, in a closed-session speech to delegates at the Twentieth Party Congress in 1956 and, openly, at the Twenty-Second Congress in 1961. He made the 1956 breakthrough speech against the wishes of some senior members of the Presidium of the Central Committee (as the Politburo was known at the time).

Among those anxious to preserve the late dictator's image intact, Vyacheslav Molotov, Lazar Kaganovich and Kliment Voroshilov were especially vocal. Molotov declared at a Presidium meeting that 'Stalin was the great continuer of Lenin's work' and that 'under the leadership of Stalin, socialism was victorious'.[18] Khrushchev replied: 'Stalin was a betrayer of socialism, and by the most barbaric means. He annihilated the party. He was no Marxist.' Rather than protect Stalin's memory, Khrushchev insisted, they needed to 'intensify the bombardment of the cult of personality'.[19] One of Khrushchev's closest allies in the party leadership on the issue of destalinization, Anastas Mikoyan, later wrote:

'He had the character of a leader: persistence, obstinacy in pursuit of a goal, courage, and a willingness to go against the prevailing stereotypes.' When Khrushchev was seized of a new idea, Mikoyan added, there would be no measured response. He 'moved forward like a tank'. That could have its disadvantages, but, said Mikoyan, it was an excellent quality for a leader engaged in the battle for destalinization.[20]

The fears of Khrushchev's opponents within the leadership about the consequences of attacking Stalin seemed to them all too justified when the February 1956 speech had huge repercussions within the international Communist movement. It shook the faith of many party members worldwide and stimulated unrest in Eastern Europe, especially Poland and Hungary. Before the end of the year, revolution against Communist rule had broken out in Hungary and it was put down ruthlessly by Soviet tanks. Blaming Khrushchev for destabilizing international Communism, a majority of the Presidium attempted to depose him in 1957. Khrushchev outmanoeuvred them by appealing over their heads to the Central Committee, the larger body in which he had more supporters, many of them recently promoted by him. In principle, the Central Committee had a still higher authority than the Presidium (Politburo), but normally it did the bidding of that smaller group. Given an open split in the inner leadership team, the Central Committee had a choice of whom to follow. In 1957 they rallied behind Khrushchev. It was a different story in 1964 when a much more overwhelming majority of the Presidium had decided to get rid of Khrushchev (with only Mikoyan prepared to put in a word for him). This time the Central Committee gave their full support to the party leader's opponents. Khrushchev had, they believed, acted increasingly capriciously and unilaterally. As they saw it, he had undermined the interests of virtually every institution and elite group within the system.

While Khrushchev deserves real credit for beginning the process of destalinization, his own progression from heading a collective leadership in the mid-1950s to making impulsive and arbitrary decisions by the early 1960s was damaging and dangerous. The decision to place Soviet missiles in Cuba, which brought the world close to nuclear war in 1962, was Khrushchev's. Domestically, he was doing more harm than good to the economy. Like Stalin, he was taken in by the quack scientist Trofim Lysenko, backing his useless nostrums for increasing agricultural production and ignoring the evidence produced by serious specialists. Infuriated by opposition from within the Academy of Sciences and the Agricultural Academy, Khrushchev called in July 1964 for the Academy of Sciences to be abolished and the Agricultural Academy to be banished from Moscow and reconstructed in the countryside.[21] These things did not happen, for already his senior colleagues were playing for time and just waiting for the optimal moment to remove a leader who had become increasingly autocratic as well as irascible and unpredictable. They struck on 14 October 1964, calling him back from vacation to Moscow to send him into compulsory retirement. A *Pravda* editorial two days later did not even mention Khrushchev by name but spoke of 'harebrained scheming, half-baked conclusions and hasty decisions and actions divorced from reality, bragging and bluster, attraction to rule by fiat' and an 'unwillingness to take into account what science and practical experience have already worked out'.[22] Although that was not the whole story of Khrushchev's leadership, it was certainly part of it.

With the elevation of Leonid Brezhnev, in succession to Khrushchev, as leader of the Soviet Communist Party in 1964, eighteen years of more collective leadership ensued. Once again the general secretary was able to use the political resources available to the holder of that office to strengthen his authority over time, and in the 1970s a series of ever more absurd honours were heaped on Brezhnev, including the Order of Victory, the highest award for military valour, for Brezhnev's role in the Second World War (which had not seemed quite so remarkable at the time) and the Lenin Prize for literature, the highest award available to writers, which Brezhnev received for his slim volumes of ghosted memoirs. Brezhnev and his Politburo colleagues were happy to allow the KGB to use a variety of methods to quell any overt manifestations of dissent within Soviet society – from warnings to lengthy imprisonment in labour camps or incarceration in mental hospitals. How could you be sane, the question seemed to be, if you thought you could challenge the power of the Soviet state? With dissidents who enjoyed great prestige, both internationally and with a significant minority of Soviet citizens, different methods were used. Thus, the writer Aleksandr Solzhenitsyn – anti-Communist but more Russian nationalist than liberal – was forcibly expelled from the country, with his Soviet citizenship revoked, and the physicist and liberal critic of many of the party leadership's actions, Andrey Sakharov, was sent into internal exile.

As these measures underline, Brezhnev was a conservative Communist. Even the anti-Stalinism that Khrushchev had set in motion was put into reverse. Stalin was not fully rehabilitated, but it became easier to praise him in print than to criticize him. Brezhnev's basic position was that all rocking of the boat should be strictly discouraged. But in dealing with the various Soviet elites – the higher echelons of the party, the military, the KGB and the ministries – his style was conciliatory. The Brezhnev era was the golden age of the Soviet bureaucrat. Stalin had threatened (and often taken) their lives. Khrushchev had threatened (and often removed) their security of tenure. With Brezhnev presiding in the Kremlin, they were allowed to grow old together, in comfort and with little to fear. With its lack of freedom, shortage of consumer goods, and long queues even for basic foodstuffs, it was far from a golden age for the average citizen, and yet when Russians were asked in a serious survey conducted at the end of the twentieth century what was the best time to have lived in Russia in those last hundred years, the Brezhnev era was mentioned more often than any other.[23] It was seen as a time of predictability and stability.

Under Stalin anyone could be arrested, even if they were not in the least critical of the regime. The secret police had quotas to fulfil, Stalin was chronically suspicious, and you could be the subject of an anonymous denunciation by a neighbour who coveted your apartment. In the Brezhnev era, you had actually to do something to attract hostile attention from the authorities. These could be activities that would be regarded as perfectly legal in a democracy, but which in the Soviet Union led to severe sanctions – such as calling for greater national autonomy (in, for instance, Ukraine or Lithuania), circulating banned creative literature in typescript, or writing a letter of protest (about, for example, the hounding of Solzhenitsyn and Sakharov). In contrast, Soviet citizens who observed all the outward proprieties could feel reasonably secure. Under Stalin, hundreds of thousands of arrests were quite arbitrary. In the Brezhnev era there were discernible rules of the game.

A number of senior figures in the Politburo in addition to Brezhnev carried weight in the 1970s, among them Mikhail Suslov, Aleksey Kosygin, Andrey Gromyko and Dmitriy Ustinov. The regime was never less than highly authoritarian, but in their own homes people were no longer afraid to speak freely, in contrast with Stalin's time. Paradoxically, there were more true believers that the Soviet Union was building a new society, one that would be vastly superior to anything in the contemporary West, during the years of Stalin's terror in the later 1930s than were to be found in the 1970s. That kind of optimism also existed, and had even taken a new lease of life, under Khrushchev. This had been, among other things, the era in which the Soviet Union put the first person in space, a source of great pride for most Russians. The Brezhnev era, in contrast, was one of growing cynicism. It was a period of 'doublethink', to use Orwell's term, in which people could simultaneously proclaim the superiority and eventual triumph of the Soviet system while envying the standard of living in the West, yearning for its products and dreaming of spending some time there. Crucially, however, essentially collective leadership was at least a vast improvement over Stalin's dictatorship. The conditions of life in 1977 were qualitatively better for Soviet citizens, whether manual workers, peasants or well-educated professionals, than they were in 1937. The collective caution of the top leadership team did not inflict remotely as much pain on their own people as Stalin had done.

PERSONAL RULE VERSUS OLIGARCHY IN CHINA

A similar pattern can be discerned in the other Communist giant, China. The greatest disasters occurred during the period when Mao Zedong wielded untrammelled power. In contrast, the Chinese Communists had some notable achievements in the early years after the success of their revolution in 1949 and again after Mao's death. Between 1949 and 1957, the new Communist government brought inflation under control, largely eliminated corruption, and made substantial strides in industrialization. During this time hundreds of thousands of people were killed by the new regime, and so the period should certainly not be idealized, but there were more real achievements and fewer premature deaths than in the years of Mao's greatest individual exercise of power.

Even in the first half of the 1950s, Mao Zedong unquestionably had a higher authority than any of his colleagues, but his individual impact on policy was quite limited. That was partly because China was drawing heavily on Soviet experience, while carefully avoiding at that stage some of the worst Soviet excesses in the collectivization of agriculture. The Chinese leadership shared a commitment to rapid economic development and technological advance, although opinions differed on the speed and manner in which this could be achieved. Mao in those years held a 'relatively centrist position' that 'served to ameliorate conflict and build a consensus rather than polarize differences within the leadership'.[24] Until the mid-1950s, as two leading specialists on Chinese politics have noted, 'Mao seemed tolerant of debate in the Politburo, even accepting defeat on economic policy.'[25] It is not accidental that in all the time China was under Mao's leadership, these years saw the most solid accomplishments. Disaster beckoned when Mao decided he knew better than any specialists and bulldozed his colleagues into approving in 1958 what was called the 'Great Leap Forward'.

The Great Leap was immediately preceded by the Hundred Flowers movement, which gained its name from Mao's remark, 'Let a hundred flowers bloom in culture' and 'let a hundred schools of thought contend'.[26] Nikita Khrushchev was not the only one who thought that what Mao wanted was to get critics to reveal themselves, so that he could identify and deal with them. Yet one impetus to this apparent liberalization had been Khrushchev's own exposure of at least some of the crimes of Stalin. It had become prudent for Mao at such a time to attempt to demonstrate that he was nothing like the Soviet dictator. Mao was willing to encourage criticism of specific errors, while having absolutely no desire to let loose fundamental critiques of the Communist system. The criticism that did ensue was clearly more than he had bargained for, with serious differences of opinion within the Communist Party revealed. Mao's own position in the Politburo was weakened in 1957, and his response was to re-emphasize the importance of class struggle and to launch an 'anti-rightist campaign'. It led to the expulsion from the party of several hundred thousand members.[27] The Great Leap Forward, which he next embarked upon, was an exercise in mass mobilization in which Mao stopped listening to engineers and technologists, including well-qualified specialists from the Soviet Union, and sidelined the institutions of the Chinese central government. Inspirational ideology, so it appeared, was about to make expertise redundant. Huge 'people's communes' were created in the countryside, as Mao sought to bring closer the ultimate goal of building Communism, as well as setting the more prosaic target of overtaking Britain economically within fifteen years. No heed was paid either to material obstacles or to professional advice. Once this mass mobilization was underway, false reporting suggested increased grain output, whereas in reality there had been a drastic drop. Mao's man-made catastrophe was not helped by nature, for there were serious floods in 1959 and 1960.

Along with the deliberate killing of tens of thousands of those who dragged their feet, rather than making the 'Great Leap', at least thirty million people – forty-five million according to a recent high-end estimate based on research in provincial Chinese archives – died prematurely between 1958 and 1961, mainly of starvation and also of disease, to which malnourished and exhausted workers were especially prone.[28] Liu Shaoqi, who was at the time the number two person in the Politburo and Mao's putative successor, went as close to criticizing Mao as was possible in a speech in January 1962 when he attributed the disastrous consequences of the Great Leap 30 per cent to bad weather and the withdrawal of Soviet aid, but 70 per cent to bad political decisions.[29] The venture had been Mao's personal initiative and was driven ruthlessly by him. The tragedy it produced was on such a scale that a more orderly government had to be reintroduced in the early 1960s to put the state and society together again. The collegiality of the first half of the 1950s was not, however, restored. In 1962, with the Great Leap Forward abandoned, Mao 'disrupted the ongoing national recovery effort by forcing his colleagues to accept renewed class struggle' and made it clear that he would tolerate no opposition.[30]

Institutions which had been downgraded, especially in the three-year period of 1959–1961, were, nevertheless, restored to something approaching Communist normality. Mao believed that it was *his* radical initiatives that were now being watered down and rendered more innocuous by the bureaucracy. Although his position in the early 1960s as the pre-eminent leader was hardly in doubt, other leaders also enjoyed considerable authority. They included such senior officials as Liu Shaoqi, Deng Xiaoping and the First Secretary of the Beijing party organization, Peng Zhen. Mao not only wanted to place himself on a still higher pedestal, he also retained an enthusiasm for ultra-radical ideas. Having been very critical of Soviet 'revisionism' under Khrushchev, he became increasingly concerned that China was losing its revolutionary élan. This was combined with an egocentric preoccupation with his own legacy which he preferred to entrust to radical revolutionaries rather than to bureaucrats or reformists. His solution was to launch what was called the 'Great Proletarian Cultural Revolution'. It lasted for a decade and during that time made life impossible for bureaucrats and for pragmatic reformers alike. Mao set about radicalizing China's youth and encouraging them to reject everything old and established and to build anew. School teachers were prime victims of revolutionary persecution. Dismissed from their jobs and abused, they were in many cases in rural areas tortured to confess to political crimes.[31] Universities stopped functioning for several years in the late 1960s, as students became emissaries of Maoism. Mao himself played an incendiary role, urging the distribution of arms to workers and students active in the revolutionary cause. 'Arm the left' became a slogan and one that was acted upon.[32] Violence got so out of hand that by 1969 the military were brought in to reduce the level of disorder. The Cultural Revolution lasted from 1966 until Mao's death in 1976, although with a lesser intensity in the first half of the 1970s than in the second half of the 1960s. In the long run, it achieved precisely the opposite of what Mao had intended. The revulsion against the turmoil was such that the pragmatists and reformers gained ascendancy in the post-Mao era, with Deng Xiaoping (as already noted in Chapter 4) playing the most decisive role.

The Chinese Communist Party has been cautious about criticizing Mao – his face still adorns the country's paper money – so crucial was his role in the party's history. He was the leader before the revolution, during the successful revolutionary struggle and for over a quarter of a century thereafter when he latterly acquired dictatorial power over the party and the rest of society. Yet the post-Mao leadership, with Deng especially prominent, could hardly avoid condemning the Cultural Revolution, since many of them had suffered from it, and as the task of repairing the damage fell to them. Nor, while propagating the idea that over his career Mao Zedong had done more good than harm, could they disguise the fact that the person who bore responsibility for the turmoil was none other than Mao. In a 'Resolution on Party History' of 1981, the Central Committee declared:

The 'cultural revolution', which lasted from May 1966 to October 1976, was responsible for the most severe setback and the heaviest losses suffered by the Party, the state and the people since the founding of the People's Republic. It was initiated and led by Comrade Mao Zedong.[33]

In reality, many more deaths were caused by Mao's earlier folly, the Great Leap Forward, but the vast majority of those who perished then belonged to the rural community who constituted at that time overwhelmingly the greater part of the Chinese population. On a global scale of suffering, that was a still greater tragedy than the 'Great Proletarian Cultural Revolution'. The Cultural Revolution, however, lasted for much longer and the people who were attacked during it included officials and the most highly educated segment of the population. Whereas the Great Leap Forward meant revolutionary turmoil in the countryside, the Cultural Revolution was both an urban and a rural phenomenon. Initially, it affected mainly the towns, but from the winter of 1968–69 the countryside was also hard hit by zealots and thugs in the name of revolution. Recent research puts the number killed in the countryside alone in a range between 750,000 and 1.5 million people and as many again afflicted with permanent injuries.[34] The number who died in the towns as a direct result of the Cultural Revolution has been estimated at 'approximately half a million Chinese, out of an urban population of around 135 million in 1967'.[35]

The Great Proletarian Cultural Revolution had a dire effect on Chinese education as well as on economic growth, and it affected the political elite adversely to a far greater extent than had the Great Leap Forward. Indeed, a higher proportion of officials were removed from their posts in the course of the Cultural Revolution than were ousted even by Stalin in the Soviet Union in the late 1930s, although a lower proportion were imprisoned or executed in China. As an illustration of the scale of the loss of office, there were thirteen members of the Secretariat of the party's Central Committee in 1966, but only four still in place in 1969, and between 60 and 70 per cent of officials in the central organs of the party were dismissed.[36] For these various reasons, nothing in Chinese history in the years since the revolution seemed worse to the post-Mao leadership than the Cultural Revolution, and they could hardly absolve Mao of responsibility for it.

From Mao to Deng

In the launch of this 'last revolution' of Mao's lifetime, his wife Jiang Qing, who was part of a group of radicals, played a major role, even though she and Mao no longer had a particularly close relationship. An actress by profession, Jiang used her position as Mao's wife to further her own political ambitions, and interpreted part of her task as encouraging Mao to be Mao, that is to say a revolutionary who would not allow time-servers and pen-pushers to get in the way of purification through conflict. In particular, Jiang reinforced Mao's belief that the country needed a cultural revolution. What ensued was in reality an *anti-cultural revolution*. Many treasures of Chinese culture were destroyed – among them historic buildings, paintings, museum exhibits and books. The youthful Red Guards were encouraged to attack the 'Four Olds' – old thought, old culture, old customs and old habits. Old party officials also had a very hard time, with the obvious exception of old Chairman Mao, whose personality cult was taken to new heights (or depths). Deng Xiaoping was condemned as a 'capitalist roader' in 1966, removed from office and put under house arrest in 1967 before being sent to work in a factory. Liu Shaoqui was removed from his posts in 1967 and condemned as a 'traitor, renegade and scab'. He died under house arrest in 1969.

Mao's death in 1976 was soon followed by the comeuppance of Jiang Qing and her three principal allies who constituted the 'Gang of Four', which (for a time, at least) had been a 'Gang of Five', with Mao as the fifth and overwhelmingly the most important. He did not, however, try to anoint any one of the four former partners-in-crime as his potential successor. When by 1976 Mao was too ill to attend government and Politburo meetings, they were chaired by Hua Guofeng whom Mao had nominated as acting premier with an eye to his succession. Hua occupied a middle position between the radical 'Gang of Four' on the one hand and Deng Xiaoping on the other. During these last months of Mao's life, Deng, according to his daughter, attended the Politburo only when summoned, for he felt 'much better at home with his children and grandchildren than having to look at the mad faces of the "Gang of Four"'. When he did attend, he practised a selective deafness. When one of the Gang of Four, such as Zhang Chunqiao, attacked him, Deng claimed not to have been able to make out what had been said. However, as Zhang complained bitterly, when Hua, at the other end of the table, announced in a low voice 'meeting adjourned', Deng immediately pushed back his chair and got ready to leave.[37] A month after Mao's death, the Gang of Four (all of them members of the Politburo) were arrested. Their ultra-revolutionary activities had depended on the acquiescence, and at times active encouragement, of Mao. With Mao gone, those in the party and government elite who had suffered at their hands were able to consolidate their forces. At their subsequent trial, Jiang Qing and Zhang Chunqiao were both sentenced to death, although the sentence was later commuted to life imprisonment. In 1991, by which time she was suffering from cancer, Jiang hanged herself. Zhang was released from prison after serving twenty years.[38]

Mao's short-term successes in leading a revolution, involving mass mobilization and violence, against the party and state establishment turned out to be wholly counterproductive. The reformism that followed Mao's death, including the creation of a substantial private sector and movement to a market economy, far exceeded the 'revisionism' of Khrushchev or of the Brezhnev leadership in the Soviet Union which Mao had found shocking. It was an unintended consequence of the Cultural Revolution that those party officials and intellectuals who had survived it were inoculated for life against the kind of crude, unthinking, ultra-left revolutionism which had been so traumatic for them personally and which had so damaged the social and economic development of China.[39]

That was at least a beneficial side-effect in the midst of the misery the Cultural Revolution heaped on China – and there was one other. Those who attempted to introduce marketizing measures in the Soviet Union, even in the Gorbachev era, ran up against tremendous opposition from entrenched bureaucracies in the economic ministries and from the party apparatus. Those bureaucratic structures had been so shattered in China during the Cultural Revolution that there could be no similar powerful bureaucratic resistance to the still bolder marketizing reforms which Deng Xiaoping espoused. The collective leadership that succeeded Mao, in which Deng quite soon emerged as the most influential member, listened to specialist opinion. The policies they pursued were far more rational than were Mao's from the late 1950s onwards, by which time he had placed himself on a higher pedestal than any of his colleagues.

Deng's role has been discussed at length in Chapter 4. The main point which needs underlining in the present context is how different was not only the content of his policy but also his style of leadership as compared with Mao. Deng, during his period of greatest influence – from 1978 until the end of the 1980s – did not hold the highest rank within the party and state. He did retain, however, until 1989 the leadership of the party's Central Military Commission, and his confidence that he could rely on the support of the army was a significant underpinning for his authority. By 1990–91, Deng's ideas were losing ground in Beijing, partly because of the developing crisis in the Soviet Union, culminating in the break-up of the Soviet state at the end of 1991, which dramatically illustrated for veteran Chinese Communists the potential dangers of liberalization. Deng was weakened also by the mass demonstrations in Tiananmen Square in 1989 and their bloody outcome. Conservative Communists and Maoist leftists alike blamed a decade of reform for whetting the appetite of young people for politically liberal change. Reform and the opening to the outside world were castigated for allowing in the evil influence of capitalism and individualism. All this strengthened the hands of those who emphasized once again the importance both of class struggle and of central planning and who made clear their hostility to further liberalization of the economic system. With a less determined, skilful and widely admired politician than Deng available to respond, the conservative backlash could have been more successful and far-reaching. Deng's contention was that only a decade of reform had enabled the party to survive the upheaval of 1989.[40] He opposed democratization but refused to be deflected from the economic course which he had presided over.

Throughout the period when Deng Xiaoping was China's paramount leader, his views prevailed more often than not. Yet, serious argument went on within the party leadership. Some leaders, notably Hu Yaobang and Zhao Ziyang, were prepared to contemplate more significant political reform than Deng would countenance, while also backing the radical economic reform which Deng espoused.* Others, such as Hua Guofeng (Mao's hand-picked immediate successor) and Li Peng (prime minister at the time of the Tiananmen Square massacre)

---

* It would be wrong to suggest that China has had no political reform in the post-Mao era. There has certainly been no embrace of liberal democracy, but there have been incremental reforms, and the political system (without having had anything like the transformation which has occurred in the economic system) works significantly differently from the way it operated under Mao. See David Shambaugh, *China's Communist Party: Atrophy and Adaptation* (University of California Press, Berkeley, 2008).

strongly opposed any political relaxation and were very suspicious of Deng's marketizing economic policy. After Deng had ceased to be the most powerful figure within the leadership, 'Deng Xiaoping theory' was added to Marxism-Leninism and Mao Zedong Thought as part of the official ideology (making it a still more heterogeneous and contradictory motley). Yet Deng, unlike Mao, saw himself as a prag-matist, not a theoretician, and had not aspired to such ideological sanctification, any more than he had (in sharp contrast with Mao) sought to promote a cult of his personality.

His immense contribution to economic systemic change apart, Deng also oversaw one very important development in China's political system. A besetting difficulty for authoritarian regimes, and for Communist systems quite specifically, has been that of managing leadership successions.* They posed two different but serious problems. On the one hand, they led to excessively long tenure of the party leadership, as the person at the top of the hierarchy appointed more and more of his favoured people to senior positions, and they, in turn, supported him out of fear for their security of tenure under his successor. On the other hand, when a leadership change became inevitable, often only as a result of the death of an elderly incumbent, intra-party conflict could become sharp enough to threaten the system's stability. One of Deng's pragmatic achievements was to pave the way for the compromise figure of Jiang Zemin to become leader of the Chinese Communist Party in 1989 (following the Tiananmen Square massacre) and from 1993 president. More importantly, he presided over an institutionalization of the succession, whereby the very highest party and state offices would be held for ten years only – through the two five-year terms which separated party congresses. Deng even managed to have a decisive influence on the choice of

---

* The most successful authoritarian regime, monarchies aside, in arranging orderly and regular leadership transition over the greater part of the twentieth century was the Institutional Revolutionary Party – the PRI – in Mexico. Mexican presidents were limited to a single term of office and the party leadership thus constantly renewed itself, retaining its single party rule over seven decades. Even after the party was finally voted out in the year 2000, it retained a lot of informal power, and in 2012 the PRI regained the presidency in the person of Enrique Peña Nieto, albeit in a more or less democratic election. See Gustavo Flores-Macías, 'Mexico's 2012 Elections: The Return of the PRI', *Journal of Democracy*, Vol. 24, No. 2, 2013, pp. 128–141.

Jiang's successor long ahead of the changeover. That person, Hu Jintao, duly attained the highest party post in 2002. Some time before Xi Jinping, in turn, succeeded Hu as party leader in November 2012, it had become clear that he would be the choice of the top leadership team. Establishing rules of the game for leadership succession has, for the time being at least, alleviated at least one of the problems faced by authoritarian regimes.

Over the period of a quarter of a century from Jiang's elevation to the party chairmanship in 1989, neither he nor his two successors have enjoyed a similar authority to Deng, not to speak of power comparable with that of Mao. The party chairmanship means that the holder of this office is the most important member of the top team, but that leadership has been collective. Not that all has been sweetness and light, as was illustrated by the fall and arrest in 2012 of the ambitious provincial leader Bo Xilai, whose wife was accused of murdering a British businessman. Possible cover-up by Bo of a real crime was used to the political advantage of those who were his rivals for promotion to the highest echelon of the party, the Standing Committee of the Politburo. He was convicted of this in 2013 and found guilty also of corruption in a trial which was closed to the public but was nevertheless reported (especially widely in the outside world). Within the leadership, the role of the party chairman has increasingly become one of balancing competing intra-party interests rather than of dominating the policy process.[41] In relation to the broader society, and especially the various elites, the system has become one of consultative authoritarianism, as the leadership (again in sharp contrast with Mao) has drawn on the knowledge of experts outside government. The system retains the faults endemic to authoritarian regimes – above all, lack of accountability of the top leadership to the wider public, given the absence of competitive elections other than at local level. Among the major problems is massive corruption, involving high party and state officials. Nevertheless, the post-Mao years have been a time of fast economic growth and dramatically improving living standards for the great majority of the population of China. Even without a leader of Deng Xiaoping's political standing, China under an essentially collective leadership has over the past two decades made much greater progress, with far less violence and loss of life than disfigured the years when Mao wielded despotic power.

THE LEADER UNDER COMMUNISM

The Soviet Union and China were far from alone in the Communist world in having an individual leader (Stalin and Mao), around whom a cult of personality was created, with that person wielding vastly more power than anyone else. This occurred even in Yugoslavia, which, under Tito's leadership, developed by the 1960s and 1970s into a far milder authoritarian regime than its Soviet and Chinese counterparts. Moreover, the leaders of Yugoslavia's constituent republics became increasingly significant political figures as the federal forms of the country acquired greater political substance. Tito's prestige had been important for holding the multi-national Yugoslav state together, and from the time of his death in 1980 the danger of its disintegration increased.

During his years in power, however, Tito did nothing to discourage the creation of a personality cult around him. It never reached anything like the absurd levels of Stalin's, Mao's, Nicolae Ceauşescu's in Romania, or Kim Il Sung's in North Korea, and, compared with a number of other Communist leaders who presided over the creation of myths of their greatness, such as Ceauşescu, there was real substance to Tito's popular standing. He had led the highly effective Partisan resistance to German occupation during the Second World War; he was the leader of the Communist Party when it seized power through its own strength (rather than by courtesy of the Soviet army); and he was the national leader who had been prepared to stand up to the Soviet Union when Yugoslavia was expelled from the Cominform. Tito went on to become an important figure among the leaders of non-aligned countries who stood apart from both the American and the Soviet camps during the Cold War. Milovan Djilas, one of the Partisan leaders who fought alongside Tito in wartime and became a prominent figure in the post-war Communist government – until he began arguing for the country's democratization – had an appropriately nuanced view of Tito. Writing shortly after Tito's death in 1980, Djilas described him as 'a politician of formidable resourcefulness, unerring instinct, and inexhaustible energy'.[42] However, he noted Tito's 'inborn sense of superiority' and 'his conviction that he deserved special care'. Moreover, 'in the end autocratic power transformed proud and decent impulses into self-serving and undemocratic ones, and [Tito's] closest and most faithful comrades became both leaders and toadies'.[43]

In Communist countries the elevation of one leader far above the collective was a striking departure from the ideas that had inspired the revolutionaries. Leader-worship was an intrinsic component of fascism, but was far removed from the ideas of Marx and Lenin, though Lenin's certitude of belief and his conviction that the Communist Party had to be strictly centralized, disciplined and hierarchical created preconditions for future personal dictatorship. Nevertheless, even under Stalin, obeisance was paid to ideas which, in principle, were higher than the leader. Stalin could hardly have launched a campaign of privatization of Soviet industry in the 1930s or 1940s, for this would have been too fundamental a break with the official ideology. Not, of course, that he had any desire to do so, for he was, in many respects, a true believer. Even when he did depart from the ideas of Marx and Lenin, he could not admit to doing so. As Alan Bullock appositely summed up the differences in relation to doctrine of Hitler and Stalin: 'In the case of Hitler, ideology was what the Führer said it was; in the case of Stalin, it was what the General Secretary said Marx and Lenin said it was.'[44]

Stalin, however, played a full part in the build-up of the cult of his personality, which set him by the 1930s far above those who had been his fellow-revolutionaries during the first two decades of the twentieth century. After Khrushchev delivered his 'secret speech' at the Twentieth Congress of the Soviet Communist Party in 1956, in which he denounced Stalin, he was sent a letter by an old Bolshevik, P. Chagin, who had joined the party in the summer of 1917. Chagin recalled an evening in April 1926 when Stalin, on a visit to Leningrad, was invited to supper by Sergey Kirov (who in that year became head of the Leningrad party organization). As the editor of a Leningrad newspaper at the time, Chagin was also a guest at the gathering. During the conversation Kirov said: 'Without Lenin, it is, of course, difficult, but we still have the party, the Central Committee, and the Politburo, and they will lead the country along the Leninist path.' Stalin, who was pacing up and down the room, responded:

Yes, it's all true – the party, the Central Committee, the Politburo. But keep in mind, our people understand little of all that. For centuries the people in Russia were under the tsar. The Russian people are tsarist. For many centuries the Russian people, and especially the Russian peasants, have been used to being led by just one person. And *now* there must be *one* [italics added].[45]

Stalin was doubtless sincere in expressing such views (which con--stituted a non-Marxist version of historical determinism), but they were also self-serving, for he was in no doubt about who was going to be the 'one'. In another private conversation a decade later, Stalin said that 'the people need a tsar', meaning 'someone to revere and in whose name to live and labour'.[46] This view was shared by many Soviet propagandists who believed that it was easier to instil and fortify admiration for a great leader than to get the majority of the people enthusiastically to embrace Marxism-Leninism. At a time when the cult of his personality was rampant, and regarded by Stalin as no less than his due, he would occasionally, and hypocritically, suggest that a publisher was overdoing it. Thus, in 1938 he told the children's literature publishing house that they should burn a book called *Stories of Stalin's Childhood* because a 'cult of personalities' and of 'infallible heroes' was inconsistent with 'Bolshevik theory'.[47]

The cult of personality of the leader was not embraced in all Communist countries. Thus, for example, János Kádár, who was the top person in the Hungarian leadership for more than three decades – from 1956 to 1988 – avoided it. Kádár was far removed from the image of a heroic leader, but his survival in the highest office for so long was based neither on extremes of oppression nor on projecting an image of his greatness. By virtue of his position at the head of the party, he was the principal arbiter of Hungarian policy, but no dictator. In the earliest years after the Hungarian revolution of 1956, he had presided over severe repression, but from the early 1960s onwards Kádár pursued a cautiously reformist course. From then until the mid-1980s Hungary underwent more economic reform and experienced greater cultural relaxation than any other European Communist state during that quarter of a century. Kádár was a master of ambiguity and of judging how far it was safe to go in deviating from Soviet orthodoxy. When Khrushchev took his denunciation of Stalin into the open at the Twenty-Second Congress of the Communist Party of the Soviet Union in October 1961, Kádár seized the opportunity to intensify Hungarian destalinization. Ideologically, he went further than was permitted within the Soviet Union itself. His declaration in late 1961 that 'whoever is not against us is with us' reflected a willingness to accept political quietism and contrasted with Khrushchev's campaigning style.[48]

Still more, it was a world away from Maoist 'Great Leaps' and 'Cultural Revolution'. Instead of mass mobilization campaigns to get everyone embracing, or at least mouthing, the official ideology, there was an acceptance that people could get on with their own lives and thoughts, so long as they did not openly challenge the system. Concessions to the market in Hungarian agriculture meant that it became a relative success story, at least in comparison with other Communist countries. Hungary had economic reformers who pushed for this and for other modifications of the economic system. It was not Kádár who was the driving force, but he did not stand in the way.[49] In comparison not only with other Communist leaders but in relation to the wide opportunities open to him, Kádár lived modestly and, in the tradition of his rural childhood, kept chickens in the garden of his home. In sharp contrast with Mátyás Rákosi, his main predecessor as Hungary's Communist leader, he entirely eschewed a personality cult.[50]

Hungary under Kádár was sometimes called 'the happiest barracks in the camp' (a reference to the Soviet bloc of European Communist states). To say the country was 'happy' is something of an exaggeration, and it was not an adjective anyone would reach for in describing Kádár himself. Moreover, Poland at various times and Czechoslovakia in 1968 were freer, but Hungary over a lengthy period was generally the *least repressive* barracks in the camp. Hungarian citizens' perceptions of Kádár himself underwent a remarkable change. He was widely regarded as a national traitor in 1956 and for the remainder of the fifties, having become the Soviet-endorsed leader charged with 'restoring order' in Hungary, following the crushing of the Hungarian revolution. Over time he came to be viewed as the 'least bad' of the various realistic options available to the country, given the external constraints imposed from Moscow. That developed into a grudging respect – or even more. When he died in the summer of 1989, over a hundred thousand people congregated for his funeral. More remarkably, one decade later (and ten years into Hungary's post-Communist democracy), the lugubrious and unheroic János Kádár emerged in more than one opinion survey as the 'greatest Hungarian' of the twentieth century.[51] While he was no liberal democrat, he was just as far removed from being a dictator in the style of Romania's Ceauşescu, a Communist potentate who, because of his deviation at times from Soviet foreign policy, was over many years treated with greater respect in Western capitals than was Kádár.

Fidel Castro in Power

Communism in Cuba has had a vigorous nationalist component, closer to the anti-colonialist Communism to be found in Asia than the Communism of the ruling parties in Eastern Europe. The patriotic aspect was certainly important for Castro who, as noted in Chapter 5, had not yet become a Communist at the time he acquired power as the leader of the successful revolutionary struggle in January 1959. His hero, José Martí, had not only sought Cuba's liberation from Spanish colonial rule, he had also warned against this being replaced by a less formal domination from the United States. In 1961 Castro merged his revolutionary July 26th Movement with the Communists. His desire for social justice and anti-capitalism, together with the sheer difficulties of running an economy in which big business had been nationalized or frightened off, led within a very few years to the adoption of orthodox (and thus highly authoritarian) Communist economic and political institutions. Castro's Cuba was officially recognized to be part of the international Communist movement in 1963.

By the time Castro, with his health declining, ceded the leadership of the country in 2008 to his brother Raúl, he had been in power for half a century. His political longevity derived in substantial part from his personal appeal, but also from the adoption of the characteristic institutions of a Communist system (with their proven instruments for control). It has additionally owed much to the counterproductive policies pursued by the United States. Early attempts to overthrow the Castro regime, followed by a policy of isolating and endeavouring to undermine it, enabled Fidel both to appeal to Cuban patriotism and to sustain a siege mentality.* So long as Cuba was a Soviet ally during the Cold War, the policy of successive American administrations was slightly more understandable than it became after the Soviet Union itself had ceased to exist and Cuba could no longer be seen as a threat

---

* The German specialist on Cuba and Castro, Volker Skierka, has described the US embargo dating back to the early 1960s as 'the longest, most uncompromising, and politically most senseless economic blockade that a large country has ever inflicted on a smaller one, and which has had the opposite of the intended effect'. See Volker Skierka, *Fidel Castro: A Biography* (Polity, Cambridge, 2005), p. 371.

to the United States other than by the most fevered imagination.* A policy of maximum engagement with Cuba would have made it harder for Castro to resist liberalizing and democratizing measures. No such liberalization took place so long as Fidel was leader, and only modest economic reform has ensued since he was succeeded by Raúl (accompanied by some limited relaxation also of American policy towards Cuba under the Obama administration). Until the demise of Communist rule in Russia, Cuba benefited from its trade with the Soviet Union, which supplied it with both energy and armaments. It had, accordingly, a hard time in the 1990s when that help was no longer forthcoming from post-Soviet Russia. Material conditions deteriorated drastically; there were food shortages and lengthy electricity blackouts.[52]

It was a surprise to many observers that Havana remained Communist after Moscow had become capitalist. A moderate degree of political relaxation probably helped, although this, in many contexts, can stimulate demand for more far-reaching change. The most important policy shift was an extension of religious tolerance, so that religious belief no longer prevented someone from holding official office.[53] Economic assistance arrived at the end of the decade, with the coming to power of Hugo Chávez in Venezuela in 1999 providing a new source of subsidized oil. Living standards in Cuba, however, remained low. The main success stories (true of a number of Communist countries but in Cuba more than most) were in health and education. It was an especially impressive achievement that Cuba in the twenty-first century has had an infant mortality rate and average life expectancy very similar to that of the United States, notwithstanding the vastly greater wealth of the USA.[54]

Improving the educational and health prospects of the poor, especially the rural poor (for there was a high level of urban literacy already in pre-revolutionary Cuba), has been matched neither by a spread of pluralist democracy nor of political liberty. Opponents of the Cuban Communist regime have over the years been repressed, although the number of

---

* Domestic political considerations apparently dissuaded Bill Clinton from adopting a more productive policy towards Cuba. He told Taylor Branch on 6 December 1993 that the Spanish prime minister 'Felipe González had given him a hard time today over the thirty-year US embargo against Fidel Castro's Cuba – calling it illogical, counterproductive, lonely, and wrong'. However, said Clinton, 'now was not the time to change'. See Taylor Branch, *The Clinton Tapes: A President's Secret Diary* (Simon & Schuster, London, 2009), p. 92.

political prisoners has greatly declined over time.[55] The use of the safety valve of emigration has meant that many potential opponents of the regime were abroad rather than in Cuba. Several hundred thousand citizens were able to leave either for other parts of Latin America or for the United States in successive waves of permitted emigration. Cuba under Fidel, having adopted a Soviet-type economic system, did not reform it even to the extent of Kádár's Hungary. Castro remained deeply suspicious of any kind of 'market socialism'. Nor did he try to emulate the political reforms of Gorbachev's perestroika. Although fully capable of taking decisions independently of the Soviet Union, Castro during the 1960s and 1970s internalized the orthodox Communist conception of 'socialism'. He stuck with it doggedly, even while it was being abandoned in Russia. Thus, for example, Castro, who over the years had many meetings with Felipe González, the leader of the democratic Socialist party in Spain and Spanish prime minister from 1982 to 1996, resisted the reforms the Spanish social democrat suggested to him.[56]

So long as he held office as party leader and president, Castro was the dominant figure in the policy-making process as well as the custodian of the ideals of the revolution. His prestige, intelligence and personality were such that he did not need an artificially constructed cult. To a perhaps surprising extent, given how long his leadership lasted and the problems ordinary Cubans faced, he retained respect and loyalty. While Cuba has been far from free of corruption, Castro personally was untainted by it. He remained contemptuous of materialism. During the 1990s, when the issue for many Cubans was obtaining the basic material necessities of life, rather than materialist excess, the survival of the system owed a good deal to residual loyalty to Castro. An American specialist on Cuba, Julia Sweig, has emphasized the importance of 'Fidel Castro's personal leadership and charisma during this time' for 'Cuba's defiance and survival', adding: 'It was through his ubiquitous presence that many Cubans, even as some of their neighbors receded into apathy or left for good, continued to see the revolution as a set of ideals in which they personally had a stake.'[57]

North Korean Extremes

Of the world's five remaining Communist states, four in Asia and one in the Caribbean, the only one in which a full-blown cult of personality of the leader is still to be found is North Korea. Three generations of the one family, albeit in descending order of adulation, have now been the subjects of myth-creation on a grand scale. The personality cult excesses are most abundant in relation to Kim Il Sung, the state's first Communist ruler. Kim did enjoy some genuine support as the North's leader during the Korean War, which (with massive Chinese assistance on the side of the North Koreans, and vast participation from the United States and other democracies on the South Korean side) ended in stalemate. Most North Koreans believed that South Koreans had started the war by invading the North and that, under Kim Il Sung's leadership, they had subsequently emerged victorious from the conflict.[58] Along with a regimented society closed to the outside world went a manufactured cult of the leader which defied parody. All of the country's advances, such as they have been, are attributed to Kim and to his family. It is difficult to imagine that outside North Korea a Communist Party would describe its late leader, as Kim Il Sung was portrayed, as being 'superior to Christ in love, superior to Buddha in benevolence, superior to Confucius in virtue and superior to Mohammed in justice'.[59]

Children, by the time they reached kindergarten age, had learned to say 'Thank you, Great Fatherly Leader' when they received a snack.[60] Typically, Kim was the 'Sun of the world, supreme brain of the nation'.[61] Moreover, he 'not only protected the political life of the people but also saved their physical life, his love cured the sick and gave them a new life, like the spring rain falling on the sacred territory of Korea'.[62] Apart from acquiring godlike attributes, Kim's most distinctive innovation in the world of Communist politics was to combine lip-service to Marxism-Leninism with the creation of hereditary rule, grooming his son, Kim Jong Il to succeed him, which he did on the father's death in 1994. This, then, has been a totalitarianism combined 'with sultanistic aspects'.[63] Interestingly, the dynastic aspiration had long been signalled by a change in the North Korean *Dictionary of Political Terminology*. The 1970 edition had the following entry: 'Hereditary succession is a reactionary custom of exploitative societies whereby certain positions or riches may be legally inherited. Originally a product of slave societies, it was later adopted by feudal lords as a means to perpetuate dictatorial rule.'[64] That definition disappeared from the 1972 edition of the book. When Kim Jong Il died in December 2011, the dynasty was carried on by his youngest son, Kim Jong Un.[65] The dictatorial rule of the three generations of Kims has done little to improve the lives of North Koreans who have suffered famines and a miserable standard of living. Teenage defectors from North Korea are 'on average five inches shorter and 25 pounds lighter than their South Korean counterparts'.[66] So oppressive and intrusive has been the regime that it has come closer than most totalitarian regimes to mirroring the kind of system and society portrayed in Orwell's *Nineteen Eighty-Four*.

THE LEADER UNDER FASCISM

The creation of myths about the greatness of the leader was a radical departure from Marxism-Leninism, an excrescence within Communist systems, however valuable its function in consolidating support for the regime within predominantly peasant societies. In contrast, the cult of the leader was central to fascist thinking and of the utmost importance in the two major fascist regimes of the twentieth century – Benito Mussolini's and Adolf Hitler's. But what all leadership cults had in common – in fascist Italy, Nazi Germany and in those Communist states which indulged in them – was their utility in generating support for the regime on the part of those least interested in ideological formulations. Mussolini, as we have seen, embraced the idea of the totalitarian state. For him and those around him it was a desired goal. Yet highly repressive though Mussolini's rule was, it was somewhat further away from the totalitarian ideal type than either Hitler's Germany or Stalin's Soviet Union.

Mussolini

Mussolini had been an anti-clerical socialist before the First World War. By the end of the war he had turned strongly against socialism and Communism, but he was still anti-Catholic. Before long, he found it prudent to drop much of his hostility to the Church, since an accommodation with the Vatican made more sense than struggle. Moreover, they shared some beliefs. Mussolini talked repeatedly about the need for reassertion of authority, discipline and order, and 'his passionate opposition to socialism, liberalism and the doctrines of materialism' was well received by many in the Church.[67] Having been a republican,

Mussolini reconciled himself also to keeping the monarchy, so long as he rather than the king wielded supreme power. Since the monarch could, in the earliest stage of Mussolini's rise, have ordered the army to crush the growing fascist movement, its leader decided that it would be unwise to make an enemy of King Victor Emmanuel III. Mussolini's fascist movement developed very quickly. With a group of like-minded war veterans, he established the nationalist Fasci di Combattimento (Fighting Leagues) in 1919, and soon the Blackshirt gangs they spawned were interpreting the name literally, fighting against socialists, liberals and other democrats. The fascist party, which Mussolini headed, had some twenty thousand members by 1920, and that number had grown to almost 220,000 by the end of 1921. Part of its appeal was the promise of jobs for those who joined the movement, but there was also a sense of mission and of sacrifice for the nation. The party appealed to young people, and especially to rural youth. A quarter of the members by 1921 were agricultural labourers; farmers counted for another 12 per cent.[68]

Mussolini became prime minister in 1922 as a result of threat and bluster. He appealed to the king not to oppose the 'fascist revolution'.[69] But he also threatened a mass march on Rome by his Blackshirts against the existing civil authority. The king refused to sign a decree presented to him by the prime minister, Luigi Facta, declaring a state of emergency in the country, which could have facilitated the use of troops against Mussolini's ragtag army of insurgents. It was not entirely clear, however, that either the army or the police could be relied upon, for within their ranks there was sympathy for Mussolini and his cause. Whether for that reason, or as an attempt simply to avoid bloodshed, the king invited Mussolini to head a coalition government.[70] Brutality continued through the 1924 election campaign that saw Mussolini's government-supported list of candidates win two-thirds of the votes. They were condemned in parliament by a well-known socialist polit- ician, Giacomo Matteotti, who complained of violence and intimidation in the election. Mussolini, he added, had made it clear that, even if he had been in a minority after the election, he would not have given up power. Less than two weeks later Matteotti was stabbed to death.[71] Mussolini had clearly sanctioned the killing, although he denied it.

Conservative opinion continued to support Mussolini both at home and abroad. In London, *The Times* noted his success in combating Bolshevism and said that his fall 'would be too horrible to contemplate'.

In January 1925 Mussolini put an end to parliamentarism and seized full dictatorial power. The king once again facilitated this, having evidently decided that right-wing authoritarian rule was preferable to weak parliamentary government and party competition.[72] By the end of 1926 Mussolini had banned all political parties other than his own and, having established a special tribunal for the purpose, either imprisoned or put under police surveillance most of the Communist leaders and other prominent anti-fascist activists in Italy.[73]

There were several attempts on Mussolini's life in 1925 and 1926, but he survived unscathed. The Pope said that Mussolini was 'truly protected by God', and the Archbishop of Naples declared in a sermon that Mussolini had been preserved for 'some high destiny' that would be 'for the greater good of our Italy and perhaps of the whole world'.[74] Robert Paxton has noted that long after Mussolini's regime had settled into a routine, he still liked to talk about the 'Fascist revolution'. What he meant was 'a revolution against socialism and flabby liberalism, a new way of uniting and motivating Italians, and a new kind of governmental authority capable of subordinating private liberties to the needs of the national community and of organizing mass assent while leaving property intact'.[75] Mussolini was, however, prepared to manoeuvre in order to get his way and secure as much assent as possible. He told an old friend of his what an effort had been involved in seeking 'equilibrium' among such influential institutions and interests within the country as the 'government, party, monarchy, Vatican, army, militzia, prefects, provincial party leaders, ministers, the head of the Confederazioni [corporatist structures] and the giant monopolistic interests'.[76] Establishing totalitarian power remained for Mussolini a rather distant aspiration.

The creation of a leadership cult was the principal mechanism for enhancing his authority and maintaining power. A powerful orator, Mussolini in the mid-1920s offered the supposed benefits of the 'strong hand' and of establishing 'order'. As Christopher Duggan has observed, 'After the turmoil of the previous few years, the myth of "order" was mesmerising. It was ironic that those who had been the chief instigators of the violence and who had done more than anyone else to undermine the rule of law and bring the state into disrepute should emerge as the principal beneficiaries of the widespread craving for stability.'[77] The project of building up an image of Mussolini's greatness came at that time largely from within the fascist party organization, for the party, which was less popular than the Duce, hoped to benefit from some of the reflected glory. Simultaneously, however, the cult of Mussolini put a distance between him and the roughhouse tactics of the Blackshirts. In general, when things went wrong, the problems could be blamed on others. During the 1930s, as Duggan notes, fascism's failings were regularly 'imputed to the Duce's incompetent, corrupt or treacherous entourage, with Mussolini himself viewed as ignorant of the sins of those around him or otherwise magnanimously forgiving of them'.[78]

Even an Italian journalist who would have liked fascism to have been *more* monolithic accepted that there had been 'various currents' within it and 'the only unifying element was the myth of the leader and his presumed infallibility'.[79] In the course of the 1930s, Mussolini himself increasingly came to believe in that myth, saying: 'I have never made a mistake when I followed my instinct; I have always gone wrong when I listened to reason.' It was characteristic of fascism to elevate 'instinct' above reason.[80] There were, however, important differences between Italian and German fascism. Whereas anti-Semitism was absolutely central to Hitler's creed, this was not the case with Mussolini. The Minister of Finance in his government from 1932 to 1935 was Jewish, and Jews had been more than proportionately represented in Mussolini's party from its earliest existence.[81] It was during the period of growing friendship with Nazi Germany in the late 1930s that the issue of Jewish influence in Italian society began to be raised sharply and legislation discriminating against Jews was introduced in the autumn of 1938.[82]

By the time it became evident during the later stages of the Second World War that Italy was on the road to defeat, Mussolini's 'contempt for his opponents' was 'extended to include his followers'.[83] His earlier enormous popularity dwindled fast when the suffering inflicted by the war appeared to be all for no purpose. When Mussolini and his mistress Claretta Petacci were captured and shot by Communist partisans in April 1945, and subsequently strung up by their feet so that large crowds could gawp, it was quickly forgotten how popular Mussolini had earlier been. One young journalist who was present summed up the rapid shift from eulogizing to cursing the fallen leader as 'Tyranny at the top, credulity and conformism at the bottom' and the change from one political mythology to another as people 'who would have rushed to any piazza in Italy to scream deliriously for Mussolini' reacted as if they had been opposed to him all along.[84]

Hitler's Rise to Power

Even though they sometimes used the language of revolution, both Mussolini and Hitler, as Robert Paxton notes, 'were invited to take office as head of government by a head of state' who did so 'in the legitimate exercise of his official functions, on the advice of civilian and military counsellors'.[85] Hitler had attempted a putsch in Bavaria in 1923, hoping to seize power in Munich as a stepping-stone to Berlin, but he was arrested and spent a year in prison. After that experience he decided to campaign for electoral office rather than grab power unconstitutionally. That was not because he had been converted to a belief in the rule of law, but because relying on his growing appeal seemed the more dependable route. Dictatorship could come later. Hitler used his time in prison to read and to work on his book, *Mein Kampf* (My Struggle), which was published in two volumes in the mid-1920s. His fixation on an imagined Aryan 'racial purity' and obsessive anti-Semitism are running themes. Hitler was able to tap into the sense of humiliation and injustice in Germany in the 1920s, following the First World War. Viewing the country as being in a state of crisis and collapse, he insisted that 'of all the causes of the German collapse . . . the ultimate and most decisive remains the failure to recognise the racial problem and especially the Jewish menace'.[86] Hitler also inveighed against pacifism, writing, 'Those who want to live, let them fight, and those who do not want to fight in this world of eternal struggle do not deserve to live.'[87]

Harsh peace terms imposed by the victorious allies in 1919, hyperinflation in the early 1920s, followed by serious unemployment enabled the National Socialist (Nazi) organization Hitler had established in 1919 to make some progress during the 1920s, but a degree of economic recovery in the second half of that decade helped to ensure that they remained a fringe party. This changed after the Wall Street crash of October 1929. The knock-on effect meant that German banks withdrew their loans to businesses and by 1932 more than one worker in three was unemployed.[88] Hitler's party was a major beneficiary of that economic crisis. In the parliamentary election of 1928 they had secured twelve seats and 2.6 per cent of the vote. In the election for the Reichstag of September 1930, that rose to 107 seats and 18.3 per cent. The Nazi Party had become the second largest in the parliament, and more than six million people had voted for it.[89] Hitler's major biographer, Ian

Kershaw, offers a generalization which has, indeed, a much wider application than to inter-war Germany when he writes: 'There are times – they mark the danger point for a political system – when politicians can no longer communicate, when they stop understanding the people they are supposed to be representing. The politicians of Weimar's parties were well on the way to reaching that point in 1930.'[90]

Two years later Hitler's support was still stronger. The aged Reich President, Field Marshal von Hindenburg, came to the end of his seven-year term of office and stood for re-election. Hitler entered the contest against him, as did the Communist leader Ernst Thälmann. Hindenburg did not have an overall majority on the first round of voting and Hitler was the runner-up. In the second round he secured 37 per cent of the votes, and more than thirteen million people voted for him.[91] Hitler believed that, as a consequence of that showing, he was entitled to be offered the Chancellorship, the main position of power as head of the government, but he was rebuffed by Hindenburg. (The latter's majority was secured partly thanks to the votes of Social Democrats, since, conservative though Hindenburg was, he was clearly preferable to Hitler.) The Nazis had mixed fortunes in 1932. There were Reichstag elections in both July and November of that year and the party got two million votes fewer in November than they had received in the summer. Hindenburg thought he was cleverly taking advantage of the Nazis' comparative weakness, therefore, when he finally acceded to their demand that Hitler be made Chancellor, appointing him to that post at the end of January 1933, but surrounding him within the government by conservatives rather than fascists. He believed that Hitler's powers would thus be constrained.

Hitler had other ideas, and he was greatly helped by the burning down of the Reichstag (parliament) building on 27 February 1933. This was a chance event, for it was the work of a young Dutch socialist who had acted alone with the intention of galvanizing German workers to struggle actively against their right-wing government and against capitalism. Hitler took the opportunity to blame the Communists collectively for the arson, cracking down especially on them but also on Social Democrats and other anti-fascists. In an election on 5 March 1933, marked by extreme intimidation, the Nazi Party won just under 44 per cent of the vote, which gave them 288 out of 647 seats in the new Reichstag. In spite of the brutal tactics used against them, with Communists and

Social Democrats beaten up and sometimes murdered, the Communist Party gathered more than 12 per cent and the Social Democrats over 18 per cent of the vote.[92] The Nazis, however, had not only emerged as by far the largest single party, they also had an overall parliamentary majority as a result of their coalition with conservatives. They did not, in fact, even need to rely on the latter's support in order to seize power, for the Nazis ensured that Communist deputies elected were not able to take their seats. They had either been arrested or taken flight. In the intimidating presence of the two paramilitary organizations, the SA and the SS, only the votes of ninety-four Social Democrats were cast against an Enabling Act, which, with 441 deputies voting for it, essentially passed power from parliament to the National Socialists.[93] (Importantly, the Centre Party – the precursor of the post-war Christian Democrats – who were not natural allies of the Nazis voted for the law.) By the summer of 1933 over one hundred thousand Communists, Social Democrats and trade unionists had been arrested, and even official estimates put 'the number of deaths in custody at 600'.[94]

Already in 1933 Hitler, with the particular assistance of the chief Nazi propagandist Joseph Goebbels, had instigated a nationwide boycott of Jewish shops and businesses. Dismissal of Jews – defined by 'racial', not religious criteria – affected the whole of cultural and educational life. By 1934 around 1,600 out of 5,000 university teachers had been hounded out of their jobs either because they were Jewish or because they were political opponents of fascism.[95] There was ample cooperation from below as well as encouragement from above. Students played a large part in hastening the expulsion of Jewish and anti-Nazi professors. The regime's ideology had become increasingly widely imbibed. Hitler, after all, had 'one great gift: the ability to move crowds with his rhetoric'.[96]

Many of Hitler's followers were eager for him to take dictatorial power, and he was now able to advance more rapidly in that direction. The one threat to his complete ascendancy was a potential alliance between conservative forces and the army, especially since senior army officers were increasingly concerned about the pretensions of the fascist party's paramilitary wing, the SA, with its four and a half million members. Not only were they arresting, beating up and sometimes killing Jews, Communists and Social Democrats, they seemed, under their ambitious leader, Ernst Röhm, to be seeking a superior authority to the army. In the circumstances, Hitler chose a crackdown on the SA leadership. This was not just a short-term concession to the army, but an enterprise he decided was to his own advantage, for he had come to suspect the loyalty of Röhm. He had him arrested and shot. Hitler's praetorian guard, the SS, previously subordinate to the SA, were now elevated above it, and the SA 'turned into little more than a military sports and training body'.[97] The showdown with the SA took place in July 1934 – at the same time as Hitler dealt with a potential threat from a quite different source. The killing of top SA leaders was paralleled by the shooting of a number of respected conservative figures, among them the former chancellor, General Kurt von Schleicher and his wife. Yet, with an emphasis on their bringing the SA to heel, Hitler and Goebbels presented the purge as a heroic measure to prevent a coup by Röhm that would have plunged Germany into continuous revolution. This spurious claim was taken sufficiently at face value by many middle-class Germans to lead them to believe that Hitler had saved Germany from chaos.

Until the death of Hindenburg at the beginning of August 1934, Hitler did not, however, attain the fully fledged 'Führer state'. While Hindenburg was dying, Hitler pushed through an important constitutional change whereby on the president's death that office would be combined with the Reich Chancellorship. Since it was the president who had been commander of the armed forces, it meant that this important power was being transferred to Hitler who in future was officially to be addressed as 'Führer and Reich Chancellor'.[98] From that time on, his absolutism became greater and ideological goals clearer. Although an egomaniac, Hitler had not been driven by lust for power alone. He was also 'an ideologue of unshakeable convictions'.[99] Accompanying his racial interpretation of historical development was an impassioned belief in a 'great man' understanding of history. He was an ardent admirer of the eighteenth-century Prussian monarch, Frederick II (Frederick the Great). For Hitler, he perfectly exemplified greatness, since he combined absolute rule at home with military success abroad, greatly expanding the boundaries of the state and making Prussia the leading military power in Europe. In the later stages of the Second World War, when it was clear to others that imminent defeat beckoned for Nazi Germany, Hitler was still taking inspiration from the German translation of Thomas Carlyle's biography of Frederick which Goebbels presented to him.[100]

By 1934 the normal way of addressing Hitler was '*Mein Führer*', while he himself, when speaking to most Nazi leaders, used just their surname. He took far greater pains over projecting his image (though that was not the term used then) than in the content of policy. The exceptions were the areas which most obsessed him – eliminating Jewish influence (which ultimately became a policy of eliminating Jews themselves), building up German military power, and foreign policy (discussed in the next chapter). One important respect in which the system was less than totalitarian is that argument on many other policies took place at a level below Hitler, with subordinates following his broad guidelines and trying to do what they thought he would approve. This merely enhanced his immense authority, although leadership by means of inaccessibility, unpredictable interventions, long-winded monologues and lack of interest in policy detail hardly made for efficient government.[101]

Hitler hated cabinet meetings in which there could be critical discussion. When in 1933 he was still heading a coalition government, containing more conservatives than Nazis, the cabinet met four or five times a month up until the summer recess, but thereafter much less frequently. He preferred one-to-one meetings, which he could be certain to dominate, and he practised strong favouritism among his ministers.[102] By the later 1930s the cabinet never met. By this time, all semblance of collective government had disappeared and no one within the system doubted that the Führer, and he alone, had the ultimate right to take decisions. Policy on which Hitler chose to focus was decided by him, in consultation with whichever individuals he decided to summon at any particular time.[103]

By 1936 Hitler's popularity in Germany could not be doubted. While an election in that year which gave almost 99 per cent of the vote to the Nazis owed much, for a significant minority within the electorate, to intimidation and fear of the consequences of a negative vote, it seems clear that by this time Hitler was supported by the greater part of the German population. The recovery of the economy, national pride in the country's renewed military might and a widespread belief in the greatness of Hitler were political realities. No one believed more in his genius than Hitler himself. As Kershaw writes, 'Hubris – that overweening arrogance which courts disaster – was inevitable. The point where hubris takes over had been reached in 1936.'[104] By early 1938 Hitler was remarking to the Austrian dictator Kurt von

Schuschnigg: 'I have achieved everything that I set out to do and have thus perhaps become the greatest German of all history.'[105]

Fascism was very much a movement of the inter-war period of the twentieth century, and Italy and Germany are the clearest examples of this movement in power. The fact that there were some dissimilarities between those two regimes does not invalidate the use of 'fascist' to describe them both; there were, after all, big differences at various times among Communist systems, including international tensions (as the Sino-Soviet dispute testified). Fascism constituted a particular type of political movement. Although the ideology could be changed by the leader far more easily than Marxist-Leninist doctrine could be discarded by their Communist counterparts, fascism was a movement with some common elements. They included glorification of war and violence, expansionism, racism, an aspiration for total control, a fixation on national solidarity and refusal to admit legitimate differences of interest and values within the society, and – not least – a belief in heroic leadership. To these Robert Paxton adds, *inter alia*, 'the belief that one's group is a victim, a sentiment that justifies any action, without legal or moral limits, against its enemies, both internal and external'; 'the superiority of the leader's instincts over abstract and universal reason', and 'right being decided by the sole criterion of the group's prowess within a Darwinian struggle'.[106]

There were fascist movements between the two world wars in many European countries, including France, Britain, Belgium, the Netherlands and Norway. They took inspiration from Italy and Germany but made, however, only a minor impact on their domestic political systems. As Paxton puts it: 'Most of these feeble imitations showed that it was not enough to don a colored shirt, march about, and beat up some local minority to conjure up the success of a Hitler or Mussolini. It took a comparable crisis, a comparable opening of political space, comparable skill at alliance building, and comparable cooperation from existing elites.'[107] There has been a tendency to stretch the meaning of fascism to cover too many different regimes, but just as dressing up as a group and beating up others did not necessarily make a political movement successful, so not every brutal and repressive right-wing regime was by that very token fascist. Thus, neither Spain under General Franco nor Portugal under António de Oliviera Salazar was, strictly speaking, fascist, although highly autocratic. In both cases the regimes began as military dictatorships and remained authoritarian, but, in the Spanish case espe-cially, some elements of pluralism had crept in even before the break-through to democracy of the 1970s. Significantly, both Spain and Portugal preserved traditional elements of conservatism more than did either Mussolini's Italy or (especially) Hitler's Germany. Both Franco and Salazar were Catholics who embraced the Church as an institution and counted on its backing. Nevertheless, Franco flirted with the major fascist dicta-tors, benefiting in the Spanish Civil War from the aid of both Mussolini and Hitler. In the aftermath of that conflict, he engaged in bloody repres-sion, in which some two hundred thousand people were killed.[108]

Hitler's 'genuine and immense popularity among the great mass of the German people' continued until the middle of the Second World War.[109] (His foreign policy miscalculations, which brought calamity to his nation and destroyed him, are one of the themes of the next chapter.) Nazi Germany combined the cult of Hitler's personality with the insti-tutions of a powerful modern state. Even after Hitler's charisma began to fade, in the midst of wartime suffering, the institutions of the state continued to function. For Hitler, however, the main purpose of the state was to promote a great leader to the position of highest authority and to serve him loyally. As early as 1920 he had declared: 'We need a dictator who is a genius.'[110] Hailed by a regional Nazi party leader as 'a new, a greater and a more powerful Jesus Christ',[111] Hitler held millions in thrall as a result of his magnetism, the apparent success until the end of the 1930s of his undertakings, and the shared myth that what Germany needed most of all was a great and strong leader. 'Success', wrote Adam Smith, when 'joined to great popular favour', often turned the heads of even the greatest of leaders, leading them to 'ascribe to themselves both an importance and an ability much beyond what they really possessed' and 'by this presumption, to precipitate themselves into many rash and sometimes ruinous adventures'.[112] While Hitler's greatness, other than in a capacity to whip up evil, was an illusion, it was an illusion that certainly generated ruinous adventures.

MYTHS OF DICTATORIAL REGIMES

In the eighteenth century Turgot wrote: 'Despotism is easy. To do what you want to do, is a rule which a king learns very quickly; art is necessary to persuade people, but none is necessary to give orders. If despotism did not revolt those who are its victims, it would never be banished from the earth.'[113] Despotism does sooner or later provoke its victims into overthrowing it (although violent revolution has often been but a prelude to a different variant of authoritarian rule). Even an autocrat, however, cannot rule by force alone, for he must be able to persuade those around him – his praetorian guard, army chiefs or head of the political police – that it is either for the good of the country or in their personal interests (or, more commonly, both) to support him loyally. As Turgot's older contemporary David Hume put it: 'No man would have any reason to *fear* the fury of a tyrant, if he had no authority over any but from fear; since, as a single man, his bodily force can reach but a small way, and all the further power he possesses must be founded either on our own opinion, or on the presumed opinion of others.'[114]

Thus, persuasion as well as force has to be part of the armoury of an authoritarian leader. Autocrats in the twentieth and twenty-first centuries have had at their disposal means and media undreamt of by Enlightenment thinkers – from the amplified mass meeting, used to such effect by Mussolini and Hitler, to electronic surveillance, to radio and television and a monopoly control over the messages they convey.* Linked to the need to influence opinion is the necessity of organization, since ruling a modern state is different from being chief of what eighteenth-century writers called a 'rude tribe'. Traditional monarchies apart, many authoritarian regimes in an age of democratization feel the need for a façade of democracy, including 'elections' offering no real choice, but which can be and are, nevertheless, presented as evidence of popular support for the regime. A monopolistic ruling party will normally play an important part in organizing such elections and mobilizing people to vote. There is evidence, indeed, that autocrats who have a party at their disposal enjoy greater political longevity than those who rely on personalistic rule without a political party. Not only is party

---

* A monopoly, at any rate, within the state. Foreign broadcasts – as, for example, those of Radio Liberty and Radio Free Europe in the case of Communist states – were jammed, but the jamming was not effective in all parts of the country. Thus, the monopoly over the dissemination of information and opinion of authoritarian and totalitarian states was incomplete, even before the intrusion of the internet presented authoritarian rulers with serious problems as well as new opportunities.

organization useful for mobilizational purposes; it may also help 'to regulate the ambitions of political rivals and bind them to the ruler'.[115]

The Baath Party was an important support for the power of Saddam Hussein in Iraq, although it was founded in Damascus by Syrians and introduced into Iraq in 1951 by a young Iraqi engineer who was later to be murdered by Saddam.[116] While Saddam was fiercely opposed to any domestic Communists – as well as to radical Islamists – the party organization was not dissimilar to that of ruling Communist parties. Like them, it played an important part in subordinating the army and the security services to the party. Political officers were inserted in the army to insure that the military became deeply imbued with the party's – and, above all, Saddam's – ideas.[117] The party was also the driving force in the building of the personality cult of Saddam Hussein. This went to extreme lengths, as did the obsequiousness of his associates and subordinates in his presence. Towns, mosques, theatres and rivers were named after Saddam. Banners declared that 'Iraq is Saddam and Saddam is Iraq', while writers gushed that 'Saddam is the peak of the mountains and the roar of the seas'.[118] Nevertheless, the author of the most detailed study of Saddam and the Baath Party argues that the regime, although undoubtedly tyrannical, should be regarded as authoritarian rather than totalitarian.[119]

Totalitarian regimes, in order to justify the aspiration for total control of the ruling party and leader, characteristically offer a vision of a glorious future, a new golden age, which, for a time at least (as happened in the Soviet Union, Italy and Germany), inspires a significant proportion of the population. More prosaic arguments used to justify both totalitarian and authoritarian regimes are that they provide order and are a source of stable government. The claim to supply order is seductive, for most people most of the time want a peaceful environment, providing a settled order in which they can bring up their families. If they are told, and believe, that the alternative to the 'order' provided by the dictatorial regime is civil war and anarchy, many will give either willing or grudging assent to the powers that be.

There are, however, several fundamental problems with this justification of 'order'. The first is that a majority of authoritarian regimes have themselves created massive disorder through contempt for a rule of law and by resort to violence and the physical break-up of families, involving the arrest, imprisonment and killing of tens of thousands (as in the case of the Chilean dictator Augusto Pinochet) or millions of their own citizens (as occurred in Stalin's Soviet Union and Mao Zedong's China). Nothing could have been further removed from order, however defined, than the Chinese Great Leap Forward and the Cultural Revolution. The second difficulty is that such regimes, through lack of accountability and responsiveness to grievances, are incapable of resolving underlying problems; they merely repress them. When reform or revolution eventually takes place, the difficulties have usually become more rather than less intractable. A third problem is related to the fact that most states are ethnically diverse and countries under authoritarian rule are no exceptions. In Africa, in particular, but also in the Middle East, national boundaries were determined by imperial powers with little or no regard for local allegiances and ethnic loyalties. As Paul Collier observes, 'Typically, in ethnically diverse societies autocrats depend upon the support of their own ethnic group' and the more diverse the society, 'the smaller the autocrat's group is likely to be'.[120] This leads the autocrat to favour his own group both politically and economically. Resources are quite disproportionately concentrated in the hands of the dominating religious or ethnic group. That exacerbates underlying inter-group tensions as well as damaging economic development.

It is no less of a myth that authoritarian rule provides stability. In an established democracy the defeat and removal of a government is a normal and healthy event. It does not imply a crisis for the system or society. The removal of a government within an authoritarian regime, in contrast, means systemic crisis. In the past few decades this has been well illustrated by the transformation of Eastern Europe in 1989 and the much more tumultuous upheaval in the Middle East since 2011. Democratic leaders until the recent past went on to enjoy a modest and well-earned retirement. Now many of them prefer an immodest and exceptionally well-remunerated retirement, in which they cash in on their celebrity. Either way, their fate has been very different from that of Mussolini (shot and strung up by his feet), Hitler (shooting himself in his Berlin bunker), Ceauşescu (shot, along with his wife, by firing squad) or Muammar Gaddafi (tortured and killed by rebel fighters), although, admittedly, many other dictators have had more natural deaths.

The most persistent myth of dictatorial regimes has been that of the great and far-seeing leader. This applies particularly to autocracies, less so to oligarchies, in which the emphasis is generally on the unique insights and wisdom of the ruling party rather than those qualities in an individual leader. The words for 'leader' in Italian (*Duce*), German (*Führer*) and Russian (*vozhd*) changed their meanings during the periods of Mussolini's, Hitler's and Stalin's rule. The word in each case came to signify *the* leader, someone of virtually superhuman strength, understanding, insight and fatherly care for his people. Credulous followers bestowed on their leaders heroic qualities, in some cases before the leader had fully invested himself with such attributes. Hitler, most notably, went from believing that Germany needed a great and heroic leader to discovering, to his great satisfaction, that he was that person. In the early 1920s – unlike Mussolini at that point – Hitler was not yet trying to build up a personality cult. His followers, however, were already declaring that they had 'found something which millions are yearning for, a leader'.[121] By the end of the 1920s Hitler was convinced that they were right, and the Nazi Party became entirely focused on its leader. 'For us,' said Hitler in 1930, 'the Leader is the Idea, and each party member has to obey only the Leader.'[122] The personality cult was sedulously promoted in all of these major dictatorships of the twentieth century by the leader himself (although part of Stalin's cult was a propagation of the fable of his supposed modesty), but they were never short of acolytes and sycophants who played their parts in the creation of the myth of the superman who led them.

*

Dictatorial power owes a vast amount to the social and political contexts in which leaders achieve governmental office, to followers who hope to gain from their patronage, to elites who accommodate them for fear of something worse (as Italian and German conservatives cooperated with Mussolini and Hitler from fear of Communism), and to the irrational belief that one person can embody the wisdom of the nation. They are testimony, in a dangerous form, to the 'emotional tail wagging the rational dog'.[123] They are the apotheosis of the illusion that what humanity needs is a strong leader and a reminder that, if unchecked, the power of such a leader will lead to oppression and carnage.

7

Foreign Policy Illusions of 'Strong Leaders'

It would obviously be misleading to suggest that bad foreign policy decisions are taken *only* by those who fancy themselves to be strong individual leaders, endowed with special insights. However, such leaders are more prone to serious error because of their willingness to discount the accumulated knowledge of people with expertise on the part of the world in question. They are characterized also by a disinclination to promote uninhibited discussion, based on full access to information, with governmental colleagues who feel free to raise objections and to insist on consideration of alternative approaches. Worse decisions on foreign policy are, on the whole, taken in authoritarian regimes than in democracies (the gulf is still wider on domestic policy), and the worst of all are within autocratic, rather than oligarchic, regimes. There the preordained lack of dissent from the views of the top leader fortifies his belief that he is supremely qualified to make the decisive judgement call. Within a democracy, the Minister of Foreign Affairs (Secretary of State in the US, Foreign Secretary in the UK) is usually a very influential figure and there will be a Cabinet, Cabinet committee or National Security Council, with senior ministers involved in the making of international policy, although to a varying extent over time and from one country to another.

Prime ministers, however, for reasons elaborated earlier in the book, have played a growing role in foreign policy and there are special pitfalls for those who come to believe in the unrivalled quality of their own judgement. Leaders who pride themselves on being 'strong', or who are anxious to appear strong, may be especially tempted by military intervention in another country. War leaders often have a higher prestige than peacetime premiers and presidents, although the risks to their reputations – and, far more importantly, to other people's lives – are also high. Leading a country into an unnecessary war, one which contravenes international law, which has been entered into on a false prospectus, or whose costs outweigh its benefits, can fatally undermine a leader's standing. David Owen has observed 'the hubris syndrome' which takes hold of over-confident and high-handed leaders. Among the symptoms, to which such leaders are prone, are 'a narcissistic propensity to see the world primarily as an arena in which they can exercise power and seek glory rather than as a place with problems that need approaching in a pragmatic and non-self-referential manner'; a belief that they need not feel accountable to mere colleagues but to something higher, 'History or God'; and a lack of curiosity about what might go wrong, which amounts to a 'hubristic incompetence', since excessive self-confidence 'has led the leader not to bother worrying about the nuts and bolts of a policy'.[1]

FOREIGN POLICY ILLUSIONS OF TOTALITARIAN AND AUTHORITARIAN LEADERS

The greater part of this chapter will focus on the foreign policy illusions of democratic leaders and, most specifically, those of three British prime ministers – Neville Chamberlain, Anthony Eden and Tony Blair. Still more striking delusions, with often devastating consequences, are to be found, however, among the dictatorial leaders discussed in Chapter 6. Not all authoritarian leaders, however, seek foreign adventures. Some maintain a focus on consolidating their domestic regime and among such authoritarian states, those of Chinese cultural heritage have been the most successful in modernizing their countries' economies.[2]

Hitler, Stalin and Mussolini could also lay claim to economic modernization, albeit with a bias towards military production, especially in the first two cases. What the three 'great dictators' of the inter-war era of the twentieth century had in common is that their most serious foreign policy misjudgements were a result of succumbing to their own myths. They came to believe in their own genius and in the triumph of their indomitable will. Self-consciously strong leaders, whether within dictatorships or democracies, have a tendency to become over time still more impressed by their own judgement, and less inclined to listen to objections even from within the executive. They also tend to be afraid of nothing so much as being perceived to be weak or to have shown weakness.

Hitler's and Mussolini's Miscalculations

Foreign interventions which achieve their immediate objectives may be seen very differently in later perspective. Thus, Hitler's takeover of Czechoslovakia was initially entirely successful. With the Munich Agreement, Hitler secured the Sudetenland territory, but in the second half of October 1938, just a few weeks after that settlement, he was planning to breach its provisions. He gave the army instructions to prepare for the 'liquidation of remainder of the Czech state'.[3] The invasion of Czechoslovakia in March 1939 was not physically opposed by other countries at the time, so it appeared to be indubitably a German gain. Yet it changed foreign opinion, not least in Britain. Thus, the lack of opposition to Hitler's expansionism fed his hubris at the very time that the realization was growing in Europe that he could not be trusted. The seizure of the whole of Czechoslovakia not only broke the promise that no further territorial demands would be made but demonstrated also the falsity of Hitler's claim that his goal was simply that of uniting German peoples in a single state.[4] As 'the most ardent believer in his own infallibility and destiny', Hitler became more reckless from 1938 onwards and led Europe into disaster.[5]

The invasion of Poland in September 1939 brought Britain and its imperial and commonwealth allies, together with France, into the war, for both the UK and France had given guarantees to Poland that, if it were attacked, they would come to its defence. Hitler believed that he had secured a free hand by his agreement the previous month with Stalin to carve up Poland and the Baltic states with the signing of what became known as the Molotov–Ribbentrop Pact, named after the Soviet and German government's foreign ministers who negotiated and put their signatures to the agreement. It did not declare eternal peace between two states which had been fierce ideological opponents, but committed them to avoid war with each other for a period of ten years. Allowing the Soviet Union a temporary share of the spoils suited Hitler, for it meant that, for the time being, Germany would not be fighting a European war on two fronts, even should Britain and France react differently to the invasion of Poland from the way they had responded to the takeover of Czechoslovakia. (And Hitler doubted whether they would.) It also suited Stalin because the Soviet Union was militarily weak at the time. That was in no small part because his pathological suspicion had led him to preside over the destruction of the high command of the Red Army.

With his customary ruthlessness and cynicism, Stalin agreed that hundreds of political refugees from Nazi Germany, including German Communists, would be handed over to the Gestapo. In many cases, they had already been arrested as part of the Soviet Great Purge. For some of them the transfer was directly from the Soviet gulag to a Nazi concentration camp.[6] And with *his* barbarism and cynical disregard for any pledges given, Hitler was the first to break the Pact, ordering the German invasion of the Soviet Union in June 1941. In terms of the Second World War's outcome, this was Hitler's most disastrous mistake of all, for German losses were far greater on the Russian front than on any other and contributed hugely to the Nazi military defeat and the consequent division of Germany, which persisted for more than four decades. Hitler's last major meeting with his generals to brief them on the forthcoming invasion of the Soviet Union took place just a week in advance of it. He told them that though the Russians would put up tough resistance, 'the worst of the fighting would be over in about six weeks'. A majority of his military audience were anxious about the implications of embarking on a two-front war, but the system was such, and the cult of the leader sufficiently internalized, that none of them raised any concerns.[7]

Hitler had written in *Mein Kampf*, with himself in mind, that 'the combination of theoretician, organizer, and leader in one person is the rarest thing that can be found on this earth' and it is this combination that 'makes the great man'.[8] While 'theoretician' was clearly an exaggeration, ideology mattered for Hitler, and he formed a few central notions which changed little from the early years after the First World War to his suicide in 1945. Among his most basic and unchangeable ideas were the belief that Germany needed more 'living space' (*Lebensraum*) and the need to dismember the Soviet Union, which Hitler linked with destruction of the Jews. Obsessed by 'Jewish Bolshevism', he believed that 'the end of Jewish rule in Russia will also be the end of Russia as a state'.[9] It was in the first half of 1941 that Hitler decided that the time had come to bring these aims to speedy fruition with a victory over Russia, which would bring that country's 'immeasurable riches' under German political and economic control. This would also facilitate the realization of what Ian Kershaw has called Hitler's 'twin obsessions' – 'removing the Jews' and *Lebensraum*.[10]

Mussolini was in power for longer than Hitler, but it was in the 1930s that his foreign policy became adventurist, and it turned into tragedy for his country when he fully allied Italy with Nazi Germany. Earlier, he gave vigorous voice to sentiments, quite widely shared by his fellow-citizens, that Italy had lost out at a time when other European powers were accumulating empires as well as in the distribution of territorial rewards at the peace conference of 1919. With the League of Nations in place, different standards were meant to prevail by the 1930s from those of the late nineteenth century. Mussolini's Italy, however, having first consolidated its control of Libya, which had been an Italian protectorate since before the First World War, invaded and conquered Ethiopia in 1935–36 and annexed Albania in 1939. Encouraged by these campaigns, Mussolini gave assistance from the outset of the Spanish Civil War to General Franco's nationalist (and close to fascist) rebels, agreeing to send fifty thousand troops. When the Italians suffered severe losses, the Duce's response was to send large quantities of aircraft, armoured vehicles and weaponry to Spain.[11] Mussolini's support for Franco, and Italy's provision of both personnel and ma-teriel, made a significant contribution to the defeat of democracy in Spain and the establishment of Franco's authoritarian regime. The commitment of Mussolini to the war in Spain was greater than that of either Hitler or Stalin.[12] He was, however, allying Italy ever closer with Hitler's Germany from 1936 onwards and brought his country into the Second World War on the Nazi side in June 1940. The fall of France had left him in no doubt that he would be an important partner on the winning side. Yet Italy was to be very much a junior, and unsuccessful, partner in the war. Mussolini had lost the support even of the fascist Grand Council by the summer of 1943, was deposed by the king, rescued by the Germans, and led only a small puppet regime until he met his grisly end in 1945.

Stalin's Mixture of Realism and Illusion

Of the trio of 'great dictators', Stalin was the most cautious foreign policy actor. Moreover, whereas violence and territorial expansion on grounds of national or racial superiority were part of the fascist creed, Communist expansion could be justified only on the grounds – usually spurious, as it turned out – that they represented the wishes of the local population to replace capitalism with Soviet-style 'socialism'. Clearly, the majority of citizens of the Baltic states of Estonia, Latvia and Lithuania did not wish to be incorporated in the Soviet Union, but following the Molotov–Ribbentrop Pact, they were first forced to host Soviet military bases in 1939 and then annexed in 1940. There, as elsewhere, however, there were enough local Communists to do the Kremlin's bidding. A determined minority, when backed by Soviet force, could install and sustain an unpopular regime. Finland had also been placed by the Nazi–Soviet agreement within the Soviet sphere of influence, but the Finns put up fierce resistance. In the Winter War of 1939–40, Finland lost territory to the Soviet Union, but Russian manpower losses were vastly greater than those of the Finns. As a result, a peace treaty was concluded in March 1940 which left Finland independent.[13]

Stalin, having seen the great difficulties the Red Army experienced in the Soviet–Finnish war, was much more reluctant than was Hitler to engage in a wider conflict. Better, in his view, for capitalist and imperialist states to fight a devastating war with each other, while the Soviet Union stood on the sidelines and benefited from their resultant weakness. What is of special relevance in the present context, however, is that Stalin's faith in his own foresight led him to disbelieve a range of warnings he received – from Soviet diplomats in Germany, from the Soviet spy Richard Sorge in Japan, and from Winston Churchill, among others – of the impending German invasion of the Soviet Union on 22 June 1941.[14] The variety of sources from which Stalin received the information that an all-out German attack was imminent should have led him to question his assumption that, for the near future, this was out of the question. One day before the Nazi invasion, the head of the NKVD, Lavrenti Beria, hoping to avoid being a future scapegoat, wrote to Stalin that 'I and my people, Iosif Vissarionovich [Stalin], have firmly embedded in our memory your wise conclusion: Hitler is not going to attack us in 1941.'[15]

It seemed that the more people warned Stalin of the coming German attack, the more he suspected a deliberate campaign of disinformation. Stalin, who is sometimes depicted as the ultimate realist in politics, was surprisingly gullible where Hitler was concerned. He evidently trusted the leader of Nazi Germany more than he trusted his own most senior officers, since three of the five Marshals of the Soviet Union were sentenced to death in 1937–38 and the two who were left were the least competent. Soviet losses in the earliest days of the war would have been nowhere near as great as they were, had the warnings been taken seriously, and had the Soviet high command not been savaged by Stalin himself. In the conduct of the war, Hitler and Stalin both added greatly to the loss of life in their own armies by refusing their commanders permission to retreat, even when they were in hopeless positions.

Stalin, however, was better than Hitler at calculating the likely reactions of Western governments – including the administration of the most powerful country, the United States – to his actions. Thus, with the ending of the Second World War, he got away with the creation of what became the Soviet bloc in Central and Eastern Europe. In the immediate aftermath of war with Germany, there was no appetite in the West – or by 1945–46 the physical resources in Western Europe – for embarking on another war, this time against their most important ally in the defeat of Nazi Germany. Stalin, moreover, knew where to draw the line. The Soviet Union was as physically and materially devastated by its wartime victory as was Nazi Germany in defeat and in no position at that time to combat American military strength. Even after Soviet hegemony in Eastern Europe had been secured, with the establishment of Communist states all loyal (initially at least) to Moscow, Stalin was opposed to helping Communists come to power in Greece. He withheld Soviet backing for them in order to avoid direct conflict with the Western powers and thus risk the loss of the Soviet Union's recent gains on the European continent.[16]

The creation of Soviet client states in Europe was in the long run of no advantage to Russians and the other nations that made up the Soviet Union. The Soviet takeover of Eastern Europe was the principal cause of the Cold War, leading to vast military expenditure on both sides, which was a greater drain on the smaller Soviet economy than on that of the United States. Stalin's insistence not simply on having regimes in East-Central Europe which would not be a threat to the Soviet Union but also on the establishment of Soviet-type oppressive systems in those countries meant there was little chance of winning hearts and minds in the 'people's democracies'. His preference for 'Muscovite' Communists (those from East-Central Europe who had spent a lot of time in the Soviet Union and had managed to avoid disappearing in the NKVD maelstrom of the late 1930s) over 'national Communists', who had actively engaged in the anti-fascist resistance of the domestic underground, only made that task harder. Popular unrest in central Europe at various times – in addition to the refusal of Tito (who *had* spent plenty of time in Moscow but, more crucially, had led the Partisan resistance to German occupation) to take orders from Moscow – brought major headaches for the Kremlin. Ultimately, the animosity towards the Soviet Union of a majority of the population of central and eastern Europe as a result of having Communism imposed on them meant that for the Soviet successor states, and Russia in the first instance, there was a legacy of distrust that was only partially redeemed by the transformation of Soviet foreign policy under Gorbachev.

Stalin showed a mixture of caution and bravado in the run-up to the Korean War. The initiator of the proposal for North Korea to attack the South and extend the Communist regime to the whole of Korea was Kim Il Sung. He had, however, to seek Stalin's agreement, for he was not only heavily indebted to the Soviet Union for bringing him to power, he also needed Soviet weaponry. When in March 1949 Kim first proposed to Stalin a North Korean surprise attack on the South to unite the country, Stalin vetoed the idea. At that time there were 7,500 American troops in the South and Stalin was anxious to avoid a direct confrontation with the United States. The Americans did not, however, expect an attack from the North and later that year their troops began a withdrawal. By the end of January 1950 Stalin was won over by Kim. Much had changed in the meantime. The withdrawal of US troops was almost complete, with only some five hundred remaining. More significantly, the Chinese Communists had emerged victorious in their civil war and had established a Communist government in Beijing. Should it turn out that the North Koreans could not achieve victory on their own, this raised the possibility of China supplying troops to ensure a successful outcome. Stalin had no intention of involving Soviet troops, but would supply materiel.[17]

Mao, for his part, was reluctant to commit China to participation in a Korean war. The country and especially the army were exhausted, and Mao in those days had to listen to opinion within the Politburo where there was a strong feeling that China should focus on domestic reconstruction. Stalin, however, was accepted even by Mao as the senior and most authoritative figure within the worldwide Communist movement (a deference he never showed to any subsequent Soviet leader). Mao also felt some obligation to the North Koreans who had sent tens of thousands of troops to fight on the Communist side in the Chinese civil war. They were now returning to Korea, battle-hardened, and ready to fight in the South.[18] Having eventually agreed in principle to supply troops, Mao was slow to follow through after North Korea launched the war on 25 June 1950. Initially, it did not seem necessary, for the element of surprise had been effective and the North Koreans had soon captured Seoul, the capital of the South. However, the tide was to turn when the US led a United Nations-sanctioned multinational force to assist the South Koreans who themselves supplied the largest contingent of troops. Neither the South (Republic of Korea) nor the North (Democratic People's Republic of Korea) was a member of the UN. More importantly, neither was the People's Republic of China. In the face of American refusal to recognize the new Chinese government and accord it the seat reserved for China in the UN, the Soviet delegation was currently boycotting the United Nations. In their absence from the Security Council, that body voted by 9 to 0 (with Yugoslavia abstaining) to condemn the North Korean attack and (two days later) to call on UN members to resist it.

The UN forces drove the North Korean troops back beyond the 38th parallel, the dividing line drawn in 1945 between the Soviet- and US-controlled zones. Stalin called on Mao to send a fighting force, writing that he did not think it would draw them into a 'big war', but if it did, this was not something they should fear 'because together we will be stronger than the USA and England'.[19] When China did commit troops, it was on an enormous scale. Three million soldiers crossed into Korea and, according to US estimates, they suffered as many as 900,000 casualties, taking together the killed, missing or wounded; among those killed, in an American air raid, was Mao's eldest son.[20] Inconclusive armistice talks began in 1951, but by 1952 Kim Il Sung had become more ready to make peace, having realized that the attempt at reunification on his terms would not succeed. With the Soviet Union supplying massive amounts of armaments but no troops, while the Americans suffered losses, Stalin, however, had no wish to call a halt. Nor did Mao, in spite of the scale of Chinese casualties. The stalemate might have gone on for much longer, with a still higher death toll, had Stalin not died in March 1953. The new collective Soviet leadership looked to improve their relations with the Western world and were ready to seek a compromise agreement to end the war. After three million Koreans had been killed (approximately a tenth of the peninsula's population), an armistice was signed in July 1953, with Korea divided along the line of the ceasefire.[21]

After his initial caution about supporting Kim Il Sung's attempt to unite Korea under Communist rule by force, Stalin had been firmly committed to continuing the struggle, however heavy the cost in other people's blood. For Stalin the Korean War had the advantage of ensuring that China was in alliance with the Soviet Union against the United States and he believed that the main loser from the conflict was the US – the 'main enemy'. Right up to the time of his death Stalin was urging Mao and Kim Il Sung to drag their feet in the cease-fire talks. Stalin's confidence in the wisdom of his support for the war was, however, misplaced. As a leading Russian historian, Vladimir Pechatnov, has observed, the Korean conflict had very negative conse-quences for the Soviet Union in the longer term. It 'led to a massive rearmament of the United States and NATO's transformation into a full-fledged military alliance' and 'it also boosted the United States' long-term military presence in the region'.[22]

Autocrats and Oligarchs in Chinese and Soviet Foreign Policy

If Mao is compared with the post-Maoist Chinese ruling group and Khrushchev compared with his successors, we find that they fit the pattern whereby the more autocratic individual leader was the readier to take major foreign policy risks than the more collective leadership.

The two men were themselves on a collision course from 1956 onwards. They were both dominating personalities and they were moving politically in different directions. That combination precipitated the Sino-Soviet split. As Khrushchev embarked on destalinization, Mao became more ideologically extreme. The Chinese leader was scarcely less ruthless than Stalin in disposing of opponents, real or imagined, within the ruling party, although his Great Leap Forward and especially the Cultural Revolution were dissimilar from Stalin's style of rule. Even after Stalin had become an object of attack in the Soviet Union, Mao continued to defend him, and the Soviet *vozhd*'s works were republished in China long after they had ceased to appear in Russia. Although Stalin had at times treated Mao less than respectfully, Khrushchev's debunking of him was not to Mao's taste and threatened his own 'cult of personality' – even though that had not yet approached the heights it reached a decade later during the Cultural Revolution when the 'Little Red Book' of quotations from Mao was treated with a reverence greater than that accorded the entire works of Marx and Lenin.

Sharp foreign policy differences also emerged. The post-Stalin Soviet Union was the first of the two major Communist powers to seek better relations with the United States and, in spite of Khrushchev's impetuousness and inconsistency, the Soviet leadership as a whole were vitally concerned to avoid nuclear war. Mao, in contrast, took a recklessly irresponsible view of the prospect of all-out war. He told the Indian prime minister Jawaharlal Nehru in 1954 that 'the socialist camp would survive a nuclear war while the imperialists would be totally wiped off the face of the earth'. Three years later he shocked East European Communists when he told a gathering of the international Communist movement in Moscow in November 1957 that, in a nuclear war, the world would lose a third, or perhaps a half, of its population, but those numbers would soon be made up, and as a result of the war the imperialists would have been utterly defeated 'and the whole world will become socialist'.[23]

In the remaining years of the 1950s following Stalin's death, Khrushchev was strengthening his position within the Soviet leadership which remained, however, essentially collective. It was from the early 1960s, by which time he had set himself above his colleagues and frequently made policy on the hoof, that Khrushchev was at his most wilful and dangerous. Of nothing was that more true than his idea of installing nuclear weapons in Cuba. This led to a stand-off with the United States which could have led, had either side refused to compromise, to catastrophic nuclear war. In the end, good sense prevailed. The Kennedy administration made major concessions, but won the public relations battle. The United States agreed that they would not in future sponsor any interventions to topple the government led by Fidel Castro in Cuba. They further promised that they would, after a decent interval, remove their missiles from Turkey, where they had been installed in easy reach of the Soviet Union. It was agreed, however, that there would be no announcement of the latter concession. Thus, when the Soviet missiles were withdrawn from Cuba, it appeared as if only Khrushchev had backed down. There had been major doubts in the Soviet leadership and in the military about placing missiles in Cuba in the first place, but being forced to ship them out was seen by the army (and by Castro) as a humiliation. When Khrushchev was deposed in October 1964, one of the major errors of which he was accused was the Cuban missile escapade.[24] More generally, his colleagues, most of whom had treated him fawningly in the years of his ascendancy, spoke of his 'impulsiveness and explosiveness, his unilateral, arbitrary leadership, his megalomania'.[25]

One of the stimuli to Mao Zedong's break with the Soviet Union was what Mao took to be Khrushchev's desire to reach an accommodation with the United States (no matter how inconsistently the Soviet leader went about it). He was to be at least as concerned by the relative cosiness of the Nixon–Kissinger relationship with the Soviet leadership in Brezhnev's time. Mao himself, though, was prepared to flirt with the United States to avoid having a simultaneously fractious relationship with both military superpowers. In common with the entire Beijing leadership, he also had the longstanding goal of shifting the US from its position of support for the Taiwanese (Republic of China) government as the one legitimate Chinese state. The belated recognition by the United States of the statehood of the People's Republic of China was accomplished by Richard Nixon in 1972, although a fuller normalization of US–Chinese relations did not occur until 1979 when it was achieved by President Jimmy Carter and Deng Xiaoping.[26] It was only after Deng emerged as Mao's most authoritative successor in 1978 that his policies of 'reform and opening' saw China begin 'the process of integrating itself, really for the first time, into the international system'.[27]

Deng's first foreign trip after returning to the centre of power was to Singapore which he had last visited almost sixty years earlier. In 1920 it had been a 'colonial backwater', now it was 'a powerhouse'.[28] It had, in the words of the major architect of that transition, Lee Kuan Yew, gone 'from Third World to First'. Lee, who had got to know a vast number of world leaders during his long political career, wrote of that 1978 conversation with Deng: 'He was the most impressive leader I had met. He was a five-footer, but a giant among men. At 74, when he was faced with an unpleasant truth, he was prepared to change his mind.'[29] Deng, for his part, was much impressed by Singapore's progress. He went on to establish good relations with Lee and to accept that his country had much to learn from those Chinese who had experience of making market economies work.

Whereas Mao aimed to dazzle the world with the power of his radical ideas and of China's revolutionary example, his successors have pursued more pragmatic policies. The course was set by Deng, even though he did approve one major military enterprise – the attack on Vietnam in 1979 in response to the Vietnamese driving the Pol Pot regime out of Cambodia. On a visit to the United States, Deng informed President Carter of China's concern about the Vietnamese occupation of Cambodia and their intention to 'teach Vietnam a lesson'. Carter was prevailed upon by his National Security Adviser, Zbigniew Brzezinski, not to try too hard to dissuade the Chinese from this action.[30] Deng told his White House interlocutors that it was China's intention that it should be a short war. It may have been even shorter than he had in mind, for it was far from a triumph for the Chinese forces. They were forced to withdraw within less than a month, in which time they had suffered an estimated 42,000 casualties in the face of fierce Vietnamese resistance.[31]

In the years since then China has modernized its armed forces, but has relied much more on its growing economic power to exert influence throughout the world. It has taken a fairly narrow view of its national interest, punishing with fewer high-level political contacts and a reduction of trade and investment opportunities those countries which offered support to the Dalai Lama, raised too vociferously abuses of human rights in China, or suggested that Taiwan might become a fully independent state. The pragmatism, however, has extended to improving relations with Taiwan – to such an extent that a majority of Taiwanese prefer their present situation of de facto autonomy within a pluralist democracy to the option of political integration with Communist China *or* to de jure independence. That last option would not only end the mutually beneficial economic relationship which the island now enjoys with mainland China but also raise the serious possibility of a Chinese invasion and the further risk of a wider conflict involving the United States. Post-Maoist China has established close economic ties with countries in every continent of the world, using the tools of direct foreign investment and also overseas aid. Much of China's international economic and diplomatic activity is related to its energy and raw material needs, but some is connected with the search for political support in international bodies. Even a small Caribbean country has, after all, a vote in the United Nations.[32] China's economic power has been used by its post-Maoist leadership as an important instrument of foreign policy in a way it never could be in Mao's time, since he so disrupted the country's economic development with the Great Leap Forward and the Cultural Revolution.*

In general, China's more collective leadership in the years since Mao's death has been quite risk-averse in its conduct of foreign policy. Being vulnerable to criticism of its own human rights record and lack of political freedoms and democracy, twenty-first-century China has been, along with Russia (which in the same period has seen an increasingly drastic curtailment of independent political activity), a firm advocate of the doctrine of non-interference in the internal affairs of other states. Yet, even that doctrine has been laced with a cautious realism. China was opposed to the 2003 US invasion of Iraq but, as Odd Arne Westad notes, it did not wish to take the lead in the campaign against something that was going to happen anyway. They were content, therefore, to leave the task of 'main opponent of unilateral

---

* More worryingly for other countries, however, China has developed cyber intrusions to such an extent that it has been described as 'the most aggressive cyber state in the world today' (although there are other strong contenders). See David Shambaugh, *China Goes Global* (Oxford University Press, New York, 2013), p. 297. Misha Glenny, however, writes: 'For the moment, the United States is the acknowledged front runner as developer of offensive cyber weapons. But the Chinese, the French and the Israelis are snapping at their heels, with the Indians and British not far behind.' (Misha Glenny, *Dark Market: CyberThieves, CyberCops and You*, Bodley Head, London, 2011, p. 178.)

US action' to Russia as well as to such European allies of the United States as France and Germany.[33] Moreover, the foreign policy team in Beijing had 'concluded that the Iraq and Afghanistan wars were weakening the United States, rather than making it stronger'.[34]

The post-Khrushchev collective leadership in the Soviet Union (as well as post-Soviet Russia) also conducted a fairly cautious international policy. Conflicts in Africa saw the United States and the Soviet Union backing different sides, fighting proxy wars with African lives, but when Cuban forces played a major part in the war in Angola, repulsing troops of the South African apartheid regime, this was on the initiative of Fidel Castro, not the Kremlin. Castro later observed: 'Never before had any Third World country acted in support of another nation in a military conflict outside its own geographic region.'[35] Even the worst Soviet foreign policy decisions of the Brezhnev era, the invasion of Czechoslovakia in 1968 and of Afghanistan in 1979, were not expansionist undertakings, although the Afghan venture was interpreted as such in Washington at the time. The use of military force was seen in Moscow to be in both cases essentially a defensive measure, designed to restore the status quo ante. In the case of Czechoslovakia, it was to put an end to an attempt to combine political pluralism with socialist ownership, while the country remained a Soviet ally, although a more enlightened Kremlin leadership would have been interested in seeing the experiment run its course. The intervention restored an orthodox Soviet-type system and served as a warning to other European Communist states of the limits of Soviet tolerance. It also helped to ensure that the break with the Soviet Union, when it came at the end of the 1980s, would be comprehensive.

Sending Soviet troops to Afghanistan had the aim of ensuring that this neighbouring country would not produce a regime hostile to the Soviet Union. The decision was only in the most formal sense made by the Politburo as a whole. It was planned in secrecy by a very small group, albeit not the edict of just one person. Indeed, the Soviet leader, Leonid Brezhnev, whose health was poor by this time, was brought into the discussions only at a late stage. By no means the most hawkish member of the group, he did not want a further deterioration of relations with the United States and had to be persuaded that the occupation of Afghanistan would be a short-lived affair. Among the senior members of the Politburo (and they alone were involved in the decision), the Chairman of the Council of Ministers, Aleksey Kosygin, was the most opposed to military intervention. When the leader of the more radical of the two factions into which the Afghan Communists were bitterly divided, Nur Mohammad Taraki, in March 1979 insistently requested direct Soviet military participation to consolidate the government that had been installed in Kabul, Kosygin said that only arms and technical assistance would be provided, adding: 'Our enemies are just waiting for the moment when Soviet troops appear in Afghanistan.'[36] It was, however, the General Secretary Brezhnev who had the last word, for on a major foreign policy decision his consent was essential. The three people who persuaded Brezhnev that the Soviet Union should intervene militarily in Afghanistan were the KGB Chairman Yuriy Andropov, the Minister of Defence Dmitriy Ustinov and the Foreign Minister Andrey Gromyko, with Andropov and Ustinov the most decisive duo.

The Afghan Communists' seizure of power in April 1978 had taken the Kremlin by surprise, for it had been achieved by the faction less connected with Moscow and less favoured there. Communists in Afghanistan were to bring far more troubles for the Soviet leadership than had the traditional leaders of the country, with whom relations had been uncomplicated. After they gained power, Afghanistan's Communists devoted as much of their energy to killing each other as to suppressing their traditional opponents. By the time of the Soviet invasion in December 1979, Taraki had been imprisoned and executed by his successor, Hafizullah Amin, a murderous rival from the same faction as Taraki. Andropov, Ustinov and Gromyko distrusted Amin, with Andropov and the KGB, in particular, fearing that he might 'do a Sadat' and switch sides to the Americans.[37] He had studied in the United States and within the chronically suspicious KGB there were those who wondered if he might have been recruited by the CIA.

Since Amin, like his predecessor Taraki, had been seeking direct Soviet military participation to consolidate Communist rule in Afghanistan, he held a lunchtime party on 27 December 1979 to celebrate the fact that the Russians had finally arrived. The KGB used the occasion to poison him. Amin survived, but was still suffering ill effects when Soviet troops stormed his palace that night and shot him dead. That was the easy part. The Soviet leadership found it much harder to get out of Afghanistan than to get in. Before Gorbachev became general secretary in March 1985, his predecessors were already aware that they were making limited progress at best and that the prolonged war had damaged their international standing. They had lost friends in the Third World and had seen a deterioration in their relations with both the US and China. From the outset of his leadership, Gorbachev intended to bring Soviet troops home but, like Western leaders in similar situations (including an American president with troops in Afghanistan in the second decade of the twenty-first century), he wanted the withdrawal to occur in a manner that would not be seen in the outside world as a humiliating retreat. Like them, he could not tell parents of dead soldiers that their sons had lost their lives in vain, although, as he observed to his foreign policy aide Anatoliy Chernyaev in the summer of 1987, he found it 'awful when you have to defend Brezhnev's policies'.[38] By the time the last Soviet soldier left Afghanistan in February 1989, over 25,000 of their comrades had died there, with more than 50,000 wounded, while many others suffered from post-traumatic stress disorder. Afghan losses were vastly greater. More than a million of them were killed during the Soviet war.[39]

Cold War paranoia led to many foolish decisions on both sides of the ideological divide, and armed interventions without major unintended consequences are rare. Time and again governments think that the military part of the operation will be over in a matter of weeks or months, after which the right kind of government will be securely installed. Outside specialists, as distinct from senior KGB officers, were given no opportunity to influence the Soviet decision to invade Afghanistan. The director of an institute for economic and political analysis, which contained more radical reformers than any other in Moscow, Oleg Bogomolov, sent a critical memorandum to the Central Committee of the Soviet Communist Party on 20 January 1980 which spoke of the 'hopelessness and harmfulness' of the military intervention.[40] By then it was too late. The decision to intervene (planned for late December) had been formally ratified at a Politburo meeting on 12 December 1979, in which all the members present had to append their signatures. The principal opponent of the intervention, Kosygin (who more than once commended to the Afghan Communists the example of the Vietnamese who, he said, had seen off both the Americans and the Chinese without the help of any foreign troops), was absent from that Politburo meeting.[41] The pros and cons of intervention were never debated in the Politburo as a whole, and the opposition of Kosygin was disregarded by the small inner group who took the decision to invade Afghanistan.

THE SELF-DECEPTION OF BRITISH 'STRONG LEADERS'

If we turn to democracies, Britain provides several examples of prime ministers intent on dominating their colleagues and coming to disastrous conclusions on the basis of a misplaced faith in their own judgement on foreign policy. The two most clear-cut cases are those of Anthony Eden and the collusion with France and Israel to invade Egypt in 1956 and of Tony Blair and the invasion of Iraq in 2003. In the latter case, the prime mover was, of course, the United States, where the decision was somewhat more consensual. The USA would have intervened militarily in any event, whether or not Blair volunteered British lives and resources to the joint effort.[42]

There are arguments about the extent to which these leaders deceived the public, that deception being especially clear in Eden's case, but they were guilty, above all, of self-deception, of believing what they wanted to believe. Eden and Blair disregarded the knowledge and judgements of those best qualified to assess the likely consequences of their actions. While the support subsequently greatly diminished, initially public opinion was fairly evenly split, with millions of British citizens prepared to take at face value the word of both prime ministers on a major international issue and especially inclined to support British troops in action.*

* On 1–2 November 1956, just after the British air attack on Egyptian military targets had begun, an opinion poll found only 37 per cent answering 'right' to the question, 'Do you think we were right or wrong to take military action in Egypt?', with 44 per cent saying it was wrong. Once British ground forces were engaged in Egypt, some rallying of support for the action occurred, with 53 per cent on 10–11 November satisfied with what Britain was doing in the Middle East and 32 per cent against (with 15 per cent undecided). See Hugh Thomas, *The Suez Affair* (Weidenfeld & Nicolson, London, 1967), p. 133. The Iraq war likewise divided the British people, but there was a clearer majority in favour of the action initially than there had been for the Suez venture. The fact that both the major political parties supported it was an important difference with 1956 when the Labour Party opposed the use of military force. A Mori

In the Suez crisis the attack on Egypt was opposed by both the main opposition Labour Party and the small Liberal Party. In the case of the Iraq war, the Conservative Leader of the Opposition, Iain Duncan Smith, appeared to be trying to outbid Blair and the Labour government in his enthusiastic support for the policy decided upon by the US government. The war was opposed in Britain by the Liberal Democrats and by the Scottish National Party, as well as by a substantial minority of Labour MPs, a much smaller group of Conservative dissidents and millions of citizens who did not belong to any party. Bad foreign policy decisions often go along with, and may be influenced by, misleading historical analogies.[43] Suez and Iraq both brought out the most hackneyed of all the comparisons to be regularly recycled since the Second World War. It has been Neville Chamberlain's posthumous misfortune to be held up time and again as exemplifying the one model which must *not* be followed – that of appeasing dictators. His style of rule provided much justification for holding him personally responsible for policies based on the belief that it was feasible to do a deal with Hitler and Mussolini. Yet in their attempts to concentrate a major foreign policy decision in their own individual hands, prime ministers who have been most anxious to distance themselves from Chamberlain have been in that respect his closest imitators.

Chamberlain and Appeasement

Chamberlain was, nevertheless, more in tune with the broad thrust of public opinion in September 1938 than were either Eden or Blair. As compared with those who opposed the British government's action in 1956 and 2003, it was a much smaller proportion of the population in 1938 who were against the appeasement policy. Few felt ashamed

---

poll taken between 28 and 31 March 2003 found 47 per cent approving of Tony Blair's handling of Iraq, as compared with 44 per cent disapproving. The military action itself was supported by a wider margin, 56 per cent for and 38 per cent against. In contrast, the war evoked a much more positive response in the United States. A poll conducted in the USA at the same time as that in the UK found 69 per cent agreeing with George W. Bush's handling of Iraq. See http://ipsos-mori.com/newsevents/ca/180/Iraq-Public-Support-Maintained-8212-The-State-Of-Public-Opinion-On-The-War.aspx. In both countries, majority support for the war turned into substantial majorities against within a very few years.

of Chamberlain's description of the conflict Hitler was stoking between Czechs and Sudeten Germans as one 'between people of whom we know nothing'. Moreover, the words with which Chamberlain prefaced those remarks had a wide resonance. He said how 'horrible, fantastic, incredible' it was that 'we should be digging trenches and trying on gas-masks here' because of a quarrel in that 'far away country'. When he returned from Munich in 1938 and proclaimed on 30 September that 'I believe it is peace for our time', Chamberlain received a rapturous reception.[44] After the carnage of the First World War, the intense desire to avoid another such conflict was more than understandable. In retrospective justification of Chamberlain, it can be also argued that it was to Britain's advantage to go to war with Germany a year later, by which time rearmament had proceeded further and Nazi Germany's subsequent aggression meant that the British population was more psychologically prepared for battle and sacrifice.

Chamberlain, however, did not sign an agreement with Hitler primarily to buy time, any more than Stalin was simply buying time with the Nazi–Soviet Pact. Both men actually trusted Hitler to keep his word, and Chamberlain believed that it was a 'peace with honour' he had secured, not a mere delay before hostilities began.[45] His predecessor, Stanley Baldwin, had been no less anxious to avoid conflict, although he was averse to maintaining a constant interest in foreign policy. He told the Foreign Secretary, Anthony Eden, in the autumn of 1936 not to bother him with foreign affairs, since he would be focusing on the problem presented by the king and his mistress, which led to the abdication of Edward VIII. As this remark followed a period of three months in which Eden had not had a comment from the prime minister, he found it 'an astonishing doctrine'.[46]

In his biography of Baldwin, Roy Jenkins suggests that Baldwin was 'as much of an appeaser as Chamberlain, but less dogmatic and self-righteous'.[47] The second part of that statement is undoubtedly true, the first part more questionable. The Earl of Swinton (Viscount Swinton at the time), who was Air Minister in both Baldwin's and Chamberlain's governments until Chamberlain dismissed him, did not dissent from the view that Baldwin 'avoided foreign affairs', declaring: 'I do not think he liked foreigners, and he certainly did not understand them.'[48] However, Swinton's own efforts, and that of others in the Air Ministry, to invest in new types of aircraft – Hurricanes and Spitfires

– and in the development of radar were never obstructed by Baldwin who allowed ministers to get on with the job. Chamberlain, who intervened constantly in policy matters, did not give a high priority to rearmament, and that was reflected in his removal of Swinton from the Air Ministry at the end of May 1938. Years later Churchill told Swinton: 'You were sacked for building the Air Force that won the Battle of Britain, and they couldn't undo what you did.'[49] Baldwin was much criticized, especially by Winston Churchill, for a speech he made in the House of Commons in November 1936 in which he said that if he had gone to the country in the previous election and said that Germany was rearming and 'we must rearm', he could not think of anything that in 'this pacific democracy' would have made electoral defeat more certain.[50] Swinton points out that at the time of the 1935 election Britain was in fact rearming (albeit more slowly than Churchill deemed necessary) and, in particular, committing itself to a vast increase in expenditure on the Royal Air Force.[51] This, of course, had more to do with the departmental minister concerned than with the prime minister.

Chamberlain's leadership style could not have been in sharper contrast with Baldwin's emollient and consensual manner. As Swinton noted, it was when Chamberlain ventured for the first time in his life into foreign affairs that he became especially 'autocratic and intolerant of criticism'. The very field in which he was most inexperienced was the one in which 'he became almost intolerably self-assertive, sometimes even making personal decisions and taking personal initiatives without consulting either his colleagues or the experts'.[52] As a Foreign Secretary who had complained about Baldwin's lack of interest in international affairs, Eden now had good reason for concern that Chamberlain was going to the opposite extreme. The relationship was strained from the outset between 'a headstrong old man and a headstrong young man' and 'Eden rightly resented the secrecy with which Chamberlain surrounded his personal contacts, his hush-hush messages from and meetings with mysterious go-betweens'.[53] The Foreign Secretary, whose emphasis on collective security and the League of Nations put him at odds with Chamberlain, nonetheless found himself often defending policies which were essentially the Prime Minister's and with which he was out of sympathy. Somewhat belatedly, he decided he could put up with this no longer and resigned in February

1938 over Chamberlain's plan to begin, without preconditions, discussions with Mussolini. The resignation stood Eden in very good stead in the longer term, for he escaped collective responsibility for appeasement and its failure. It led to his being Churchill's choice as Foreign Secretary (after a brief period as War Minister) in 1940, a post he held for the remainder of the Second World War and in the government which Churchill led from 1951 to 1955.[54]

Chamberlain preferred to surround himself with people who would support his foreign policy views and kept out of the government the most vigorous Conservative critics of appeasement. Thus, he was happy to appoint Lord Halifax as Eden's successor. Alfred Duff Cooper, the most anti-appeasement member of the Cabinet, deplored the change, writing in his diary that 'Halifax will be a bad Foreign Secretary', for he 'knows very little about Europe, very little about foreigners, very little about men.' Halifax was also a 'great friend' of Geoffrey Dawson, the editor of *The Times*, whose influence was 'pernicious'.[55] Harold Nicolson, a member of the government coalition as a 'National Labour' MP (and an anti-appeaser with a strong international background whose views became increasingly close to those of his fellow backbencher Winston Churchill) wrote of the prime minister in his diary entry of 26 August 1938: 'Chamberlain has no conception really of world politics. Nor does he welcome advice from those who have.'[56]

One of the most pro-rearmament Labour MPs, Hugh Dalton, wrote of Chamberlain that not only was he 'inexperienced, gullible and ill-informed' in foreign affairs, but that he also 'preferred advisers with these same qualities to men of experience, shrewdness and knowledge'. Thus, when he went to negotiate with Hitler, he did not take with him any senior official from the Foreign Office, but instead Sir Horace Wilson whose expertise was in industrial disputes, not in international relations.[57] Chamberlain had, said the Earl of Swinton, 'a personal faith that he could handle the dictators and make them see reason'.[88] As Swinton observed: 'Neville was running a one-man band, and became angry if anyone appeared to question his judgment. All the negotiations and secret or official contacts with Mussolini were his own. Munich was his own. He was convinced that he, and he alone, could understand and get on with the dictators and secure a peaceful settlement with them.'[89] Already out of office by the time of the Munich agreement, Swinton was, nevertheless, asked for his view of it by Chamberlain.

He answered that he thought it had been worthwhile 'buying a year's grace', for in the course of a year much of the aircraft production programme would come to fruition. Provided the prime minister would do everything possible to advance rearmament, he would support Munich on that basis. 'But I have made peace,' replied Chamberlain.[90]

Until the point that it became clear that Hitler cared nothing for any apparent agreement he had reached with Chamberlain, only a minority in parliament opposed the prime minister's efforts to avoid war. The Labour Party had failed to resolve its dilemma of being both strongly anti-war and vehemently anti-fascist and had actually voted against the sharp rise in expenditure on the air force proposed by Swinton when the Air Estimates came to the House of Commons in 1935.[91] Although there was a minority of Labour MPs in favour of accelerated rearmament, the official Opposition opposed the government primarily on the grounds that an arms race was leading to war.[92] Chamberlain was personally and politically disliked by Labour politicians, but he had more than enough doting followers on his own benches. None more so than Sir Henry ('Chips') Channon, the American who, after his marriage to Lady Honor Guinness, became a leading London socialite and a Conservative MP.* When Chamberlain proudly announced to the House of Commons on 28 September that Hitler had 'invited him to Munich tomorrow morning', Channon recorded in his diary that he felt 'an admiration for the PM which will be eternal' and 'longed to clutch him'. He described the scene in the House: 'We stood on our benches, waved our order papers, shouted – until we were hoarse – a scene of indescribable enthusiasm – Peace must now be saved, and with it the world.'[93] In his diary Duff Cooper provides a more balanced picture: 'The scene was remarkable, all Government supporters rising and cheering while the Opposition sat glum and silent.'[94]

Duff Cooper was one of the very few people in the Cabinet who was prepared to stand up to Chamberlain in the face of the prime minister's utter self-belief. He had been Secretary of State for War

---

* A characteristic entry (of 19 June 1938) in Channon's diaries reads: 'The "Sunday Express" today published a most extraordinary paragraph to the effect that I am really 41 instead of 39, and hinted that I had faked my age in the reference books. The awful thing is that it is true'. (*Chips: The Diaries of Sir Henry Channon*, edited by Robert Rhodes James, Penguin, Harmondsworth, 1970, p. 198.)

when Baldwin was Prime Minister and was moved from being the minister in charge of the army to charge of the navy by Chamberlain. As First Lord of the Admiralty, Duff Cooper's discontent with Chamberlain grew. Noting in his diary that Chamberlain 'hates any opposition', he took it upon himself to provide some.[95] Within the Foreign Office there was a range of opinion, but its best-informed members tended to take a firmer and more realistic line on the dictators of Germany and Italy than did the prime minister. Duff Cooper refers to an 'admirable' Foreign Office telegram he read on 11 September 1938 which instructed the British ambassador, Sir Nevile Henderson, 'to make it quite plain to the German government where we should stand in the event of war'. Henderson, who was an archappeaser, sent a series of messages back which were 'almost hysterical, imploring the Government not to insist upon his carrying out these instructions which he was sure would have the opposite effect to that desired. And the government had given way.'[96] By 'the government', Duff Cooper noted, was now meant just four people – the Prime Minister, the Chancellor of the Exchequer Sir John Simon, Foreign Secretary Lord Halifax and the Home Secretary Sir Samuel Hoare.[97]

As the crisis in relations with Germany developed in late September 1938, Chamberlain spoke on the radio at eight o'clock on the evening of 27 September. For Duff Cooper, 'It was a most depressing utterance. There was no mention of France in it nor a word of sympathy for Czechoslovakia. The only sympathy expressed was for Hitler whose feeling about the Sudetens the Prime Minister said that he could well understand. And he never said a word about the mobilization of the Fleet. I was furious.'[98] A Cabinet meeting was held later in the same evening. Duff Cooper wrote in his diary that night: 'I spoke at once. I thought it important to get my oar in before the Big Four, as once they had spoken I knew that the yes men who are the majority of the Cabinet would agree with them.'[99] He said that Henderson in Berlin 'had shown himself a defeatist from the first' and expressed his disappointment that Chamberlain in his broadcast had been unable to give any encouragement to the Czechs and 'reserved all his sympathy for Hitler', adding: 'If we now were to desert the Czechs, or even advise them to surrender, we should be guilty of one of the basest betrayals in history.'[100] On 29 September Chamberlain flew to Munich and came back with the 'agreement' that allowed the Germans to march into Czechoslovakia and gave

Hitler the concessions he wanted, albeit accompanied by assurances that Britain and Germany would never go to war with each other. Chamberlain was greeted in London the following day with what Duff Cooper called 'scenes of indescribable enthusiasm'. He added that he 'felt very lonely in the midst of so much happiness that I could not share'. Duff Cooper condemned the agreement at a Cabinet meeting that same day and resigned from the government.[101]

Even after Hitler had annexed the rest of Czechoslovakia the following year, Chamberlain was seen by his critics, such as Harold Nicolson, to be following a 'dual policy', an overt stance of arming and a covert practice of appeasement, using Horace Wilson as his personal envoy. Chamberlain reorganized the government in April 1939, but in his diary entry of the 20th, Nicolson wrote that 'Chamberlain's obstinate refusal to include any but the yes-men in his Cabinet caused real dismay'.[102] There were no easy choices for a British government in the late 1930s, faced by the expansionism of Nazi Germany and fascist Italy, especially since the choice of Stalin's Soviet Union as a potential ally was unpalatable for most members of the government headed by Chamberlain and certainly anathema for the Prime Minister himself.*

Chamberlain's guilt did not lie in trying to prevent a war. There are grounds for deep scepticism about Churchill's belief that war with Hitler's Germany could have been avoided if it had been made clear much earlier that Britain (and its still-existent empire) was prepared to fight and had armed itself adequately for that purpose. What might deter a rational actor, even if that person was an authoritarian ruler, would not necessarily have had the same effect on Hitler, given his

---

* His successor, Winston Churchill, who was second to none in his anti-Communism, was profoundly relieved when the Soviet Union in June 1941 did enter the war. The American ambassador to London, Gilbert Winant, who had succeeded Joseph Kennedy in that role, spoke with Churchill on 21 June 1941, the day before Nazi Germany invaded Russia but when Churchill was certain it was about to happen. To his aide John Colville's suggestion that Churchill as an 'arch anti-Communist' would be in an awkward position supporting the Soviet Union, the prime minister's response was: 'Not at all. I have only one purpose, the destruction of Hitler, and my life is much simplified thereby. If Hitler invaded Hell I would at least make a favourable reference to the Devil in the House of Commons.' See Churchill, *The Second World War, Volume III: The Grand Alliance* (Cassell, London, 1950), p. 331; and Colville, *The Fringes of Power: Downing Street Diaries 1939–1955* (Hodder and Stoughton, London, 1985), p. 404.

personality and the nature of Nazi ideology. It was Chamberlain's illusion that he understood foreign policy better than those with far greater knowledge and experience of the world beyond British shores, and that he was uniquely capable of preserving peace through establishing a constructive relationship with the dictators, that was blameworthy. This involved him in playing down the foreign aggression and domestic crimes of the German and Italian regimes. Not least important, Chamberlain's exclusion of formidable critics and potential rivals in his own party from membership of the Cabinet stifled debate at the highest governmental level, making his conduct of foreign policy a still pertinent illustration of the dangers of a prime minister concentrating an excessive power in his (or her) own hands.

Eden and the Suez Crisis

Sir Anthony Eden, who succeeded Winston Churchill as Prime Minister in 1955, had a very different background from that of Neville Chamberlain. Whereas Chamberlain's previous political experience had lain in domestic policy, Eden was very much a foreign policy specialist. He was also someone with long experience of the Middle East and a Persian and Arabic speaker. Yet in the year after he entered 10 Downing Street it was a calamitous error of judgement in foreign policy, in relation to the Middle East in particular, that did permanent damage to his reputation. His folly could not be put down to ignorance of the wider world, as Chamberlain's could. A major part of the problem was that Eden, having been perceived as a weak leader, wished to show that he was strong. Writing in his diary during Eden's short prime ministership, Sir Evelyn Shuckburgh (who had earlier been Eden's Private Secretary and by this time was Under-Secretary in the Foreign Office dealing with the Middle East) observed: 'He is far away, thinking largely about the effect he is making, not in any way strengthened in character, as I had hoped, by the attainment of his ambition' of having become prime minister.[103] Eden was acutely sensitive to press criticism which included the charge that he was indecisive. As Keith Kyle, the author of the major book on Eden and the Suez crisis of 1956, noted: 'He became obsessive about not appearing to dither'.[104]

Colonel Gamal Abdel Nasser had come to power in Egypt, following an officers' coup of 1952, in which he was before long to emerge as the most determined and popular political figure. Following a power struggle, he became Egyptian president in 1954. He was an Arab nationalist opposed both to the Muslim Brotherhood in Egypt (one of whom tried to assassinate him) and to domestic Communists. The fact that he imprisoned Egyptian Communists, however, did not prevent him from developing within a very few years friendly relations with the Soviet Union. Eden as Foreign Secretary had initially sought good relations with Nasser and had adopted a relatively conciliatory policy towards Egypt. The UK and Egyptian governments had reached an agreement in 1954 that all British troops based in Egypt would leave the Suez Canal zone by 1956. Churchill was far from enthusiastic about this policy of 'scuttle', but went along with it. Some right-wing Conservative backbench MPs, who became known as the 'Suez group', were outspokenly critical.[105] Just six weeks after the last of the British troops left Egypt, Nasser nationalized the Suez Canal.[106] This was partly triggered by Egyptian disappointment that the United States and Britain had the previous year changed their minds about financing the Aswan Dam on the River Nile, a project dear to Nasser's heart. It was later to be built with the support of the Soviet Union.

The nationalization of the Suez Canal, which had previously been owned by the Suez Canal Company, in which there were British and French interests, was announced by Nasser in a speech on 26 July when he stated that Egypt had begun 'to take over the Canal Company and its property and to control shipping in the Canal . . . which is situated in Egyptian territory, which is part of Egypt and which is owned by Egypt'.[107] Although Nasser offered compensation to the shareholders, Eden reacted with outrage, which was shared by a large part of the British establishment. Even the Labour Party leader, Hugh Gaitskell, who was to become an outspoken and effective critic of the subsequent Israeli-Anglo-French invasion of Egypt a little over two months later, said in a speech in the House of Commons: 'It is all very familiar. It is exactly the same as we encountered from Hitler and Mussolini.'[108] It was a popular but highly misleading analogy, used by the Prime Minister, Anthony Eden, and by the Foreign Secretary, Selwyn Lloyd, both at the time and in retrospect.[109] Eden was aware that he was seen in some Conservative circles as an irresolute leader, too ready to make concessions to those opposed to British interests to have the full approval of his own parliamentary party. The dubious references to history, portraying the Suez crisis of 1956 as analogous to the appeasement dilemmas and viewing Nasser as a new Hitler or Mussolini, added to the muddle. Egypt, in contrast with Nazi Germany, was not a major industrial power, and Nasser was neither a fascist nor a Communist, but a nationalist.

The British and French governments decided that they would not only take the Suez Canal back under international ownership but that they would also topple Nasser, by force if necessary. After the nationalization of the canal, an 'Egypt Committee' of the British Cabinet was established, and only four days after Nasser had effected the Canal takeover, made clear its readiness to advocate the use of force to achieve what would now be called regime change. The minutes of the meeting of 30 July of this committee – which was to become, in effect, a War Cabinet – stated: 'While our ultimate purpose was to place the Canal under international control, our immediate [purpose] was to bring about the downfall of the present Egyptian Government.'[110] There was much talk about how important the free flow of maritime traffic through the Canal was to Britain and to the international community, and patronizing aspersions were cast on Egypt's ability to maintain this. However, no disruption of shipping actually occurred, and life proceeded normally outside the hothouse atmosphere of 10 Downing Street.

There was no similar appetite for military action in the White House. President Eisenhower and his Secretary of State, John Foster Dulles, took scarcely a more favourable view of Nasser than did their British counterparts, although they were more concerned about his possible tilt towards the Soviet bloc and Communism than with historical comparisons with fascism. Eden merged his own particular obsessions with the different preoccupations of the US administration in his communications with Eisenhower. Thus, in a telegram dispatched to the President on 1 October 1956, he wrote: 'There is no doubt in our minds that Nasser, whether he likes it or not, is now effectively in Russian hands, just as Mussolini was in Hitler's. It would be as ineffective to show weakness to Nasser now in order to placate him as it was to show weakness to Mussolini.'[111] In the political context of the Cold War, Eisenhower was aware that international opinion would not take kindly to operations that smacked of old-fashioned imperialism on the part of Britain and France, and he made plain that he was opposed to a military invasion of Egypt. In 1956 he had, moreover, a presidential election to fight, in which the former general was concerned to be seen as a peacemaker. Eden was aware of Eisenhower's opposition – he had it in black and white in letters from him – but he deceived himself into believing that the American president would accept the outcome of military intervention once it was presented to the United States as a fait accompli.

Nasser was an authoritarian leader, but one whose brand of pan-Arab nationalism was for a time hugely popular at street-level in the Middle East, particularly because of his championship of the Arab cause vis-à-vis Israel, which would eventually suffer a heavy blow in the Six-Day War of 1967. What Eden in 1956 had in common with Chamberlain in 1937–39 had far less to do with a struggle against fascist dictators than with a similar domination of the decision-making process and disregard of the views of those best qualified to give advice – most notably, in Eden's case, the Middle Eastern specialists within the Foreign Office and the government's Law Officers.[112] Nasser's nationalization of the Canal was not illegal. It was Britain and France, together with Israel, who were to be in breach of international law. Britain's ambassadors in the Middle East, the Foreign Office specialists and the principal law officers within the government were opposed to the military intervention in Suez, even without knowledge of the most dishonest element in the policy, the collusion with Israel, although some of them suspected it.[113]

Eden and Lloyd had already agreed on a policy proposed by their French counterparts that Israel would attack Egypt and that Britain and France would then intervene, ostensibly to separate the warring parties, while going on to finish the job by reasserting control over the Suez Canal and removing Nasser from power. It became known as the Challe plan, for it was first elaborated to Eden at Chequers on 14 October 1956 by General Maurice Challe, deputy head of the French General Staff.* This method of bringing down Nasser had been thought up in Paris and discussed with leading figures in Israel,

---

* In 1961 Challe became the leader of an attempted military coup to oust President de Gaulle, for which he was sentenced by a military court to fifteen years of imprisonment. See Charles de Gaulle, *Memoirs of Hope: Renewal and Endeavour* (Simon & Schuster, New York, 1971), pp. 105–111; and Kyle, *Suez*, pp. 296–297.

including General Moshe Dayan, the Chief of the General Staff. The Israeli Prime Minister, David Ben-Gurion, persisted in calling it 'the British plan'. Initially he viewed it warily, regarding it as 'the best of British hypocrisy', but he came round to it.[114]

The details of the plan were worked out at a meeting on 22–24 October in Sèvres, on the outskirts of Paris.[115] The Israeli delegation was headed by Ben-Gurion, the French team was led by the premier Guy Mollet. The head of the British group was the Foreign Secretary Selwyn Lloyd (rather than the prime minister), although Lloyd did not stay for all three days of the conference.[116] The meeting was so sensitive and secret that Eden was adamant that no written record of it should be kept. He was dismayed, therefore, when he discovered that the senior Foreign Office official present, Sir Patrick Dean, had after Lloyd's departure signed a document summarizing what had been agreed.[117] Eden dispatched another diplomat to Paris the next day to retrieve it, and that British copy was then destroyed. It was Ben-Gurion who had proposed that a protocol binding on all three parties be drawn up, partly to make sure that the British, of whom he was suspicious, did not double-cross him.[118] The French government's copy of the Sèvres protocol was subsequently lost, but the Israeli one was deposited in the Ben-Gurion Archive and surfaced only in the year of the fortieth anniversary of the Suez affair, 1996.[119]*

On 29 October 1956 Israeli troops began their attack on Egypt. The next morning the French premier Guy Mollet and Foreign Minister Christian Pineau flew to London, supposedly to draw up an Anglo-French ultimatum to the belligerents, telling them to stop fighting otherwise British and French forces would intervene to separate them and to seize the Canal. The document had, in fact, been drawn up

* By the time of the 1959 general election in Britain, Suez was no longer an especially salient issue. If the contents of the Sèvres protocol had been revealed in the late 1950s, the combination of deceit and debacle which Suez represented would have been very damaging for the Conservative Party. Harold Macmillan, who led the party in that victorious election, had played a curious role in the Suez crisis, which was aptly summarised as 'first in, first out'. He had been among the most hawkish of ministers in supporting military intervention, but as Chancellor of the Exchequer, he was the first to see that pressure on the pound, and the unwillingness of the American government to help until the military action was stopped, meant that the troops would have to be speedily withdrawn.

five days earlier.[120] During the night of 31 October–1 November, British aircraft, fulfilling a promise that had been made to Ben-Gurion, attacked four Egyptian airfields, destroying most of Egypt's bomber force.[121] British and French paratroops were dropped on Port Said on 5 November and, following fierce fighting, controlled the area before the end of the day. By 6 November the Secretary General of the United Nations, Dag Hammarskjöld, was able to announce that both Egypt and Israel had accepted an unconditional ceasefire and Britain and France were asked to do likewise. There had been threats and bluster from the Soviet Union, although the Soviet leadership were secretly delighted by the Anglo–French folly, for it took attention away from the suppression of the Hungarian revolution on which they were simultaneously engaged and about to brutally intensify. Khrushchev had flown to Yugoslavia to seek Tito's support for the crackdown in Hungary. He told Tito that Britain, France and Israel had 'provided a favourable moment' for the further intervention of Soviet troops. The uproar in the West and at the UN about Soviet actions in Hungary would be less because of the distraction of Suez.[122]

Far more decisive than Soviet criticism, more crucial even than condemnation at the UN or from large-scale opposition at home, was the pressure on the pound sterling and American insistence that there would be no financial bailout for Britain unless and until hostilities in Egypt ceased. At that time the pound was still a reserve currency and a flight from sterling was underway. Harold Macmillan had hoped that his wartime friendship with Dwight Eisenhower would lead the president to offer a helping hand, but though they were to go on to re-establish excellent relations after Macmillan had succeeded Eden as prime minister, it did not lead to a softening of Eisenhower's opposition to the Suez venture. In a letter to an old army friend on 2 November, Eisenhower wrote that Britain was reacting 'in the manner of the Victorian period'. He went on: 'But I don't see the point in getting into a fight to which there can be no satisfactory end; and in which the whole world believes you are playing the part of a bully, and you do not even have the firm backing of your entire people.'[123] In a telephone call to Macmillan, Secretary of the Treasury George Humphrey told the Chancellor of the Exchequer: 'You'll not get a dime from the US Government until you've gotten out of Suez.'

Macmillan, taken aback, said: 'That's a frosty message you have for me, George.' Humphrey had, for the sake of privacy, retreated to a refrigerated domestic meat safe to make the call, so he replied: 'Well, it's a frosty place I'm ringing from.'[124]

The British Cabinet, much influenced by Macmillan's total turn-around, now prevented Eden from continuing with the military option. As Keith Kyle put it: 'Throughout the three-month build-up of the crisis Eden had played an absolutely determining role. He dominated those around him, according to his Chairman of the Chiefs of Staff, to a greater extent even than Churchill in time of war, and he had taken on the detailed direction of every move in the game.' Although he did not wish to abort the operation, 'he felt he could not go against the voices of his Cabinet'. That was all the more so because of the seniority of those who had decided that the game was up. Not only Macmillan but also Butler (more sceptical from the outset) and Lord Salisbury were among those now firmly against continuing with the Suez operation in defiance of the United States, the Commonwealth and the United Nations.[125]

As General Sir Charles Keightley, the Commander-in-Chief of Middle East Land Forces, who had been put in charge of the military side of the Suez operation, concluded: 'The one overriding lesson of the Suez operation is that world opinion is now an absolute principle of war and must be treated as such.'[126] Two junior ministers resigned from the government in protest at Britain's military intervention in the Middle East, Sir Edward Boyle and Anthony Nutting. The latter's resignation was potentially the more damaging, for he was Minister of State at the Foreign Office and had negotiated the Anglo-Egyptian Agreement of 1954. The Suez venture achieved almost the precise opposite of what had been intended. It was meant to show that Britain was still a power in the world, not least in the Middle East. It demon-strated instead its comparative weakness and accelerated the ending of its pretensions to imperial grandeur. The aim had been to show that Britain could take military action even when the United States stood aloof or was opposed, whereas the speed at which the govern-ment succumbed to American pressure suggested the opposite. It was intended to ensure that the Suez Canal remained open, whereas the Egyptians had closed it at the outset of the hostilities. The toppling of Nasser was supposedly going to send an encouraging lesson to the conservative Arab leaders who counted as Britain's friends in the Middle East, for they had felt threatened by the Egyptian president's ambitions and popularity. Instead, Nutting observed, by 'making Nasser a martyr and a hero, we had raised him to a pinnacle of power and prestige unknown in the Arab world since the beginning of the eighteenth century'.[127]

The Canal was not reopened to shipping until April of the following year. Eden, who had hoped to consolidate his own national and international standing by playing the leading role in the overthrow of Nasser, was himself undermined, both politically and in his fragile health. He resigned the prime ministership on 9 January 1957 and retired from active politics. On 18 January he boarded a ship for a holiday of recuperation in New Zealand. Nigel Nicolson, one of the band of Conservative MPs on the opposite wing of the party from the 'Suez Group' who had opposed Britain's military intervention in Egypt, wrote to his father, Sir Harold Nicolson, on 22 January: 'I suppose you know that Eden left on Saturday to go to New Zealand the other way round, via the Panama Canal, because, for some reason, the Suez Canal was not open.'[128]*

Blair and the War in Iraq

For the second time since the Second World War, in 2003 a British prime minister led his country into a war fought on a false prospectus, with Tony Blair following in the footsteps of Eden in 1956. There were, of course, major differences. Eden took this action against the wishes of a Republican administration in the United States, whereas Blair acted as the junior partner of a much less knowledgeable Republican president than Eisenhower. Moreover, thanks in no small part to the American opposition, the Suez war of 1956 was short-lived. The Iraq conflict, in contrast, led to a new spiral of violence. Following the removal from power of a secular dictator, internecine and sectarian conflict was still taking a heavy daily toll of lives and limbs more than a decade after the US-led invasion occurred. A study, led by Gilbert

---

* Nigel Nicolson's own political career was halted by his opposition to Eden. He was deselected by his Conservative constituency association in Bournemouth East and thus his parliamentary life ended with the election of 1959.

Burnham (a public health specialist, medical doctor and former military officer), conducted at the Hopkins Bloomberg School of Public Health in the US, estimated an excess mortality of 655,000 in the first forty months after the invasion of Iraq. This high figure has tended to be either ignored or dismissed by those who supported the invasion, but has stood up to further professional scrutiny.[129] Even the Iraqi government's estimates put the number of civilians killed in the first five years after the invasion as between 100,000 and 150,000. By 2009 over 4,300 Americans and 170 Britons had been killed in Iraq, while more than 31,000 foreign soldiers had been wounded by the insurgents.[130]

The decision to invade Iraq was very much an American one, and already in the summer of 2002 it seemed highly probable that it was going to take place, with or without the participation of Britain or other countries. Saddam Hussein headed a viciously authoritarian regime, but one which the United States had assisted, with Donald Rumsfeld as President Reagan's special envoy, when it was at war with Iran.* The attacks of 11 September 2001 on the twin towers in New York and on the Pentagon were seized upon by those within the US administration who were looking for a pretext to attack Iraq. That these particular crimes had nothing whatsoever to do with Saddam Hussein, who was no friend of radical Islamists, was confirmed by the Central Intelligence Agency. As Condoleezza Rice, Bush's National Security Adviser in the run-up to the invasion, observes in her memoirs, 'the CIA felt strongly that there had been no complicity between Saddam and al Qaeda in the 9/11 attacks and said so'.[131] Ever since the Gulf War of 1991 a no-fly zone had been imposed on Iraq and enforced, mainly by American aircraft but with UN support. Vice-President Dick Cheney had been Secretary of Defense at the time of that earlier war

---

* That visit in 1983 was at a time when Iraq was developing weapons of mass destruction and when Saddam had demonstrated just how dangerous the foreign policy of an overweening leader could be. He it was who initiated the war with Iran which lasted from 1980 until 1988, killed more than half a million people, and ended with neither country gaining any territory or changing the other's regime. During Reagan's first term, it was deemed, however, that Saddam was one of the 'less bad' Middle Eastern rulers, in comparison especially with those of Iran and Syria. See Donald Rumsfeld, *Known and Unknown: A Memoir* (Sentinel, London, 2011), pp. 3–8, especially p. 4.

and he regarded Saddam Hussein's continuing rule in Iraq, however constrained and even intermittently bombed by international forces, as 'unfinished business'. From the outset of the Bush presidency in January 2001 Iraq was for him a high priority.[132] President Bush was receptive, especially after 9/11, to the view that Saddam Hussein, with his supposed weapons of mass destruction, constituted a threat which must be confronted.[133] The fact that he was a tyrant, although far from the only one among contemporary world leaders, did not provide a reason consonant with international law for his removal.

International law, however, was the least of the concerns of Cheney, Defense Secretary Rumsfeld and Deputy Secretary of Defense Paul Wolfowitz who were the most intent on regime change in Iraq. Wolfowitz refused to believe that an organization headed by Osama bin Laden could have carried out the 2001 attacks in New York and Washington without a state sponsor and, furthermore, that Saddam Hussein must be the sponsor.[134] The 9/11 attacks were used as ammunition in the campaign of Cheney, Rumsfeld and Wolfowitz to move towards an invasion of Iraq. Despite the CIA's position that 'there was simply no convincing case' for the linkage, Condoleezza Rice noted: 'The Vice President and his staff, however, were absolutely convinced that Saddam was somehow culpable.'[135] Cheney, in his memoirs, offers a lame retrospective rationalization of that position, writing, 'When we looked around the world in those first months after 9/11, there was no place more likely to be a nexus between terrorism and WMD capability than Saddam Hussein's Iraq. With the benefit of hindsight – even taking into account that some of the intelligence we received was wrong – that assessment still holds true.'[136]

When Tony Blair, because of his eagerness to commit British troops to the coming war in Iraq, faced strong opposition in the UK and an impending difficult debate in the House of Commons, President George W. Bush called him at the beginning of March 2003 and 'made clear that he would think no less of the prime minister if Britain did not participate in the invasion'. Blair's response was: 'I absolutely believe in this. I will take it up to the very last.' Bush 'heard an echo of Winston Churchill in my friend's voice'.[137] Blair evidently heard the same echoes. He told an official who urged caution on Iraq: 'You are Neville Chamberlain, I am Winston Churchill and Saddam is Hitler.'[138]

To win the support of the House of Commons for the UK joining in the attack on Iraq, Blair felt obliged to rest his case on Saddam having weapons of mass destruction which posed a threat not only to his region but to Britain. To invade another country in order to change its regime is, after all, a clear contravention of international law.[139] Blair thus said: 'Iraq continues to deny that it has any weapons of mass destruction, although no serious intelligence service anywhere in the world believes it.' Although he listed a number of the iniquities of the Saddam Hussein regime – adding 'I accept fully that those who are opposed to this course of action share my detestation of Saddam' – Blair insisted: 'I have never put the justification for action as regime change.'[140] In a memorandum to his chief of staff Jonathan Powell exactly one year earlier, however, Blair had written (in a document that has now been declassified): 'Saddam's regime is a brutal, oppressive military dictatorship. He kills his opponents, has wrecked his country's economy and is a source of instability and danger in the region. I can understand a right-wing Tory opposed to "nation-building" being opposed to it [military invasion] on grounds it hasn't any direct bearing on our national interest. But in fact a political philosophy that does care about other nations . . . and is prepared to change regimes on the merits, should be gung-ho on Saddam.'[141] Blair himself was certainly 'gung-ho'.

In the House of Commons debate on Iraq three days before the invasion took place on 20 March 2003, Robin Cook, who had been Foreign Secretary for four years before becoming Leader of the House, made a speech which more than a decade later has withstood the test of time.[142] Cook said that if the uncertain American presidential election of 2000 had gone the other way and Al Gore had been president, he suspected the issue of committing British troops to Iraq would not have arisen. He added that the British people 'do not doubt that Saddam is a brutal dictator, but they are not persuaded that he is a clear and present danger to Britain. They want inspections to be given a chance, and they suspect that they are being pushed too quickly into conflict by a US Administration with an agenda of its own.'[143] Pointedly, Cook said:

Ironically, it is only because Iraq's military forces are so weak that we can even contemplate its invasion . . . We cannot base our military strategy on the assumption that Saddam is weak and at the same time justify pre-emptive action on the claim that he is a threat. Iraq probably has no weapons of mass destruction in the commonly understood sense of the term – namely a credible device capable of being delivered against a strategic city target. It probably still has biological toxins and battlefield chemical munitions, but it has had them since the 1980s when US companies sold Saddam anthrax agents and the then British government approved chemical and munitions factories. Why is it now so urgent that we should take military action to disarm a military capacity that has been there for twenty years, and which we helped to create?[144]

Cook could without qualms reproduce in full his resignation speech of 17 March 2003 in the memoir he published later that year, whereas Blair's speech in the same Commons debate, much acclaimed at the time, has not worn well. One hundred and thirty-nine Labour MPs voted against the Iraq war. A senior member of the 10 Downing Street press office, Lance Price – subordinate to the formidable Alastair Campbell – later wrote: 'Had every Labour MP, including those with ministerial jobs, voted with his or her conscience it is almost certain that Blair would have been the one to go . . . He survived thanks to the Conservative Party's backing for the war.'[145] The number of opponents of the invasion grew when it turned out that much of the intelligence on Saddam Hussein's 'weapons of mass destruction' was outdated, misleading or fabricated by unreliable informants, and that any weapons in that category which Iraq formerly possessed had been destroyed. Moreover, the way the intelligence was used by Blair, and also by President Bush, went beyond, in its certainty of tone, what the intelligence analysts themselves could vouch for at the time.

Tony Blair referred to critics of his intention to commit British troops to the invasion of Iraq as the 'anti-Americans'.[146] If understanding the folly of the enterprise and the false premises which underlay the decision were to be criteria of anti-Americanism, their ranks would include the current President of the United States, Barack Obama, and his Secretary of State, John Kerry. The latter, in November 2005, accused President Bush of orchestrating 'one of the great acts of misleading and deception in American history' and of manipulating flawed intelligence to fit a political agenda.'[147] In 2006 – and in the same week as Tony Blair described as 'madness' what he called 'anti-American feeling' of some European politicians – former President Jimmy Carter said in a BBC interview: 'I have been really disappointed in the apparent subservience of the British government's policies related to many of the serious mistakes that have been originated in Washington.' Carter, who opposed the war in Iraq, added: 'No matter what kind of radical or ill-advised policy was proposed from the White House, it seems to me that almost automatically the government of Great Britain would adopt the same policy without exerting its influence.'[148]

Two years earlier Carter's former National Security Adviser, Zbigniew Brzezinski, had made that point especially cogently:

That the US, led by a president who likes simplistic Manichean slogans, might err in a region unfamiliar to it – and that it might do so especially because of the shock effects of the 9/11 attacks – is perhaps understandable, even if still deplorable. It is up to us, Americans, to correct our own missteps. It is more difficult to understand why an ally with an intimate knowledge of the Arab world and a deep grasp of Islamic culture would have been so feckless as not to urge a wiser course of action. Had the UK, America's most trusted ally, spoken firmly as the stalwart voice of Europe instead of acting as the supine follower in an exclusive Anglo-American partnership it could have made its voice heard. The US would have had no choice but to listen.[149]

The problem was that, while Britain did have greater expertise on the Arab world both in the Foreign Office and in academia, Blair was not prepared to take seriously views that contradicted his own certitude or got in the way of his desire always to be close to the American president, whichever president that might happen to be. Charles Tripp, a leading specialist on Iraq, was among those who attended a 10 Downing Street meeting in November 2002, at which Tony Blair and the Foreign Secretary Jack Straw met with academics familiar with the Middle East. Tripp noted that 'ominously, Blair seemed wholly unin-terested in Iraq as a complex and puzzling political society, wanting confirmation merely that deposing Saddam Hussein would remove "evil" from the country'.[150] A former British ambassador in the Arab world, who could see in 2002 that the war was likely to happen, said: 'It will be a disaster. They've got no idea what they are getting into. Iraq is a terribly complicated country. And they are not listening to us.'[151] There was deep disquiet among the Middle Eastern specialists in the Foreign Office, among senior army officers,[152] and in MI5, the security service with the major responsibility for countering terrorism within the UK. The head of MI5, Baroness Manningham-Buller, said that prior to Blair's gamble, there had been a 'very limited' threat posed by Saddam Hussein and that invading Iraq would 'substantially' increase it. Since then the radicalization of many young Muslims in Britain had left MI5 'pretty well swamped' by terrorist threats. She regarded the Iraq conflict as a distraction from combating al-Qaeda. Unfortunately, her warning that the UK would be at greater risk of terrorist attack if Blair pursued the military option against Saddam Hussein's regime has been borne out. 'What Iraq did was produce a fresh impetus of people prepared to engage in terrorism,' Manningham-Buller told the Chilcott Inquiry into the Iraq War. She was dismayed by the bombings in London of 7 July 2005, but said in 2010 that she had predicted such an event.[153]

Former senior civil servants and ambassadors were free to make public their view that the invasion of Iraq was likely to be a disastrous error in a way in which officials still in post were not. Sir Michael Quinlan, who was the top official in the Ministry of Defence when the Cold War came to an end, could see in August 2002 the way things were going in Washington, and observed that the time had come for Britain to oppose the US administration. He wrote: 'No definite proposition is on the table. But anyone who has worked within government, and particularly with the US, knows that once one is tabled, the time for effective influence is past; minds have been made up and domestic consensus negotiated; psychological if not public commitment will often have gone too far for reversal.'[154] As Quinlan noted more than half a year before the invasion of Iraq:

A majority of people polled in a recent survey of opinion on the Arab street believed that a Zionist conspiracy was behind the September 11 attacks; given such sentiment, it would be naïve to assume that a US-led overthrow of Mr Hussein would be hailed with general relief. And there remains the problem of governing Iraq afterwards. Claims about viable regimes-in-waiting, especially ones likely both to please the US and to enjoy popular support, carry little conviction.[155]

Sir Rodric Braithwaite, who chaired the Joint Intelligence Committee in the Cabinet Office in the early 1990s, wrote in 2003 that 'if Blair has had any influence on US policy in the last six years, it has been on packaging only' and 'his blind adherence to the US position on Iraq has left his wider policy in tatters'. Braithwaite is sceptical of the influence that the 'special relationship' gives Britain in the US even at the best of times, regarding it as flattering mainly for the egos of prime ministers and their entourage. It had made Blair 'a hero in America' (although not, it should be said, in the most liberal circles), adding: 'He and his advisers like that.'[156]

Most Cabinet Secretaries who served during the period when Blair was prime minister have been critical of the way he did business – and in relation to Iraq quite specifically. Lord Wilson, Cabinet Secretary from 1998 to mid-2002, in the last meeting he had with Blair before leaving that post warned him of 'the dangers of what was going on and I reminded him of the legal position'. On Blair's attitude to military action, he recalled: 'I would have said there is a gleam in his eye which worries me.' Lord Turnbull, who succeeded Wilson, said that the Cabinet was not shown 'crucial material during the countdown to war, including a March 2002 paper laying out the UK's strategic options regarding Iraq and a July 2002 document outlining military alternatives'. By the time they were given a supposed choice at a meeting in March 2003, it was too late to turn back. It would have led to Blair's resignation and the Cabinet 'were pretty much imprisoned'. The prime minister's 'favourite way of working', said Turnbull, 'was to get a group of people who shared the same endeavour and to move at pace'.[157]

Lord (Robin) Butler, who was Secretary of the Cabinet from 1988 to 1998 and thus worked in that position with three prime ministers – Margaret Thatcher, John Major and Tony Blair – has been critical of Blair's style of rule on a number of occasions. The forums included the official committee of inquiry which produced, under Butler's chairmanship, a Review of Intelligence on Weapons of Mass Destruction.[158] Concerned to protect intelligence judgements from political pressures, the committee recommended that the post of Chairman of the Joint Intelligence Committee be held by 'someone with experience of dealing with Ministers in a very senior role, and who is demonstrably beyond influence, and thus probably in his last post'. The final recommendation in the report was still more pertinent in its aspersions on Blair's style of rule. Butler and his colleagues said that 'we are concerned that the informality and circumscribed character of the Government's procedures which we saw in the context of policy-making towards Iraq risks reducing the scope for informed collective political judgement. Such risks are especially significant in a field like the subject of our Review, where hard facts are inherently difficult to come by and the quality of judgement is accordingly all the more important.'[159]

US Secretary of Defense Rumsfeld embarrassed Blair by saying in public less than a month before the invasion what President Bush had indicated to the prime minister in private, namely that the attack could perfectly well go ahead without British participation.[160] This was a war of choice for the United States and it was the Bush administration as a whole, with some members much more enthusiastic about the impending action than others, which had made the choice. In Britain, it was essentially Blair's choice because of the degree to which he had concentrated foreign policy-making power in 10 Downing Street. Although Blair, at a moment when it had been politically convenient to do so, admitted that statutory powers are conferred directly on Secretaries of State and other ministers and not on the prime minister, the Cabinet Office was reorganized to serve the prime minister personally rather than the Cabinet as a whole.[161] The Defence and Overseas Committee of the Cabinet, which had traditionally been the key body for collective decision-making on foreign policy, fell into desuetude during Blair's premiership and did not meet at all in the months preceding the Iraq war.* Instead, there were ad hoc committee meetings summoned by Blair, in many of which no minutes were taken. The Cabinet itself was not shown documents that were essential if they were to come to an informed judgement. These included the provisional legal opinion of the Attorney-General, Lord Goldsmith, that without a UN resolution specifically authorizing an invasion of

---

* A National Security Council was created as recently as 2010. The functional equivalent of the old Defence and Overseas Policy Committee of the Cabinet, it is chaired by the prime minister and based in the Cabinet Office, with a National Security Secretariat, headed by a former senior member of the Foreign Office who has the title (new in UK politics) of National Security Adviser. The ministerial membership includes the Foreign Secretary, Home Secretary, Defence Secretary, International Development Secretary, Secretary of State for Energy and Climate Change and, in the Coalition Government formed in 2010, the Deputy Prime Minister (the leader of the minority party in the coalition).

Iraq, the occupation of that country would be illegal under international law. (Following a visit to the United States, Goldsmith changed his mind.)[162]

When the military might of the USA was brought to bear, it is not surprising that the aim of overthrowing Saddam Hussein was accomplished. But his removal did not, and could not, carry the legitimacy that it would have done if achieved by his own people. The invasion of Iraq underlined the relevance of the already-quoted lesson General Sir Charles Keightley drew from the unsuccessful Suez venture that 'world opinion is now an absolute principle of war and must be treated as such'. The Iraq invasion and occupation was condemned by the Secretary-General of the United Nations,[163] by most of its member states, by international lawyers and, as survey research has shown, by the overwhelming majority of Arabs.[164] The initial support in the United States evaporated as the conflict continued and American lives were lost. In Britain, where opinion was more evenly divided at the time the troops went in, the war became progressively more unpopular. It did not eliminate Saddam's weapons of mass destruction, for they had already been destroyed. The invasion led to inter-communal conflict in Iraq and switched the balance of power from Sunni to Shia Muslims and hence brought Iraq closer to Shia Iran.

Moreover, the chances of the Taliban being defeated in Afghanistan and the prospects for the political success of that military intervention were seriously undermined. Victory in Afghanistan was always going to be a dubious prospect in the long term, but the dispatch of an international force there had a legitimacy at the outset which the Iraq invasion lacked. The intervention in Afghanistan was given United Nations backing in late 2001, since an attack on al-Qaeda bases in that country was seen as a valid response to the 9/11 attacks in the United States. However, the extension of the 'war on terror' to an Arab country made more plausible the idea that the United States and its coalition partners were waging an anti-Islamic 'crusade'.[165] The one-sidedness of US support for Israel in the Arab–Israeli disputes lent credence to that view.[166] As most of those best qualified to judge, including the head of the agency charged with countering terrorism in Britain, have testified, the invasion of Iraq was a stimulus to Islamist extremism and led to a great increase, not reduction, in the number of small groups planning murder and mayhem (most of which MI5 in the UK succeeded in foiling). The response to 9/11, which, *inter alia*, was supposed to bring culprits 'to justice', involved degrading ill-treatment of prisoners in Iraq and the indefinite imprisonment without trial of others in Guantánamo Bay. Al-Qaeda, which had no chance to be effective in Saddam's Iraq, has become more active there since the invasion. Its greatest setback occurred when the 'Arab spring', brought about by citizens of Middle Eastern countries themselves, produced the first real hope of democracy – thus far, only very partially fulfilled – in the region.

These consequences of the invasion were, of course, unintended, but they did immense damage to the international reputation of the United States and, to the extent that it too was involved, Great Britain. For politicians who supported the invasion it is not good enough to say that the idea of attacking Iraq was right and the errors were only in implementation. In their memoirs, the American protagonists, in particular, blame other officials and agencies for incompetence and lack of foresight. Rumsfeld, for example, writes: 'In the list of intelligence shortcomings, the failure to highlight the dangers of an insurgency was among the more serious. Intelligence reports occasionally discussed the possibility of post-war disorder and instability, but I don't recall seeing a briefing that anticipated the likelihood of a sustained guerrilla campaign against the coalition.'[167] That the invasion would be regarded as illegitimate in Iraq and the foreign troops treated as hostile occupiers did not come as a surprise to specialists on the Arab world. Many of the ill-effects of the invasion of Iraq were not only predictable but were indeed predicted by critics in advance of the war, not least in Britain. For Charles Tripp the sectarian conflict and armed resistance against the occupying powers appeared 'a surprise only to those in the United States and the UK who had engineered the military occupation in the first place'.[168]

Lessons of Iraq: Policy, Process, and 'Strong Leaders'

Saddam Hussein could have avoided the invasion. He bore a huge responsibility for the suffering that was imposed by the intervention as well as for the regime which preceded it. His spokesmen had denied that Iraq had weapons of mass destruction, but Saddam had been more than content to maintain ambiguity. Obstacles were put in the way of the UN weapons inspection team led by Hans Blix sufficiently often to feed the suspicion that Saddam had something to hide. Blix himself believed that some weapons of mass destruction probably still existed, but he wanted time to track them down and was against the invasion. Saddam had, as it turned out, something he felt he must hide or concerning which he must, at least, keep the outside world guessing – the fact that he no longer had such weapons. He had spent all his years as Iraqi leader *burnishing his image as a strongman* and the main reason he was unwilling to demonstrate clearly that Iraq no longer had chemical and biological weapons was that *he did not wish to appear weak*, especially in the eyes of Iran. That was what Saddam told his FBI interrogators after his capture.[169] It was almost certainly true.

Western leaders, including those who opposed the war, assumed that Saddam had some weapons of mass destruction because he had them in the past and he behaved as if they still existed. Opponents of the war did not see that as a reason to abort the Blix mission or to invade and occupy Iraq, thus assuming responsibility for what followed. David Fisher, who, after working in the UK Ministry of Defence for many years was the senior defence official in the Cabinet Office from 1997 to 1999, with access to all the intelligence reports, likewise believed that Saddam still had some chemical and biological weapons. The big mistake made, he now argues, was to analyze Saddam's behaviour as if the Iraqi leader had been governing in a democracy, since no sane politician there would incur 'the penalties of immensely damaging economic sanctions against his people and the threat of military action'. But though no Western democratic leader could survive after behaving the way Saddam did, 'a ruthless Arab dictator could or, at least he could for twelve years'.[170] A leading specialist on Saddam and on the Baath party, Joseph Sassoon, has written that 'the principle of being strong at all times and at any cost accompanied Saddam Hussein throughout his life'. Process is important even within an authoritarian regime. Compounding his obsessive need to show strength, Sassoon writes, was Saddam's 'stubbornness once he had reached a decision and his reluctance from the mid-1980s until his demise to accept negative views'.[171]

Contrary views to those of the US president and the British prime minister could, of course, be raised within the executive and, it goes without saying, outside it in the United States and in Britain. There were, however, flaws in the policy process which contributed to ill-conceived policy in both countries in the run-up to the military intervention in Iraq. In the United States it has not been uncommon for the State Department and the Defense Department to be at logger-heads. It happened during the Reagan administration, but, ultimately, on the big issues Reagan preferred the judgement of the former (and specifically George Shultz over Caspar Weinberger) when it came to dealing with Gorbachev's Soviet Union. In the approach to Iraq the alliance between Cheney, an unusually influential vice-president, and Rumsfeld gave the Defense Department an advantage over State. Although Bush could override the objections of both Cheney and Rumsfeld (as he did when he went along with Tony Blair's wish to get a UN resolution specifically authorizing the attack, a diplomatic effort which predictably failed), he allowed the Defense Department to determine, to a significant extent, Iraq policy before and especially after the invasion. Condoleezza Rice, one of whose main tasks as National Security Adviser in the White House was to facilitate cooperation between the relevant departments and agencies of government, reports the response of the vice-president when she tried to impress on him the need for inter-agency coordination just after US forces had entered Baghdad. 'The Pentagon just liberated Iraq,' Cheney said. 'What has the State Department done?'[172]

Secretary of State Colin Powell, as a former army general, had far more experience of real war than the others, in addition to his background as National Security Adviser to the first President Bush. He was, though, less of a master of Washington turf wars than were Cheney and Rumsfeld. Rice, who was often caught in the middle, witnessed the extreme distrust between Powell and Rumsfeld, with the former 'a cautious consensus builder in international politics' and the latter 'confrontational'.[173] Within the National Security Council, Rumsfeld argued that the US was not obliged to have a view on what would come next in Iraq after the ousting of Saddam Hussein – 'If a strongman emerged, so be it.'[174] Rice surmised that a major reason why Powell did not put more strongly and directly to the president his complaints that the Defense Department, aided and abetted by the vice-president, were encroaching on matters which should primarily belong to State, was his reluctance as a former professional soldier to challenge the commander-in-chief. There was also the more delicate factor in Colin Powell's relationship with Bush that, as Rice puts it, Powell 'had to be aware that he probably would have been President had he chosen to run'.[175] Drawing on his experience as British Foreign Secretary until 2001, Robin Cook observed that one reason why the UK Foreign Office's influence was limited, so far as decision-making on Iraq was concerned, was 'the fact that the State Department itself had little influence on what was happening in Washington'.[176]

Cook's successor, Jack Straw – unlike the four UK Foreign Secretaries who were his immediate predecessors (three Conservative, one Labour) – supported the invasion, although with far less 'gung-ho' enthusiasm than did the prime minister. Straw takes the view, however, that Blair's reputation has justly suffered from his preferring informal methods of decision-making to proper use of the Cabinet and Cabinet Committees. In his memoirs, Straw writes that 'it would have been far better – for Tony and his reputation, as well as for good government – if he, and I, and the Defence Secretary, had had to discuss progress with, and seek decisions from, a National Security Council, in turn reporting to the Cabinet – and on paper, not by way of oral briefing'.[177] Straw adds that he is confident that the decision to join with the US in the invasion would ultimately have been the same. However, an unnamed senior British minister was quoted as saying soon after the 2003 invasion that 'If Colin Powell had been US president and Jack Straw the prime minister you can be pretty sure there would not have been a war.'[178] If the departments they actually headed had been the prime institutional actors, the same would still more surely have applied.

Given the extent to which Blair's colleagues had allowed him to get away with the strange and egocentric notion that whether or not Britain would go to war was a matter for him to decide, even due process might not have prevented the same decision being reached. There was, moreover, a vast difference between the political stature and public standing of Geof Hoon, Secretary of State for Defence in Blair's Cabinet at the time of the invasion, and that of Denis Healey who held the office from 1964 to 1970 during Harold Wilson's prime ministership. Wilson has been given credit for keeping Britain out of the Vietnam War – which did him no favours in Washington – but in an interview in 2006 Healey said that 'Wilson was tempted and I said "Absolutely not".'[179] That was the proper relationship between a minister and prime minister. If either one of them had been sufficiently dissatisfied with the position of the other, then the pros and cons needed to be argued out in a properly constituted Cabinet committee and subsequently in the Cabinet. In this case, Wilson had enough sense to bow to the superior judgement of the senior minister departmentally responsible who had deep knowledge and long experience of foreign and defence policy (following active service as an army officer in the Second World War). In a non-presidential system, a prime minister should have to work hard to persuade colleagues of high party and national standing on the merits of a policy he or she favours, and not be allowed to pull rank. Better-informed collective judgement, in the case of the Iraq war, should have led to serious scrutiny of easy assumptions about what would follow the overthrow of Saddam Hussein.*

*

Lack of due process places more power in the hands of a premier and of his unelected advisers and has an impact on policy outcomes. In the three cases looked at here, Chamberlain, Eden and Blair all acted high-handedly and kept colleagues inadequately informed about important discussions and documents. Bypassing the appropriate government structures becomes all the more dangerous when the prime minister concerned is desperately anxious to be seen as a strong leader. Of the three, Eden was the most guilty of deceiving the British public, but he circumvented correct procedures slightly less than did

---

* David Fisher who, as a senior defence official, did not oppose the invasion of Iraq at the time, reached the conclusion some years later that it did not meet the criteria of a just war. Fisher writes: 'As casualties have mounted in the years since 2003, it has become increasingly difficult to maintain that more good than harm was produced by military action, however evil and oppressive the Saddam regime had undoubtedly been. Moreover, however the balance sheet is scored, what is clear is that the careful assessment of consequences required by the just war tradition before a war is embarked on was not undertaken. Nor was there adequate planning to ensure the prompt restoration of peaceful conditions after military operations and the establishment of a just peace.' (David Fisher, *Morality and War: Can War be Just in the Twenty-first Century?*, Oxford University Press, Oxford, 2012, p. 213.)

Chamberlain and Blair. While Chamberlain resented opposition, it was Eden and Blair who were the most preoccupied with being *perceived* to be strong leaders. A British journalist who has followed Tony Blair's career closely and (in the main) sympathetically since the 1990s, Andrew Rawnsley, wrote as early as Blair's first year as prime minister: 'Mr Blair has many strengths. Among his greatest weaknesses is an obsession with not looking weak.'[180] That has been accompanied by Blair's unsubstantiated faith in his own judgement.

The way intelligence was interpreted in the lead-up to the invasion of Iraq, by Blair in Britain, and also by Cheney, Rumsfeld and, ultimately, Bush in the United States, was a good illustration of 'premature cognitive closure'. Beliefs simplify reality and mould the way in which information is processed. They screen out inconvenient facts and are systematically more receptive to information consonant with prior beliefs than to information that runs contrary to those convictions.[181] If a head of government – whether a Chamberlain, Eden or Blair – becomes so wedded to his beliefs that all he wants is for them to be reinforced by those whom he consults, he finishes up a victim of self-deception and illusion. It is, therefore, essential that foreign policy decision-making should not be the province of one leader, helped by his or her loyal advisers. Undoubtedly, developments discussed in an earlier chapter – not least, the dramatic increase in speed of travel and communications – have led to more direct interaction between premiers and presidents, requiring them to speak on behalf of their countries. This makes it more, not less, important that the policies they espouse should have been worked out collectively within the elected government. Determination of policy is not a task that should be left to a premier's placemen, but is the responsibility, which they should not shirk, of politicians of independent standing and appropriate departmental responsibilities who, in many cases, will not share all of the leader's predispositions.

8

What Kind of Leadership is Desirable?

Of all the books that have been written on leadership, a very high proportion have emanated from the United States. In the political literature, this usually means a focus on the American presidency, with other countries receiving only passing mention. Moreover, as Hugh Heclo has complained, many presidential studies implicitly lean towards a 'great man' conception of history and politics. Success 'means prevailing over opponents and ostensibly shaping the course of public policy'; success or failure 'is a matter of whether or not the president gets his way'. Thus, presidential studies often become advocacy of presidential power.[1] This point, as I have argued, has applied for some time now to assessments of political leaders more generally. Too often those who seek ascendancy over their colleagues in government and try to dominate them are regarded as strong and, by that very token, successful, and those who work within a more collective leadership are deemed to be weak and less successful.

It is, though, unsurprising that special attention should be devoted to leaderships, individual or as a group, which play a decisive role in effecting great change. I have distinguished the rare *transformational* leaders who have been crucially important in producing *systemic* change from *redefining* governments, still far from common, which alter the terms of the debate and stretch understandings of what is politically possible. Sometimes, to take the British example, that redefining was done by what was very much a collective leadership, in which the prime minister's main task was coordination of the work of others. That was the case with the Labour government headed by Clement Attlee from 1945 to 1951. There are other instances where the prime minister has been the driving force, as may fairly be said of the Conservative government headed by Margaret Thatcher between 1979 and 1990.

In the United States there is a widespread tendency to expect the president to do too much, more than is possible for any chief executive within a system with as many checks and balances.[2] In recent decades there has been a similar tendency for commentators to demand that premiers in parliamentary democracies should do still more than they are already doing. They are urged to wield power with greater vigour, including power over their colleagues and political party. Many a premier and party leader has attempted to oblige, having been goaded by the mass media (and by political opponents with their own agenda) into a demonstration of political virility, eager to prove 'he is his own man'. In the UK some observers and former insiders believe that British prime ministers do not have enough powers. From time to time they advocate the creation of a prime minister's department, being dissatisfied with the extent to which recent incumbents of 10 Downing Street have already colonized the Cabinet Office.[3] In the United States, the gradual increase in size of the executive office of the presidency, created by Franklin D. Roosevelt, has led, as we have seen, to plaintive cries from other parts of government of 'too many people trying to bite me with the president's teeth'. In fact, because of the way power is dispersed within the United States, with an especially powerful legislature, there was and remains far more justification for the presidential back-up in Washington than there would be for a prime minister's department in London. That would mean acolytes guessing (even more than at present) what the prime minister wanted, which would often be conveniently close to their own opinions, as they attempted to bite members of parliament and even ministers with the prime minister's teeth.

When an increasing number of issues are referred to a prime minister for adjudication, this is unlikely to lead to their successful resolution. Problems can become more intractable as responsibility for making decisions is transferred to the head of government, thus delaying matters until that person can give the issue a necessary minimum (but often inadequate) amount of attention.[4] Heclo sees wisdom in the words of the ancient Chinese philosopher Lao-tzu who said that 'a leader is best when men barely know he is there, not so good when men obey and acclaim him'.[5] That, he admits, is an unrealistic counsel of perfection for a modern chief executive, but he is right when he urges that presidents (and this goes for premiers, too) who ensure that other people get together and themselves work out answers to the problems may be exercising 'a more subtle and productive form of leadership' than the 'hyped-up kind of "follow me" drama' familiar in popular culture.[6]

When the United States is put into comparative perspective, it is clear that it is virtually impossible for a modern president to be 'transformational' in the sense in which that term has been used in Chapter 4 of this book. To change the system is scarcely feasible. Even to redefine the limits of the possible is not easy. Franklin D. Roosevelt and Lyndon B. Johnson are the clearest twentieth-century examples of such redefining leadership, and what they achieved was generally positive.[7] (The huge and most tragic exception was Johnson's embroilment in war in Vietnam.) Both presidents made ample and effective use of their 'power to persuade', in Roosevelt's case with particular appeal to a broad public, while Johnson fully exploited his links to individual senators and intimate knowledge of Congress as a whole.[8]

Some presidents have been at their most effective when they let others take the lead in important policies. The role of Secretary of State George Marshall, and the Marshall Plan, in Harry Truman's presidency was, as noted in the Introduction, an example of this style of leadership. Truman, though, stood full-square behind Marshall in his support for the European recovery programme. The civil rights breakthrough, limited and bitterly contested as it was, which occurred on Eisenhower's watch – ending racial segregation of state schools – owed much more to the attorney-general Herbert Brownell than to the president (and, as was seen in Chapter 2, Eisenhower was generally the more hesitant of the two). Ronald Reagan acquired a reputation as a hardliner, but it was when he behaved more collaboratively that he had some legislative success in changing social security and the federal tax code.[9] The same could be said of Reagan's foreign policy. He was content for George Shultz and the State Department to take the lead in responding to the radical change underway in Moscow, and Reagan himself entered into a constructive relationship with Mikhail Gorbachev.

Nevertheless, in the light of the constraints which the American political system imposes on the president, there is more of a case for an occupant of the White House making the most of the powers he has than for prime ministers in parliamentary democracies to be similarly assertive, given that there is normally a majority in parliament (whether of the same party or a coalition of parties) ready to sustain the government. Thus, Alfred Stepan and Juan Linz are among those who argue that President Obama should, on coming to office in 2009, have worked closely with the Democratic majority in the Senate 'to eliminate, or greatly reduce' that institution's blocking power through filibuster. As the Senate has the right to make its own rules at the beginning of a new Congress, a simple majority vote would have eliminated the filibuster during 2009–2010.[10] Given that the United States political system has been described as a 'vetocracy', and has more veto power embedded in it than most, Obama was perhaps unduly cautious about using the legitimacy of his freshly conferred democratic mandate to seek 'the elimination of the extreme majority-constraining filibuster rules'. One result of this would almost certainly have been the passing of his health reforms in less diluted (and less complicated) form, giving him a more convincing message to take to the mid-term 2010 election. In reality, the messy process of passing the complex and compromised health legislation contributed to the defeat of the Democrats.[11] The Patient Protection and Affordable Care Act that was eventually approved could be counted as a 'legislative success', in light of the fierce opposition and misrepresentation it encountered in the United States, but such a 'success' in the British context would have been deemed a failure liable to undermine the authority of the prime minister.[12]

There has not been a *transformational American president* since Abraham Lincoln. Readmission to the Union of the eleven Confederate states that had seceded and granting citizenship to black Americans constituted a transformation of the federal republic. Lincoln has been mentioned only in passing earlier in this book, for its focus is on the twentieth and twenty-first centuries. He is, however, an outstanding example of how collaborative and collegial leadership could be combined with attachment to principle and the achievement of path-breaking change. In an important sense, the republic was refounded on a new basis. It is likely, as the leading authority on the Lincoln presidency James McPherson has written, that 'without Lincoln's determined leadership the *United* States would have ceased to be'.[13] Lincoln's leadership and Union victory in the Civil War, the same author observes, resolved two fundamental problems that had been left unsettled by the American Revolution and the Constitution alike. The first was the survival of the republic as one nation and the second was the 'monstrous injustice' (in Lincoln's words) of a country 'founded on a charter that declared all people deserving of the inalienable right of liberty' which had become 'the largest slaveholding nation in the world'.[14] On the latter issue, Lincoln came under strong pressure to drop abandonment of slavery as a condition of peace, but he refused to do so. After noting that more than a hundred thousand black soldiers were fighting for the Union as he spoke, he said: 'If they stake their lives for us they must be prompted by the strongest motive – even the promise of freedom. And the promise being made, must be kept.'[15] Lincoln went on to employ a combination of high principle and low politics to get the votes needed to pass the Thirteenth Amendment, abolishing slavery, through Congress.[16]

As Doris Kearns Goodwin has demonstrated particularly well, Lincoln's 'political genius' lay not only in the brilliance and profundity of his speeches and in his resolve. It rested also on his feel for timing, an ability to be ahead of public opinion but not so far ahead of it in the policies he pursued as to undermine the chances of success.[17] And, as much as anything, it rested on Lincoln's willingness to work collegially with the most capable politicians of the day, including those who had been his most formidable rivals. A less assured or less magnanimous leader than Lincoln would have been disinclined to surround himself by a group of men, each of whom thought, at the outset of his presidency, that he had a stronger entitlement to the White House. A lesser leader would have been more inclined to appoint to cabinet positions 'personal supporters who would never question his authority'.[18] Instead, Lincoln gave the most senior posts to his principal rivals for the 1860 Republican presidential nomination, Senator William H. Seward of New York, Governor Salmon P. Chase of Ohio, and the Missouri elder statesman Edward Bates. Seward came to regard Lincoln as 'the best and wisest man' he had ever known and observed that his 'magnanimity is almost superhuman'.[19] Chase, who never quite got over what Lincoln called his 'White House fever', on four occasions sent the president letters of resignation, and the fourth time Lincoln surprised him by accepting it. Even so, Lincoln later appointed Chase, who had frequently intrigued against him, to the office of Chief Justice. Subsequently Lincoln told Senator Zachariah Chandler that he 'would rather have swallowed his buckhorn chair than to have nominated Chase', but that the decision was right for the country.[20]

Lincoln often said that 'he, and not his Cabinet, was in fault for errors imputed to them', observed Gideon Welles, a member of that Cabinet. A notable case involved Simon Cameron, the Pennsylvanian political boss who has been credited with the definition of an honest politician as 'one who, when he is bought, stays bought'.[21] Lincoln found it necessary to remove Cameron as Secretary for War after extensive corruption in the War Department had been exposed. However, the president then wrote a long letter to Congress explaining that the unfortunate contracts had been 'spawned by the emergency situation facing the government' and that he and his entire Cabinet 'were at least equally responsible with [Cameron] for whatever error, wrong, or fault was committed'.[22] Cameron was for ever after devoted to Lincoln and, as Goodwin notes, 'appreciated the courage it took for Lincoln to share the blame at a time when everyone had deserted him'.[23]

In a system which invests executive power in a president, that leader generally has the power to make a bigger difference than has a prime minister in a parliamentary democracy. Yet the USA, if we leave aside foreign policy, scarcely fits into that generalization. The modern American political system is one in which power is so divided – among the White House staff, the other government departments and agencies, Congress, the judiciary and the fifty states that make up the federation – that the president has far less power domestically than most prime ministers possess, provided (and it is an important proviso) they can carry with them their Cabinet colleagues. This applies especially to countries with majoritarian electoral systems, rather than proportional representation. The party of which the prime minister is the leader normally has an overall majority in the legislature.

Yet, there are occasions, especially in the field of foreign policy, when the election of an American president has much more far-reaching consequences than the choice of government within parliamentary democracies. The US presidential election of 2000 was a clear illustration of the point. It showed that even when individuals as unexceptional in talent as George W. Bush become leaders of a country, when it is one as powerful as the United States, they can make a significant difference, whether for better or for worse. Yet that election also illuminated the part which chance and sheer luck can play in one, rather than another contender, reaching the highest office. It would not have taken many more Democrat-inclined voters in one or two crucial states to have voted for Al Gore rather than for the more radical (but no-hope) candidate, Ralph Nader, to have put Gore in the White House. Or Palm Beach County in Florida might have used a more reliable voting mechanism than its butterfly ballots (the 'hanging chads', whose existence it thrust into the consciousness of an unsuspecting world).[24] Or Gore might have won Arkansas 'if he had been willing to let Bill Clinton's popularity work for him'.[25] In fact, it was Bush's good fortune to scrape victory in the electoral college as a result of factors such as these, even though he lost the popular vote nationally. And this was surely one of the cases where the choice of leader in a democracy had a huge impact on the lives, and deaths, of others in countries far from the United States. As Nannerl Keohane puts it: 'Gore might well have pursued a course in Afghanistan not too different from that of George W. Bush. But he would almost certainly not have invaded Iraq, and on this score alone the world today would be a different place.'[26]

'NAPOLEONIC' RULE IN BRITAIN?

Setting the top leader far above and apart from the ruling group within an authoritarian regime, or above and apart from his or her Cabinet in a democracy, serves the purpose of strengthening the leader's power at the expense of party colleagues. It has, therefore, a real utility for the leader and for the leader's entourage, if the purpose is maximization of personal power rather than good government. In an autocracy, obedience to a dictator's command and the absence of overt opposition feeds his vanity. There is often also more than a touch of vanity involved in the attempts of democratic leaders to maximize their personal power. Daily and hourly, Max Weber wrote, a politician has to overcome 'a quite vulgar vanity, the deadly enemy of all matter-of-fact devotion to a cause and . . . of distance towards one's self'.[27] Weber sees lack of objectivity and irresponsibility as 'deadly sins' in politics, and vanity, 'the need personally to stand in the foreground as clearly as possible', something which tempts the politician to commit those offences and to be 'constantly in danger of becoming an actor', concerned, above all, with the impression that he is making.[28]

Margaret Thatcher, although described as an 'egotist' even by her sympathetic major biographer,[29] was more concerned with power as a means to uphold values she held dear than with seeking the limelight out of personal vanity. As was argued in Chapter 3 of this book, she helped to redefine the terms of political debate in British politics in a way in which Tony Blair did not. Blair accepted the new centre ground of British politics which Thatcher and like-minded colleagues had helped to create. Kenneth Clarke, who served in the Conservative cabinets headed both by Margaret Thatcher and then by John Major, remarked that Major's government 'was destroyed from within by people who considered themselves to be the most loyal to Margaret' and it 'was left to Tony Blair to take over Thatcherism with a human face'.[30] Domestically, this included a bias in favour of the private over the public sector in the economy and increasing the private sector component and application of market criteria in health, social and educational provision. In foreign policy Blair went beyond Thatcher in his acceptance of the views of the right wing of the US Republican party, reaching a position which on the Middle East was difficult to distinguish from that of American neocons. Blair influenced only the form, but not the substance, of the Bush administration's approach to Iraq, whereas Thatcher did not hesitate to take Ronald Reagan to task on certain issues, although they enjoyed good relations and an ideological affinity. In particular, and after listening both to advisers within government and to outside specialists, she played an important part in reinforcing Reagan's desire to engage with a new Soviet leadership, helping to convince him that it made sense to do so in the person of Gorbachev.[31] Over time, however, Mrs Thatcher listened much less and would not hesitate to explain to

Hungarians what was happening in Hungary.* She did concede, however, when she visited a Moscow housing estate in 1987, that the people living there 'knew the system even better than I did'.[32]

Although far more polite to, and emollient with, Cabinet colleagues than was Mrs Thatcher, Tony Blair attempted to emulate or even outdo Thatcher in the centralization of power in 10 Downing Street. Thatcher had as her right-hand man and Private Secretary Charles Powell. Blair appointed his brother Jonathan Powell who asked for, and was given, the grander title of chief of staff.[33] (Both of them highly capable officials, they came to these posts from the Foreign Office.) Interviewed in 1996, six years after Thatcher left office, Charles Powell said: 'I've always thought there was something Leninist about Mrs Thatcher which came through in the style of government – the absolute determination, the belief that there's a vanguard which is right and if you keep that small, tightly knit team together, they will drive things through . . . They could go out and really confront people, lay down the law, bully a bit.'[34] Jonathan Powell, before Blair had yet entered 10 Downing Street, in a remark at an off-the-record seminar which was leaked to the press, said that 'we wanted to move from a feudal to a Napoleonic system'. Explaining what he had in mind in a book written much later (its hero is Machiavelli rather than Napoleon), Powell wrote: 'The British system of government is traditionally a feudal system of barons (Cabinet ministers) who have armies and funds (civil servants and budgets), who pay fealty to their liege but really get on with whatever they want to do. There is very little that

---

* Whereas in the earlier years of her premiership, Mrs Thatcher was capable both of asking good questions and of listening to the answers, especially if they came from people with specialist knowledge, this had changed by her last years in office. Ivan Berend, an important Hungarian reformer and President of the Hungarian Academy of Sciences at the time of his meeting with Thatcher in August 1990, recalls that immediately after he was introduced to her, she grabbed his arm, took him to a corner and asked him about the exciting events in Hungary. However, 'she did not wait until I began speaking, and immediately started answering her own questions and explained to me what was really happening in Hungary'. Berend contrasted this with a meeting he had in the same year with the Spanish prime minister Felipe González 'who expressed a deep interest and excellent understanding of what was happening in Hungary, and asked brilliant questions'. See Ivan T. Berend, *History in my Life: A Memoir of Three Eras* (Central European University Press, Budapest and New York, 2009), p. 225.

the prime minister can do to make the government consistent or coherent. The only weapon he has in his armoury, a very blunt one, is hiring and firing people . . . We needed to have greater coordination at the centre on both policy development and implementation.'[35]

Whether either Lenin or Napoleon were appropriate models for a political leader in a democracy, or whether a leader who had never held even the most junior ministerial office (Blair's case, although not Thatcher's) need have other ministers regard him as their 'liege' (master), are questions that should have only one answer. Nothing remotely Napoleonic occurred, but at the beginning of the Labour government's second term, a new institutional mechanism for monitoring the implementation of policy was introduced. Its initiator was Michael Barber who argued that if a government had an objective or target, there should be a plan for achieving it and means created for ensuring delivery.[36] Blair appointed Barber head of this new Delivery Unit, which reported to the prime minister. The targets it set for reducing hospital waiting times, reducing crime and improving school performances were highly controversial, and had some unintended as well as intended consequences. Nevertheless, in a book in which he reflects on his experience in government, Barber argues strongly that the pluses outnumbered the minuses (although the 'targets culture' remains contentious).

Whatever Napoleonic ambitions Blair may have harboured, and in spite of his sense of entitlement to take decisions on behalf of the government, he could never achieve his imperial goal, for if he was the Napoleon of 10 Downing Street, exercising significant control over foreign policy and influencing the social agenda, there was another Napoleon next door where Gordon Brown dominated economic policy-making and hence a large swath of domestic policy. Writing in the last days of the Blair premiership, Barber was just one among many insiders who noted that ministers had to decide 'whether they are predominantly in the Brown camp or the Blair camp or whether they will seek to be in both'. The unusually powerful chancellor was a constant constraint upon Blair's power and, as that power 'ebbed away' during the prime minister's third term, this constraint became still greater.[37]

When Margaret Thatcher died in April 2013, much admiration for her achievements was expressed. Not the least of these was her becoming the first woman prime minister in Britain, and doing so, moreover, as leader of the Conservative Party, which had consistently lagged well behind Labour in bringing women into parliament and government (although it, too, fell far short of the degree of gender equality attained in Scandinavia). There was also much emphasis on Thatcher's 'strong leadership' and praise for her being a 'conviction politician'. There is, indeed, much to be said for a politician having a thought-through political philosophy and firm values. Such a person will not be excessively driven by opinion polls or focus groups, though she or he may take them into account in deciding how to present policy. Convictions, however, and a determination to act on them, are not necessarily an unalloyed blessing. Lenin, Mussolini, Hitler, Stalin and Mao, to take a few obvious examples, were 'strong' and domineering leaders, and they all (even Stalin) had exceedingly firm convictions. A majority of the Conservative Cabinet (and a large section of the parliamentary party) finally decided that they would put up no longer with one of Mrs Thatcher's convictions in particular – the belief that she was always right. Almost a quarter of a century later, the cabinet ministers who told the prime minister she would have to go were still being scorned by those nostalgic for the lost leader. The latter included the historian Andrew Roberts who, in language strangely reminiscent of that used by Stalin's minions about the victims of the show trials of the 1930s, described the Cabinet ministers who saw off Margaret Thatcher in 1990 as 'an over-ambitious cabal of cowards, fools and traitors'.[38]

Geoffrey Howe, whose resignation speech triggered the forced resignation of Margaret Thatcher from the premiership in 1990, wrote of how the prime minister had come to dominate the reactions of her colleagues to the extent that meetings in Whitehall and Westminster were 'subconsciously attended, unseen and unspoken' by her. He notes: 'The discussion would always come around somehow to: how will this play with the prime minister? That gradually grew, to the point where she was so accustomed to getting her own way that she became over-confident; less and less dependent on consultation with colleagues, more and more dependent on a narrow circle. It tends to happen. It happened to Ted Heath. It happened to Tony Blair.'[39] Kenneth Clarke recalled that on one occasion the prime minister said in Cabinet: 'Why do I have to do everything in this government?' Clarke says: 'To which I think I wasn't the only person sitting round the table thinking: "The trouble is, Margaret, that you believe that you do have to. And you shouldn't. And you can't."'[40]★

Thatcher may have tried to bludgeon her Cabinet, and it was ultimately her undoing, but she bypassed it rather less than did Blair. Alistair Darling, who was not only a Cabinet member continuously from 1997 to 2010 but also a politician well disposed towards the 'New Labour' emphasis on 'Middle Britain', is among those who have been critical of the lack of collective discussion, and thus of genuine collective responsibility, for policy during those years. He notes that a reader of Blair's memoirs might be forgiven for thinking that 'for Tony it meant, "New Labour, *c'est moi*"'. Embracing in his generalization Brown's premiership as well as Blair's, Darling says that on too many occasions 'we didn't discuss issues, in principle, well before the die was cast'. As examples of bypassing of the Cabinet, Darling notes: 'Tuition fees [for universities], a policy which has worked, was never discussed properly, so the result was no collective ownership. On Lebanon there was little discussion. And because he thought it was the right thing to do, [Blair] was prepared to ignore public opinion and any reservations there may have been in the Cabinet.'[41]

LEADERS AND PARTIES

It is easier to define *effective* leadership than to get anything remotely approaching consensus on what is *good* or (the rarer) great leadership. An evaluation of a leader as good will depend either on a subjective judgement about that person's likeability or on whether one approves

---

★ That in a democracy senior politicians should feel the need to subordinate their convictions to the will of one person is lamentably reminiscent of life under autocracy in which, when the leader is absent or has not given explicit instructions, trying to divine the will of the dictator becomes the guide to action. In Hitler's Germany this was called 'working towards the Führer'. As Ian Kershaw has written: 'In the Darwinist jungle of the Third Reich, the way to power and advancement was through anticipating the "Führer will", and, without waiting for directives, taking initiatives to promote what were presumed to be Hitler's aims and wishes.' (Ian Kershaw, *Hitler*, Penguin, London, 2009, p. 321.) Cabinet ministers in a democracy, behaving in a similarly supine manner for the sake of promotion (or avoidance of demotion), could usefully be reminded that many of those who have come to occupy the highest political office within their countries were at one time critics, and even rebels, within their parties.

or disapproves of the policies the leader has promoted. Different situations, however, call for different styles and qualities of leadership. Thus, 'the most effective leader in a given context is the group member who is best equipped to assist the group in achieving its objectives'.[42] In Joseph Nye's concise definition a leader is someone 'who helps a group create and achieve shared goals'.[43] In an organization other than a political party a leader may also 'determine or clarify goals',[44] but *determination* of *goals* is not an appropriate function of a party leader in a democracy. The broad objectives – for 'goals' have become less grandiose than they were for some political parties in the first half of the twentieth century – should be the prerogative of the membership of the party in a dialogue with the party leadership, for why otherwise should they give up their time to work for it? In a democracy, effective political leadership will involve helping a political party to win power and, after attaining governmental office, helping to implement the policies the party has espoused.

The relationship between the leadership group as a whole and the party's members in the legislature (as well as the leadership's relationship with the party membership in the country) is normally, and should be, a two-way process. The leadership team have the advantage of being able to determine priorities, but if their actual policies are more influenced by media tycoons or by financial lobbies, this is neither effective nor democratic leadership, but a different form of followership. It is much easier for a party leader – certainly in Britain – to get a good press by distancing himself from his own party than by standing up to media proprietors. Stanley Baldwin was much more robust in his attitude to newspaper owners than have been his late twentieth-century and twenty-first-century successors (with the partial exception of the current Labour Party leader, Ed Miliband). In a speech in 1929, Baldwin said: 'The papers conducted by Lord Rothermere and Lord Beaverbrook are not newspapers in the ordinary acceptance of the term. They are engines of propaganda for the constantly changing policies, desires, personal likes and dislikes of two men.' Continuing his attack on the press barons, he famously went on: 'What the proprietorship of these papers is aiming at is power, and power without responsibility – the prerogative of the harlot throughout the ages . . .'[45]

Tony Blair, in contrast, was much more solicitous towards wealthy newspaper proprietors and business interests than to members of his party, the only people, apart from his Sedgefield constituents in the north-east of England, who had voted directly for him. As noted in Chapter 2, he dismissed them – and not in an offhand remark, but in his memoirs – as 'exiled for years in the Siberia of party drudgery far from the centre of government' and re-emerging in the run-up to a general election 'in the halls of the Kremlin with renewed self-importance'.[46] In what *was* an off-the-cuff remark, an unnamed close ally of prime minister David Cameron was widely quoted in May 2013 describing Conservative Party activists in the constituencies as 'mad, swivel-eyed loons'.[47] Such a disconnection between party members and their leaders, and disdain for the rank-and-file by their leaderships, is not only unbecoming. It is also dangerous for democracy.

Leaders should view their parties not just as a vehicle for their ambitions but as a shared undertaking to advance the most widely shared objectives and values of that party. This obviously requires the serious pursuit of electoral success. Parties which put purity of principle ahead of all compromise are likely to remain in the political wilderness. This need not mean disregarding the views or disparaging the beliefs of the generality of party members. Those are not likely to be identical to the opinions (or apathy) of the broader electorate, but any member of a legislature as well as a party leader has some necessary room for manoeuvre in negotiating between the active and inactive, between the committed and the sceptical.

There are, though, two conclusions on which students of democracies and of countries in transition from authoritarian rule are widely agreed. One is that a viable party system is an indispensable pillar of a democracy and that when parties are manipulated from above, rather than allowed to develop an independent and influential existence, a country in transition from autocratic or oligarchic rule has got little or no chance of becoming a consolidated democracy. A majority of the successor states to the Soviet Union, including post-Soviet Russia, are cases in point. The other finding is that political parties throughout most of the world have seen substantial declines in their membership in the period since the mid-twentieth century and that survey research shows them to be held in low esteem. As the authors of a major comparative study of political parties noted, 'Large majorities of citizens in most countries acknowledge that "Without parties there can be no democracy", but those same individuals often criticize parties for their "divisive" behaviour'.[48] Another of the dilemmas parties in many countries face is pithily summed up by Juan Linz as 'Parties Cost Money: But Not Mine, Not from my Taxes, and Not from Interest Groups'.[49] Interestingly, one country in which democracy has thrived more than most in recent decades is reunited Germany (and, indeed, West Germany before that) where parties do receive state funding and where their membership has increased, although that owes a good deal to the incorporation of the former German Democratic Republic in the united German state.

Given that it is reasonable to expect leaders of political parties in a free and pluralistic political system to have a prior commitment to democracy as such, and granted their need to connect with the wider electorate, it is dangerous if they regard the rank-and-file membership of their party as little more than a necessary evil. The authors of a study of party organizational change in the twentieth century noted that, in order to assert their supremacy, one 'answer is for the leadership to marginalize the party on the ground, and even to let it wither away'. Whether consciously planned or not, at the beginning of the twenty-first century, this appeared to reflect 'the recent experiences of the mainstream parties in Denmark and the Netherlands'.[50] In Britain, in contrast, there was a major membership drive by the Labour Party in the early years of Tony Blair's leadership. Successful though it was at the time, many of those members, as well as other long-standing ones, subsequently left the party in disillusionment, the Iraq war being the last straw for a significant number. Too great a concentration of power in the hands of a party leader debilitates the internal life of the party, while its members are caught between a reluctance to criticize the party leadership in a way that would give succour to political opponents and an equal reluctance to delegate excessive power to the leader.[51]

Criticism of the leader from within the parliamentary party or from the rank-and-file membership will, of course, lead to complaints that the leader has 'lost control' of the party, but we need to question how much 'control' it is appropriate for a leader to have over the people who put him where he is. Equally, a party leadership has a responsibility not to allow intolerant extremists to take over the party. Thus, the UK Labour Party, under the leadership of Neil Kinnock, expelled from their ranks the Militant Tendency organization which had been taking over a number of local party branches, intimidating, berating or boring other members into submission or exit. A similarly 'hostile takeover', as Moisés Naim puts it, of the US Republican Party by the Tea Party has endangered that political organization.[52] The prestige of political parties has declined cross-nationally for a number of reasons. One, as Naim observes, is an unintended consequence of a healthier development, freer media and more independent scrutiny, which has exposed corruption that was previously hidden or silently tolerated.[53] But the 'public tarnishing', he argues, is also connected with political parties having become less able to distinguish themselves from their opponents ideologically.* As a result, they have 'relied less on the popular appeal of their ideals and ideas and more on marketing techniques, the media prowess of candidates, and, of course, the money they could raise'.[54]

None of the criticism of overmighty or presumptuous leaders should be taken to suggest that leadership does not have a distinctive and important role to play. Members of the top leadership team, and not just the top individual leader, have a responsibility to explain and justify why a particular action is being taken, even if it is one unanticipated by party members or one which does not fare well in opinion polls. The polls themselves have a significant part to play in a democracy – countries on the way to authoritarian rule can be relied upon to stifle independent survey research – but they do not relieve leaderships of the duty to give a lead. They need, however, to engage with their parties, giving *them* a leadership role in public discourse, rather than fob them off with sham consultation, for if political parties become moribund, so will democracy.

---

* The United States has partly bucked that trend, gravitating in certain respects towards the opposite danger. It is moderate Republicanism which has been under threat, as has the necessary modicum of consensus on what constitutes civilized democratic discourse. Rather than see implementation of the Patient Protection and Affordable Care Act, which had gone through due process in Congress and had been upheld by the Supreme Court, the Tea Party conservatives showed themselves willing in October 2013 to shut down the federal government, lay off hundreds of thousands of workers, halt medical research, and seriously undermine not only the dollar but their country's international standing. While their extremism, and their misrepresentation of a modest and long overdue social reform, could no longer come as a surprise, what was more remarkable was their success in intimidating more mainstream Republican leaders into going along with an action which, if prolonged, was liable to do profound damage not only to American society but also to the global economy.

It is easy for a leader to have his (or her) own beliefs reinforced by his immediate entourage. It is not too difficult, other than in the time it consumes, for a leader to speak individually to a majority of cabinet members and get their agreement on a particular issue. Most of them will not have given much thought to the matter because they have their own departmental responsibilities and, in a one-to-one conversation with the head of the government, they will be disposed to acquiesce. If, however, this is an important matter of policy principle for the government and the governing party, it is more conducive to good governance and more in keeping with democratic values for the issue to be presented to a Cabinet committee or, if need be, the Cabinet as a whole. There may be one or two people present who have thought seriously about the issue, have come to a quite different conclusion from the premier, and who may have the more cogent arguments. Whether that minority then becomes a majority depends on other members of the top leadership team. They will need not only to have been convinced of the merits of that opposing argument and the desirability of a different policy decision, but also to possess enough backbone to reject the view of the prime minister.

To the extent that political parties decline, their place will be taken by those both within the society and from without who have the most wealth to deploy in the exercise of economic and political leverage. Notwithstanding the great political and social change that has occurred since the eighteenth century, the words of Adam Smith and John Millar quoted in Chapter 1 have not lost their relevance. 'The authority of fortune', observed Smith, is 'very great even in an opulent and civilized society.' His pupil Millar similarly noted that the influence derived from wealth 'is not only greater than that which arises from mere personal accomplishments, but also more stable and permanent'.[55] It is political parties, with a mass membership and strong organization – as well as, importantly, trade unions – which have exercised a democratic countervailing power to that wielded by wealthy individuals, rich families, big business and financial institutions.* If leaders pay more attention to

---

* Smith's and Millar's emphasis on family wealth and connections as a 'source of authority' appears all too relevant two and a half centuries later. The point applies in contemporary authoritarian regimes, not least China, while in parliamentary democracies political parties need to be on their guard against having the best-connected candidates foisted on them, rather than seeking breadth of experience, ability and

the latter than the former, they pave the way for two dangerous outcomes. One is that their countries will more and more become plutocracies rather than democracies. The other is that the place of political parties will increasingly be taken by direct action groups. They are often not particularly interested in democratic norms and procedures and are liable to fall into the same mistaken trap as revolutionaries a century earlier of believing that only ends matter, and that whatever means are deployed to achieve those ends are justified. Even when moved by righteous anger against evident injustice, as in the 'leaderless revolutions' of recent years in the Middle East, they may – given the absence of organization, policy coherence and commitment to political pluralism which a democratic party can provide – pave the way for a new authoritarianism.

LEADERSHIP UNDER AUTHORITARIANISM AND DEMOCRACY

A myth may contain an element of truth, and yet be greatly misleading. Some of the people who have been thought of as strong leaders – Hitler, Stalin, Mao Zedong, Kim Il Sung or Saddam Hussein – did indeed wield enormous power. In that sense they *were* strong leaders. The myth here consists of the idea, sedulously promoted by these leaders and their propagandists, that each of them was singularly wise, gifted and far-seeing. Vast resources are devoted in many totalitarian and authoritarian

---

commitment to the party's values. The danger is readily discernible in Britain. Even in the United States, which still cherishes the 'log cabin to White House' parable (which has occasionally, as in Lincoln's case, been a reality), 'keeping it in the family' has become a pronounced trend in recent decades. It beggars belief – and statistical probability – that within a population of over three hundred million people, the best presidential candidates should turn up in the immediate family of President George H.W. Bush. Family fortunes have counted for much, as in the case of Joseph Kennedy's sons. Still more significant, however, are family members of a president inheriting the latter's wealthy friends, fund-raisers and backers in a system in which more money is required to win an election than in any other democratic country. The United States, moreover, remains the most unequal of the world's democracies. It was at its least unequal, as noted in Chapter 3, when Johnson's Great Society reforms were having an impact. Even then, however, the US was more unequal than other democracies for which comparable data are available.

states to spreading the message of the people's good fortune to have such a great leader. In the absence of alternative sources of information and criticism, the regime's narrative can be, and often has been, widely believed for a time. The fabrication lies also in the idea that concentrating enormous power in the hands of an individual leader brought great benefit to their countries. In reality, their tyrannical rule had disastrous consequences.

There is a qualitative difference between the possibilities open to even the most high-handed and overweening leader within a democracy and such a leader in an authoritarian or totalitarian regime. However hard a leader in a democracy tries to dominate the political process, that person and, more pertinently, his or her party are ultimately accountable to the electorate. There are, however, lessons to be learned, and warnings to be heeded, from looking at leadership in authoritarian as well as democratic systems.* The idea that one leader knows best, and is entitled to have a quite disproportionate share of executive power within his or her hands, is not confined to dictatorial regimes. And even authoritarian systems, as has been suggested in earlier chapters, tend to be less dangerously adventurous abroad and less murderous at home when they are led by an oligarchy rather than an autocrat.

The cult of the leader, which emerged in fascist and in many (not all) Communist states, was pernicious. But there have been unconscious echoes of what in Nazi Germany was the *Führerprinzip* (the leader principle) and what in Stalin's Soviet Union, from the early 1930s onwards, was known as *edinonachalie* (one-person command) also in democracies. We encounter it in the attitudes of politicians and political commentators who want to place more powers in the hands of the top leader nationally and who also prefer one-person rule at the local level to more collective leadership. Both in Nazi Germany and in the Soviet Union, especially under Stalin, this big boss principle applied,

---

* That is all the more so because in the contemporary world there are many regimes which have been described as 'electoral democracies', inasmuch as they have elections of a sort, but in which the opposition is given no access to the major mass media, and opposition parties and independent political movements are restricted and harassed. These hybrid regimes – which, in most cases, fit the description of 'electoral authoritarianism' (or 'competitive authoritarianism') better than 'electoral democracy' – occupy a middle ground (although a far from golden mean) between genuine democracies and indisputably authoritarian regimes.

above all, to the *Führer* or, in the Russian case, the *vozhd* at the apex of the system, but it went all the way down the hierarchy, so that little Hitlers and little Stalins at the regional and local level could justify their arbitrary decision-making on the basis of one-man leadership (and they *were* men, not women). After Stalin's death the need to balance *edinonachalie* with *kollegialnost* (collegiality) began to be stressed.[56]

A leader in a highly authoritarian political system who wishes to introduce radical reform has a justification for bypassing the party organization not open to a party leader in a democracy. Since the party itself has generally seized the reins of government by force, proceeded to monopolize power, and then retain that power with a mixture of rewards for conformism and punishments for deviation (all the way up to the death penalty or, at best, long imprisonment for opposition), it cannot convincingly claim either a moral or a democratic right to rule. Thus, neither Gorbachev attempting to liberalize and, ultimately, democratize the political system of the Soviet Union nor Deng Xiaoping aiming to liberalize and marketize the Chinese economic system was under an obligation to abide by the norms of the system each man was trying to supplant. In fact, as a matter of political prudence, they worked within the existing system for as long as it took to make the changes and, in Deng's case, beyond.

In the Politburo chaired by Gorbachev, there was, as even members of it who became his enemies admitted, freer and lengthier discussion, with every opportunity for critical voices to be raised, than had existed under his predecessors. Not knowing what policies he would pursue, the Politburo had selected Gorbachev as party leader. At the time, this meant his automatically becoming the country's leader. Until there was qualitative change in the political system, that same group had the power to remove him from the first of these posts and, as a necessary consequence, from the other. Thus, it made sense for Gorbachev to use his 'power to persuade' within the Politburo, carrying more conservative colleagues with him and, when he could not do so, making tactical retreats. From the point at which an executive presidency was created in the Soviet Union – in March 1990 – Gorbachev increasingly bypassed the Politburo to the fury of its members. By then the Politburo was no longer the functional equivalent of the Cabinet in a system such as that of Britain. It was merely the highest policy-making committee within the Communist Party, which was rapidly losing support in the country and was no longer the centre of power in the Soviet state.[57]

*

Finally, several important misconceptions underlying the myth of the strong leader are worth reiterating. Within parliamentary democracies there is a tendency to believe that the top leader counts for more than he or she actually does. Policy outcomes which have been brought about mainly by others are frequently attributed to the premier. No less often electoral victories are misleadingly hailed as the party leader's achievement, whereas only very rarely has the leader made the difference between victory or defeat. The more fundamental error is to view the top individual leader who asserts his or her political pre-eminence, bypassing senior colleagues and the machinery of government, relying more on a coterie of personal attendants than on his or her political party, as the kind of leader we should wish to see. Usurpation of powers that more properly belong to individual ministers, and which, in matters of intra-governmental or intra-party contention, are more appropriately settled in the course of collective consideration by Cabinet members, are not, and should not be regarded as, the mark of a successful democratic head of government. Leaders who believe they have a personal right to dominate decision-making in many different areas of policy, and who attempt to exercise such a prerogative, do a disservice both to good governance and to democracy. They deserve not followers, but critics.

Acknowledgements

Some of my debts are immediately related to this book and some are of a much longer-term character. Starting with the latter, I am grateful to a number of institutions in which I have studied and worked, but two in particular should be singled out – the London School of Economics and Political Science and St Antony's College, Oxford. Degree courses in Britain have become somewhat narrower and more specialized than they were more than fifty years ago when I was an undergraduate and graduate student at the London School of Economics. Therefore, I still appreciate the fact that in the B.Sc.Econ. at LSE, I was able to study not only politics and economics but also political and economic history, social psychology and sociology and to attend lecture courses that ranged from Michael Oakeshott on the history of political thought and Lionel Robbins on the history of economic thought to Hilde Himmelweit and Bram Oppenheim on theories and concepts in social psychology and Leonard Schapiro on the government and politics of the Soviet Union. As a student I bene-fited particularly from the encouragement of Jack Hayward, Keith Panter-Brick, Alan Beattie and Leonard Schapiro. The institution to which I am even more indebted is St Antony's College, Oxford – and Oxford University more generally – for, notwithstanding Visiting Professorships and Fellowships in, and numerous study visits to, other countries, it has been my academic home for more than forty years. St Antony's, as a graduate college with a special focus on the social sciences and modern history, is distinctive for the strength of its centres of research on particular regions of the world – Russia and Eurasia,

Europe, Africa, the Far East, the Middle East, and Latin America, among them. It has been of great benefit to be able to discuss particular countries – and, in the context of this book, particular leaders – with first-rate specialists on the politics and history of those states. Many of them, as my individual acknowledgements will illustrate, have been Fellows of St Antony's, although friends and colleagues from the wider Oxford academic community and from further afield have also been generous with their time and insights.

In addition to St Antony's being very much in touch with the real political world, I have benefited from a lot of direct contact with political practitioners, both in Britain and in a number of other countries over the years. Some of these meetings arose from ad hoc consultation by prime ministers, party leaders or foreign secretaries; some from participation in meetings of the World Political Forum and the InterAction Council, which bring together former heads of government and a number of academic specialists; while many flowed from the Visiting Parliamentary Fellowship at St Antony's. I mention here by name only a few of the participants in public and political life with whom I have had interesting conversations of direct relevance to the subject of this book – leadership, power and influence in high politics. They include Sir Michael Barber, Ivan Berend, (Judge) William Birtles, Sir Rodric Braithwaite, Sir Bryan Cartledge, Anatoliy Sergeyevich Chernyaev, Patrick (Lord) Cormack, Sir James Craig, the late Ralf (Lord) Dahrendorf, Mark Fisher, Andrei Serafimovich Grachev, former Senator Gary Hart, Geoffrey (Lord) Howe, Derry (Lord) Irvine, the late Rita Klímová, Nigel (Lord) Lawson, Jack F. Matlock, Jr, Vadim Andreyevich Medvedev, the late Zdeněk Mlynář, Joyce (Baroness) Quin, Sir Malcolm Rifkind, MP, the late Georgiy Khosroevich Shakhnazarov, Gillian (Baroness) Shephard, Stuart (Lord) Wood and the late Aleksandr Nikolaevich Yakovlev.

If that is part of the background to the book, it is even more important to highlight the foreground. A work which ranges as widely as this volume incurs many debts to other authors. Those which derive from my reading are, I trust, fully acknowledged in the endnotes. But I have also had more direct help from fellow academics. For answering specific queries, I am particularly grateful to Professor Alan Barnard (Edinburgh University), Professor John Curtice (Strathclyde University), Professor Graeme Gill (University of Sydney), Professor Leslie Holmes (University of Melbourne), Dr Philip Robbins (St Antony's College), Professor Arthur Stockwin (St Antony's) and Dr Ann Waswo (St Antony's). I appreciate even more the kindness of those friends and colleagues who read one or more chapters of this book in manuscript and offered invaluable comments and, in some cases, made necessary corrections. My particular thanks for doing so go to Alan Angell (St Antony's), Professor William Beinart (St Antony's), Professor Geoffrey Best (St Antony's), Dr Nic Cheeseman (Jesus College, Oxford), Malcolm Deas (St Antony's), Professor Rosemary Foot (St Antony's), Peter Fotheringham (Glasgow University), Dr Sudhir Hazareesingh (Balliol College, Oxford), Professor Alan Knight (St Antony's), Professor Rana Mitter (St Cross College, Oxford), Professor Kenneth (Lord) Morgan (Queen's College, Oxford), Professor Tony Nicholls (St Antony's), Dr Alex Pravda (St Antony's), Dr Eugene Rogan (St Antony's), Professor Avi Shlaim (St Antony's), Professor Steve Smith (All Souls College, Oxford), Professor Alfred Stepan (Columbia University, New York), Professor Arne Westad (LSE) and Professor Stephen Whitefield (Pembroke College, Oxford). I am especially grateful to Al Stepan for many stimulating conversations as well as for his valuable comments on several chapters.

It is perhaps more than usually necessary to add that no one mentioned in these acknowledgements should be blamed for my views or assumed to be in agreement with what I have written. In a few cases I can be fairly sure that they *disagree*, since I am arguing against things they have written or said.

I have been extremely fortunate to have as my UK literary agent Felicity Bryan and the splendid team she leads (in exemplary style) at Felicity Bryan Associates in Oxford and I am no less lucky to have as my American agent George Lucas of Inkwell in New York. I have enjoyed a happy and collaborative relationship with my publishers, the Bodley Head in London and Basic Books in New York, and have appreciated very much the encouragement and support of, first, Will Sulkin and then Stuart Williams, publishers at the Bodley Head, and of Tim Bartlett at Basic Books. I am greatly indebted to Lara Heimert, publisher at Basic, who took a keen interest in the book from the outset and saw the US edition through to publication. I am very conscious also of how much indispensable work has been done by Katherine Ailes and Joe Pickering in London and by Michele Jacob and Leah Stecher in New York. Special thanks are due, above all, to

Jörg Hensgen of the Bodley Head who did the detailed editing of this book and made many excellent suggestions. They included very good advice on points which could do with further elucidation and elaboration, and so he shares a modicum of blame for making what was not a short book somewhat longer. Finally, I am, as ever, hugely indebted to my wife Pat who has also read every word of the book in manuscript, been supportive in every way, and has put up with the long hours I have spent working on it. By the time anyone reads this in print, we'll have had the long holiday I've been promising.

Notes and Sources

Preface

1. A.H. (Archie) Brown, 'Prime Ministerial Power', Part I, *Public Law*, Spring 1968, pp. 28–51; and Part II, Summer 1968, pp. 96–118. In an abbreviated version, it was republished in Mattei Dogan and Richard Rose (eds), *European Politics: A Reader* (Macmillan, London, 1971), pp. 459–482.
2. The interview was conducted for a Jesuit journal and reported in the *New York Times*, 19 September 2013.

Introduction

1. To take an example at random, the first sentence of a recent article in a respected newspaper reads: 'For years, it has been a matter of common agreement that what Japan needs, above all, is a strong leader.' See David Pilling, 'Why a strong leader in Japan is a plus not a minus', *Financial Times*, 18 July 2013.
2. John Rentoul, *Tony Blair* (Little, Brown, London, 1995), p. 427.
3. Miliband, who appears to be sufficiently balanced not to be an overbearing leader, rose to the bait rather more than was necessary. Perhaps overly concerned that he might be perceived as weak, he remarked in an interview: 'You discover things about yourself in this job [Leader of the Labour Party], which is that I am someone of real steel and grit . . .', *Guardian*, 7 January 2012. Miliband's use several times of '*my* government' (in the context of what the next Labour government would and would not do), during a generally impressive speech on 24 September 2013 to the Labour Party annual conference, may have been a similar response to exhortation to project an image

of strength. However, no Labour leader or prime minister before Tony Blair (who used the first person singular much *more* than his successor but one) would have employed the constitutionally incorrect and politically imperious terminology, 'my government'.

4. 'David Cameron and Ed Miliband clash over Lords reform', http://www.bbc.co.uk/news/uk-politics-18798683.

5. Donald J. Savoie, *Power: Where Is It?* (McGill-Queen's University Press, Montreal, 2010), p. 96.

6. Jonathan Malloy, 'Prime Ministers and their Parties in Canada', in Paul Strangio, Paul 't Hart and James Walter (eds.), *Understanding Prime-Ministerial Performance: Comparative Perspectives* (Oxford University Press, Oxford, 2013), pp. 151–171, at p. 168.

7. Savoie, *Power*, p. 96.

8. I am extremely grateful to Stephen Whitefield of Oxford University, under whose supervision the investigations of public attitudes were conducted, for generously making available to me the survey data on these post-Communist European states. The italics in the proposition, as well as the interpretation of the differences between one country and another, are my own.

9. Max Weber, *From Max Weber*, translated, edited and with an introduction by H.H. Gerth and C. Wright Mills (Routledge & Kegan Paul, London, 1948), pp. 245–250, esp. p. 245.

10. S. Alexander Haslam, Stephen D. Reicher and Michael J. Platow, *The New Psychology of Leadership: Identity, Influence and Power* (Psychology Press, Hove and New York, 2011), p. 103.

11. Margaret Thatcher, *The Downing Street Years* (HarperCollins, London, 1993), pp. 6–7.

12. The Lord Chancellor, Derry Irvine, chaired four Cabinet committees which formulated policy on constitutional reform – on Scottish and Welsh legislative devolution; on Human Rights legislation; on the Freedom of Information Act; and on reform of the House of Lords. Irvine had, along with David Miliband, drafted the 1997 Labour Party election manifesto and helped to make sure that these issues of constitutional reform, which he cared about, were included. The commitment to hold a referendum on the establishment of a Scottish parliament had become firm Labour policy under Blair's predecessor as party leader, John Smith, and to have reneged on it would have been too damaging to the Labour Party in Scotland for Blair to contemplate. (Blair at the time thought that there was overlap among this legislation and that they, therefore, needed the same guiding hand. That was a major reason why Irvine chaired all four of these important committees.)

13. Tony Blair, *A Journey* (Hutchinson, London, 2010), p. 516.

14. Brown's economic adviser (later a Member of Parliament and minister),

Ed Balls, played an important role in the devising of the tests, and Lord Chancellor Derry Irvine lent his legal skills to their drafting.

15. Alistair Darling, 'The lure of common sense', *Guardian*, 11 September 2010.

16. Jonathan Powell, *The New Machiavelli: How to Wield Power in the Modern World* (Bodley Head, London, 2010), p. 112. Powell adds that there were no 'really big ideological differences' between Blair and Brown on economic policy – 'just a refusal on Gordon's part to involve Tony and Number 10 in the process' (ibid., p. 113). As Peter Mandelson aptly noted: 'Any Chancellor wields major influence on all aspects of government, through control of tax and spending'. But Brown's influence was much greater than that of most Chancellors. It was, Mandelson contends, 'of an entirely different order'. Brown 'believed that his own acumen, and the talents of his inner circle, served the government's policy-making far better than anything in Number 10'. See Mandelson, *The Third Man: Life at the Heart of New Labour* (Harper Press, London, 2010), p. 240.

17. Blair, *A Journey*, p. 522.

18. See Richard Gunther, José Ramón Montero and Juan J. Linz (eds.), *Political Parties: Old Concepts and New Challenges* (Oxford University Press, Oxford, 2002).

19. When John Major resigned his leadership of the British Conservative Party, while prime minister, in June 1995 in order to force a re-election for the party post, this was an exception to that generalization. Major did not pretend to a monopoly of wisdom, but, faced by very persistent sniping at the government from his back benches, especially on policy towards Europe, he deemed it necessary to show who had the greater support. His opponent in the election, John Redwood, received 89 votes as compared with Major's 218. It was a sufficient vote against a sitting prime minister (especially when one adds in eight abstentions and twelve spoiled papers) by his own side in the House of Commons to be of only modest help in consolidating his authority. It was, however, enough to enable Major to continue until the next general election in May 1997. See John Major, *The Autobiography* (HarperCollins paperback, 2000), pp. 617–647.

20. Blair, *A Journey*, p. 545.

21. Powell, *The New Machiavelli*.

22. Ibid., p. 59.

23. Thomas Carlyle, *On Heroes, Hero-Worship, and The Heroic in History* (Chapman & Hall, London, 3rd ed., 1846), p. 1.

24. Louis Fisher, *Presidential War Power* (University of Kansas Press, Lawrence, 2nd ed., 2004); and David Gray Adler, 'Louis Fisher on the Constitution and War Power', *PS: Political Science and Politics*, Vol. 46, No. 3, 2013, pp. 505–509.

25. Fisher, *Presidential War Power*, esp. pp. 278–279.

26. Ibid., pp. 261–262.

27. Cf. James Blitz, 'A long week: Putin's diplomatic gambit', *Financial Times*, 14 September 2013.

28. Fisher, *Presidential War Power*, pp. 81–104.

29. For Fisher, however, resolutions passed by the UN Security Council matter less than the US Constitution, with the former no more than 'a beguiling but spurious source of authority' (ibid., p. 81).

30. Many, however, would regard Truman's decision to use the atomic bomb on two heavily populated Japanese cities as a major blot on his record. It has been argued that 'a test demonstration in an unpopulated area would have been a far more humane means of achieving the same objective', which was to bring to a rapid end the prolonged suffering on both sides caused by the war with Japan. See Richard F. Haynes, *The Awesome Power: Harry S. Truman as Commander in Chief* (Louisiana State University Press, Baton Rouge, 1974), p. 269.

31. Robert L. Beisner, *Dean Acheson: A Life in the Cold War* (Oxford University Press, Oxford, 2006), p. 27.

32. Percy Cradock, *In Pursuit of British Interests: Reflections on Foreign Policy under Margaret Thatcher and John Major* (John Murray, London, 1997), p. 24.

33. Richard E. Neustadt, *Presidential Power and the Modern Presidents: The Politics of Leadership from Roosevelt to Reagan* (Free Press, New York, 1990), p. 10.

34. Ibid.

35. Harry S. Truman, *Off the Record: The Private Papers of Harry S. Truman*, edited by Robert H. Ferrell (Harper & Row, New York, 1980), p. 96. In a farewell address by radio and television to the nation in January 1953, Truman said: 'When Franklin Roosevelt died, I felt there must be a million men better qualified than I, to take up the Presidential task. But the work was mine to do, and I had to do it.' Quoted in David McCullough, *Truman* (Simon & Schuster, New York, 1992), pp. 919–920.

36. Truman, *Off the Record*, p. 207.

37. Ibid., p. 211.

38. Roy Jenkins, *Truman* (Collins, London, 1986), p. 187.

39. Haynes, *The Awesome Power*, p. 255.

40. There was, however, a 'Truman Doctrine'. That was the name given to the policy, enunciated by Truman in March 1947, of containment of Communist expansion, by military means if necessary. It initially and specifically referred to the need to prevent the Communist subversion of Greece and Turkey after the British had admitted that they no longer had the economic strength to provide military underpinning of those efforts.

41. Stephen Graubard, *The Presidents: The Transformation of the American Presidency from Theodore Roosevelt to George W. Bush* (Allen Lane, London, 2004), p. 326.

42. Thus, on the basis of an unsupported assumption that the smaller membership of British political parties as compared with the 1950s makes them less representative of the wider population, one prominent political commentator worries that this makes the parties 'even more difficult for leaders to lead'. See Andrew Rawnsley, 'The numbers that add up to trouble for all political parties', *Observer*, 14 July 2013. It is not clear, to take a case cited by Rawnsley, why one leader, chosen by an electorate which included the mass membership of his party, should be more 'representative' than the one hundred and ninety thousand members of the Labour Party as of 2013. And, in reality, successive Labour leaders John Smith, Tony Blair, Gordon Brown and Ed Miliband have been given a much easier ride by the smaller and supposedly less representative membership of their party than was Hugh Gaitskell as leader of a much larger Labour Party (over a million members) in the 1950s.

43. In the financial crisis and prolonged economic difficulties which began in 2008, there was more of a tendency to look to technocrats than to charismatic 'strongmen'. That is not an evil on the scale of the rise of Mussolini and Hitler, but it is also a threat to, and no substitute for, democracy.

44. Ed Pilkington, '"The Taliban thought the bullet would silence us. But they failed", defiant Malala tells the UN', *Guardian*, 13 July 2013.

45. In that speech, Malala Yousafzai said that 'the extremists are afraid of books and pens' and that 'the power of the voice of women frightens them'. Making clear her own loyalty to Islam, describing it as 'a religion of peace, humanity and brotherhood', she said that the religion not only asserted the right of each child to receive an education but made this a duty. She scorned the Taliban conception of their deity as 'a tiny little conservative' who would send girls to hell 'just because of going to school' (ibid.).

46. Ibid.

47. David Remnick, *The Bridge: The Life and Rise of Barack Obama* (Picador, London, 2010), p. 574.

48. Jean Blondel, *Political Leadership: Towards a General Analysis* (Sage, London, 1987), pp. 19–26.

49. The 'transforming' and the 'transactional' is the favoured dichotomy of James MacGregor Burns. See Burns, *Leadership* (Harper & Row, New York, 1978); and Burns, *Transforming Leadership: A New Pursuit of Happiness* (Atlantic Books, London, 2003).

1   Putting Leaders in Context

1. Ronald L. Meek, *Social Science and the Ignoble Savage* (Cambridge University Press, Cambridge, 1976).

2. See Christian Marouby, 'Adam Smith and the Anthropology of the

Enlightenment: The "Ethnographic" Sources of Economic Progress' in Larry Wolff and Marco Cipolloni (eds), *The Anthropology of the Enlightenment* (Stanford University Press, Stanford, 2007), pp. 85–102; Alan Barnard, *Social Anthropology and Human Origins* (Cambridge University Press, Cambridge, 2011); and Barnard, *History and Theory in Anthropology* (Cambridge University Press, Cambridge, 2000).

3. Meek, *Social Science and the Ignoble Savage*, pp. 238–239.

4. Emma Rothschild, *Economic Sentiments: Adam Smith, Condorcet, and the Enlightenment* (Harvard University Press, Cambridge, Mass., 2001), p. 242.

5. Adam Smith, *Lectures on Jurisprudence*, edited by R.L. Meek, D.D. Raphael and P.G. Stein (Clarendon Press, Oxford, 1978). I have used throughout this most scholarly edition of the complete works of Smith (known as the Glasgow Edition and published by the Clarendon division of Oxford University Press). However, when quoting from these works, I have modernized and corrected the spelling, whereas the editors retained some archaic spellings of Smith himself and the misspellings of his student note-takers. Smith was such a perfectionist that, when he was dying, he caused the book manuscript on law and government which he had not succeeded in finishing to his own satisfaction to be destroyed. He would have been horrified had he known that student notes of the lectures on which the book was based were to be published instead. However, these sets of notes do more than enough to indicate the value of the manuscript which was lost. Smith taught at Glasgow from 1751 until early 1764 (as Professor of Moral Philosophy from 1752).

6. Smith, *Lectures on Jurisprudence*, pp. 201–202.

7. As John Locke had earlier argued (*Two Treatises of Civil Government*, Everyman Edition, Dent, London, 1953, p. 180; first published 1690).

8. Agriculture began earlier than Smith assumed, and mixed forms of subsistence were more common than he and his contemporaries knew or acknowledged. Archaeological evidence suggests that as long ago as 7000 BC, the hunter-gatherers of New Guinea also practised agriculture. See Jared Diamond, *Guns, Germs and Steel: A Short History of Everybody for the Last 13,000 Years* (Vintage, London, 2005), p. 148. Moreover, Christian Marouby observes: 'We now know that except in the marginal conditions of sub-artic regions, hunter-gatherers the world over relied on the collection of plant foods for more than half, and frequently more than 70 per cent of their diet. Of course . . . Adam Smith cannot be faulted for ignoring studies in economic anthropology that were only undertaken in the 1960s' (Marouby, 'Adam Smith and the Anthropology of the Enlightenment', p. 90).

9. *Turgot on Progress, Sociology and Economics*, translated and edited by Ronald L. Meek (Cambridge University Press, Cambridge, 1973), p. 72. I pay attention in this chapter to the four-stages theory mainly because those who expounded it were vitally concerned with the development of government and of

political leadership. The stadial theory itself, especially in the light of more recent research, can be seen to be a great oversimplification. Yet, bold generalization is a useful antidote to the particularism of the kind of anthropological research that seeks to emphasize the utter uniqueness of every tribe or to fit their experience into ever more complex and variegated typologies.

10. David Hume, 'Of the First Principles of Government', in Hume, *Essays and Treatises on Several Subjects Containing Essays, Moral, Political and Literary: A New Edition*, Vol. 1 (Cadell, London, 1788), p. 37.

11. Hume, 'Of the Origin of Government', in Hume, *Essays*, p. 43.

12. Ibid. Some anthropological research of recent decades provides empirical support for Hume's supposition. Thus, in the Highlands of Papua New Guinea, 'certain military "leaders" begin behaving like big men, particularly by relying on a wider network of acquaintances than the ordinary mass of individuals', and a 'warrier-organizer' gradually 'turns into a manipulator of social relations and wealth'. See Pierre Lemonnier, 'From great men to big men: peace, substitution and competition in the Highlands of New Guinea', in Maurice Godelier and Marilyn Strathern (eds.), *Big Men and Great Men: Personifications of Power in Melanesia* (Cambridge University Press, Cambridge, 1991), pp. 7–27, at p. 19.

13. Adam Smith, *An Inquiry into the Nature and Causes of the Wealth of Nations*, edited by R.H. Campbell and A.S. Skinner (Clarendon Press, Oxford, 1976), Vol. 2, p. 711.

14. Ibid.

15. Anthropological research carried out in the twentieth century was consonant with a number of Smith's generalizations. Thus, for example, discussing the emergence of leaders among the Neur of southern Sudan, Lucy Mair writes: 'The kind of man who attracts people to attach themselves to him will probably be . . . the eldest of a group of brothers who themselves have adult children living in the village.' Such an informal leader would be comparatively wealthy – measured by ownership of cattle – and would have gained prestige 'from a reputation for prowess in fighting in his youth, for skill in debate, or for ritual powers (which are believed to be inherited)'. See Mair *Primitive Government* (Penguin, Harmondsworth, 1962), p. 64. The Neur, however, did not have chiefs. There was no single person with ultimate power. Rather, some individuals gained authority as people 'worth listening to'. Here, and elsewhere in Africa, colonial administrators (not least British District Commissioners) set about creating chiefs, bringing with them their own culture of hierarchy and a desire to have a recognized leader with whom to interact (Mair, ibid., pp. 257–258). Mair's work remains unusual in that she brought together the findings of anthropological research on many different tribes in geographically dispersed countries of Africa, focusing on their leadership, distribution of power, and conflict resolution. She makes clear that

chieftainship was by no means a universal phenomenon. The Alur of western Uganda had 'recognized hereditary chiefs', but neighbouring peoples, the Lendu and Okebu, had no chiefs of their own. The Alur chiefs supposedly had the mystical power of controlling rain, but their secular function was to settle disputes that had led to fighting. Accordingly, neighbours without chiefs would turn to them, and sometimes request one of their chief's sons to come to them as a chief in order to resolve conflict (Mair, ibid., pp. 120–121). Even within a particular group of people with a common sense of identity, the absence of authoritative means of settling serious disputes can be deadly. By the end of the 1970s, the Fayu hunter-gatherers of New Guinea had reduced themselves from around 2,000 people to about 400, divided into four clans, as a result of killing each other in the absence of social or political mechanisms for conflict-resolution. See Diamond, *Guns, Germs and Steel*, pp. 205–266.

16. Smith, *An Inquiry into the Nature and Causes of the Weatlh of Nations*, p. 712.

17. Ibid.

18. Ibid., pp. 712–713.

19. Ibid., p. 713.

20. Ibid. There never was, Smith adds, 'a great family in the world' whose illustriousness 'was entirely derived from the inheritance of wisdom and virtue' (ibid., p. 714).

21. Smith, *Lectures on Jurisprudence*, p. 323.

22. Ibid.

23. Ibid. The Russian 'revolutions' to which Smith refers, insofar as they were successful, were more in the nature of palace coups. Peasant risings in eighteenth-century Russia ended very badly for the rebels. Interestingly, this course of lectures, in which Smith referred to recent Russian experience, was attended by two Russian students, Semyon Efimovich Desnitsky and Ivan Andreevich Tretyakov, who spent six years at the University of Glasgow. Both of them subsequently became professors of law at Moscow University. See A.H. (Archie) Brown, 'Adam Smith's First Russian Followers' in A.S. Skinner and T. Wilson (eds), *Essays on Adam Smith* (Clarendon Press, Oxford, 1975), pp. 247–273.

24. John Millar, *The Origin of the Distinction of Ranks*, 3rd edition, 1779, reprinted in William C. Lehmann (ed.), *John Millar of Glasgow 1735–1801: His Life and Thought and his Contributions to Sociological Analysis* (Cambridge University Press, Cambridge, 1960), p. 254. John Locke had earlier justified people's right to rebel against tyrannical government (with characteristic concern for property rights). 'The end of government is the good of mankind,' he wrote, 'and which is best for mankind, that the people should be always exposed to the boundless will of tyranny, or that the rulers should be sometimes liable to be opposed when they grow exorbitant in the use of their power, and employ it for the destruction, and not the preservation, of the properties of their people?' (Locke, *Two Treatises of Civil Government*, p. 233.)

25. Millar, *The Origin of the Distinction of Ranks*, p. 250.

26. Ibid., p. 271.

27. Ibid., pp. 263 and 271 (italics in the original).

28. Locke surmised in 1690 that 'if we look back, as far as history will direct us, towards the original of commonwealths, we shall generally find them under the government and administration of one man' (*Two Treatises of Civil Government*, p. 168).

29. The most ambitiously comprehensive scholarly account of government from its origins until the twentieth century is that of S.E. Finer, *The History of Government From the Earliest Times*, 3 volumes (Oxford University Press, Oxford, 1997).

30. Finer, *The History of Government*, Vol. III, p. 1476.

31. The phrase, 'democracy on the installment plan' is that of Dankwart A. Rustow, 'Transitions to Democracy: Toward a Dynamic Model', *Comparative Politics*, Vol. 2/3, 1970, pp. 337–363, at p. 356. On the argument in nineteenth-century Britain that further democratization would be a threat to liberty, see Albert O. Hirschman, *The Rhetoric of Reaction: Perversity, Futility, Jeopardy* (Harvard University Press, Cambridge, Mass., 1991), pp. 86–101.

32. It was Sir Walter Scott, rather than James Boswell, who reported this particular exchange in a conversation between Johnson and Alexander Boswell (Lord Auchinleck). The great Boswell scholar Frederick Pottle was not prepared to vouch for the accuracy of Scott's account of the Auchinleck–Johnson conversation. See *Boswell's Journal of a Tour to the Hebrides with Samuel Johnson, LL.D.*, edited by Frederick A. Pottle and Charles H. Bennett (Viking Press, New York, 1936), pp. 375–376.

33. Robert A. Dahl notes that only one delegate at the constitutional convention, Alexander Hamilton, looked favourably on monarchy, and this stance reduced his influence. See Dahl, *How Democratic Is the American Constitution?* (Yale University Press, New Haven, 2nd ed., 2003), p. 11.

34. Dahl, *How Democratic is the American Constitution?*, p. 16.

35. Ibid., p. 31. Dahl is referring to the election of George W. Bush for his first term as President when his Democratic opponent, Al Gore, obtained about 540,000 more votes nationally than Bush (approximately 0.5 per cent of all votes cast) but lost narrowly to his Republican opponent in the electoral college.

36. Alexis de Tocqueville, *Democracy in America*, translated by George Lawrence, edited by J.P. Mayer (Anchor Books, New York, 1969), p. 101.

37. Finer, *The History of Government*, Vol. III, p. 1526.

38. The proposed legislation was not very radical to begin with, and it was further watered down in its passage through Congress, with numerous concessions made to legislators and special interests. More generally, as John Kay noted, 'Americans . . . engage in a healthcare debate on issues that in Europe are not even open to discussion. Yet experience around the world is that only the rich can buy physical or economic security for themselves. Others must look to the state, more successfully in Sweden than Somalia' (Kay, 'Only market evangelists can reconcile Jekyll with Hyde', *Financial Times*, 6 June 2012).

39. Edward Luce, 'Obama wins a healthcare battle, but the war rages on', *Financial Times*, 2 July 2012.

40. Dworkin's suggestion was that Chief Justice Roberts wanted 'to blunt the anticipated accusations of political partisanship' in a series of contentious matters – including abortion and the Voting Rights Act 1965 – which before long would be coming to the Supreme Court. See Ronald Dworkin, 'A Bigger Victory Than We Knew', *New York Review of Books*, Vol. LIX, No. 13, 16 August–26 September 2012, pp. 6–12, at p. 8.

41. Tocqueville, *Democracy in America*, p. 270.

42. While the French Revolution divides opinion to this day, there is also a school of thought which sees its break with the past as nothing like as momentous as the revolutionaries insisted. Tocqueville stands out as the first and most famous of those who have emphasized continuities between the *Ancien Régime* and post-revolutionary France. His emphasis on the 'futility' of the French Revolution, Hirschman suggested, did not endear him to either set of protagonists or to later historians who were devoting their lives to the study of the Revolution and perceiving it to be the pivotal event of modern times. See Hirschman, *The Rhetoric of Reaction*, pp. 48–49 and 138–139.

43. See, for example, Stephen F. Cohen, *Bukharin and the Bolshevik Revolution: A Political Biography 1988–1938* (Wildwood House, London, 1974), especially pp. 131 and 144; and Baruch Knei-Paz, *The Social and Political Thought of Leon Trotsky* (Clarendon Press, Oxford, 1978), pp. 392–410.

44. Finer, *The History of Government*, Vol. III, p. 1540.

45. Jonathan I. Israel, *Democratic Enlightenment: Philosophy, Revolution, and Human Rights 1750–1790* (Oxford University Press, New York, 2011), p. 928.

46. The statistic is based on a comparison of 2004 and 2008 exit polls. See Kate Kenski, Bruce W. Hardy and Kathleen Hall Jamieson, *The Obama Victory: How Media, Money, and Message Shaped the 2008 Election* (Oxford University Press, New York, 2010), p. 103. The authors add that they 'found evidence that race-based perceptions played a role in the votes of some. But Obama's campaign boosted black turnout and white votes outside the Deep South enough to compensate for these anti-Obama ballots' (ibid.). It is worth noting that the Republicans have had the support of a majority of white American voters ever since 1968, but that this is a declining asset for them, as the ethnic

composition of the United States changes. Not only did more black and Hispanic voters go to the polls in 2008, but they supported the Democratic candidate still more strongly in that year than in 2004 with 7 per cent more of the African-American vote going to Obama, as compared with their votes for the Democratic candidate in 2004, and a remarkable 14 per cent more of Hispanics voting for Obama than they did for Kerry four years earlier.

47. If, as John Dunn, argues, 'democracy is above all the name for political authority exercised solely through the persuasion of the greater number', then democratization indeed made important strides in the nineteenth century, in part under the impact of both the American and the French Revolutions. See Dunn, Setting the People Free: The Story of Democracy (Atlantic Books, London, 2005), p. 132.

48. Cf. W.G. Runciman, The Theory of Cultural and Social Selection (Cambridge University Press, Cambridge, 2009), pp. 42–45; and Diamond, Guns, Germs and Steel, pp. 271–278.

49. Barnard, Social Anthropology and Human Origins, pp. 49–50.

50. Diamond, Guns, Germs and Steel, p. 272. Diamond also observes: 'In traditional New Guinea society, if a New Guinean happened to encounter an unfamiliar New Guinean while both were away from their respective villages, the two engaged in a long discussion of their relatives, in an attempt to establish some relationship and hence some reason why the two should not attempt to kill each other' (ibid., pp. 271–272).

51. Sahlins was influenced at the time by a Marxism that he later abandoned. This summary of his view of the transition from big-men to chiefs is drawn from Adam Kuper, Culture: The Anthropologists' Account (Harvard University Press, Cambridge, Mass., 2001), pp. 163–164.

52. Diamond, Guns, Germs and Steel, p. 273.

53. Thus, chiefs emerged in the highlands of Mexico, Guatemala, Peru and Madagascar, but not in New Guinea. Ibid., p. 423.

54. Paul Chaisty, Nic Cheeseman and Timothy Power, 'Rethinking the "presidentialism debate": conceptualizing coalitional politics in cross-regional perspective', Democratization (2012) DOI: 10.1080/13510347.2012.710604.

55. Paul Collier, War, Guns and Votes: Democracy in Dangerous Places (Bodley Head, London, 2009), pp. 230–231. Collier also observes that fashionable enthusiasm for multiculturalism has tended to obscure the point that 'the rights of minorities rest on systems that depend upon the prior forging of an overriding sense of common nationality' (ibid., p. 185). Anti-colonialism made a useful contribution to building national unity. A factor specific to Julius Nyerere's success in promoting a sense of common nationality was the presence of a lingua franca in Tanzania – Swahili in this case. That was an asset that many other African leaders did not possess. In some cases the attempt to create a single nation, as distinct from state-building, is

counterproductive. On this, see Alfred Stepan, Juan J. Linz and Yogendra Yadav, *Crafting State-Nations* (Johns Hopkins University Press, Baltimore, 2011).
56. Collier, *War, Guns and Votes*, pp. 51–52.
57. Ibid., p. 52.
58. That does not, of course, invalidate it. If lack of agreement in delineating a concept were to be enough to damn it, we should have to stop taking seriously such fundamentally important notions as freedom and democracy. An influential formulation has been that of Clifford Geertz: 'Believing, with Max Weber, that man is an animal suspended in webs of significance he himself has spun, I take culture to be those webs, and the analysis of it to be therefore not an experimental science in search of law but an interpretive one in search of meaning.' See Geertz, *The Interpretation of Cultures* (Basic Books, New York, 1973), p. 5. For an interesting critique of both 'the deployment of the attitude survey method by positivists' *and* the deployment of 'semiotic "reading" of culture by interpretivists', see Stephen Welch, *The Theory of Political Culture* (Oxford University Press, Oxford, 2013).
59. Or, as Richard W. Wilson observes: 'In the most general sense political cultures are socially constructed normative systems that are the product of both social . . . and psychological . . . influences but are not reducible to either. They have prescriptive qualities that stipulate not only desirable ends but also appropriate means to achieve those ends. The norms are not coterminous with legal codes, although they often overlap.' See Wilson, 'The Many Voices of Political Culture: Assessing Different Approaches', *World Politics*, Vol. 52, No. 2, 2000, pp. 246–273, at p. 264.
60. Values need to be distinguished from mere attitudes. Far fewer in number than attitudes, they are, as Stanley Feldman puts it, nevertheless 'more numerous than the single ideological dimension that is typically used to understand political conflict'. Feldman observes that while value priorities 'may change slowly over time' as people adapt to a changing environment, they tend to be 'inertial enough . . . to lend stability to evaluations and behavior'. See Feldman, 'Values, Ideology, and the Structure of Political Attitudes', in David O. Sears, Leonie Huddy and Robert Jervis (eds.), *Oxford Handbook of Political Psychology* (Oxford University Press, New York, 2003), pp. 477–508, at p. 479.
61. Strong evidence to support that contention (in the context of culture, more broadly) is to be found in Geert Hofstede, *Culture's Consequences: International Differences in Work-Related Values* (Sage, Beverly Hills and London, 1980).
62. *Le Monde*, 13 September 2010; and *Financial Times*, 14 September 2010.
63. Robert Putnam, in a notable study, has compared historically conditioned political cultures in different regions of Italy and documented the importance of public engagement in northern Italy and the link between the strength

of civic associations and more effective democratic institutions. See Robert D. Putnam, *Making Democracy Work: Civic Traditions in Modern Italy* (Princeton University Press, Princeton, N.J., 1993).

64. *Vztah Čechů a Slováků k dějinám* (ČSAV, Prague, 1968), p. 7; and Archie Brown and Gordon Wightman, 'Czechoslovakia: Revival and Retreat' in Brown and Jack Gray (eds.), *Political Culture and Political Change in Communist States* (Macmillan, London, 1977), pp. 159–196, at p. 164.

65. It was the Chairman of the Council of Ministers of the Soviet Union, Aleksey Kosygin, who referred to Dubček as the 'Number One Scoundrel'. See Archie Brown, *The Rise and Fall of Communism* (Bodley Head, London, and Ecco, New York, 2009), pp. 395–396.

66. Ivan Krastev and Stephen Holmes, 'An Autopsy of Managed Democracy', *Journal of Democracy*, Vol. 23, No. 3, 2012, pp. 32–45, at pp. 35–36.

67. Boris Dubin, 'Stalin i drugie. Figury vysshey vlasti v obshchestvennom mnenii sovremennoy Rossii', *Monitoring obshchestvennogo mneniya*, No. 2 (64), March–April 2003, pp. 26–40, at p. 34.

68. Timothy J. Colton and Michael McFaul, *Popular Choice and Managed Democracy: The Russian Elections of 1999 and 2000* (Brookings Institution, Washington, DC, 2003), pp. 220–223.

69. Jeffrey W. Hahn, 'Yaroslavl' Revisited: Assessing Continuity and Change in Russian Political Culture', in Stephen Whitefield (ed.), *Political Culture and Post-Communism* (Palgrave Macmillan, Basingstoke, 2005), pp. 148–179, at p. 172.

70. Dubin, 'Stalin i drugie', esp. p. 34.

71. Yuriy Levada, *Ishchem cheloveka. Sotsiologicheskie ocherki, 2000–2005* (Novoe izdatel'stvo, Moscow, 2006), p. 140. There is evidence supporting the idea of 'political generations' as a more general phenomenon, partly based on testing the hypothesis that individuals are particularly susceptible to influence on their political attitudes in late adolescence and early adulthood. See David O. Sears and Sheri Levy, 'Childhood and Adult Political Development', in Sears, Huddy and Jervis (eds.), *Oxford Handbook of Political Psychology*, pp. 60–109, at pp. 84–87.

72. Sears and Levy, ibid., p. 77.

73. The autocratic modernizer tsar, Peter the Great, has been consistently mentioned more often than any other person when Russians have been asked at five-yearly intervals to name the 'most outstanding people of all times and nations'. See Boris Dubin, 'Stalin i drugie. Figury vysshey vlasti v obshchestvennom mnenii v sovremennoy Rossii', *Monitoring obshchestvennogo mneniya*, No. 1 (63), 2003.

74. Daniel Kahneman, *Thinking Fast and Slow* (Allen Lane, London, 2011), p. 342.

75. Adam Smith, *The Theory of Moral Sentiments* (Clarendon Press, Oxford, 1976 [first published 1759]), p. 52.

76. Ibid.

77. Ibid., p. 62.

78. Barbara Kellerman is a notable case in point. See, for example, *Bad Leadership: What It Is, How It Happens, Why It Matters* (Harvard Business School Press, Boston, Mass., 2004); and Kellerman, *The End of Leadership* (HarperCollins, New York, 2012).

79. S. Alexander Haslam, Stephen D. Reicher and Michael J. Platow, *The New Psychology of Leadership: Identity, Influence and Power* (Psychology Press, Hove and New York, 2011), p. 199.

80. Jean Lipman-Blumen, *The Allure of Toxic Leaders: Why We Follow Destructive Bosses and Corrupt Politicians – and How We Can Survive Them* (Oxford University Press, New York, 2005), p. 241.

81. Barbara Kellerman, *Reinventing Leadership: Making the Connection between Politics and Business* (State University of New York Press, Albany, 1999), p. 46.

82. James Fallows, cited in James MacGregor Burns, *Running Alone. Presidential Leadership – JFK to Bush II. Why It Has Failed and How We Can Fix It* (Basic Books, New York, 2006), pp. 126–127.

83. Drew Westen, *The Political Brain: The Role of Emotion in Deciding the Fate of the Nation* (Public Affairs, New York, 2007), p. 125.

84. Haslam, Reicher and Platow, *The New Psychology of Leadership*, p. 200.

85. Ibid., p. 201.

86. Ibid., p. 200.

87. Kahneman, *Thinking Fast and Slow*, p. 217.

88. Harold Seidman, who worked for many years as a senior official in the Bureau of the Budget before becoming a Professor of Political Science at the University of Connecticut, coined the term 'Miles's law' for this aphorism of Rufus Miles who was assistant secretary for administration within the Department of Health, Education and Welfare of the US government. In Seidman's formulation it is: 'Where one stands depends on where one sits.' See Seidman, *Politics, Position, and Power: The Dynamics of Federal Organization* (Oxford University Press, New York, 3rd edition, 1980), p. 21. (The first edition of Seidman's book was published in 1970.)

89. Roy Jenkins, *Churchill* (Pan Macmillan, London, 2001), pp. 219–222 and p. 397. It should be added that the circumstances, as well as Churchill's institutional affiliation, had also changed. Before 1914 Germany had challenged Britain's naval supremacy. In the mid-1920s that was not the case.

90. Jennifer L. Hochschild, 'Where You Stand Depends on What You See: Connections among Values, Perceptions of Fact, and Political Prescriptions', in James H. Kuklinski (ed.), *Citizens and Politics: Perspectives from Political Psychology* (Cambridge University Press, Cambridge, 2001), pp. 313–340.

91. Ibid., p. 321.

92. Ibid., p. 320.

93. Much of this comes under the heading of cognitive dissonance, on which there is a large body of experimental and theoretical literature. See, for example, J. Richard Eiser, *Cognitive Social Psychology: A Guidebook to Theory and Research* (McGraw-Hill, London and New York, 1980), esp. pp. 127–163; and Robert A. Baron and Donn Byrne, *Social Psychology: Understanding Human Interaction* (Allyn and Bacon, Boston, 5th ed., 1987), esp. pp. 132–138.

94. Howard G. Lavine, Christopher D. Johnston and Marco R. Steenbergen, *The Ambivalent Partisan: How Critical Loyalty Promotes Democracy* (Oxford University Press, New York, 2012), p. 125; and Charles S. Taber, Milton Lodge and Jill Glathar, 'The Motivated Construction of Political Judgments', in Kuklinski (ed.), *Citizens and Politics*, pp. 198–226, at p. 213.

95. See especially Westen, *The Political Brain*; and Roger D. Masters, 'Cognitive Neuroscience, Emotion, and Leadership', in Kuklinski (ed.), *Citizens and Politics*, pp. 68–102.

96. Westen, *The Political Brain*, p. 121.

97. Ibid., pp. 121–122.

98. See Rajmohan Gandhi, *Gandhi: The Man, His People and the Empire* (Haus, London, 2007); Louis Fischer, *The Life of Mahatma Gandhi* (HarperCollins, New York, 1997); B.R. Nanda, *Mahatma Gandhi: A Biography* (Allen & Unwin, London, 1958); Nelson Mandela, *Long Walk to Freedom* (Abacus, London, 1995); Nelson Mandela, *Conversations with Myself* (Macmillan, London, 2010); Tom Lodge, *Mandela: A Critical Life* (Oxford University Press, Oxford, 2006); Aung San Suu Kyi, *Freedom from Fear* (edited and introduced by Michael Aris, Penguin, London, new ed., 2010); Justin Wintle, *Perfect Hostage: Aung San Suu Kyi, Burma and the Generals* (Arrow, London, 2007); Bertil Lintner, *Aung San Suu Kyi and Burma's Struggle for Democracy* (Silkworm Books, Chiang Mai, Thailand, 2011); Peter Popham, *The Lady and the Peacock: The Life of Aung San Suu Kyi* (Random House, London, 2011); and John Kane, *The Politics of Moral Capital* (Cambridge University Press, Cambridge, 2001).

99. Robert A. Caro, *The Years of Lyndon Johnson, Volume 3: Master of the Senate* (Vintage, New York, 2003), p. xxii.

100. Robert A. Caro, *The Years of Lyndon Johnson, Volume 4: The Passage of Power* (Bodley Head, London, 2012), p. 110.

101. Doris Kearns, *Lyndon Johnson and the American Dream* (Signet, New York, 1976), p. 171.

102. In his memoirs, Bush observed: 'I didn't look at the vice-president as another senior adviser. He had put his name on the ballot and gotten elected. I wanted him to be comfortable with all the issues on my desk. After all, it could become his at any moment . . . I hadn't chosen [Cheney] to be a political asset; I had chosen him to help me do the job. That was exactly what he had done. He accepted any assignment I asked. He gave me his unvarnished opinions. He understood that I made the final decisions. When

we disagreed, he kept our differences private. Most important, I trusted Dick. I valued his steadiness. I enjoyed being around him. And he had become a good friend.' See George W. Bush, *Decision Points* (Crown, New York, 2010), pp. 86–87. For his part, Cheney notes: 'History is full of examples of vice-presidents who were kept far from the center of power. Indeed, I've known a few personally. But at the beginning George W. Bush had said that I would be part of governing. He had been – as I had known he would be – a man of his word' – Dick Cheney (with Liz Cheney), *In My Name: A Personal and Political Memoir* (Threshold, New York, 2011), p. 519.

103. See Caro, *The Years of Lyndon Johnson: The Passage of Power*, pp. 112–115.

104. Condoleezza Rice, *No Higher Honour: A Memoir of My Years in Washington* (Simon & Schuster, London, 2011), p. 23. After admitting to these errors of judgement, Rice somewhat disarmingly adds: 'Fortunately, no one remembers that we wrote policy guidance questioning Gorbachev's motives and setting up careful "tests" of Moscow's intentions months before the collapse of Soviet power in Eastern Europe and the unification of Germany' (ibid.).

105. Jack F. Matlock, Jr, *Reagan and Gorbachev: How the Cold War Ended* (Random House, New York, 2004), p. 314.

106. B. Guy Peters, *Institutional Theory in Political Science: The 'New Institutionalism'* (Pinter, London and New York, 1999), p. 115. Although party structures have somewhat weakened, there has been no let-up in party partisanship. Recent evidence suggests that among American citizens it has, if anything, 'grown stronger over the past two decades'. See Lavine, Johnston and Steenbergen, *The Ambivalent Partisan*, p. 2.

107. Peters, *Institutional Theory in Political Science*, p. 115.

108. As the Australian political scientist Judith Brett notes: 'Since 1990 Labor has twice ejected electorally popular prime ministers, and John Howard [who led the Liberal Party to four election victories] worked hard to prevent a challenge in his last term in office.' See Brett, 'Prime Ministers and their Parties in Australia', in Paul Strangio, Paul 't Hart and James Walter (eds.), *Understanding Prime-Ministerial Performance: Comparative Perspectives* (Oxford University Press, Oxford, 2013), pp. 172–192, at p. 177.

109. Neil Hume, 'Rudd ousts Gillard as Labor leader', *Financial Times*, 27 June 2013. In contrast to the cases noted by Judith Brett in note 108, Gillard's public opinion poll standing was low at the time of her removal from the party leadership.

110. Brett, 'Prime Ministers and their Parties in Australia', p. 189.

111. 'Australian PM Gillard in reshuffle after "unseemly" vote', http://www.bbc.co.uk/news/world-asia-21920762, 25 March 2013.

112. *Financial Times*, 25/26 February 2012; and ibid., 28 February 2012. Judith Brett noted Rudd's 'general unavailability to parliamentary colleagues and senior bureaucrats, his mania for control, and his rudeness to everyone from

members of cabinet to airhostesses' (Brett, 'Prime Ministers and their Parties in Australia', p. 188). In the view of Andrew Hughes, an analyst of Canberra politics from the Australian National University, Julia Gillard was 'very efficient as prime minister. But that message hasn't got through to the Australian public'. He added: 'The problem is the way she seized power. It's been an albatross round her neck and it's still there' (*Financial Times*, 22 March 2013). One observer of Australian politics, Erik Jensen, wrote soon after Rudd's short-lived return to the premiership: 'Rudd stands atop the ruins of a government he played no small part in wrecking.' Jensen noted that a number of ministers had resigned rather than work with Rudd and that a former Labor leader had called for him to be expelled from the party. See Jensen, 'The people's psychopath', *New Statesman*, 5–12 July 2013, p. 14.

113. The editors of a recent comparative study of prime ministers note that even before the Australian Labor Party's election victory in 2007, 'Rudd had signalled that he would not be beholden to his party in the way he led his government' and announced that he would appoint ministers rather than have them elected by the parliamentary party (Strangio, 't Hart and Walters, *Understanding Prime-Ministerial Performance*, p. 8). Following Labour's defeat in 2013, election of the cabinet and shadow cabinet was restored to the parliamentary caucus.

114. The senator was Steve Hutchins; the Cabinet minister was speaking off the record. See the well-informed article by Annabel Crabb in the Australian journal *The Monthly*, August 2011, pp. 30–41. When the global financial crisis hit, decision-making became concentrated in what was, in effect, an inner Cabinet dominated by Rudd. Called the Strategic Priorities and Budget Committee, it contained just three Cabinet ministers in addition to the prime minister but was attended by a growing number of non-elected advisers. This body did not exist prior to Rudd's first becoming prime minister. It was formed in late 2007 and abolished by Julia Gillard in 2010. However, Gillard had been a member of the 'Gang of Four' who belonged to the SPBC, and 'she defended this system right up until the point at which she declared it intolerable' (ibid., p. 37).

115. See, for example, Arend Lijphart (ed.), *Parliamentary versus Presidential Government* (Oxford University Press, New York, 1992); Alfred Stepan, *Arguing Comparative Politics* (Oxford University Press, Oxford, 2001), esp. Part III, 'The Metaframeworks of Democratic Governance and Democratic States'; and Robert Elgie, *Semi-Presidentialism: Sub-Types and Democratic Performance* (Oxford University Press, Oxford, 2011).

116. Elgie, *Semi-Presidentialism* (p. 24) lists fifty-two countries with semi-presidential constitutions, as of December 2010.

117. This is one of the main arguments of Elgie, ibid., for which he provides much supporting evidence.

118. Elgie, ibid., pp. 151–152. Political scientists, including Elgie, use the term 'premier-presidential' for systems in which the prime minister and cabinet are responsible only to the legislature and 'president-parliamentary' for the form of semi-presidentialism in which prime minister and cabinet are responsible both to the parliament *and* to the president. The latter case prevails in Russia. On Putin as leader, see Richard Sakwa, *Putin: Russia's Choice* (Routledge, London, 2004); Alex Pravda (ed.), *Leading Russia: Putin in Perspective* (Oxford University Press, Oxford, 2005), Chapters 2 and 6–13; Lilia Shevtsova, *Putin's Russia* (Carnegie Endowment for International Peace, Washington, DC, revised and expanded ed., 2005); Angus Roxburgh, *The Strongman: Vladimir Putin and the Struggle for Russia* (Tauris, London, 2012); and Fiona Hill and Clifford G. Gaddy, *Mr Putin: Operative in the Kremlin* (Brookings Institution, Washington, DC, 2013).

119. Cf. Lilia Shevtsova and Andrew Wood, *Change or Decay: Russia's Dilemma and the West's Response* (Carnegie Endowment for International Peace, Washington, DC, 2011); and Angus Roxburgh, *The Strongman.*

2   Democratic Leadership: Myths, Powers, Styles

1. Tony Blair, *A Journey* (Hutchinson, London, 2010), p. xvi.
2. Ibid., p. 50.
3. Anthony King (ed.), *Leaders' Personalities and the Outcomes of Democratic Elections* (Oxford University Press, Oxford, 2002), p. 216.
4. See, for example, Lauri Karvonen, *The Personalisation of Politics: A Study of Parliamentary Democracies* (ECPR Press, Colchester, 2010), esp. pp. 4–5. Television has been a major new factor in the personalization of politics, for people are easier to portray than the issues. However, the way newspapers report politics has also changed. A study of how *The Times* reported British politics in the years since 1945 found that the 'overall visibility of prime ministers has grown; references to their leadership qualities have become more common; and they are today referred to in clearly more personal terms than three decades ago' (Karvonen, ibid., pp. 87–93, esp. p. 93).
5. See especially Thomas Poguntke and Paul Webb (eds.), *The Presidentialization of Politics: A Comparative Study of Modern Democracies* (Oxford University Press, Oxford, paperback 2007).
6. Occasionally political commentators recognize this – as, for example, Rafael Behr who wrote: 'The view that Britain holds presidential elections disguised as parliamentary ones is commonplace in Westminster – and wrong, . . . It is the media coverage that is presidential but voters see beyond that' ('Project "Ed's Charisma" – the mission to help Miliband loosen up', *New Statesman*, 28 September–4 October 2012, p. 10).
7. Karvonen, *The Personalisation of Politics*, p. 102.

8. Amanda Bittner, *Platform or Personality? The Role of Party Leaders in Elections* (Oxford University Press, Oxford, 2011), p. 73. Bittner is, nevertheless, among the academic authors who emphasize the importance of leader evaluations, especially in closely contested elections. She observes that 'the scholarly literature to date on party leaders is undecided as to whether or not party leaders *actually matter in the first place*' (p. 139). It would be difficult, though, to find a serious scholar who argued that leaders were of *no* account. What the evidence-based literature does suggest, however, is that their role is much exaggerated by most political journalists – who *have* embraced a personalization of politics – and by many politicians.

9. Karvonen, *The Personalisation of Politics*, p. 20.

10. Ibid.

11. Sören Holmberg and Henrik Oscarsson, 'Party Leader Effects on the Vote', in Kees Aarts, André Blais and Hermann Schmitt (eds.), *Political Leaders and Democratic Elections* (Oxford University Press, Oxford, 2011), p. 47.

12. King (ed.), *Leaders' Personalities and the Outcomes of Democratic Elections*, p. 214. King adds: 'If anything, Kennedy as an individual was a handicap to his party. As a Catholic, he cost the Democrats substantial numbers of votes, mostly among southern Protestants.' A recent scholarly study of American voters concludes: 'As central as individual actors are, it is the political *parties* that are the enduring foundation of American political conflict. Political leaders enter and exit the public stage, but the parties and their symbols, platforms and group associations provide a long-term anchor to the political system.' See Howard G. Lavine, Christopher D. Johnston and Marco R. Steenbergen, *The Ambivalent Partisan; How Critical Loyalty Promotes Democracy* (Oxford University Press, New York, 2012), p. 2.

13. Peter Brown of Quinnipiac University Polling Institute, cited in Kate Kenski, Bruce W. Hardy and Kathleen Hall Jamieson, *The Obama Victory: How Media, Money, and Message Shaped the 2008 Election* (Oxford University Press, New York, 2010), p. 14.

14. Kenski, Hardy and Jamieson, *The Obama Victory*, p. 289. The Democrats' advertisements hammered home the 'McSame' message, but it was reinforced also in the mass media. Kenski *et al.* note: 'The more one watched television news, read the newspaper, or went online for campaign information, the more likely one was to embrace the notion of McCain as McSame' (pp. 288–289).

15. Ibid., p. 16.

16. Dieter Ohr and Henrik Oscarsson, 'Leader Traits, Leader Image, and Vote Choice', in Aarts, Blais and Schmitt, *Political Leaders and Democratic Elections*, pp. 187–214, at p. 197.

17. Roy Pierce, 'Candidate Evaluations and Presidential Election Choices in France', in King (ed.), *Leaders' Personalities and the Outcome of Democratic Elections*, pp. 96–126, at pp. 124–126.

18. Ibid., p. 126.
19. Sören Holmberg and Henrik Oscarsson, 'Party Leader Effects on the Vote', in Aarts, Blais and Schmitt (eds.), *Political Leaders and Democratic Elections*, pp. 35–51, at p. 50.
20. Ibid., p. 49.
21. John Bartle and Ivor Crewe, 'The Impact of Party Leaders in Britain: Strong Assumptions, Weak Evidence', in King (ed.), *Leaders' Personalities and the Outcomes of Democratic Elections*, pp. 70–95, esp. pp. 77–78.
22. Neil O'Brien, 'The Language of Priorities', *New Statesman*, 9 July 2012, pp. 22–25, at p. 22.
23. Ibid.; and Dennis Kavanagh and Philip Cowley, *The British General Election of 2010* (Palgrave Macmillan, Houndmills, 2010), p. 378.
24. David Butler and Michael Pinto-Duschinsky, *The British General Election of 1970* (Macmillan, London, 1971), pp. 24 and 64.
25. See Kenneth O. Morgan, *Callaghan: A Life* (Oxford University Press, Oxford, 1997), pp. 692–693. See also Anthony King in King (ed.), *Leaders' Personalities and the Outcomes of Democratic Elections*, pp. 214–215.
26. Ohr and Oscarsson, 'Leader Traits, Leader Image, and Vote Choice', in Aarts, Blais and Schmitt (eds.), *Political Leaders and Democratic Elections*, pp. 197–198. An interesting finding that holds good across countries and over time is that leaders of Conservative parties tend to be rated more highly on 'competence' and leaders of Left parties on 'character' (Bittner, *Platform or Personality*, pp. 78–84). In a reversal, however, of the general cross-national Left–Right trend, Howard was rated more highly than Keating for empathy (Ohr and Oscarsson, 'Leader Traits, Leader Image, and Vote Choice', p. 197).
27. Blair interview with Lionel Barber, 'Waiting in the Wings', *ft.com/magazine*, 30 June / 1 July 2012.
28. Bartle and Crewe, 'The Impact of Party Leaders in Britain', p. 94.
29. John Major, *The Autobiography* (HarperCollins paperback, London, 2000), p. 312.
30. Peter Mandelson, *The Third Man: Life at the Heart of New Labour* (Harper Press, London, 2010), p. 150.
31. John Curtice and Michael Steed, 'The Results Analysed', in David Butler and Dennis Kavanagh (eds.), *The British General Election of 1997* (Macmillan, Houndmills, 1997), pp. 295 and 320.
32. Bartle and Crewe, 'The Impact of Party Leaders in Britain', p. 90.
33. David Butler and Dennis Kavanagh, *The British General Election of 2001* (Palgrave Macmillan, Houndmills, 2002), p. 241. Elaborating the point, Butler and Kavanagh write: 'An analysis by ICM found that, out of a number of issues determining the vote, Labour's economic performance was most influential, followed by education, health, law and order, with Europe the least significant.'

34. David Butler and Dennis Kavanagh, *The British General Election of 2005* (Palgrave Macmillan, 2005), p. 204.

35. Dwight Eisenhower made a similar distinction, but without Macmillan's or Truman's irony, when, after retiring from the presidency, he wrote of Nikita Khrushchev: 'In our use of the word, he is not . . . a statesman, but rather a powerful, skillful, ruthless, and highly ambitious politician.' See Jim Newton, *Eisenhower: The White House Years* (Doubleday, New York, 2011), p. 195.

36. Quoted by Bill Clinton in his speech to the Democratic Party Convention of 1984, cited in Stephen Graubard, *The Presidents: The Transformation of the American Presidency from Theodore Roosevelt to George W. Bush* (Allen Lane, London, 2004), p. 626.

37. Harold M. Barger, *The Impossible Presidency: Illusions and Realities of Executive Power* (Scott, Foreman & Co., Glenview, 1984), p. 227.

38. Harold Seidman, *Politics, Position, and Power: The Dynamics of Federal Organization* (Oxford University Press, New York, 3rd ed., 1980), pp. 85–86.

39. See Bill Clinton, *My Life* (Hutchinson, London, 2004), pp. 523–524; and Taylor Branch, *The Clinton Tapes: A President's Secret Diary* (Simon & Schuster, London, 2009), p. 70.

40. 'Obama's trust wasn't enough to save Rice appointment', *International Herald Tribune*, 15–16 December 2012. Obama did, however, see off congressional resistance in 2013 to his nomination of Chuck Hagel (himself a Republican) as Secretary for Defense in succession to Leon Panetta.

41. William E. Leuchtenburg, 'Franklin D. Roosevelt: The First Modern President', in Fred I. Greenstein (ed.), *Leadership in the Modern Presidency* (Harvard University Press, Cambridge, Mass., 1988), pp. 7–40, at pp. 13 and 23. See also Charles M. Cameron, 'The Presidential Veto', in George C. Edwards III and William G. Howell (eds.), *The Oxford Handbook of the American Presidency* (Oxford University Press, Oxford, 2009), pp. 362–382.

42. George C. Edwards III, 'The Study of Presidential Leadership', in Edwards and Howell (eds.), *The Oxford Handbook of the American Presidency*, pp. 816–837, at p. 833. Roosevelt was also losing the confidence of many Southern Democrats, but that (as is discussed in Chapter 3) was because of their concern that the longer-term effect of some New Deal legislation was to undermine the racist order over which they reigned in the South. See Ira Katznelson, *Fear Itself: The New Deal and the Origins of Our Time* (Norton, New York, 2013), esp. pp. 156–194.

43. Graubard, *The Presidents*, pp. 807–808; and Jim Newton, *Eisenhower: The White House Years* (Doubleday, New York, 2011), p. 86.

44. Newton, *Eisenhower: The White House Years*, p. 218.

45. Ibid., pp. 250–252.

46. Ibid., p. 202.

47. Randall Woods, *LBJ: Architect of American Ambition* (Harvard University Press paperback, Cambridge, Mass., 2007), p. 440.

48. Ibid., pp. 512 and 570.

49. Joseph S. Nye, Jr, *The Powers to Lead* (Oxford University Press, New York, 2008), p. 80.

50. Michael Schaller, *Ronald Reagan* (Oxford University Press, New York, 2011), p. xiii.

51. William K. Muir, Jr, 'Ronald Reagan: The Primacy of Rhetoric', in Greenstein (ed.), *Leadership in the Modern Presidency*, pp. 260–295, at p. 260.

52. Schaller, *Ronald Reagan*, pp. 45–46.

53. Ibid., p. 39.

54. Ibid., p. 78.

55. Ibid., pp. 77–80.

56. Alonzo L. Hamby, 'Harry S. Truman: Insecurity and Responsibility', in Greenstein (ed.), *Leadership in the Modern Presidency*, pp. 41–75, at pp. 73–74.

57. Joe Klein, *The Natural: The Misunderstood Presidency of Bill Clinton* (Hodder & Stoughton, London, 2002), pp. 123–124.

58. Klein, *The Natural*, pp. 179–180. Clinton's approval rating for the performance of his presidential duties was around 60 per cent at the end of his second term, and when voters were asked how they would vote if the 1996 election were to be run again, 'the results were almost the same as they'd been: 46 percent said Clinton, 36 percent said Dole, 11 percent said Perot' (ibid., p. 180). The term 'special persecutor', applied to Starr, appears in Drew Westen, *The Political Brain: The Role of Emotion in Deciding the Fate of the Nation* (Public Affairs, New York, 2008), p. 372.

59. Klein, *The Natural*, p. 209.

60. Earl of Swinton (in collaboration with James Margagh), *Sixty Years of Power: Some Memories of the Men Who Wielded It* (Hutchinson, London, 1966), p. 49.

61. Lord Beaverbrook, *The Decline and Fall of Lloyd George: And Great Was the Fall Thereof* (Collins, London, 1963), p. 40.

62. Philip Ziegler, 'Churchill and the Monarchy', in Robert Blake and Wm. Roger Louis (eds.), *Churchill* (Oxford University Press, Oxford, 1993), pp. 187–198. 'But for the war,' Ziegler observes, 'it seems likely that George VI would have continued to view Churchill with some unease as a man to be, if not kept at arms' length, then at least not embraced as a trusted confidant' (p. 194).

63. Swinton, *Sixty Years of Power*, p. 116.

64. Iain Macleod, *Neville Chamberlain* (Muller, London, 1961), p. 165.

65. A.G. Gardiner, *Certain People of Importance* (Jonathan Cape, London, 1926), p. 58.

66. Robert Blake, 'How Churchill became Prime Minister', in Blake and Louis (eds.), *Churchill*, pp. 257–273, at p. 264.

67. Ibid., p. 266.

68. Robert Blake, *The Conservative Party from Peel to Churchill* (Fontana, London, 1972), p. 248.

69. John Colville, *The Fringes of Power: Downing Street Diaries 1939–1955* (Hodder and Stoughton, London, 1985), pp. 126–127.

70. David Reynolds, 'Churchill in 1940: The Worst and Finest Hour', in Blake and Louis (eds.), *Churchill*, pp. 241–255, at p. 254.

71. Attlee's involvement in the allocation of posts is confirmed in his brief and rather dry autobiography, *As It Happened* (Odhams, London, 1954), pp. 132–133.

72. Robert Crowcroft, *Attlee's War: World War II and the Making of a Labour Leader* (Tauris, London, (2011), p. 231.

73. Ibid., p. 174.

74. Roy Jenkins, *Churchill* (Pan Macmillan, London, 2002), pp. 775–777.

75. Colville, *The Fringes of Power*, p. 555.

76. Ibid., p. 554.

77. Ibid., pp. 554–555.

78. Jenkins, *Churchill*, p. 777.

79. Lord Moran, *Winston Churchill: The Struggle for Survival, 1940–1965* (Constable, London, 1966).

80. My interview with R.A. (Lord) Butler, when he was Master of Trinity College, Cambridge, on 23 September 1966. (It was on a non-attributable basis during Butler's lifetime.)

81. Ibid.

82. Lord Butler, *The Art of the Possible: The Memoirs of Lord Butler K.G., C.H.* (Hamish Hamilton, London, 1971). p. 164.

83. Moran, *Winston Churchill*, p. 404.

84. Ibid., p. 553.

85. Alan Bullock, *Ernest Bevin: Foreign Secretary 1945–1951* (Oxford University Press, Oxford, 1985), p. 87.

86. Ibid.

87. Ibid., p. 89.

88. Ibid., p. 55.

89. Bernard Donoughue and G.W. Jones, *Herbert Morrison: Portrait of a Politician* (new edition, Phoenix, London, 2001), p. 490; and Attlee, *As It Happened*, p. 239. Donoughue and Jones express doubts about Attlee's ability in this case to calm the troubled waters, saying 'it is difficult to see how Attlee or anyone else could have devised a formula which would enable Bevan to stay without forcing Gaitskell to go'.

90. Clement Attlee, Leader's Speech to Labour Party Conference at

Scarborough, 1948, http://www.britishpoliticalspeech.org/speech-archive.htm?speech=158.

91. Ibid.

92. David Cameron has been the most overtly constrained of the four leaders mentioned, as he is the first prime minister since the Second World War to be presiding over a coalition government in Britain. This has also added to tensions and discontent among backbench MPs in his own Conservative Party.

93. Harold Wilson, *The Governance of Britain* (Weidenfeld & Nicolson and Michael Joseph, London, 1976), p. 9.

94. David Cameron conducted a reshuffle of ministerial responsibilities in the late summer of 2012, and Lansley was moved from the Department of Health to the non-departmental role of Leader of the House of Commons.

95. Butler, *The Art of the Possible*, p. 184.

96. D.R. Thorpe, *Supermac: The Life of Harold Macmillan* (Pimlico, London, 2010), p. 86.

97. Ibid., pp. 345–346. Hoosier is the popular name for a native of the mid-Western state of Indiana.

98. My source for this was Selwyn Lloyd. I interviewed him on 7 July 1966, on a non-attributable basis at the time. He is cited, as 'a very senior member of Macmillan's Cabinet', saying this in my article, 'Prime Ministerial Power', *Public Law*, Part I, Spring 1968, pp. 28–51, at p. 41. In the same interview, Lloyd, who had served under all three men, described Churchill and (perhaps more surprisingly) Eden as 'more Cabinet-minded than Macmillan'.

99. My 7 July 1966 interview of Selwyn Lloyd.

100. Thorpe, *Supermac*, p. 519.

101. *The Macmillan Diaries, Volume II: Prime Minister and After, 1957–1966*, edited with an introduction by Peter Catterall (Pan Macmillan, London, 2012), p. 89.

102. Reginald Bevins, *The Greasy Pole: A Personal Account of the Realities of British Politics* (Hodder and Stoughton, London, 1965), pp. 137–138. Lord (R.A.) Butler made a similar point, albeit less dogmatically, when he wrote that such an action could stimulate countervailing forces within the government party 'because all the people who go out have friends who mobilize round them' (*The Listener*, 16 September, 1965, p. 409). Lloyd later remarked on Macmillan's 'utter ruthlessness', which led him to attempt to conciliate him not out of friendship but 'because I had become a possible danger' (Thorpe, *Supermac*, p. 524).

103. Percy Cradock, *In Pursuit of British Interests: Reflections on Foreign Policy under Margaret Thatcher and John Major* (John Murray, London, 1997) pp. 100 and 201.

104. Margaret Thatcher, *The Downing Street Years* (HarperCollins, London, 1993), p. 840.

105. Ibid., p. 851.

106. Ibid., p. 847.

107. Ibid., pp. 860–861.

108. Blair, *A Journey*, p. 119.

109. Ibid., p. 201.

110. Ibid., p. 287.

111. Ibid., p. 486. Blair claimed an emotional link with the British people, and he felt this dissipating the longer he was in office. 'For me and for the people', he writes, 'this was sad. My relationship with them had always been more intense, more emotional, if that's the right word, than the normal relationship between leader and nation' (p. 658). He attributed the disenchantment to his increasing unwillingness to modify policy in the face of opposition and disagreement: '"Being in touch" with opinion was no longer the lodestar. "Doing what was right" had replaced it' (ibid., p. 659).

112. Ibid., p. 609.

113. Ibid., p. 117.

114. Tony Wright, *Doing Politics* (Biteback, London, 2012), p. 31.

115. Ibid.

116. Holmberg and Oscarsson, 'Party Leader Effects on the Vote', in Aarts, Blais and Schmitt (eds.), *Political Leaders in Democratic Elections*, p. 50.

3   Redefining Leadership

1. Jean Blondel uses the term 'redefiners', but differently. He regards leaders in that category as promoters of 'moderate change' as distinct from 'reformists' who produce 'large change'. In the way I use the term, redefining leaders *are* radical reformers. Cf. Blondel, *Political Leadership: Towards a General Analysis* (Sage, London, 1987), p. 97.

2. Theodore Roosevelt's tenure of the White House added lustre to the presidency, and his grasp of foreign policy and the world beyond America's shores was much greater than that of many of his predecessors and not a few of his successors.

3. Cf. James MacGregor Burns, *Leadership* (Harper & Row, New York, 1978); and Burns, *Transforming Leadership: A New Pursuit of Happiness* (Atlantic Books, London, 2003).

4. James MacGregor Burns, *Roosevelt: The Soldier of Freedom* (Harcourt Brace Jovanovich, New York, 1970), p. 351.

5. Ibid., p. 352.

6. Stephen Graubard, *The Presidents: The Transformation of the American Presidency from Theodore Roosevelt to George W. Bush* (Allen Lane, London, 2004), p. 272. There was no love lost between Franklin Roosevelt and Joe

Kennedy, and Harry Truman, for his part, retained to the end of his life an intense dislike for the elder Kennedy. Referring to Jack Kennedy's Catholicism, when JFK became a serious contender for the Democratic nomination as presidential candidate, Truman quipped to his daughter: 'It's not the pope I'm afraid of, it's the pop' (David McCullough, *Truman*, Simon & Schuster, New York, 1992, p. 970).

7. Ira Katznelson, *Fear Itself: The New Deal and the Origins of Our Time* (Norton, New York, 2013), pp. 302–303.

8. Ibid., pp. 336–337.

9. Quoted by Katznelson, ibid., p. 337.

10. George McJimsey, *The Presidency of Franklin Delano Roosevelt* (University Press of Kansas, Lawrence, 2000), p. 41.

11. Ibid.

12. Ibid., p. 288.

13. Ibid., pp. 287 and 293.

14. Katznelson, *Fear Itself*, p. 162.

15. Ibid., p. 486.

16. McJimsey, *The Presidency of Franklin Delano Roosevelt*, p. 154.

17. Ibid., p. 163.

18. Katznelson, *Fear Itself*, pp. 178–179.

19. McJimsey, *The Presidency of Franklin Delano Roosevelt*, p. 169; and more generally on the role and influence of Eleanor Roosevelt, pp. 151–170.

20. Graubard, *The Presidents*, pp. 258–259.

21. Harold M. Barger, *The Impossible Presidency: Illusions and Realities of Executive Power* (Scott, Foresman & Co., Glenville, Ill., 1984), pp. 101–102.

22. Ibid., p. 102.

23. David McCullough, *Truman* (Simon & Schuster, New York 1992), p. 972; and Taylor Branch, *Pillar of Fire: America in the King Years 1963–65* (Simon & Schuster, New York, 1998), p. 295.

24. See Alfred Stepan and Juan J. Linz, 'Comparative Perspectives on Inequality and the Quality of Democracy in the United States', *Perspectives on Politics*, Vol. 9, No. 4, December 2011, pp. 841–856, at p. 843. Since the early 1970s, the same authors note, inequality in the USA has got much worse, both by comparison with the 1960s and by international standards: 'From an all-time best measure on the Gini index of .388 in 1968, by 2009 the US Census Bureau had put the US Gini at .469, America's worst Gini index in many decades' (ibid., p. 844).

25. Graubard, *The Presidents*, pp. 456–457.

26. Randall B. Woods, *LBJ: Architect of American Ambition* (Harvard University Press, Cambridge, Mass., paperback, 2007), pp. 440 and 442.

27. Robert A. Caro, *The Years of Lyndon Johnson, Volume 4: The Passage of Power* (Bodley Head, London, 2012), p. 352. On Johnson's relative lack of education (Southwest Texas State Teachers College versus Harvard or Oxford Rhodes

33333333333333333

Scholars), Caro adds, 'Nothing the Kennedys felt about Lyndon Johnson could be any worse than what Lyndon Johnson felt about himself.'

28. Robert A. Caro, *The Years of Lyndon Johnson, Volume 3: Master of the Senate* (Vintage paperback, New York, 2003), p. xxiii.

29. Ibid., pp. xv–xvi.

30. Caro, *The Years of Lyndon Johnson, Volume 4*, p. xvi.

31. Robert A. Caro, *The Years of Lyndon Johnson,Volume 2: Means of Ascent* (Bodley Head, London, 1990), p. xxi.

32. Caro, *The Years of Lyndon Johnson, Volume 4*, pp. 419–420. By including 'the Johnsons of Johnson city', Johnson was talking also about poor whites – and about his own far from privileged youth.

33. Ibid., p. 488.

34. Ibid., p. 484.

35. Ibid., pp. xvii–xviii.

36. Randall B. Woods, *LBJ*, p. 884.

37. Michael Schaller, *Ronald Reagan* (Oxford University Press, New York, 2011), pp. 88–89.

38. Ibid., p. 90.

39. Brian Harrison, *The Transformation of British Politics 1860–1995* (Oxford University Press, Oxford, 1996), p. 69.

40. Ibid.

41. Quoted in Roy Jenkins, *Churchill* (Pan Books, London, 2002), p. 146.

42. Rhodri Walters, 'The House of Lords', in Vernon Bogdanor (ed.), *The British Constitution in the Twentieth Century* (Oxford University Press for the British Academy, Oxford, 2003), pp. 189–235, at p. 192.

43. Jenkins, *Churchill*, p. 160.

44. Ibid., p. 144.

45. Kenneth O. Morgan, *Labour in Power 1945–1951* (Clarendon Press, Oxford, 1984), p. 37.

46. Ibid., p. 37.

47. Kingsley Martin, *Harold Laski: A Biography* (Jonathan Cape, London, new edition, 1969), p. 153.

48. Ibid., p. 173. I can add one anecdote on Attlee and Laski. When I was studying at the London School of Economics, I attended a function organized by the Department of Government at which Reginald Bassett – a professor in that department (and author, *inter alia*, of a notable book, *The Essentials of Parliamentary Democracy*, first published in 1935) – told a small group of us about a return visit Attlee made to the School when he was Prime Minister. Attlee, who had done a lot of practical social work in East London, lectured on local government to prospective social workers at the LSE in the years just before the First World War (for which he immediately volunteered and served as an officer, being several times wounded). Bassett

was in the circle around Attlee when another member of the staff, a former military man who had drunk more than was wise, came up to Attlee and said: 'Clem, Clem, I believe I'm the only man alive who has ever kicked Harold Laski up the arse.' The deference accorded prime ministers was greater then than now, and the familiarity of this address to someone as formal as Attlee embarrassed the speaker's (and Laski's) colleagues. Attlee was unperturbed. 'Good,' he said. 'We need more men like you.'

49. Morgan, *Labour in Power*, pp. 99 and 117.

50. Ibid., pp. 370–371.

51. Ibid., p. 172.

52. Nicklaus Thomas-Symonds, *Attlee: A Life in Politics* (I.B. Tauris, London, 2010), p. 167.

53. Archie Brown, 'The Change to Engagement in Britain's Cold War Policy: The Origins of the Thatcher–Gorbachev Relationship', *Journal of Cold War History*, Vol. 10, No. 3, 2008, pp. 3–47. (I used the UK Freedom of Information Act to have Cabinet Office and Foreign Office documents, as well as the papers of the academics for the Chequers seminars discussed in that article, declassified. They contain revealing annotations by Thatcher.) See also Rodric Braithwaite, 'Gorbachev and Thatcher', *Journal of European Integration History*, Vol. 16, No. 1, 2010, pp. 31–44; and Archie Brown, 'Margaret Thatcher and Perceptions of Change in the Soviet Union', ibid., pp. 17–30.

54. Richard Aldous, *Reagan and Thatcher: The Difficult Relationship* (Hutchinson, London, 2012), p. 207.

55. Quoted in Geoffrey Howe, *Conflict of Loyalty* (Macmillan, London, 1994), p. 332.

56. See Howe, *Conflict of Loyalty*; and Douglas Hurd, *Memoirs* (Little, Brown, London, 2003). It is worth noting that although not even Nelson Mandela's personal advocacy, when he met with her, could shift Margaret Thatcher's opposition to sanctions against the apartheid South African regime, Mandela was pleasantly surprised by her. In a recorded interview he said: 'She was very warm, you know; she was just the opposite of what I was told . . . I was also tremendously impressed by her . . . I was impressed by her *strength* of character – really an iron lady . . .' See Nelson Mandela, *Conversations with Myself* (Macmillan, London, 2010), p. 385.

57. The reluctance of political commentators to see governments as other than extensions of the political will of their party leaders means that even Attlee, a consensus-seeking leader of the Labour Party and a prime minister who did not attempt to dictate to ministers, is all too often portrayed as if *he* were the dominant figure in all areas of policy during the Labour governments of 1945–51. Thus the BBC's political editor, Nick Robinson, writing on the eve of the 2012 Labour Party conference, in an article headed 'Is Ed Miliband a Churchill or an Attlee?', writes: 'It was the Labour man, as his successor may

well remind us on Tuesday, who built the NHS, strengthened the welfare state and created the Arts Council even at a time when there was "no money left"' (http://www.bbc.co.uk/news/uk-politics-19773185, 29 September 2012).

58. Ian Gilmour, *Dancing with Dogma: Britain under Thatcherism* (Simon & Schuster, London, 1992), p. 5. Gilmour also observes: 'Faced with a Prime Minister who disliked cabinet government and sought to evade it in order always to prevail, her most senior colleagues had either to acquiesce in what was going on – in so far as they knew what it was – or to present her with an ultimatum that unless she changed tack they would resign their offices. Since to act in such a way might well have split the Conservative party, they would have been in a serious dilemma, had they ever confronted it. In fact they did not' (ibid., p. 33).

59. For accounts, *inter alia*, of their political relations with Margaret Thatcher, see Nigel Lawson, *The View from No. 11: Memoirs of a Tory Radical* (Transworld, London, 1992); and Michael Heseltine, *Life in the Jungle: My Autobiography* (Hodder and Stoughton paperback, London, 2001).

60. In his resignation speech to the House of Commons on 31 October 1989, Lawson also said that 'for our system of Cabinet government to work effectively, the Prime Minister of the day must appoint Ministers whom he or she trusts and then leave them to carry out the policy. When differences of view emerge, as they are bound to do from time to time, they should be resolved privately and, whenever appropriate, collectively' (Lawson, *The View from No. 11*, p. 1063).

61. Charles Moore, *Margaret Thatcher: The Authorized Biography. Volume One: Not for Turning* (Allen Lane, London, 2013), p. 423.

62. Tony Blair was less willing to spend time in the House of Commons than was Margaret Thatcher and other earlier prime ministers. During his premiership, prime minister's questions were reduced from twice a week to once a week (although the session itself became longer) and so they have remained.

63. Moore, *Margaret Thatcher*, p. 424.

64. Ibid., p. 422.

65. The fullest account of the rise of Margaret Thatcher and of her premiership from 1979 to 1982 is to be found in Moore's authorized biography, *Margaret Thatcher*, which contains much fresh information. In addition to Moore's substantial volume, Gilmour's critical assessment, *Dancing with Dogma*, and the memoirs of other ministers who served in governments headed by Mrs Thatcher, two especially valuable accounts of the Thatcher years, from quite different points of view, are those of Geoffrey K. Fry, *The Politics of the Thatcher Revolution: An Interpretation of British Politics, 1979–1990* (Palgrave Macmillan, Houndmills, 2008); and Hugo Young, *One of Us: A Biography of Margaret Thatcher* (Macmillan, London, 1989).

66. Anthony King, *The British Constitution* (Oxford University Press, Oxford, 2007), p. 316.

67. David Butler and Michael Pinto-Duschinsky, *The British General Election of 1970* (Macmillan, London, 1971), p. 195.

68. Lawson, *The View from No. 11*, p. 7.

69. Peter Hennessy, *The Prime Minister: The Office and its Holders since 1945* (Penguin, London, 2001), pp. 105–106.

70. Lawson, *The View from No. 11*, p. 561.

71. Ibid., p. 574. Describing the poll tax as Margaret Thatcher's greatest political blunder of her eleven years as prime minister, Lawson adds that 'at the time of its initiation in 1986, she had openly boasted to her favourite journalists about how she had "seen me off". Ironically in the end it played a large part in seeing *her* off as Prime Minister' (ibid., p. 584).

72. David Butler and Dennis Kavanagh, *The British General Election of 1992* (Macmillan, London, 1992), pp. 10 and 72–75.

73. D.R. Thorpe, *Supermac: The Life of Harold Macmillan* (Pimlico, London, 2011), pp. 321–322.

74. The Macmillan government accepted the Robbins Report in principle. It was left to the Labour government, elected in 1964 and headed by Harold Wilson, to find the money to implement a dramatic increase in the number of universities and of students attending them. 'This', noted Ben Pimlott, 'it unflinchingly did . . . and the result was the biggest proportionate increase in the number of students in full-time higher education ever'. See Pimlott, *Harold Wilson* (HarperCollins paperback, London, 1993), p. 513.

75. Roy Jenkins, *A Life at the Centre* (new edition, Politico, London, 2006), p. 206. As Jenkins pointed out, the law had long been different in Scotland where majority verdicts were allowed.

76. As Patricia Hollis noted, 'Wilson, characteristically, was not very keen on lifting censorship – he thought playwrights might say rude things about the royals.' See Hollis, *Jennie Lee: A Life* (Oxford University Press, Oxford, 1997), p. 274.

77. Soskice was a relatively conservative Home Secretary and much less ready to challenge the views of his department and, in particular, loath to overrule his formidable Permanent Secretary, Sir Charles Cunningham. Jenkins, from the outset, made clear that he would be running the Home Office, not the department running him.

78. See Emrys Hughes, *Sydney Silverman: Rebel in Parliament* (Charles Skilton, London, 1969), esp. pp. 96–112 and 171–192.

79. See Roy Jenkins, *The Labour Case* (Penguin, Harmondsworth, 1959), esp. pp. 135–146; and Jenkins, *A Life at the Centre*, esp. pp. 175–213. The House of Lords amended Silverman's abolition bill, so that it would apply only for five years, after which it would have to be reviewed. By that time James Callaghan had succeeded Jenkins as Home Secretary. Although more socially conservative than Jenkins, Callaghan was a firm opponent of capital punishment of long standing. He said that he 'would resign rather than order any more executions'. And on a free vote in the House of Commons the abolition of the death penalty was made permanent (by a majority of 158) in December 1969. See Kenneth O. Morgan, *Callaghan: A Life* (Oxford University Press, Oxford, 1997), p. 297.

80. Jenkins, *A Life at the Centre*, p. 196.

81. Ibid., pp. 208–209. The Cabinet was divided on both issues. Although a substantial majority of ministers favoured both reforms, 'three or four were opposed, and another larger group wished the issues would go away' (ibid., p. 208).

82. Jennie Lee was a national figure and highly regarded by many Labour Party activists. She was less popular with her own local electorate and the party members in the Staffordshire constituency of Cannock. A Scots miner's daughter, she had a somewhat regal style, and did not much concern herself with local issues or her constituents' particular problems (Hollis, *Jennie Lee*, pp. 371–380).

83. See Hollis, *Jennie Lee*, pp. 297–359; Ben Pimlott, *Harold Wilson*, pp. 513–515; and Philip Ziegler, *Wilson: The Authorised Life of Lord Wilson of Rievaulx* (Weidenfeld & Nicolson, London, 1993), p. 201. On the Open University, Ziegler sums up: 'Bevan's widow, Jennie Lee, was put in charge of the enterprise. Without her energy and enthusiasm it would have got nowhere, but without Wilson's continued support she would have had no chance to do what she did' (ibid.). This new educational institution was granted university status in 1969 and admitted its first students in 1971. Within the next four decades more than one and a half million people were to become Open University students.

84. Vernon Bogdanor, *The New British Constitution* (Hart, Portland, Oregon, and Oxford, 2009), p.62.

85. Tony Blair, *A Journey* (Hutchinson, London, 2010), pp. 516–517. Even at the time, one senior Cabinet minister from those years told me, Blair made it clear that he was ill-disposed towards the Freedom of Information Act, and the original draft was watered down by two ministers, David Clark and Jack Straw. 'Fortunately,' said the same minister, 'Parliament restored some of the substance to the Act which had been taken out of it.' In his memoirs, Straw makes clear that he was personally horrified by the implications of the Freedom of Information Act and was active in reducing its scope, but he portrays the minister in charge, Clark, as having become evangelical in support of the FoI Act, under the strong influence of his special adviser, James Cornford. See Jack Straw, *Last Man Standing: Memoirs of a Political Survivor* (Macmillan, London, 2012), pp. 275–282 and 285–287.

86. Derry Irvine has written illuminatingly on the background to the constitutional legislation. See Lord Irvine of Lairg, PC, QC, *Human Rights, Constitutional Law and the Development of the English Legal System: Selected Essays* (Hart, Oxford and Portland, Oregon, 2003); and on Scottish devolution specifically in 'A Skilful Advocate' in Wendy Alexander (ed.), *Donald Dewar: Scotland's first First Minister* (Mainstream, Edinburgh and London, 2005), pp. 125–129. Irvine and Dewar (the latter became Secretary of State for Scotland and subsequently the first of the First Ministers of Scotland after devolution was enacted) had 'a shared view that the renaissance in Scotland's sense of its national identity demanded the amplest devolution of legislative authority to a Scottish Parliament consistent with the maintenance of the Union'. They were, however, over-optimistic in their belief that a consequence would be 'the marginalization of the SNP [Scottish National Party]' (p. 127).

87. Kenneth O. Morgan, *Ages of Reform: Dawns and Downfalls of the British Left* (I.B. Tauris, London, 2011), p. 75. Irvine had been picked out as Labour's future Lord Chancellor while Neil Kinnock still led the Labour Party. As a brilliant Labour-supporting barrister who was a close friend of John Smith, his central role in constitutional reform would have been even more assured had Smith not died in 1994. Irvine was also the person who gave Blair his first job – as a pupil in the legal chambers he headed. The other young pupil he took on in 1975 was Cherie Booth who married Blair five years later. While noting this, Philip Stephens gets the chronology and Blair's supposed patronage of his former mentor wrong when he writes: 'After the 1997 election, Irvine was amply rewarded by his young pupil with a seat in the House of Lords and the post of Lord Chancellor, the head of the nation's judicial system' (Philip Stephens, *Tony Blair: The Price of Leadership*, Politico's, London, revised edition 2004, pp. 44–45). In fact, Irvine became a life peer when Margaret Thatcher was Prime Minister and Neil Kinnock was Leader of the Opposition – in 1987.

88. The constitutional implications are that, increasingly, the euro's longer-term survival is seen as likely to depend on less fiscal disparity and on movement towards still closer economic and political union of the member states.

89. Hennessy, *The Prime Minister*, p. 477.

90. Giles Radice, *Trio: Inside the Blair, Brown, Mandelson Project* (Tauris, London, 2010), pp. 174–176.

91. Tony Blair was quite explicit in his approval of much of what Margaret Thatcher achieved as prime minister. In his memoirs he writes that 'Britain needed the industrial and economic reforms of the Thatcher period' (Blair, *A Journey*, p. 99).

92. Robin Cook, *The Point of Departure* (Simon & Schuster, London, 2003), p. 121. Cook added: 'Part of Gordon's tragedy is that he is an old believer in redistribution, but stuck within a Blairite ideology which only allows him to do it by stealth.'

93. Blair, *A Journey*, pp. 116 and 508. As Chancellor, Brown had blocked or severely modified a number of changes to public services that Blair favoured and which were, in many ways, a logical extension of the remodelling of the welfare state begun by Thatcher. Brown successfully resisted changes, backed by Blair, which Alan Milburn as Secretary of State for Health attempted to introduce, to 'deliver genuine competition and choice' in the National Health Service. See Peter Mandelson, *The Third Man: Life at the Heart of New Labour* (HarperPress, London, 2010), pp. 364–365.

94. Radice, *Trio*, p. 220. For very distinctive accounts of how the Labour government dealt with the impact of the global financial crisis which became apparent in 2008, see Gordon Brown, *Beyond the Crash: Overcoming the First Crisis of Globalisation* (Simon & Schuster, London, 2010); and Alistair Darling, *Back from the Brink* (Atlantic Books, London, 2011).

95. The deputy leader of the party, in particular – Nicola Sturgeon – established a reputation as a very able minister and talented politician.

96. David Torrance, *Salmond: Against the Odds* (revised ed., Birlinn, Edinburgh, 2011), p. 227

97. On Harold Wilson as a 'role model' for Salmond, ibid., pp. 339–340.

98. As noted in Chapter 1, that is a central argument of Drew Westen, *The Political Brain: The Role of Emotion in Deciding the Fate of the Nation* (Public Affairs, paperback edition, New York, 2008).

99. Frank Brettschneider and Oscar W. Gabriel, 'The Nonpersonalization of Voting Behavior in Germany', in Anthony King (ed.), *Leaders' Personalities and the Outcomes of Democratic Elections* (Oxford University Press, New York, 2002), pp. 127–157, at p. 138.

100. Robert Elgie, *Political Leadership in Liberal Democracies* (Palgrave Macmillan, Houndmills, 1995), pp. 81–86.

101. Peter Pulzer, *German Politics 1945–1995* (Oxford University Press, Oxford, 1995), pp. 46–47.

102. Mary Fulbrook, *History of Germany 1918–2000: The Divided Nation* (Blackwell, Oxford, 2nd ed., 2002), p. 52. Immediate post-war Germany was divided into zones administered by the occupying powers. In the American zone, the overseers were presented with a dilemma when in one town a Nazi mayor was re-elected by majority vote. As Fulbrook observes (pp. 115–116): 'It was not immediately clear whether the most "democratic" thing to do would be to reject the democratic vote for an undemocratic person, or to install, undemocratically, a democratic candidate against the wishes of the majority. What was clear, however, was that many Germans had little conception of what was meant by "democracy": it was associated for all those who were old enough to have experienced it as adults in the Weimar Republic with national defeat and humiliation, economic crisis, and political chaos.'

103. Cologne was within the British zone of Germany when the country

was administratively divided up at the end of the war. Adenauer was actually dismissed as Mayor of Cologne by the British in 1945. Freed to devote more time to the Christian Democratic Party, he took full advantage of the opportunity and became the party's Chairman.

104. Germany has, indeed, been described as 'Europe's oldest welfare state'. See Pulzer, *German Politics 1945–1995*, pp. 63–64.

105. Ibid.

106. Gordon A. Craig, cited by Giles Radice, *The New Germans* (Michael Joseph, London, 1995), p. 79.

107. Willy Brandt, *My Life in Politics* (Penguin, London, 1993), p. 74.

108. Ibid., p. 78.

109. Thomas A. Bayliss, *Governing by Committee: Collegial Leadership in Advanced Societies* (State University of New York Press, Albany, 1989), p. 76.

110. Fulbrook, *History of Germany 1918–2000*, p. 168.

111. I say this partly on the basis of personal experience and countless conversations in Russia in those years. I spent three months in the Soviet Union in 1966, ten months in 1967–68 and two months in 1976, and noted the big difference in attitudes to Germany in the third of these academic exchange visits as compared with the first two. There is little reason to doubt that it was Willy Brandt and his change of German foreign policy which played a major role in bringing about that development.

112. Archie Brown, 'Did Gorbachev as General Secretary Become a Social Democrat?', *Europe-Asia Studies*, Vol. 65, No. 2, 2013, pp. 198–220.

113. Shortly after Brandt's death, Gorbachev published a journal article of warm tribute to his German colleague in the broader context of the role of the individual in the making of politics and history. See Mikhail Gorbachev, 'Delaet li chelovek politiku? Delaet li chelovek istoriyu: razmyshleniya o nasledii Villi Brandta', *Svobodnaya mysl'*, No. 17, 1992, pp. 17–21. Of Brandt's *Ostpolitik*, Gorbachev wrote: 'There is no doubt that it exerted an appreciable influence on the spiritual and political atmosphere not only in Germany itself, but also in Europe as a whole, including on us. The "Eastern Policy" promoted deepening reflection in our society, reflection on the relationship between freedom and development, on democracy and the future of our country' (p. 19).

114. Brandt, *My Life in Politics*, p. 200.

115. Ibid.

116. Ibid., p. 6.

117. Kohl's *Newsweek* interview is quoted in Helga Haftendorn, 'The Unification of Germany, 1985–1991', in Melvyn P. Leffler and Odd Arne Westad (eds.), *The Cambridge History of the Cold War, Volume III: Endings* (Cambridge University Press, Cambridge, 2010), pp. 333–355, at p. 335.

118. Timothy Garton Ash, *The Magic Lantern: The Revolution of '89 Witnessed*

in *Warsaw, Budapest, Berlin and Prague* (Random House, New York, 1990), p. 72.

119. Haftendorn, 'The Unification of Germany, 1985–1991', p. 351.

120. Bush later wrote that 'Thatcher's lack of sympathy for and even distrust of reunification was obvious', but added: 'While I did not agree with Margaret's concern about the implications of a united Germany, to some degree I did share her worry about the adverse political effect reunification could have on Gorbachev.' See George Bush and Brent Scowcroft, *A World Transformed* (Knopf, New York, 1998), pp. 192–193. See also Philip Zelikow and Condoleezza Rice, *Germany Unified and Europe Transformed: A Study in Statecraft* (Harvard University Press, Cambridge, Mass., 1995).

121. Frederick Taylor, *The Berlin Wall 13 August 1961–9 November 1989* (Blooms-bury, London, 2006), p. 645.

122. George C. Edwards III, *The Public Presidency: The Pursuit of Popular Support* (St Martin's Press, New York, 1983), p. 208.

123. Stephen Skowronek, 'The Paradigm of Development in Presidential History', in George C. Edwards III and William G. Howell (eds.), *The Oxford Handbook of the American Presidency* (Oxford University Press, Oxford, 2009), pp. 749–770, at p. 761.

124. Richard Rose, *The Postmodern President: George Bush Meets the World* (Chatham House, Chatham, N.J., 2nd ed., 1991), p. 183.

125. Ibid.

126. Hugh Heclo, 'Whose Presidency is This Anyhow?', in Edwards and Howells (eds.), *The Oxford Handbook of the American Presidency*, p. 776.

127. That was scarcely less true even a generation ago. See Edwards, *The Public Presidency*, pp. 187–210.

128. I have in mind the readmission to the Communist Party of the Soviet Union of Stalin's right-hand man, Vyacheslav Molotov, and the proposal at a Politburo meeting presided over by Chernenko to restore to the city of Volgograd its famous wartime name of Stalingrad. The idea was to do this as part of the celebration of the fortieth anniversary of the victory over Nazi Germany in May 1985. These were symbolic gestures (Molotov himself was aged ninety-three by that time), but of political significance – moves towards rehabilitation of Stalin which would bolster anti-reformist forces within the party and society. However, although Molotov was duly readmitted to the party in 1984, by May 1985 Gorbachev was General Secretary. The principal advocate of a return to 'Stalingrad', Marshal Dmitriy Ustinov, was dead, and no such name-change took place. See Archie Brown, *The Rise and Fall of Communism* (Bodley Head, London, 2009), p. 484.

129. For this quotation and a much more detailed study of Cardoso's leader-ship, I am indebted to Alfred Stepan's forthcoming chapter, 'Cardoso as Academic Theoretician and Democratic Leader', in Dietrich Rueschemeyer and Richard Snyder (eds.), *Cardoso and Approaches to Inequality* (Lynne Rienner, Boulder, 2014).

130. As Adrian Guelke put it, the government led by the National Party in South Africa had become 'increasingly reliant on anti-communism to justify its policies internationally, particularly as any residual sympathy for racial oligarchy in the Western world faded' (Guelke, 'The Impact of the End of the Cold War on the South African Transition', *Journal of Contemporary African Studies*, Vol. 14, No. 1, 1996, p. 97).

131. Nelson Mandela, *Long Walk to Freedom: The Autobiography of Nelson Mandela* (Abacus, London, 1995), p. 660.

132. See David Welsh and Jack Spence, 'F.W. de Klerk: Enlightened Conservative', in Martin Westlake (ed.), *Leaders of Transition* (Macmillan, London, 2000), pp. 29–52. The fact that in the years following Mandela's retirement, South African politics and society have hardly lived up to the high hopes of 1994 does not lessen the scale of Mandela's – and, indeed, de Klerk's – achievement.

133. Ching-fen Hu, 'Taiwan's Geopolitics and Chiang Ching-Kuo's Decision to Democratize Taiwan', *Stanford Journal of East Asian Affairs*, Vol. 5, No. 1, 2005, pp. 26–44, at p. 43.

134. See *The Memoirs of Richard Nixon* (Grosset & Dunlap, New York, 1978), pp. 544–580; Henry Kissinger, *The White House Years* (Little, Brown, Boston, 1979), pp. 684–787; Margaret MacMillan, *Seize the Hour: When Nixon Met Mao* (John Murray, London, 2006); Jimmy Carter, *Keeping Faith: The Memoirs of a President* (Bantam Books, New York, 1982), pp. 186–211; and Zbigniew Brzezinski, *Power and Principle: Memoirs of the National Security Adviser 1977–1981* (Weidenfeld & Nicolson, London, 1983), pp. 401–425.

135. Ching-fen Hu, 'Taiwan's Geopolitics and Chiang Ching-Kuo's Decision to Democratize Taiwan', p. 38.

136. Ibid., p. 42.

4   Transformational Political Leadership

1. Charles de Gaulle, *The Complete War Memoirs of Charles de Gaulle* (Carroll & Graf, New York, 1998), p. 3.

2. Ibid., p. 233. Writing about himself in the third person was characteristic of de Gaulle.

3. Winston S. Churchill, *The Second World War: Volume II: Their Finest Hour* (Cassell, London, 1949), pp. 136–137, 141–142.

4. Churchill, *The Second World War: Volume II*, p. 142.

5. Quoted by Philip M. Williams and Martin Harrison, *De Gaulle's Republic* (Longmans, London, 1960), p. 75.

6. Vincent Wright, *The Government and Politics of France* (Unwin Hyman, London, 3rd ed., 1989), p. 4.

7. Williams and Harrison, *De Gaulle's Republic*, pp. 3–4.

8. Ibid., p. 35.

9. Ibid., p. 41.

10. John Gaffney, *Political Leadership in France: From Charles de Gaulle to Nicolas Sarkozy* (Palgrave Macmillan paperback, Houndmills, 2012), p. 15.

11. Especially memorable was de Gaulle's opening sentence of his war memoirs: *'Toute ma vie, je me suis fait une certaine idée de la France'* (quoted by Sudhir Hazareesingh, *Le Mythe gaullien*, Gallimard, Paris, 2010, p. 58).

12. Gaffney, *Political Leadership in France*, p. 11.

13. See Michel Debré, *Entretiens avec le général de Gaulle 1961–1969* (Albin Michel, Paris, 1993).

14. Gaffney notes (*Political Leadership in France*, p. 32): 'Opinion polls at the time suggested that 50 per cent of the French – as with most texts of this kind – had not even looked at the draft constitution they would vote upon, and only 15 per cent claimed to have properly read it at all.'

15. Wright, *The Government and Politics of France*, pp. 53–54.

16. Ibid., p. 60.

17. Gaffney, *Political Leadership in France*, pp. 33–34.

18. Presidential power was also drastically reduced during the times when the incumbent did not have the support of a majority in the legislature and had to 'cohabit' with a prime minister of a different political persuasion. This did not happen, however, during de Gaulle's eleven years in the presidency.

19. Robert Elgie, *Political Leadership in Liberal Democracies* (Palgrave Macmillan, Houndmills, 1995), p. 64.

20. Wright, *The Government and Politics of France*, p. 37.

21. Williams and Harrison, *De Gaulle's Republic*, p. 209.

22. Wright, *The Government and Politics of France*, p. 28.

23. Sudhir Hazareesingh, *In the Shadow of the General: Modern France and the Myth of De Gaulle* (Oxford University Press, Oxford, 2012), pp. 172–173.

24. Ibid., pp. 179 and 182.

25. Ibid., p. 104.

26. De Gaulle advised Presidents Eisenhower and Kennedy not to become embroiled in Vietnam and subsequently publicly opposed Lyndon Johnson's escalation of the war (Gaffney, *Political Leadership in France*, pp. 54–55).

27. Hazareesingh, *In the Shadow of the General*, p. 107.

28. Wright, *The Government and Politics of France*, pp. 18–20.

29. Survey research showed that de Gaulle's standing remained relatively high. When in April 1968 French citizens were asked whether, all things considered, de Gaulle's return to power in 1958 had been a good thing or a

bad thing, 67 per cent said it had been good. Even in November 1969 when respondents were asked if they were satisfied with what de Gaulle did in the years 1958–1969, 53 per cent were either 'very satisfied' or 'more satisfied than dissatisfied'. See Jean Charlot, *Les Français et de Gaulle* (Plon, Paris, 1971), pp. 165–166.

30. González, who had become Socialist Party leader while his party was still a banned organization under Franco's rule, was one of Suárez's strongest critics and himself a politician who played an important part in the transition from authoritarianism and a still greater role in the *consolidation* of Spanish democracy. He was to become Spain's longest-serving democratic prime minister, holding the premiership continuously for fourteen years – from 1982 until 1996. His popularity at home and impact abroad was much greater than that of Suárez, but it was the latter who played the most indispensable part in the transition from authoritarian rule.

31. The 'Eurocommunist' parties distinguished themselves by being prepared to criticize some of the actions of the Soviet Union. Most notably, they were critical of the Soviet invasion of Czechoslovakia in August 1968, having been themselves sympathetic to the Prague Spring reformers. See Paulo Filo della Torre, Edward Mortimer and Jonathan Story (eds.), *Eurocommunism: Myth or Reality?* (Penguin, Harmondsworth, 1979); and Richard Kindersley (ed.), *In Search of Eurocommunism* (Macmillan, London, 1981).

32. Simon Parlier, 'Adolfo Suárez: Democratic Dark Horse', in Martin Westlake (ed.), *Leaders of Transition* (Macmillan, London, 2000), pp. 133–155, at p. 144.

33. Quoted in Juan Linz and Alfred Stepan, *Problems of Democratic Transition and Consolidation: Southern Europe, South America, and Post-Communist Europe* (Johns Hopkins University Press, Baltimore, 1996), pp. 96–97.

34. The quotations are from Adolfo Suárez González, *Un nuevo horizonte para España: Discursos del Presidente del Gobierno 1976–1978* (Imprenta del Boletín Oficial del Estado, Madrid, 1978). I owe these references to Alfred Stepan. The entire section on Suárez has benefited greatly from my conversations with Professor Stepan and from his generous sharing of the insights he gained from his long interview with Suárez on 24 May 1990.

35. Ibid., p. 101.

36. Should Catalonia, or even the Basque country, become independent states in the future, there is every reason now to suppose that both they and the Spanish state would still be democracies.

37. Parlier, 'Adolfo Suárez, pp. 148–149.

38. Quoted in Linz and Stepan, *Problems of Democratic Transition and Consolidation*, p. 114.

39. Parlier, 'Adolfo Suárez', p. 149.

40. Ibid., p. 150. The Basque National Party called on its supporters to abstain and 50 per cent of the electorate did so.

41. Linz and Stepan, *Problems of Democratic Transition and Consolidation*, p. 89. Some evidence came to light as recently as early 2012 which suggested that the king had become somewhat disenchanted with Suárez by the time of the attempted coup. He told the German ambassador to Madrid on 26 March 1981, in documents declassified only in February 2012, that the military plotters had 'wanted what we are all striving for, namely, the re-establishment of discipline, order, security and calm'. He also blamed Suárez for failing 'to establish a relationship with the military'. See Fiona Govan, 'Juan Carlos was "sympathetic" to 1981 coup leaders', http://www.telegraph.co.uk/news/worldnews/europe/spain/9072122/Juan-Carlos, 9 February 2012. The quoted remarks notwithstanding, the heading does not do justice to the king's role at the time when his actions spoke louder than his later words.

42. Many of the points made briefly in the Gorbachev section of this chapter I have elaborated at length elsewhere. Beginning with a volume published in the early 1980s (Archie Brown and Michael Kaser, eds., *Soviet Policy for the 1980s*, Macmillan, London, 1982), I have written extensively about Gorbachev and perestroika in books and articles over the years. See especially Archie Brown, *The Gorbachev Factor* (Oxford University Press, Oxford, 1996); Brown, *Seven Years that Changed the World: Perestroika in Perspective* (Oxford University Press, Oxford, 2007); and Brown, 'The Gorbachev Factor Revisited', *Problems of Post-Communism*, Vol. 58, Nos. 4–5, 2011, pp. 56–65.

43. *New York Times*, 13 March 2010.

44. The head of Soviet space research, Roald Sagdeev, was among the specialists extremely sceptical about SDI. When, at a meeting with Gorbachev, a representative of the Soviet space industry told the Soviet leader that 'We are losing time while doing nothing to build our own counterpart of the American SDI program', Sagdeev says, 'I nearly died from suppressing my laughter.' See Sagdeev, *The Making of a Soviet Scientist: My Adventures in Nuclear Fusion and Space From Stalin to Star Wars* (John Wiley, New York, 1994), p. 273.

45. Ronald Reagan, *An American Life* (Simon & Schuster, New York, 1990), p. 608.

46. He had, however, shared some of his critical views with Eduard Shevardnadze, the First Secretary of the Georgian party organization and a candidate (or non-voting) member of the Politburo, and, still more, with Aleksandr Yakovlev, the Director of the think-tank IMEMO and a former high official of the Central Committee. Two years earlier, at Gorbachev's behest, Yakovlev had been brought back to Moscow after a ten-year dignified exile as Soviet ambassador to Canada.

47. On the process by which Gorbachev became General Secretary in March 1985, see Brown, *Seven Years that Changed the World*, pp. 29–67, esp. 39–40.

48. Mikhail Gorbachev, *Zhizn' i reformy* (Novosti, Moscow, 1995), Volume 1, p. 395.

49. Mikhail Gorbachev in *XIX Vsesoyuznaya konferentsiya Kommunisticheskoy partii Sovetskogo Soyuza: Stenograficheskiy otchet* (Politizdat, Moscow, 1988), Volume 1, p. 43.

50. Jean Blondel makes the general point that 'leaders whose goals change are among those who are the most important', suggesting that they are 'drawn primarily from the relatively small group who stay in office for substantial and even very long periods'. See Blondel, *Political Leadership: Towards a General Analysis* (Sage, London, 1987), p. 85. Gorbachev's goals, however, changed within quite a short time – in a period of little more than three years after he had become Soviet leader.

51. Mikhail Gorbachev, *Ponyat' perestroyku . . . Pochemu eto vazhno seychas* (Al'pina, Moscow, 2006), p. 180.

52. Aleksandr Yakovlev, *Predislovie, Obval, Posleslovie* (Novosti, Moscow, 1992), p. 267.

53. 'Zasedanie Politbyuro TsK KPSS, 15 Okybrya 1987 goda', Volkogonov Collection, National Security Archive, Washington, DC, pp. 149–150 and 155. Gorbachev had already used the term 'socialist pluralism' at a meeting with representatives of the mass media, reported in *Pravda* on 15 July 1987. Once he had given the hitherto taboo word 'pluralism' his imprimatur, reformist intellectuals began to use it, sometimes dropping the 'socialist' qualifier. Gorbachev himself, by February 1990, was speaking not of 'socialist pluralism' but of 'political pluralism'.

54. The top foreign policy officials whom Gorbachev replaced were the Minister of Foreign Affairs, the heads of the International Department and the Socialist Countries Department of the Central Committee, and his own principal foreign policy adviser. Especially important were the first of these and the last (Eduard Shevardnadze replacing Andrey Gromyko as Foreign Minister and Anatoliy Chernyaev taking the place of Andrey Aleksandrov-Agentov as foreign policy aide to the General Secretary). It was much harder to replace the key officials in the economic sector, there were so many of them. Half of the more than twenty departments of the Central Committee were concerned with the economy. (In the autumn of 1988, three and a half years after he became Soviet leader, Gorbachev managed to abolish all but two of them.) There were dozens of economic ministries, and every regional party official and manager of a large factory was involved in the implementation of economic policy, in most cases representing an obstacle to reform.

55. V.I. Vorotnikov, *I bylo eto tak . . . Iz dnevnika chlena Politbyuro TsK KPSS* (Sovet veteranov knigoizdanie, Moscow, 1995), p. 260. See also pp. 460–461.

56. Aleksandr Yakovlev, *Sumerki* (Materik, Moscow, 2003), p. 501.

57. Ibid.

58. Vorotnikov, *I bylo eto tak*, p. 461.

59. Ibid., p. 260.

60. By the time he came to write his memoirs (*The Making of a Soviet Scientist*), Sagdeev was living in the United States. An event in his personal life had occurred which, earlier than the late perestroika era, would have been unimaginable for a high-ranking Soviet scientist who had close contacts with the Soviet military-industrial complex. Sagdeev had become the husband of Susan Eisenhower, the granddaughter of President Dwight D. Eisenhower.

61. Sagdeev, *The Making of a Soviet Scientist*, p. 272. Gorbachev came up against the limits of his powers of persuasion when he tried to convince Lithuanians in 1990–91 that they would be better off in a democratized and genuinely federal Soviet Union than in the separate state they were seeking.

62. Ibid.

63. According to the survey research of the most reliable investigators of public opinion in those years, VTsIOM, led by Tatiana Zaslavskaya, Boris Grushin and Yuriy Levada. See *Reytingi Borisa Yel'tsina i Mikhaila Gorbacheva po 10-bal'noy shkale* (VTsIOM, Moscow, 1993).

64. These were not yet multi-party elections, and most of the deputies elected were members of the Communist Party. However, what was decisively important was that they competed against one another on fundamentally different political platforms, thus revealing the full extent of the political differences within the party which lay behind the monolithic façade that the party leadership had hitherto maintained before its own society and the outside world (and that had been justified by the doctrine of 'democratic centralism', which was now as dead as the dodo). An intra-party pluralism prepared the way for the rapid development of competing political parties which were fully legalized by a change to the Soviet Constitution in March 1990.

65. Georgiy Shakhnazarov, *Tsena svobody: Reformatsiya Gorbacheva glazami ego pomoshchnika* (Rossika Zevs, Moscow, 1993), pp. 77–78.

66. Ryzhkov claimed to have read Stalin's copy of Machiavelli's *The Prince* (in the Russian translation of 1869), complete with Stalin's underlinings and annotations. See Nikolay Ryzhkov, *Perestroyka: Istoriya predatel'stv* (Novosti, Moscow, 1992), pp. 354–355.

67. Ryzhkov, *Perestroyka*, p. 364.

68. Mikhail Gorbachev and Zdeněk Mlynář, *Conversations with Gorbachev: On Perestroika, the Prague Spring, and the Crossroads of Socialism* (Columbia University Press, New York, 2002), p. 15.

69. Archie Brown, 'Did Gorbachev as General Secretary Become a Social Democrat?', *Europe-Asia Studies*, Vol. 65, No. 2, 2013, pp. 198–220. Of all the foreign heads of government with whom he came in contact while he was Soviet leader, Gorbachev's favourite was the Spanish democratic socialist prime minister, Felipe González.

70. From time to time the absurd suggestion that Gorbachev was himself complicit in the coup is floated by Gorbachev's enemies and by ill-informed authors, sometimes given more publicity than such nonsense deserves. For refutations of the conspiracy theories, see Anatoly Chernyaev, *My Six Years with Gorbachev* (Pennsylvania State University Press, University Park, 2000), 'Afterword to the U.S. Edition', pp. 401–423; and Brown, *Seven Years that Changed the World*, pp. 319–324.

71. Aleksandr Dugin, 'Perestroyka po-evraziyski: upushchennyy shans', in V.I. Tolstykh (ed.), *Perestroyka dvadtsat' let spustya* (Russkiy put', Moscow, 2005), pp. 88–97, at p. 96.

72. Aleksandr Yakovlev, 'Eto krupneyshiy reformator', *Ogonek*, No. 11, March 1995, p. 45.

73. Ezra F. Vogel, *Deng Xiaoping and the Transformation of China* (Harvard University Press, Cambridge, Mass., 2011), pp. 18–24 and 487.

74. Rana Mitter, *A Bitter Revolution: China's Struggle with the Modern World* (Oxford University Press, Oxford, 2004), p. 161.

75. See Vogel, *Deng Xiaoping and the Transformation of China*, pp. 15–36.

76. Ibid., p. 38.

77. See Frank Dikötter, *Mao's Great Famine* (Bloomsbury paperback, London, 2011), pp. 88, 92 and 118–119.

78. Roderick MacFarquhar and Michael Schoenhals, *Mao's Last Revolution* (Harvard University Press, Cambridge, Mass., 2006), pp. 358–359.

79. Ibid., p. 359.

80. Vogel, *Deng Xiaoping and the Transformation of China*, p. 313.

81. Ibid., p. 247.

82. Ibid., p. 377.

83. *Khrushchev Remembers: The Last Testament*, translated and edited by Strobe Talbott (Deutsch, London, 1974), p. 253.

84. MacFarquhar and Schoenhals, *Mao's Last Revolution*, p. 457.

85. Peter Nolan, *China at the Crossroads* (Polity Press, Cambridge, 2004), p. 3.

86. Ibid., p. 1.

87. For an excellent analysis of the 'insurance policy' against regime change which a number of senior Chinese officials maintain through businesses abroad, whereby publicly owned productive and financial assets are turned into private property (with the overseas enterprises run more often than not by their children), see X.L. Ding, 'Informal Privatization Through Internationalization: The Rise of Nomenklatura Capitalism in China's Offshore Business', *British Journal of Political Science*, Vol. 30, No. 1, 2000, pp. 121–146.

88. Vogel, *Deng Xiaoping and the Transformation of China*, pp. 703–704.

89. Zhao Ziyang, *Prisoner of the State: The Secret Journal of Zhao Ziyang*, translated and edited by Bao Pu, Renee Chiang and Adi Ignatius (Simon & Schuster, London, 2009), pp. 25–34, esp. p. 28.

90. Some military commanders refused to take part in the violent suppression of young demonstrators, among them a general who was, as a consequence, court-martialled and sentenced to five years of imprisonment. See Richard McGregor, *The Party: The Secret World of China's Communist Rulers* (Penguin, London, 2011), pp. 109–110.

91. Green Cross International, *Mikhail Gorbachev: Prophet of Change. From Cold War to a Sustainable World* (Clareview, East Sussex, 2011), p. 243. De Klerk also notes that, quite apart from the changes in Europe, under Gorbachev's leadership 'the Soviet Union played a constructive role in the negotiations between South Africa, Angola and Cuba, which resulted in the withdrawal of Cuban forces from Angola and the successful implementation of the United Nations independence process in Namibia' (ibid.).

92. Nelson Mandela, *Long Walk to Freedom* (Abacus, London, 1995), p. 24.

93. Ibid.

94. Ibid., p. 25.

95. Ibid., p. 134.

96. Ibid., p. 436.

97. Ibid.

98. William Beinart, *Twentieth-Century South Africa* (Oxford University Press, Oxford, 2nd ed., 2001), p. 166.

99. Tom Lodge, *Mandela: A Critical Life* (Oxford University Press, Oxford, paperback edition, 2007), p. 82.

100. Also banned was the Pan African Congress, a militant group which had broken away from the ANC and had been involved in the protests that led up to the Sharpeville killings (ibid.).

101. Ibid., pp. 90 and 92.

102. Nelson Mandela, *Conversations with Myself* (Macmillan, London, 2010), p. 413.

103. Ibid.; and Lodge, *Mandela*, p. 99.

104. Mandela, *Long Walk to Freedom*, p. 438.

105. Frederick Cooper, *Africa since 1940: The Past of the Present* (Cambridge University Press, Cambridge, 2002), p. 153.

106. Mandela, *Conversations with Myself*, p. 344.

107. Ibid., pp. 344–345.

108. Lodge, *Mandela*, p. 205.

109. Ibid., p. 211.

110. Ibid.

111. Ibid., p. 213.

112. Taylor Branch, *The Clinton Tapes: A President's Secret Diary* (Simon & Schuster, London, 2009), pp. 303–304.

113. Stefan Hedlund, *Russia's "Market" Economy: A Bad Case of Predatory Capitalism* (ICL Press, London, 1999). See also Hedlund, *Invisible Hands, Russian*

Experience, and Social Science: Approaches to Understanding Systemic Failure (Cambridge University Press, New York, 2011).

114. See Peter Reddaway and Dmitri Glinski, *The Tragedy of Russia's Reforms: Market Bolshevism Against Democracy* (United States Institute of Peace, Washington, DC, 2001); and for a more sympathetic view of Russia's first post-Communist president, Timothy J. Colton, *Yeltsin: A Life* (Basic Books, New York, 2008).

5   Revolutions and Revolutionary Leadership

1. Ludvík Vaculík speech at Writers' Congress in Prague, June 1967: *IV Sjezd Svazu československých spisovatelů, Praha 27–29 června 1967* (Československý spisovatel, Prague, 1968), p. 141 (translated in Dušan Hamšík, *Writers Against Rulers*, Hutchinson, London, 1971, p. 182).

2. Samuel P. Huntington, *Political Order in Changing Societies* (Yale University Press, New Haven, 1968), p. 266.

3. John Dunn, *Modern Revolutions: An Introduction to the Analysis of a Political Phenomenon* (Cambridge University Press, Cambridge, 2nd ed., 1989), p. 12.

4. See, for example, Sharon Erickson Nepstad, *Nonviolent Revolutions: Civil Resistance in the Late 20th Century* (Oxford University Press, New York, 2011). In contrast, Chalmers Johnson has written that '"nonviolent revolution", so long as these words retain any precise meaning whatsoever, is a contradiction in terms'. See Johnson, *Revolutionary Change* (University of London Press, London, 1968), p. 7. At the same time, Johnson defines 'violence' quite broadly to include revolutions accomplished 'without any blood flowing in the gutters or a single death being caused' (ibid.).

5. Nepstad, *Nonviolent Revolutions*, pp. 4–5. One survey of the use of the concept of revolution concluded that 'there is a general consensus that violence is a necessary characteristic of revolution', with only one author (Charles Tilly), among those surveyed, who did 'not make it a defining characteristic'. See Christoph M. Kotowski, 'Revolution', in Giovanni Sartori (ed.), *Social Science Concepts: A Systematic Analaysis* (Sage, Beverly Hills, 1984), pp. 403–451, at p. 414.

6. For a useful review of these attempts, see Jack A. Goldstone, 'Comparative Historical Analysis and Knowledge Accumulation in the Study of Revolutions', in James Mahoney and Dietrich Rueschemeyer (eds.), *Comparative Historical Analysis in the Social Sciences* (Cambridge University Press, Cambridge, 2003), pp. 41–90.

7. I have used the term 'institutional relationships' to convey the meaning of what Marx called 'the relations of production'.

8. See especially Karl Marx, *Critique of the Gotha Programme* (Foreign Languages Publishing House, Moscow, 1959), p. 22. (Marx's critique of the 'Gotha Unity

Congress' of the German Social Democrats was written in London in 1875, and first published by Friedrich Engels in 1891.) Marx, it should be added, only rarely used the expression 'dictatorship of the proletariat'. It was Lenin who turned it into a much more central tenet of 'Marxist-Leninist' revolutionary theory.

9. Although not claiming the comprehensive explanatory power which Marx sought, two notable studies of revolutionary change written in the second half of the twentieth century were Barrington Moore's *Social Origins of Dictatorship and Democracy: Lord and Peasant in the Making of the Modern World* (Peregrine, London, 1969); and Theda Scocpol, *States and Social Revolutions: A Comparative Analysis of France, Russia, and China* (Cambridge University Press, Cambridge, 1979). Moore offers a non-Marxist class analysis, in which he is especially concerned to explore the circumstances in which peasants become the major revolutionary force. Scocpol's emphasis is on the state, viewed as relatively autonomous from class interests. She compares both the state crises that paved the way for the three major revolutions within her purview – those of France, China and Russia – and the post-revolutionary use of state power.

10. Eric Hobsbawm, *Revolutionaries* (Abacus paperback, London, 1999), p. 295.

11. I have drawn here on several articles by the leading historian of the Mexican revolution, Alan Knight.

12. Alan Knight, 'The Myth of the Mexican Revolution', *Past and Present*, No. 209, November 2010, pp. 223–273, esp. p. 228; see also Knight, 'The Mexican Revolution: Bourgeois? Nationalist? Or just a "Great Rebellion"?', *Bulletin of Latin American Research*, Vol. 4, No. 2, 1985, pp. 1–37. The Mexican revolution, writes Knight, 'was justified less as a leap into an unknown future, than as a restoration of a preferred status quo ante' ('The Myth of the Mexican Revolution', p. 231).

13. When we speak of a 'revolution from above', such as occurred within the Soviet Union between 1985 and 1989, this is a figurative use of revolution. Similarly, 'revolutionary change by evolutionary means' indicates *fundamental* change, introduced gradually, rather than revolution more strictly defined.

14. Knight, 'The Mexican Revolution: Bourgeois? Nationalist? Or just a "Great Rebellion"?', p. 8.

15. Knight, 'The Myth of the Mexican Revolution', pp. 237–238.

16. Alan Knight, 'Populism and Neo-Populism in Latin America, especially Mexico', *Journal of Latin American Studies*, Vol. 30, No. 2, 1998, pp. 223–248, at pp. 235–236.

17. Ibid., p. 237.

18. Jonathan D. Spence, *The Search for Modern China* (Norton, New York, 2nd ed., 1999), pp. 244–253.

19. Ibid., pp. 262–263; and Jonathan Fenby, *The Penguin History of Modern China: The Fall and Rise of a Great Power, 1850–2008* (Allen Lane, London, 2008), p. 121.

20. Fenby, *The Penguin History of Modern China*, pp. 125–126.

21. Spence, *The Search for Modern China*, pp. 274–276.

22. Fenby, *The Penguin History of Modern China*, p. 123.

23. Spence, *The Search for Modern China*, pp. 276–277; Margaret MacMillan, *Peacemakers: Six Months that Changed the World* (John Murray paperback, London, 2002), pp. 331–353; and Rana Mitter, *A Bitter Revolution: China's Struggle with the Modern World* (Oxford University Press, Oxford, 2004), pp. 35–36.

24. See Spence, *The Search for Modern China*, pp. 277–289.

25. On the May Fourth movement, see Spence, ibid., pp. 299–313; and Mitter, *A Bitter Revolution*, pp. 6–11.

26. Spence, *The Search for Modern China*, pp. 284–285.

27. Ibid., p. 314.

28. Mitter, *A Bitter Revolution*, pp. 141–142.

29. Spence, *The Search for Modern China*, pp. 314–322.

30. Fenby, *The Penguin History of Modern China*, p. 144.

31. Andrew Mango, *Atatürk* (John Murray, London, 1999), p. 76.

32. Ibid., p. 176.

33. MacMillan, *Peacemakers*, p. 445.

34. Mango, *Atatürk*, pp. 300–304.

35. Albert Hourani, *The Emergence of the Modern Middle East* (Macmillan, London, in association with St Antony's College, Oxford, 1981), p. 17. As Hourani noted: 'Many of the early leaders (although not Atatürk himself) came from the families of the officers and bureaucrats who had been at the centre of Ottoman government and reform', ibid.

36. Mango, *Atatürk*, p. 364.

37. Ibid., p. 406.

38. Erik J. Zürcher, *Turkey: A Modern History* (Tauris, London, 1993), p. 178.

39. Ibid., pp. 176–180.

40. Mango, *Atatürk*, p. 403.

41. Ibid., pp. 407 and 434–435.

42. Zürcher, *Turkey*, pp. 227–228; and Mango, *Atatürk*, p. 531.

43. Imperial Russia in 1917 was thirteen days behind the rest of Europe in its measurement of time. Until 1920 Russia used the Julian calendar (still employed by the Orthodox Church) before switching to the more generally used Gregorian calendar.

44. This was a recently invented tradition, established by socialist parties in several different countries, to focus attention on equal rights for women.

45. Ronald Grigor Suny, *The Soviet Experiment: Russia, the USSR, and the Successor States* (Oxford University Press, New York, 1998), p. 35.

46. The Bolshevik name dated back to 1903 when there was a split within the Russian revolutionary movement, instigated by Lenin, between the Bolsheviks and Mensheviks, with the former taking a harder and more

uncompromising line than the latter. The official name of the party, led by Lenin, at the time of the 1917 revolutions was the Russian Social Democratic Labour Party (Bolsheviks). In 1918 the name was changed to Communist Party (although 'Bolsheviks' was retained in brackets until 1952).

47. S.A. Smith, 'The Revolutions of 1917–1918', in Ronald Grigor Suny (ed.), *The Cambridge History of Russia: Volume III, The Twentieth Century* (Cambridge University Press, Cambridge, 2006), pp. 114–139, at pp. 124 and 138.

48. Suny, *The Soviet Experiment*, p. 38.

49. Ibid.; and Smith, 'The Revolutions of 1917–1918', pp. 114–115.

50. Sheila Fitzpatrick, *The Russian Revolution* (Oxford University Press, New York, 3rd ed., 2008), p. 49.

51. Fitzpatrick, *The Russian Revolution*, p. 47.

52. Robert Service, *Lenin: A Biography* (Pan, London, 2002), pp. 300–301.

53. See Leon Trotsky, *The Permanent Revolution and Results and Prospects* (Pathfinder Press, New York, 3rd ed., 1972).

54. Fitzpatrick, *The Russian Revolution*, pp. 49–50.

55. Suny, *The Soviet Experiment*, p. 59.

56. Ibid., p. 52.

57. Ibid., pp. 64–65.

58. Leonard Schapiro, *The Communist Party of the Soviet Union* (Methuen, London, 2nd ed., 1970), p. 183. Sheila Fitzpatrick, while accepting that in electoral democratic politics 'a loss is a loss', has noted a rationalization for the Bolsheviks' spurning of the result of the election to the Constituent Assembly. She writes that 'they could and did argue that it was not the population as a whole that they claimed to represent. They had taken power in the name of the working class'. And the elections both to the Second Congress of Soviets and to the Constituent Assembly suggested that in October–November 1917 the Bolsheviks 'were drawing more working-class votes than any other party' (Fitzpatrick, *The Russian Revolution*, p. 67).

59. Phyllis Auty, *Tito: A Biography* (Longman, London, 1970), pp. 29–39.

60. Bertram D. Wolfe, *A Life in Two Centuries: An Autobiography* (Stein and Day, New York, 1981), p. 441.

61. See *The Diary of Georgi Dimitrov 1933–1949* (introduced and edited by Ivo Banac, Yale University Press, New Haven, 2003).

62. Ibid., p. 474.

63. F.W.D. Deakin, *The Embattled Mountain* (Oxford University Press, London, 1971), pp. 79–80.

64. Deakin, having fought alongside him, noted Djilas's 'outstanding physical courage' (ibid., p. 84).

65. Milovan Djilas, *The New Class: An Analysis of the Communist System* (Thames and Hudson, London, 1957), p. 47.

66. Milovan Djilas, *Tito: The Story from Inside* (Weidenfeld & Nicolson, London, 1981), pp. 13–15.

67. Auty, *Tito*, p. 266.

68. Apart from Tito, its members were Edvard Kardelj, a Slovene; the Serbs Moša Pijade (who was also of Jewish origin) and Aleksandar Ranković; and Djilas, who was a Montenegrin.

69. *The Artful Albanian: The Memoirs of Enver Hoxha*, edited and introduced by Jon Halliday (Chatto & Windus, London, 1986).

70. Jürgen Domes, 'The Model for Revolutionary People's War: The Communist Takeover of China', in Thomas T. Hammond (ed.), *The Anatomy of Communist Takeovers* (Yale University Press, New Haven, 1975), pp. 516–533, at pp. 520–521.

71. Spence, *The Search for Modern China*, pp. 463–464.

72. Milovan Djilas, *Conversations with Stalin* (Rupert Hart-Davis, London, 1962), pp. 164–165.

73. Spence, *The Search for Modern China*, p. 467.

74. Roderick MacFarquhar in MacFarquhar (ed.), 'Introduction', in *The Politics of China: The Eras of Mao and Deng* (Cambridge University Press, Cambridge, 2nd ed., 1997), pp. 1–4, at p. 1.

75. Ho's original name was Nguyen Tat Than, but for many years he achieved fame as Nguyen Ai Quoc (Nguyen the Patriot). The last time he used that name was when he signed an 'appeal to the people' in 1945, calling for Vietnamese independence from France. See William J. Duiker, *Ho Chi Minh* (Hyperion, New York, 2000), p. 306.

76. Ibid., p. 75.

77. Ibid., p. 95.

78. Patrick J. Heardon, *The Tragedy of Vietnam* (Pearson Longman, New York, 3rd ed., 2008), pp. 18–19.

79. Ibid., pp. 20–23.

80. Ibid., p. 29.

81. Ibid., p. 181.

82. David W.P. Elliott, 'Official History, Revisionist History, and Wild History', in Mark Philip Bradley and Marilyn B. Young (eds.), *Making Sense of the Vietnam Wars: Local, National, and Transnational Perspectives* (Oxford University Press, New York, 2008), pp. 277–304, at p. 278.

83. Duiker, *Ho Chi Minh*, pp. 5 and 572. The author notes that he had been fascinated by Ho Chi Minh ever since he served as a young foreign service officer at the US Embassy in Saigon in the mid-1960s, when he was 'puzzled by the fact that the Viet Cong guerrillas fighting in the jungles appeared to be better disciplined and more motivated than the armed forces of our ally, the government of South Vietnam' (ibid., p. ix).

84. Ibid., p. 572.

85. Jean-Louis Margolin, 'Cambodia: The Country of Disconcerting Crimes', in Stéphane Courtois *et al.*, *The Black Book of Communism: Crimes, Terror, Repression* (Harvard University Press, Cambridge, Mass., 1999), pp. 577–635, at p. 581.

86. Nicholas Shakespeare, 'Letter from Cambodia: How the dead live', *New Statesman*, 15–21 February 2013, pp. 37–41, at p. 38.

87. Margolin, 'Cambodia', p. 582.

88. Ibid., pp. 630 and 635.

89. Ibid., p. 577.

90. Bradley K. Martin, *Under the Loving Care of the Fatherly Leader: North Korea and the Kim Dynasty* (St Martin's Press, New York, 2006), pp. 30–31. A Korean Communist Party had been set up in secret in 1925, but it was disbanded by the Comintern in 1928.

91. Christopher Bluth, *Korea* (Polity, Cambridge, 2008), p. 12.

92. Martin, *Under the Loving Care of the Fatherly Leader*, pp. 56–57.

93. Volker Skierka, *Fidel Castro*, translated by Patrick Camiller (Polity, Cambridge, 2004), p. 30.

94. Castro, *My Life*, edited by Ignacio Ramonet and translated by Andrew Hurley (revised ed., Allen Lane, London, 2007), p. 157.

95. Skierka, *Fidel Castro*, p. 5.

96. Castro, *My Life*, pp. 80–81.

97. Skierka, *Fidel Castro*, p. 20.

98. Ibid., p. 24.

99. Ibid., pp. 35–36.

100. Fidel Castro, *History Will Absolve Me: The Moncada Trial Defence Speech, Santiago de Cuba, October 16th, 1953* (Jonathan Cape, London, 1968).

101. Skierka, *Fidel Castro*, pp. 38–39.

102. Ibid., p. 51.

103. Ibid.

104. Ibid., pp. 53–54.

105. Ibid., p. 69.

106. Ibid., p. 183.

107. Ibid., pp. 96–97.

108. Ibid., p. 378.

109. Castro, *My Life*, p. 85.

110. For documentation of Gorbachev's abandonment of Communist ideology and embrace of social democratic values while he was still Soviet leader, see Archie Brown, 'Did Gorbachev as General Secretary Become a Social Democrat?', *Europe-Asia Studies*, Vol. 65, No. 2, 2013, pp. 198–220.

111. See, for example, Jacques Lévesque, *The Enigma of 1989: The USSR and the Liberation of Eastern Europe* (University of California Press, Berkeley, 1997), pp. 133 and 186.

112. The figure of 1,000 for those who took part in the main opposition movement, Charter 77, is given in H. Gordon Skilling, *Charter 77 and Human Rights in Czechoslovakia* (Allen & Unwin, London, 1981), p. 79.

113. Timothy Garton Ash, *The Magic Lantern: The Revolution of '89 Witnessed in Warsaw, Budapest, Berlin and Prague* (Random House, New York, 1990), p. 90.

114. Ibid., pp. 89–90.

115. It is understandable that many of those who took part in the systemic transformation of Central and Eastern Europe in 1989 wish to call what occurred a revolution, since it would mean that they themselves were the main agents of change. They are joined, though, by a substantial number of academic authors who include the East European systemic transformations of 1989–90 under the rubric of revolution. See, for example, Goldstone, 'Comparative Historical Analysis and Knowledge Accumulation in the Study of Revolutions'; Nepstad, *Nonviolent Revolutions*; and Stephen K. Sanderson, *Revolutions: A Worldwide Introduction to Political and Social Change* (Paradigm, Boulder and London, 2005). For my own interpretation of the events of 1989–91 in Eastern Europe, see Brown, *The Rise and Fall of Communism* (Bodley Head, London, and Ecco, New York, 2009), esp. ch. 26, 'The End of Communism in Europe', pp. 522–548.

116. Timothy Garton Ash has observed that, compared with the events elsewhere in Eastern Europe, in its 'immediate outcome (the transfer of power from one set of communists to another)', what happened in Romania 'was in substance one of the least revolutionary of them all'. Garton Ash retains sufficient attachment to the revolutionary ideal to wish to broaden its scope to include 'new-style, non-violent transfers of power over states' within 'a new genre of revolution, qualitatively different from the Jacobin-Bolshevik model of 1789 and 1917'. See Garton Ash, 'A Century of Civil Resistance: Some Lessons and Questions', in Adam Roberts and Timothy Garton Ash (eds.), *Civil Resistance and Power Politics: The Experience of Non-Violent Action from Gandhi to the Present* (Oxford University Press, Oxford, 2009), pp. 371–390, esp. pp. 375–377.

117. International (Western) intervention has also played a part in the reconfiguration of the map of former Yugoslavia, especially in the case of Kosovo, which had the status of an 'autonomous province' within the republic of Serbia in Communist Yugoslavia. As Charles King has observed: 'Kosovo is the first instance in the postcommunist world of a newly independent state that (1) achieved de facto independence in large measure because of the intervention of external powers, (2) has boundaries reflecting something other than the internal borders of a highest level administrative component of a preexisting federation, and (3) has achieved widespread de jure recognition'. See King, *Extreme Politics: Nationalism, Violence, and the End of Eastern Europe* (Oxford University Press, New York, 2010), p. 127.

118. The official figures for casualties from clashes between demonstrators and the army in Romania were 1,033 dead and 2,383 wounded, of whom a quarter were soldiers. See Robin Okey, *The Demise of Communist East Europe: 1989 in Context* (Hodder Arnold, London, 2004), p. 97.

119. See Christopher de Bellaigue, *Patriot of Persia: Muhammad Mossadegh and a Very British Coup* (Bodley Head, London, 2012).

120. Ervand Abrahamian, 'Mass Protests in the Iranian Revolution, 1977–79', in Roberts and Garton Ash (eds.), *Civil Resistance and Power Politics*, pp. 162–178, at p. 166.

121. Ibid., pp. 166–167.

122. Ibid., p. 168.

123. Ibid., pp. 173–174. See also Charles Tripp, *The Power and the People: Paths of Resistance in the Middle East* (Cambridge University Press, Cambridge, 2013), pp. 77–82.

124. Abrahamian, 'Mass Protests in the Iranian Revolution', p. 177.

125. Ibid., pp. 174–177.

126. Jeremy Bowen, *The Arab Uprisings: The People Want the Fall of the Regime* (Simon & Schuster, London, 2012), p. 25.

127. Sudarsan Raghaven (for the *Washington Post*), 'Powerful elite cast a shadow over reforms in Yemen', republished in *Guardian Weekly*, 22 February 2013. Yemen's branch of al-Qaeda has also been among the most threatening in the region.

128. Farhad Khosrokhavar, *The New Arab Revolutions That Shook the World* (Paradigm, Boulder and London, 2012), p. 154. The author notes that 'Al Jazeera has not only voiced Arab public opinion but literally contributed to its shaping, helping to establish it by providing a vehicle for free expression.' Khosrokhavar adds: 'Of course, as it is financed by Qatari capital, when it comes to Saudi Arabia or the United Arab Emirates, Al Jazeera loses its edge and becomes much less incisive and critical. On the major issues concerning the Arab world, however, it has played a crucial role in raising the public's awareness and its capacity for critical assessment and reflexive thought' (ibid.).

129. David Gardner, Preface to the Paperback Edition of *Last Chance: The Middle East in the Balance* (Tauris paperback, London, 2012), p. xxi.

130. Khosrokhavar, *The New Arab Revolutions That Shook the World*, p. 267.

131. Bowen, *The Arab Uprisings*, p. 293.

132. Khosrokhavar, *The New Arab Revolutions That Shook the World*, pp. 91–93.

133. Olivier Roy's article is (controversially) titled 'There Will Be No Islamist Revolution', *Journal of Democracy*, Vol. 24, No. 1, 2013, pp. 14–19, at p. 15. Eugene Rogan, in contrast, emphasizes 'the power of Islam' as the inspirational force leading Arabs to believe that they 'could overthrow autocrats and stand up to superpowers' (Rogan, *The Arabs: A History*, Penguin, London, 2010, at p. 497; see also pp. 498–550). Except in relation to the West and, still more, to Israel, however, Islam divides as well as unites. As with all the world's major religions, it contains many different strands. It has long been said that there are no Arab democracies, although this may or may not be changing, but, as Alfred Stepan has emphasized, even when it was clearly true as a generalization about the Arab world, that did not demonstrate an incompatibility between Islam and democracy. There are democracies in overwhelmingly Muslim countries (with Turkey probably the most successful example) and at least 435 million Muslims living under democracy, if 'fragile' and 'intermittent' democracies are included. Islam itself is not immune from change in an evolving global culture. See 'The World's Religious Systems and Democracy: Crafting the "Twin Tolerations"', in Stepan, *Arguing Comparative Politics* (Oxford University Press, Oxford, 2001), pp. 213–253, esp. p. 237.

134. Mark Tessler, Amaney Jamal and Michael Robbins, 'New Findings on Arabs and Democracy', *Journal of Democracy*, Vol. 23, No. 4, 2012, pp. 89–103, at p. 97.

135. Ibid., pp. 95–101.

136. Heba Saleh, 'A revolution betrayed', *Financial Times*, 28 June 2013. This prescient article, written a week before a military coup toppled the Muslim Brotherhood government in early July 2013, convincingly outlined the failures of the Morsi government and the grave tensions it had generated.

137. I am very grateful to Professor Stephen Whitefield of Oxford University for the survey data and for his interpretation of them.

6   Totalitarian and Authoritarian Leadership

1. Abbot Gleason, *Totalitarianism: The Inner History of the Cold War* (Oxford University Press, New York, 1995), pp. 13–30; see also Leonard Schapiro, *Totalitarianism* (Pall Mall, London, 1972), pp. 13–17.

2. Schapiro, *Totalitarianism*, p. 13.

3. Richard Overy, *The Dictators: Hitler's Germany and Stalin's Russia* (Penguin, London, 2005), p. 294.

4. Schapiro, *Totalitarianism*, pp. 13–14.

5. In the summer of 1991 the draft programme of the Communist Party of the Soviet Union, overseen and strongly influenced by Gorbachev, did imply that the regime had been totalitarian. It included the statement that 'our party indisputably bears responsibility for the fact that it was not able to erect a barrier to despotism and allowed itself to be used as an instrument of totalitarianism'. That programme itself, however, which a majority of party officials had no intention of implementing (and which was shortly thereafter overtaken by the August 1991 attempted coup, with Gorbachev placed under house arrest at his holiday home), was more social democratic than Communist. The draft, 'Sotsializm, demokratiya, progress', was published in *Nezavizimaya gazeta*, 23 July 1991. The Soviet Union had ceased to have a Communist system in the course of 1989–90.

6. The Communist Party of the Soviet Union, as a political institution, was even more powerful within Soviet society than was the National Socialist Party within the German system. Yet Stalin had acquired a position of such power by the mid-1930s that, like Hitler, he could play off one institution against another. The party had a superior authority in principle to the political police, but Stalin was able to use the latter against the former, so that even members of the highest echelons of the party were liable to arrest and execution at his behest.

7. The differences between Hitler's Germany and Stalin's Russia were also very great, and in a number of respects Germany in the 1930s was further removed from ideal typical totalitarianism than was the Soviet Union. In any event, the concept of totalitarianism, while of some classificatory utility, is of only limited explanatory value. As Ian Kershaw has observed, totalitarianism has become less fashionable as 'an interpretation of the behaviour of ordinary Germans during the Third Reich'. Recent research has, rather, 'increasingly tended to place the emphasis upon the enthusiastic support of the German people for the Nazi regime, and their willing collaboration and complicity in policies that led to war and genocide'. See Kershaw, *The End: Hitler's Germany* (Penguin, London, 2012), p. 9. For an authoritative exploration of the regime–society relationship, see Richard J. Evans, *The Third Reich in Power 1933–1939* (Penguin, London, 2006). Two notable comparative studies of Hitler and Stalin by historians also largely eschew using the notion of totalitarianism. See Alan Bullock, *Hitler and Stalin: Parallel Lives* (Fontana edition, London, 1993); and Overy, *The Dictators*.

8. Orwell's novel was written in 1948 (hence 1984 was a reversal of the last two digits) and first published in 1949. For a scholarly edition of the book, see George Orwell, *Nineteen Eighty-Four*, with a Critical Introduction and Annotations by Bernard Crick (Oxford University Press, Oxford, 1984).

9. *From Max Weber: Essays in Sociology*, translated and edited by H.H. Gerth and C. Wright Mills (Routledge & Kegan Paul, London, 1948), pp. 196–244.

10. See Jeane J. Kirkpatrick, 'Dictatorship and Double Standards', *Commentary*, November 1979. Kirkpatrick suggested that no 'revolutionary "socialist" or Communist society' had ever been democratized, but that 'right-wing autocracies do sometimes evolve into democracies' (p. 37). She turned the historical generalization into a prediction when she wrote that 'the history of this century provides no grounds for expecting that radical totalitarian regimes will transform themselves' (p. 44). Not surprisingly, the title of a book she published just over a decade later was *The Withering Away of the Totalitarian State . . . and Other Surprises* (American Enterprise Institute, Washington, DC, 1990).

11. This remark of Smith in one of his Glasgow lectures is cited in part in

Chapter 1 of this volume. For the full context, see Adam Smith, *Lectures on Jurisprudence*, edited by R.L. Meek, D.D. Raphael and P.G. Stein (eds.) (Clarendon Press, Oxford, 1978), pp. 322–323.

12. R.W. Davies, 'Stalin as economic policy-maker', in Sarah Davies and James Harris (eds.), *Stalin: A New History* (Cambridge University Press, Cambridge, 2005), pp. 121–139, at p. 138.

13. David R. Shearer, 'Stalinism, 1928–1940', in Ronald G. Suny (ed.), *The Cambridge History of Russia. Volume III: The Twentieth Century* (Cambridge University Press, Cambridge, 2006), pp. 192–216, at pp. 196–197.

14. Davies, 'Stalin as economic policy-maker', p. 131.

15. Oleg V. Khlevniuk, 'Stalin as dictator: the personalization of power', in Davies and Harris (ed.), *Stalin: A New History*, pp. 108–120, at p. 109.

16. The figures are those of the Russian NGO Memorial, which is dedicated to investigating the repression and preserving the memory of its victims (reported in Johnson's Russia List, No. 203, 27 September 2007).

17. Shearer, 'Stalinism, 1928–1940', p. 214.

18. 'Protokol No. 185. Zasedanie 1 fevralya 1956 g.' in A.A. Fursenko (ed.), *Presidium TsK KPSS, Tom 1: Chernovye protokol'nye zapisi zasedaniy. Stenogrammy* (Rosspen, Moscow, 2004), pp. 96–97.

19. Ibid., p. 97.

20. Anastas Ivanovich Mikoyan, *Tak bylo: razmyshleniya o minuvshem* (Vagrius, Moscow, 1999), pp. 597–598.

21. William Taubman, *Khrushchev: The Man and His Era* (Simon & Schuster, London, 2003), p. 616.

22. Ibid., p. 620.

23. The Brezhnev era fared best, for example, in a survey of 1999 conducted by the most professional of Russian pollster organizations, headed by Yuriy Levada. See Levada, *Ishchem cheloveka: Sotsiologicheskie ocherki, 2000–2005* (Novoe izdatel'stvo, Moscow, 2006), p. 68.

24. Frederick C. Teiwes, 'The Establishment and Consolidation of the New Regime, 1949–1957', in Roderick MacFarquhar (ed.), *The Politics of China: The Eras of Mao and Deng* (Cambridge University Press, Cambridge, 2nd ed., 1997), pp. 5–86, at pp. 14–15.

25. Roderick MacFarquhar and Michael Schoenhals, *Mao's Last Revolution* (Harvard University Press, Cambridge, Mass., 2006) pp. 9–10.

26. Rana Mitter, *A Bitter Revolution: China's Struggle with the Modern World* (Oxford University Press, Oxford, 2004) p. 189.

27. Lorenz M. Lüthi, *The Sino-Soviet Split: Cold War in the Communist World* (Princeton University Press, Princeton, 2008), p. 72.

28. Frank Dikötter, *Mao's Great Famine: The History of China's Most Devastating Catastrophe, 1958–62* (Bloomsbury paperback, London, 2011) p. 277. Dikötter's is the most recent, specialist study of the Great Leap Forward and it is he who

estimates (p. 325) that it was the cause of some forty-five million 'excess deaths'.

29. Kenneth Lieberthal, 'The Great Leap Forward and the Split in the Yan'an Leadership 1958–65', in MacFarquhar (ed.), *The Politics of China*, pp. 87–147, at p. 117.

30. MacFarquhar and Schoenhals, *Mao's Last Revolution*, p. 10.

31. Andrew G. Walder and Yang Su, 'The Cultural Revolution in the Countryside: Scope, Timing and Human Impact', *The China Quarterly*, No. 173, 2003, pp. 74–99, at p. 76.

32. MacFarquhar and Schoenhals, *Mao's Last Revolution*, pp. 215–216.

33. Quoted in ibid., p. 3.

34. Walder and Su, 'The Cultural Revolution in the Countryside', pp. 95–96.

35. Harry Harding, 'The Chinese State in Crisis, 1966–1969', in MacFarquhar (ed.), *The Politics of China*, pp. 148–247, at p. 244.

36. Ibid., pp. 242–243.

37. MacFarquhar and Schoenhals, *Mao's Last Revolution*, p. 417.

38. Ibid., pp. 444–455.

39. Harding, 'The Chinese State in Crisis', pp. 246–247.

40. Joseph Fewsmith, 'Reaction, Resurgence, and Succession: Chinese Politics since Tiananmen', in MacFarquhar (ed.), *The Politics of China*, pp. 472–531, at p. 497.

41. Joseph Fewsmith, *China Since Tiananmen: From Deng Xiaoping to Hu Jintao* (Cambridge University Press, Cambridge, 2nd ed., 2008), p. 284.

42. Milovan Djilas, *Tito: The Story from Inside* (Weidenfeld & Nicolson, London, 1981), p. 179.

43. Ibid., p. 23.

44. Bullock, *Hitler and Stalin*, p. 451.

45. 'Sekretaryu TsK N.S. Khrushchevu', APRF, f. 3, op. 24, Volkogonov Papers, National Security Archive (Washington, DC), R 1217. The date at the bottom of Chagin's letter looks like 14.2.56, but it was evidently written in March 1956 (probably 14 March), for the letter opens by referring to Khrushchev's speech to the Twentieth Congress on the cult of personality, which he delivered on 24–25 February. Chagin, who in 1926 was editor of the newspaper, *Krasnaya gazeta*, says he regarded it as his party duty to draw Khrushchev's attention to Stalin's remark. The document has the Central Committee stamp of 22 March 1956, consigning it to the archives of the General Department.

46. David Brandenberger, 'Stalin as symbol: a case study of the personality cult and its construction' in Davies and Harris (eds.), *Stalin: A New History*, pp. 249–270, at p. 250.

47. Ibid., p. 261.

48. For Kádár's declaration, and its context, see Roger Gough, *A Good Comrade: János Kádár, Communism and Hungary* (Tauris, London, 2006), p. 135. Fedor Burlatsky, a reformist intellectual within the Communist Party of the Soviet

Union, quoted approvingly in the Soviet press Kádár's 'who is not against us is with us', and (as Burlatsky told me some years later) he was severely rebuked by Leonid Ilyichev, a Secretary of the Central Committee with responsibility for ideology, for 'trying to teach *us* lessons'.

49. Gough, *A Good Comrade*, pp. 249–253.

50. Ibid., p. 139.

51. Ibid., pp. xi and 255–256.

52. Julia E. Sweig, *Cuba: What Everyone Needs to Know* (Oxford University Press, New York, 2009), pp. 127–128.

53. Ibid., p. 128.

54. Gloria Giraldo, 'Cuba Rising in Major UN Indices', *MEDICC Review*, 9 April 2007; Marc Schenker, 'Cuban Public Health: A Model for the US?', *CIA World Facebook, 2001* and schenker.ucdavis.edu/CubaPublicHealth.ppt; and Fidel Castro, *My Life*, edited by Ignacio Ramonet and translated by Andrew Hurley (Allen Lane, London, 2007), p. 585.

55. Sweig, *Cuba*, pp. 65–68.

56. Castro did not count González as a socialist and, certainly, González's political outlook was far removed from Marxism-Leninism. Fidel, therefore, was surprised when Gorbachev told him 'how much he admired Felipe González', and strongly disagreed with the Soviet leader when he referred to him as 'a Socialist'. Castro told Ignacio Ramonet (his questioner in an interview-based autobiography) that 'Felipe was no socialist'. Castro, *My Life*, p. 487.

57. Sweig, *Cuba*, p. 130.

58. Bradley K. Martin, *Under the Loving Care of the Great Fatherly Leader: North Korea and the Kim Dynasty* (Thomas Dunne, New York, 2006), p. 4.

59. Jasper Becker, *Rogue Regime: Kim Jong Il and the Looming Threat of North Korea* (Oxford University Press, New York, 2005), p. 77.

60. Martin, *Under the Loving Care of the Great Fatherly Leader*, p. 166.

61. Bruce Cumings, 'Democratic People's Republic of Korea', in Bogdan Szajkowski (ed.), *Marxist Governments: A World Survey*, Vol. 2 (Macmillan, London, 1981), pp. 443–467, at p. 453.

62. Becker, *Rogue Regime*, p. 77.

63. Juan J. Linz, *Totalitarian and Authoritarian Regimes* (Lynne Rienner, Boulder, 2000), p. 35.

64. Quoted by Martin, *Under the Loving Care of the Fatherly Leader*, p. 194.

65. Another Communist leader who succeeded in arranging a dynastic succession was Heidar Aliev who for many years headed the Communist Party organization in Azerbaijan. However, by the time he did this, it was 1993 and he was president of *post-Soviet* Azerbaijan. He was succeeded by his son, Ilham Aliev. On the broader issue of hereditary succession in countries other than monarchies, see Jason Brownlee, 'Hereditary Succession in Modern Autocracies', *World Politics*, Vol. 59, No. 4, 2007, pp. 595–628.

66. Carl Gershman, 'A Voice from the North Korean Gulag', *Journal of Democracy*, Vol. 24, No. 2, 2013, pp. 165–173, at p. 171.

67. Christopher Duggan, *Fascist Voices: An Intimate History of Mussolini's Italy* (Bodley Head, London, 2012), p. 81.

68. Ibid., p. 30.

69. Ibid., pp. 50 and 57.

70. Ibid., pp. 59–60.

71. Ibid., pp. 87–90.

72. Ibid., pp. 91–94.

73. Donald Sassoon, *One Hundred Years of Socialism: The West European Left in the Twentieth Century* (Fontana, London, 1997), p. 75.

74. Duggan, *Fascist Voices*, p. 108.

75. Robert O. Paxton, *The Anatomy of Fascism* (Penguin, London, 2005), p. 63.

76. Quoted by Linz in *Authoritarian and Totalitarian Regimes*, p. 166.

77. Duggan, *Fascist Voices*, p. 70.

78. Ibid., p. 101.

79. Ibid., p. 231.

80. Ibid., p. 280.

81. Ibid., p. 305. Mussolini was listed in 1933 by American Jewish publishers among the world's 'twelve greatest Christian champions' of the Jews (Paxton, *The Anatomy of Fascism*, p. 166).

82. Duggan, *Fascist Voices*, p. 305.

83. F.W. Deakin, *The Brutal Friendship: Mussolini, Hitler and the Fall of Fascism* (Weidenfeld & Nicolson, London, 1962), p. 795.

84. Duggan, *Fascist Voices*, pp. 416–417.

85. Paxton, *The Anatomy of Fascism*, p. 96.

86. Adolf Hitler, *Mein Kampf*, translated by Ralph Manheim with an introduction by D.C. Watt (Pimlico, London, 1992; 2009 reprint), p. 296.

87. Ibid., p. 262.

88. Evans, *The Third Reich in Power 1933–1939*, p. 8.

89. Ian Kershaw, *Hitler* (Penguin, London, new edition, 2008), p. 204.

90. Ibid., p. 206.

91. Ibid., p. 227.

92. Ibid., pp. 276–277.

93. Ibid., pp. 281–282.

94. Evans, *The Third Reich in Power*, p. 11; and Kershaw, *Hitler*, pp. 274–282.

95. Evans, *The Third Reich in Power*, p. 16.

96. Ibid., pp. 7 and 16.

97. Kershaw, *Hitler*, p. 313; and for a fuller account of the showdown with the SA and the assassination also of leading conservative figures at Hitler's behest in July 1934, ibid., pp. 301–319.

98. Ibid., pp. 317–318.

99. Ibid., pp. xl and 320–321.

100. Hitler, *Mein Kampf*, pp. 194, 217 and 137; and Kershaw, *Hitler*, pp. 909–910.

101. Kershaw, *Hitler*, pp. 212–215.

102. Ibid., p. 324; and Evans, *The Third Reich in Power*, p. 27.

103. Kershaw, *Hitler*, p. 511.

104. Ibid., p. 356.

105. Evans, *The Third Reich in Power*, p. 649.

106. Paxton, *The Anatomy of Fascism*, pp. 219–220.

107. Ibid., p. 75.

108. Ibid., p. 149.

109. Ian Kershaw, *The End: Hitler's Germany, 1944–45* (Penguin, London, 2012), p. 13.

110. Overy, *The Dictators*, p. 100.

111. Ibid., p. 120.

112. Adam Smith, *The Theory of Moral Sentiments* (Clarendon Press, Oxford, 1976), p. 251.

113. *Turgot on Progress, Sociology and Economics*, translated and edited by Ronald G. Meek (Cambridge University Press, Cambridge, 1973), p. 76.

114. David Hume, 'Of the First Principles of Government', in *Essays and Treatises on Several Subjects Containing Essays Moral, Political and Literary: A New Edition*, Vol. 1 (Cadell, London, 1788), p. 39.

115. Jason Brownlee, *Authoritarianism in an Age of Democratization* (Cambridge University Press, Cambridge, 2007), pp. 202–205.

116. William R. Polk, *Understanding Iraq* (Tauris, London, 2006), p. 109.

117. Joseph Sassoon, *Saddam Hussein's Ba'th Party: Inside an Authoritarian Regime* (Cambridge University Press, New York, 2012), pp. 130–131.

118. Ibid., pp. 5 and 181.

119. Ibid., p. 5. Sassoon's book is based on a detailed study of Baath Party documents, captured by the American occupying forces after the invasion of Iraq in 2003.

120. Paul Collier, *The Bottom Billion: Why the Poorest Countries are Failing and What Can Be Done About It* (Oxford University Press, Oxford, 2008), p. 49.

121. Kershaw, *Hitler*, p. 111.

122. Ibid., p. 201.

123. Daniel Kahneman, *Thinking Fast and Slow* (Allen Lane, London, 2011) p. 140.

7 Foreign Policy Illusions of 'Strong Leaders'

1. David Owen, *The Hubris Syndrome: Bush, Blair and the Intoxication of Power* (Methuen, revised edition, York, 2012), pp. 1–2.

2. Francis Fukuyama observes that 'virtually all of the world's successful authoritarian modernizers, including South Korea, Taiwan, Singapore and modern China itself, are East Asian countries sharing a common Chinese cultural heritage'. See Fukuyama, *The Origins of Political Order: From Prehuman Times to the French Revolution* (Profile, London, 2011), p. 313. In the cases of Taiwan and South Korea, some of that modernization has, of course, come after authoritarian rule gave way to democracy.

3. Cited by Ian Kershaw, *Hitler* (Penguin, London, 2009), p. 473.

4. Kershaw, *Hitler*, p. 479.

5. Ibid., pp. 420 and 422.

6. Richard J. Evans, *The Third Reich in Power 1933–1939* (Penguin, London, 2006), pp. 692–695.

7. Kershaw, *Hitler*, p. 619.

8. Ibid., pp. 157–158.

9. Ibid., pp. 154–155.

10. Ibid., p. 588.

11. Christopher Duggan, *Fascist Voices: An Intimate History of Mussolini's Italy* (Bodley Head, London, 2012), p. 298.

12. Stanley G. Payne, *The Spanish Civil War, the Soviet Union, and Communism* (Yale University Press, New Haven, 2004), p. 172.

13. Archie Brown, *The Rise and Fall of Communism* (Bodley Head, London, and Ecco, New York, 2009), pp. 91–92.

14. For the plethora of warnings of the imminence of the German invasion which Stalin received and ignored, see Winston S. Churchill, *The Second World War, Volume IV: The Hinge of Fate* (Cassell, London, 1951), p. 443; John Erickson, *The Road to Stalingrad: Stalin's War with Germany* (Weidenfeld & Nicolson, London, 1975), pp. 87–98; and Christopher Andrew and Vasili Mitrokhin, *The Mitrokhin Archive: The KGB in Europe and the West* (Allen Lane, London, 1999), pp. 122–125.

15. Andrew and Mitrokhin, *The Mitrokhin Archive*, p. 124.

16. See *The Diary of Georgi Dimitrov 1933–1949*, introduced and edited by Ivo Banac (Yale University Press, New Haven, 2003), pp. 434–441; and Milovan Djilas, *Conversations with Stalin* (Rupert Hart-Davis, London, 1962), pp. 164–165.

17. William Stueck, 'The Korean War', in Melvyn P. Leffler and Odd Arne Westad (eds.), *The Cambridge History of the Cold War, Volume I: Origins* (Cambridge University Press, Cambridge, 2010), pp. 266–287, esp. 273–276. See also Odd Arne Westad, *The Global Cold War* (Cambridge University Press, Cambridge, 2005), p. 66.

18. Stueck, 'The Korean War', p. 274.

19. Letter of Stalin to Mao, dated 4 October 1950, sent via Soviet Ambassador to Bejing, 5 October 1950, *Cold War International History Project Bulletin*, No. 14/15, pp. 375–376.

20. Craig Dietrich, *People's China: A Brief History* (Oxford University Press,

New York, 3rd ed., 1998); and Jung Chang and Jon Halliday, *Mao: The Unknown Story* (Vintage, London, 2006), p. 394.

21. Stueck, 'The Korean War', p. 283.

22. Vladimir O. Pechatnov, 'The Soviet Union and the World, 1944–1953', in Leffler and Westad, *The Cambridge History of the Cold War, Volume 1: Origins*, pp. 90–111, at pp. 109–110.

23. Lorenz M. Lüthi, *The Sino-Soviet Split: Cold War in the Communist World* (Princeton University Press, Princeton, 2008), p. 77.

24. For the major biography of Khrushchev, which gives full weight to both his merits and demerits, see William Taubman, *Khrushchev: The Man and His Era* (Free Press, New York, 2003). On Khrushchev and the Cuban missile crisis, see Aleksandr Fursenko and Timothy Naftali, *Khrushchev's Cold War: The Inside Story of an American Adversary* (Norton, New York, 2006), pp. 409–508.

25. William Taubman, 'The Khrushchev Period, 1953–1954', in Suny (ed.), *The Cambridge History of Russia. Volume III*, pp. 268–291, at p. 290.

26. See Margaret MacMillan, *Seize the Hour: When Nixon Met Mao* (John Murray paperback, London, 2007).

27. David Shambaugh, *China Goes Global: The Partial Power* (Oxford University Press, New York, 2013), p. 309.

28. Odd Arne Westad, *Restless Empire: China and the World since 1750* (Bodley Head, London, 2012), pp. 419–420.

29. Lee Kuan Yew, *From Third World to First. The Singapore Story: 1965–2000* [volume two of Memoirs of Lee Kuan Yew] (Times, Singapore, 2000), p. 667.

30. Zbigniew Brzezinski, *Power and Principle: Memoirs of the National Security Adviser 1977–1981* (Weidenfeld & Nicolson, London, 1983), pp. 409–414.

31. Shambaugh, *China Goes Global*, pp. 275–276. Shambaugh observes: 'Instead of "teaching Vietnam a lesson" . . . it was Vietnam that administered the lessons.'

32. Benedict Mander and Robin Wigglesworth, 'China's Caribbean influence grows', *Financial Times*, 21 May 2013.

33. Westad, *Restless Empire*, p. 437.

34. Ibid., pp. 437–438.

35. Fidel Castro, *My Life* (Allen Lane, London, 2007), p. 322.

36. 'Zapis' besedy A.N. Kosygina, A.A. Gromyko, D.F. Ustinova, B.N. Pomomareva s N.M. Taraki 20 marta 1979 goda', Hoover Institution Archives, Fond 89, 1.1003, opis 42, file 3, p. 3.

37. Westad, *The Global Cold War*, p. 316. Muhammad Anwar al-Sadat, Nasser's successor as President of Egypt, set about improving his country's relations with the United States and expelled around 20,000 Soviet advisers. He also made dramatic overtures to Israel and following peace negotiations brokered by the Carter administration in the US, he signed the Camp David peace

agreement of 1978. He received the Nobel Peace Prize that same year, and was assassinated in 1981.

38. Artemy M. Kalinovsky, *A Long Goodbye: The Soviet Withdrawal from Afghanistan* (Harvard University Press, Cambridge, Mass., 2011), p. 118.

39. Westad, *The Global Cold War*, p. 356; and Rodric Braithwaite, *Afgantsy: The Russians in Afghanistan 1979–1989* (Profile, London, 2011), pp. 329–331.

40. Bogomolov was Director of the Institute of Economics of the World Socialist System. It was not until the perestroika era that he first drew public attention to the existence of that memorandum – in the newspaper, *Literaturnaya gazeta*, 16 March 1988. On the significance of Bogomolov's institute and on the impressive array of radical reformers who worked there, see Archie Brown, *Seven Years that Changed the World: Perestroika in Perspective* (Oxford University Press, Oxford, 2007), pp. 172–178.

41. Westad, *The Global Cold War*, p. 321; and Brown, *The Rise and Fall of Communism*, p. 353.

42. David Gardner, the International Affairs editor of the *Financial Times* and a specialist on the Middle East, dismisses Britain's role as that of 'spear-carrier' and 'a sideshow', while noting that Iraq was also a demonstration of 'a pitilessly public spectacle of the limits to US power'. See *Financial Times*, 9/10 March 2013.

43. For broader discussion of historical analogy in the process of political perception, see Robert Jervis, *Perception and Misperception in International Politics* (Princeton University Press, Princeton, 1976) and Richard E. Neustadt and Ernest R. May, *Thinking in Time: The Uses of History for Decision Makers* (Free Press, New York, 1986). See also Yuen Foong Khong, *Analogies at War: Korea, Munich, Dien Bien Phu, and the Vietnam Decisions of 1965* (Princeton University Press, Princeton, 1992).

44. Keith Feiling, *The Life of Neville Chamberlain* (Macmillan, London, 1946), p. 381. Iain Macleod, in his sympathetic biography of Chamberlain, argues that too much can be made of what Chamberlain, in the elation of the moment, said to the crowd in Downing Street. In what Macleod called his 'more measured words to the House of Commons', Chamberlain expressed the hope that Members of Parliament would 'not read into those words more than they were intended to convey', adding: 'I do indeed believe that we may yet secure peace for our time, but I never meant to suggest that we should do that by disarmament, until we can induce others to disarm too . . .' See Iain Macleod, *Neville Chamberlain* (Muller, London, 1961), p. 256.

45. R.A. Butler, in his memoirs, presents as one of the justifications of the Munich agreement that it bought time for the British rearmament programme and suggests that this was part of his own motivation for strongly supporting – and, as a junior minister at the Foreign Office, implementing – the policy of appeasement. See *The Art of the Possible: The Memoirs of Lord Butler K.G.,*

C.H. (Hamish Hamilton, London, 1971), esp. p. 63. Patrick Cosgrave, in his *R.A. Butler: An English Life* (Quartet Books, London, 1981) observes: 'Butler argues that the Munich agreement was consciously made out of a realization of Britain's weakness and an awareness that time was needed to strengthen her defences; and this is not true' (p. 53). Cosgrove, whose account of Rab Butler's political career is more nuanced than hostile, notes also that 'Butler did not merely go along with appeasement: he worked hard, long and enthusiastically for it, and there is very little evidence in the public records for the time that he took the slightest contemporary interest in the rearmament programme to which he devotes such emphasis in his memoirs' (p. 43).

46. Roy Jenkins, *Baldwin* (Papermac, London, 1987), pp. 147–148.

47. Ibid., p. 164.

48. Ibid., p. 81.

49. Earl of Swinton, *Sixty Years of Power: Some Memories of the Men Who Wielded It* (Hutchinson, London, 1966), p. 120.

50. Winston Churchill quotes at length from that House of Commons speech of Baldwin in his war memoirs, *The Second World War: Volume 1, The Gathering Storm* (Cassell, London, 1948), pp. 169–170. Although Churchill did not compile the index to the book, he doubtless made an exception for the entry to those pages which reads '[Baldwin] confesses putting party before country' (p. 615).

51. Swinton, *Sixty Years of Power*, pp. 86 and 89.

52. Ibid., p. 111.

53. Ibid., pp. 115–116.

54. Avi Shlaim, Peter Jones and Keith Sainsbury, *British Foreign Secretaries since 1945* (David & Charles, Newton Abbot, 1977), p. 82. Lord Cranborne, the future fifth Marquis of Salisbury and a junior minister in the Foreign Office in 1938, resigned from the government along with Eden.

55. *The Duff Cooper Diaries 1915–1951*, edited by John Julius Norwich (Weidenfeld & Nicolson, London 2005), p. 245.

56. Harold Nicolson, *Diaries and Letters 1930–1939*, edited by Nigel Nicolson (Fontana, London, 1969), p. 351.

57. Hugh Dalton, *The Fateful Years: Memoirs (Volume 2), 1931–1945* (Frederick Muller, London, 1957), p. 176.

88. Swinton, *Sixty Years of Power*, p. 121.

89. Ibid., p. 116.

90. Ibid., p. 120. Swinton adds that Chamberlain did confirm that rearmament would go ahead, to which he responded that he accepted Munich on that basis but had 'no illusions about peace'.

91. Ibid., p. 123.

92. Among Labour MPs, Hugh Dalton, who was to become a member of the wartime coalition government and a prominent Cabinet minister in the first post-war Labour administration, was one of those pressing most strongly

for an anti-appeasement policy and for faster rearmament. He had a number of discussions with anti-Chamberlain Conservatives, including Winston Churchill and Harold Macmillan, on making common cause against Chamberlain's foreign policy. See Dalton, *The Fateful Years*, pp. 161–221.

93. *Chips: The Diaries of Sir Henry Channon*, p. 213.

94. Duff Cooper adds: 'And then, when Attlee gave the plan his blessing, our side all rose again and cheered him – cheers with which the opposition had to join, though looking a little foolish', *The Duff Cooper Diaries*, p. 269.

95. *The Duff Cooper Diaries*, p. 258.

96. Ibid., pp. 257–258.

97. Ibid., p. 258.

98. Ibid., p. 268.

99. Ibid.

100. Ibid., pp. 268–269.

101. Ibid., p. 271.

102. Nicolson, *Diaries and Letters 1930–1939*, p. 392.

103. Quoted in Wm. Roger Louis, *Ends of British Imperialism: The Scramble for Empire, Suez and Decolonization* (Tauris, London, 2006), p. 638.

104. Keith Kyle, *Suez: Britain's End of Empire in the Middle East* (2nd ed., Tauris, London, 2003), p. 68. Max Beloff similarly observed: 'Press criticism of his alleged indecisiveness tended to make Eden more determined to show himself as tough.' See Lord Beloff, 'The Crisis and its Consequences for the British Conservative Party', in Wm. Roger Louis and Roger Owen (eds.), *Suez 1956: The Crisis and its Consequences* (Clarendon Press, Oxford, 1989), p. 320.

105. Louis, *Ends of British Imperialism*, pp. 609–626. Churchill retained some of the racial stereotypes and imperialist assumptions of a politician who had first stood for Parliament when Queen Victoria was on the throne. While he was still prime minister, Churchill's advice to Eden as Foreign Secretary on 'how to handle the Egyptians' was: 'Tell them that if we have any more of their cheek we will set the Jews on them and drive them into the gutter, from which they should never have emerged' (ibid., p. 635).

106. Gill Bennett, *Six Moments of Crisis: Inside British Foreign Policy* (Oxford University Press, Oxford, 2013), p. 38.

107. Kyle, *Suez*, p. 134.

108. Cited by Nigel Nicolson, *People and Parliament* (Weidenfeld & Nicolson, London, 1958), p. 108.

109. *The Memoirs of Sir Anthony Eden: Full Circle* (Cassell, London, 1960), p. 431; and Selwyn Lloyd, *Suez 1956: A Personal Account* (Jonathan Cape, London, 1978), p. 192.

110. Quoted in Louis, *Ends of British Imperialism*, p. 632.

111. Eden, *Full Circle*, p. 498.

112. The area specialists in the Foreign Office were denied access to many

of the crucial papers and 'the overwhelming majority of the Foreign Office' considered the Suez adventure to be a 'bad mistake' from which Britain must 'urgently extract herself'. That confidential note was written on 2 November 1956 and addressed to the Permanent Under-Secretary Sir Ivone Kirkpatrick who had been at least as committed to the enterprise as was Eden. See Kyle, *Suez*, p. 397.

113. Kyle, *Suez*, pp. 391 and 397.

114. Kyle, *Suez*, p. 299.

115. For a detailed and scholarly account of the Sèvres meeting, see Avi Shlaim, 'The Protocol of Sèvres, 1956: anatomy of a war plot', *International Affairs*, Vol. 73, No. 3, 1997, pp. 509–530.

116. Ibid. For Selwyn Lloyd's account of the meeting, in a book he wrote not long before his death, see his *Suez 1956*, pp. 180–190.

117. Shlaim, 'The Protocol of Sèvres 1956', p. 522.

118. Ibid. A.J.P. Taylor was to observe of the Suez venture: 'The moral for British Governments is clear. Like most respectable people, they will make poor criminals and had better stick to respectability' (quoted by Kyle, *Suez*, p. 585).

119. Avi Shlaim, *The Iron Wall: Israel and the Arab World* (Penguin, London, 2001), pp. 174–177.

120. Anthony Nutting, *No End of a Lesson: The Story of Suez* (Constable, London, 1967), p. 115.

121. Ibid., pp. 126–127.

122. Veljko Mićunović, *Moscow Diary*, translated by David Floyd (Chatto & Windus, London, 1980), p. 134. Mićunović, who was the Yugoslav ambassador to the Soviet Union, attended this meeting of Khrushchev and Malenkov with Tito at the Yugoslav leader's villa on the island of Brioni.

123. Kyle, *Suez*, p. 427.

124. D.R. Thorpe, *Supermac: The Life of Harold Macmillan* (Pimlico, London, 2011), p. 350. For a fuller account of the economic dimensions of the Suez crisis, see Diane B. Kunz, 'The Importance of Having Money: The Economic Diplomacy of the Suez Crisis', in Louis and Owen (eds.), *Suez 1956*, pp. 215–232.

125. Kyle, *Suez*, pp. 467–468.

126. Keith Kyle, 'Britain and the Suez Crisis, 1955–1956', in Louis and Owen (eds.), *Suez 1956*, pp. 103–130, at p. 130.

127. Nutting, *No End of a Lesson*, p. 171.

128. Harold Nicolson, *Diaries and Letters 1945–1962* (Fontana, London, 1971), p. 301.

129. John Tirman, *The Deaths of Others: The Fate of Civilians in America's Wars* (Oxford University Press, New York, 2011), pp. 324–336, esp. p. 327. Tirman is Principal Research Scientist and Director of the Center for International Studies at the Massachusetts Institute of Technology.

130. Eugene Rogan, *The Arabs: A History* (Penguin, London, 2010), p. 615.

131. Condoleezza Rice, *No Higher Honour: A Memoir of My Years in Washington* (Simon & Schuster, London, 2011), pp. 170–171.

132. Bob Woodward, *Plan of Attack* (Simon & Schuster, London, 2004), p. 9.

133. George W. Bush, *Decision Points* (Crown, New York, 2010), p. 229.

134. Richard A. Clarke, *Against All Enemies: Inside America's War on Terror* (Free Press, New York, 2004), pp. 231–232.

135. Ibid., p. 170.

136. Dick Cheney, with Liz Cheney, *In My Time: A Personal and Political Memoir* (Threshold, New York, 2011), p. 369.

137. Rice, *No Higher Honour*, pp. 202–203; and Bush, *Decision Points*, p. 246.

138. Simon Jenkins, 'Blair may itch to return, but he faces a cruel reality check', *Guardian*, 27 July 2012. Jenkins adds: 'We can see why Blair admitted to Roy Jenkins that he regretted not having studied history.' Peter Stothard, a former editor of *The Times* who was allowed to shadow the British prime minister for thirty days in March–April 2003, publishing a fairly sympathetic account of life in 10 Downing Street in the run-up to and immediate aftermath of the invasion of Iraq, wrote that 'when Tony Blair finally meets his judge, he may find himself compared neither with Churchill nor Eden, nor Macmillan nor any of the other names that have been called up in all the pre-war debates, but with earlier figures, nineteenth-century missionary imperialists, or much earlier ones, the Romans who created deserts and called them peace' (Stothard, *30 Days: A Month at the Heart of Blair's War*, HarperCollins, London, 2003, p. 173).

139. The great majority of international lawyers regarded the invasion of March 2003 as being against international law. The case for its illegality is made very clearly by the late Lord Bingham who was Lord Chief Justice of England and Wales and Senior Law Lord of the UK. See Tom Bingham, *The Rule of Law* (Penguin, London, 2011), pp. 120–129. See also Roy Allison, *Russia, the West, and Military Intervention* (Oxford University Press, Oxford, 2013), especially pp. 106–112.

140. House of Commons Hansard Debates for 18 March 2003, Blair speech, at columns 763 and 772.

141. http://www.iraqinquiry.org.uk/media50751/Blair-to-Powell-17March2002-minute.pdf.

142. Cook was Foreign Secretary from 1997 to 2001 when Blair replaced him in that office by Jack Straw. Cook remained in the Cabinet as Leader of the House until he resigned over the Iraq war.

143. Robin Cook, *Point of Departure* (Simon & Schuster, London, 2003), pp. 361–365, at p. 364.

144. Ibid., pp. 361–365.

145. Lance Price, *Where Power Lies: Prime Ministers v. the Media* (Simon & Schuster, London, 2010), p. 370.

146. Stothard, *30 Days*, p. 8.

147. Menzies Campbell, 'No More Evasions', *Observer*, 27 November 2005. Former Vice-President Dick Cheney's response to Kerry in his memoirs is that the Democrats 'did not, apparently, want to admit that they too had accepted and relied on faulty intelligence'. See Cheney, *In My Time*, pp. 412–413.

148. 'Ex-president blasts Blair US role', http://news.bbc.co.uk/1/hi/world/americas/5346976.stm, 14 September 2006.

149. Zbigniew Brzezinski, 'America's policy blunders were compounded by Britain', *Financial Times*, 6 August 2004. Brzezinski added, with reference to Blair, 'Superior personal eloquence in making the case for a historically reckless course is no badge of merit but a disservice not only to America but ultimately to the democratic West as a whole.'

150. Charles Tripp, 'Militias, Vigilantes, Death Squads', *London Review of Books*, Vol. 29, No. 2, 25 January 2007, pp. 30–33, at p. 30.

151. Sir James Craig, in conversation with the author in late 2002.

152. The important principle that the military are subject to political control meant that serving officers could not publicly criticize the decision to invade Iraq, but retired senior officers were not similarly constrained. One of the most distinguished of them, General Sir Michael Rose (who was UN commander in Bosnia) said that Tony Blair's actions were 'somewhere in between' getting the politics wrong and acting illegally. He went on: 'The politics were wrong' and 'he rarely declared what his ultimate aims were . . . harping continually on weapons of mass destruction when actually he probably had some other strategy in mind. And secondly, the consequences of that war have been quite disastrous both for the people of Iraq and also for the west in terms of our wider interests in the war against global terror' (http://news.bbc.co.uk/1/hi/uk_politics/4594216.stm, 9 January 2006).

153. See Alex Barker, 'Security chief exposes Blair's gamble on Iraq', and James Blitz, 'MI5 head dismayed by stance on Saddam felt ignored by premier', *Financial Times*, 21 July 2010; and Tim Ross, 'Iraq was not a threat to Britain before invasion, says former head of MI5', *Daily Telegraph*, 29 August 2011. Many others, with highly relevant experience, came to the same judgement before the invasion as that reached by Baroness Manningham-Buller. Lord (Patrick) Wright, who chaired the Joint Intelligence Committee from 1982 to 1984 and was Head of the Diplomatic Service, 1986–1991, wrote that he was far from alone in a House of Lords debate on 26 February 2003 in saying that 'an attack on Iraq . . . will be seen as a direct attack against Islam and will fuel further terrorist attacks against the west'. He also requested that the advice received on this question 'from British heads of mission in Arab and Islamic posts' be made public (letter to *Financial*

Times of Lord Wright of Richmond, 13/14 September 2003). See also Avi Shlaim, 'It is not only God that will be Blair's judge over Iraq', *Guardian*, 14 May 2007. Shlaim, a specialist on the Middle East who is at home in both Hebrew and Arabic, argues that 'Blair's entire record in the Middle East is one of catastrophic failure'.

154. Michael Quinlan, 'War on Iraq: a blunder and a crime', *Financial Times*, 7 August 2002.

155. Ibid.

156. Rodric Braithwaite, 'End of the affair', *Prospect*, Issue 86, May 2003, pp. 20–23 at p. 22.

157. Lord Wilson and Lord Turnbull were giving evidence to the Chilcott Inquiry. See http://www.bbc.co.uk/news/uk-politics-12278788, 25 January 2011.

158. *Review of Intelligence on Weapons of Mass Destruction: Report of a Committee of Privy Counsellors. Chairman: The Rt Hon The Lord Butler of Brockwell* (Stationery Office, London, 2004).

159. Ibid., pp. 159 and 160.

160. Tony Blair, *A Journey* (Hutchinson, London, 2010), pp. 432–433; and Stothard, *30 Days*, pp. 20–21.

161. Peter Hennessy, *The Prime Minister: The Office and its Holders Since 1945* (Penguin, London, 2001), p. 532; and Owen, *The Hubris Syndrome*, pp. 80–81.

162. On this, see Philippe Sands, 'A Very British Deceit', *New York Review of Books*, 30 September 2010.

163. Kofi Annan with Nader Mousavizadeh, *Interventions: A Life in War and Peace* (Allen Lane, London, 2012), esp. pp. 344–358.

164. Especially importantly, this was true of Iraq itself. A leading American academic specialist on the Middle East, writing in 2005, noted that 'a recent independent public opinion poll holds that only 2 per cent of Iraqi Arabs view the United States as liberators'. See William R. Polk, *Understanding Iraq* (Tauris, London, 2006), p. 190.

165. On this, see Sherard Cowper-Coles, *Cables from Kabul: The Inside Story of the West's Afghanistan Campaign* (Harper Press, London, 2011). The author, who was UK ambassador to Kabul, speaks of 'the tragic diversion of attention and then resources from Afghanistan to Iraq' (p. xxiii). See also pp. 4 and 59–60.

166. Rogan, *The Arabs*, esp. pp. 607–625; and David Gardner, *Last Chance: The Middle East in the Balance* (Tauris, London, paperback ed., 2012), pp. 16–17 and 86–90.

167. Rumsfeld, *Known and Unknown*, p. 520.

168. Charles Tripp, *The Power and the People: Paths of Resistance in the Middle East* (Cambridge University Press, Cambridge, 2013), p. 42.

169. Bush, *Decision Points*, p. 269; and Joseph Sassoon, *Saddam Hussein's Ba'th Party: Inside an Authoritarian Regime* (Cambridge University Press, Cambridge, 2012), p. 165.

170. David Fisher, *Morality and War: Can War be Just in the Twenty-first Century?* (Oxford University Press paperback, Oxford, 2012), p. 202.

171. Sassoon, *Saddam Hussein's Ba'th Party*, p. 165.

172. Rice, *No Higher Honour*, p. 208.

173. Ibid., p. 20. Cf. Bush, *Decision Points*, pp. 87–88.

174. Rice, *No Higher Honour*, p. 187.

175. Ibid., pp. 21–22.

176. Cook, *Point of Departure*, p. 323.

177. Jack Straw, *Last Man Standing: Memoirs of a Political Survivor* (Macmillan, London, 2012), pp. 544–545.

178. Philip Stephens, *Tony Blair: The Price of Leadership* (Politico, London, revised edition, 2004), p. 319.

179. Archie Brown, 'The myth of the boundless debt Labour owes Blair', *Financial Times*, 11 September 2006.

180. Andrew Rawnsley, 'Tony Blair's obsession with size', *Observer*, 14 December 1997.

181. Jack S. Levy, 'Political Psychology and Foreign Policy', in David O. Sears, Leonie Huddy and Robert Jervis (eds.), *Oxford Handbook of Political Psychology* (Oxford University Press, New York, 2003), pp. 253–284, at pp. 264–265.

8   What Kind of Leadership is Desirable?

1. Hugh Heclo, 'Whose Presidency is This Anyhow?', in George C. Edwards III and William G. Howell (eds.), *The Oxford Handbook of the American Presidency* (Oxford University Press, New York, 2009), pp. 771–796, at p. 782.

2. That, moreover, applies to 'checks [English 'cheques'] and balances' in a monetary as well as political sense.

3. Michael Barber, *Instruction to Deliver: Tony Blair, Public Services and the Challenge of Achieving Targets* (Politico, London, 2007), pp. 291–340. This is a long chapter (in an interesting book) called 'Enhancing the power of the Prime Minister'. Having worked with Tony Blair, Barber came to the conclusion that the prime minister's powers were insufficient. While enhancing the power of government to achieve its objectives, subject to criticism and scrutiny in parliament and outside, is doubtless desirable, that does not mean – here I disagree fundamentally with Barber – that it is at all desirable to strive for 'strengthening the Prime Minister's capacity to exercise his power' (p. 339).

4. Cf. Heclo, 'Whose Presidency is This Anyhow?', p. 791.

5. Ibid.

6. Ibid.

7. I am not persuaded that it is necessary to attempt a strict separation of fact and values when discussing political leadership, so long as this is done consciously and openly. Thus, I have argued that 'transformational', as in 'transformational leadership', does in everyday speech have a positive connotation, and it is in that sense it has been used in this book. Adolf Hitler played the principal part in effecting profound change in the German political system and German society in the 1930s, but the category of 'transformational leader' would become too disparate to be meaningful if this accorded him a place alongside de Gaulle, Gorbachev and Mandela. 'Redefining leadership', as I have used the term, is value-neutral. Redefining the limits of the possible within any particular system can be in a direction of which one approves or, on the contrary, disapproves.

8. One notable specialist on the American presidency has remained surprisingly sceptical even of the president's ability to persuade. George C. Edwards III believes that the evidence for this is too anecdotal, adding: 'There is not a single systematic study that demonstrates that presidents can reliably move others to support them' (Edwards, 'The Study of Presidential Leadership', in Edwards and Howell (eds.), *The Oxford Handbook of the American Presidency*, pp. 816–837, at p. 821). A 'systematic' study, if by that is meant a study which separates the influence of the president from every other communication and source of information in citizens' environment, is, of course, virtually impossible to operationalize.

9. Heclo, 'Whose Presidency is This Anyhow?', p. 791.

10. Alfred Stepan and Juan J. Linz, 'Comparative Perspectives on Inequality and the Quality of Democracy in the United States', *Perspectives on Politics*, Vol. 9, No. 4, 2011, pp. 841–856, at pp. 848–849.

11. Ibid., p. 849.

12. Keith Dowding, 'Prime Ministerial Power: Institutional and Personal Factors', in Paul Strangio, Paul 't Hart and James Walter (eds.), *Understanding Prime Ministerial Performance: Comparative Perspectives* (Oxford University Press, Oxford, 2013), pp. 56–78, at p. 61.

13. James P. McPherson, *Abraham Lincoln* (Oxford University Press, New York, 2009), p. 62.

14. Ibid., p. 64.

15. Ibid., p. 57.

16. Doris Kearns Goodwin, *Team of Rivals: The Political Genius of Abraham Lincoln* (Penguin, London, 2009), pp. 686–690.

17. Ibid., pp. 571–572. Goodwin quotes a contemporary of Lincoln, John Forney of the Washington *Daily Chronicle*, arguing that Lincoln was 'the most truly progressive man of the age, because he always moves in conjunction with propitious circumstances, not waiting to be dragged by the force of events or wasting strength in premature struggles with them' (p. 572). On the momentous issue of Emancipation, James McPherson concludes that if

Lincoln 'had moved decisively against slavery in the war's first year, as radicals pressed him to do, he might well have fractured his war coalition, driven border-state Unionists over to the Confederacy, lost the war, and witnessed the survival of slavery for at least another generation' (McPherson, *Abraham Lincoln*, p. x).

18. Goodwin, *Team of Rivals*, p. 319.

19. Ibid., pp. 364 and 507.

20. Ibid., pp. 633 and 680.

21. Ibid., p. 217.

22. Ibid., pp. 412–413.

23. Ibid., p. 413.

24. Nannerl O. Keohane, *Thinking about Leadership* (Princeton University Press, Princeton, 2010), p. 12.

25. Ibid.

26. Ibid. Keohane adds that there is plenty of evidence that Gore would 'have pursued a very different set of goals in office, particularly in environmental policy but also in international and domestic policy more generally', although how much of this he would have been able to accomplish remains questionable, given the constraints imposed by Congress.

27. Max Weber, 'Politics as a Vocation', in *From Max Weber: Essays in Sociology*, translated and edited by H.H. Gerth and C. Wright Mills (Routledge & Kegan Paul, London, 1948), pp. 77–128, at p. 116. Weber acknowledges that vanity is far from being a distinctive sin of politicians, observing: 'In academic and scholarly circles, vanity is a sort of occupational disease, but precisely with the scholar, vanity – however disagreeably it may express itself – is relatively harmless; in the sense that as a rule it does not disturb scientific enterprise.'

28. Ibid. In April 2000, in a private note to his staff, Tony Blair asked them to produce 'a series of eye-catching initiatives' (especially on issues like crime, the family, and defence), and, he continued, 'I should be personally associated with as much of this as possible.' Philip Stephens, who reported this, adds: 'Translated, the prime minister wanted more headline-grabbing initiatives and wheezes to keep him in the public eye.' See Stephens, *Tony Blair, The Price of Leadership* (Politico, London, 2004), p. 188.

29. Charles Moore, *Margaret Thatcher. The Authorized Biography. Volume One: Not for Turning* (Allen Lane, London, 2013), pp. xiv and 432.

30. *Guardian*, 9 April 2013.

31. Archie Brown, 'Margaret Thatcher and the End of the Cold War', in Wm Roger Louis (ed.), *Resurgent Adventures with Britannia: Personalities, Politics and Culture in Britain* (Tauris, London, 2011), pp. 259–273.

32. Rodric Braithwaite, *Across the Moscow River: The World Turned Upside Down* (Yale University Press, New Haven and London, 2002), p. 45.

33. Jonathan Powell, *The New Machiavelli: How to Wield Power in the Modern World* (Bodley Head, London, 2010), p. 2.

34. Peter Hennessy, *The Prime Minister: The Office and its Holders since 1945* (Penguin, London, 2001), p. 397.

35. Powell, *The New Machiavelli*, p. 78.

36. Barber, *Instruction to Deliver*, p. 84.

37. Ibid., pp. 306–307.

38. *Guardian*, 9 April 2013.

39. Ibid. Howe adds: 'In Margaret's case, she became prepared to test her will to destruction. First Michael Heseltine walked out, followed by Leon Brittan, then Nigel Lawson, then me.'

40. *Guardian*, 9 April 2013.

41. *Guardian*, 11 September 2010.

42. Michael A. Hogg, 'Influence and Leadership', in Susan T. Fiske, Daniel T. Gilbert and Gardner Lindzey (eds.), *Handbook of Social Psychology* (Wiley, Hoboken, N.J., 5th ed., 2010), pp. 1166–1207, at p. 1190.

43. Joseph S. Nye, *The Powers to Lead* (Oxford University Press, New York, 2008), p. 18.

44. Keohane, *Thinking about Leadership*, p. 23.

45. Roy Jenkins, *Baldwin* (Papermac, London, 1987), p. 120.

46. Tony Blair, *A Journey* (Hutchinson, London, 2010), p. 287.

47. See, for example, George Parker, 'PM "losing control" of his party', *Financial Times*, 20 May 2013.

48. José Ramón Montero and Richard Gunther, 'Introduction: Reviewing and Reassessing Parties', in Richard Gunther, José Ramón Montero and Juan J. Linz (eds.), *Political Parties: Old Concepts and New Challenges* (Oxford University Press, New York, 2002), pp. 1–35, at p. 31.

49. Juan J. Linz, 'Parties in Contemporary Democracies: Problems and Paradoxes', in Gunther, Montero and Linz (eds.), *Political Parties*, pp. 291–317, at p. 307.

50. Richard S. Katz and Peter Mair, 'The Ascendancy of the Party in Public Office', in Gunther, Montero and Linz (eds.), *Political Parties*, pp. 113–135, at p. 126.

51. Linz, 'Parties in Contemporary Democracies: Problems and Paradoxes', in Gunther, Montero and Linz (eds.), *Political Parties*, pp. 291–317, at p. 303. Recent work by Robert Rohrschneider and Stephen Whitefield has underlined how important mass organization of political parties is to democratic representation and also how much more effective it still is, in spite of a decline in party partisanship, in Western Europe than in Central and Eastern Europe. See Rohrschneider and Whitefield, *The Strain of Representation: How Parties Represent Diverse Voters in Western and Eastern Europe* (Oxford University Press, Oxford, 2012), esp. pp. 174–183.

52. Moisés Naim, *The End of Power* (Basic Books, New York, 2013), p. 239. See also Richard McGregor, 'America Goes Dark', *Financial Times*, 5–6 October 2013.
53. Naim, *The End of Power*, p. 240. Naim adds: 'It is impossible to ascertain whether political corruption actually increased in the past decades, but it certainly has been more publicized than ever before.'
54. Ibid., pp. 239–240.
55. Adam Smith, *An Inquiry into the Nature and Causes of the Wealth of Nations*, edited by R.H. Campbell and A.S. Skinner (Clarendon Press, Oxford, 1976 [first published 1776]), Vol. 2, p. 712; and John Millar, *The Origin of the Distinction of Ranks*, 3rd ed., 1779, reprinted in William C. Lehmann (ed.), *John Millar of Glasgow 1735–1801: His Life and Thought and His Contribution to Sociological Analysis* (Cambridge University Press, Cambridge, 1960), p. 250.
56. Elena Viktorovna Shorina, *Kollegial'nost' i edinonachalie v sovetskom gosudarstvennom upravlenii* (Yuridicheskaya literatura, Moscow, 1959).
57. In the end neither Gorbachev nor his opponents who had become a majority within the party apparatus, at both higher and lower levels of the organization, prevailed. The August coup of 1991 by conservative Communists and hardline Russian nationalists merely accelerated the break-up of the Soviet Union and hence the end both of the Communist Party of the Soviet Union and of Gorbachev's political leadership, for he had become on 15 March 1990 the president of a country which by 31 December 1991 had ceased to exist. I have written about this much more fully elsewhere. See, for example, Archie Brown, *The Gorbachev Factor* (Oxford University Press, Oxford, 1996) and Brown, *Seven Years that Changed the World: Perestroika in Perspective* (Oxford University Press, Oxford, 2007).

Index